DATE DUE

ALSO BY EDITH EFRON

THE NEWS TWISTERS

A TIME FOR TRUTH
(In collaboration with William Simon)

THE
APOCALYPTICS

Cancer and the Big Lie

by
EDITH EFRON

HOW ENVIRONMENTAL POLITICS CONTROLS
WHAT WE KNOW ABOUT CANCER

SIMON AND SCHUSTER
New York

1 3 5 7 9 10 8 6 4 2

Library of Congress Cataloging in Publication Data

Efron, Edith, date.
The apocalyptics: cancer and the big lie.

Includes bibliographies and index.
1.Cancer—Prevention—Social aspects   2.Cancer—
Prevention—Political aspects.   3.Environmentally induced
diseases—Prevention—Social aspects.   4.Medical policy.
5.Science and state.   I.Title.
RC268.E35   1984   362.1'96994   83-20208

ISBN 0-671-41743-6

The author and publisher gratefully acknowledge permission to reprint poems, tables, and excerpts from the following:

Frederick Winsor, *The Space Child's Mother Goose* by Frederick Winsor and Marian Parry, Simon and Schuster, 1968. Reprinted by permission of Margaret Winsor Stubbs.

Rocky Mountain Suite (Cold Nights in Canada) by John Denver. Copyright © 1973 Cherry Lane Music & Publishing Co., Inc. All rights reserved. Used by permission.

Drinking Water and Health, National Academy Press, Washington, D.C., 1977.

Particulate Polycyclic Organic Matter, National Academy Press, Washington, D.C., 1978.

The Tropospheric Transport of Pollutants and Other Substances to the Oceans, National Academy Press, Washington, D.C., 1978.

The Tropospheric Transport of Pollutants and Other Substances to the Oceans, National Academy Press, Washington, D.C., 1978.

Toxicology: The Basic Science of Poisons, edited by Louis J. Casarett and John Doull. Copyright © 1975 by Macmillan Publishing Company. Used by permission.

P. B. Medawar and J. S. Medawar, *The Life Science: Current Ideas of Biology,* Harper & Row, Inc. Copyright © 1977 by Peter and Jean Medawar.

(Continued on the last page)

To Alexander Efron and Rose Efron, who built a bridge between "the two cultures" so that their children might cross it.

CONTENTS

8   CONTENTS

Preface

This book is an intellectual detective story, I am the detective, and I shall not give away the "plot." I shall simply say here that I discovered a cultural crime which should not be possible in a free society: a complex corruption of science and a prolonged deception of the public. The crime emerged from the sciences of environmental cancer and cancer prevention, and it has all the superficial characteristics of "The Purloined Letter": It has been committed under our very eyes, its details are publicly recorded in documents which are within hand's reach, and yet it remains invisible to most of the people of this country who are its victims. It is rendered invisible by one thing above all: the phenomenon of "the two cultures"—the dangerous barrier which separates the scientific and the humanist cultures and which may leave even the most educated layman incapable of differentiating between serious science and ideology in a white smock. The cultural crime I discovered *was* perpetuated by ideology in a white smock—and that is all I shall say about the "plot," for if the lay reader is to extricate himself from this complex deception, he must make his discoveries step by step as I did: He, too, must be prepared to be a detective.

There is one aspect of this corruption of science which can and should be identified in advance. It is a manifestation of a much wider cultural problem—an insidious assault on reason, science, and the value of objectivity, which has taken place in every field of scholarship since the 1960s. In all branches of the humanities and the social sciences, there has been a rejection of the criteria and disciplines of the field and a slide into a subjectivity which serves as a vehicle, overt or covert, for ideological values. These trends are now institutionalized and are well known to a generation of scholars in the humanist world, whether they have capitulated to the irrationalists or are fighting them. Most humanists, however, have not realized that the same trends have infiltrated science. I did not know it. In my reading in the environmental sciences and later in environmental cancer, I bumped into evidence of such hostility to the objective disciplines of science, evidence of so aggressive a rejection of facts and logic, that I could scarcely credit my senses. I began to investigate this phenomenon, much as one would investigate an outbreak of bubonic plague in a community one had supposed to be healthy.

I gradually discovered that scientific intellectuals were aware of the problem. I learned from Ernest Nagel, a philosopher of science, that many biologists in the 1960s had rejected the analytical and abstractive disciplines of

9

science.[1] I learned from a discussion of a book entitled *Science, Technology and Society*, edited by Ina Spiegel-Rosing and Derek DeSolla Price, that many biologists in the 1970s were rejecting the most crucial "norms" of science: "universalism, communality, disinterestedness, organized skepticism, and more lately originality and humility."[2] I discovered a paper by Bernard Davis of Harvard, a prominent geneticist, observing that "some scientists appear to be losing confidence in the objectivity of scientific knowledge . . ."[3] I learned from a vehement defense of peer review and publication by Philip Abelson, editor of *Science*, that, by the late 1970s, there was indeed a need to protect those disciplines—two of the most crucial requirements for integrity and objectivity in the scientific enterprise.[4] I discovered a 1980 speech by Philip Handler, then President of the National Academy of Sciences, warning against the "antiscientific" and "antirationalistic" trends which were infiltrating both the humanist and scientific cultures, and calling upon scientists to confront those trends and to identify the "charlatans" in their midst.[5] It was obvious from these analyses and others like them that the revolt against reason and objectivity which I had believed to be restricted to the humanities was present in every branch of biology.

I had found precisely those patterns in the science of cancer prevention, which is controlled by the government. In that field, too, scientists were making similar analyses and protesting the presence of strong antireason and antiscience trends in their own ranks. When I was certain that the blatant irrationality I had discovered was not an isolated aberration but a deeply rooted trend—and that it was now lodged within the state itself—the subject became the focus of my book. It is a "detective story" precisely because I did not know this before; it is the story of what I discovered, and how I discovered it.

I have spent a good deal of time trying to understand why there has been little or no press coverage of much of the information I present—information which has been widely available in some cases for decades. While "the two cultures" may be the most fundamental explanation, it is not the only one. There are other reasons which are directly relevant to the particular science to which this book is devoted. A veritable wall stands between the citizen and the science of cancer prevention, although he is usually unaware of it. Since in the course of my research I raised certain questions which had the unexpected effect of knocking over that wall, I can describe some of its components.

The first thing that keeps the layman in a chronic state of ignorance is his inability to differentiate between the various cancer sciences and the kinds of information they produce. While such ignorance is not universal, it is extraordinarily common, and more often than not the layman, even the occasional doctor, cannot identify the specific science of "cancer prevention." In part, this confusion is due to the fact that all cancer sciences ultimately seek to become sciences of prevention. That is certainly the goal of basic science which studies the mechanisms of cancer, but despite continuing and brilliant advances, the same judgment that James Watson made in 1982 can be repeated today: For the purpose of prevention, the information is still "hopelessly inadequate" and the mechanisms of cancer are still "inherently unknown."[6] Prevention is also the goal of the science of epidemiology, which studies human mortality and incidence patterns and investigates groups of people at high risk for specific cancers. It is epidemiology which has identified every known risk factor for cancer in human beings (e.g., tobacco, asbestos, vinyl chloride) and is most commonly mistaken for the science of prevention. Epidemiology, however, can only conduct its studies *after* people have died of cancer. Once the epidemiologist has definitively discovered a risk factor for cancer, his knowledge can be applied to protect men in the future, but the science itself can only begin with cancer deaths; it cannot prevent cancer in advance. There is actually only one science which seeks to prevent cancer in advance: the science which exposes animals (or bacteria or cells) to chemicals, which identifies "potential" or "suspected" carcinogens and extrapolates the findings to man. Animal-man extrapolation *is* "cancer prevention," and it is applied by the state. The layman who cannot clearly differentiate the politically applied science of the "suspected" from the other sciences of cancer can neither understand nor judge cancer prevention and the cancer prevention establishment.

Another block to the layman's understanding is the conceptual approach to the problem of environmental carcinogens adopted by the press. Shaped by the regulatory process, it is actually a tripartite formula: (1) A "suspected" carcinogen is announced along with a proclamation of its danger; (2) a controversy between a regulatory agency and an incriminated industry is reported; and (3) a regulatory solution to the problem is promulgated. That is almost the only approach to environmental carcinogens known to the layman. For twenty years, but most intensively during the last decade, he has heard this formula over and over again—always applied to single instances: to a carcinogenic drug (diethylstilbestrol); to a carcinogenic food additive (Red Dye #2); to a carcinogenic pesticide (DDT); to a carcinogenic pollutant (dioxin); to a carcinogenic waste dump (Love Canal). The individual carcinogens merge with each other, as do the warnings of danger, the denunciations of "industry," the calls for regulatory solutions. Ultimately, details are forgotten, and only the formula itself remains: "Carcinogen! Industrial evil! Pass a law!" The mind is frozen, the mouth is agape, nothing new is ever learned.

This book is not dominated by the tripartite formula. The difference is so great that the lay reader should be prepared for it, point by point. First, unlike regulators and press, I report on every *category* of carcinogen that has ever been recorded in the literature. There are more reported carcinogens in this book, and more categories of carcinogens, than the layman has ever dreamed of. The resultant perspective is so drastically different from that habitually communicated by regulators and press that it does permit one to learn something new: One learns that the phenomenon of the environmental carcinogen has been profoundly misrepresented to the public.

Second, unlike regulators and press, I do not monotonously recreate the standard regulator-industry controversies. I do not report them at all. Data produced by industrial firms have been exiled from this book, because they have largely been discredited. While this is unfair to some excellent industrial scientists, and I apologize for it, it does not damage the scientific analysis, be-

cause the full spectrum of scientific positions is present in the academic literature. This expulsion of industry hurls one into the academic world, where one
discovers an entirely different set of controversies—the theoretical controversies that lie concealed behind the regulatory facade. This perspective, too, is so
different that one learns something new. What one learns above all is that the
government has systematically fed the public the views of one faction in the academic world while the views of others have been largely withheld. This official selectivity has generated a misleading view of the science.

And third, unlike regulators and press, I do not promulgate regulatory solutions. I do not even discuss them. I discovered quite early that regulation—
the "preventive" part of cancer prevention—was virtually nonexistent and that
its nonexistence had been kept a secret from the public. Only after I finished
this book did I find a published concession of the hopeless chaos and paralysis
of the regulatory process. It came from a prominent adviser to a regulatory
agency—Roy Albert, Chairman of the Environmental Protection Agency's
Carcinogen Assessment Group. Caught in an illiterate public controversy over
the Reagan administration's policies, this scientist finally told the unvarnished
truth in a public forum. Writing in *Science* in 1983, he pointed out that the
issue was not whether the administration was more or less conservative in its
approach to cancer prevention, but that there had never been a government
cancer policy that had actually functioned. The most striking aspect of the last
twelve years of carcinogen regulation, he said, was that there had been so little
of it. The essential problem, according to Albert, was the "hodgepodge of laws"
produced by a succession of congresses, each of which had had different
theories about how to deal with carcinogens. Albert illustrated his point with a
long list of those theories, e.g., outright banning, comparing risks with benefits,
protecting people by using the best existing technology, providing safety for everyone, etc. In the face of this varied and self-contradictory "hodgepodge of
laws," he said that cancer regulators had been provided with little direction—
thus the strangely small number of carcinogens which had ever been regulated.[7]

This is an accurate picture of cancer regulation in America, which is to say
that cancer prevention is almost an institutionalized public illusion. Unlike the
press, I do not perpetuate that illusion by reflexively invoking regulation. Instead, I report on the deepest source of the conceptual chaos and paralysis: the
science of animal-man extrapolation itself.

Finally, the incessant focus of the press on political regulation keeps the
layman ignorant in one other way. He rarely, if ever, has the experience of encountering a neutral presentation of the controversies in the field. It is impossible to be neutral in the face of a regulator-industry conflict. One is watching a
policeman collar a defensive suspect whose deepest concern is his balance
sheet. By contrast, it is impossible *not* to be neutral in the face of academic
conflict. Only the pathologically ignorant layman presumes to hold opinions
where serious academic scientists differ. In this book, I make no scientific
judgments whatever; the presentation of the scientific controversies is implac-
ably neutral. Only when both sides in a controversy finally agree on a disputed

issue, or when a finding is universally accepted do I accept a conclusion or identify a discovery as "established." Paradoxically, one learns vastly more from militant neutrality than one can by taking sides. One discovers the existence of a profoundly polarized and ideologized science.

These are some of the discoveries hidden by the tripartite formula of regulator and press. No mind trapped by that formula can make such discoveries. To an extraordinary degree, this book is the result of abandoning the conventional approach of the press. The result is a report on a series of mind-boggling misrepresentations.

Many of the misrepresentations are simply the result of the profound indifference of the cancer prevention establishment to public education; they are due to defaults in communication, not to an intent to deceive. That is by no means true in all cases, however. Serious falsehoods have been disseminated. Information on critical issues has been deliberately withheld by government agencies, resulting in false implications. Misinformation has poured through the nation because premature studies were deliberately released. Finally, actual myths and distortions of scientific history have been systematically pumped into this culture. In each of these cases, government agencies and high officials in the scientific bureaucracies are implicated. They are not alone in misinforming the country, but they are the most significant sources, for they alone have been blindly trusted by the lay press. The discovery that an abnormal number of untruths had emerged from the cancer prevention establishment, combined with the discovery of an entrenched scientific irrationalism, also shaped this book. One of its functions is to disentangle myth from scientific fact.

Because I was a media critic before writing this book and began investigating the environmental sciences and environmental cancer in order to evaluate television coverage of those subjects, I was particularly interested in understanding the role of the press in disseminating a group of major myths in which environmental cancer is now embedded. Press coverage is not an issue in the book, but at the very end, in an epilogue, I track down those myths and briefly discuss the press. I will only say here that the manipulation of the press by scientists, above all by some government scientists, has been so severe that the issue that should concern us is the manipulation, not the press.

There are a few other details which should be called to the reader's attention:

In one way or another, the material in this book covers a span of fifty years, with most attention given to the first decade of cancer prevention, 1970 to 1980. I have concentrated intensely on the middle and late 1970s, when the American public received its basic and fallacious education on environmental cancer.

The research and writing itself took a good many years. After preliminary research in 1975 and 1976, I researched and wrote the first draft of this book between 1978 and 1981. It took me an additional year to have the manuscript reviewed by scientists and to integrate their suggestions and corrections. The final draft went to press in 1983. Because the book was written over a long period of time, I was often reporting on events as they occurred, and the data grow more recent as the book progresses. Each section has a different cutoff date, which is made quite clear in both text and footnotes. Given the time lag in publishing, I have made little attempt to provide the very latest data. For that one must read journals. The reader who is particularly interested in following up on any given type of information will find that, perhaps for the first time, he has a context into which he can integrate it.

I interviewed some 200 scientists in the course of working on this book, but, with a few exceptions, I do not use interview material, much of which was off the record. Because of the nature of the analysis, I rely on verifiable documents.

I quote a great many scientists, and, for the sake of simplicity, *I have frozen job histories.* I usually identify scientists in terms of the positions they held when they made the statements quoted, and the same policy is applied to institutions; they are called by the names they held when they produced the documents I cite. I do this even when, for stylistic reasons, I write in the present tense. Should any scientist-reader wish to update the whereabouts of his colleagues, he is cordially invited to scribble their new jobs in the margins of this book. Laymen who wish to know the whereabouts of any particular scientist are advised to consult the latest edition of the *Current Bibliographic Directory of the Arts and Sciences*, published by the Institute for Scientific Information, with the warning that many of the entries will already be out of date. It is far more important for the reader to know with what institutions scientists were affiliated when they made the statements in this book than to know about their most recent career moves.

With this, I leave the lay reader to begin my detective story. Should he suffer from "science anxiety," I can only reassure him: This is a book written by a humanist for other humanists, and it is written in English. It is certainly about a scientific enterprise, but in the last analysis it is a story of a cultural phenomenon, a story which has been untold for too long.

Edith Efron
Research Associate, Center for Research
    in Government Policy and Business
Graduate School of Management
University of Rochester
Rochester, N.Y.
March 1983

ACKNOWLEDGMENTS—
AND SOME ADDITIONAL INFORMATION

In the course of a review process which took one year, I received assistance, comment, and helpful criticism from twenty scientists, but I can give public thanks to only four of them—all basic scientists in carcinogenesis and genetics:

Isaac Berenblum, Weizmann Institute, Israel; Takashi Sugimura, Director, and Takashi Kawachi, Vice-Director, of the Japanese National Cancer Center Research Institute; and Lee Wattenberg, University of Minnesota.

I can express my gratitude to these scientists because they have seen only self-contained and specialized sections of my manuscript—parts, or all, of the basic science chapters and, in the case of the Japanese Institute, the survey of carcinogens in Chapter 4. It is even possible that Dr. Sugimura has not actually read the survey of carcinogens; he certainly knew its nature and generously arranged that it be read by Dr. Kawachi. These scientists do not know what is in the rest of the book, they do not know its integrating themes and conclusions, and cannot in any way be perceived as endorsing them.

The manuscript was also reviewed in its entirety by sixteen other scientists who do know its integrating themes and conclusions and who do endorse them. I cannot thank them by name, however, because they explicitly requested anonymity or because it became clear that they expected it. It is so unorthodox to thank anonymous reviewers—as unorthodox as it is to quote them on the jacket—that it requires explanation.

The book itself is the best explanation. What can be said here is that by the time I finished it, I hypothesized that it might be difficult to get major scientists to discuss it openly. Although laymen rarely realize it, scientists are the most vulnerable intellectuals in the United States. If they do not wish to work for industry, they are entirely dependent for jobs or for grants on the state—and my book, I knew, was not liable to please the American Biologist-State. My hypothesis was instantly confirmed when the review process began. I immediately found myself facing a bizarre combination of extravagant praise and demands for anonymity. To appreciate the situation, one must have a few examples. Here are some of the reactions from scientific reviewers of international reputation:

One expert in carcinogenesis and animal testing declared my book a "scientific work of art." When asked for a written assessment, he agreed but insisted that his name be kept secret. I asked him why. "Your book will come out before I retire," he said.

One cancer epidemiologist said my book was an "intellectual tour de force." He then warned that neither he nor any other "senior scientist" would publicly endorse my book. He was willing only to whisper his praise into my editor's ear.

One basic scientist in genetics wrote a letter saying that my book was "on the whole very good and remarkably thorough." He had labored generously on the manuscript. He then added: "Please do not acknowledge my help publicly."

One basic scientist in cancer research wrote a letter declaring that my book was "great" and granted me an interview in which he confirmed my most devastating conclusions about the science of cancer prevention. He then looked deeply into my eyes and said, "You understand, of course, that I cannot help you publicly." I nodded numbly. By then I understood.

And I did understand—up to a point. In my research, I had discovered the phenomenon of the publicly silent scientist and had described it in my book. I had quoted a 1980 lecture by Philip Handler (referred to in the Preface and discussed at the end of the book) in which he said that many scientists had been "intimidated" in the past decade. In the course of the year, four of my reviewers—three of them basic scientists—had made equivalent statements. One referred to "persecution"; another to "environmental McCarthyism"; a third to the "destruction of reputations"; and a fourth to "Lysenkoism." This was not new to me. What I did not understand was how this "persecution" or "intimidation" worked. What exactly happened to a scientist who opened his mouth to inform the public of what I had discovered?

Finally, yet another basic scientist explained it to me. He did it in terms of Thomas Kuhn's paradigm theory—and any reader who wants a deeper understanding of what he said should read *The Structure of Scientific Revolutions.* He told me exactly what would happen to a leading scientist who publicly endorsed this book. It was the equivalent, he said, of rejecting the ruling paradigm or conceptual model of his field—an act which is dangerous to a scientist. The scientist is free to quarrel eternally within the confines of that model, and on occasion point out its flaws and anomalies, but he is ill-advised to reject the model itself. We were at lunch, and the basic scientist scribbled a numbered list of the punitive consequences on a paper napkin. Here it is:

1. No longer in the "in-group" of American scientists.
2. Loss of prestige, approval of peers and respect.
3. More criticism of his own work area than he has previously experienced and increasing resistance to publication of his work.
4. No invitations to: (a) symposia; (b) address scientific societies; (c) be visiting professor; (d) travel.
5. Loss of income. If a scientist is tenured, he derives 30–50 percent of his income from item 4.
6. Ultimate problems: (a) difficulty in getting funding in epochs when money is tight; (b) losing funding and subsequent loss of students, postdoctoral students, etc., professional isolation, ultimate loss of identity.

He then observed that these were the penalties in "normal" science, where the ruling paradigms of the "in-group" usually have no political significance. When those paradigms did have political implications, he said—as in the case of cancer prevention—yet another penalty was incurred. The basic scientist scribbled an addition to item 2 and held it up silently. It was: "POLITICAL SMEARS."

That was the missing explanation. As a humanist, I had not known all of it. I had made an ironic mistake, and so had my humanist editor. We knew that my book needed protection by "in-group" scientists; we learned that "in-group" scientists needed protection from my book.

Under these difficult circumstances, I would have preferred to leave my reviewers in peace and say nothing about them. I cannot do so, however. As a layman, and particularly a layman who is challenging the state-imposed conventional wisdom, I must inform readers that my book has been subjected to a detailed review process by competent academic scientists in every specialized field that I discuss. The only solution which protects both my reviewers and my book is to describe them in a way that does not identify them, but does identify their fields of expertise and indicate their professional status. I hereby do so.

Of the sixteen scientists who have read and criticized the entire manuscript, three are foreign (from the United Kingdom and Canada); the rest are American. Seven are internationally known figures, and six are authors of scientific texts. They are eight basic scientists in different fields of biology, including carcinogenesis, genetics, immunology, molecular biology, and biochemistry; two toxicologists; one pathologist; one radiation expert; one specialist in nuclear medicine; and three cancer epidemiologists.

At the time of the review process, their positions were as follows: Eight were at U.S. universities (e.g., Harvard, Cornell, New York University, University of California at Berkeley)—seven of them full professors and one a contract member of a famous research team. Five were members of state, national, and international health agencies (e.g., the National Cancer Institute and the International Agency for Research on Cancer). Three were or had recently been members of institutions specializing in cancer research (e.g., Memorial Sloan-Kettering); one of this group now works for a foreign government. Fourteen of the sixteen have served as scientific consultants. Twelve have worked or presently work as consultants to American health agencies, and to America's most prominent scientific institutions (e.g., the National Academy of Sciences, the National Research Council, the National Cancer Institute, the Environmental Protection Agency, the National Institute of Environmental Health Sciences) and to international agencies (e.g., to the World Health Organization and to the International Agency for Research on Cancer). Three have also worked as industrial consultants.

I am deeply indebted to all for advice and criticism, but I am passionately grateful to five of the academic scientists—three basic scientists, one toxicologist, and one epidemiologist, all specialists in carcinogenesis and genetics—who voluntarily turned themselves into my scientific editors, commenting on every section in detail.

The above descriptions of these scientists, their positions, and their fields of expertise will be attested to by my editors, Erwin Glikes and Bob Bender, of Simon and Schuster; Professor William Meckling, Dean of the Graduate

School of Management of the University of Rochester; Professor Karl Brunner, head of the Center for Research in Government Policy and Business of that graduate school; and my agent, Owen Laster of the William Morris Agency. All have copies of my correspondence with each scientist; all will honor the pledges of confidentiality made to those scientists. These are the sole guardians of the scientists' identities; they alone had a "need to know." Mr. Glikes in particular will testify to the strange and often anguishing details of the reviewing process.

I now turn to the non-biologists who played a role in this project. I thank Allen Wallis, former President and Chancellor of the University of Rochester, and Professors Meckling and Brunner, identified above, who invited me to do this work as Research Associate of the Center for Research in Government Policy and Business of the Graduate School of Management.

I am also grateful to those who supported this project economically. I thank Simon & Schuster for a helpful advance. I thank a group of foundations which gave the Graduate School of Management grants to support the research for two and a half years: the Schultz Foundation, the Sarah Scaife Foundation, the Scaife Family Charitable Trust, the Olin Foundation, and the Pepsico Foundation. And I thank the readers of earlier books for the royalties they provided, which allowed me to finance this project myself for almost four years.

I also wish to express my appreciation to all those who worked with me. I am deeply grateful to Judith Engerman, then graduate student in environmental studies, who was my science researcher and shared the remarkable adventure which changed us both. I thank my former research assistants Henry Constantine and Pamela Blanpied; the librarians at the University of Rochester's Medical School, who endured our incessant demands for their services; James Newman, Arlene Shaner, and Christine Brudevold, also graduate students at the time, who helped me put a hundred pages of footnotes in order; the part-time helpers who clipped, pasted, filed, checked, and copied: John Blanpied, Lisa Kunitz, Nan Wood, Nancy Cornmesser, and Nancy Mitchell. And, finally, I thank my secretary-assistants Lynn McCoy, Holly Goldseth, and Amy Gunn, who among them produced innumerable drafts of the manuscript and kept my world moving on its axis.

PART

I

THE APOCALYPSE

Chapter 1

The Apocalyptic Movement

Man is the original and basic pollutant.[1]
—J. O'M. Bockris, editor,
Environmental Chemistry, 1977

At the recent American Association for the Advancement of Science Annual
Meeting ... there were other eruptions too, more impassioned and divisive,
whose echoes still resound. ... What pushes scientists ... to plunge into social
and political controversies which are not central to the search for and application of knowledge? What is politics doing in the house of science?[2]
—William D. Carey,
editorial in *Science*, 1978

On December 12, 1975, Dr. Irving Selikoff, known nationally today as an
authority on asbestos-related cancers, delivered an address at a meeting of the
Scientific Committee on Occupational Medicine in Milan. In it he described
what he called the Paradox of Rehn—the strange fact that since the early
1900s, it had been suspected, on theoretical grounds, that industrial chemicals
should be causing a large amount of cancer in human beings, but that as of
1975, that had not been found to be the case. Here is what he said:

In 1895, Rehn reported the first three cases of cancer of the bladder among aniline
workers. When additional cases of this association were identified in the next 15 years
in Germany and Switzerland, it was projected that the developing chemical industry,
with its increasing number of synthetic chemicals new to the human environment,
would bring with it a host of problems and an unhappy harvest of cancer. This prediction, in the next decades, seemed far from unreasonable when our laboratory colleagues
demonstrated carcinogenicity of literally hundreds of chemicals in animal test programs. Yet, by and large, the prophecy was not seen to be fulfilled in the first half of the
20th century. Even until recently, human chemical cancers have been relatively few and
seemingly restricted in type and number, almost as exceptions to the broad spectrum of
human cancer, viz. betanaphthylamine and benzidine bladder cancer, radium neoplasms, coal tar skin cancers, etc.

Thus, until recent years, we were faced with something of a paradox; Rehn and his
contemporaries had shown that human cancer could result from chemical industry exposure, laboratory studies indicated that the agents could be varied and numerous, yet

21

human experience had not demonstrated this to be a major problem. In recent years, the question has again been put before us in pressing terms.

Do experiences with vinyl chloride, bischloromethyl ether, chromates, etc., demonstrate that the prophecies were really correct, merely premature? We do not yet know, but the question is an important one and must be now addressed.[3]

One month later, on January 12, 1976, an informal symposium was conducted by the Environmental Study Conference of the House of Representatives, a private group with about 160 members. During the symposium, various witnesses presented their views on the same subject. They were strikingly different in tone and content from those of Dr. Selikoff. In fact, one might have suspected on listening to them that there had been an unannounced breakthrough in the knowledge of chemical cancer causation. Dr. Samuel Epstein, then director of the environmental health program at Case Western Reserve University in Cleveland, was well equipped with statistics; he told the conference that, according to experts, one out of five Americans was dying in an "epidemic" of cancer, that 70 to 90 percent of human cancers are environmentally induced, and that a majority "are due to chemical carcinogens in the environment"; he declared that most cancer, accordingly, is "preventable," and that federal agencies must move swiftly against polluting industries.[4] Consumer advocate Ralph Nader was a wrathful prophet. He assured the Congressmen that the world was clearly entering "the carcinogenic century," that this was due to the "historic abuse" of the environment by corporations which had polluted the land, air, and water, and he baptized environmental cancer "corporate cancer."[5] How, in one month, Selikoff's ignorance had turned into Epstein's statistics and Selikoff's "Paradox of Rehn" into Nader's "carcinogenic century" these gentlemen did not say.

Still another month later, however, even Epstein and Nader were made to look diffident and uncertain by Russell E. Train, then Administrator of the Environmental Protection Agency. On February 26, 1976, Train addressed an audience of newsmen at the National Press Club in Washington, D.C., and he made a startling announcement. He declared that because of the toxic chemicals in use in industry, all American lives were in peril; he said that the nation must stress "the prevention, rather than the treatment of disease," and that such industrial dangers must be dealt with before, not after, they entered the environment. He concluded his analysis of the dangers in this society with this statement:

Most Americans had no idea, until relatively recently, that they were living so dangerously. They had no idea that when they went to work in the morning, or when they ate their breakfast—that when they did the things they had to do to earn a living and keep themselves alive and well—that when they did things as ordinary, as innocent and as essential to life as eat, drink, breathe or touch they could, in fact, be laying their lives on the line. They had no idea that, without their knowledge or consent, they were often engaging in a grim game of chemical roulette whose result they would not know until many years later.

It is time we started putting chemicals to the test, not people. It is time we gave the people of this country some reason to believe that, every time they breathe or eat or drink or touch, they are not taking their life into their own hands.[6]

These last paragraphs of Train's statement were perceived as historically significant by an anonymous legal scribe and were later incorporated into the legislative history of the Toxic Substances Control Act of 1976, where they will now stand for the duration of recorded history. And the statement merits a place in history, for that was the first time that an American government official had told the entire nation that the sources of industrial danger were, for all practical purposes, beyond counting; that we were all now teetering chronically on the verge of slow physiological disintegration and death. How relevant cancer was to this prophecy, however, no one could know. Train had also told his audience of newsmen, according to the EPA report, that "of the more than 2 million known chemicals, only a few thousand have been tested for carcinogenicity. . . ." The "Paradox of Rehn" was still in force.

That same year, the "Paradox of Rehn" was dissolved. Once suspended by the "Delaney Clause" of 1959, which forbade the addition of animal carcinogens to the food supply, that "paradox" was entirely abrogated by the passage of the Toxic Substances Control Act, which was intended to protect both citizens and the environment from industrial chemicals which posed "an unreasonable risk"—the "environment" defined as the water, the air, the land, "and the interrelationship which exists among and between water, air, and land and all living things." From that time on, the American public was ceaselessly bombarded by findings of "potential" cancer threats from industrial sources. The "carcinogenic century" had indeed arrived. Unfortunately, it arrived in a form that Congress may not have anticipated: that of an unintelligible menace.

An unintelligible menace did not inspire human beings with intellectual self-confidence. It did not trigger thought at all but, rather, emotional response. The fearful were severely afflicted, trying desperately to make little lists of what was safe to eat, to drink, to do. A certain number paid no attention to the unintelligible menace once they ascertained that it was unintelligible. Others converted it into morbid humor: "Everything causes cancer." Yet others liked to imagine themselves knowledgeable, which is to say that they blindly repeated the latest formulae on the unintelligible menace from trusted sources. And, finally, some came slowly to suspect that the menace was unintelligible because those who had deposited it on the public agenda did not understand it themselves.

From the layman's point of view, the single most striking aspect of the problem of industrial carcinogenicity was the squabbling of scientists, which had rapidly acquired a ritual quality. If one scientist informed us that substance X was carcinogenic, we were likely to be informed by another that it was not. If, by chance, many scientists agreed that a substance was "potentially" carcinogenic, we soon learned that one group believed that it was inconceivably dangerous and should be banned, while another group believed that it was inconsequential and that one might breathe it, drink it, or roll around in it with impunity. And if a particularly vehement warning was tendered about the lethal properties of a substance, one needed only to wait patiently until a distinguished voice pointed out that that very substance occurs naturally in one's lights and liver. After a while the haggling seemed to fade away, and many of these ostensibly crucial issues simply vanished. Where did they go? The layman hadn't the faintest idea. He had all he could do to keep up with the latest bout of haggling.

If the layman was unable to judge a specific carcinogen, he was doomed to greater confusion if he sought answers to broader questions. On consulting Authority to ascertain the magnitude of the problem of industrially induced cancer, he learned that Authority was in a state of high confusion. If he consulted Dr. Thomas Corbett, the public health official who won an award from the Environmental Protection Agency for discovering the PBB contamination in Michigan, the layman learned that synthetic chemicals were responsible for "at least 80 percent of all cancers."[7] If he consulted Dr. John Cairns, a molecular biologist, former Director of the Cold Spring Harbor Laboratory of Quantitative Biology in New York and at that time Director of the Imperial Cancer Research Fund's Mill Hill Laboratory in London, the layman learned that "there is little evidence that the chemical industry causes much of the current total cancer incidence," and that "with the exception of lung cancer, none of the common cancers are much commoner now than they were 50 years ago. . . ."[8]

Predictions by experts were not more helpful. If one went to books to discover whether the problem was worsening or improving, one discovered works called *The Politics of Cancer* and *Cancer and Chemicals*, written respectively by Dr. Samuel Epstein and Dr. Thomas Corbett. Epstein informed us that we were in the grip of a cancer epidemic which was growing ever more serious, and Corbett declared that the epidemic would reach catastrophic proportions by the year 2000.[9] One also discovered a book by Dr. Elizabeth Whelan, then a research associate of the Harvard School of Public Health; it was called *Preventing Cancer*, and it said there was no cancer epidemic at all and that, in fact, "the overall incidence of cancer has decreased slightly since 1950."[10]

In sum, the layman who made a modest effort to inform himself quickly learned that the "carcinogenic century" was in an intellectually parlous state. It had acquired all the characteristics of a social science convention and was hopelessly divided into competing theoretical and ideological camps. And a little more research indicated that it had been thus from the very beginning, that the problem had grown steadily worse, and that scientists of every persuasion were quietly desperate about it.

The ideologization of the field became visible to the public in 1975–1976, the very period in which Ralph Nader and Dr. Samuel Epstein were seeking to convince Congressmen that our political and economic institutions were preventing proper recognition of the carcinogen problem and Russell Train was announcing that all Americans were risking their lives every time they breathed, ate, drank, or touched. In 1975, Ralph Nader's Center for the Study of Responsive Law decided to conduct an investigation into the scientific objectivity of the National Academy of Sciences, the loftiest body of scientists in America. The investigation was conducted by Phillip Boffey, then a young writer for *Science* magazine. The book he wrote was called *The Brain Bank of America: An Inquiry into the Politics of Science.* Primarily on the basis of interviews conducted with critics and staff, with some participants in academy activities, and on the basis of analyses of academy membership and academy studies, Boffey charged the academy and its president, Philip Handler, with being too frequently biased in favor of government policy and industrial interests. The broadest conclusions of the Nader-sponsored study, however, transcended the academy; Boffey warned that most public policy decisions on scientific issues emanating from "advisory groups" were not objective:

The public tends to assume that these expert advisers dispense some sort of objective truth, the "right" answer to the problem under consideration. But such implicit trust is misplaced. There are relatively few public policy questions whose answers are purely technical. In almost all cases, an element of informed judgment is required, and what comes out strutting as "objective" wisdom is actually the subjective opinion of those who prepared the advice.[11]

Three years later, in 1978, after Nader's values had triumphed on a variety of political and legal fronts, after President Jimmy Carter had professed himself an admirer of Nader and had hired a group of Nader lieutenants for top regulatory positions, and after Boffey himself had become an editor of the *New York Times*, Philip Handler, the President of the National Academy of Sciences, made a startlingly similar observation about the subjective nature of public policy on scientific issues:

We have seen a spate of regulations and there are more in the offing. Each one of them, it seems to me, is very well intentioned. Each of them seemingly is designed to protect us from some hazard, small or large, and perhaps one could live with any one of them. The sum of them constitutes a failure of nerve, a desire to stop our technological progress.... In some aspects of these debates, like that on nuclear power, the arguments which have been made by quite respectable, successful competent scientists become suffused with an ideology which makes it difficult for the rest of us to know where the scientific argument ceases and the ideology begins.[12]

In 1978, David L. Sills of the Social Science Research Council made yet another such statement to the annual meeting of the American Association for the Advancement of Science. He was describing the specific ideological debates that pertained to the "environmental movement":

... the environmental movement is a part of—or at least closely related to—two other contemporary movements: the *citizens movement,* a term used broadly to refer to such activities as the consumer movement, the access-to-information movement, Naderism, etc. and the *antiscience/antitechnology movement,* which attracts people who feel that technology and complexity have gotten out of control....
    Many of the debates that characterize the environmental movement—perhaps any social movement—are on the surface "factual" or "technical" in nature. But closer inspection often reveals them to be debates over values. However, scientists are unsure over how to debate about values—indeed, how to measure or choose between values. So they use the language of facts and technology to express their ideological positions. (I should note that the term "ideology" is used neutrally here; we all act and speak out of ideological convictions.) ...
    The values that intrude into environmental debates are generally related to preferences concerning an ideal (or at least an improved) society.[13]

Comparable statements were already on the record from Paul Ehrlich and Anne H. Ehrlich of Stanford University, and from John P. Holdren of the University of California, Berkeley. In the 1977 edition of their textbook *Ecoscience* they observed that some method was required to allow the public and makers of policy to differentiate the moral and political opinions of scientists from their scientific statements:

One suggestion for opening up the process of ethical decision-making in science has been put forward by physicist Arthur Kantrowitz. He proposed that in science policy disputes . . . the technical aspects of the cases be, in essence, tried in a scientific court. The first step would be to separate the scientific from the moral and political questions. . . . Once the separation had been accomplished, then advocates of the different scientific points of view would "try" them before scientific judges. . . .

In many cases today, disputes concern the negative direct or indirect effects of technology on humanity or on the ecosphere. The split within the scientific community on this is deep and bitter, and finding judges satisfactory to both technologists and environmentalists (for want of better terms) might often prove exceedingly difficult.

In spite of the difficulties, we support Kantrowitz's proposal for the test establishment of an institution for making scientific judgments as described above. The present methods of making such judgments are so bad that any promising alternative or modification deserves a chance.[14]

As these statements clearly reveal, the central problem for the layman, as well as for the scientist, was not the question of which ideological faction to support, but rather the fact that there was no longer a way to differentiate between ideology and science. Clearly, in a situation where the President of the National Academy of Sciences on the one hand and ecologist Paul Ehrlich on the other were frequently unable to tell where science left off and politics began, the layman was totally helpless. Or, rather, he was totally helpless if he expected the participants in this imbroglio to clarify it for him. In fact, he had only two rational choices: He could either believe nothing at all, or he could seek to clarify the situation for himself.

In 1978, I concluded that there was a way to arrive at a judgment of the problem of carcinogenicity in particular. I could stage an end run around public policy, so to speak, and go to the scientific literature to discover what scientists had reported, and over what they were in conflict, *before* any question of public policy had arisen. I could also check on the selective processes of American public policy by comparing the pattern of information I had been receiving from the government and press with the pattern of information that existed in the literature. I knew I could never assess any particular carcinogen, of course, but I certainly could discover what scientists were saying to their peers before they ever got to the stage of seeking to convey their views to the public. Once I was within the ivory tower itself, I quickly learned that the discussions were extraordinarily different from the public policy wrangling, and infinitely more illuminating. This book is a report on what I learned from just such a project. I concentrated on the years that immediately preceded and immediately followed the passage of the Toxic Substances Control Act, and eventually the trail led me to discoveries made fifty years ago. I learned that if one does not know what happened in the past, one cannot understand what is happening now, and one will not understand what happens in the future.

. . .

One must begin the analytic process by identifying the ideological conflict itself, both because it is a barricade against understanding and because the untangling of it leads directly to the context in which the problem of industrially caused cancer must be set. What is that ideological conflict? The people quoted above all named it in their own ways. Nader and Boffey, before the Toxic Substances Control Act was passed, saw the problem as the tendency of "establishment" scientists to resist evidence that American industry was producing dangerous and deadly substances. Handler, the President of the National Academy of Sciences, identified the problem as the desire by unidentified people "to stop our technological progress." Sills introduced half the movements of the 1960s and 1970s into the picture, but later labeled the movement that was generating debate as "environmentalism" and linked it to the "antiscience/antitechnology movement." And the Ehrlichs and Holden stated the division clearly: They said a "deep and bitter" split existed within the scientific community and between "technologists and environmentalists (for want of better terms)."

It is not particularly difficult to grasp one side of this ideological battle. Whether one describes them as protective of industry, in favor of technological progress, in favor of science and technology, or as "technologists," it is clear that some scientists are sympathetic to industrial civilization, wish to see it flourish, and presumably are very cautious about indicting any industrial substance, product, or process as a cause of human disease. But what, precisely, is the other side? It is by no means clear what an "antiscience/antitechnology" position is, *if held by a scientist.* And "environmentalism" is not clear at all. It may, in fact, be the most meaningless term in common use in America today, for it applies to most of the citizens in the country. If an environmentalist is someone who wants pure drinking water, sparkling rivers, fresh air, and uncontaminated food and who resists the notion of erecting factories and casinos on the brink of the Grand Canyon, then most Americans are environmentalists. If an environmentalist is one who is moved by the great whales and their "songs" and wants to protect winsome baby seals, then again, great numbers of Americans are environmentalists. If an environmentalist is one who would like to see industrial cancer vanish from the earth, then all Americans are environmentalists.[15] But one may be all these kinds of environmentalist and be in favor of "science and technology" and industrial civilization. Who then is the opposition? Of whom was Ehrlich speaking when he referred to environmentalists?

When one conducts a search for the identity of these "environmentalists," one discovers why Paul Ehrlich had such difficulties in naming this group. Those citizens who were concerned over the industrial damage to biological life were something more than the word "environmentalist" conveys—so incredibly much more that it will take an entire chapter to describe it. In all cases, these "environmentalists" were concerned with problems that had essentially the same attributes as those of the problem of industrially caused cancer: The problems were all of catastrophic proportions; they were all being caused by industry; and all threatened to destroy life on a huge scale. And the best way to understand what these "environmentalists" were saying about these problems, and what was so extraordinary about what they were saying, is to read them. Here are the voices of "environmentalists" who made their views known over a period of almost twenty years:

Not war, but a plethora of man-made things . . . is threatening to strangle us, suffocate us, bury us, in the debris and by-products of our technologically inventive and irresponsible age.[16]

> —Margaret Mead, anthropologist,
> in a review of Rachel Carson's
> *Silent Spring*, 1962

As a biologist, I have reached this conclusion: we have come to a turning point in the human habitation of the earth. The environment is a complex, subtly balanced system, and it is this integrated whole which receives the impact of all the separate insults inflicted by pollutants. Never before in the history of this planet has its thin life supporting surface been subjected to such diverse, novel, and potent agents. *I* believe that the cumulative effects of these pollutants, their interactions and amplification, can be fatal to the complex fabric of the biosphere. And, because man is, after all, a dependent part of this system, I believe that continued pollution of the earth, if unchecked, will eventually destroy the fitness of this planet as a place for human life.[17]

> —Barry Commoner, biologist, 1963

. . . surely no creature other than man has ever managed to foul its nest in such short order. . . . More science and more technology are not going to get us out of the present ecologic crisis until we find a new religion, or rethink our old one. The beatniks, who are the basic revolutionaries of our time, show a sound instinct in their affinity for Zen Buddhism, which conceives of the man-nature relationship as very nearly the mirror image of the Christian view.[18]

> —Lynn White, historian, 1967

To me it seems possible that the new amount of technological power let loose in an overcrowded world may overload any system we might devise for its control; the possibility of a complete and apocalyptic end of civilization cannot be dismissed as a morbid fantasy.[19]

> —Don K. Price, Dean of the John F. Kennedy
> School of Government, Harvard University;
> former President, AAAS, 1969

Scientists of all kinds are warning us most urgently that we are using our technology disastrously, eating up all the natural resources of the earth . . . altering the biochemical balances of the soil, spawning unbelievable amounts of detergent froth which will eventually engulf cities, overpopulating ourselves because of the success of medicine, and thus winning our war against nature in such a way as to defeat ourselves completely.[20]

> —Alan Watts, philosopher, 1969

Nothing less than a profound re-orientation of our vaunted technological "way of life" will save this planet from becoming a lifeless desert. . . . For its effective salvation mankind will need to undergo something like a spontaneous religious conversion: one that will replace the mechanical world picture with an organic world picture, and give to the human personality, as the highest known manifestation of life, the precedence it now gives to its machines and computers.[21]

—Lewis Mumford, *The Myth of the Machine*, 1970

... man-made changes in the biosphere threaten the integrity of the life-support system essential for the survival of human life. ... I believe that the present threat to the life-support system demands changes in values, institutions, and societal goals. ...[22]

—Robert Disch, editor,
The Ecological Conscience,
1970

The natural conditions of human health and safety are being subjected to complex and savage assaults. ... They are now threatening the physiological integrity of our citizens. ... During the past decade, this country has begun to show that it can destroy itself inadvertently from within.[23]

—Ralph Nader, 1970

The institutions we have created are destroying the liveability of the whole world; and the young people know it. They may not articulate it well, but they sense it. They feel it.[24]

—Senator Gaylord Nelson, 1970

Modern society is literally undoing the work of organic evolution. If this process continues unabated, the earth may be reduced to a level of biotic simplicity where humanity ... will no longer be able to sustain itself as a viable animal species. ... This centuries-long tendency finds its most exacerbating development in modern capitalism: a social order that is orchestrated entirely by the maxim "Production for the sake of production". ... The plundering of the human spirit by the market place is paralleled by the plundering of the earth by capital.[25]

—Murray Bookchin,
Ramparts, 1970

Many people ... are concluding on the basis of mounting and reasonably objective evidence that the length of life of the biosphere as an inhabitable region for organisms is to be measured in decades rather than in hundreds of millions of years. This is entirely the fault of our own species.[26]

—G. Evelyn Hutchinson, biologist, 1970

Responsible scientific opinion holds that, unless present trends are not merely halted but reversed, there will be not more than 35 to 100 more years to the end of all human life on earth.[27]

—Lee Loevinger, Commissioner of the
Federal Communication Commission, 1970

The ecology of Earth's life-support system is disintegrating.[28]

—Michael McCloskey, Executive Director, Sierra Club, 1970

... it is clear that the ravaging and raping of the earth that has gone on must stop. ... Population pressures mount; littering and pollution remain a scourge; the powerful lobbies seem bent on destroying our last few sanctuaries.

For things to change, there must be a spiritual awakening. Our people—young and old—must become truly activist—and aggressively so—if we and the biosphere on which we depend are to survive.[29]

—Justice William O. Douglas, 1972

Relentlessly accumulating evidence suggests that human life on the planet is headed for a catastrophe. Indeed, several disasters are possible, and if we avert one, we will be caught by another. At present rates of population growth, another century will put 40 billion people on Earth, too many to feed. If industrial production grows at present rates during the next century, resource requirements will multiply by a thousand. And energy emission, some scientists say, will over a longer period of time raise Earth's temperature to a level unsuitable for human habitation. All this assumes that a nuclear catastrophe does not spare us the long anguish of degeneration.[30]

—Charles Lindblom, economist, Yale University, 1977

Modern science . . . made man the master of cosmic forces and speeds that are out of proportion to his own. This made all previous thinking and institutions antiquated and placed man on a crossroads, one of which leads to wealth and health while the other leads to self-destruction. . . .

We either adapt to the new situation, revamp our thinking and human relations, exchange our outdated ideas of glory, force, domination and exploitation for mutual understanding, respect, help and collaboration, or else perish.

At present we are heading for extinction and who will shed tears for us? Who regrets the dinosaur?[31]

—Albert Szent-Györgyi, Nobel laureate in biochemistry, 1975

In spite of all its frightening groans and rattles, the great world machine can still be made to work, but not unless it comes to be accepted that the long-term welfare of human beings cannot be secured by policies that promote the interests of some people at the expense of others or even the interests of mankind at the expense of other living things. The *unity* of nature is not a slogan but a principle to the truth of which all natural processes bear witness. The lesson has been learnt too late to save some living creatures, but there may just be time to save the rest of us.[32] [Stress in original]

—P. B. Medawar, Nobel laureate in biology, 1977

These, as the reader will recognize, are the voices of an intellectual movement that surged through the educated classes in the United States and other countries in the late 1960s and the first half of the 1970s, and that continues to this day. It is certainly the movement that launched the national concern for the "environment." But the term "environmental" is a misnomer for this movement, since it had many other attributes which are not communicated by that concept, and which, indeed, are obliterated by it. As the quotations reveal, there were some very unusual and non-"environmental" themes running through the thought of this movement. There was an obvious element of anger, even of scorn, directed against several targets. One was clearly America, the America that was "destroying itself," and the American "institutions" which were "destroying the liveability of the whole world." Another target was the constellation of science, technology, industrial production, the marketplace, and capitalism. Yet another target was "Man," for it was his innovative intelligence, his productivity, his appetite for material goods, and his numbers that were responsible for this destruction. A final target was "Man's" immorality: It was "Man's" own "fault" that he was destroying life on earth, including his own. And if "Man" wanted to survive, he would have to undergo—and *immediately*—an intellectual, spiritual, moral, and political conversion. Salvation was promised to "Man" if he renounced his evil ways; annihilation was guaranteed if he did not. *This was not just "environmentalism"—this was the voice of the apocalypse in new secular attire.*

It is apparent from this why Paul Ehrlich found it so difficult to define "environmentalists." In this book, those who hold such views will not be called "environmentalists," they will be called "apocalyptics"—and as a group, they will be called "the apocalyptic movement." It is also apparent from both the style and substance of these statements that there was nothing extraordinary about Ralph Nader's declamations against "corporate cancer" or his prophecy of a "carcinogenic century," or about Russell Train's vision of nationwide physiological disintegration caused by industrial chemicals. They were entirely consistent with the apocalyptic mode of the movement.

It is unreasonable, however, to bump into an apocalyptic movement by accident and say nothing further about it. An apocalyptic movement is not the sort of thing one overlooks, particularly when it explodes among the most sophisticated and secular class in America. There is one aspect of this particular apocalyptic movement, furthermore, which is unlike any other that has ever existed in history: It was spearheaded by scientists. The laymen who were predicting the apocalypse were, with no exception, relying on information that had been given to them by scientists. It was "environmental" scientists alone who had granted intellectual legitimacy to the apocalypse, and since in this book we are concerned with one branch of this science, the science of "environmental cancer," it is the scientists we must look at most closely. First we will listen to their apocalyptic philosophy and the scientific conclusions on which that philosophy is based. And then we will look at their data. On the basis of both, we will be in a far better position to assess the apocalyptic movement, its acceptance by educated laymen, and the effects that acceptance had on the nation—and ultimately, on the problem of industrially caused cancer.

Here, then, is a close look at the views of five leading apocalyptic scientists—Rachel Carson, Paul Ehrlich, Barry Commoner, René Dubos, and George Wald—as well as those of a group of scientists at MIT who conducted a study for the Club of Rome. They will be considered in the order of their greatest impact on the country—determined, in all but two cases, by the dates of their best-selling books.

· · ·

RACHEL CARSON: 1962

The first apocalyptic of national importance was Rachel Carson, a biologist who worked at the Fish and Wildlife Service, and whose perspective was that formed by ecology. Her book *Silent Spring* was written with a lyrical passion, was read by millions, and is still a living classic. In it Carson warned that man might destroy the biosphere and himself along with it. Although Carson was not the first to reach this conclusion—a group of ecologists had preceded her— she was the first to present this thesis to the broad national audience. Standing alone on a page, at the opening of her book, is a quotation from Albert

Schweitzer: "Man has lost the capacity to foresee and to forestall. He will end by destroying the earth."[33] Carson opened her own text with an apocalyptic fantasy. Her first chapter was a fable, and it portrayed the sudden eerie disappearance of the living creatures of earth. Everywhere, she wrote, was the sign of death. People grew ill. The birds vanished. Hens ceased to have chicks. Baby pigs died. There were no bees to pollinate the apple blossoms. The fish in the streams had died. It had not been a supernatural event, said Carson: It had been done by man.[34]

Man had done it, presumably, by spraying with pesticides. Carson had planned out her fable to symbolize the poisoning of the food chain on which human life depends. Without birds, without fish, without pollination by insects, without the reproduction of livestock, man would die. And when all were poisoned, man too would die of poison. Carson portrayed only the beginning illness of the human race. Unlike some who were to follow her, she delicately omitted the corpses. But they were there by implication. That fable, Carson warned, might readily become reality.

Although Carson's primary focus was ecological, she clearly had a political perspective on the problems she was describing. She attributed the cause of this fantasied catastrophe to our profit-making economic system. She criticized salesmanship and advertising, "the soft sell and the hidden persuaders" which, she said, manipulated and pressured people into purchasing and using dangerous poisons. She held industry responsible for the fact that most people did not read the warnings printed on the poison containers.[35] She also condemned the regulatory agencies as tacit protectors of industry, and charged them with providing false reassurances of safety to the public.[36] She made these points strongly, but briefly. She preferred, on the whole, to weave a condemning moral perspective into chapter after chapter in which she listed the lethal products of human intelligence. Thus, she said, industry was producing an unbroken chain of "evil" and death. The chief damage, she said, was being done by two "sinister" partners: man-made radiation and man-made chemicals, both of which were "unnatural" and "synthetic" creations, and were rendering toxic the air, the water, and the soil.[37] Chemicals in particular were threats to life, and she warned that all lives were now in peril. For the first time since man had been on earth, she said, he was exposed to hazardous chemicals from the moment he emerged from the womb to the moment of death.[38]

The chemicals on which Carson focused most extensively were pesticides. She reported on a series of extremely toxic pesticides and relayed a great many reports of poisoned fish, poisoned birds, poisoned animals, and poisoned men. Her greatest concern was about DDT, which, she said, had the "sinister" attribute of passing through all the links of the food chain, magnifying in concentration as it moved, and culminating in the greatest intensity in man.[39] Another important target of her attack was the American food supply. We were, said Carson, being progressively poisoned by the food from farm, market, and grocery, which had been contaminated by chemical pesticides, by additives and preservatives, all of which were interacting in unknown ways in our bodies. Because of this, she said, it was futile to speak of safe amounts of any one toxic substance; it was this that constituted the great deception of the regulatory agencies.[40] She compared the situation of all Americans to that of victims of the Borgias.[41]

Carson offered a political solution to the technological problem she had raised; she indicated that more regulation of industry was needed. She did not call for the banning of all toxic agents and was careful to say, several times, that she understood the need for pest control. It was not her view, she said, that chemical insecticides should be abolished.[42] Nor did she deny that there was an insect problem in need of control. Her point, she said, was that the means of control must be so selected that they do not kill man as well as insect.[43] Nonetheless, Carson was imbued with a profoundly ecological perspective and bore a deep animus against modern technology. She detested the concept of man's mastery of nature, declaring it an illusion of false pride and a reflection of biological and philosophical primitivism.[44] The bulk of her book was a passionate denunciation of the life-destroying evils of modern industrial technology.

Toward the end of her book, she warned once again, this time indirectly, that technology could wipe out the entire human race in twenty-odd years. She quoted one scientist, Dr. David Price of the U.S. Public Health Service, as expressing the dread that some man-made substance might so contaminate the environment as to make man as obsolete as the dinosaur. And what was particularly frightening, he said, referring to a long latency disease—although he did not name cancer—was that this annihilation of the species might be determined some twenty years before a symptom had appeared.[45]

The influence of Carson on our era can hardly be overstated. Russell Train's warning that all Americans were on the verge of destruction by toxic and carcinogenic chemicals was a simple rewrite of Rachel Carson, and the Toxic Substances Control Act under which we live today is a monument to her thought.

PAUL EHRLICH: 1968

Paul Ehrlich was the second apocalyptic to make a thunderous impact on the public. An entomologist and ecologist, and a student of population theory, he burst upon the scene in 1968 with an extraordinary announcement. In at least nine years, he said—perhaps in the early 1970s, but surely in the early 1980s—there would be worldwide death and famine on a scale previously unimaginable.[46] Not only was industrial technology endangering biological life on earth, he warned, but man himself had so overpopulated the planet that nature herself would eliminate him, if man did not act first. Ehrlich's thesis appeared in a gigantic best-seller called *The Population Bomb: Population Control or Race to Oblivion?*, jointly published by the Sierra Club and Ballantine Books, and prefaced by David Brower, then President of the Sierra Club and one of the most prestigious conservationists in the country.

The world's population, warned Ehrlich, was now doubling every thirty-seven years: "If growth continued at that rate for about 900 years, there would be some 60,000,000,000,000,000 people on the face of the earth. Sixty million billion people. This is about 100 persons for each square yard of the Earth's

surface, land and sea."[47] This, however, was absurd, he said, because man
would die long before such a thing occurred. In fact, the starvation and death
of huge masses of men was now imminent, because population growth was far
exceeding the rate of production of food. In 1966, Ehrlich reported, only ten
countries were growing more food than they consumed: the United States,
Canada, Australia, Argentina, France, New Zealand, Burma, Thailand, Ru-
mania, and South Africa. China, India, and Russia were unable to feed themselves without imports. Three countries alone were keeping much of the world
fed—the United States produced more than half of the surplus, and most of the
rest came from Canada and Australia.[48] Ehrlich did not conclude from this that
high-technology agriculture under capitalism was the solution; he concluded,
rather, that "mankind" had been horrifyingly defeated in the battle against
hunger.[49]

The population explosion, however, was only one of Ehrlich's themes; his
second was an attack on the conventional belief that technology could solve the
problem. According to Ehrlich, modern technological agriculture with its pesticides and fertilizers was destroying the soil; and modern technology, generally, was introducing lethal poisons and carcinogens into the food chains. He
recapitulated the essence of Carson's message to the world and further illustrated his thesis with several new examples of industrial threats to the biosphere—e.g., the increases in the carbon dioxide level because of combustion
of fossil fuels threatened us with a greenhouse effect, the SST was damaging
the atmosphere, and Lake Erie was dead.[50] After completing his list of examples, he traced the "causal chain of the deterioration" to its source: There were,
he said, too many factories, too many machines—above all, "too many people."[51] In the last analysis, for Ehrlich the sheer number of people on earth was
the root source of the destruction. Man himself was a corrupter and defiler of
the biosphere.

Ehrlich proposed political solutions to those problems with abandon. He
compared the growth of population to cancer and demanded surgery. A cancer,
he said, was "an uncontrolled multiplication of cells"; the population explosion, he said, was "an uncontrolled multiplication of people." He called for
"the cutting out of the cancer," an "operation," he said, that would require
"many apparently brutal and heartless decisions."[52] Government, he said, had
to be the surgeon. Ehrlich called for the creation of a "powerful government
agency" which would research and impose such solutions as "compulsory birth
regulation," "the addition of temporary sterilants to water supplies or staple
food," "financial rewards and penalties designed to discourage reproduction,"
"luxury taxes . . . placed on layettes, cribs, diapers, diaper services."[53] The critical goal, he said, was reducing the population growth rate to zero, and later,
reducing the population levels.[54] As for foreign policy, Ehrlich said, continuing
to advocate surgery, the proper principle in distributing food abroad was
"triage." Countries which had resources should not be given food; countries
which could manage to survive if they got aid should be given food; but countries like India, whose population problems were hopeless, should be given no
food.[55] How such "apparently brutal" goals were to be achieved without actual
brutality, Ehrlich has never said.

As for man's technological destruction of the biosphere, said Ehrlich, there had to be a spiritual revolution in our relationship with nature in order to save the earth. He shared Carson's revulsion against the tradition of man's dominance over nature and saw it as the root of the imminent ecological catastrophe. He also agreed with medieval historian Lynn White, who traced the concept of man's mastery over nature to the Judeo-Christian tradition and, like White, said that the "hippie movement, which was committed to Zen Buddhism, sexual love and contempt for wealth, had an answer, if not the only answer."[56] In 1968, Ehrlich doubted that science and technology could solve the ecological crisis. He has ceased to be tentative about this. He teaches at Stanford University, and the 1977 edition of his 1,000-page textbook *Ecoscience*, written with Anne H. Ehrlich, also of Stanford, and John P. Holdren of the University of California at Berkeley, advocates "zero economic growth," adding that the wealth should be equitably redistributed.[57] He elaborated elsewhere: "What economic growth there is to be in the future should be concentrated on the poor countries and carefully controlled and directed there."[58] In 1977, Ehrlich was quoted by CBS science reporter Fred Warshofsky as saying: "There is no, I repeat, no conceivable technological solution to the problems we face."[59]

Ehrlich, who is intensely political but whose politics can only be described as ecological totalitarianism (for want of a better term), played a powerful role in feeding the apocalyptic fever which was building in the country. He almost single-handedly launched the "Zero Population Growth" movement and convinced many in the upper middle class that it was immoral to have children. "Man," above all, was Ehrlich's enemy. He became well known in the youth movements of the 1960s for his extraordinarily lurid and detailed "scenarios" of the deaths of millions of people which appeared in *The Population Bomb* and also in *Ramparts* magazine in September 1969, under the title "Eco-Catastrophe!" That issue of *Ramparts*, published by young radicals, was a pure apocalyptic document. Its cover was a photograph of a tombstone standing in a limitless expanse of sand. The tombstone was engraved:

THE OCEANS

Born: Circa
3,500,000,000 B.C.
Died: 1979 A.D.

"The Lord Gave,
and Man Hath Taken
Away, Cursed Be the
Name of Man."

BARRY COMMONER: 1969

By 1969, the ecological "crisis" was part of the repertoire of many of those who were considered enlightened. Indeed, Senator Edmund Muskie, a major Democratic Party contender for the next presidential nomination, had made the apocalypse his own. He launched a series of Senate hearings to investigate the charge that American industrial technology was destroying life on earth; and one of his most startling witnesses was biologist Barry Commoner of Washington University in St. Louis. Commoner had been predicting environmental disaster ever since the early 1960s, and because he was a scientist he had aroused widespread interest. But this was his first appearance in America's most prestigious political forum. He testified before Muskie, accompanied by W. H. Ferry, Vice-President of the Center for the Study of Democratic Institutions, who was also an apocalyptic.[60] Their testimony was reported in the *New York Times* of April 28, 1969, under the headline "Technology and Environment: Senators Hear Gloomy Appraisals." The word "gloomy" did not quite capture the revolutionary nature of their testimony, in either its scientific or its political dimension. Here is how the reporter, Robert H. Phelps, presented the story quite accurately:

Is the United States set on an irreversible course that will destroy the natural base on which it has built the highest standard of living in the world?

This is one of the questions that the Senate Subcommittee on Intergovernmental Affairs, headed by Senator Edmund S. Muskie, has been looking into for months. While at least another round of hearings is scheduled, the answers so far are pessimistic.

The gloomiest appraisals of all came last week from Barry Commoner, director of the Center for the Biology of Natural Systems, at Washington University in St. Louis, and W. H. Ferry, vice-president of the Center for the Study of Democratic Institutions, Santa Barbara, Calif.

Both witnesses said that nothing less than a change in the political and social system, including revision of the Constitution, was necessary to save the country from destroying its natural environment.

Both agreed, too, that the peril came from uncontrolled technology. In the process of creating new goods and services, they said, technology is destroying the country's "capital" of land, water and other resources as well as injuring people.

Dr. Commoner said, "Our present system of technology is not merely consuming this capital, but threatening—probably within the next 50 years—to destroy it irreparably."

Mr. Ferry . . . said, "We may have passed the point of no return in some areas."

Dr. Commoner cited the success of inorganic fertilizers, high-compression automobile engines and insecticides as examples of "progress" that damages the environment. . . .

Referring to Dr. Commoner's testimony, Mr. Ferry asked: "What good will color television in every room and outposts on the moon be to the grandchildren, if their air is unbreathable, their water undrinkable and their dwellings half buried in their own debris? . . .

Mr. Ferry offered what he called a "wildly absurd" proposal for a two-year moratorium on most technological research and innovation. He suggested creation of an international body to halt pollution of the oceans and a national ecological authority with wide powers over all major construction and technological projects.

Noting that such proposals might be unconstitutional, Mr. Ferry suggested that the Constitution be completely revised. . . .

Agreeing with Mr. Ferry, Dr. Commoner said . . . the problems are so profound that they call for "not a new legislative base, but a new constitutional one."

In response, Senator Muskie, referring to technology as "the modern Trojan Horse," told Dr. Commoner and Mr. Ferry that their proposals, even if they served no other purpose, would "open a lot of eyes that are still closed to the problem."

This news story reveals the degree to which apocalyptic thought had penetrated the highest levels of the political culture by 1969. While Senator Muskie was careful to disassociate himself from proposals for "revising" the Constitution, he nonetheless had given Commoner and Ferry one of the most important political platforms in the land and praised their testimony as enlightening.

Commoner's conviction that the Constitution stood in the way of solutions to ecological problems was paralleled by his conviction that "our system of production" stood in the way of such solutions. That same year, he was invited to contribute a paper for the 13th National Conference of the U.S. National Commission for UNESCO. The conclusion of a lengthy analysis of the same general problems he was discussing above can be cited here:

Our technology is enormously successful in producing material goods, but too often is disastrously incompatible with the natural environmental systems that support not only human life, but technology itself. Moreover, these technologies are now so massively embedded in our system of industrial and agricultural production that any effort to make them conform to the demands of the environment will involve serious economic dislocations. If, as I believe, environmental pollution is a sign of major incompatibilities between our system of production and the environmental system that supports it, then, if we are to survive, we must successfully confront these economic obligations, however severe and challenging to our social concepts they may be.[61]

It was not until 1976, in a book entitled *The Poverty of Power,* that Commoner explicitly identified the political solution he envisioned. To survive, he said, our society would have to repudiate its present productive system and substitute a system organized in harmony with the global ecosystem using the second law of thermodynamics as its guiding standard: ". . . it may be time to view the faults of the U.S. capitalist economic system," he wrote, "from the vantage point of a socialist alternative."[62]

In 1978, Commoner was identified by Rae Goodell in an MIT study of scientists who dominated the media as a "guerrilla" and one of the most "visible scientists" in the country.[63] And in 1979, he abandoned his primary identity as a scientist and founded a new leftist party in the United States, called the Citizens Party, which would direct its efforts to achieving greater government control of industry in the name of the environment. In 1980, he ran for President, as the candidate of that party.

RENÉ DUBOS: 1972

Unlike his predecessors in this story, René Dubos entered the apocalyptic-ecological movement with an entirely different perspective. A microbiologist and experimental pathologist who had worked at the Rockefeller University for forty-four years. Dubos was a pure scientist with an unimpeachable institutional affiliation. He was also one other thing: a strong mystic and a utopian theorist. He may, in the long run, have been the most continuously powerful influence in the apocalyptic movement. The only reason, in fact, for assigning him to the year 1972 is that after almost a decade of influencing evolving apocalyptic thought within the United States itself, this mystic bacteriologist culminated his career in 1972 by weaving a strand of his apocalyptic vision into the very fabric of American foreign policy.

Dubos is so prolific and gifted a writer—he won a Pulitzer Prize for his book *So Human an Animal* in 1967—that to summarize all of his views here is not possible. But one can isolate the specifically apocalyptic elements in his thinking. By the early 1960s, Dubos had concluded that biological life was threatened by modern technology. In his book *Man Adapting,* published in 1965, he declared that man's biological and psychological characteristics were essentially unchangeable because they had been inscribed in his genetic code in the course of evolution and that there were stringent limits to his adaptive capacity.[64] In a later essay called "The Limits of Adaptability" he elaborated on this idea and described man as the victim of his own technological development: Man, he said, could adapt to his "technological environment" only to the degree that adaptive mechanisms are "potentially" inscribed in his genetic code. It could almost be taken "for granted," he said, that such evolutionary adaptive mechanisms had not developed to permit man to cope with the noises of modern machinery and with the synthetic substances that now entered his food, water, and air. According to Dubos, the limits of technological development had to be determined by man's "potential" genetic nature.[65]

By 1969, Dubos took it "for granted" that the time for imposing those limits had come and declared that they would result in new social and economic systems based on an arrest of growth. In order to "survive," he said, man would have to develop a new social and economic system, which he described as a "steady state formula," a formula which was entirely different from the "philosophy of endless quantitative growth" which had dominated Western civilization. His statement stands as a thematic quote at the head of a chapter in *Ecoscience* by Ehrlich, Ehrlich, and Holdren.[66]

By 1972, Dubos was convinced that technological solutions to the ecological problems were futile and that for most fundamental human purposes, "technological magic" was not much more useful than "primitive magic."[67] In that same year, he published *A God Within,* an eloquent plea to mankind to abandon "Faustian Civilization" for "Arcadian Life"—a utopian vision of a society guided by a "theology of the earth" in which society would be organized to conform with the ecosystem and in which man would serve as the steward of the earth. He passionately attacked the Western concept that man was the "master" of nature as an expression of "the criminal conceit" that nature existed above all as a source of materials to fulfill human needs. It was, he said, "a perversion" which would, if continued, "become a fatal disease of technological societies."[68] Over and over, Dubos issued warnings that Western society, based on science, technology, and economic growth—"the Faustian way of individual life"—was careening toward "racial death."[69] And he declared it "certain" that economic and technologic growth "would lead to collective suicide."[70]

As Dubos acquired increasing renown for his views, he, like Barry Commoner, was given an opportunity to influence the international intelligentsia of the United Nations. The role offered to Dubos, however, was far more significant. He was asked by Maurice F. Strong, Secretary General of the United Nations Conference on the Human Environment, to prepare the "conceptual framework" for the Stockholm Conference on the Environment in June 1972. It was to be a study of global environmental problems. Dubos accepted the charge, and shortly thereafter the British economist Barbara Ward (Lady Jackson), then Albert Schweitzer Professor of International Economic Development at Columbia University, was chosen to be his coauthor.[71] If Maurice Strong's intention was to produce an objective study of global environmental problems, it was a remarkable choice of authors, for not only was René Dubos a well-known apocalyptic who since 1969 had advocated the cessation of technical and economic growth in the advanced industrial states, but Barbara Ward, too, was an apocalyptic who advocated the redistribution of the wealth of the advanced industrial states to the underdeveloped countries. Together, their ideas added up to an explosive political position—the precise equivalent on the international front of Paul Ehrlich's position on the domestic front. That position emerged forcefully in the study itself, later published under the title *Only One Earth: The Care and Maintenance of a Small Planet.* The scientific aspect of the study pertaining to the global damage caused by industrialization will be described later. Here, it is rather the philosophy communicated by the authors in the course of writing the study that is relevant.

Within the first dozen pages of the study, Dubos warned that "technological man" was on a course that could destroy "the natural system" of this planet on which his existence depended.[72] He stressed two concepts: the unity of life and its acute fragility. Life, he said, was one vast food chain. He warned that even the "sudden removal of one small component in a food chain" could have tragic effects; that "the unities of dynamic balance we call ecosystems cannot survive indefinite overloading or mistreatment"; and that there were innumerable "potential paths towards points of irreversible no return." He declared that "the deliberate equilibrium" of these ecosystems might be imperiled by almost anything—by natural disturbances like a volcanic eruption or an ice age, or by man-made disturbances: "A new species introduced, a chemical balance upset. . . ." The lessons learned from the study of the universe and of earth, he said, teach us how complex are these natural systems and how vulnerable their "egg-shell delicacy."[73]

This "unity" and "egg-shell delicacy" proved, Dubos declared, that the moral teachings of "the philosophers"—by which he clearly meant Eastern philosophers—were actually scientific truths. They had taught us that "we were one, part of a greater unity which transcends our local drives and needs." Their condemnations of aggression and violence, which were paths to death, were actually "factual descriptions" of the workings of the universe.[74]

Dubos, accordingly, condemned "arrogant and unheeding power" in Western man and cited warnings against such power in Western tradition itself:

For the Greeks, it is Prometheus, stealer of fire, who is chained to the rock. Nemesis in the shape of shrieking, destroying harpies follows the footsteps of the overmighty. In the Bible, it is the proud who are put down from their seats; the exalted are those of humble spirit. At the very beginnings of the scientific age, in the Faustian legend, it is the man of science who sells his soul to secure all knowledge and all power.[75]

It was science, said this man of science, that was the source of the evil.

Finally came Dubos' own prophecy: "If man continues to let his behavior be dominated by separation, antagonism and greed, he will destroy the delicate balances of his planetary environment. And if they were once destroyed, there would be no more life for him."[76] In fact, Dubos was willing to place a time limit on the problem. If man did not alter his "scientific drive," his economic greed, and his nationalism, he said, "then we cannot rate very highly the chances of reaching the year 2000 with our planet still functioning safely and our humanity securely preserved."[77] Dubos was giving the apocalypse, or at least its dramatic entrance, twenty-five years.

The text, finally, contained a series of political prescriptions consistent with this scientific and moral analysis. Dubos' political and economic views were as impassioned as his moral views. Together with Barbara Ward, he denounced the Industrial Revolution—both "the vile slums" of nineteenth-century Europe and America—and the "urban degradation in affluent countries" and the "squalid slums."[78] Above all, the authors criticized the production- and consumption-oriented market and profit system, which, from its inception, they said, had resulted in what was eventually to be described as "private affluence and public squalor."[79]

The essential solution, they said, was that the haves of the world must seek out "nonconsumptive joys"—e.g., "the non-polluting pleasures of great art," and playing games on "unpolluting sports grounds." The have-nots, however, must be protected from "the worst of all pollutions"—"pollution" now a sociological metaphor—that of "bitter, hopeless, neglected poverty."[80]

Thus was the perception of the "unity" and the "egg-shell delicacy" of the planet converted into the position that life on earth might end if the rich did not sacrifice themselves to the poor—which, as Barbara Ward was to explain forthrightly in a speech at the Stockholm Conference, meant: if the industrial nations did not sacrifice themselves to the undeveloped nations. That, in essence, was Dubos' contribution to international affairs. In collaboration with Barbara Ward, he provided a rationale for the surging movement in the Third World that was already clamoring for redistribution of Western wealth. The gentle mystic who wrote A God Within had done his best to bring about the social and economic "change" he had predicted in 1969.

MIT: 1972

Other apocalyptics, too, were advocating the stoppage of growth and the redistribution of Western wealth to the undeveloped nations, and a particular group of them at MIT were reaching these conclusions at the same time as Dubos. Seventeen comparatively unknown professionals—ten of them Americans—had been asked by a group called the Club of Rome to do a study on "the predicament of man." The Club of Rome had been founded in 1968 by an Italian businessman named Dr. Aurelio Peceii and consisted of internationalists from many countries who had come together to discuss their shared belief that the problems facing the human race were so grave that existing institutions could no longer deal with them.[81] One of the questions to which the Club of Rome wanted an answer was this: How long, on a finite planet, could we expect our resources to hold out, at the present rate of growth? The factors to be investigated were population, agricultural production, natural resources, industrial production, and pollution. The data were to be evaluated by systems analysis with the assistance of MIT's giant computer.

In 1972, the findings of the MIT group were published under the title *The Limits to Growth*. The authors were Project Director Dennis L. Meadows, Donella H. Meadows, Jørgen Randers, and William W. Behrens III. Because MIT was a symbol of "science" to the world, the study caused an international furor, and three million volumes were sold. It was yet another apocalyptic best-seller to hit the United States. The principal predictions of the study were expressed in deliberately dry and understated language:

If the present growth trends in world population, industrialization, pollution, food production, and resource depletion continue unchanged, the limits to growth on this planet will be reached sometime within the next one hundred years. The most probable result will be a rather sudden and uncontrollable decline in both population and industrial capacity.[82]

One graph—Figure 35—accompanying the dry text actually showed the "uncontrollable decline" beginning in about thirty years: It showed natural resources, the industrial output, the food supply, and the population crashing somewhere near the year 2005 and continuing to crash for years—the ungraspable death rate assisted by a pollution level peaking around the year 2003. MIT's computers had borne out the most hair-raising prophecies of the apocalyptics.

On the basis of these findings, the study called for an immediate cessation of all economic growth on a finite earth, and compounded it with the call for a moral transformation in man that always accompanied the apocalyptic vision:

We are convinced that realization of the quantitative restraints of the world environment and of the tragic consequences of an overshoot is essential to the initiation of new forms of thinking that will lead to a fundamental revision of human behavior and, by implication, of the entire fabric of present-day society. . . .

For the first time, it has become vital to inquire into the cost of unrestricted material growth and to consider alternatives to its continuation. . . . Short of a world effort, today's already explosive gaps and inequalities will continue to grow larger. The outcome can only be disaster, whether due to the selfishness of individual countries that continue to act purely in their own interests, or to a power struggle between the developing and developed nations. The world system is simply not ample enough nor generous enough to accommodate much longer such egocentric and conflictive behavior by its inhabitants. The closer we come to the material limits to the planet, the more difficult this problem will be to tackle.[83]

The data in this study precipitated a violent controversy which will be discussed later, along with other studies. One result of the controversy, however, was a change of policy by the Club of Rome, which, four years later, shifted its goal from the cessation of growth to "selective growth." The major industrial nations, the group proposed, should shrink their growth while the Third World expanded, with the goal of reaching eventual equilibrium.[84] This was the same solution that was already being proposed to the world by Dubos and Ward.

The undeveloped nations, who were not in the least interested in moral transformation but in material, understood the solution perfectly. In 1976, at the Lima Conference, they invoked the concept of "a finite earth" and demanded that 25 percent of world manufacturing output be in their hands by the year 2000.[85] It was not just a political demand. The converging views of Dubos, the apocalyptic from the Rockefeller University; Ward, the apocalyptic from Columbia University; and the team of apocalyptics from MIT had given it scientific status.

GEORGE WALD: 1975

The apocalyptic revolutionary movement, in both its domestic and international manifestations, had long had the sympathy of George Wald. Wald was Higginson Professor of Biology at Harvard University, winner of the Nobel Prize for Physiology and Medicine in 1968, and one of the most brilliant scientists in the country. He was a known leftist who detested the capitalist system, and like others already cited here, he was also in rebellion against the lethal impulses of Western society guided by "Christianity."

In 1975, Wald published an article entitled "There Isn't Much Time" in *The Progressive* magazine which contained the most vehement warning of his apocalyptic career. He foresaw a series of calamities converging on mankind at the same time, and he found it difficult, he said, "to see how the human race will get itself much past the year 2000." He observed that no human society had ever created such technology of "killing and destruction" as had Western Christian society. And he listed the dangers launched under Christian auspices that concerned him most: nuclear weapons, nuclear energy, plutonium-239, and nuclear wastes; oil residues in the upper layers of the ocean, which according to one estimate, he said, "exceeded in bulk all the photosynthetic organisms" in the sea; the destruction of the ozone layer by propellant gases; the automobile, a "major killer"; industrial accidents and death from lung diseases and cancer from a variety of causes; the population explosion; and famine, which, he said, could be averted were U.S. livestock not consuming "enough feed materials to nourish 1.3 billion persons," and were world livestock not consuming "enough to nourish 15 billion persons." If the industrial nations stopped eating meat and subsisted on cereals, they could stave off worldwide starvation.[86]

Wald explained that the solution was not scientific, but political. Scientific research, he said, was not the answer. It was necessary to reorganize society. Political power, he said, must be exercised "by an aroused people who insist on taking their lives back into their own hands."[87] The chief obstacle to such a social revolution, said Wald, was the fact that the world was ruled by a group of powerful corporations. The "so-called free world," he said, was now wholly controlled by multinational "super-enterprises." Under their rule, he said, the role of the middle class was to serve these masters, to foster the acceptance of their power "through education, indoctrination, and religious exhortation," and to divide and crush any significant opposition. This, he said, was the political system under which we lived, one that was ruled by "an obsessive pursuit of short-term profit" and threatened to terminate "the human enterprise." Wald summoned the middle class to refuse to serve "the power elite"; it must rebel and "serve the people." In sum, said Wald, American capitalism was a threat to human existence and only by a revolution led by the upper middle class against the corporations could life on earth be saved.[88]

Although he made no scientific points that all the others did not make, George Wald was the most frantic of all the apocalyptic scientists. He was unique in one particular respect—in his estimate of the time left to man before he vanished from the earth. Other estimates of the kind had been made. Carson had suggested that one chemical might wipe out the entire human race within twenty years. Evelyn Hutchinson had said that the life of the biosphere might terminate in "decades." Ehrlich had predicted mass death by the end of the 1970s. Commoner, speaking to the Senate, had set a moderate fifty years as the beginning of the irreversible destruction of the earth. The MIT systems analysts had given civilization about thirty years before it began its hideous collapse. Dubos had given the world about twenty-five years before man would cease to be safe on earth. But Wald, possibly the most distinguished scientist in the group, was expecting The End even sooner. He had started his essay by giving mankind twenty-five years, but the time left shrank appreciably before Wald completed his warning. In the course of his exposition, he paused for a personal comment. He still had young children, he said, and he taught about two hundred "magnificent young people at Harvard." He could not, however, find reason to believe that they had a "future"; he could find no reason to believe "that they will be in physical existence ten, twenty, twenty-five years from now."[89] With that statement, George Wald proved himself to be the crowning apocalyptic of them all. As his estimate stands, life on earth may end as early as 1985.

These, then, were the ideas of leading scientists of the apocalyptic movement. And only a reader who is too young to remember, or an older reader with amnesia, can fail to recognize in these "scientific" writings some of the major philosophical and political themes that have been coursing through this country since the explosion of the atomic bomb in the late 1940s, and reaching their climactic pitch in the last twenty years. These leading apocalyptics were extremely different kinds of people, however—as even brief excerpts from their writings reveal. They had also arrived at their conclusions by different professional and philosophical routes—their philosophies ranging from a vision of man as a vile intruder into the biosphere, to a vision of the interdependence of life taught by Eastern mysticism through Judeo-Christian-Pantheist revisionism, to conventional Marxism. But despite their differences, all shared certain themes: All were hostile to the science and technology that were threatening the life of the biosphere; and all perceived industrial civilization primarily as a producer of torrents of toxic and carcinogenic substances that were threatening all life on earth. Most were explicitly opposed to capitalism and its profit system. And all, save Carson, who died before this development occurred, ended up, however they may have begun, with a commitment to the stoppage of economic growth and to the redistribution of American wealth, and the wealth of other great industrial nations, to the Third World countries. Finally, and most important, all strongly indicated that it was the discoveries of science that had led them directly to their political conclusions.

This is rather astonishing material to find in a collection of works by scientists. Normally, scientific research leads to scientific conclusions, not to metaphysical manifestos, prophetic outbursts, utopian reorganizations of society, and political positions, let alone to a set of internationalist positions on the redistribution of wealth from rich to poor nations, which are clearly identifiable as positions taken by the far left portion of the political spectrum. Nonetheless, while we must take due note of this phenomenon, it is nowhere writ that a scientist ceases to be a scientist because he holds religious beliefs and takes political positions. And it is certainly not a precondition of good science that its practitioner be an admirer of the capitalist system; one finds brilliant scientists in communist nations, in socialist nations, and in capitalist nations. The only reasonable question, at this point, is to ask how these scientists arrived at their certainty that the biosphere was in immediate peril and that The End could be calculated in decades. Thus, we must now look at the data that supported their collective announcement of the apocalypse.

• • •

Apart from the population crisis, which pertained primarily to the Third World, the entire argument presented by the apocalyptic scientists rested on a few premises:

—that life on earth was a unity,
—that the planet was finite,
—that industrial technology was ravaging the finite planet,
—that industrial technology was destroying the unity that is life.

If, indeed, industrial technology was ravaging the planet and destroying life on earth, one could understand the desperate solutions being promulgated. Was it true that industrial technology was destroying the global ecosystem or the biosphere? What scientific knowledge was available to the apocalyptics that allowed them to formulate such a charge? Clearly, the random examples of industrial damage or the speculative dangers they all cited did not constitute an answer. Only systematic studies could provide such knowledge, and several global studies were done between 1970 and 1972—triggered by the apocalyptic movement itself. A brief survey of some of the major conclusions of the global studies gives us some idea of the state of the apocalyptics' knowledge.

The first strikingly curious thing that one learns about the available knowledge of the globe's operation was that an abnormal amount of it came from a small number of people at the Massachusetts Institute of Technology, was linked to the Club of Rome, and was siphoned directly to the UN. The first study was conducted by MIT (and is not to be confused with MIT's *Limits to Growth* study, which was undertaken two years later). Published in 1970, it was known as SCEP. Its full title was *Man's Impact on the Global Environment: Assessment and Recommendations for Action,* with the subtitle "Report of the Study of Critical Environmental Problems (SCEP)." The director of the study was Professor Carroll Wilson of the Alfred P. Sloan School of Management of MIT, a member of the Club of Rome. The preface of the study explained that "several of us" had concluded that such a study should be prepared for the UN conference. The "several" were a steering committee headed by the Club of Rome member at MIT, and of the eleven members of the committee, six were on the faculty of MIT. The work was done, with the assistance of computer analysis, by forty scholars and scientists including representatives of such fields as engineering, physics, geology, oceanography, ecology, aeronautics, astro-geophysics, meteorology, and atmospheric sciences. The preface of the study also informed the reader that participants in the project acted individually and not as members of any institution with which they were associated.[90] Many of its members were apocalyptics, whose speculations about the dangers of "irreversible planetary damage" filled the pages of the study. Despite this, the broad summary section of the study contained the following concluding paragraphs. And they should be read carefully, for they give one a vivid understanding of the state of the scientific knowledge that had produced the conclusion that life on earth was on the verge of ending.

THE QUALITY OF AVAILABLE DATA AND PROJECTION

Before discussing the findings, conclusions, and recommendations of the Study, it is important to note the deficiencies in the data and projections related to problems of global concern. In the process of making judgments we found that critically needed data were fragmentary, contradictory, and in some cases completely unavailable. This was true for all types of data—scientific, technical, economic, industrial, and social. These conditions existed despite a year of planning, extensive preparation of background materials, the presence among Study participants of some of the world's leading scientists, and the generous access to data provided by virtually every relevant federal agency.

With respect to economic and industrial statistical data and projections needed to determine trends of environmental contamination, we found firm data only up to 1967 or 1968 for the United States. International compilations of such data are often incomplete and are of questionable reliability because of uncertainties and inconsistencies in reporting, and because of lack of mechanisms to verify or standardize reports of cooperating nations. Very few projections exist for rates of growth of various industrial sectors, relevant domestic and agricultural activities of man, and energy demands. Those that are available are often based on different and sometimes questionable assumptions and methodologies.

Data on important physical, chemical, and ecological phenomena and parameters are also inadequate for providing the foundation for definitive statements about environmental effects. Specific recommendations for obtaining these data appear throughout this Report. The present data base for global problems is so poor, however, that three general recommendations are necessary.

Recommendations:

1. We recommend the development of new methods for gathering and compiling global economic and statistical information, which organize data across traditional areas of environmental responsibility, such as air and water pollution. We further recommend the propagation of uniform data-collection standards to ensure, for example, that industrial production data collection across the world will be of comparable precision and focus.
2. We recommend a study of the possibility of setting up international physical, chemical, and ecological measurement standards, to be administered through a monitoring standards center with a "real time" data analysis capability, allowing for prompt feedback to monitoring units in terms of monitoring or measurement parameters, levels of accuracy, frequency of observation, and other factors.
3. We recommend an immediate study of global monitoring to examine the scientific and political feasibility of integration of existing and planned monitoring programs and to set out steps necessary to establish an optimal system.[91]

What this meant, in plain English, is that the preconditions for making a scientific analysis of "Man's impact on the global environment" did not exist. Over and over again, in the various subsections of the "findings and recommendations," the refrain was repeated: Data did not exist.

- On the possible warming of the earth due to the rise of CO_2 in the atmosphere: "CO_2 seems to have been increasing throughout the world at about 0.2 percent per year, or 0.7 ppm out of 320 ppm . . . but the length of record is too short to place much emphasis on the deviations from a linear trend."[92]
- On the possible cooling or warming of the earth caused by industrial particles in the troposphere: "The area of greatest uncertainty in connection with the effects of particles on the heat balance of the atmosphere is our current lack of knowledge of their optical properties in scattering or absorbing radiation from the sun or the earth."[93]
- On contrail (condensation trail) formation: "There are very few, if any, statistics that permit us to determine whether the advent of commercial jet aircraft has altered the frequency of occurrence or the properties of cirrus clouds. We do not know whether the projected increase in the operation of subsonic jets will have any climate effects."[94]
- On damage by a projected fleet of 500 supersonic transports (SSTs) to the stratosphere: ". . . we have concluded that no problems should arise from the introduction of carbon dioxide and that the reduction of ozone due to interaction with water vapor or other exhaust gases should be insignificant. . . ." But, added SCEP, "Very little is known about the way particles will form from SST-exhaust products."[95]
- On the depletion of oxygen: SCEP defined it as a "non-problem."[96]
- On thermal pollution: "Although by the year 2000 global thermal power output may be as much as six times the present level, we do not expect it to affect global climate."[97]

- On the effects of oil spills on marine life in the oceans: "Very little is known about the effects of oil in the oceans on marine life. Present results are conflicting."[98]
- On the industrial discharge of minerals into the oceans, as compared to the natural discharges: "Better estimates of natural processes, and of man-induced rates ... would be very useful. If total production rates of materials are small in comparison with natural rates, problems may be locally intensive but are not expected to be large on a global scale. Where technological exploitation or production rates are high, data on loss rates to the environment are needed. In the absence of such data it is impossible to ascertain the effects of technology on the environment."[99]
- On the monitoring and analysis of global problems: "For every one of the global problems that have been identified, we find we have insufficient knowledge of either the workings or the present state of the environmental system. ... This hinders us as we attempt to design monitoring that will not only warn us of change but also provide information upon which we can base rational and efficient remedial action. ... Research is most needed in providing a closer specification of the present state of the planet and in developing a more complete understanding of the mechanisms of interaction between atmosphere, ocean, and ecosystem. ... Nor is our knowledge of the functioning of particular ecosystems sufficient to allow us to quantify effects of a particular pollutant when it, for example, eradicates one or a group of species within the ecosystem. This has meant that we lack information on which to base projections and models for decision making. It has also meant that the organization of data on which to base an analysis of the global environment problems considered by this conference has been a tedious, often approximative, and sometimes impossible task."[100]

These quotations alone nullify the evidence offered by the apocalyptics to support the conclusion that industrial technology was inexorably destroying life on earth and that technology itself could not correct the problem. According to SCEP, no scientific information existed to support such a conclusion. The SCEP scientists had indeed found ample evidence of serious pollution problems; they expressed a "feeling of genuine concern" over the SST, and recommended a "drastic reduction" in the use of DDT;[101] but they named no problem that technological civilization could not correct. Above all, they could not reach any solid conclusions about the state of the global ecosystem because scientists did not yet understand much about how it worked, because computer models of the planetary systems had serious deficiencies,[102] and because many data did not exist. This did not stop SCEP panelists from engaging in apocalyptic speculation; they published a great many agitated guesses about what disastrous events might occur if the effects of unknown chemical reactions on ill-understood aspects of various planetary systems were of this order rather than that. Indeed, had the tissue of speculations been omitted, the SCEP study could have been published on a postcard. But despite the dose of catastrophic theorizing, in the last analysis, the document always returned to reality; to every major question about the state of the global system, SCEP's basic response was: no data or insufficient data. There is no such thing as scientific knowledge without adequate data, and replicable data at that. As of 1970, the apocalyptic premises about man's impact on the globe hung in thin air.

Two years later, in 1972, the second MIT study appeared, this time a computer study commissioned by the Club of Rome. It was called *Limits to Growth*, and, as already indicated, its authors informed the world that the population crisis, the food crisis, and the natural resources crisis would interact and peak, possibly in thirty years, producing the collapse of civilization and human death on an inconceivable scale. Unlike the SCEP study which preceded and followed all its speculations with the anticlimactic statement that little or nothing was known, *Limits* presented its findings as truth. The study was immediately subjected to violent attack. As sympathizers Ehrlich, Ehrlich, and Holdren were to put it, the use of a computer model "provided a target for indignant economists and others who saw the outcome as an illustration of the syndrome known in the computing trade as 'garbage in, garbage out.' "[103] Thus Norman Macrae, Deputy Editor of the *Economist,* in Britain, declared that "by extrapolating present trends and yet assuming no change in technology it would have been possible in every human lifetime to prophesy some such ineluctable disaster." An Englishman in the horse-and-buggy era of the late 1800s, he said, might have proved with such a method of extrapolation that the cities of the 1970s would be buried under mountains of horse manure.[104]

In Stockholm, in 1972, at the height of the international agitation over the MIT study, Gunnar Myrdal, the Nobel Prize–winning economist also made devastating criticisms of *Limits.* Myrdal, a socialist, believed in large-scale government planning for environmental as well as for other purposes. He also believed that there were limits to "a growth whose component elements all follow an exponential curve." He might have been expected to be sympathetic to the study, but he was, on the contrary, outraged by it. He criticized the "inexcusably careless manner in which so-called futuristic research is now often pursued," and said that the "estimates upon which the warnings for depletion and pollution are founded are utterly uncertain. . . ." He reinforced his point with a quotation from another lecturer at the Stockholm series, René Dubos: "The existing knowledge of the natural sciences is not sufficient to permit the development of effective action programs."[105]

Myrdal curtly dismissed the claim of the MIT systems analysts that this "sort of model is actually a new tool for mankind." That was not true, said Myrdal; "It represents quasi-learnedness. . . ."

One year after the publication of *Limits* in 1973, yet another detailed critique was done by four British scholars who entitled their work *Models of Doom.*[106] The essential criticisms of *Limits,* once again, were that the model was simplistic and flawed; that the authors had not reckoned with the complex and changing adjustments of people and societies, to technology itself, and to changing events. Again, in 1974, two other analysts sought to construct a more complex model than the one used in *Limits* and presented their findings in "Mankind at the Turning Point: The Second Report to the Club of Rome."[107] In this work, the authors also criticized the flaws of *Limits* and its conclusions of global disaster, and concluded that what were more likely to occur in the future were differentiated regional problems which might lead to wars. Its conclusions were scarcely cheerful, but they did not constitute either a political or a metaphysical novelty. According to this particular model, too, neither the planet nor "Man" was in danger of expiring.

The simplest and most telling criticism of *Limits*, however, was an observation of a factor that was missing in the MIT computer analysis. The observation was made at the Stockholm Conference by Lord Zuckerman, who had served as Chief Scientific Adviser to the British Government. He was an anatomist, the Honorary Secretary of the Zoological Society in London, the author of books on anatomy and ethology, and a dedicated "environmentalist." Lord Zuckerman gave *Limits* the back of his hand. It had been lauded, he said, "mainly by the scientifically uninitiated." He summed up its thesis scornfully: "Its authors led themselves through the circuits of a computer to the conclusion that the only way out for mankind is to slow down economic growth abruptly and to change human nature drastically." He dismissed their thesis as "unscientific nonsense." His principal objection was that "the only kind of exponential growth with which the book does not deal . . . is that of the growth of human knowledge . . ." and he demanded: "What are we—ants, lemmings, or rational human beings?"[108]

In the heat of their demands for the transformation of human nature, this prominent biologist observed, the MIT scholars had forgotten the existence of the human mind.

One last scientific study reflects the state of knowledge of the apocalyptic movement. It was the scientific aspect of *Only One Earth*, the study conducted for the United Nations by biologist René Dubos and economist Barbara Ward and published in 1972. Because of the views of its authors, the study was, as already indicated, awesomely apocalyptic. But because Dubos had little scientific data and was required by the arrangements made with the UN to record the observations of a group of consultants from forty different countries and since, as he said, "The spectrum of views among our consultants was much wider than we expected,"[109] it was also awesomely inconclusive.

The same global issues that were examined by SCEP were examined by Dubos, with similar results. In fact, Dubos used a certain amount of material taken from the SCEP study, since there was nothing much better available. He reported on pollution problems, and he, too, reproduced the various speculations that the earth might heat up, grow cold, that the SSTs might destroy the ozone layer, that oil might kill the photosynthetic organisms in the oceans, etc. Dubos, too, repeatedly conceded that scientists were in substantial ignorance about the workings of the major global systems. Nature, said Dubos, also used the ocean as a dump for minerals and toxic wastes, but what happened to the natural runoff was as little understood as what happened to the man-made.[110] And, he said, no one knew what happened to all the carbon dioxide generated in the biosphere,[111] or what effects, whether heating or chilling, might be produced on the climate by industrial effluents in the atmosphere.[112]

Even more difficult, however, was to get the world's scientists to agree on some of the issues most essential to the apocalyptic vision. Scientists did agree, said Dubos, that severe pollution problems existed all over the world—in preindustrial as well as in industrial nations. They agreed, for example, that the dumping of sewage and oil in the ocean should be stopped. The world's governments had already agreed, before the Stockholm Conference, that dumping of radioactive wastes in the ocean should stop. But on many other issues there was no agreement at all. There were, said Dubos, deep conflicts on nuclear power, some perceiving it as a threat to the biosphere, others arguing that the threat had been exaggerated.[113] Similarly, there was intense conflict between the supporters of pesticides and their opponents—the supporters predicting the rapid death of millions of people from infectious disease or of malnutrition if pesticides were drastically limited, the opponents predicting that the earth would become increasingly inhospitable to life if present trends in pesticide use were to continue.[114] And on the issue of fertilizer use, Dubos reported, scientists disputed over the degree of risk that the soil might be depleted.[115]

The most dramatic disagreements, however, were not about scientific issues at all. Dubos pointed out that the scientists were in strong conflict over the manuscript of *Only One Earth*, which some criticized as "a fear story" while others criticized it for making it insufficiently clear that life on earth would be destroyed. The scientists were also torn by value disagreements of a particularly intense kind. The authors' descriptions of two important disagreements were of particular interest. One was about "life," the other about "Man." The scientists who argued about "life" were divided into two camps—those who perceived life as sturdy, and those who perceived it as delicate. As Dubos, a passionate advocate of the "delicate" school, put it: "Some are more impressed by the stability and resilience of ecosystems than by their fragility."[116]

The argument about man pertained to his metaphysical status. Dubos and Ward reported that one African correspondent had urged them to spell "man" with a capital M throughout their manuscript, and agreed that the issue was not minor, for it represented a problem that lay at the base of all environmentalist debates—namely, the role of man in nature: Was man simply a more complex ape, or did he play a special metaphysical role on the planet? Ecologists, said Dubos, demanded that we focus on the ecosystem as a whole, "man being considered chiefly as a disturbing element in it." And Dubos agreed at least that man's ecological "misbehavior" was the cause of most environmental problems.[117] Man's ecological "misbehavior," for many ecologists, was the equivalent of human action. The ecological view—voiced by Dubos himself, and one to be found in ecology textbooks—is that *any* damage done to *any* aspect of the interacting unity of life, no matter how slight, may have catastrophic consequences. Since man cannot build a road, pave a street, erect a house, or plow the land, let alone create an advanced technological civilization, without damaging various aspects of the interlocking ecosystem, the ecological view, accordingly, elicited—in some people, at least—an emotion that can only be described as "man hatred." It was rarely voiced explicitly. Only very young apocalyptics tended to envisage tombstones engraved "Cursed Be the Name of Man!" Their elders preferred on the whole to defend man's place in the ecosystem but to denounce him morally and to demand the destruction of his most intellectually advanced form of civilization. In the last analysis, the strange quarrel over life and "Man" was a highly subjective quarrel over the apocalyptics' basic premises—that life was a fragile unity and that technological man was destroying it.

Dubos' own study did not offer any scientific support for the apocalypse. He wrote it shortly after the SCEP study had appeared, and there had not been time to discover how the globe worked. He declared that the first job was to create a planetary strategy, for which all nations were to be responsible, to learn about the global system and man's impact upon it.[118] In the absence of such a strategy, he embroidered the book with the apocalyptic prophecies already described—but he had neither data nor scientific consensus to support them.

These studies, then, exemplified the state of scientific knowledge at the peak period of apocalyptic thought in the culture. It was clear that serious pollution problems existed and required action. It was clear that "technological fixes" could be—and were being—undertaken. And it was clear that research into the operations of the global ecosystem was both desirable and necessary. But there was not enough knowledge of the operations of the biosphere as a whole to permit scientific prediction. No one alive at that time had the capacity or knowledge to justify the kind of apocalyptic prophecies that were surging over the United States and across the world. Above all, the principal method on which such prophecies rested—extrapolations done by computers—had proved itself to be inadequate. The apocalypse was, quite simply, baseless.

What is particularly strange is that some of the most influential apocalyptics were fully aware that their predictions had no scientific basis. At the Stockholm Conference, right after *The Limits to Growth* had been published, Barbara Ward repeated that the planet was finite and that eventually its resources would disappear. She granted that one could put numbers into a computer "and come up with the answers that match the figures put in in the first place." Thus, no one, she said, actually knew when the fatal cataclysm would arrive, and she asked, rhetorically, "Shall we collapse by 2010, or 2050, or, by a longer reach of the imagination, the year 3000, or by further centuries still?"[119]

Ward was using MIT numbers before they had been systematically refuted—and before it had been widely observed that the computer programmers had ignored such details as human intelligence and technological innovation. The Albert Schweitzer Professor of Economics at Columbia University had not, herself, observed these omissions. Had she done so, she might as well have asked: Shall we collapse one million years from now, or one billion years from now? Nonetheless, even her awareness of "garbage in, garbage out" did not cause Barbara Ward to desist from predicting global disaster.

Dubos, too, was well aware of the lack of a data base for his apocalyptic views. At Stockholm, Myrdal quoted him as saying: "The existing knowledge of the natural sciences is not sufficient to permit the development of effective action programs."[120] In *A God Within*, written that same year, Dubos made it clear that he did not rely on computers for assistance. "The really modern students of the future . . . program various combinations of known facts about the present world and read out from computers' analyses the social and ecological consequences of various courses of action. But, in fact, the real future is likely to be very different from any of the predictable futures."[121] He said quite clearly on what his position rested: "Now as in the past, seminal decisions will be made not on the basis of computerized abstract planning but through the vision and faith of men who have a holistic sense of what is feasible and enough courage to impose their will on events."[122] Thus Dubos candidly proclaimed his "vision and faith" to be cognitively superior to science.

Similarly, Ehrlich, Ehrlich, and Holdren have made it quite clear in their textbook that they were fully aware of the limitations on both analytical and computer studies. They wrote:

Systems ecology has concentrated on constructing computer models of ecosystems. . . . The most famous model of this class was the world model developed by Donella and Dennis Meadows and their colleagues at Massachusetts Institute of Technology and published in *The Limits to Growth.* . . .

The computer models of the systems ecologists tend to be high in precision and low in generality and to lose reality as they become more general. . . . One of the major drawbacks of systems ecology is the relative paucity of data available with which to develop and test models.[123]

This knowledge of the "paucity of data" has never kept Paul Ehrlich from predicting global disaster with monotonous regularity.

Whether other apocalyptic scientists made such concessions or not, it is obvious that all apocalyptics had arrived at their conclusions by means other than scientific and maintained their views by means other than scientific. Both before any global studies existed and afterward, they had been serenely indifferent to the absence of global data in issuing their pronouncements of global disaster. This was a departure of no small proportions from the classic disciplines of science. Indeed, it appears to be outright scientific nihilism, and it requires some explanation. It would be simple enough to postulate that the apocalyptic scientists were exploiting a few bits of ill-comprehended data in order to rationalize the philosophical and political positions they held. And that possibility cannot be ruled out. Dubos, if no other, was absolutely candid about his nonreliance on science, but on a "holistic" vision of the problem.

It seems likely, however, that it was not Dubos alone who was relying on a "holistic" vision. That is a fallacy that has been commonplace in modern biology for at least twenty years—the very period in which the "scientific" apocalypse emerged. Ernest Nagel, a distinguished philosopher of science, has analyzed the "holistic" fallacy as follows:

Organismic biologists sometimes write as if any analysis of vital processes into the operation of distinguishable parts of living things entails a seriously distorted view of these processes. For example, E. S. Russell has maintained that in analyzing the activities of an organism into elementary processes "something is lost, for the action of the whole has a certain unifiedness and completeness which is left out of account in the process of analysis." Analogously, J. S. Haldane claimed that we cannot apply mathematical reasoning to vital processes, since a mathematical treatment assumes a separability of events in space "which does not exist for life as such. We are dealing with an indivisible whole when we are dealing with life." And H. Wildon Carr, a professional philosopher who subscribed to the organismic standpoint and wrote as one of its exponents, declared that "Life is individual; it exists only in living beings, and each living being is indivisible, a whole not constituted of parts."

Such pronouncements exhibit an intellectual temper that is as much an obstacle to the advancement of biological inquiry as is the dogmatism of intransigent mechanists. In biology as in other branches of science knowledge is acquired only by analysis or the use of the so-called "abstractive method"—by concentrating on a limited set of properties things possess and ignoring (at least for a time) others, and by investigating the traits selected for study under controlled conditions. Organismic biologists also proceed in this way, despite what they may say, for there is no effective alternative to it. . . . Like everyone else who contributes to the advance of knowledge, organismic biologists must be abstractive and analytical in their research procedures. They must study the operations of various prescinded parts of living organisms under selected and often artificially instituted conditions—*on pain of mistaking unenlightening statements liberally studded with locutions like "wholeness," "unifiedness," and "indivisible unity" for expressions of genuine knowledge.*[124] [Emphasis added]

This analysis of the holistic fallacy appeared in Nagel's *The Structure of Science: Problems in the Logic of Scientific Explanation*, published in 1961. That fallacy, which may have emerged from a legitimate desire for an integrated view of phenomena, was obviously transferred intact from the individual organism to the entire ecosystem, which is identified by all ecologists as a "web" or a "chain" or a "grid" of life, and which was hypothesized by some scientists (Loren Eiseley[125] and J. P. Lovelock[126]) to be a gigantic living organism. In ecology, too, the holistic scientists clearly imagined that the statement "Life is a unity" was an expression of genuine knowledge. They recited those words incessantly, and they believed that they could reach conclusions on the basis of that "knowledge" in the absence of analytical and abstractive processes. In fact, they could not do so. The moment they leaped over the processes of abstraction and analysis—i.e., over the fundamental processes of reason and science—they were actually left with little but emotions, feelings about "man" and the "fragility" of life, meaningless extrapolations from ill-understood givens, apocalyptic fantasies—and ultimately with "vision and faith" in their particular religious and political solutions. They thought they knew something concrete when they said, "Life is a unity." In fact, they didn't.

This criticism of the concept "Life is a unity" requires a little more explanation, because there is a sense in which it is true. It is, however, a very special kind of truth. It is exactly like "All men are mortal," which is also true. Unfortunately such immensely broad abstractions lack substantive content and are not applicable to concrete reality, save in the vaguest of fashions. The statement "All men are mortal" says that he who is born must someday die; but it does not allow one to differentiate between a four-year-old with the sniffles who needs a handkerchief, a fifty-year-old with kidney failure who needs a dialysis machine, and a ninety-year-old with a fulminating heart attack who needs nothing that man can give him. That truth, in other words, is not a substitute for a science of medicine. Similarly, "Life is a unity," while true in that same broad sense, is not a substitute for an authentic science of planetary or ecological systems. If one is to act, one must know what specific technological actions affect specific aspects of the biosphere in what specific ways. One cannot simply intone, "Life is a unity," and vault lightly over the need for specific analysis.

Yet again: "The planet is finite" is another one of those vast but vacuous truths. It is true, in the sense that every material entity is finite; but it is no substitute for the science of geology, for the phenomena of exploration and invention, or for the innovative intelligence of man.

In scientific terms, the apocalyptic scientists were juggling empty abstractions, and in the minds of those who imagined they were knowledge, they gave birth to other equally empty abstractions called political solutions, such as "One must organize society to conform to the needs of the global ecosystem," or "One must organize society to conform with the second law of thermodynamics," or "One must immediately stop industrial growth and divide the world's wealth equally among men, for there will never be any more wealth to be had."

There is another and apparently friendlier explanation for the apocalyptics' addiction to empty abstractions and their bizarre indifference to data. It comes from one of their number, Lord Eric Ashby, one of Britain's most influential "environmentalists." After twenty years as a plant biologist, Lord Ashby became one of Britain's most prestigious academic administrators. A Fellow of the Royal Society, who has received twenty-one awards for his contributions to education and to science, he was Vice-Chancellor of Cambridge and is now Chancellor of Queens University, Belfast, and he has also taught at Harvard. During the years of the apocalyptic explosion, he was Professor-at-Large at Cornell University (1967–1972) and Professor of Human Understanding at the University of Michigan (1976–1977). In a group of lectures at Stanford University published as *Reconciling Man with the Environment*, Lord Ashby described the "environmental" movement as a welcome manifestation of modern man's return to the equivalent of the primitive animist beliefs of his ancestors. Although Ashby believed the "web of nature" to be hardier than "some sentimentalists would have us believe," his other beliefs were standard: Life is a unity, the planet is finite, men must live as brothers, gratuitous destruction of an ecosystem is "vandalism," neither industrial capitalism nor industrial socialism can be reconciled with the needs of the ecosystem, resources must be equitably redistributed, etc.[127] In the context of giving public policy advice to legislators, Ashby identified what he perceived to be the essentials of "environmentalist" thought:

It is significant that the most effective defenders of nature today are not humanists; they are scientists, helped by a few social scientists. The message preached by Blake and Wordsworth is now preached (with inferior eloquence) by writers such as Dubos, Schumacher, and Thorpe. The reason is simple: some scientists have arrived (on a lower path, doubtless, than the one philosophers and theologians have used) at an I-Thou relationship with nature.

The signposts that have led them along this path are these. Scientists have become more and more impressed—awed is perhaps a better word—by the interdependence of things in nature. Animals, green plants, insects, bacteria are partners with man in the same ecosystems. No one can predict the full consequences of tinkering with any part of an ecosystem. Even the nonliving environment has properties without which life as we know it would be inconceivable. The idea of man as lord of nature is, in the minds of scientists, replaced by the idea of man in symbiosis with nature. Hamlet's comment "We fat all creatures else to fat us, and we fat ourselves for maggots" is a curt but accurate summary of man's place in the biosphere.[128]

Ashby endorsed the views of Justice Douglas that "the rights of nature" should be protected by law. Such law has, he said (quoting Harvey Brooks), "a social function analogous to that of taboos or religious beliefs in more traditional cultures."[129]

Ashby also said unequivocally that the methods available to science are unable to justify any statements about the operations of the total ecosystem offered by those scientists who have acquired the "I-Thou" relationship with nature: "The technique of reductionism in science, although it has been enormously successful, does not (and cannot) illuminate the behavior of whole interdependent systems. For the analysis of complexity new techniques are being worked out: information theory, catastrophe theory, systems analysis. But these techniques cannot yet begin to deal with anything so complex as an ecosystem, and the techniques of reductionism are irrelevant for this order of complexity."[130] Since teleological explanation was long ago "excommunicated from conventional scientific inquiry," said Ashby, "it has left an embarrassing gap in the methodology for studying *the overall behavior of complex biological systems*"[131]—the italicized phrase being Ashby's version of a "holistic" view of life.

In summary, although Ashby conceived of these statements as a defense of the mental processes of his apocalyptic colleagues, he was actually defending them on the interesting grounds that they were *not* relying on science, that they were second-rate mystics, less eloquent than Blake and Wordsworth, and that they were hampered in making their generalizations because the concept of purposefulness—presumably divine purposefulness—had been "excommunicated" from science. Ashby's criticism of the apocalyptics was equally interesting. It pertained to the realm in which Ashby had actually worked for many decades—the delicate realm of high-level academic politics. Where political action was concerned, Ashby saw that the apocalyptics were engaging in "empty rhetoric," but this time he defended it neither as mystical nor as "evolutionary":

If I have one paramount misgiving about books on the so-called ecological crisis, it involves their use of the word "must." "Economic and technologic considerations," writes René Dubos, "must be made subservient to the needs, attributes, and aspirations that have been woven into the fabric of man's nature." "We must," writes E. F. Schumacher, "learn to think in terms of an articulated structure that can cope with a multiplicity of small-scale units." "Long-term goals," write Meadows and his co-workers, "must be specified and short-term goals made consistent with them." And "modern man," write Paul and Anne Ehrlich, "must come soon to a better understanding of the Earth and of what he has been doing to it." The sentiments are not misguided; it is just that they are empty rhetoric unless they are accompanied by specific and politically feasible—and I repeat *specific and politically feasible*—plans for turning "must be" into "can be." That politics is the art of the possible is a cliché, but those who have not mastered that art cannot expect their political prescriptions to be taken seriously.[132]

In fact, the feverish attempts to describe, without data, the "finite planet," the "holistic" view that life was a "unity," and the "empty rhetoric" in the political realm were epistemologically identical. In all areas the apocalyptics were manipulating contentless abstractions with almost no anchor in reality.

Whether one identifies this juggling of vacant abstractions as a logical fallacy that generates ersatz science or more affectionately as an intuitive "I-Thou" relationship with nature which seeks a modern substitute for primitive animism, religion, and taboo makes little difference. What is essential is that in either case, the apocalyptic movement spearheaded by scientists—specifically, the movement that declared on the basis of *unknowns* that life on earth was about to end, that the Industrial Revolution had to be arrested, reversed, or destroyed, and that pollution problems could not be solved by technological means—rested on faith, not on analytical science. It was, in fact, a repudiation of science by scientists.

In 1977, two legal historians got a serious shock. They were James E. Krier of UCLA and Edmund Ursin of the University of San Diego, authors of a scholarly book called *Pollution and Policy*. Both were themselves strong supporters of the "environmental" movement, their work had been generously funded by the Environmental Protection Agency, and they were analyzing the development of public policy in the realm of air pollution. When they sought to identify the origins of the "great environmental crisis" that had suddenly swept the U.S. with force during the years 1969–1970, they found they were unable to do so. The reason, they said with some bewilderment, was that there had never been a "great environmental crisis."

And then there was the great environmental crisis; it most of all is a mystery. That, like crises in the past, this one contributed to further intervention seems unquestionable, but there similarity ends. Crises in the past concerned particular pollution episodes and generated, if anything, rather focused response. But that was not the case with the great environmental crisis of 1969–1970. Its roots were not in any specific cause, and it spawned not narrow response but an entire movement (or the movement spawned it; the connection is hardly clear)—a general "environmental consciousness." **Some observers appear to attribute the new crisis to the same forces largely behind the old: growth in population, production, consumption, affluence, and pollution. Surely these factors played a part, but more must also have been at work. For this crisis had no episode to trigger it (unless one lays it all on a few oil spills) and, in any event, if growth factors were the cause, why did not the crisis, and the movement, occur sooner—or later?** We cannot answer that question; we do not know what "more" was at work. We only know that this new crisis was different. Those of the past were crises in action; they merely signified that government should do more of the same, take that next small step in policy. The great environmental crisis was rather a crisis in thought. . . . In this sense, the environmental crisis may simply have been part of a larger whole, a general "loss of

citizen confidence in governmental institutions ... generating a crisis of its own."
Whether the environmental crisis arose from this larger sense of unrest, or from efforts
of crusaders finally bearing fruit, or from growth, or the need for a new issue now that
the "urban crisis" had quietly died, or from all or none of these is an open question.[133]
[Emphasis added]

Indeed, there had never been a "great environmental crisis." Even Lord Ashby,
for all his rejoicing over the return by modern man to primitive animism, had
referred to it as the "so-called ecological crisis." The apocalyptic movement
had been an intellectual hallucination. The scientists who had led that movement and legitimized it as a serious intellectual position had not had a sau-
cerful of data.

From this, we learn a number of crucially important things about the scientists who have shaped the views of this country on the subject of the threat of
industrial civilization to the living "environment" and to man. We can make
five specific generalizations now that we could not make before—and they shed
light on the ideological battles that we have sought to understand:

1. There are scientists in existence today who are deeply distrustful of, or even
   hostile to, science as well as technology. They are guided by the belief that
   Western industrial civilization will, if not arrested and reversed, destroy life
   on earth.
2. The idea of the apocalypse has greater power over such scientists than any
   attachment to the disciplines of science, and in the name of that idea they
   are entirely willing to reject those disciplines. Even when they are fully
   aware that the known data do not support that idea, they do not tolerate rational limits on their knowledge. They aggressively convert not-knowing
   into a kind of knowing, a pseudo-knowing that Myrdal in one instance
   called "quasi-learnedness" and Nagel in another describes as an "unenlightening" substitute for "genuine knowledge." The spurious knowledge is
   always used to rationalize their expectation of catastrophe. The characteristics of the spurious knowledge—vacant abstractions, arbitrary extrapolations, conclusions based on inadequate or nonexistent data; the rejection of
   logic; and the incorporation of moral attitudes into the very core of their
   "scientific" thought—are so standardized that they constitute a pseudo-sci-
   entific paradigm. It will be called, henceforth, the "apocalyptic paradigm."
3. From the moment that this "apocalyptic paradigm" appeared, "traditional"
   scientists have been clashing with the apocalyptic scientists—actually clashing over the "apocalyptic paradigm" itself.
4. These conflicts among scientists emerge in many issues involving real or
   imagined damage by industrial technology to biological organisms. The
   warring camps are known as the "environmentalists" versus the "technologists"; the "antiscience/antitechnology" movement versus the advocates of
   science and technology; and the advocates of economic growth versus those
   who would "stop growth."
5. These same ideological conflicts are now present in the realm of industrially
   caused cancer.

We can now, at last, arrive at an overview of this "environmental movement," which is the necessary background for our investigation of "environmental cancer." One aspect of the movement is perfectly intelligible. It was
based on one real phenomenon—pollution problems, in some cases severe,
throughout the industrial and preindustrial world. When the problem became
known, and was emotionally dramatized for millions in all industrialized nations by the first televised voyage to the moon which allowed people to see their
own planet, "spaceship earth"—"tiny," delicately blue-green and wreathed in
mist, floating in the black void of space—it generated an almost universal demand for correction. In the United States, that demand was symbolized by a
series of symbolic "Earth Days," which, as interpreted by citizens from coast to
coast, took the homely form of earnestly cleaning up garbage in their own lo-
calities, and in the serious political demand that industry be legally required to
clean up its own garbage, both toxic and nontoxic, and cease spewing it into
rivers and lakes or dumping it into unsightly and dangerous heaps on various
land sites. For the broad American public, the obvious problem was one of
garbage disposal; it took an elite educational system to endow garbage with
metaphysical significance. The public response also took the form of a heightened concern for the conservation of the dramatically beautiful areas in the
United States which had been left in their natural state, and for the preserva-
tion of wildlife—a value to which individuals in affluent industrialized societies
are particularly sensitive, since the human beings in those societies are not in
direct competition with animals for food. That was the "environmental" movement to which most Americans subscribed, and it was, and remains, a transpo-
litical movement, in that its goals are shared by people of every conceivable
political and nonpolitical persuasion. There never was any mystery about *this*
"environmental" movement, linguistic or otherwise; its meaning, if not its regulatory interpretation, has been known to all.

Then there was the "mysterious" aspect of the environmental movement
for which no descriptive concept in the English language could be found by
Paul Ehrlich, although it is sometimes, inadequately, called the "stop growth"
movement by critics. To recapitulate: It consisted of a set of denunciations and
of solutions. The objects of denunciation were "Man," America, science, technology, industrial production, the profit and market system, and economic
growth and capitalism. The solutions were the arrest of technological and economic development and the redistribution of American wealth and the wealth
of other industrialized nations to the preindustrial world. This was a purely political movement, influenced by both the counterculture and the new left. And
it was characterized by the astoundingly impoverished moral repertoire that
has always characterized the left—namely, the single Biblical injunction that
the rich must give to the poor, the "haves" to the "have-nots." The novelty, this
time, was that the injunction must be applicable to the entire globe and that
once the ultimate global redistribution of wealth was made, and all were
equally wretched, new productive activity in industrialized states must cease
forever. And underlying this Biblical-utopian movement, and propping it up,
was the apocalyptic hard core—a group of scientists, mainly Americans, who
rushed frantically with no data to inform the book-reading world and the

United Nations that the biosphere itself was imperiled; that industrial technology was ravaging the "finite" planet; that life on earth might end within several decades—and that the only conceivable solutions were . . . see above.

Several writers have captured the apocalyptic-utopian aspect of the movement at various moments of its history, both from inside the movement and without, and their observations about its dynamics, taken together, are illuminating. One of the earliest descriptions comes from within the movement, from Barbara Ward, the British economist who taught at Columbia, who eagerly embraced the scientific apocalypse, and who served as coauthor with René Dubos of the UN study of the dateless global peril. In an address at Stockholm in 1972—a gathering of scientists and humanists who argued about whether the world was or was not on the verge of expiring, and when it would expire if it did—Barbara Ward observed (referring to her coauthorship with René Dubos of *Only One Earth*) that she found it "fascinating" to note the rapidity with which ideas about danger to the planet were spreading:

There are ideas and concepts which, when I wrote them in our preliminary draft, last year, made me wonder how far out I could be. Yet today Ministers of the Crown are saying them and that is surely about as far in as you can get. . . .

Just the year before, she said, the notion that the oceans were in danger was a novel one, but:

Now, it is a *lieu-commun,* a near-platitude. . . . The progress toward truism means that the new ideas are penetrating human consciousness with incredible rapidity.[134]

It is true that the death of the ocean (1979) was announced on the cover of the radical *Ramparts* magazine—an issue prepared at the time of a ritual Earth Day—but there is no evidence that the ocean's imminent demise formed any part of "the popular wisdom" in America or in any other country. Barbara Ward (Lady Jackson) was a member of the British upper class, as well as a professor of economics at Columbia University, and the "consciousness" she spoke of that was being so rapidly penetrated by the new apocalyptic "platitudes" and "truisms" was an upper-class consciousness. Her ingenuous language—only last year it had been so "far out" to speak of the endangered planet, while it was now as "far in as you can get"—tells us more about the dynamics of this phenomenon than perhaps she intended. Clearly, just as there had been a "radical chic" during this epoch, so was there an "apocalyptic chic."

A second "report" from within the movement—a cultural document of sorts—is sharply reminiscent of Barbara Ward's status-consciousness assessment of the apocalypse. It is a song by John Denver about The End. Composed one year later, in 1973, it was Paul Ehrlich set to music, and it was much beloved by members of the counterculture:

> And one is a teacher and one a beginner
> Just wanting to be there and wanting to know
> And together they're trying to tell us a story
> That should have been listened to long, long ago

How the life in the mountains is living in danger
From too many people, too many machines
And the time is upon us, today is forever
Tomorrow is just one of yesterday's dreams[135]

What both this song and Barbara Ward tell us is that for many, this was just a symbolic apocalypse. It is a little difficult to accept the notion that in the grip of an *authentic* belief that life on earth is coming to an end, a British aristocrat will finely calibrate her shifting social status or up-to-the-minute "hippies" will sit around strumming guitars, bidding a harmonious and self-pitying farewell to existence. "Apocalyptic chic" may have been vastly more widespread than any authentic belief in the apocalypse.

Two years later, in 1975, Daniel Moynihan, who had been Ambassador to the UN during the early 1970s, offered a disbeliever's view of the phenomenon. He reported that when he arrived at the UN, he had found that a relatively small group of Americans had literally talked a large portion of the UN intelligentsia into accepting the idea that the planet was in peril. He said that America's "elite" was manufacturing the global crisis for export: ". . . we have become great producers and distributors of crisis. The world environment crisis, the world population crisis, the world food crisis, are in the main American discoveries—or inventions—opinions differ."[136] It was entirely clear from the context and the documentation offered that Moynihan thought them inventions. Moynihan, however, did not explain why the American "elite" was engaging in this curious manufacture and export of an invented global crisis.

Two years after that, in 1977, Paul Johnson, former editor of the *New Statesman*, did offer an explanation. He had discovered that the "environmental" apocalypse was widespread among the intellectuals of the entire Western world. He reflected on changing styles in secular apocalyptic thought:

[In the past, the] apocalyptics and millenarians . . . constantly predicted the event and the precise form it would take; and, this strain of human nature being what it is, the repeated failures of such precise prophecies in no way deterred men from framing and believing in new ones. What is even more remarkable is that apocalyptic prophecy survived the coming of the secular age, and took on a more materialist form. Marx, with his highly detailed and imaginative presentation of the eschatology of capitalism, can be described as the last of the Judeo-Christian prophets, or the first of the secular ones. Nor, as one would expect, has the discrediting of Marx's vision by the actual unrolling of events prevented fresh generations of the millenarian-minded from modifying and updating it, or indeed from devising new secular eschatologies. Any unexpected, brutal or ominous conjunction of events is enough to conjure up new visions of the end. . . .

[Today,] in relation to the future of the international free economy, it takes the particular form of ecological eschatology. The Four Last Things are to be the poisoning of the air, the exhaustion of the soil, the final consumption of the earth's natural resources, and mass-starvation of an overpopulated planet.[137]

This appears to be a reasonable explanation of the apocalyptic aspect of the movement—of its hard-core "scientific" component, of the lay true believers, and of "apocalyptic chic" itself. The discredited Marxian eschatology had, apparently, been replaced by an ecological eschatology. And since a large portion of the educated world in all industrialized countries had been so saturated by Marxist thought, often without knowing it was Marxist thought, there may, in many, have been an imperative need for a new conceptual mold into which one might pour one's expectations of—or yearnings for—a cataclysmic collapse of American capitalism, and the winged emergence of a Judeo-Christian egalitarian utopia from its ashes. In 1979, Charles Frankel, President of the National Humanities Center in North Carolina and Old Dominion Professor of Philosophy and Public Affairs at Columbia University, made an observation of the American university which supported Johnson's analysis:

Our citadels of reason stand alongside certain fundamentalist sects in their susceptibility to the hope that, through some new revelation of truth, human nature can be freed of its corruptions and society made over as it was intended to be.[138]

It was certainly from the American "citadels of reason" that the apocalypse emerged, and this leaves us with one final question. Whatever the political bitterness and yearnings may have been in many during this period—a period in which America's technology, for the left and the counterculture, was symbolized by the nuclear bomb, by the chemical carcinogen, by the technological race to "colonialize" space, and by bodies blazing in napalm fire—one must still account for the fact that a large group of highly educated humanists, the "elite," accepted the word of a relatively small group of scientists that the *biosphere* was in desperate and immediate peril—although no data existed anywhere in the world to substantiate such a claim. And even many who were in no sense apocalyptic accepted the notion that some fearful "environmental crisis" was upon us—a crisis which the EPA-subsidized Krier and Ursin were unable to discover, "unless one lays it all on a few oil spills."

A fundamental reason for this blind acceptance—there are, as we will see, many others—is that all educated humanists, whether susceptible to the apocalypse or not, were almost totally ignorant of science and could not recognize a serious corruption of science when one was flaunted before their eyes. As Lord Zuckerman observed in 1972, it was primarily the "scientifically uninitiated" who were swallowing whole the unsubstantiated projections of global catastrophe which were emerging from a tiny fragment of the scientific community. The literary and political intellectuals had been warned in the late 1950s by C. P. Snow, in his famous essay "The Two Cultures," that their ignorance of science was both unjustifiable and dangerous, but they had denounced him for his pains. In fact, the political and literary intellectuals have always viewed scientists and technologists as highly skilled plumbers. They have trusted them blindly, have used their gifts unthinkingly, and have looked down upon them, and have not considered them to be "intellectuals." In 1972, Charles Kadushin, writing for a scholarly journal called *The Public Interest*, devised a master list of 172 American intellectuals considered to be highly influential in American society. It was the twentieth century, and only one scientist was on the list.[139] Edward O. Wilson, the Frank B. Baird, Jr., Professor of Science and a curator at the Museum of Comparative Zoology at Harvard University, whatever the

controversiality of his views in the realm of sociobiology, has observed of most
"intellectuals" with unpleasant accuracy:

In the United States intellectuals are virtually defined as those who work in the prevailing mode of the social sciences and humanities. Their reflections are devoid of the
idioms of chemistry and biology, as though humankind were still in some sense a nu-
minous spectator of physical reality. In the pages of *The New York Review of Books,
Commentary, The New Republic, Daedalus, National Review, Saturday Review,* and
other literary journals articles dominate that read as if most of basic science had halted
during the nineteenth century. Their content consists largely of historical anecdotes,
diachronic collating of outdated, verbalized theories of human behavior, and judgments of current events according to personal ideology—all enlivened by the pleasant
but frustrating techniques of effervescence. Modern science is still regarded as a prob-
lem-solving activity and a set of technical marvels, the importance of which is to be
valuated in an ethos extraneous to science.[140]

Insulated by their own textured world of art and social theory, the "intellectuals" did not appreciate the magnitude of their own ignorance, and many
were bowled over, or at least were intimidated, by the apocalyptic charges. Invariably, they assumed that the scientists knew more than was known—because they underestimated the complexity of what scientists did know. Above
all, they did not appreciate the rigorous disciplines to which an authentic claim
to scientific knowledge is subjected. They inhabited a universe in which such
disciplines did not exist, or worse, in which such disciplines were crudely mim-
icked. And since, as Wilson observed, they assumed they could assess the importance of science by an ethos extraneous to science, they assessed the
apocalyptics' statements the way they assessed each other's prose and social
and political positions—that is, "according to personal ideology." It occurred
to few to judge the scientists' statements by the standards of science itself. Thus
few discovered the scientific void, the logical fallacies, and the actual rejection
of science that lay beneath the apocalyptic rhetoric.

In this intellectual vacuum, the apocalyptic message was sanctified for
many when such cultural and political leaders as Margaret Mead, Don Price,
and Senator Edmund Muskie clambered aboard this "avant-garde" band-
wagon. By 1969–1970, the apocalyptics' views were widely accepted as "enlightened" thought—and that thought automatically coursed through the
communications arteries of the land. Thus, the scientifically baseless assertion
that man and the global ecosystem were in acute peril was rapidly converted
into the conventional wisdom of the "elite."

And it was rapidly converted into law. The legislation that emerged in this
period shows quite clearly that the values of the intellectual opinion leaders
had made a profound impact on the legislators. Starting in 1969, there was an
extraordinary proliferation of laws:

1969   National Environmental Policy Act
1970   Environmental Protection Agency Reorganization
1970   Poison Prevention Packaging Act
1970   Amended Federal Hazardous Substances Act

1970   Clean Air Act Amendments
1970   Resource Recovery Act
1970   Occupational Safety and Health Act
1971   Federal Boat Safety Act
1972   Amended National Traffic and Motor Vehicle Safety Act
1972   Technology Assessment Act
1972   Amended Federal Water Pollution Control Act
1972   Marine Protection, Research, and Sanctuaries Act
1972   Noise Control Act
1972   Drug Listing Act; Amended Federal Food, Drug and Cosmetic Act
1972   Federal Insecticide, Fungicide and Rodenticide Act
1972   Consumer Product Safety Act
1973   Endangered Species Act
1974   Safe Drinking Water Act
1975   Federal Coal Leasing Act
1975   Amended Federal Insecticide, Fungicide, and Rodenticide Act
1976   National Science and Technology Policy, Organization and Priorities
        Act
1976   Amended Federal Food, Drug and Cosmetic Act
1976   Amended Public Health Services Act
1976   National Consumer Health Information and Health Promotion Act
1976   Medical Device Amendments
1976   Toxic Substances Control Act
1976   Resource Conservation and Recovery Act
1976   Amended Solid Waste Disposal Act
1976   Environmental Research and Development Demonstration Act
1977   Amended Clean Air Act
1977   Amended Federal Water Pollution Control Act
1977   Amended Federal Mine Safety and Health Act
1977   Surface Mining Control and Reclamation Act

These laws were, in all cases, a response to real problems. But when one reads them, one does not see a straightforward and confident concern to acknowledge and to resolve those problems—one sees a hysterical conviction that life itself was under siege and that life was losing the battle. The many documents that offer the history of those laws, from the congressional hearings to the formal acts themselves with their legislative histories, preambles, policy declarations, and lists of prescriptions, make it vividly clear that a substantial majority of our elected representatives—or the intellectual staff that actually did the work—had become thoroughly convinced, or thought it "enlightened" to be convinced, that all of our 222,000,000 citizens were in physical peril, that the peril emerged from our industrial system, that the peril was accelerating, and that it ultimately extended to all biological existence. Only a few illustrations of the language used in legal documents prepared in the 1970s need be given to convey the sense of frantic urgency and the extraordinary willingness to equate fearful speculation with knowledge.

In the legislative history of the Occupational Safety and Health Act of 1970, its authors reported:

In the field of occupational health the view is particularly bleak, and, due to the lack of information and records, may well be considerably worse than we currently know.

Occupational diseases which first commanded attention at the beginning of the Industrial Revolution are still undermining the health of workers. Substantial numbers, even today, fall victim to ancient industrial poisons such as lead and mercury. Workers in the dusty trades still contract various respiratory diseases. Other materials long in industrial use are only now being discovered to have toxic effects. In addition, technological advances and new processes in American industry have brought numerous new hazards to the workplace. Carcinogenic chemicals, lasers, ultrasonic energy, beryllium metal, epoxy resins, pesticides, among others, all present incipient threats to the health of workers. Indeed, new materials and processes are being introduced into industry at a much faster rate than the present meager resources of occupational health can keep up with.[141]

In the 1977 Amendments to the Clean Air Act, the Congress found that:

. . . the growth in the amount and complexity of air pollution brought about by urbanization, industrial development, and the increasing use of motor vehicles, has resulted in mounting dangers to the public health and welfare, including injury to agricultural crops and livestock . . . and that . . . halocarbon compounds introduced into the environment potentially threaten to reduce the concentration of ozone in the stratosphere; ozone reduction will lead to increased incidence of solar ultraviolet radiation at the surface of the Earth; increased incidence of solar ultraviolet radiation is likely to cause increased rates of disease in humans (including increased rates of skin cancer), threaten food crops and otherwise damage the natural environment. . . .[142]

In the Toxic Substances Control Act of 1976, the Congress found that:

. . . human beings and the environment are being exposed each year to a large number of chemical substances and mixtures; among the many chemical substances and mixtures which are constantly being developed and produced, there are some whose manufacture, processing, distribution in commerce, use, or disposal may present an unreasonable risk of injury to health or the environment. . . . The term "environment" includes water, air, and land and the interrelationship which exists among and between water, air, and land and all living things.[143]

Finally, in the Endangered Species Act of 1973, the Congress found that:

. . . various species of fish, wildlife and plants in the United States have been rendered extinct as a consequence of economic growth and development untempered by adequate concern and conservation; other species of fish, wildlife, and plants have been so depleted in numbers that they are in danger of or threatened with extinction. . . . the United States has pledged itself as a sovereign state in the international community to conserve to the extent practicable the various species of fish or wildlife and plants facing extinction. . . .[144]

Many of the specifics were true, but the totality was set in a framework of metaphysical hysteria. Within less than a decade, the Congress in its collective wisdom had reached this conclusion: that the entire producing and consuming population of the United States; plants, fish, birds, animals; and the air, water, and land itself, as well as their "interrelationship" with all living things, were in peril. The sources of the global peril, just to name those identified in the four laws cited above, were "technological advances," "new processes in American industry," and "industrial development." Congress had actually accepted and built into the legislation the principal assumptions of the apocalyptic movement. The concept that industrial civilization and economic growth were an intrinsic threat to biological existence had been enshrined in American law, and the state was now, incredibly, committed to protect the barely understood global ecosystem—i.e., "the interrelationship which exists among and between water, air, and land and all living things," a statement which is pure apocalyptic gibberish. Whatever practical qualifications and conditions Congress had added to these amazing concepts—and there were many—it is an uncontestable fact that one decade of American legislation bears the brand of the apocalyptics.

During this same period, we saw certain regulatory agencies acquire unprecedented power. The Food and Drug Administration and the new regulatory triad—the Environmental Protection Agency, the Occupational Safety and Health Administration, and the Consumer Product Safety Commission—were charged with protecting the public, the air, water, land, and all living creatures from industrial hazards. They ran on a parallel course with the Congress, executing and interpreting its mandates, manufacturing "suspected" threats by the carload, supplying Congress with new grounds for alarm, investigation, and legislation, and generating so many tens of thousands of regulations that no sampling can possibly convey their magnitude. Between 1967 and 1977 the FDA, the EPA, the OSHA, and the CPSC had warned the public, by means of notices to the press, about the potential threats to health and life of about 2,000 manufactured products and processes in all categories of heavy and consumer industries.[145] In addition, the FDA had warned the public about the potential hazards of 10,000 food additives.[146] And the EPA had reported that 35,000 pesticide formulations were potentially hazardous and required testing.[147] And unknown legions of industrial projects were delayed or blocked entirely by a proliferating network of "environmental" regulations, all guided by the concept that virtually any human action might imperil a crucial aspect of the "web of life."

As the years passed, one class of industrial hazard to human beings came to transcend all others in importance. An examination of the entire list of warnings disseminated by all the protective agencies between 1967 and 1977 makes this quite understandable. Whatever the almost 50,000 dangerous industrial products, substances, processes, and by-products might have been called (e.g., "foods," "drugs," "cosmetics," "pesticides," "pajamas," "automobile exhaust," "industrial solvents," "electrical capacitors," "nuclear power," "coal dust"), the overwhelming majority of them had been found to be hazardous because they contained or released toxic substances or had been shown, usually in animal experiments, to be cancer-causing agents. Inevitably, the problem of industrially caused cancer moved to the front stage of public health considerations and has remained there ever since. As the apocalyptic Ralph Nader had prophesied, the "carcinogenic century" had arrived—and the war against "corporate" cancer had begun.

With this war came the disturbing phenomenon that until so recently Americans had always associated with such countries as Soviet Russia and Nazi Germany—scientists charging each other with ideological distortion. But now the charges of ideological distortion pertained not to a hallucinatory apocalypse, but to a hideous and ravaging disease that was actually causing one out of every four deaths. And the laymen were caught in the middle, with nothing to do but to take one faction or another on faith, to believe no one at all—or to investigate the issue independently. Thus, this book.

Chapter 2

The Apocalyptic Heritage

Cancer is now a killing and disabling disease of epidemic proportions in the United States. More than 53 million persons (over 25 percent of the U.S. population) will develop some form of cancer in their lifetimes, and approximately 20 percent will die from it. . . . cancer deaths in 1975 alone were approximately five times higher than the total U.S. military deaths in the Vietnam and Korean war years combined.[1]

—Samuel S. Epstein, cancer researcher,
Bulletin of the Atomic Scientists, 1977

It is extraordinary that we have just now become convinced of our bad health, our constant jeopardy of disease and death . . . when the facts should be telling us the opposite. In a more rational world, you'd think we would be staging bicentennial ceremonies for the celebration of our general good shape. In the year 1976, out of a population of around 220 million, only 1.9 million died, or just under 1 percent, not at all a discouraging record once you accept the fact of mortality itself.[2]

—Lewis Thomas, cancer researcher,
The Medusa and the Snail, 1979

To know that the problem of environmental cancer is a branch of the "environmental movement" is to face an immediate and disagreeable question: Has the issue of industrially caused cancer been contaminated by the apocalyptic ideology? It is a reasonable question, given the history of the "environmental" movement, and yet one knows, even before one asks it, that there will be several significant differences between "environmentalism" and the study of environmental cancer.

One of those differences has already been named: The pronouncement that all life on earth was in peril and that The End was upon us was a cultural hallucination propped up by an industrial garbage problem, while the ravaging of human life by cancer is a fact. There is another difference of importance: The science of ecology, from which the apocalypse directly emerged, is yet so young that its very existence was hardly known to the public before the publication of *Silent Spring*, while the field of cancer research is an old and established branch of science. What is more, the phenomenon of the exogenous

67

carcinogen—the substance outside the body that may induce cancer in human beings who have been exposed to it—was discovered long before anyone dreamed of the "environmental" apocalypse: Soot and coal tars were first suspected to be carcinogenic by Sir Percival Pott, who observed, in the late eighteenth century, that many of his patients with cancer of the scrotum were chimney sweeps. Thus, we can be certain that even if the issue of environmental carcinogens has been subject to some form of apocalyptic contamination, the phenomenon is a real one, and some aspect of the problem will be firmly anchored in reality.

On the surface, any attempt to answer the question of whether any science is ideologically contaminated may seem to pose insuperable difficulties for a layman. How, after all, can a layman presume to assess the integrity of a complex science in which he has not been trained? The answer is: He cannot do so. He can, however, as this book will show, do a great many other things; and the first thing is to listen intently to those who told him immediately and repeatedly before and after the passage of the Toxic Substances Control Act (TSCA) that the apocalypse had invaded the terrain. Without prior knowledge of the pattern of the apocalyptic "environmental movement," he could easily have failed to understand what he was being told at the time; with knowledge of that pattern, he cannot fail, retroactively, to recognize it. With the birth of TSCA a powerful apocalyptic strain in the field of environmental cancer announced itself instantly and in unmistakable fashion. It also announced itself in terms a layman could readily grasp, because those terms either came from scientists through the press or were directly chosen by scientists for laymen. Only a small number of sources of information available to the public will be quoted in this chapter.[3] In no sense is this a systematic study. But the nature and prominence of the sources are such that one may assume that they reliably reflect the kind of information that was being beamed at American citizens.

CANCER APOCALYPTICS: THE PRESS

In 1976, TSCA was passed, and during the years 1975 to 1978, the American public was given its basic education on environmental cancer by the press. The apocalyptic themes rang out from journalists who were reporting on the frightening news as the journalists themselves had come to understand it—from scientists at the National Cancer Institute, from other governmental scientists, and from academic scientists. The themes were exactly the same as those which appeared in the preceding chapter, but now they had been adapted to cancer. Here are some examples:

It was America which was the most culpable for giving its people cancer. That was the message beamed out to the nation by Dan Rather, of CBS, after a briefing at the National Cancer Institute. His documentary, entitled "The American Way of Death," aired on October 15, 1975 and opened with this stunning statement from unidentified NCI sources: "The news tonight is that the United States is number one in cancer. The National Cancer Institute estimates that if you're living in America your chances of getting cancer are higher than anywhere else in the world."[4]

It was Man who had created most human cancer, said James Bishop, Jr., National Energy and Environmental Correspondent of *Newsweek* magazine, who was serving as an authoritative panelist on CBS' "Face the Nation" on April 18, 1976. What was more, he said, everyone knew it: ". . . it's now generally accepted that about 60 to 90 percent of all human cancer is caused by manmade toxic chemicals of various sorts."[5] Bishop did not cite any specific source for that estimate. But journalist Larry Agran did, in a book called *The Cancer Connection*, published in 1977. This time the 90 percent figure was attributed to sources at the National Cancer Institute, once again anonymous: "The man-made nature of the problem is underscored by National Cancer Institute estimates that the vast majority of all human cancers—perhaps up to 90 percent—are attributable to environmental carcinogens."[6]

It was the Faustian sin of science and technology that had created the chemicals which were destroying the lives of Americans, said *Newsweek,* in a long review article entitled "The Chemicals Around Us" published on August 21, 1978—a title evoking an early work by Rachel Carson, *The Sea Around Us.* The article was pegged to the problem of Love Canal, a community near Niagara Falls, N.Y., which had been infiltrated by toxic and carcinogenic wastes. *Newsweek*'s team of reporters said: "The only certainty is that the people of Love Canal are simply the latest victims of a burgeoning menace to technologically sophisticated man—toxic chemicals. In a grim update of the Faustian legend, the products and by-products of industrial efforts to improve consumers' standards of living are threatening those same people with disease and death. Chemicals vital to packaging, paints, perfumes, plastics, and preservatives are causing ailments that range from headaches and skin rashes to sterility and cancer."[7]

It was the chemical industry that was giving people cancer, declared a labor leader invited to interpret the problem for the public by reporter Lesley Stahl in a "CBS Reports Special" documentary entitled "The Politics of Cancer," aired on June 22, 1976. Anthony Mazzocchi, of the Oil, Chemical and Atomic Workers Union, called the chemical industry "mad bombers" and declared: "That's the big crime in the street story. It's not your local mugger, it's an industry that mugs people by the thousands."[8]

A slow and/or rapid cancer epidemic was occurring and/or would explode in the future, journalists told the country. In 1975, Dan Rather of CBS, whose stated source of information was the National Cancer Institute, said in "The American Way of Death": "Meanwhile, the slow epidemic goes on. . . . It's been said that we are suffering a cancer epidemic in slow motion."[9] In 1976, Lesley Stahl of CBS, in "The Politics of Cancer," reported that the cancer rates caused by industry were "soaring."[10] In 1976, Betty Furness of NBC said in a documentary called "What Is This Thing Called Food?" that a calamity to the human species might be on its way: "Some scientists worry over the kind of safety tests being done today. They even talk about genetic disaster."[11] And in 1977, journalist Larry Agran, in *The Cancer Connection,* informed his readers that the emerging epidemic was of appalling proportions: "In truth, what we are witnessing is the unmistakable emergence of a national cancer epidemic.

An epidemic of frightful proportions. A cancer pox. The numbers and the trends point clearly to the calamity that is already upon us."[12]

While most of the above statements by journalists and laymen do not indicate their sources, save for references to the anonymous National Cancer Institute, the context, in most cases, revealed clearly that they were repeating lessons from scientists. Journalists have their inadequacies, but inventing gigantic cancer epidemics out of thin air is not one of them. Who, then, were these scientists who were pouring the cancer apocalypse into the ears of the press? Once again, when one looks at a few of the most vocal, one finds them expressing the same, familiar themes.

CANCER APOCALYPTICS: THE SCIENTISTS

It was man—producing, consuming man—who was creating the chemical pollution that was causing 80 percent of human cancer. That was the thesis of Thomas Corbett, in one of the earliest books published for laymen on cancer, *Cancer and Chemicals*, in 1977. Corbett, at the University of Michigan, was, to many, the very symbol of the idealistic science-fighter against chemical cancer. He had received an award from the EPA, according to the cover of his book, for "exposing a scandalous mass contamination of animal and human food by PBBs (polybrominated biphenyls) throughout the state of Michigan." Corbett declared that "the United States has one of the world's highest incidences of cancer associated with environmental pollution." The fundamental reason for this disaster, he said, was that "there are too many of us." The great mass of human beings, he said, contributed nothing to civilization: "They only exist, and in the process are a detriment to society. They eat, produce wastes, and when they die they leave a decomposing corpse behind." People, said Corbett, were the cause of cancer-causing chemical pollution by "using modern machines or their products." It was "now believed," he said, "that at least 80 percent of all cancers are caused by synthetic chemicals with unfamiliar names like polyvinyl chloride, styrene oxide, urethane, diethylstilbestrol, and methylcholanthrene." Such chemicals, he said, were found in familiar household products and in industrial wastes, and caused "birth defects, tumors, and death." The teeming, useless millions, he said, are "polluting the environment to a degree that threatens man's existence."[13]

It was the capitalist system that had allowed the post–World War II chemical industry to produce most of the cancer that was killing Americans. This was the message of Barry Commoner, who was speaking in 1977 at an unusual cancer conference designed for laymen. Because a number of the scientists who spoke at that conference will be quoted in this chapter, it should be described. Funded primarily by the National Cancer Institute, which stressed its own neutrality on the issues discussed, the conference was laden with stellar government scientists: Marvin Schneiderman and Robert Hoover of the National Cancer Institute, David Rall of NIEHS, and Eula Bingham of OSHA. Nongovernmental scientists included Samuel Epstein (who had assisted in organizing the conference), Barry Commoner, Irving Selikoff, and John Higginson, Founding Director of the International Agency for Research on Cancer. There were lay participants, including Representative Andrew Maguire of New Jersey and Judge Miles Lord of the U.S. District Court in Minnesota. Finally, there was a host of less well-known scientists and laymen, including representatives of the Sierra Club and the Environmental Defense Fund. It was a remarkable gathering of spokesmen for the little world that had first formed around the environmental cancer issue. At the end of the conference, the climactic summation of the principal ideas and the conclusions of the discussion was offered by Barry Commoner. Commoner had simply adapted his prior views about the destruction of life on earth to the destruction of man by cancer. He declared that "the issue of environmental cancer is largely the issue of all cancer"; that cancer in the United States was caused by the carcinogenic agents in the environment; and that "most of these agents are synthetic organic chemicals." The issue of cancer was synonymous with the issue of the chemical industries, said Commoner: "When you talk about carcinogens you are talking about the economic life of the petrochemical industry, which now largely dominates the American economy." The judgments which had led to this deadly problem, he said, were the judgments normally made in the "private enterprise system," which allowed an entrepreneur to produce anything he wanted by "sacred right," "the right of private property."[14] Thus, the conference on cancer causation for laymen ended with a rousing attack on capitalism.

It was corrupt industrial scientists, intent on protecting profits, who were responsible for the blocking of cancer prevention. This was the theme of the talk by Samuel Epstein of the University of Illinois, who also spoke at the Urban Environment Conference, which he had helped to organize. Epstein had been one of the earliest campaigners for the Toxic Substances Control Act. Much of his book *The Politics of Cancer*, published in 1978, is dedicated to the same theme. At the Urban Environment Conference, Epstein declared: "Cancer is largely environmental in origin and hence, preventable." The most important piece of legislation to guard public health, he said, was TSCA, and the Manufacturing Chemists Association and Dow Chemical Company had "fought tooth and nail" to prevent it. Worse yet, he reported, TSCA depended on a data base furnished by industry, which "is suspect until proven otherwise." According to Epstein, the "overwhelming majority of industry data" which he had examined for "congressional committees, federal agencies, and the media" had been defective, the defects ranging from "suppression of information to manipulation of data to gross inadequacy." He declared there were "no major mysteries or problems" about reducing cancer incidence; "the constraints are primarily economic and political." The actors in the drama of cancer prevention changed from industry to industry, he said, but the pattern was always the same, revealing a disregard for long-term effects on human health and "a high degree of regard for short-term economic profits."[15] Again, the laymen attending this conference of luminaries of the chemical cancer world were told that the disease was political—and could be cured only by politics.

A great cancer epidemic was arriving and/or had arrived because of the post-World War II buildup of industrial chemicals. Depending on the scientist, we were told that a cancer epidemic was an absolute certainty, a possibility, or had already appeared. In 1977, Corbett predicted a terrifying epidemic which would be caused by "the thousands of untested new chemicals introduced into the environment each year." Cancer incidence, he said, "should skyrocket to epidemic proportions by the beginning of the twenty-first century."[16] In 1978, *Newsweek*, whose reporters had interviewed EPA Administrator Douglas Costle, warned that a "chemical plague" was coming; the "plague" image was Costle's. Costle, who spoke with the scientific voice of the EPA, had said: "We look back on the Middle Ages, and we say, 'No wonder they had Bubonic Plague—they used to throw their garbage in the streets.' " Costle hoped, he said, that in the year 2025, his "grandchildren don't look back at this generation" and at the problems caused by "all the chemicals just carelessly introduced into the environment, uncontrolled."[17] And in 1978, Samuel Epstein announced that the epidemic had begun. It was "clear," Epstein said in his new book, that there had been a definitive increase in cancer incidence and mortality in the past hundred years which could not be talked out of existence by statistics about increased cancer caused by smoking. A real "acceleration" in cancer mortality was going on, he announced.[18]

These, then, were some of the scientists who were giving basic instruction in the new discoveries of cancer causation to the laymen of this country. All were apocalyptics. And theirs were the themes one finds in the press and in most of the books of the period which were addressed to laymen. The press, however, was not the only institution to absorb the new apocalypse of cancer. A certain portion of the "elite" had also accepted it. No study has been done on the subject, but one need merely read the endorsements that appeared on the covers of the early books for laymen on cancer to get a picture of the ardent response, in some, to this new variant of the apocalypse. Those who enthusiastically endorsed or reviewed *The Cancer Connection* by Larry Agran (who had informed them that cancer was largely a man-made disease, that as much as 90 percent of American cancer was coming from industry, and that a cancer epidemic of "frightful proportions" was imminent) were, in order of their appearance on the back cover, *Publishers Weekly*, Jane Fonda, *The Nation*, *Columbia Journalism Review*, and David Cohen, President of Common Cause. All found Agran's analysis entirely reasonable—"good sense," as Jane Fonda put it. The President of Common Cause informed the world that Agran's book "makes me cry and makes me angry."[19]

Similarly, the book by the EPA-award-winning Corbett (the apocalyptic who blamed the eventual destruction of the human race on the number of useless people, who attributed 80 percent of cancer to synthetic chemicals, and who warned that cancer incidence would "skyrocket" by the twenty-first century) was hailed on his back cover by *Library Journal*, an important guide to American libraries, as an "important book"—and was passionately endorsed by Minnesota Judge Miles W. Lord, who declared: "If we are to save mankind, we must heed the work of those like Dr. Corbett."[20] Miles Lord did not confine his enthusiasm for this thesis to Corbett's back cover. He was, the reader will recall, yet another speaker at the Urban Environment Conference in 1977, at which he had denounced the corrupt industrial scientists and industrial consultants, "the hired guns of the scientific world," hired, he said, "to misconstrue, to skew, to overlook, and to fabricate." He demanded that the "new Magna Carta of human rights" be applied to American citizens defending "their right not to be killed in the name of profit, not to be sacrificed on the altar of technology."[21]

Finally, another leader of the "elite," a scientist, but one whose field was not cancer, made his appearance on the front cover of a book. It was George Wald, the Harvard apocalyptic, and he endorsed the 1979 paperback edition of Epstein's *The Politics of Cancer.*[22] It was undoubtedly a helpful endorsement to Epstein, since it was a signal to Wald's following that the book was worthy of purchase. But this particular endorsement may create a little confusion in the mind of the reader of this book, since Wald believed that life on earth might end in 1985. It hardly seemed worthwhile to worry about cancer, under the circumstances, given its long latency period. The problem in logic is unsolvable, and it applies not only to Wald, but to Barry Commoner, who even as the planet was expiring decided to run for President. One must generously assume that both men were prepared to go down fighting the corporations until the last protozoan expired beneath their feet, and that they were inviting their admirers to emulate them.

In sum, as TSCA was being born, and for several years afterward, a good portion of the "elite" had no more difficulty accepting the cancer apocalypse than it had accepting the ecological apocalypse. Both were seen as the same issue. The leading apocalyptic scientists, and some eternally unidentified authority or authorities at the National Cancer Institute, had simply transferred the established ideology to a new front. Scientists had legitimized the cancer apocalypse as well.

Or, more precisely, in the case of industrial cancer, they had also legitimized their right to proclaim a cancer apocalypse without any reason to do so. There was one other thing that the press and the "elite" had been told over and over again by scientists, but since the scientists themselves seemed indifferent to it, the laymen too learned to pay it no heed. It was the problem of an extreme shortage of data. This information was often communicated by scientists even as they made their horrifying speculations and prophetic announcements. In 1976, the year of the passage of TSCA, when Russell Train made his announcement to the press that because of industrial chemicals, Americans were now risking their lives by breathing, eating, drinking, and touching, he simultaneously informed the press that most of the chemicals in industries had never been tested. In 1977, when Corbett was predicting a "skyrocketing" cancer explosion from industrial chemicals, he too reported that there were "literally thousands" of those chemicals that had never been tested.[23] Again in 1978, when EPA Administrator Douglas Costle speculated to *Newsweek* on the possibility of a chemical "plague," he told *Newsweek* reporters that there were "an awful lot of chemicals out there that we know very little about."[24] Finally, in the same year, Samuel Epstein considered the lack of data on the effects of industrial chemicals so important that he published the information in a footnote. The majority of industries, he said, had not been "evaluated" for cancer-causation: "This alone makes it impossible to estimate the number of cancers that are industrially related."[25]

As for the genetic damage done by synthetic chemicals, the same coexistence of terrifying speculations and professions of ignorance was found. In the NBC documentary "What Is This Thing Called Food?" Marvin Legator, a prominent geneticist, aired his views to the nation that mutagenic chemicals in food might cause such diseases as schizophrenia, diabetes, and mental retardation. To this, reporter Jim Polk asked: "Of the thousands of chemicals we eat in our food today will they have harmful effects?" And Legator replied: "Well, the great majority of these food additives have not been specifically tested for genetic effects."[26]

To cap the climax, no one even had any idea of the degree of human exposure to the synthetic chemicals. At the Urban Environment Conference of 1977, David Rall, Director of the National Institute of Environmental Health Sciences (NIEHS), informed the audience while arguing for the similarity of rodent and human sensitivity that "good exposure data in the human situation" existed for "only six chemicals."[27]

How, then, did anyone know that industrial substances in general or synthetic chemicals in particular were causing most (60, 80, 90 percent) human cancer? No one did know. That, doubtless, was why the anonymous NCI sources for such statements were anonymous. Someone or some group of scientists at the NCI was certainly feeding journalists these estimates, and the source or sources had obviously asked for confidentiality. There was good reason for this peculiar secrecy in imparting scientific information: It wasn't scientific information. There was no way, given the shortage of data, that a scientist could make a calculation of the percentage of cancer being caused by industrial chemicals. Nor could any scientist have calculated, from *chemicals* alone, that they would cause a cancer epidemic: Every one of the statements on percentages of cancer causation extrapolated from industrial chemicals was unsupported by data, for most industries had never been studied by epidemiologists to discover whether or not they had carcinogenic effects on *people*. To requote Samuel Epstein: "This alone makes it impossible to estimate the number of cancers that are industrially related."

Like the scientific ecological apocalyptics, the scientific cancer apocalyptics were aware of, and indifferent to, the acute shortage of data. It was irrelevant to the emotions and intuitions from which they actually extrapolated the cancer apocalypse. And thus we find ourselves looking right at the "apocalyptic paradigm"—that mysterious "scientific" paradigm which rejected facts, logic, and scientific disciplines; which engaged in the fabrication of imaginary percentages; which projected vast extrapolations from fragments of real or alleged data; and which disseminated terrifying and baseless conclusions to the nation. That very "apocalyptic paradigm" was present in the informal education being given to laymen.

There is only one aspect of that "paradigm" that has not yet been mentioned—the substitution of moral concepts for missing data. That moral constituent of the "paradigm" was supplied to the press and to the nation by a few government scientists and heads of research agencies. It took the form of solutions to problems of industrially caused cancer. Two moral concepts, above all, were communicated to laymen.

The first concept was that it was unethical to wait until the science of epidemiology, the science which studies people *after* they have gotten cancer, had made its discoveries; and that the moral solution was to *prevent* cancer before anyone got it. There was a way to do this, said government scientists: One could simply use animal tests to predict cancer in man. Animals had been used for decades in all biological research, in pharmacology, in medicine, and in industrial toxicology because the physiology of all mammals is broadly similar. Quite suddenly, the public was told, it had been found that animals could predict and prevent human cancer. Thus, on April 18, 1976, Russell Train, then EPA Administrator, made these very points to the reporters on CBS's "Face the Nation."[28] And in 1976, David Rall, Director of NIEHS, told Lesley Stahl of CBS, on "The Politics of Cancer": "Mice and rats predict very well for human cancer. If you don't accept the mouse and rat data, you only have one alternative, and that's letting the human population be exposed for about 25 years and if in fact the compound was carcinogenic you can have a small epidemic of chemical carcinogenesis in man after that 25 years. So I think there's no alternative. We have to view the mouse and rat data as predictive for man."[29] Rall did not explain why we "have" to view the mouse and rat data "as predictive for man," if mice and rats *do* "predict very well" for man. He made the same double moral-scientific point when addressing the Urban Environment Conference in 1977. After repeating that "animal and microbiological tests do predict well for man," he added: "There are other compelling arguments in favor of animal tests. The epidemiological approach requires at least 30 to 40 years of human exposure; it is insensitive to small changes in rates; it is susceptible to confounding and confusing factors; and, finally and simply, it is to me morally wrong to use the human population as the test animals."[30] Again, the slight mystery about invoking morality to justify the use of a good scientific prediction was left dangling. One does not customarily invoke morality as a "compelling argument" for accepting the prediction that water, at a given temperature, will boil, or for accepting the law of gravity. Rall's morality was irreproachable, but it undercut his claims to scientific prediction.

The second moral concept taught to laymen by government scientists pertained to the amount or dose of exposure to a carcinogen that might endanger human beings. How much *was* dangerous? Here is how various government scientists answered this question directly or indirectly to CBS-TV News, and to the audience at the Urban Environment Conference for laymen.

1975: Marvin Schneiderman of the National Cancer Institute told Dan Rather of CBS: "It's certainly possible that minute amounts can be dangerous."[31]

1976: CBS reporter Lesley Stahl thus summed up what she had been told by unnamed NCI scientists: "But scientists at the National Cancer Institute say cancer may start with one single molecule and every extraneous risk that can be eliminated must be eliminated."[32]

1977: Marvin Schneiderman, speaking again at the Urban Environment Conference, said: "Several methods for making calculations of risk have been considered and used, but the most prudent method available to us today is to assume no threshold for a carcinogen (i.e., no proven 'safe' dose). . . ."[33]

1977: Eula Bingham, Assistant Secretary of Labor for Occupational Safety and Health, speaking at the same conference, said: "Under the proposed theories of cancer, only one molecule may cause cancer, although many molecules are usually necessary to get to the target cell."[34]

Although clearly some NCI scientists were skittish about being quoted as saying that on moral grounds they were assuming that one molecule of a carcinogen might cause cancer, that, in fact, is what many were assuming, and it was to become official policy. This is called the "one-molecule" theory of carcinogenesis, and the reader may as well be warned right now that it has an unimaginable significance in cancer prevention and will show up in different ways and forms throughout this book. Whether scientists use the concept "no safe dose," "no threshold," or the "one-molecule theory," they mean precisely the same thing—that even the most minute dose, even a single molecule, may trigger a lethal change in a cell that will cause it to multiply malignantly. This was, as Eula Bingham put it candidly, the expression of a "proposed theory of cancer." Or, as Marvin Schneiderman put it equally candidly, it was "prudent" to assume it. It was thus not a proved principle—it was moral stuffing for the void of ignorance.

And here we stop—with the "apocalyptic paradigm" complete, paraded before our eyes in the earliest scientific communications to laymen around the time of the passage of the Toxic Substances Control Act.

In 1975, one year before the passage of the Toxic Substances Control Act, the apocalyptic typhoon was still blowing through the brains of the press and the "elite." The sources quoted in this chapter tell us clearly that the apocalypse provided the intellectual framework for the interpretation of the deluge of "suspected" carcinogens descending upon us and that, once again, it was scientists both in and out of government who were legitimizing the interpretation. The apocalypse had indeed invaded the realm of environmental cancer. Indeed, it had obviously invaded the realm of cancer prevention.

It was this discovery that influenced the course of my investigation and set my general goals. I would hunt for the genuinely scientific dimension of the field; I would try to establish what chemical carcinogens had been identified; I would try to assess the government's program of cancer prediction and prevention by animal testing in order to discover how and whether it worked; and I would try to ferret out the "apocalyptic paradigm" and discover exactly where it was lodged and what purpose it served.

PART

II

THE PLANET DISAPPEARS

Chapter 3

Lethal Industry

In other words, for a prudent toxicological policy, a chemical should be considered guilty until proven innocent.[1]
—Umberto Saffiotti, National Cancer Institute, May 1976

In effect, the government can now regard chemicals as guilty until proven innocent.[2]
—Newsweek, August 1978

I started this intellectual voyage by considering the phenomenon of chemical carcinogenicity, for, like most laymen, I had heard of nothing else. My immediate goal was to get an independent perspective on the kind of data that had been reported on chemical carcinogens, and that goal was, to some degree, achievable; such a survey constitutes one-half of this chapter. But the voyage itself was surprising; I encountered unexpected obstacles and I made two very strange discoveries.

THE OBSTACLE COURSE

The chief problem pertained to the nature of experimental science itself. It is a discipline in which men, like an army of diligent ants, bite off microscopic bits of a problem, study those bits, and publish reports on what they have discovered; one is consequently confronted by the minutiae of acute specialization. The nature of the minutiae characteristic of most carcinogenesis research can be best communicated to the reader by subjecting him to a portion of the bibliography on one single substance. In this case, it is PCBs, but it might as well be anything else. Here are just a few of the references cited by a single source—Vol. 7 of the IARC monographs (1974):

Curley, A., Burse, V. W. & Grim, M. E. (1973a) Polychlorinated biphenyls: evidence of transplacental passage in Sherman rat. *Fd Cosmet. Toxicol., 11*, 471–476

Dahlgren, R. B., Greichus, Y. A. & Linder, R. L. (1971) Storage and excretion of polychlorinated biphenyls in the pheasant. *J. Wildlife Management, 35*, 823–828

Fries, G. F., Marrow, G. S., Jr. & Gordon, C. H. (1973) Long-term studies of residue retention and excretion by cows fed a polychlorinated biphenyl (Arochlor 1254). *J. agric. Fd. Chem., 21*, 117–120

Gardner, A. M., Chen, J. T., Roach, J. A. G. & Ragelis, E. P. (1973) Polychlorinated biphenyls: hydroxylated urinary metabolites of 2,5,2',5'-tetrachlorobiphenyl identified in rabbits. *Biochem. Biophys. Res. Commun., 55,* 1377–1384

Goto, M., Sugimura, K., Hattori, M., Miyagawa, T. & Okamura, M. (1973) *Hydroxylation of dichlorobiphenyls in rats.* In: Coulston, F., Korte, F. & Goto, M., eds., *New Methods in Environmental Chemistry and Toxicology,* Tokyo, Academic Scientific Book Inc., pp. 299–302

Grant, D. L., Villeneuve, D. C., McCully, K. A. & Phillips, W. E. J. (1971) Placental transfer of polychlorinated biphenyls in the rabbit. *Environm. Physiol., 1,* 61–66.

Ito, N., Nagasaki, H., Makiura, S. & Arai, M. (1974) Histopathologic studies on liver tumorigenesis in rats treated with technical polychlorinated biphenyls. *Gann* (in press)

Kimbrough, R. D. & Linder, R. E. (1974) The induction of adenofibrosis and hepatomas of the liver in mice of the BALB/cj strain by polychlorinated biphenyls (Arochlor 1254). *J. nat. Cancer Inst.* (in press)

Kimura, N. T. & Baba, T. (1973) Neoplastic changes in the rat liver induced by polychlorinated biphenyls. *Gann, 64,* 105–108

Nagasaki, H., Tomii, S., Mega, T., Marugami, M. & Ito, N. (1972) Hepatocarcinogenicity of polychlorinated biphenyls in mice. *Gann, 63,* 805

Norbach, D. H. & Allen, J. P. (1972) Chlorinated aromatic hydrocarbon induced modifications of the hepatic endoplasmic reticulum: concentric membrane assays. *Environm. Hlth Perspect., 1,* 137–143

To compound the problem, such papers exist by the thousands, each usually dealing with one particular chemical. One is thus faced not with minutiae alone, but with a veritable mountain of minutiae. Shortly after the passage of TSCA, the most efficient way for a layman to get a sense of the magnitude of this mountain was to scan a publication called *Suspected Carcinogens* produced in 1976 by the National Institute for Occupational Safety and Health (NIOSH). It is a catalogue of all substances reported, validly or not, to be carcinogens as of that date, plus a group of "suspected" substances—2,413 in all. In this catalogue, the entire bibliography on one substance—e.g., PCBs—is reduced to one or two mentions of each of the compounds tested, along with a few coded symbols referring to the findings. The catalogue is large, it includes 238 pages of very fine type, and the substances are listed alphabetically. To illustrate the contents, on the next page I list some—not all—of the substances to be found under the letter A.

The parade of chemicals continues for every letter of the alphabet—and it just scratches the surface of the problem of carcinogenicity; as Samuel Epstein observes, "The majority of industries has not been evaluated for cancer. . . ."[3]

The number of documents is a serious problem for the layman until he grasps that scientists suffer from it chronically, and have devised a variety of systems which allow them to slash their way through the "knowledge explosion" to the most essential findings. They prepare "literature reviews" in which scientists, individually or in groups, review and screen the data in specific areas; they prepare "abstracts" summing up the major findings of their experi-

ABIETYLAMINE,BIS(DEHYDRO-,ACETATE*ABIETYLAMINE,DEHY
DRO-,ACETATE*ACENAPHTHENE*ACENAPHTHENE,5-NITRO-*AC
ETAMIDE*ACETAMIDE,N-ACETYL-N-(2-METHYL-4-((2-METHYLPH
EYL)AZO)PHENYL)-*ACETAMIDE,2-AMINO-N-FLUOREN-2-YL-*AC
ETAMIDE,N,O-BIS(TRIMETHYLSILYL)-*ACETAMIDE,N-(CARBAMO
YLMETHYL)-2-DIAZO-*ACETAMIDE,N-(7-CHLORO-2-FLUORENYL)
*ACETAMIDE,N-3-DIBENZOFURANYL-*ACETAMIDE,N-2-DIBENZO
THINYL-*ACETAMIDE,N-3-DIBENZOTHTENYL-*ACETAMIDE,N-3-
DIBNZOTHIENYL-,5-OXIDE*ACETAMIDE,2,2-DICHLORO-N(beta-HY
DROXY-alpha-(HYDROXYMETHYL)-p-NITROPHENETHYL-D-(-)-thre
o-*ACETAMIDE,N,N-DIETHYL-*ACETAMIDE,N-(9,10-DIHYDRO-2-P
HENANTTHRYL)-*ACETAMIDE,N,N-DIMETHYL-2,2-DIPHENYL-*A
CETAMIDE,N-3-FLUORANTHENYL-*ACETAMIDE,N-FLUOREN-1-Y
L*ACETAMIDE,N-FLUOREN-2-YL-*ACETAMIDE,N-FLUOREN-4-YL
-*ACETAMIDE,N-FLUOREN-2-YLDI-*ACETAMIDE,N,N'-FLUOREN-
2,5-YLENEBIS-*ACETAMIDE,N,N'-FLUOREN-2,7-YLENEBIS-*ACETA
MIDE,N,N'-FLUOREN-2,7-YLENEBIS(TRIFLUORO-*ACETAMIDE,N-
FLUOREN-2-YL-2,2,2-TRIFLUORO-*ACETAMIDE,N-(1-FLUOROFLU
OREN-2-YL)-*ACETAMIDE,N-(3-FLUOROFLUOREN-2-YL)-*ACETA
MIDE,N-(4-FLUOROFLUOREN-2-YL)-*ACETAMIDE,N-(5-FLUOROF
LUOREN-2-YL)-*ACETAMIDE,N-(6-FLUOROFLUOREN-2-YL)*ACET
AMIDE,N-(7-FLUOROFLUOREN-2-YL)*ACETAMIDE,N-(8-FLUOROF
LUOREN-2-YL)-*ACETAMIDE,N-(9-HYDROXYFLUOREN-2-YL)-*AC
ETAMIDE,N-(4-((2-HYDROXY-5-METHYLPHENYL)AZO)PHENYL)-*
ACETAMIDE,N-(3-IODO-2-FLUORENYL)-*ACETAMIDE,N-(1-METHO
XYFLUOREN-2-YL)-*ACETAMIDE,N-(7-METHOXYFLUOREN-2-YL)
-*ACETAMIDE,N-METHYL-N-NITROSO-*ACETAMIDE,5-(3-(5-NITR
O-2-FURYL)-6H-1,2,4-OXADIAZINYL)-*ACETAMIDE,N-((3-(5-NITRO-
2-FURYL)-1,2,4-OXADIAZOLE-5-YL)METHYL)-*ACETAMIDE,N-(5-(5-
NITRO-2-FURYL)-1,3,,4-THIADIAZOL-2-YL)-*ACETAMIDE,N-(4-(5-NI
TRO-2-FURYL)-2-THIAZOLYL)-*ACETAMIDE,N-(4-(5-NITRO-2-FUR
YL-2-THIAZOLYL)-*ACETAMIDE,N-(4-(5-NITRO-2-FURYL-2-THIAZ
OLYL)-2,2,2-TRIFLUORO-*ACETAMIDE,N-(9-OXO-2-FLUORENYL)-*
ACETAMIDE,N-2-PHENANTHRYL-*ACETAMIDE,N-3-PHENANTHR
YL-*ACETAMIDE,N-9-PHENHNTHRYL-*ACETAMIDE,N-PYREN-2-Y
L-*ACETAMIDE,p-TERPHENYL-4-YL-*ACETAMIDE,THIO-*ACETAM
IDE,2,2,2-TRIFLUORO-N-(9-OOOFLUOREN-2-YL)*ACETANILIDE,3'-
AMINO-4'-ETHOXY-*ACETANILIDE,4'-(CHLOROACETYL)-*ACETA
NILIDE,4-((p-(DIMETHYLAMINO)PHENYL)AZO)-N-METHYL-*ACET
ANILIDE,N,N'-DIMETHYL-4,4'-AZODI-*ACETANILIDE,2'-FLUORO-4
'-PHENYL-*ACETANILIDE,4'-(m-FLUOROPHENYL)-*ACETANILIDE,
4'-(p-FLUOROPHENYL)-*ACETANILIDE,4'-(p-HYDROXYSTYRYL)-*
ACETANILIDE,4-(p-METHYLAMINOPHENYLAZO)-N-METHYL-*AC
ETANILIDE,2'-PHENYL-*ACETANILIDE,3'-PHENYL-*ACETANILIDE
,4'-PHENYL-*ACETANILIDE,4'-PHENYLAZO-*ACETANILIDE,4'-STY
RYL-*ACETANILIDE,4'4'''-SULFONYLBIS-*ACETANILIDE,m-TOLYL

ments; they hold conferences at which the scientists who are deemed by their colleagues to be doing the most important work are invited to present their findings; individuals writing papers often provide rapid surveys of the findings on their particular subject as a part of the paper itself; anthologies are published which compile the seminal papers on specific subjects. The same systems that assist scientists assist the lay researcher as well. Most of the reported data in the survey that appears later in this chapter come from just such overviews of the literature provided by scientists.

THE FIRST DISCOVERY

Bulk and detail were the biggest mechanical obstacles in this voyage, but the most startling obstacle was an intellectual discovery: There was no way to make even the most limited generalizations about the significance of the animal data and still remain neutral in the controversies one was attempting to assess. The dilemma can be quickly stated, although it takes the entire book to unravel. It rests on the fact that there are essentially two kinds of data on chemical cancer—comparatively few studies on human beings and a gigantic number of studies on animals. The meaning for man of the few human studies is self-evident. The meaning for man of the huge body of animal studies is not; it requires interpretation. One cannot, however, find any interpretation of the significance of the animal data without entering the regulatory world and accepting regulatory theory as a guide. For all practical purposes, the available organized thought on the human implications of animal data *is* regulatory thought. Its original premise was that most, if not all, cancer could be prevented by identifying carcinogens in animal tests and by regulating the industries that produce them or by banning them. The regulatory institutions of cancer prevention in the United States are expressions of this very belief. In sum, "environmental" cancer *is* "corporate" cancer, and cancer prevention *is* the regulation of industry. That means that the intellectual world we are about to enter is the very regulatory and public policy world we are trying to transcend and judge. But we cannot escape it. If one is to find even a handful of guiding ideas to help us understand the significance of animal data to man, it is to "official" theory that one must turn.

In this chapter, therefore, we will view the animal data with the eyes of "official" science. This is a strange situation, since it is roughly akin to saying that we are about to check on the translation of a document in an alien tongue by using a dictionary devised by the very translator on whom we wish to check. It is a circular process; it sounds like an impossible intellectual trap, and it would be one save for two facts: The government's approach itself, once identified, can be evaluated in some respects; in addition, later bodies of data will assist us in gaining further perspective on it. But for now, there is no alternative. We must approach the animal data as do those who create or follow regulatory theory, and that means that, in short order, we must learn to *think* in their terms.

In practice, that means that we must acquire some of the major assumptions with which the government theoreticians and the academic scientists who share their views interpret the animal data. The man we shall select as our primary instructor is Umberto Saffiotti of the National Cancer Institute. Saffiotti's full title is Chief of the Laboratory of Experimental Pathology, Carcinogenesis Intramural Program, Division of Cancer Cause and Prevention of the National Cancer Institute; and he, perhaps more than any other contemporary scientist, has translated the problems of carcinogenesis into an organized body of theory. In the field of chemical carcinogenesis, Saffiotti is an intellectual's intellectual. He is not known to the wide public, nor is he a "visible scientist" or a media cult figure, so a few words should be said about his influence and how he acquired it. There are doubtless a number of versions of the story, but we will settle here for the account supplied by one of his early allies and admirers, Jacqueline Verrett of the FDA. According to Verrett, Saffiotti was one of the prominent participants in a rebellion of scientists that took place within the government's scientific bureaucracies in the 1960s, a rebellion allied from the beginning with a few members of the world of academic research, with the environmental and consumer movements, and with certain political figures. This "dissenting vitality," as Verrett described it, consisted of those "scientists . . . who could be counted on to strongly disagree with 'establishment' policy when it was scientifically untenable."[4] At the National Cancer Institute, the leaders of the rebellion included Wilhelm Hueper, former Chief of the Environmental Cancer Section, and Saffiotti, then Associate Director for Carcinogenesis. At the FDA, she said, they included Dr. Marvin Legator, Dr. Herman Kraybill, and Dr. Kent Davis. Chief among the academic allies, according to Verrett's account, were geneticist Joshua Lederberg, Samuel Epstein, and Matthew Meselson, a biologist at Harvard. The "public interest" allies were numerous. There were Ralph Nader and the leaders of his many interlocking organizations: James Turner, Director of Consumer Action for Improved Food and Drugs; Anita Johnson and Dr. Sidney Wolfe of the Health Research Group; and Harrison Wellford of the Center for the Study of Responsive Law (which sponsored the exposé of the National Academy of Sciences by Philip Boffey). In addition, there were David Hawkins of the National Resources Defense Council, Inc.; Peter Schuck of the Consumers Union; Ruth Desmond of the Federation of Homemakers, Inc.; and Michael F. Jacobson of the Center for Science in the Public Interest. Finally, said Verrett, the important congressional allies were Senators Edward M. Kennedy, Gaylord Nelson, and Abraham A. Ribicoff, as well as Representative H. L. Fountain.[5]

Saffiotti, in sum, was one of the founding fathers of the contemporary crusade against industrial cancer; he was an integral part of a strong political-scientific movement in the 1960s, and the success of that movement in both the lay and the regulatory world greatly magnified his influence. He played an instrumental role in the formulation of the original cancer prevention program: In 1970, he was chairman of the "Ad Hoc Committee on the Evaluation of Low Levels of Environmental Carcinogens" which informed the Surgeon General that "the mass" of cancer could be prevented by legislation. That document is, so to speak, the original bible of the world of cancer prevention, and it is reproduced in its entirety in the appendix of Samuel Epstein's *The Politics of*

Cancer. Rare is the American regulatory document dealing with interpretation of the animal data on carcinogens that does not quote, paraphrase, or footnote Saffiotti or depend, historically, on some of his thoughts: He is one of the authors of the National Cancer Institute's *Guidelines for Carcinogenesis Bioassay in Small Rodents,* published in 1976[6]—this, too, the official U.S. bible on the conduct of animal testing. In the work of Samuel Epstein, Saffiotti's role as a molder of the government's toxicological policy on industrial carcinogens is written about in detail and in a manner that communicates Epstein's profound admiration.[7] It is certainly Saffiotti who has most clearly stated the philosophical ideas of the regulatory world—and since we are about to embrace those ideas, there is no better teacher.

Saffiotti's most fundamental assumption is that industrial chemicals are the primary source of American cancer. In 1976, while campaigning for the passage of the Toxic Substances Control Act, he delivered a paper at a Canadian cancer conference in which he identified the culpability of the industrial system, and that paper has become something of a classic. Calling himself a spokesman for cancer prevention, he described cancer as "largely preventable" and said:

I consider cancer as a social disease, largely caused by external agents which are derived from our technology, conditioned by our societal lifestyle and whose control is dependent on societal actions and policies.[8]

Enormous investments, said Saffiotti, had been made in products and technologies which have "conditioned" us into "induced needs" and had become "powerful economic and social factors." But, he added, science and technology had also made it possible to discover that "certain aspects of technological 'progress' may bring grief, disease, and death." The solution, he said, was to adopt "less dangerous technological alternatives."

Saffiotti's originality did not lie in his social theories. There was nothing new about his view of modern technology, or the "progress" that he put within quotation marks, or, for that matter, about the view that powerful economic forces were manipulating consumers into "induced needs" and addictions. These beliefs have been common coin among critics of the American social system since the 1950s, they had all been expressed by Rachel Carson a decade earlier, and by the 1970s, they were a set piece in the "environmental," radical, and counterculture movements. Similarly, Saffiotti's belief that cancer was a political disease whose cause was "largely" rooted in our economic system was not new; that idea was more than several decades old and, as we shall soon discover, was taught to Rachel Carson by the late Wilhelm Hueper of the National Cancer Institute. Saffiotti's immense originality lay in stating his ideas openly and in print. As we saw, in the last chapter, the idea attributed to anonymous whisperers at the National Cancer Institute that industrial technology was causing most of the cancer that was killing Americans roared through the major media like a revelation. Saffiotti did not whisper his ideas; he stood up and said them aloud. His own formulation, that cancer is a "social disease," was transmitted to the layman by such writers as Agran in *The Cancer Connection* (1977)[9] and Bil Gilbert in *Audubon* (1979).[10]

Unlike many of his devout followers in science and journalism, however, Saffiotti knew the limits of his own statement that industrial chemicals were the primary source of human cancer. He had never presented this as a scientific conclusion that had emerged from a disciplined study of the facts; he could hardly have done so, since he was fighting for a program which would make it possible to acquire the facts; what is more, he knew that most industrial substances had never been tested. He had offered the idea that most cancer came from our technology and the manipulation of the marketplace as a personal belief—"I consider . . ."—and had not misrepresented its status. In his Canadian paper, he did something additional, however, that was considerably more audacious. He proposed, in effect, that his personal belief be endowed with the status of a toxicological axiom. Given his personal assumption that most cancer was coming from industrial chemicals, Saffiotti indicated the kind of policy that would be logically consistent with that assumption. The critical core of that policy, he said, lay in the approach to the carcinogen data that fell into "a gray area." Saffiotti explained this by breaking all data down into three categories, and formulating a policy based on the third—an apparently dry little academic exercise which had explosive implications. Here were Saffiotti's three categories of data:

1. Data were positive, he said, when exposure to the substance was conclusively shown to cause tumors in humans or in animals of one or more species.
2. Data were negative, he said, when no tumors were induced, but this observation was "only valid within the conditions of the observations" (meaning that another experiment might be designed in which the same substance would induce tumors).
3. Data were inconclusive, he said, when observations were "lacking," when they were of "poor quality," or because of their "excessively limited extent"; this, he said, was the "gray area" in which results could range from "uninformative to highly suggestive."

Most data, including the "data" which were "lacking," said Saffiotti, fell into that third "gray area," and he went on to define the toxicological policy he would like to see applied to that area:

The most "prudent" policy is to consider all agents, for which the evidence is not clearly negative under accepted minimum conditions of observation, as if they were positive. . . . *In other words, for a prudent toxicological policy a chemical should be considered guilty until proven innocent.*[11] [Emphasis added]

In his paper, Saffiotti made no mention of the number of chemicals that would be so interpreted, but at that very time, David P. Rall, Director of the National Institute of Environmental Health Sciences, had put the figure of industrial chemicals at 10,000,[12] and few of them had ever been tested for carcinogenicity. The assumption that "external agents . . . derived from our technology" were the primary cause of most cancer and a guilty-until-proven-innocent policy thus meant, in 1976, that almost 10,000 chemicals were to be presumed "guilty" of causing cancer in the United States and that almost none could be considered "innocent." What Saffiotti was actually saying here was both scientifically and politically revolutionary. Biologically, he was postulating that a disease, understood by no one, might have 10,000 possible causes. And that same unusual biological postulate implicated most American manufacturers as presumed generators of cancer. Saffiotti was aware that his own mental processes were of interest. Although he made no observations on the implications of his biological postulate, he did observe that the political implementation of his proposed toxicological policy reflected a certain "Utopianism."[13]

Biologically unusual and utopian or not, these were the very ideas that flooded through the nation. In 1976, the national press excitedly informed the country that industrial chemicals were responsible for as much as 90 percent of the cancer in this country. The idea that chemicals should be presumed "guilty" until proved "innocent" quickly became a rallying cry for "activists." In 1976, CBS-TV News scooped its colleagues in its documentary called "The Politics of Cancer" with the revelations of three EPA "whistle-blowers," a group of angry lawyers who had quit the agency because, as CBS put it: "Chemicals on the market have the same right as people. They must be considered innocent until proven guilty."[14] By 1978, Newsweek was reporting, approvingly, that "the government can now regard chemicals as guilty until proven innocent."[15] Almost overnight it seemed, Saffiotti's deepest personal assumptions about how to approach toxicological data had become the law of the land and the bromides of the enlightened. To what degree this can be attributed to Saffiotti is a matter for a scientific historian. According to informed sources of the period, he was extremely influential, and that is enough for our purposes.

Although the seminal idea—that industrial chemicals were presumed in advance to be "guilty" of causing most cancer—was never explicitly written into regulation or law, many of the policies that logically emerged from that premise were accepted by the cancer prevention establishment. Among the most important were those that applied to the interpretation of the animal data. Five of those policies are particularly critical; they are elaborations of ideas the reader has already heard in headline form, and they are the basic conceptual repertoire to bring to the animal data if one is to approach the data with any concepts at all. In most cases, they are candidly stated by those who voice them to be assumptions. They are not scientific principles; their primary purpose is to permit conclusions to be drawn in the "gray area" of animal research where knowledge is inadequate, inconclusive, or lacking. In this sense, they are five undemonstrable postulates about the unknown or the largely unknown. Nonetheless, they have serious scientific content, for the very formulations that describe the unknown emerge from the most advanced frontiers of carcinogenesis. They are, consequently, very sophisticated professions of ignorance.

Some of these assumptions overlap, to some degree; but each stresses an idea of importance. Each will be stated first in clear English, and it will be followed by several expressions of that same assumption in "scientific English." Despite a certain opacity of verbiage, the five ideas themselves are not particularly complex, and they are presented as they appear in the original texts because it is imperative that the lay reader be liberated from secondhand versions that are less precise—and far less startling. More than one version of each assumption is given because the nuances are informative and because we cannot depend on one expert, however authoritative. Those quoted, in addition to Saffiotti, are government and academic scientists who are active in the cancer prevention field, and many of the following citations are from government documents.

Assumption No. 1: Since there is evidence that most known human carcinogens are also carcinogenic in animals, we shall assume, despite the absence of proof, that small groups of laboratory animals can serve as biological stand-ins for our entire society.

In 1972, Saffiotti, then NCI's Associate Director for Carcinogenesis, stated that despite man-animal correlations, animal findings did not constitute proof of cancer causation in human beings. But, he said, animals had to be used anyway:

Over one thousand chemical substances have been shown to be carcinogenic by tests in animals (although some of the "positive" tests reported in the literature—particularly the older ones—are not quite satisfactory by present standards). Several individual chemicals or mixtures of chemicals have also been shown conclusively to be carcinogenic by direct observation in man. . . . With the exception of arsenic, still under experimental study, all the main products that were found to be carcinogenic by direct evidence in man have also been proven carcinogenic in animals. *On the other hand, proof that a substance, which had been recognized as carcinogenic in animals, actually causes cancer in man would require in most cases extremely complex and lengthy epidemiologic studies. In many cases, it may be impossible to obtain such proof because of the complexity of controls that would be needed for a satisfactory demonstration. Therefore, the only prudent course of action at the present state of our knowledge is to assume that chemicals which are carcinogenic in animals could also be so in man, although the direct demonstration in man is lacking.*[16] [Emphasis added]

The same essential statement can be found, seven years later, in a 1979 Staff Paper by the Office of Sciences and Technology, adapted for publication in the *Journal of the National Cancer Institute:*

Virtually every chemical shown to be carcinogenic in humans has also been shown to be carcinogenic in other mammals (arsenic and benzene are the major apparent exceptions). *Although proof is impossible that the converse is true, it is prudent to view a positive test result in a carefully designed and well-conducted mammalian study as evidence of potential human carcinogenicity.*[17] [Emphasis added]

Several paragraphs later, the OST staff scientists also stated that animals did not necessarily predict for each other, and that scientists had no idea on which species they could rely in making extrapolations to man. Interpretations of conflicting data, said the staff, should be made "taking into account the frequent occurrence of inter-species variation and the inability to determine which species experience is most relevant to that of humans."[18]

(This is not what David Rall of the NIEHS had said in 1976 to CBS or to the Urban Environment Conference in 1977. He had flatly declared that animals predicted very well for man, and beamed the news all over the nation. We are not yet in a position to account for this disparity of views, but we duly note it.)

Assumption No. 2: Since no one knows what amount of a carcinogen is required to trigger the growth of a malignancy, it must be assumed that there is no threshold dose—i.e., that no amount of any carcinogen is safe.

This idea is clearly of immense importance to government scientists, since it was widely circulated throughout the country at the time of the passage of the Toxic Substances Control Act. Usually it appeared in its simplest form—that expressed in the last chapter by Marvin Schneiderman of the NCI, who declared that where risk of cancer was concerned, "the prudent method available to us today is to assume no threshold for a carcinogen (i.e., no proven 'safe' dose)." "Prudence" in the face of uncertainty is an easy idea for the public to understand, but it is not the only reason scientists give each other for the assumption that no threshold dose of a carcinogen can be identified. There are actually many different reasons for this "prudent" assumption, as we will learn as this book progresses. But several of the arguments for the no-threshold theory will be presented here, for the capsule argument is an adequate guide to the issue. If we are going to adopt a biological assumption, we must have some idea what it is. Here are three of the basic scientific arguments. They often appear in the same documents, but they will be presented separately, for clarity.

The first argument for the no-threshold theory is statistical. It pertains to the limitations of what can be learned from a small number of animals used to test a *single carcinogen*. The standard version of this explanation was offered in 1972 by the Committee on Biologic Effects of Atmospheric Pollutants in a work published by the National Academy of Sciences:

Although dose-response studies have been carried out with many chemicals and the problem of quantitative carcinogenesis has been extensively studied for a few selected carcinogens, it has not been possible to reach agreement as to whether there is a threshold dosage above which carcinogenesis is produced. The dilemma is related to the shape of the dose-response curve. . . . *Because it is impossible, at very low doses, to obtain reliable data without enormous numbers of animals . . . the concept of a threshold dose is probably meaningless, and it would be prudent, because of these uncertainties of measurement, to extrapolate dose-response curves to zero in a linear fashion.*[19] [Emphasis added]

The second argument is broader. It may include the first, and it still pertains to a single carcinogen, but here the stress is on the limitations in the understanding of the human response. In 1973, Saffiotti presented the reasoning as follows, again basing it on uncertainty or ignorance:

. . . if a threshold exists for each *individual* (even a heavy smoker may not get lung cancer), we are not in a position to predict it in advance with certainty, and we cannot extrapolate it to the whole population.[20]

The third argument is even more complex, for this time the rejection of a threshold rests not on the limitation of what can be extrapolated from mice, and not on the limitation of our understanding of man, but on the phenomenon of chemical interactions—and it pertains to *non*carcinogens as well as carcinogens as they may affect *the cell*. Several examples of this particular reason for rejecting thresholds will be given, for they offer us slightly different views of the role of the *non*carcinogenic chemical in cancer causation.

In the 1973 paper cited above, Saffiotti, observing that the area of synergism was "essentially unpredictable," touched for one moment on the carcinogenic hazard of *non*carcinogenic chemicals:

Our knowledge of combined effects of different chemicals in carcinogenesis is still quite scanty. . . . I can best summarize our knowledge in this field by saying that the extent by which several chemicals may potentiate each other in carcinogenesis is still essentially unpredictable and subject to a variety of host factors; however, there is an increasing list of examples from animal experimentation as well as human observation which show that a considerable level of potentiation may occur in the induction of certain cancers, *even between agents that are not known to produce a given type of cancer by themselves.* [Emphasis added]

In this passage, Saffiotti had actually said something extraordinary—namely, that cancer could be caused by the interaction of two or more substances, neither of which was known to be a cancer-causing agent. He did not develop this fascinating idea, but immediately added:

The scientific data available to us today do not allow us to arrive at an estimate of a safe level for a carcinogen in man.[21]

In a 1977 explanation of the dangers of even the lowest levels of exposure, Roy Albert, chairman of the Carcinogen Assessment Group of the EPA, discussed the role of the *non*carcinogenic chemical as an inducer of cancer:

Studies dealing with the carcinogenic effects of air pollutants suggest that the conventional approach of characterizing cancer risks in an exposed population by extrapolating dose-tumor-incidence curves to define an explicit probability of developing cancer from a given low level of carcinogen exposure may be inaccurate. The sounder view may be that, *at very low dose levels, there is an important additional component of risk involving a heightened susceptibility to cancer induction by a variety of agents that would otherwise be relatively innocuous.* . . .

Initiation by a subtumorigenic dose of a carcinogen has the attributes of the induction of a mutation. It occurs abruptly. It is irreversible. *Initiation is also nonprogressive and is therefore latent unless promoted by an agent which by itself may be virtually noncarcinogenic.* . . .

Thus low level carcinogen exposure that, by conventional extrapolation models, might be expected to produce a rare cancer may actually cause a much larger incidence of irreversible and latent damage. *Although the cancer risks from carcinogen exposure per se may be very low, the realistic cancer risk may be much higher, depending on the kinds and extent of exposures to substances which have the capability of translating the latent changes into neoplastic disease. . . . Low-level carcinogen exposure may therefore act as a corrosive to health by heightening the susceptibility to cancer induction by otherwise noncarcinogenic substances.*[22] [Emphasis added]

And in 1978, Samuel Epstein's *Politics of Cancer* appeared, in which this expert in carcinogenesis, who had often acted as an adviser to government, gave precisely equal stress to the dangers of noncarcinogens and carcinogens. Here is his version of the argument against thresholds:

... there is also substantive evidence of interactions between individual carcinogens making the carcinogens together much more potent than either separately. *Also interactions between carcinogens and a wide range of non-carcinogenic chemicals may increase the potency of the carcinogens. For example, the incidence of liver cancers induced in trout by feeding as little as 0.4 parts per billion (ppb) of aflatoxin is sharply increased by addition of various non-carcinogenic oils to the diet. Similarly, the carcinogenic effects of low concentrations of benzo(a)pyrene on mouse skin are increased 1,000-fold by the use of the non-carcinogenic n-dodecane as a solvent.* Benzo(a)pyrene and ferric oxide injected in the trachea of adult rodents induce a high incidence of lung tumors, only if the animals are pretreated at birth with a single low dose of another carcinogen, diethylnitrosamine. *The quantitative response to a particular carcinogen can be substantially influenced by a wide range of factors, including interaction with other carcinogenic and non-carcinogenic chemicals.* Thus, these so-called synergistic effects further confound attempts to find safe levels of carcinogens. Such interaction studies clearly confirm that threshold levels of carcinogens cannot possibly be predicted by calculations based on setting a dose arbitrarily lower than the lowest apparently carcinogenic animal dose in a particular experimental situation. *Epidemiology has given important clues on interactive effects between carcinogens, such as smoking and asbestos or uranium, and between carcinogens and non-carcinogenic chemicals, such as arsenic and sulfur dioxide.* There are now critical needs for large-scale interactive tests designed to elucidate such additive and synergistic interactions as they occur in daily life, particularly when suggested by epidemiological observations.[23] [Emphasis added]

It is clear from Epstein's even-handed shuttling back and forth between his examples of carcinogens-interacting-with-carcinogens and carcinogens-interacting-with-noncarcinogens—both kinds of interactions increasing the potency of the most minute doses of carcinogens—that by 1978 scientists who derived their views of environmental cancer from animal studies, and a few human studies, had come to perceive the entire chemical environment to be a potential carcinogenic hazard.

These, then, are some of the biological arguments offered for the proposition that there is no safe or threshold dose for a carcinogen. For the time being, we will accept the theory as a working assumption. It should be noted that some of the arguments adopt the theory out of "prudence," on the grounds that scientific information is nonexistent; others present scientific information to support the position. Again, we can only observe the contradiction.

Assumption No. 3: Given the capacity of chemicals to interreact with and to compound the effects of carcinogens, and given a cumulative barrage of carcinogenic molecules in the environment, one must assume that even one molecule of any carcinogen is a potential hazard.

The "one-molecule theory" of cancer first attracted the attention of the public at hearings in the early 1970s conducted by Congressman H. L. Fountain into DES (diethylstilbestrol), an anti-miscarriage drug that had been shown to act transplacentally and had induced cancer of the vagina in some of the daughters of the women who had taken the drug. DES was also being used as a growth stimulant in cattle feed, and a controversy took place between the FDA, which did not think that practice hazardous to the population if DES residues in beef were restricted to two parts per billion, and NCI scientists, including Umberto Saffiotti, who considered even this amount hazardous and wished the substance to be banned. In 1975, Jacqueline Verrett of the FDA, who also consulted Saffiotti for theoretical information and supported the ban, reported on the controversy—providing one of the earliest explanations of the one-molecule hazard published for the layman:

And as far as cancer specialists know, it may take only a molecule or so at the cellular level to stimulate the runaway growth that is cancer. It is easier to understand if you think of these few molecules of DES entering, not a body that has been previously free of carcinogenic exposure, but one that through the years has been receiving and "storing" other carcinogens. Thus it is probably not a single infinitesimal dose of a carcinogen that alone and by itself induces cancer, but a cumulative effect, as was amply brought out by cancer researchers during the DES controversy. *The "predisposition," if one can call it that, to cancer builds up over a period of time, perhaps from constant exposures to carcinogens along with individual susceptibility, and there may come the day when that extra molecule of a carcinogen may overload the system and cancer begins to grow. Researchers from the National Cancer Institute assured Congressmen that it might be possible for only one molecule of DES in the 340 trillion present in a quarter of a pound of beef liver to trigger human cancer, as far as they know.*[24] [Emphasis added]

The "one-molecule theory" of cancer may have surfaced dramatically during the DES controversy, but it is the same one-molecule theory of cancer that, in 1976, Lesley Stahl of CBS-TV, citing NCI sources, reported to the nation; it is the same one-molecule theory of cancer that Eula Bingham of OSHA reported as a general postulate to the Urban Environment Conference in 1977; and it will appear, again, in this book in a number of other contexts. Against a background of presumed cumulative assaults by carcinogens and by synergistic reactions, the logic applies not only to the food supply, but to one molecule of any carcinogen, however it may be ingested. The one-molecule theory is the ultimate implication of the no-threshold theory; "no threshold" *means* no safe dose, not even the minutest dose—not even one molecule. Scientists express it in different ways, however, depending on whether they are talking about the "cumulative" aspect of carcinogenesis, or exposure to any given carcinogen. Thus, Saffiotti (like many of the scientists who paraphrase and cite him)[25] and Roy Albert, adviser to the EPA, are more inclined to issue broad warnings that long-term exposure to "low-level doses" of carcinogens may be one of the most important sources of cancer in the general population. By contrast, a 1980 Government Accounting Office study of FDA decision-making states: "Many assumptions are required when making a quantitative estimate of a cancer risk in humans on the basis of animal studies." One of those "necessary" assumptions, says the GAO, is the idea that *"each exposure* to a carcinogen can cause cancer"[26] (emphasis added). In the final analysis, whatever the formulation used, the end point is the same: No safe dose exists, and each exposure to any amount of a carcinogen, even to one molecule, may be the trigger of death.

Assumption No. 4: Since no one knows which single or several molecules will give someone cancer, one must assume that all carcinogenic molecules are hazards and that, consequently, they must be banned or a technological barrier erected to protect workers and public.

This is the assumption that links the no-threshold/one-molecule theory to the practical regulatory process. It is shared by all scientists who would like to extend the "Delaney Clause," which, in principle, bans every carcinogenic additive from the food supply, to all other aspects of our productive system. The 1970 "Ad Hoc Committee on the Evaluation of Low Levels of Environmental Carcinogens," the committee of experts in carcinogenesis chaired by Saffiotti, included it as one of its recommendations to the Surgeon General—recommendations that were republished in the transcript of Senate hearings in 1971:

The principle of a zero tolerance for carcinogenic exposures should be retained in all areas of legislation presently covered by it and should be extended to cover other exposures as well. *Only in the cases where contamination of an environmental source by a carcinogen has been proven to be unavoidable should exception be made to the principle of zero tolerance.* Exceptions should be made only after the most extraordinary justification, including extensive documentation of chemical and biological analyses and a specific statement of the estimated risk for man, are presented. All efforts should be made to reduce the level of contamination to the minimum. Periodic review of the degree of contamination and the estimated risk should be made mandatory.[27] [Emphasis added]

In an independent paper published two years later, Saffiotti quoted this recommendation and again stressed its importance.[28]

This is still, today, the position of many scientists in cancer prevention: "Zero tolerance," which is to say "zero exposure," meaning exposure to zero molecules, must be required unless there is "incontrovertible evidence" that the contamination has been "proven" to be unavoidable.

Assumption No. 5: Since scientific findings in the realm of chemical carcinogenesis often contradict one another, data showing "guilt" must be considered truer than data showing "innocence."

This is the last assumption which the reader must know, and it is the one invoked in the face of contradictory data. As is often the case, some experiments report that a substance causes cancer, and others report that it does not—but in all cases the regulatory scientist maintains that "prudence" requires the acceptance of the "guilty" result. As the Ad Hoc Committee, chaired by Saffiotti, put it in 1970:

Evidence of negative [noncarcinogenic] results, under the conditions of the test used, should be considered superseded by positive [carcinogenic] findings in other tests. Evidence of positive results should remain definitive, unless and until new evidence conclusively proves that the prior results were not casually related to the exposure.[29]

The balanced structure of this paragraph may lead the reader to suppose that all that is being said here is that data, whether positive or negative, are valid until proved invalid. That is not the meaning of this passage. It actually says that only "evidence"—not conclusive proof—of carcinogenic findings is to be viewed as "definitive"; noncarcinogenic findings, however, can only be viewed as "definitive" if conclusive proof is offered. The two groups of data are unequal in value.

A more explicit statement of the nonequity of positive and negative data comes four years later from Jacqueline Verrett of the FDA, who learned it from Saffiotti. As she put it, speaking only of well-designed and well-conducted animal studies:

Negative studies simply cannot be given equal or more equal weight in the presence of contrary positive evidence. Particularly in cancer testing, Dr. Saffiotti points out, weak cancer-causing agents would show up negative because current tests fail to detect cancer incidence below 5 to 10 percent. "Accordingly," he stresses, "we must pay great attention to the warning signal represented by a positive animal test."[30]

By 1979, the cognitive priority accorded to positive over negative findings was well established, and the Office of Science and Technology stated it this way, simultaneously observing that a poor animal study was "less meaningful" than a good animal study—i.e., that a bad study still had some meaning:

Divergent results may occur either among tests on different species or among different tests on the same species. *Any test that is poorly designed or poorly conducted must be viewed as less meaningful than one that is done properly. If appropriate testing procedures are followed, however, it is generally sound to let positive results supersede negative results in tests involving different species,* taking into account the frequent occurrence of interspecies variation and the inability to determine which species experience is most relevant to that of humans. In the interpretation of divergent results from separate studies within the same species, all of the data should be considered.[31] [Emphasis added]

And by 1980, the authors of the GAO study of the FDA wrote even more simply:

FDA's current policy, as stated in the discussion of the GLP [Good Laboratory Practices] regulations in the Federal Register, provides that a technically bad study can never establish the absence of a safety risk, but may establish the presence of a previously unsuspected hazard.[32]

In sum, the idea enunciated by Saffiotti and his 1970 Ad Hoc Committee remained unchanged: When in the "gray area," the presumption of "guilt" must prevail. But it had acquired a curious new potency: According to FDA policy, the diagnosis of possible "guilt" no longer even required *good* experimental science; it could now be established by *bad* experimental science.

This brief roster of basic assumptions by no means exhausts the subject of regulatory theory, nor does it give us more than a passing glance at what the researchers in basic science are thinking. But we can be confident that these are the first ideas that government scientists consider most important for us to learn, since they are the very ideas they have popularized so insistently. In fact, the only significant difference between the ideas expressed in this chapter and those expressed in the last is that here, some of the reasons for the heavily publicized ideas have been given.

It is this set of ideas, above all, which allows one to make a preliminary assessment of the survey of reported chemical carcinogens that follows. At a minimum, with this information in hand, the layman, faced with a mass of animal data, can adopt the following interpretive policies:

1. Wherever a substance is identified in an animal test as a possible, probable, or proved carcinogen (or a cocarcinogen or a "promoter" of carcinogenicity), one may assume that it is or may be killing some number of human beings, somewhere.

2. One need not worry overly about the quality of the carcinogenic data, for animal experiments with positive results may be assumed to be "meaningful" and capable of alerting us to the risk of cancer even if they are not particularly good experiments or even if they are actively bad ones.

3. One may allow oneself, at least temporarily, to be indifferent to the fact that other animal experiments may exist somewhere that contradict these carcinogenic findings, because findings of "guilt" are generally held to be truer than findings of "innocence."

However embarrassing they may sound—in any other field of thought, this would be a formula for rigging the conclusions—these are the practical applications of the five basic assumptions once the complex scientific rationale has been stripped away.

THE SECOND DISCOVERY

The survey itself contains the second discovery. It emerged when I left the world of alphabetized chemicals. While the alphabet may be invaluable to file clerks and computers, it does not give one a picture of the role that industrial chemicals play in our lives. I therefore abandoned the alphabet and looked for material that would illustrate the impact that industrial chemicals were having on the country. By the time I had collected a mass of data, I found I was not only confronting the chemical industry, but *all* the most basic industries on which our civilization rests. But let us put aside for the moment the implications of this discovery. The survey that follows here lists each of these industries and presents a collection of reported carcinogens associated with each field. Like the NIOSH catalogue, I do not vouch for the validity of the data, only that they come from government and academic scientists. Some information is given on mutagens—chemicals that cause mutations in bacteria and cells—because many scientists believe that mutations, heritable changes in the DNA of a germ or somatic cell, cause cancer. Several agents reported to cause cancer in man are also mentioned. The primary focus of the survey, however, is on animal tests that have reported carcinogenicity.

The survey is written in English: Save for the names of the chemicals themselves, there is no technical language here; the concept "carcinogen," unless otherwise stated, refers to an animal carcinogen. When numbers are given at all, it is because they reveal clearly understandable relationships, i.e., "more," "less," "about the same." Although some exposition appears, the material consists essentially of lists, of tables (which are lists), and of charts (which are lists)—many of these composed by scientists seeking overviews of the findings in their own fields. It is above all by lists that one can scan a great mass of data, and however simplified this type of condensation may be, it is used continually by scientists. An effort has been made to provide as large a number of reported findings as can be fitted into the available space. It is only when one has some idea of what scientists claim to have discovered in the most fundamental areas of our industrial system that one can begin to think efficiently about the problem.

INDUSTRIAL CARCINOGENS: A SURVEY

NOTE

The term "survey" is used here to mean a large collection or compilation of examples of reported animal carcinogens, as well as some examples of reported human carcinogens and mutagens, and a few teratogens (chemicals that damage the fetus). It should provide the reader with the perspective he might gain by browsing in a library. The selection and number of references given for each entry are necessarily unsystematic, and are not a measure of the validity of the findings.

Most reports come from reviews of the literature, thus unless explicitly indicated it is not to be assumed that the National Cancer Institute, the National Academy of Sciences, the International Agency for Research on Cancer, or any other research or regulatory institution or individual scientist is necessarily vouching for the validity of the data. The appearance of a carcinogen, mutagen, or teratogen in this survey means only that such findings have been reported by scientists.

In Appendix A of this book, the reader will find a paginated and indexed bibliography which will allow him to identify the precise source of every finding. In the survey itself, findings are often grouped to make them readable, and the sources of the data are referred to as briefly as possible. Usually, when papers or books are mentioned, only the first scientist is named (with apologies to coauthors who are buried in an "et al."). Initials, second authors, and key words of titles are given if required to avoid confusion, when consulting the bibliography, between similar names, titles, or papers published in the same year. Finally, when the author himself, his editor, or his translator uses variants or different spellings of a name on different papers, those inconsistencies are reproduced, as published, in the bibliography.

I.   CHEMICALS

The tabulation of findings for the chemical industry, which overlaps with all other industries, will be restricted here to data pertaining to chemicals in the aggregate. Various aspects of the universe of chemicals have been tallied and analyzed as follows:

All the Chemicals That Are Known to Exist

1976:   Russell Train, then Administrator of the EPA, put the number at 2,000,000.

1977:   The EPA document entitled *Potential Industrial Carcinogens and Mutagens* put the number at 3,500,000.

1978:   The Chemical Abstracts computer registry of chemical compounds put the number at more than 4,000,000, and reported that the number was growing at the rate of 6,000 compounds per week.

1978:   Joseph E. Califano, then Secretary of the Department of Health, Education, and Welfare, put the number at 7,000,000.

All the Chemicals in Commercial Use

1975:   David P. Rall, Director of the National Institute of Environmental Health Sciences, put the figure at approximately 10,000 and said, in addition, that between 500 and 1,000 new chemicals entered the market each year.

1977:   The EPA, in *Potential Industrial Carcinogens and Mutagens,* put the number at 25,000 and said the number was increasing at the rate of about 700 a year.

1977:   David S. Sundin, Chief of the Hazard Section, Surveillance Branch, of the National Institute for Occupational Safety and Health (NIOSH), reported that NIOSH had "approximately 46,000 product formulations" on file.

1978:   Samuel S. Epstein reported that the Chemical Abstracts Computer Registry had submitted to the EPA a list of about 33,000 chemicals which it believed to be in common use.

1979:   R. Jeffrey Smith (January 5) quoted EPA Administrator Douglas Costle as putting the number of chemicals in use at 70,000.

Carcinogenic and Mutagenic Classes

In 1977, the EPA published *Potential Industrial Carcinogens and Mutagens,* a study of 90 organic compounds widely used in industry, the chemical structures of which were reportedly carcinogenic or mutagenic. They represented 16 major classes of chemicals, and 19 "structural subsets." In 52 of the 90 compounds, both carcinogenicity and mutagenicity were reported; 31 were reported to be mutagenic and noncarcinogenic; and 7 were reported to be carcinogenic and nonmutagenic.

The EPA reported: "The largest number of industrial agents that have been reported to be carcinogenic and/or mutagenic are *alkylating and acylating agents* classified under 12 structural headings, viz., *epoxides, lactones, aziridines, alkylsulfates, sultones, aryldialkyl triazenes, diazoalkanes, phosphoric acid esters, alkane halides, halogenated alkanols, halogenated ethers,* and *aldehydes.* The major industrial class of demonstrated carcinogenic and/or mutagenic activity are the *halogenated hydrocarbons* comprising saturated and unsaturated derivatives including: *alkanes, alkanols, ethers, vinyl and vinylidene analogs, alkyl, aryl and polyaromatic derivatives*" (emphasis added).

Numbers of Chemical Carcinogens

At various intervals in the past few years, different attempts have been made to survey all the data, with a view of determining how many carcinogens have been discovered. Here are some of the numbers given, between 1967 and 1979:

1967:   Berenblum, in *Cancer Research Today,* put the number of synthetic substances reported to cause cancer in laboratory animals at 500.

1975:   Maugh and Marx in *Seeds of Destruction,* the report by *Science* magazine on cancer research, put the number of cancer-causing substances at 1,000—adding "and many times that number are suspect."

1976:   The National Institute for Occupational Safety and Health (NIOSH), which is the research arm of the Occupational Safety and Health Agency (OSHA), published a volume entitled *Suspected Carcinogens* and put the combined number of chemicals that had been reported to be tumorigenic (causing benign tumors) and carcinogenic (causing cancers) at 1,905 and listed another 510 that were suspected—2,415 in all.

1977:   The Environmental Protection Agency (EPA) published *Potential Industrial Carcinogens and Mutagens,* reporting that 1,000 chemicals had been shown to be tumorigenic (causing benign tumors) and 100 had been "definitely" shown to cause cancers.

1979:   *The Surgeon General's Report on Health Promotion and Disease Prevention* put the number of suspected carcinogens at "over 2,300"—clearly the NIOSH master list.

Carcinogens by Percentage

1976:   HEW (*Survey of Compounds*) reviewed all the chemicals tested (1974–1976)—7,000—and said that 17 percent of them had been reported to be tumorigenic.

1979:   Davis and Magee said that 7,000 chemicals had been tested and that 1,500 of them—more than 20 percent—had been reported to be carcinogenic.

1979:   Smith (January 5) said that according to Douglas Costle, EPA Administrator, a review of all the substances ever tested by the EPA indicated that 20 percent had been found carcinogenic.

II. ENERGY

Energy: Coal

Carcinogens in Coal Combustion

Elemental carcinogens: *arsenic, beryllium, cadmium, chromium, cobalt, lead, mercury, nickel, selenium, uranium, zinc* (Falk et al., 1979; Young et al., 1978).

Polynuclear aromatics: *benz* (a) *anthracene, chrysene, pyrene, benzo* (a) *pyrene, benzo* (e) *pyrene, perylene, benzo* (b) *fluoranthene, benzo* (j) *fluoranthene, benzo* (ghi) *perylene, indeno* (1, 2, 3,-cd) *pyrene, coronene* (Falk et al., 1979; Young et al., 1978). Some of these are potentiated by other chemicals.

Polycyclic and heterocyclic aromatic compounds: *benzo* (f) *quinoline, benzo* (h) *quino-*

line; benz (a) *acridine, benz* (c) *acridine, 11 H-indenol (1, 2-b) quinoline, dibenz* (a, j) *acridine* (Falk et al., 1979).

Radioactive substances: The burning of coal releases *uranium* on an average of about 1.5 parts per million (Cohen, "Disposal," 1977). Radioactivity also emerges from decay products of both uranium and thorium, especially *radium-226* and *radium-228.* Coal fly ash contains 10 times as much radium as fly ash from oil-powered generators (WHO, *Health Implications,* 1977).

Sulfur particulates: *Dimethyl and monomethyl sulfate* are found in high concentrations (as high as 1,000 ppm) in fly ash and in airborne particulate matter from coal combustion processes. Both compounds are reported to be carcinogenic and mutagenic (Druckrey et al., 1966; Druckrey et al., 1970; A. Hollaender, 1971; P. D. Lowley, 1976; D. B. Couch et al., 1978—all cited by Lee et al., 1980).

Nitrosamines: These compounds, reported to be extremely potent carcinogens, may be formed by elements in conventional coal effluents in combination with other chemicals in the air or in mammalian tissue (Falk et al., 1979) and are potentially present in gasified and liquefied coal (Bridbord et al., 1978).

Carcinogens in Gasified and Liquefied Coal

A breakdown of the carcinogens identified in the "process streams" of gasified and liquefied coal is reported by K. Bridbord and his colleagues, at NIOSH, 1978:

Diethylamines	Alkyl cresols	Dibenzo(*a*,1)pyrene	Beryllium
Methylethylamines	Anthracene	Dibenzo(*a*,*n*)pyrene	Cadmium
Pyridines	Benzo(*a*)pyrene	Dibenzo(*a*,i)pyrene	Arsenic
Pyrroles	Chrysene	Indeno(1,2,3-*c*,*d*)	Nickel carbonyl
Benzene	Benzo(*a*)anthra-	pyrene	Sulfur particulates
Cresols	cene	Benzoacridine	Coke
	Benzo(*a*)anthrone	Nickel	Coal dust

Mutagens in Coal

Particles in coal fly ash of a size that can be inhaled have been reported to be mutagenic (Chrisp et al., 1978). The finest coal fly ash fractions, and consequently those easiest to inhale, are reported to be more mutagenic than coarser fractions (Fisher et al., 1979).

Mutagens have also been reported in the effluent from coal gasification and liquefaction processes. Those identified were *benz*(a)*anthracene, benz*(b)*anthracene, 1, 2, 3, 4-dibenzanthracene, 1, 2, 5, 6-dibenzanthracene, benzo*(a)*pyrene, chrysene, 2,3-benzofluorene, 2-aminoanthracene, acridine,* a-*naphthylamine, 2,5-dimethylaniline, quinoline, 7-methylquinoline, 8-hydroxyquinoline, 8-aminoquinoline, 8-nitroquinoline* (Epler et al., 1978).

Energy: Fossil Fuels

Many studies of petroleum and oil production are subsumed under the broader category of "fossil fuels," which may also include coal and, occasionally, wood, peat, and lignite. Often the information is presented as applicable to the entire "fossil fuel" category; sometimes it appears in comparisons of aspects of coal and oil and sometimes the information is specific to oil and gas, together or alone.

Elemental Carcinogens in Petroleum Ash and Coal Ash

A comparison between the concentration of trace metals in petroleum ash and coal was tabulated from information in the literature by Eisenbud et al., 1971. Among the substances listed were *nickel, chromium, and lead,* all reported carcinogens (see COAL). The authors also report the presence, at lower levels, of *beryllium and mercury,* both reported carcinogens (NIOSH, 1976); nickel, however, found "typically" in concentrations of 7 percent of petroleum ash, exists in striking amounts. The International Agency for Research on Cancer identified nickel as a human as well as an animal carcinogen, and cited various studies indicating that nickel has been a significant air pollutant. IARC wrote: "Nickel compounds, e.g. sulphides, oxides and carbonyl, enter the atmosphere as a result of the combustion of coal, diesel oil and fuel oil." Nickel sulphides, nickel oxides, and nickel carbonyl are all reported carcinogens (IARC, Vol. 11, 1976; NIOSH, 1976).

Radioactivity in Petroleum Ash and Coal Ash

Two studies done a decade apart—one American, one international—both conclude that the burning of coal releases greater quantities of radioactivity into the atmosphere than does the burning of oil.

1964:   Merril Eisenbud and Henry G. Petrow published "Radioactivity in the Atmospheric Effluents of Power Plants that use Fossil Fuels." They analyzed the fly ash from the combustion of pulverized Appalachian coal and found that a 1,000-megawatt coal-burning power plant will discharge between 28 millicuries to nearly 1 curie per year of radium-226 and radium-228; an oil-burning plant of similar size will only discharge about 0.5 millicuries of radium per year.

1977:   The World Health Organization Regional Office for Europe ("Health Implications") similarly concluded on the basis of worldwide studies: "The fly ash from coal and oil-fueled plants contains trace quantities of uranium and thorium and their radioactive decay products, especially radium-226 and radium-228. The actual amounts depend on the efficiency of fly ash removal and the composition of the coal. The quantities of radium released by an oil-fired power plant are much less, because oil fly ash contains about a tenth as much radium as coal fly ash and, in addition, coal has a higher ash content than oil."

Carcinogenic Additives in Fossil Fuels

Oil contains the solvent *1,4-dioxane* which produces cancers of the nasal cavity and liver in rats, and tumors of the liver and gallbladder in guinea pigs (IARC, Vol. 11, 1976).

Leaded gasoline contains *ethylene dibromide* and is widely found in self-service pumps. Carter, in *Science* magazine (February 9, 1979), reported that EDB was a known carcinogen in animals.

Rocket fuel contains various compounds of the group *hydrazines,* which produce cancers of the lung and liver in mice, angiosarcoma in mice and hamsters, and intestinal cancer in rats (Hoffmann et al., 1978).

Rocket fuel also contains *2-methylaziridine,* an intermediate and solvent. It is also used as an oil additive for viscosity control and resistance to oxidation and in flocculants used in petroleum refineries. The compound produces a variety of malignant tumors in rats (IARC, Vol. 9, 1975).

Survey of Carcinogens in Fossil Fuels

1978:   D.F.S. Natusch of Colorado State University searched the literature and published "Potentially Carcinogenic Species Emitted to the Atmosphere by Fossil-Fueled Power Plants." For the purpose of his analysis, he classified the compounds as known or "recognized" carcinogens, "suspected" carcinogens, and "reactants"—"reactants" being those which may result in the production or removal of carcinogenic species or which may react synergistically with known carcinogens. Here is the portion of his table which identifies the incriminated substances:

KNOWN AND SUSPECTED CARCINOGENS EMITTED BY FOSSIL-FUELED POWER PLANTS

Substance	Status	Substance	Status
Inorganic cases		n-Pentane	Reactant
SO_X	Reactant	2-Methylbutane	Reactant
NO_X	Reactant	Alkenes	
O_3	Reactant	2-Butene	Reactant
Hg	Suspected	1, 3-Butadiene	Reactant
Inorganic particulates		Propene	Reactant
Arsenic	Recognized	Aldehydes and ketones	
Asbestos	Recognized	Formaldehyde	Suspected
Beryllium	Recognized	Acrolein	Suspected
Cadmium	Recognized	Nitrosamines	
Cobalt	Suspected	Dimethylnitrosamine	Recognized
Chromium	Recognized	Peroxides	
Copper	Suspected	Peroxyacylnitrates	Suspected
Fluorine	Suspected	Aromatic hydrocarbons	
Iron	Suspected	Benzene	Recognized
Nickel	Recognized	Toluene	Reactant
Lead	Suspected	1, 2-Dimethylbenzene	Suspected
Selenium	Suspected	1, 3-Dimethylbenzene	Suspected
Uranium	Recognized	1, 4-Dimethylbenzene	Suspected
Vanadium	Suspected	Polyaromatic hydrocarbons	
Total particulates	Reactant	Anthracene	Reactant
Radionuclides		Benzo(a)pyrene	Recognized
210_{Pb} (lead)	Recognized	Benzo(e)pyrene	Suspected
212_{Pb} (lead)	Recognized	1, 2-Benzanthracene	Recognized
226_{Ra} (radium)	Recognized	1, 12-Benzperylene	Reactant
222_{Rn} (radon)	Recognized	Coronene	Reactant
228_{Th} (thorium)	Recognized	Chrysene	Suspected
230_{Th} (thorium)	Recognized	Pyrene	Reactant
232_{Th} (thorium)	Recognized	Polycyclic nitrogen compounds	
$234_{U}+238_{U}$ (uranium)	Recognized	Acridine	Suspected
Gaseous and particulate		Fluorene carbonitrile	Suspected
organic species		Lead tetraalkyls	
Alkanes		Tetraethyllead	Suspected
n-Butane	Reactant	Benzene-soluble organics	Recognized

Energy: Electricity

Various aspects of the generation and transmission of electricity are reported to have cancer-causing properties. Three examples are given here of very different types of problems found in the literature.

Condensers

Electrical capacitors, condensers, transformers, air conditioners, and fluorescent lights are leaking *PCBs* into the environment (Eisenbud, 1978). PCBs are reported to be potential carcinogens (WHO, 1976; Douglas Costle, Administrator of the EPA, 1977; Allen et al., 1977).

Rectifiers

High-voltage industrial rectifiers have contained *selenium,* reported above as a carcinogen. Selenium has recently been replaced with silicone, in heavy industry, but in 1975, selenium rectifiers were still in demand for home entertainment equipment (IARC, Vol. 9, 1975).

Circuits

Stabilizers in electrical-insulating silicone circuits contain *N-phenyl-2-naphthylamine.* In 1976, NIOSH reported that the compound was contaminated with the reported carcinogen *2-naphthylamine.* According to IARC (Vol. 16, 1978), which cited the NIOSH report, the findings in mice suggest that the compound is carcinogenic.

Energy: Nuclear

Ionizing radiation is a proved cancer-causing agent. In 1979, the Interagency Task Force of HEW estimated the exposure of the general population to ionizing radiation. Only the section of the Task Force table pertaining to man-made sources is reproduced:

U.S. GENERAL POPULATION EXPOSURE ESTIMATES — 1978

Source	Person-rems per year (in thousands)
Technologically enhanced	1,000
Healing arts	17,000
Nuclear weapons	
fallout	1,000–1,600
weapons development, testing, and production	.165
Nuclear energy	56
Consumer products	6

Energy: Solar

There is not much data yet on solar energy, which is still in its theoretical and practical infancy. Already, however, there are reports that carcinogenic elements may be incorporated into solar technology.

Solar Heating and Cooling Systems

In 1976, EPA's Office of Energy, Minerals and Industry published a document entitled "Potential Environmental Impacts of Solar Heating and Cooling Systems." It contained a list of 18 chemical substances called "solar system working fluids" and reported on their toxicity. Thirteen of the 18 were reported to have low or moderate toxicity. According to the NIOSH master catalogue, however, two of the four "solar system heat storage materials" are reported carcinogens, namely *diphenyl and diphenyl oxide.* Also, says NIOSH (1976), one of the eight "absorption refrigeration fluids" is a reported carcinogen: *sodium chromate.*

Solar Cells

In *Science,* February 10, 1978, Henry Kelly, technical assistant to the director of the Office of Technology Assessment, reported that *cadmium* and *arsenic* compounds (CdS/Cu_2S and GaAs) would be utilized in some commercial cells. Cadmium and arsenic are reported to be carcinogens (see Metals below). Kelly wrote that "both CdS and GaAs contain toxic materials, and, although it may be possible to reduce the hazards they present to manageable proportions, it clearly will be necessary to examine this issue with some care before their widespread use can be contemplated."

III.   METALS AND MINERALS

The following metals and minerals (and/or their compounds) have been reported to be carcinogens or suspected carcinogens in animal tests. Arsenic and asbestos, both universally acknowledged human carcinogens, are also on the list.

Antimony (T. Norseth, 1977)

Arsenic (Dutra et al., 1950; Oswald and Goerttler, cited in Sunderman, 1976; Bencko, 1977; Norseth, 1977; Wildenberg, 1978)

Asbestos (Anderson et al., 1976; Selikoff, 1977; IARC, Vol. 14, 1977; Nicholson, 1977; Vianna et al., 1978)

Beryllium (Dutra et al., 1950; Janes et al., 1954; Kelly et al., 1961; Higgins et al., 1964; IARC, Vol. 1, 1972; Sunderman, 1978; Reeves, 1978)

Cadmium (Heath et al., 1962; Sunderman, 1971; Norseth, 1977; IARC, Vol. 11, 1976; Sunderman, 1978)

Chromium (Sunderman, 1971, 1978)

Cobalt (Heath et al., 1962; Sunderman, 1971; Norseth, 1977)

Hematite—iron oxide, iron ore (Sunderman, 1971, 1978)

Lead (Sunderman, 1971; IARC, Vol. 1, 1972; WHO, 1977; New York Academy of Sciences, 1977; Shimkin et al., 1978; Sunderman, 1978, 1979)

Manganese (Shimkin et al., 1978)

Molybdenum (Shimkin et al., 1978)

Nickel (Sunderman, 1973; IARC, Vol. 11, 1976; Sunderman, 1978)

Palladium (Brubaker et al., 1975)

Selenium (Sunderman, 1971; NAS, *Drinking*, 1977)

Titanium (Sunderman, 1971, 1978)

Yttrium (Battelle Memorial Institute, Dartmouth Medical School, 1972)

Zinc (Sunderman, 1971, 1978)

Mutagenic Metals and Minerals

C. Peter Flessel (1978) reported that the following metals and minerals, and/or their compounds, were mutagens or induced chromosome aberrations: *aluminum, antimony, arsenic, cadmium, chromium, copper, hematite (iron oxide, iron ore), lead, manganese, mercury, molybdenum, nickel, platinum, selenium, tellurium.* F. W. Sunderman, Jr. (1978) added *rhodium and ruthenium* to the list of mutagenic metals. Philip H. Abelson, editor of *Science*, 1972, has also reported that *mercury* induces chromosome aberrations and birth defects.

IV.   TRANSPORTATION

Transportation, domestic and military, is dependent on the reportedly carcinogenic energy sources, metals, minerals, and mining which have been surveyed above. In addition, here are a few other carcinogenic aspects of this industry:

Airplanes

Turbojet and turboprop engines release polyaromatic hydrocarbons, above all the reported carcinogen *benzo*(a)*pyrene* (Shabad et al., USSR, 1976).

Ships

One of the major materials used in shipbuilding has been *asbestos,* reported to be a proved human carcinogen (Selikoff et al., 1978).

Automobiles

Storage batteries: *Lead* is primarily used in the manufacture of storage batteries and as an antiknocking agent in gasoline. As a result of combustion, it is converted to lead salts. Various lead salts have been reported to be carcinogenic in rats and mice (IARC, Vol. 1, 1972).

Catalytic converters: Platinum and *palladium* are the catalytic materials used to reduce carbon monoxide and hydrocarbon emissions from light-duty motor vehicles. Palladium salts are reported to induce malignant tumors in mice (Brubaker et al., 1975).

Air bags: *Sodium azide* is a gas-generating agent for inflating protective air bags. It has been reported to be "a powerful and efficient mutagen" (EPA, *Potential Industrial,* 1977).

Exhaust: *Sulfur dioxide,* emitted in automobile exhaust, is reported to potentiate the carcinogenic effects of polycyclic hydrocarbons in rats (Brubaker et al., 1975).

Diesel Engines

Extracts of *diesel particulates* have been reported to give laboratory animals skin cancer and to be mutagenic (EPA, "Precautionary Notice," 1977).

Transportation Areas

The *asphalts* and *tars* used on streets and highways are reported to be carcinogens, i.e., polyaromatic hydrocarbons (Sawicki, 1976).

Automobile exhaust, airport runways, and tunnels contain high concentrations of *benzo*(a)*pyrene,* reported to be a carcinogen (Sawicki, 1976).

V. CONSTRUCTION

Essential materials used in construction—stone, plastics, cement, and fiberglass—are reported to cause cancer in animals.

Stone

Serpentinite rock deposits contain *asbestos;* crushed serpentinite rock is used in the construction of roadways (EPA, Nov. 20, 1977). Asbestos is reported to be a proved animal and human carcinogen causing mesothelioma, and laryngeal cancer in workers who smoke (IARC, Vol. 14, 1977; Selikoff et al., 1978; Morgan et al., 1976).

Plastics

Plastics—specifically *polyvinyl chloride resins*—are used in the building and construction industries. In 1972, 42 percent of the total production of PVC resins was used in these industries in the U.S.A. (IARC, Vol. 7, 1974); the percentage may be higher today. PVC resins are used in piping, conduits, water pipes, flooring, windows, rigid structures, pipe fittings, sidings, swimming pool liners, and wire and cable coating.

   Vinyl chloride gas (monomer) is universally reported to be a proved human carcinogen (IARC, Vol. 7, 1974), causing angiosarcoma of the liver. In addition, Kenneth Bridbord of NIOSH (1978) reports that plastic workers develop excess brain cancer, and in another study, white women PVC workers are reported to have developed excess cancers of the breast and urinary organs (Chiazze et al., 1977). Vinyl chloride monomer may be mutagenic, as well as carcinogenic (Heath et al., 1977).

Cement

Asbestos cement is used extensively in the building industry for ceilings, roofing, insulation, soundproofing, high-pressure pipes, and water pipes. Asbestos cement products come in sheets: They must be cut, sawn, drilled, and machined, producing dust which can be inhaled. Goldstein et al. (1978) reported that baboons who inhaled asbestos cement showed atypical metaplasia of the bronchiolar epithelium and possibly bronchioalveolar carcinoma, implying a risk to construction workers.

Fiberglass

Animal tests report that fiberglass, widely used in the construction industry for insulation, is carcinogenic. Fiberglass, like asbestos, is reported to produce mesothelioma in rats; the finer fibers are more carcinogenic (Pott et al., 1974; Wagner et al., 1974).

VI.   COMMUNICATIONS

The industries which produce newspapers, magazines, and books; radio, television, and radar; the graphic arts; and recorded music—all the major forms of communication in the United States—have important constituents that are reported to be causes of cancer.

Publishing

On page 107 are a few examples of the suspected or established animal carcinogens and mutagens used in the process of publishing newspapers, magazines, and books:

Television

The picture tube, the shunt regulator tube, and the rectifier tube of the television set emit a certain amount of *ionizing radiation*. Policies on emissions and on tolerated exposures have been formulated by the government (National Council on Radiation Protection [NCRP], 1960; Neill et al., 1971; HEW, *Television*, 1976); Committee on the Biological Effects of Ionizing Radiation [BEIR], 1980).

Radio, Television, Radar, Microwave

Some of our major communications systems—radio, television, and radar—operate in the electromagnetic spectrum. *Electric fields and electromagnetic radiation*—which includes radio and microwave radiation—are reported to damage growth and to cause tumors in living organisms (Cleary, 1977; James H. McElhaney, cited by Marino et al., 1978; Solon, 1979). Radio-frequency radiation is also reported to produce chromosomal anomalies in the hamster and the fruit fly, and mutagenesis in mice (Solon, 1979).

Arts and Crafts

Artists and craftsmen work with a wide range of toxic substances, many of which are reported carcinogens and mutagens: *asbestos, benzene, vinyl chloride, lead, cadmium, metallic and silica dusts* (McCann, 1978). Paints are based on pigments including the reported carcinogens *chromium, cadmium, nickel, arsenic, and vinyl chloride*, which was used as an aerosol propellant in many art products until banned (Epstein, 1978). Vinyl chloride is also a reported mutagen (Heath et al., 1977; EPA, *Potential Industrial*, 1977).

Music

The recording industry is heavily dependent on plastics. *Vinyl chloride monomer* (VCM) and its primary end product, *polyvinyl chloride (PVC) resins*, are used in the manufacture of records. It is during the process of conversion of VCM to PVC that workers are exposed to the risk of contracting the rare liver cancer angiosarcoma (EPA, *Potential Industrial*, 1977; IARC, Vol. 7, 1974) and cancer of liver and brain (Bridbord, 1978).

Record Players

As late as 1975, *selenium* rectifiers were still in demand for home entertainment equipment (IARC, Vol. 9, 1975).

Use	Substance or compounds	Carcinogen	Mutagen
Pulp			
Paper pulp	Hydroxylamine		EPA, 1977*
Paper			
Sizing agents	Epichlorohydrin	IARC, Vol. 11, 1976	EPA, 1977
Additive	Aziridines	IARC, Vol. 9, 1975	EPA, 1977
Sterilizer	Hydrogen peroxide		EPA, 1977
Solvent, finishing	Acetaldehyde		EPA, 1977
Treatment	Acrolein		EPA, 1977
Dyeing	Azo dyes	EPA, 1977	EPA, 1977
Printing			
Duplicating paper	PCBs	WHO, 1976; EPA, 1977	
Inks	Azo dyes, PCBs	EPA, 1977	EPA, 1977
Photography			
Color photography	Azo dyes	EPA, 1977	EPA, 1977
Color developers	Hydroxylamine		EPA, 1977
Processing	Chloroform	EPA, 1977	

* All references to "EPA, 1977" refer to *Potential Industrial Carcinogens and Mutagens.*

VII. FOOD: UNINTENDED ADDITIVES

A great number of unintended carcinogenic additives are reported in the food supply, in the form of residues from agricultural chemicals, drugs given to food animals, food packaging, and assorted industrial practices and leakages. Many of these substances are reported to be mutagenic.

Carcinogenic Pesticides in Food

Among the more thoroughly studied sources of unintended food contamination are the pesticides which are sprayed on crops in the field, residues of which are found in the food supply itself. The classes of pesticides in which carcinogens have been most frequently reported are *chlorinated hydrocarbons, organophosphates, and carbamates* (Turk et al., 1978).

1977:   Samuel Epstein reviewed the literature and published a table of chlorinated hydrocarbon pesticides used in agriculture. Only those he identified as carcinogens are listed here. There were 18 of them:

Chlorobenzilate	DDT	Chlordane
Dieldrin	Lindane	Ethylene dichloride
Endrin	Pentachloronitrobenzene	Heptachlor
Kepone	Perthane	Mirex
Methoxychlor	TDE	Strobane
BHC	Aldrin	Toxaphene

1978:   Within a year the number of reported carcinogens in pesticides was estimated at 30 (Robert Chambers, GAO, 1978).

1972–1979:   Over the years, yet other agricultural substances—fumigants, fertilizers, herbicides, etc.—have also been reported to contain carcinogens:

Substance	Reference
Carbon tetrachloride	IARC, Vol. 1, 1972
Uranium	Eisenbud, 1973
Vinyl chloride gas	EPA, May 1974
Monuron	IARC, Vol. 12, 1976
Diallate	IARC, Vol. 12, 1976
Cadmium	IARC, Vol. 11, 1976
Oxychlordane	NAS, *Drinking*, 1977
TCDD (contaminant)	Nebert et al., 1979

1979: R. Jeffrey Smith in *Science* (January 5) quoted EPA Administrator Douglas Costle as reporting that 25 percent of the 1,500 active ingredients of registered pesticides are carcinogens.

Mutagenic Pesticides in Food

1977: Shirasu et al. reported that the following pesticides were mutagens:

Captafol	ETU	NNN
Captan	Ferbam	TMTD
Dexon	Folpet	TTCA
Dichlofluanid	HEH	Vamidothion
Dichlorvos	NBT	Ziram
EMSC		

1978: In the Subcommittee on Oversight and Investigation Report on cancer-causing chemicals contaminating food, the General Accounting Office supplied a list of randomly sampled mutagenic pesticides (GAO Appendices, 1978). Those not on the above list are cited here:

Atrazine	Guthion	Pyrazon
Benefin	Lanstan	Rogor
Carbophenothion	Malathion	Silvex
Dalapon	Methoxychlor	Sodium trichloracetate
Diazinon	Norea	Thiodemeton
Dimethylarsenic acid	Paraquat	Thiram
Diuron	Piperonyl butoxide	Zineb
Endrin		

1979: Two other pesticides were reported on. *Toxaphene* was reported mutagenic (Hooper et al., 1979). *Diallate* was reported mutagenic (Schuphan et al., 1979).

Carcinogenic Drugs in Food Animals

1978: The GAO, at Congressional hearings on cancer-causing chemicals, identified carcinogenic drugs used to treat food animals (e.g., cattle, chickens) that had been or might be leaving residues in the meat that reached the marketplace: *arsenic, carbadox, diethylstilbestrol* (banned by FDA, August 2, 1972), *ipronidazole, sulfamethazine, sulfathiazole, chlormadinone acetate, dimetridazole, estradiol benzoate, estradiol monopalmitate, furazolidone, gentian violet* (not an approved animal drug but reported as being used), *melengestrol acetate, progesterone, testosterone.*

Carcinogenic and Mutagenic Food Containers

A variety of containers and packaging constituents are reported to be leaching carcinogenic and mutagenic substances into food.

PCBs, identified both as carcinogens and as mutagens, have been reported to be migrating from grayboard and cardboard containers into various foods: seafood, shredded wheat and other cereals, and cashew nuts (IARC, Vol. 7, 1974).

Polyvinyl chloride gas, identified as a carcinogen, has been reported to be leaching into alcoholic beverages from containers by the FDA, May 9, 1973.

Phthalate esters are reported by S. I. Shibko (1974) to migrate from plastic packaging into a variety of foods and beverages; phthalate esters are reported to be carcinogens (NIOSH, 1976).

Cadmium, copper, iron, lead, manganese, and zinc, all reported above to be carcinogens, are said to be leaching out of tin cans into evaporated milk and infant products (Murthy et al., 1971).

Lead and *cadmium* have been reported in a wide variety of British canned baby foods (Snodin, 1973). Both are reported to be carcinogens and mutagens (see above). In the United States, lead and cadmium have been found in canned fruits and vegetables: canned tomatoes, currants, pineapples, damsons, apricots, prunes, grapefruit, apples, oranges, peaches, rhubarb, plums, spinach, baked beans (Thomas et al., 1973, 1975).

Lead has been reported to be leaching from glazed ceramic surfaces into fruit juices and other beverages (Gegiou et al., 1975); from glazed glasses, vessels, and containers into cola, commercial orange drink, apple and orange juice, beer, instant and fresh coffee, tea, and milk (Yoon et al., 1976; EPA, July 15, 1977); from aluminum products such as foil, pans, and pie plates, and ceramic dishes (Henderson et al., 1975); and from silver-plated hollowware, baby cups, tankards, coffee sets, tea sets, goblets, salad bowls, gravy bowls, serving trays (FDA, "Hollowware," 1975).

Other Carcinogenic Additives

Trichloroethylene was used as an extraction solvent in decaffeinated soluble (instant) coffee until it was reported to be a carcinogen by the NCI (FDA, September 27, 1977).

Asbestos filters and talc, which may contain asbestos, have been used in the manufacture of processed foods, e.g., sugar, vegetable oil, lard, and coated rice (IARC, Vol. 14, 1977).

PCBs have been reported as contaminants of milk and dairy products: of poultry, eggs, shellfish, and freshwater fish such as bass and lake trout. PCBs cause liver tumors in laboratory animals (FDA, *Talk Paper*, March 25, 1977).

In addition to the categories of unintended additives to the food supply already named, Kraybill (1974) has mentioned still others: *heavy metals, radioactive tritium* and *fall-out radionuclides, nitrates-nitrites from fertilizers, polycyclic hydrocarbons from oil spillage,* "and others too numerous to mention." The named contaminants have already been identified in the survey as reported carcinogens, or will be named later in the survey.

VIII.   FOOD: INTENDED ADDITIVES

In addition to the unintended carcinogenic and mutagenic residues likely to be found in the food supply, many carcinogens have been reported to exist in the chemical additives which are deliberately added to food. The categories of intentional additives are preservatives, antioxidants, sequestrants, surfactants, stabilizers-thickeners, acidulants, leavening agents, food colors, nutrient supplements, flavoring material, flavor enhancers-potentiators, basic taste modifiers, enzymes, functional protein additives, and "miscellaneous" including sorbital, anticaking agents, yeast foods, and dough conditioners (Miller, 1977).

Carcinogenic Additives: FDA list

The Delaney Clause allows no substance found to be carcinogenic in animal tests to be used as a food additive. Here is the list of food additives identified as carcinogens by the FDA, prepared in 1979 by R. A. Merrill, former chief counsel of the FDA. The following substances were either banned, or approval for their use was withdrawn, or authorization to use was refused. The substances were banned, successively, in the following order:

Chroanaline
DES in cattle and sheep
Diethylpyrocarbonate
Mercaptins
Violet No. 1
FD&C Red No. 2
Chloroform

DES
Dulcin and P-4000
Coumarin
Safrole
Flectol H
Oil of calamus
Cyclamate

Nitrofurans
Acrylonitrile copolymers
    used to fabricate
    beverage containers
Orange B
Saccharin
Polyvinyl chloride in
    contact with food

In 1977, the FDA announced its intention to ban *trichloroethylene (TCE)* from foods. TCE, reported to cause liver cancer in mice, has been used to extract flavoring from hops to enhance the taste of beer, in the production of spices, in the manufacture of food-packaging products, and in the processing of instant coffee (FDA, September 27, 1977).

Other Carcinogenic Additives

Another group of food additives has been reported to be carcinogenic in animal studies:

Additive	Reference
Flavoring	
Menthol	NIOSH, 1976
Dyes	
Fast green FCF	IARC, Vol. 16, 1978
Light green SF	IARC, Vol. 16, 1978
Rhodamine B	IARC, Vol. 16, 1978
Guinea green (banned)	IARC, Vol. 16, 1978
Fermentation Inhibitors	
Diethyl pyrocarbonate (DEPC), capable of synergistic reaction with other ingredients to form urethan, "a known carcinogen"	FDA, February 10, 1972
Preservatives	
Nitrite	Newberne, 1979
Sweeteners	
Xylitol	Smith, *Science* (February 10) 1978; Shubik,
Saccharin	1979; P. Handler, NAS, letter to J. Califano, 1978

Mutagenic Additives

Various food additives have been reported in the literature to produce mutagens or chromosome aberrations in microbiological tests: *butylated hydroxytoluene, butylated hydroxyanisole, coumarin, sucaryl, hexachlorocyclohexane, isopropylphenyl carbamate* (Epstein et al., 1971). *Saccharin* is a reported mutagen (Batzinger et al., 1977; Wolff et al., 1978).

The Synergistic Additive: Nitrite + Amines = N-Nitroso Compounds

Nitrite-cured meats: One source of carcinogenic N-nitroso compounds is meat cured with the additive nitrite, e.g., bacon, ham, sausage, corned beef, canned luncheon meat (Lijinsky, 1977).

Nitrite-cured meats plus amine compounds: Along with the nitrites in cured meat, Americans ingest a great many amine compounds as components of food, food additives, agricultural residues on crops, and drugs. Together, the nitrites and amines interact to form N-nitroso compounds in the stomach (Lijinsky, 1977).

As a class, N-nitroso compounds have been carcinogenic in every species tested, including rats, mice, guinea pigs, rabbits, dogs, monkeys, parakeets, pigs, hedgehogs, mink and trout (NAS, *Nitrates,* 1978). N-nitroso compounds have induced almost every type of tumor in almost all organs of experimental animals (Lijinsky, 1977). In laboratory tests on rats, for example, they produce the following cancers: liver, esophagus-pharynx, nasal cavities, respiratory tract, kidney, tongue, forestomach, bladder, central and peripheral nervous system, earduct, testis, ovary, mammary glands, intestine, glandular stomach, skin, jaw, uterus, vagina, haemopoietic system (WHO, *Nitrates,* 1978). In other experiments, the following tumors have also been produced: colon, bronchi, pancreas, brain, spinal cord, thymus, lymph nodes, blood vessels, bone (NAS, *Nitrates,* 1978).

N-nitroso compounds have also been reported to be mutagenic (Olajos, 1977).

IX. MEDICINE

Carcinogens in Drugs

DRUGS PRESCRIBED FOR HUMANS, AND CHEMICALS USED IN THEIR PRODUCTION, THAT ARE REPORTED TO CAUSE CANCER IN ANIMALS

Drug	Reference	Drug	Reference
Actinomycin-D	Adamson et al., 1977; NIOSH, 1976	Methylthiouracil (MTU)	IARC, Vol. 7, 1974
Adriamycin	NIOSH, 1976	Nitrogen mustard	Adamson et al., 1977; NIOSH, 1976
Busulfan	Adamson et al., 1977 NIOSH, 1976	Progesterone	IARC, Vol. 6, 1974
		Penicillin	NIOSH, 1976

Drug	Reference	Drug	Reference
Bis (2-chloro-ethyl) ether	IARC, Vol. 9, 1975	Propylthiouracil	IARC, Vol. 7, 1974
		Phenacetin	Vaught et. al., 1979
		Streptozotocin	NIOSH, 1976
Boric acid	NIOSH, 1976	Sulfacombin	NIOSH, 1976
Cytoxan	Adamson et al., 1977	(includes sul-fathiazole, sul-	
Chlorambucil	NIOSH, 1976	fanilamide,	
Chloroform	EPA "Potential In-dustrial," 1977	sulfonamide, and many	
Daunomycin	Adamson et al., 1977	other sulfa drugs)	
Diethylstilbestrol	IARC, Vol. 6, 1974	2, 4, 6-Tris(l-	IARC, Vol. 9, 1975
Ethinylestradiol	IARC, Vol. 6, 1974	aziridinyl)-s-	
Griseofulvin	Adamson, 1979	triazine	
Imuran	Adamson et al., 1977	Tris(aziridinyl)-para-benzo-	IARC, Vol. 9, 1975
Isoflurane	IARC, Vol. 11, 1976	quinone	
Isoniazid	Goldman et al., 1977	Triethylinemela-mine (TEM)	Adamson et al., 1977; NIOSH, 1976
Melphalan	Adamson et al., 1977	Thio-tepa	Adamson et al., 1977; NIOSH, 1976
6-Mercapto-purine	Adamson et al., 1977	Trichloroethy-lene (solvent)	IARC Vol. 11, 1976;FDA, Sept. 27, 1977
Mitomycin C	NIOSH, 1976		
Methapyrilene	FDA, June 8, 1979		
Metronidazole	Goldman et al., 1977		
Medroxyproges-terone acetate	FDA, July 26, 1979		

X. CLOTHING

Clothing consists, essentially, of textiles used to make dresses, suits, coats, raincoats, underwear, and sleepwear. These, too, are reported to be potential sources of cancer, both for those who manufacture them and those who wear them.

Carcinogens in Textiles

REPORTED CARCINOGENS IN TEXTILES

Aspect of Production	Reference
Textile fibers	
Acrilonitrile	OSHA, January 16, 1978
Asbestos	(See *METALS AND MINERALS*)
Beryllium	(See *METALS AND MINERALS*)
Fiberglass	(See *CONSTRUCTION*)

Aspect of Production	Reference
Chemicals used in processing and/or coloring of fibers and textiles	
Auramine dye	IARC, Vol. 1, 1972
Azo dyes	EPA, 1977*
Benzidine dye	IARC, Vol. 1, 1972, EPA, 1977
Copper-8-hydroxyquinoline	EPA, 1977
2-Methylaziridine	EPA, 1977
Fabric coatings and finishes: coatings for durable-press, water-repellent and crease-resistant fabrics; and for flocking, shrinkproofing and wrinkleproofing	
2-(1-Aziridinyl)-ethanol	EPA, 1977
Bis(chloromethyl)ether (BCME)	EPA, 1977
Epichlorohydrin	EPA, 1977
Lactones (e.g. β-propiolactone)	EPA, 1977
N-propylcarbamate	IARC, Vol. 12, 1976
Urethane	EPA, 1977
Coatings for flameproofing	
Pyroset TKP (carcinogen promoter)	Loewengart et al., 1977
Tetrakis (hydroxymethyl)phosphonium chloride (THPC) (carcinogen promoter)	Loewengart et al., 1977
Tris(2, 3-dibromopropyl)phosphate (TRIS)	CPSC (banned) 1977
Chemicals used in dry cleaning	
Chloroform	EPA, 1977
Perchloroethylene	EPA, 1977
Trichloroethylene	EPA, 1977

* EPA, 1977, always refers to *Potential Industrial Carcinogens and Mutagens.*

Mutagens in Textiles

Some of the carcinogenic substances reported above are also mutagens, and other mutagens as well are reported to be present in textiles:

Chemicals used in processing and/or coloring of fibers and textiles: *acetaldehyde* (cellulose), *chloroprene, diethyl and dimethyl sulfate* (cellulose), *ethylene oxide* (polyester), *formaldehyde, hydrazine, semi-carbazide* (acrylic) (EPA, *Potential Industrial,* 1977).

Fabric bleaching, sterilizing, fumigating, dyeing, and eradicating fungi: Many *anthraquinones and nitroanthraquinones, azobenzene-azo dyes, benzidine dyes; ethylene dichloride, hydrogen peroxide, hydroxylamine, peracetic acid* (EPA, *Potential Industrial,* 1977).

Fabric coatings and finishes (coatings for durable press, water-repellent, and crease-resistant fabrics, and for flocking, shrinkproofing, and wrinkleproofing): *acrolein, aziridine, bis(chloromethyl)ether (BCME), epichlorohydrin, glycidol, lactones* (e.g., *β-propiolactone), styrene oxide, urethan* (EPA, *Potential Industrial,* 1977).

Chemicals used in dry-cleaning: *trichloroethylene* (EPA, *Potential Industrial,* 1977).

Coatings for flameproofing: Tris(2,3-dibromopropyl)phosphate (TRIS) is a reported mutagen (Prival et al., 1977). In 1978, Gold et al. reported that tris-(1,3-dichloro-2-propyl)phosphate (Fyrol Fr 2) was a mutagen as well as a carcinogen, and could be absorbed through human skin. Both chemicals have been widely used in children's sleepwear.

XI. AIR

In an industrial system which is riddled with carcinogenic substances, it is inevitable that carcinogens should be found in great number in the air itself. Here are some of the major findings:

Energy Carcinogens in the Air

Every carcinogen, suspected carcinogen, or carcinogen promoter reported in Section II of this survey has also been reported in the air. In 1978, D.F.S. Natusch listed more than 50 of them.

Inorganic cases: *sulfur oxides, nitrogen oxides, ozone, mercury.*
Inorganic particulates: *arsenic, asbestos, beryllium, cadmium, cobalt, chromium, copper, iron, nickel, lead, selenium, uranium, vanadium.*
Radioactive particulates: various forms of *lead, radium, radon, thorium, and uranium.*
Gaseous and particulate organics: *alkanes (n-butane, n-pentane, 2-methylbutane), alkenes (2-butene, 1,3-butadiene), propene, aldehydes and ketones (formaldehyde, acrolein), nitrosamines (dimethylnitrosamine), peroxides (peroxyacylnitrates), aromatic hydrocarbons (benzene, toluene, 1,2-dimethylbenzene, 1,3-dimethylbenzene, 1,4-dimethylbenzene), polyaromatic hydrocarbons (anthracene, benzo(a)pyrene, benzo(e)pyrene, 1,2-benzanthracene, 1,12-benzperylene, coronene, chrysene, pyrene), polycyclic nitrogen compounds (acridine, fluorene carbonitrile), lead tetraalkyls (tetraethyllead), benzene-soluble organics.*

Other Carcinogens in the Air

Nitrogen oxides (NO_x) are major air pollutants and reported carcinogen promoters. They are frequently reported to interact with amines in the air to produce *nitrosamines*, which are also reported, independently, as carcinogenic air pollutants (Padgett, 1975; Fine et al., 1977; Althoff et al., 1977; Natusch, 1978). Nitrosamines induce cancers in more than 20 different animal species (Epstein, 1978).

Sulfur oxide is one of the major air pollutants. It has been identified as a potentiator of the carcinogenic properties of polycyclic aromatic hydrocarbons (Brubaker et al., 1975).

Ozone, a photochemical oxidant, one source of which is ozonized gasoline, is found in substantial concentrations in the air. It has been reported in several studies to be carcinogenic (WHO, *Photochemical Oxidants,* 1979).

Vinyl chloride, emitted from vinyl chloride monomer, polyvinyl chloride resins, and polyvinyl chloride fabricating plants, has been identified as a hazardous air pollutant (EPA, September 16, 1974). It has been banned as an ingredient of aerosols (CPSC, August 16, 1974).

Palladium is emitted from catalytic converters in automobiles. It has been reported to be a potentiator of carcinogenicity in mice, producing adenocarcinoma of the lung (Brubaker et al., 1975).

Chloroform, reported above by the EPA to be carcinogenic in test animals, has been identified as an air pollutant (EPA, Office of Water Supply, 1978).

Cigarette smoke is a known air pollutant. In 1970, F. W. Sunderman, Jr., reported that *nickel* was a significant component of cigarette smoke. In 1972 the NAS (*Particulate Polycyclic*) reported that cigarettes also contained such carcinogenic agents as *polycyclic hydrocarbons* (e.g., benzo (a)pyrene), *arsenic, polonium, and nitrosamines.*

Carcinogenic Indoor Air

Homes are presumed to offer protection from outside pollutants. In fact, they often trap external pollutants that have seeped in, and prevent internally generated pollutants from escaping.

Indoor pollution may be greater than outdoor pollution. *Hydrocarbons* are persistent indoor pollutants. The major source of aromatic hydrocarbons, many of which are reported to be carcinogens (e.g., benzo(*a*)pyrene), is cooking. In addition, hydrocarbons emerge from paints, cleaning fluids, artificial leather, linoleum, asphalt tiles, rubber, and plastic cement (Sterling et al., 1977).

Carcinogenic dusts and particulate matter: Many of the pollutants from the combustion of coal and petroleum are carcinogenic and are absorbed into the particulate matter in the air of the home. Lead is consistently found in household dust. Benzene-soluble organic matter adheres to the particles breathed in the home. Workers bring home carcinogenic fibers and dusts (e.g., *asbestos and beryllium*) which also adhere to the particulate matter. Carcinogenic particulate matter is also released into indoor air by cigarette smoking (Sterling et al., 1977; Cuddeback et al., 1976).

Formaldehyde, identified above by the EPA as a reported mutagen and by NIOSH as a reported carcinogen, is also found in enclosed living spaces. Health officials have reported that formaldehyde pollution is a particular health hazard in mobile homes (news story, *Wall Street Journal*, August 15, 1979).

Respiratory Carcinogens

In a 1970 review of the literature, F. W. Sunderman, Jr., tabulated those substances which had been identified as respiratory carcinogens in various animals, i.e., mouse, rat, hamster, guinea pig, rabbit, duck or fowl, dog, monkey:

Polycyclic aromatic hydrocarbons:
   3,4-Benzpyrene
   Methylcholanthrene
   Dimethylbenzanthracene
Nitrosodialkylamines:
   Dimethylnitrosamine
   Diethylnitrosamine
   Diamylnitrosamine
N-Nitroso compounds:
   N-Nitrosopiperidine
   N-Nitrosomorpholine
   N-Nitrosomethylurethan
Aromatic amines:
   Trifluoroacetamidofluorene
Dietary factors:
   Aflatoxin
   Cycasin

Other organic compounds:
   Urethan
   Uracil mustard
   4-Nitroquinoline-*N*-oxide
Nonmetallic inorganic compounds:
   Diazomethane
   Hydrazine
Minerals:
   Asbestos
Metals:
   Nickel
   Chromium
   Beryllium
Radioactive chemicals:
   Strontium-90
   Cerium-144
   Plutonium-239

XII. WATER

For almost two decades, studies have been published reporting the existence of substances in the water supplies that were thought at the time to be carcinogens, or were later identified as carcinogens. Here are some of the findings:

1962:   A study of finished drinking water in 100 United States cities reported the presence of trace elements including the following: *chromium, iron, lead, manganese, molybdenum, nickel, and titanium* (Skougstad, 1971). All are reported to be carcinogenic (see Section II, Energy: Fossil Fuels; and Section III, Metals, Minerals).

1962-1967:   During this period, 380 finished municipal water samples were listed, and again, trace metals were found, including: *zinc, cadmium, iron, manganese, lead, chromium, molybdenum, beryllium, nickel, and colbalt* (NAS, "Drinking," 1977). All are reported to be carcinogenic (see Section III).

1971:   Various radioisotopes—*uranium, iodine-131, cesium-129, and radon*—were reported to be in U.S. drinking water (Skougstad, 1971).

1974:   Iron ore wastes—*taconite tailings,* with high concentrations of *asbestos*—were being dumped into the water of Lake Superior from which many communities took their drinking water, by the Reserve Mining Company of Minnesota. Since asbestos had been linked to lung cancer, the EPA declared that drinking such fibers constituted a hazard (EPA, March 29, 1974). In April 1974, Federal District Judge Miles Lord issued an injunction in Minnesota forbidding the company to continue its dumping (Epstein, 1978).

1975:   The EPA studied drinking water in 79 cities and reported that U.S. drinking water contained six carcinogens: *chloroform, bromodichloromethane, dibromochloromethane, bromoform, carbon tetrachloride, and 1,2-dichloroethane.* The first four chemicals are formed during the process of chlorination employed to protect the citizens from waterborne diseases such as typhoid, cholera, and dysentery (EPA, April 18, 1975; NAS, "Chloroform," 1978).

1977:   The EPA, in *Potential Industrial Carcinogens and Mutagens,* reported that *vinyl chloride* was migrating from rigid PVC water pipes into municipal water supplies in the United States.

1977:   A letter to *Science* reported that thousands of municipal water tanks and pipelines used for drinking water had been coated with *asbestos* and *coal tar,* both reported carcinogens (Ford, September 30, 1977).

1977:   *PBBs* were reported to be contaminating water supplies. PBBs were identified by the EPA as suspected carcinogens (EPA, June 17, 1977; September 13, 1977).

1978:   *PCBs* were reported to be contaminating the water (DHEW Subcommittee on PCBs, 1978). PCBs have also been identified as suspected carcinogens by WHO (1976) and by Costle, EPA Administrator (May 22, 1977).

1978:   It was reported that chlorination was oxidizing plutonium in drinking water and might cause it to be more readily absorbed into the gastrointestinal tract (Larsen et al., 1978).

1978:   Arthur Upton, Director of the National Cancer Institute, reported that U.S. drinking water contained 23 carcinogens or suspected carcinogens, 11 carcinogen promoters, and 28 mutagens or suspected mutagens (letter to Costle, April 10, 1978). Here is his list:

Carcinogens and Sus- pect Carcinogens in Drinking Water (USA)	List of [Carcinogen] Promoters in Drink- ing Water (USA)	Mutagens and Suspect Mutagens in Drinking Water (USA)
Benzo(a)pyrene	Ortho-Cresol	1,1,1-Trichloroethane
Carbon tetrachloride	2,4-Dimethylphenol	Bromomethane (methyl bromide)
Chloroform	Phenol	Methyl chloride
Vinyl chloride	n-Dodecane	Bromochloromethane
1, 4-Dioxane	Eicosane	Methylene chloride
Methyl iodide	2,4-Dichlorophenol	Bromoform
DDE	n-Decane	Bromodichloromethane
DDT	Limonene	2-Chloropropane
Chlordane	Octadecane	1,2-Dichloropropane
Lindane	n-Tetradecane	1-Chloropropene
Dieldrin	n-Undecane	1,2-Dichloroethane
Benzene		Bis(2-chloroisopropyl)ether
		Chlorodibromomethane
Vinylidene chloride		1,3-Dichloropropene
Heptachlor		2,6-Dinitrotoluene
1,1,2-Trichloroethane		Dichloroacetonitrile
1,1,2-Trichloroethylene		Methylene bromide
Bis(2-chloroethyl)ether		Chlordane
Simazine		Vinylidene chloride
Tetrachloroethylene		n-Butylbromide
Heptachlor epoxide		Bis(2-chloroethyl)ether
Acrylonitrile		Acrylonitrile
Aldrin		Benzo(a)pyrene
Butyl bromide		Methyl iodide
		Vinyl chloride
		1,3-Butadiene
		1,2-Bis(chloroethoxy)ethane
		Pyrene

XIII.　WASTES

The problem of toxic wastes is the problem of soil pollution—the pollution caused by those wastes and effluents which end up not in the air or water, but in the ground. The EPA estimates that 30–40 million tons of hazardous wastes are produced each year (EPA, November 21, 1978). There are approximately 18,500 sites for disposal of munic- ipal solid wastes, another 23,000 for the disposal of sewage sludge, and about 100,000 sites for industrial wastes. Some 10–15 percent of industrial wastes are estimated to be toxic and an unknown percentage is carcinogenic (Maugh, 1979).

Radioactive Wastes

One-third of the nation's low-level radioactive waste comes from biomedical research laboratories and the nuclear medicine departments of hospitals, most of which are in the Northeast (Marshall, 1979). Two-thirds come from nuclear power. A small portion of this waste is strikingly long-lived. According to physicist Bernard L. Cohen ("High Level," 1977), some fission products endure for 1 to 10 years, some from 10 to 100 years, and some from 100 to 4×10^{10} years.

Long-Lived vs. Indestructible Wastes

In 1979, comparing low-level radioactive wastes to chemical wastes, Thomas Maugh wrote in *Science* magazine (May 25): ". . . some of the more reactive chemicals will be degraded after a few months or a few weeks of storage. But the more stable materials, such as PCBs, may retain their chemical identity—and their toxicity—for decades, perhaps for centuries. Still other toxic materials are permanent hazards—a cadmium atom or a beryllium atom will remain that forever. From this perspective, the much-bruited half-lives of radioactive wastes from nuclear power plants seem almost transient. The volume of nuclear wastes also seems small in comparison. Only about 5,000 metric tons of nuclear waste have been accumulated since the beginning of the nuclear era, four orders of magnitude less than the amount of toxic wastes generated in one year."

Indestructible Wastes

Several analyses have been made by the EPA's Office of Solid Waste Management of the types of substances that show up in toxic wastes. One (SW-115, 1974) is presented here. Eight of the 11 categories tallied—the metals—are indestructible elemental carcinogens.

REPRESENTATIVE HAZARDOUS SUBSTANCES WITHIN INDUSTRIAL WASTE STREAM*

Industry	As	Cd	Chlorinated hydrocarbons	Cr	Cu	Cyanides	Pb	Hg	Misc. organics	Se	Zn
Mining and metallurgy	X	X		X	X	X	X	X		X	X
Paint and dye		X		X	X	X	X	X	X	X	
Pesticide	X		X			X	X	X	X		X
Electrical and electronic			X		X	X	X	X		X	
Printing and duplicating	X			X	X		X		X	X	
Electroplating and metal finishing	X			X	X	X					X
Chemical manufacturing			X	X	X			X	X		
Explosives	X				X		X	X	X		
Rubber and plastics			X			X		X	X		X
Battery		X					X	X			X
Pharmaceutical	X							X	X		
Textile				X	X				X		
Petroleum and coal	X		X				X				
Pulp and paper							X		X		
Leather				X					X		

* All italicized substances and/or their compounds have been reported to be carcinogens in this survey.

• • •

We can now consider some of the implications of this survey. Although the layman may not assume the validity of these reported data and is not competent to judge any of them, he can make two important discoveries here.

First, if these data, or any significant proportion of them, are accurate, the problem of chemical cancer seems to be enormous. If the reader has used the set of regulatory assumptions about the reported animal data—above all, if he has assumed that any chemical that causes cancer in an animal may be carcinogenic to man, and that any exposure to a carcinogen, no matter how minute, can cause cancer—he can only reach a harrowing conclusion. The survey suggests that the American citizen from birth to death apparently can draw no breath, swallow no water, walk on no soil, and eat no food that is not, or may not be, contaminated by reported cancer-causing agents and mutagenic agents which themselves are believed by many scientists to cause cancer. The job the American holds, the clothing he wears, the newspapers and books he reads, the television set he watches, the photographs he takes, the pictures he paints, the records he listens to, the car he drives, the gas station where he fills its tank, the medical care and drugs he receives, the factories in the neighborhood he inhabits, the construction materials of the house he lives in, the occupations of the relatives he lives with, the fuel he burns in his basement, the fumes from his kitchen, the fluorescent lights in his bathroom, the invisible motes of dust in his living room—all, according to scientists, are possible sources of cancer.

The survey gives no information on how extensive is the exposure to any carcinogen in any single group, nor does it give any specific risk calculations; but on the assumption that even the minutest amount of a carcinogen can trigger a cancer in a population that is constantly being assaulted by chemical carcinogens, the situation appears to be catastrophic. In fact, the survey, if interpreted with the "official" assumptions, portrays our society exactly as the apocalyptics portray it—as a carcinogenic hell. Given such findings in the literature, one is not surprised to learn that Barry Commoner, in 1978, demanded a nationwide search for the victims of "environmental degradation"—"Nothing short of a massive survey of the entire population is needed";[33] that Samuel Epstein charges that our work places are sites of "the carnage of chemical-cancer";[34] and that Irving Selikoff predicts that "millions" may die in the future of industrially caused cancer.[35] And given the fearful number of reported chemical carcinogens, not to mention the mutagens which this survey considers only incidentally, one can also see how Umberto Saffiotti and others hypothesize that most human cancers are coming from industry. In sum, to accept the "official" assumptions about the reported industrial data is virtually to accept the apocalyptics' conclusions.

And yet that is not all we learn from this survey. It tells us one other startling thing. The alphabetized list of chemicals was misleading. The concept "chemical" was, in fact, being used in two different ways: (1) to mean synthetic compounds invented by the chemical industry; and (2) to mean *any* substance used in industry—for any substance on earth can be legitimately identified in chemical terms. There had either been mass equivocation in the use of the word "chemicals" or an extremely peculiar mistake had been made. I had started out to look for synthetic chemicals, and I had certainly found them; but I had ended up with a survey of the major aspects of industrial civilization—and the very pillars of industrial civilization had also been reported to be carcinogenic.

And, most startling of all, what underlay some of the oldest and most basic industries, which had simply dug up or chopped down the earth's own materials, was *nature*. A great many of those chemicals came out of fossil fuels—coal, oil, peat, lignite—which are the fossilized remains of living entities. There was stone on this list of compounds, there were minerals and metals—the very elements of the earth. There was tobacco, a plant. There was progesterone, a sex hormone. Nature keeps peering out at us from that survey of industrial substances, as an independent source of carcinogens.

Clearly, the problem of environmental carcinogenicity as presented to the public at the time of the passage of the Toxic Substances Control Act was incomplete. I had followed the lead of the researchers in chemical carcinogenesis, with a little instruction from government theorists and advisers, and most of what I had found were synthetic substances, because that is what they were dominantly studying and that is what I was looking for. But the decision to break down the information by industries had led me in a direction I had not been prepared for by any of these theorists, or the apocalyptic movement which had generated them. I ended up finding evidence that nature itself was carcinogenic.

And that raised a few interesting questions. What if I had not been guided by government theory? What if those alphabetized chemicals, which as a layman I cannot identify, also included natural chemicals? What if I had hunted for natural carcinogens as diligently as I had hunted for synthetic carcinogens? Surely the ones on this list, acquired almost by accident, could not be all that exist. So I decided to look with equal diligence for natural carcinogens. And I found them. Somehow, the theoreticians, the regulators, and the apocalyptic movement itself had misplaced them. The natural carcinogens were sitting there quietly in the literature on carcinogenesis, along with the synthetics. The only difference was that they had not been publicized. In fact, in the national uproar over "chemicals," and the presentation to the public of the concepts that science, technology, industry, profits, and capitalism were the causes of as much as 90 percent of human cancer, they had hardly been noticed.

Thus, in the next chapter, I will present another collection of carcinogens—one which includes those that peered out at us in the industrial survey. They will allow us to examine the problem from a new perspective, for this new collection offers an unusual analytical advantage. Although the scientific methodologies remain the same, and although the "official" assumptions remain the same, one variable is changed: The reported carcinogens in question are marvelously invulnerable to ideological prejudice; all are attributes of the planet and the universe in which we live. No sinful Faust or economic system can be blamed for creating these carcinogens. The moral stature of their inventor cannot be threatened. No earnest reformer can demand that they be eliminated.

And no one can use them as fuel for a battle against the status quo in the name of an arcadian ideal, for these are, so to speak, the ultimate status quo: They are arcadian carcinogens. We may accordingly learn something by applying the "official" assumptions to these carcinogens that we do not or cannot learn when we apply them to carcinogens that were invented by modern science and technology. In the next chapter, then, we will look at the earth itself through the same "official" eyes. Or rather, we will look at the earth through those eyes as if they had been open, for, in fact, they had been tightly shut. And one of the questions we will try to answer is *why* they were shut. In fact, these reports on nature's carcinogens were so easy to find once I started looking for them that that is the first question to answer.

Chapter 4

Benevolent Nature

Nature Knows Best.[1]
—Barry Commoner, *The Closing Circle*, 1971

One can readily infer the view of earth's carcinogens held both by apocalyptic and by "official" scientists from their other opinions which burst upon the national scene around the time of the Toxic Substances Control Act. They have two distinct sets of opinions, and both have been presented respectively in Chapter 2 and Chapter 3 of this book. The first set pertains to causation: The apocalyptics, in the very act of avowing that such data were nonexistent, said that carcinogens, in the form of synthetic chemicals produced after World War II, are responsible for as much as 90 percent of cancer deaths. The second set of opinions pertains to solution or prevention: "Official" science has postulated that to prevent most cancer one must test all industrial chemicals for carcinogenicity, plug up the incriminated test tubes, and protect people from exposure to even a single carcinogenic molecule. This vision of the problem and its cure clearly implies that carcinogens are, for the most part, artificial inventions and do not ordinarily appear in nature.

This is a straightforward inference, and there is no reason to doubt its accuracy. People who think that the carcinogen is essentially an artifact of the chemical industry must also think that nature's contribution to the stockpile of carcinogens is insignificant. Similarly, people who think most carcinogens were produced during and after World War II must also think that nature's role in the matter is insignificant, since nature is somewhat older than World War II. That apocalyptics think this is unquestionable; one runs into a curious problem, however, when one tries to discover why they think it. They do not say. One may peruse apocalyptic statements, articles, papers, and books by the kilo, and all one discovers is that both apocalyptics and "official" scientists hold the view, usually implicit, that nature is rarely carcinogenic, but offer no data to support that view. I looked in vain for studies comparable to those made of industrial chemicals indicating that several thousand natural chemicals had been tested and that some given number was carcinogenic. How, then, I wondered, did the apocalyptics and government theorists conclude that natural carcinogens were rare phenomena? Could this be yet another of the "official" assumptions?

This hypothesis was jarring to the nerves, for I already had enough "official" assumptions to investigate, and desired no others. Nonetheless, the question had to be confronted. What was the genesis of the conviction that nature was not particularly carcinogenic?

Since at the time I was conducting this investigation and producing the survey which appears in this chapter the government was mute on the subject and the contemporary apocalyptics declined to say, I could think of nothing to do but consult their most popular ancestors. The most reasonable ancestors to consult were Rachel Carson and Barry Commoner, whose combined intellectual influence spans almost twenty years, and when I did consult them, I found the missing explanation. Both Carson and Commoner made it quite clear what they thought about natural carcinogens and why they thought it, and their explanation appears to account quite fully for their intellectual descendants' views on the matter. In this chapter, then, we will review the original apocalyptic vision of the earth's carcinogens and will bring that vision up to date—specifically, up to the years surrounding the passage of the Toxic Substances Control Act; after that, we will look at the data on natural carcinogens; and finally, with both industrial and natural data in hand, we will be in a position to reach a few conclusions and raise a few new questions.

We shall begin with Rachel Carson's ideas about the essential noncarcinogenicity of nature. They were expressed in *Silent Spring*, and her vision of the problem is by far the most important, because it was the first to reach a national audience and it set many of the terms of public discourse. One commonly credits the ideas in *Silent Spring* to Carson, and since it was her book, we will do so here. But in fact, the ideas it presented on carcinogens were not Carson's. Although she was a biologist and an ecologist, she was not an expert in carcinogenesis. She worked at the Fish and Wildlife Service, and *Silent Spring* was the result of intensive interviewing and reporting. In her chapter on carcinogens she relied heavily on the guidance and ideas of the late Wilhelm Hueper, then Chief of the Environmental Cancer Section of NCI, a distinguished occupational toxicologist who has already been identified as one of the leaders of the scientists' rebellion against government policy in the 1960s. Carson quoted and paraphrased Hueper extensively, particularly on the subjects of the potential chemical catastrophe confronting mankind and on the need for political solutions, and Hueper was one of the scientists who reviewed her material on cancer before publication.[2] Carson's voice is thus, in some measure, the voice of the cancer prevention establishment in America before it acquired its present political power, and as such it merits close attention.

Carson's vision of nature's role in cancer causation is easily conveyed. That role, said Carson, was negligible. Her presentation of that thesis was so brief she could state it in two paragraphs[3] and restate it, in one paragraph.[4] The explanation embedded in these paragraphs was itself exceedingly sparse. In fact, to find it, one must prune away nine-tenths of the verbiage, for Carson was a talented and poetic writer, and she could spin entrancing webs of words with relatively little content. She offered her readers only one piece of factual information: Natural carcinogens were "few in number"; there were, for example, a few radioactive rocks, arsenic, and the ultraviolet rays of the sun. Carson did not say how that limited number of natural carcinogens had been established, and she cited no data to substantiate the statement. She explained nature's striking lack of carcinogens with evolutionary theory. The environment shaped and directed; life adapted; eons of time passed; balance was reached; and the result of all the shaping, directing, adapting, and balancing, said Carson, was that there were very few carcinogens.

This was her first premise, and Carson proceeded immediately to its corollary: It was man who had created his own cancerous universe, for man, she said, was the only living entity that could create cancer-causing substances.[5] The major damage, she said, had been done since the early 1940s, the period of World War II, when the world, she said, had become contaminated by an "unnatural" production of radiation, and by great numbers of "sinister" chemicals, which, in partnership, were altering the very nature of the biosphere.[6] The reason for the "sinister" qualities of the chemicals, said Carson, lay in the fact that they were "synthetic" artifacts of human intelligence; they had been manufactured in test tubes and were substances which had no natural equivalents and to which no life could adjust.[7] This concept was Carson's second premise, and however veiled in lyricism, it was actually a reformulation of her first. Synthetic chemicals, Carson had actually said, were "sinister" *because* they were synthetic. Life, she said, had adapted only to the natural.

These were the "axioms" of Carson's thought, and from them she launched her analysis. By producing "unnatural" substances in huge quantities, she said, man had turned the world in which he lived into "a sea of carcinogens" that was now taking almost one of every four lives. Man was absorbing them into his body through the air and the water and, particularly in the form of pesticides, in his food. She transmitted a powerful warning from Hueper that man might be destroyed by synthetic chemicals in food; there had been an epidemic of liver cancer in trout poisoned by a synthetic chemical, and, Hueper said, what had happened to the trout could happen to man.[8] Carson suggested that it was probably already happening. We were, she said, being poisoned by our food supply, and the poisoning was primarily from the chlorinated hydrocarbon pesticides.[9]

Chlorinated hydrocarbons were not the only carcinogens Carson identified, but they were her chief symbol of the "sea of carcinogens" with which we were surrounded. And it was largely by means of her discussion of chlorinated hydrocarbons in general and DDT in particular that Carson dramatized her view that nature and synthetic chemicals were in fundamental conflict. She gave her readers a close-up view of the chemists who constructed the "sinister" synthetics in their laboratories.[10] In one chapter, she showed how chlorinated hydrocarbons were invented. She chose a natural chemical, methane, with a simple structure, consisting of one carbon atom to which four hydrogen atoms were attached, and she illustrated it thus:

$$H \quad H$$
$$C$$
$$H \quad H$$

If one substituted one atom of chlorine for an atom of hydrogen, she said, one created a chemical called methyl chloride. If one took away three hydrogen atoms and substituted chlorine atoms, one created the anesthetic chloroform. Finally, if one substituted chlorine atoms for all the hydrogen atoms, one created the cleaning fluid carbon tetrachloride. Her choices are of interest, for all three of these chemicals are listed as reported carcinogens by NIOSH (*Suspected Carcinogens,* 1976). Far more complex manipulations, she said, had produced DDT. Thus, she said, was the chemistry of living entities converted into an instrument of destruction.[11] And Carson pleaded for the living. She preferred, she said, to see the sight of the clover, the lily, and the bracken growing wild by the roadside than to see the earth scorched by man and his pesticides. Carson was asking her readers to make a moral choice between the earth itself, which gave us such lovely spectacles as the bracken fern that "lifted high its proud lacework,"[12] and the "unnatural" chemicals like methyl chloride and carbon tetrachloride, which represented the "hideous" and artificial universe of modern technology.[13]

By man, of course, Carson primarily meant a few kinds of men: the organic chemists who manipulated the structures of nature into deadly substances, the businessmen who sold those deadly substances for profit, the advertisers who seduced the citizens into purchasing those substances with "the soft sell and the hidden persuader," and finally, the captive regulator who falsely reassured the citizen that these deadly substances, in minute doses, were safe. Although Carson did not say so explicitly, her charges against these particular categories of man added up to the single charge that what was causing most of the cancer that was killing our citizens was the American economic system. Given the "axiom" of nature's lack of culpability for most of these deaths, the conclusion was irreproachable. Clearly, if natural substances were not killing the vast majority of the cancer victims, the creators, manufacturers, and salesmen of unnatural substances were killing them, and equally clearly, the political and economic system that allowed this to happen was killing them. The "axiom" of nature's innocence was thus not a minor matter: On it rested a political theory of cancer causation and a powerful political indictment of "the system."

Accordingly, Carson's solutions were political. She was the first to present to the broad public the contemporary idea that political action—in the form of cancer prevention—is the solution for the bulk of the cancer problem. She cited Hueper on the subject at length, explaining his "germ theory" of cancer. Carcinogens, Hueper had told her, could be compared to germs, and just as preventive action—e.g., hygienic water supplies—had solved the nineteenth-century problem of combating many pathogenic microorganisms, so could preventive action solve the problem of carcinogens.[14] In one sense, she said after presenting his views, the problem was more solvable than that of germ-causing infectious disease, for man did not create those germs but, said Carson, man *had* created "the vast majority of carcinogens" and could therefore get rid of many of them.[15] And it was imperative that they be eliminated, she said, for no dose of a man-made carcinogenic "germ" was safe, and she recommended that wherever practically possible, such carcinogenic "germs" be legally banned. And the reason she gave is the precise reason offered as the most sophisticated justification for the no-threshold theory, which is the linchpin of contemporary regulation: She demanded the eradication of the carcinogens that were invading food, water, and air in order to avoid the cumulative buildup of tiny doses which, she said, constituted the crucial threat to our lives.[16]

It is entirely apparent that Carson's analysis of the carcinogen problem is the very analysis that now prevails among American regulators; and it is also apparent that among some at the National Cancer Institute, the concept of cancer as a political disease requiring a political solution had been fully crystallized at least two decades ago. But more important yet, Carson's analysis tells us that the apocalyptic approach to cancer rests, fundamentally, on the "axiom" of a largely benevolent nature—on a vision of a largely noncarcinogenic Garden of Eden now defiled by the sins of pride and greed.

Another presentation of this same vision of nature came from the biologist Barry Commoner. He and Carson had actually been communicating similar doctrines for the same length of time, but his own influence apparently reached its peak after he published *The Closing Circle*, in 1971. In that book, and in much of his work that followed it, Commoner dedicated himself to reinforcing the idea that life had adapted to the natural, but that the unnatural was dangerous. He took the idea further than Carson; he defined a "law of ecology" that stated it, and he entitled the law "Nature Knows Best."[17] It, too, was couched in the form of evolutionary theory. Evolution, Commoner informed his readers, was actually a vast experiment in "R and D" that had been going on for some two to three billion years. In that time an incalculable number of living things had been produced, and each had been given the opportunity to experiment with some random genetic change. If that change killed the organism, it did not transmit its genetic characteristics to future generations. "In this way," said Commoner, "living things accumulate a complex organization of compatible parts; those possible arrangements that are not compatible with the whole are screened out over the long course of evolution."[18] Given this evolutionary compatibility, said Commoner, any change in nature's arrangements was hazardous; "the artificial introduction of an organic compound that does not occur in nature, but is man-made and is nevertheless active in a living system, is very likely to be harmful."[19] Artificial substances, he also said, "are usually toxic and frequently carcinogenic."[20] Commoner offered no data on the "frequency" of carcinogenicity in synthetic substances, nor did he offer any data on the non-"frequency" of carcinogenicity in natural substances. Like Carson, he used evolutionary theory to account for his "law of ecology." The belief that "Nature Knows Best" was Commoner's "axiom."

That "axiom" had the same implications for Commoner that it did for

Carson. If nature was not responsible for the presence of most carcinogens in the world, the responsibility was necessarily man's. Commoner, however, did not waste his time blaming man in the abstract, nor did he focus on the pesticide industry. He went right to the source of all synthetic chemicals—the chemical industry. That industry, he said, had been flourishing since World War II, and had enthroned the synthetic in our society with its massive production of synthetic organic chemicals.[21] For the rest of the decade, with time out for proposing that socialism could solve both energy and pollution problems,[22] Commoner continued to campaign against the chemical industry and its synthetic substances. At the 1977 cancer conference cited in an earlier chapter, Commoner recapitulated his basic thesis: The chemical industry, he said, was a source of cancer because it was "deliberately designed to produce evolutionary rejects"; it was "largely based on producing organic chemicals which do not occur in living things." The problem, he said, was economic: "When you talk about carcinogens, you are talking about the economic life of the petrochemical industry, which now largely dominates the American economy." And the solution, he said, was political; the choice was either to ban the carcinogens or to take over the chemical industry, for "if we rely on a risk-benefit analysis instead of the Delaney Amendment approach [banning], the petrochemical industry must be socially governed—that is, the people who will decide what the factories produce and how they are used will be us, not the owners of the factory."[23]

Thus we see that for both apocalyptic theorists, the "axiom" of nature's minimal role in cancer causation led to a political conception of the disease of cancer and to a political solution. A decade and a half separated the analyses cited here, and yet they were almost identical. Much had changed in science during those years, but one thing had remained the same: the descriptive theory of evolution, which both of these authors had used to account for the essential noncarcinogenicity of nature.

Carson and Commoner were not the only ones to present these views on carcinogens, but they expressed them in clear, vivid prose, and both moved with brio from their evolutionary base to a moral-political conclusion. Their works provoked scientific controversy, but the controversy was always about technical details; their shared "axiom" of nature's benevolence was not challenged.[24] On the contrary, as we have already seen, their charge that most carcinogens were synthetic was accepted with almost explosive speed by a large portion of the world of educated laymen. What is more, events seemed to prove them right. Synthetic chemical carcinogens did indeed exist, the number of identified and suspected carcinogens was increasing at an appalling rate, evidence emerged that men had died of chemical cancer, and the likelihood was great that many more would die. In the face of this new and frightening problem, few were interested in evaluating the validity of the theory that purported to account for it. The underlying "axiom" of nature's virtual noncarcinogenicity was tacitly accepted, and the little packet of ideas that followed from that "axiom" soon became the conventional wisdom: "Man," not nature, was responsible for the evil . . ."man" meant the men who made and used chemicals . . ."man" meant industry . . . cancer was fundamentally a political disease.

A political disease required a political solution, and among the many solutions adopted by the Congress was the Toxic Substances Control Act. Unsurprisingly, the campaigners for the law invoked both the "axiom" of nature's innocence and the corollary of "man's" guilt. By the mid-1970s, in fact, both "axiom" and corollary had been institutionalized; they had two organized sets of partisans and two formal bases of political power, each with a slightly different stress. The "environmentalists" and ecologists, whose base was the EPA, demanded control of industry in the name of nature's innocence, while experts in chemical carcinogenesis and occupational toxicologists, whose base was OSHA, demanded control of industry on the grounds of "man's" guilt; and "public interest" groups emerged to do battle for both factions. The advocates of the act often seemed to be reciting straight from the pages of Carson and Commoner, and among "environmentalists," the flow of evolutionary language was intense. For example, in 1975, John R. Quarles, Jr., Deputy Administrator of the EPA, prefaced his congressional testimony on synthetic chemicals with the following words:

Since Darwin man has recognized the ability of living things to adapt to their environments. The great diversity of life in our biosphere reflects the successful resistance of man and other species to the myriad of chemicals found in nature. However, the advent of chemical technology in the past decades has introduced billions of pounds of new chemicals that are often alien to the environment, persistent, and unknown in their interactions with living things.[25]

Many of those who evaluated the act after its passage also talked in evolutionary terms. In 1976, an analysis of the law and the issues with which it dealt appeared in the *Environmental Law Reporter*. One paragraph read:

Finally, at least with respect to synthetic chemicals, the evolutionary perspective suggests a per se need for caution. Any chemical molecule not found in nature may be said to have the potential to harm biological organisms from bacteria to man. This is because living organisms' internal defense and waste removal systems are not likely to be prepared to cope with substances of a kind that they and their evolutionary precursors never had to contend with in the natural universe.[26]

As for those who proclaimed "man's" guilt, we know already that many, like Carson and Commoner, identified that guilt in political and economic terms. Samuel Epstein linked cancer to the profit motive; Umberto Saffiotti of the NCI pronounced cancer a "social disease" determined by "powerful social and economic factors"; and Ralph Nader rebaptized cancer as "corporate cancer."

These two groups—those who primarily talked in terms of evolutionary concepts and those who primarily talked in terms of political-economic concepts—seemed to be intellectually remote from each other, but in fact they were not. All the political critics named above were also Carsonian "environmentalists" who had been gripped by Carson's vision of a world poisoned by pesticides. Samuel Epstein had been one of the most redoubtable foes of DDT and had testified to its carcinogenicity at the Consolidated DDT Hearings which had culminated in the ban of that pesticide by EPA Administrator William D. Ruckelshaus.[27] Umberto Saffiotti, then Associate Scientific Director for Carcinogenesis, Etiology Area, of the National Cancer Institute, had also testified at those hearings, and was singled out in the *Federal Register* by Ruckelshaus as one of the "specialists in cancer research" whose "expertise" had contributed to Ruckelshaus' decision.[28] Ralph Nader, too, was a child of Carson whose crusading impulses were intensified, he says, as he walked on campus and watched men spray trees with poisons as indifferent students strolled by.[29] The concerns and activities of the two groups had always overlapped, and, philosophically, they were interdependent. Although those who engaged in political analysis did not customarily talk about nature, the "environmentalists" who did provided the necessary basis for the claim that cancer was essentially man-made: The evolutionary theory rationalized the political theory.

Ultimately, the act itself reflected the interdependent themes. Its content was chiefly political: It consisted of pages of rules, among them rules pertaining to the marketing of chemicals. Its justification was evolutionary: The goal of the act, said the act itself, was to protect the "environment," defined as "water, air and land and the interrelationship which exists among and between water, air and land and all living things." No one could imagine, on reading this evocation of the serenely interlocking harmony of the biosphere, that water and air and land and living things might themselves be deadly substances, might even be causes of cancer. TSCA was a silent monument to the "axiom" of a benevolent nature.

Even as that vision of nature was being embraced, tacitly, by the Congress of the United States, it was also being embraced by the molders of public opinion. The National Resources Defense Council, Inc., one of the most prominent public interest groups in the country, published an article in its newsletter entitled "Is Cancer the Price of Technological Advancement?" In it, the NRDC dismissed nature as a significant contributor to the human cancer rate. It assured its readers that sources of cancer other than industry were minor and stated that "if 8 out of 10 cancer cases are attributable to environmental factors, then it is obvious that cancer is not, except in a minority of cases, inevitable." The primary cause of most cancer, said the NRDC, was "the 'chemical revolution' of the past fifty years." It was to that "chemical revolution" that one could attribute "the rapid rise in the incidence of cancer." What is more, the worst was yet to come; "we may be seeing only the tip of the iceberg, because most of the suspected chemical carcinogens did not come into widespread use until after World War II. . . ."[30] That was the complete apocalyptic position, and it was to gush into the press and through the television tube into every American home.

During this period, scientists in the field of "environmental health" began to transmit the Carsonian "axiom" in their papers. Some were careful to identify it as a belief, others simply repeated it as fact, and an example of each approach should be seen. In 1976, publishing in the *Journal of Toxicology and Environmental Health*, Lawrence Fishbein of the National Center for Toxicological Research observed that both natural and synthetic carcinogens existed,

then wrote a cautious little paragraph in which the references were more interesting than the text:

Although the etiology of human neoplasia, with rare exceptions, is unknown, it has
been estimated that 50–90% of cancer in man is caused by exposure to chemicals
(Anon., 1975a; Epstein, 1974; Hammond, 1975). *Most of the known chemical carcinogens
are considered to be the product of increasing agricultural and technological sophistication*
(Anon., 1975a).[31] [Emphasis added]

Two anonymous references out of four is a somewhat startling percentage;
more startling yet is that in 1976, Fishbein could only cite "Anon." for the belief that most chemical carcinogens were products not of nature, but of technology. Other scientists, however, appeared to think that nature's lack of
responsibility for most cancer had been scientifically established. That view is
illustrated by a grant report to the National Institute of Environmental Health
Sciences written in 1977 by Norton Nelson, Director of the Institute of Environmental Medicine at the New York University Medical Center. Nelson
discussed the public health problem of chronic degenerative diseases, including
cancer, and declared them to be caused by "chemical and physical agents in the
environment": "A few of these agents arise from natural sources," he wrote in
an introductory passage, "but most are the by-products of our highly industrial
and urbanized society."[32] No data were offered to support the statement that
there were only a few natural carcinogens. It was simply asserted as a known
truth.

Inevitably, the "axiom" of nature's noncarcinogenicity left its mark on a
large portion of the American public. In fact, it was the layman above all who
was supremely conscious of that "axiom." His ignorance of the scientific issues
was so profound that he could not be distracted by details. For millions, after
years of "environmentalist" instruction, all that was really graspable was the
fact that "nature" was good and "chemicals" were evil. And particularly in the
upper middle class, many engaged in an almost obsessive pursuit of the "natural"—in food, in recreation, and in "life-style"—a pursuit frequently combined
with acute moral righteousness. Two years after the passage of the Toxic Substances Control Act, a caustic essayist in *Harper's*, Gene Lyons, was to write:
"The word 'natural' is on the way to becoming *the* cant term of the decade, replacing 'human' as an all-purpose modifier testifying to the moral seriousness
of whoever utters it."[33]

It was at the height of the triumph of the doctrines launched by Carson
and Commoner and their many intellectual heirs that the first serious books on
carcinogens appeared, written by apocalyptics for lay audiences. Those read
for this research project—by Corbett, Epstein, and Agran—have already been
mentioned, but they must be looked at more closely in this context. These first
apocalyptic books on carcinogens all reflected the idea that most cancer was
caused by industrial chemicals. All were, apparently, in full harmony with the
view of nature established by Carson and Commoner. But that harmony was
only apparent. If one read them carefully, one discovered that they contained
a strange dimension that their own authors did not acknowledge or, more

precisely, did not integrate into their abstract terminology and abstract explanations. In every case, these books contained evidence that nature was substantially more carcinogenic than had ever been suggested by the apocalyptic
theorists. Corbett was the most open about the phenomenon. He was clearly
curious about it, had done a little research, had discovered that a surprising
number of living things were carcinogenic, and had devoted a tiny chapter of
his book to the subject.[34] The discoveries listed in his chapter are included in
the survey that follows, so they will not be mentioned here. But in the context
of Corbett's total analysis, it was a very strange chapter. The natural carcinogens just sat there, like irrelevant oddities, in the middle of the author's frantic
warnings about synthetic carcinogens.

Epstein's book was even stranger. He, too, had a little list of natural carcinogens, commenting on them—particularly in his revised edition of 1979—
mainly at the beginning and at the end of the book, with occasional references
in between. His carcinogens, too, will appear in the survey that follows. But
Epstein was actively uninterested in the phenomenon and devoted only a few
pages in a 500-page book to it. After referring to carcinogenic plants, fungi, and
bacteria, and citing a few natural substances that caused cancer in the Bantu
and the Zambians, as well as in Asia, in Guam, and in one area of France—a
selection that suggested that such problems were alien to our shores—Epstein
largely dismissed the issue and turned to the carcinogenicity of industrial
chemicals.[35] But there was something strange even in Epstein's use of the concept "chemicals." He offered one list of such "chemicals" which he considered
particularly dangerous, citing a study which claimed that they might account
for as much as 38 percent of total cancer mortality over the next three decades.[36] The "chemicals" were asbestos, arsenic, benzene, chromium, nickel
oxides, and petroleum fractions. Asbestos is a natural mineral; arsenic and
chromium are elements and natural metals; and petroleum is a natural fossil
fuel. These carcinogens, like many others listed in the industrial survey in the
previous chapter, are processed by industry, but they are actually natural substances. One cannot dispute Epstein's right to call elements, metals, minerals,
and fossil fuels "chemicals." They are chemicals; everything is chemicals; Epstein is chemicals. But those ancient substances, some as old as the earth itself,
did not appear on his list of natural carcinogens. They were buried in the term
"chemicals."

Epstein was not unique in this matter. Agran had done precisely the same
thing. He had given a brief history of the development of industrialization
during the World War II years and the decade thereafter which had produced
such cancer-causing substances as plastics, metals (he named nickel and chromium), fibrous minerals (he named asbestos), and radioactive substances.
These, he said, were the carcinogens that converted human cells into the malignancies that destroyed life.[37] Agran's historical information was correct.
Carcinogenic metals and minerals had been reported since the 1940s and
1950s—long before Carson and Commoner had enunciated their "axioms" ex-
onerating nature from significant carcinogenicity. Agran, however, stressed the
industrial use of these substances and, citing the anonymous NCI's 90 percent,

identified cancer as "a disease of man-made origin." From one point of view, he was using the term correctly; "man-made" can mean "manufactured" as well as "synthetic." But under no circumstances can "man-made" mean "created by nature." The choice of "man-made" to describe metals, minerals, and radioactive substances was equivocation. Just as major natural carcinogens were hiding in Epstein's book under the term "chemicals," so they were hiding in Agran's book under the term "man-made." Agran, however, appeared to be sensitive to his own equivocation and felt compelled, immediately after the above passage, to acknowledge the existence of at least some natural carcinogens. The only ones he acknowledged were the identical ones originally named by Carson: arsenic, ultraviolet rays, and radioactive rocks.[38]

In sum, of the three apocalyptic authors whose books came out in 1977 and 1978—one and two years, respectively, after the passage of the Toxic Substances Control Act—all three seemed to be traumatized by the issue of natural carcinogens. The first acted as if his own natural carcinogens weren't there; the second named some, but declined to name others; and the third used the English language in such a way as to suggest that the National Association of Manufacturers had invented some of the most basic attributes of the planet. All three had published data suggesting that nature had a powerfully carcinogenic dimension, but not one of the three had said so.

Such mysterious taciturnity could not last for long, however. While these very books were being written, new data on natural carcinogens were emerging from the laboratories, in addition to old data, that clashed violently with the "axiomatic" belief in their rarity. It was only a small fraction of the new research, for the apocalyptic beliefs that had swept the nation and shaped the law itself had also determined the pattern of research. Most scientists had been given grants to study industrially produced substances, above all synthetic chemicals. But not all were doing so. Some were curious about natural carcinogens. Some, in the course of studying industrial substances, were well aware that they were studying nature and continued to do so. Some thought they were studying industrial chemicals and bumped into nature by accident. Some learned from studies done abroad that foreign scientists were making unusual discoveries about nature. The experiments increased and the natural data grew, and quite suddenly, by virtue of the fundamentality of the findings, the carcinogenicity of nature was an issue. In 1978, in the *Annual Review of Genetics*, a review of the literature appeared entitled "Environmental Mutagens and Carcinogens." Commissioned by the National Cancer Institute, it was written by three prominent Japanese cancer researchers, Minako Nagao, Takashi Sugimura, and Taijiro Matsushima. In the introduction to their paper, they said:

Modern industry has introduced many mutagens and carcinogens into our environment, but nature itself also created many mutagens and carcinogens, which can be found in molds and plants. In addition, environmental mutagens and carcinogens were recently discovered that have been produced ever since the first adoption of fire by our ancestors. This review attempts to give a balanced account of all these factors.[39]

The authors did not define the term "balanced," but it is of interest to note that their review of the data was almost evenly divided between industrial and natural substances. It may be the first time such a thing had ever happened. The findings reported by these scientists are also included in the survey that follows. The strange truth is that within three years of the passage of the Toxic Substances Control Act, conceived to protect the earth from Faustian man, the earth itself had been reported to be carcinogenic beyond anyone's wildest imaginings.

With this as background, we can now examine the data. A word should be said about this second survey. Although some substances are the same in both the industrial and the natural data, the survey of natural carcinogens is quite different. The data fall spontaneously into the ancient divisions of the Greek philosophers: *Earth, Fire, Air* and *Water*. In addition, *Earth* is further broken down into *Animate* and *Inanimate*.

The reader is asked to remember that the methodology used to discover natural carcinogens is *exactly* the same as that used to discover such substances in industry. The information, again, comes mostly from animal tests, and in some cases from mutagen tests.

THE EARTH'S OWN CARCINOGENS: A SURVEY

NOTE

The term "survey" is used here to mean a large collection or compilation of examples of reported animal carcinogens, as well as some examples of reported human carcinogens and mutagens, and a few teratogens (chemicals that damage the fetus). It should provide the reader with the perspective he might gain by browsing in a library. The selection and number of references given for each entry are necessarily unsystematic, and are not a measure of the validity of the findings.

Most reports come from reviews of the literature, thus unless explicitly indicated it is not to be assumed that the National Cancer Institute, the National Academy of Sciences, the International Agency for Research on Cancer, or any other research or regulatory institution or individual scientist is necessarily vouching for the validity of the data. The appearance of a carcinogen, mutagen, or teratogen in this survey means only that such findings have been reported by scientists.

In Appendix B of this book, the reader will find a paginated and indexed bibliography which will allow him to identify the precise source of every finding. In the survey itself, findings are often grouped to make them readable, and the sources of the data are referred to as briefly as possible. Usually, when papers or books are mentioned, only the first scientist is named (with apologies to coauthors who are buried in an "et al."). Initials, second authors, and key words of titles are given if required to avoid confusion, when consulting the bibliography, between similar names, titles, or papers published in the same year. Finally, when the author himself, his editor, or his translator uses variants or different spellings of a name on different papers, those inconsistencies are reproduced, as published, in the bibliography.

I. AN OVERVIEW

The Universal Disease

In the scattered findings of many different scientific disciplines we learn that from the beginning of time, cancer has occurred in every entity that lives and grows. Only those cancers that left permanent marks—on bone—can be identified today; organs and tissues are gone.

200,000,000 Years Ago: The Great Reptiles

1968:   In *A Short History of Medicine*, Erwin H. Ackerknecht, Director of the Institute of Medical History at the University of Zurich, reported that the great reptiles of 200,000,000 years ago—the dinosaurs, mesosaurs, and crocodiles, as well as fossil mammals—had tumors such as osteoma and hemangioma.

1977:   In one of the earliest books on natural carcinogens, a paper appeared written by H. P. Burchfield and Eleanor E. Storrs of the Gulf South Research Institute in Louisiana. They observed that "cancerlike changes have been found in million-year-old dinosaur bones."

1979:   At a cancer conference, James Cleaver of the Laboratory of Radiobiology at U.C., San Francisco, opened a paper with these words: "In the Natural History Museum in London, there is a skeleton of a Tyrannosaurus Rex which has in its tail a slipped disc and an osteosarcoma."

6,000 Years Ago: Human Beings

1968:   In Ackerknecht's history, mentioned above, he reported that at least 36,000 Egyptian mummies had been studied, many of them 6,000 years old. Tumors had been found among them, notably osteoma and osteosarcoma. In the Americas, Peruvian mummies dating from pre-Columbian times had been found with bone tumors, osteosarcoma, and multiple myeloma.

Plants

1970:   Many types of plant tumors exist, according to F. W. Went (1970). Called "galls," they are localized abnormal growths that appear on the buds, stems, leaves, and roots of plants as varied as oak trees and roses. They are caused by living agents: bacteria, nematodes, fungi, and a variety of insects (wasps, midges, psyllids, and saw flies) which lay their eggs in the plants' tissues. The author called for more extensive research into plant tumors as a means of illuminating the fundamental mechanisms of cancer causation.

1977:   F. Meins, in the Department of Botany at the University of Illinois, reported that he was doing just such research. His paper analyzes "the neoplastic state"—i.e., the cancerous state—in plants, in particular the mechanisms involved in crown-gall tumors.

Fish

1978:   A. Anders, a German geneticist, reports that certain wild swordfish spontaneously develop various neoplasms, including melanomas, pterinophoromas, neuroblastomas, thyroid carcinomas, kidney carcinomas, and reticulosarcomas.

Animals

1979:   L. A. Griner, a pathologist at the Zoological Society in San Diego, reported that some creatures are unusually likely to develop cancer. Eighteen Tasmanian devils were necropsied in one zoo, and a 50 percent incidence of spontaneous neoplasms and preneoplastic hyperplasia was discovered. This, the author observed, was "unusually high for any mammalian species."

Insects

1977: A National Academy of Sciences publication, called *Drinking Water and Health*, reported that insects as well as fish, plants, and animals are subject to cancer. The disease, said the authors, afflicts "every form of multicellular organisms."

The Universality of Carcinogens

In recent years, some scientists have concluded that natural carcinogens are ubiquitous. Here are a few of their general observations:

1978: Carcinogens are everywhere, reported toxicologist Elizabeth F. Rose of the Republic of South Africa in a paper on soil and plants: "Potential carcinogens are not hard to find in any community. . . . The universal presence of carcinogens, to a greater or lesser extent, is probable."

1979: The goal of eliminating all carcinogens is unrealistic, concluded Bruce Ames, geneticist, in one of the rare papers to be published by *Science* reporting on the widespread existence of natural carcinogens: "With the large number of environmental carcinogens and mutagens, both man-made and natural, it is clearly impractical to ban or eliminate every one of them."

1979: Carcinogens have been present throughout the earth's history and may have played a role in the evolution of life forms, said James A. Miller, cancer researcher at the University of Wisconsin. In comparing the types of carcinogens produced by nature with those produced by men, Miller said: "A wider variety of carcinogens occurs in our natural environment; the term 'naturally occurring' is used here in its broadest sense. The great majority of these agents have undoubtedly been present throughout evolution, some may even have facilitated the speciation of living systems." He listed the broad categories in which natural carcinogens are found:

1. Physical agents (e.g., radiation)
2. Inorganic substances
3. Organic substances
4. Mixtures of inorganic and organic
5. Products of the physical decomposition of organic substances

Miller's list constitutes the essential outline of the following survey.

II. RADIATION

The Source

The Birth of the Universe

The universe is pervaded with 3K microwave radiation. That discovery was made by A. A. Penzias and R. W. Wilson, who won a Nobel Prize for it in 1978, and provided academic cosmology with evidence for the big bang theory of the creation of the universe. According to this theory, as explained by physicist Paul S. Henry in *Science*, 1980, a primeval fireball of unknown origin expanded and nuclear explosions occurred which hurled a hot spray of protons, electrons, and photons in all directions and created the constituent parts of the galaxies—one of which is inhabited by man.

The Birth of the Earth

The sun, like other stars, is a fiery entity, eternally erupting and hurling blazing filaments into space. As physicist James S. Trefil describes it in *Smithsonian*, 1978, the sun is actually a gigantic nuclear fusion "reactor" from which nuclear energy and light stream out, perpetually, from the surface. From one such gigantic nuclear explosion in the heart of the sun, the earth was born—itself a radioactive fireball which has been cooling throughout the eons.

The Unending Reverberations

Born of a nuclear explosion that may, in turn, have been born of the explosion of a primeval fireball, the earth is constantly being bombarded by radiation from interstellar space, and is constantly emitting radiation. Man thus inhabits an environment which is eternally simmering in low-level radioactivity. Both the cosmic radiation and the terrestrial radiation that impinge on man will be described.

Galactic Radiation

Our galaxy continually emits radiation which permeates our solar system, in the form of primary cosmic rays. According to Beninson et al., 1977, these rays consist of high-energy protons. When the particles enter the earth's atmosphere, those with higher energy undergo nuclear reactions, while those with lower energy lose that energy by ionization.

Lists of the radionuclides that are produced in the earth's atmosphere by cosmic rays appear in all works on natural radioactivity, but vary slightly depending on the date. Here are the cosmic-ray-produced radionuclides and their half-lives, as reported by the National Council on Radiation Protection and Measurements in 1975:

Radionuclide	Half-life	Radionuclide	Half-life
10_{Be} (beryllium)	2.5×10^6 years	33_P (phosphorus)	24.4 days
26_{Al} (aluminum)	7.4×10^5 years	32_P (phosphorus)	14.28 days
		28_{Mg} (magnesium)	21.2 hours

Radionuclide	Half-life	Radionuclide	Half-life
36_{Cl} (chlorine)	3.08×10^5 years		
81_{Kr} (krypton)	2.1×10^5 years	24_{Na} (sodium)	14.96 hours
14_C (carbon)	5730 years		
32_{Si} (silicon)	280 years	38_S (sulfur)	2.87 hours
39_{Ar} (argon)	269 years		
3_H (hydrogen)	12.262 years	31_{Si} (silicon)	2.62 hours
22_{Na} (sodium)	2.62 years	18_F (fluorine)	109.7 minutes
		39_{Cl} (chlorine)	55.5 minutes
35_S (sulfur)	87.9 days		
7_{Be} (beryllium)	53.6 days	38_{Cl} (chlorine)	37.29 minutes
37_{Ar} (argon)	35.1 days	$34m_{Cl}$ (chlorine)	31.99 minutes

According to NCRP, the cosmogenic radionuclides that contribute a "measurable" dose of radiation to man are carbon-14, tritium (^{3}H), beryllium-7, and sodium-22.

Cosmic Radiation and Altitude

The effect of cosmic radiation is correlated with altitude. In 1962, a UN report on the effects of atomic radiation said: "The increase in cosmic radiation dose rate with altitude is such that above about 2 kms, cosmic radiation becomes the major dose rate contributor in man."

Beninson et al. (1977) also observe that people who live at high altitudes above sea level or spend an "appreciable fraction" of their time flying aircraft are exposed to significantly higher doses from cosmic rays than people living at slightly above sea level. Some of the most exposed populations on earth live in Brazilia, Nairobi, and Teheran, which are between 1 and 2 km above sea level; Mexico City and Quito, which are between 2 and 3 km; and La Paz, Bolivia, which is about 3.7 km above sea level.

Within the U.S. the same correlation holds. Merril Eisenbud writes: "For example if you live in Brooklyn, you are exposed to perhaps 20 percent less radioactivity than if you live in Washington Heights in northern Manhattan. This is due to the fact that Washington Heights is higher in altitude as well as to the fact that the igneous rocks of northern Manhattan are more radioactive than the Brooklyn sands. At sea level we say we are exposed to about .10 milliroentgens per hour. At Denver it is perhaps twice the East Coast intensity.... Converted to annual rates of exposure, New Yorkers receive about 100 milliroentgens [and] Denver about 200 milliroentgens per year ..." (Eisenbud, personal communication, 1979).

Solar Radiation

"The solar component of cosmic radiation becomes particularly significant following solar flares associated with sunspot activity, which follow an 11-year cycle. On rare occasions, once or twice during the cycle, a giant solar event may deliver dose equivalents in the range of 1–10 rem/hr with a peak of as high as 5 rem during the first hour—at altitudes of 60,000 to 80,000 feet, i.e., at the upper limit of high-performance aircraft such as the SST. During one giant solar flare in 1956, dose rates in excess of 100 mrem/hr were identified at altitudes as low as 35,000 feet. Under normal circumstances, the occupants of such aircraft would receive a dose of from 1 to 2 mrem/hr from galactic and solar radiation" (Eisenbud, 1973).

UV radiation is universally identified by scientists as a cause of skin cancer. It is far more common among fair-skinned people than among races with dark skin, the pigment of which filters out UV radiation. It is correlated with the amount of exposure to the sun. It is also correlated with latitudes; as one moves toward the equator, one finds an increase in the amount of solar radiation and in the intensity of that radiation, and both are linked to an increase of skin cancer among Caucasians (Upton, 1977; Scott et al., 1977; NAS, *Nitrates*, 1978; Branda et al., 1978; Galvan Aguilera, 1978).

UV radiation causes various types of skin cancers: keratoses, basal cell carcinomas, squamous cell carcinomas, kerato-acanthomas, and malignant melanomas (Suskind, 1977).

In recent years, a number of epidemiological studies have reinforced the association between exposure to solar radiation and malignant melanoma (Anaise et al., 1978, in Israel; Eklund et al., 1978, in Sweden; Herrmann, 1978, in Germany).

Ultraviolet radiation is mutagenic (Ames, 1971; Herriott, 1971).

Terrestrial Radiation

Man Cannot Escape Radioactivity

1973: Merril Eisenbud reports that naturally occurring radioactivity is ubiquitous: It is in the oceans, the atmosphere, in air, water, rocks and soil, and in the tissues of plants, animals, and man: "Traces of naturally occurring radioactivity can be demonstrated in all substances, living and non-living."

1975: The National Council on Radiation Protection and Measurements similarly reports that natural radioactivity is ubiquitous on earth and is to be found in air, water, rocks, soil, and in the tissues of plants, animals, and man.

1977: Beninson et al. again report:
"Man has been continuously exposed to natural radiation since his appearance on earth. . . . Terrestrial radiation is emitted from radioactive nuclides present in varying amounts in all soils and rocks, the atmosphere and the hydrosphere, and from those radionuclides that, transferred to man through food chains or by inhalation, are deposited in his tissues. Terrestrial radioactivity, therefore, leads to both external and internal exposure. . . ."

Impact on Man

According to geologist John A. S. Adams, 1977, most of the ionizing radiation impinging on terrestrial organisms arises from three primordial nuclides which were formed at least five billion years ago: potassium-40, thorium-232, and uranium-238.

According to Beninson et al., 1977, man is irradiated *externally* by cosmic rays and terrestrial radiation, and *internally* by cosmogenic radionuclide carbon-14 and primordial radionuclides potassium-40, rubidium-87, lead-210, polonium-210, radon-220, thallium-208, radon-222, polonium-214, radium-226, radium-228, radium-234, uranium-238, uranium-234, and thorium-232. Gonads, lung, bone-lining cells, and bone marrow are all irradiated in varying degrees.

Exposure: Natural Radiation vs. Other Sources

All works on natural radioactivity are in agreement that man's exposure to natural radiation is greater than his exposure to any other source of radiation.

In 1975, NCRP wrote: "Radiation in the environment from natural sources is the major source of radiation exposure to man. For this reason it is frequently used as a standard of comparison for exposure to various man-made sources of ionizing radiation."

In 1977, Beninson et al. wrote: "Even now, despite the widening use of radiation-producing devices, the widespread radioactive contamination from nuclear weapon tests and the increasing applications of nuclear energy and radio-isotopes, natural sources are the main contributors to the radiation exposure of most of the human population and are likely to remain so in the foreseeable future."

In 1979, the Department of Health, Education and Welfare (HEW, *Summary*) estimated radiation exposure to all Americans from all sources. Their table has already appeared in the industrial survey, but in that survey, the data on natural radiation were omitted. Here are the same comparisons, this time using natural radiation as the standard:

U.S. GENERAL POPULATION COLLECTIVE DOSE ESTIMATES—1978

Source	Person-rems per year (in thousands)
Natural background	20,000
Technologically enhanced	1,000
Healing arts	18,000
Nuclear weapons:	
Fallout	1,000–1,600
Weapons development, testing, and production	.165
Nuclear energy	56
Consumer products	6

It is clear from this that, barring local accidents at nuclear plants, the only technological source of radiation that remotely compares to the natural is medical—"the healing arts." The comparisons between the collective doses received from natural radiation and the collective doses received from nuclear energy plants are particularly striking: *natural, 20,000; nuclear energy, 56.*

III. THE CRUST OF THE EARTH

Metals

Metallic Carcinogens: 45 Years Old

The first carcinogenic finding, chromate, was reported in 1935 (Hueper, 1979). Beryllium was reported in the 1940s (Dutra et al., 1950). Throughout the 1950s and 1960s other carcinogenic metals were identified by scientists. In the 1970s, reviews of the literature indicated that the number was considerable, and new ones are still being identified today.

Carcinogenic Metals

The bulk of the research on metal carcinogens takes the form of studies of industrial *compounds.* But in certain literature reviews, metals are described as carcinogens either because (1) the metal alone has been reported to produce cancers in animals; (2) the metal has been reported to be carcinogenic in so many forms, combinations, and compounds that some scientists identify it as the common carcinogenic element; or (3) the metal has been reported to be a human carcinogen. Occasionally, a scientist refers to a metal as a carcinogen or as a suspected carcinogen for a number of the above reasons. And occasionally, a scientist (e.g., Hueper) uses the terms "metals and metal compounds" as synonymous with "metal carcinogens."

In 1979, Wilhelm Hueper wrote: "Among the various environmental carcinogens, metal carcinogens are the most recently recognized additions. They have, moreover, the distinction of being exclusively of natural origin. . . ." Here, taken from reviews of the literature by scientists, is a list of metals which have been reported to be carcinogens:

NIOSH (1976) published the following list of reported metallic carcinogens: *arsenic, beryl ore and beryllium; cadmium; chromite* (iron chromate); *chromium, colbalt, mercury, silver,* and various types of iron: *limonite* (*brown hematite, brown iron ore, brown ironstone clay*), *magnetite* (*micaceous iron ore, black iron oxide, iron black, black gold*), and *iron oxide* (*bauxite residues, sienna, burnt sienna, ocher, burnt umber, rouge, yellow oxide* of *iron*, all natural iron oxides); *hematite* (iron ore).

LITERATURE REVIEWS OF METAL CARCINOGENS

Carcinogenic metal	References
Aluminum	Furst, 1977.
Antimony	Norseth, 1977.
Arsenic	Battelle Memorial Institute–Dartmouth Medical School, 1972; NIOSH, 1976; Hernberg, 1977; Norseth, 1977; Hopps, 1978; Rawson, 1978; Sunderman, 1979.
Beryllium	Battelle Memorial Institute–Dartmouth Medical School, 1972; NIOSH, 1976; Weisburger, 1976; Hernberg, 1977; Norseth, 1977; Hopps, 1978; Rawson, 1978; Hueper, 1979; Sunderman, 1979.
Cadmium	Weisburger, 1976; Hernberg, 1977; Norseth, 1977; Rawson, 1978; Hopps, 1978; Furst, 1978; Hueper, 1979; Sunderman, 1979.
Chromium	NIOSH, 1976; Weisburger, 1976; Hernberg, 1977; Hopps, 1978; Rawson, 1978; Shimkin et al., 1978; Sunderman, 1979.
Cobalt	Heath et al., 1962; NIOSH, 1976; Weisburger, 1976; Norseth, 1977; Furst, 1978; Shimkin et al., 1978; Hueper, 1979; Sunderman, 1979.
Copper	Hopps, 1978.
Gold	Hueper, 1979.
Iron (hematite)	NIOSH, 1976; Hernberg, 1977; Hopps, 1978.
Lead	Sunderman, 1971; Weisburger, 1976; Hopps, 1978; Rawson, 1978; Hueper, 1979; Sunderman, 1979.
Manganese	Weisburger, 1976; Sunderman, 1979.
Mercury	NIOSH, 1976; Furst, 1977; Hopps, 1978; Hueper, 1979.
Nickel	Battelle Memorial Institute–Dartmouth Medical School, 1972; Weisburger, 1976; Hernberg, 1977; Furst, 1978; Hopps, 1978; Rawson, 1978; Hueper, 1979; Sunderman, 1979.
Selenium	Battelle Memorial Institute–Dartmouth Medical School, 1972; Norseth, 1977; Hopps, 1978; Shimkin, et al., 1978; Hueper, 1979.
Silver	NIOSH, 1976; Furst, 1977; Hopps, 1978.
Titanium	Weisburger, 1976; Hopps, 1978.
Yttrium	Battelle Memorial Institute–Dartmouth Medical School, 1972.
Zinc	Hopps, 1978; Shimkin et al., 1978; Hueper, 1979; Sunderman, 1979.

Metals: Mutagenesis, Chromosome Aberrations

The mutation theory of cancer hypothesizes that cellular malignancy is initiated by a heritable change in cellular DNA—by a change, deletion, or rearrangement of the primary structure of DNA, often accompanied by or causing chromosome aberrations. Here is a table prepared by F. W. Sunderman, Jr., in 1979, which integrates findings in metal carcinogenesis with findings reported by a variety of bacterial and cellular tests. (Sunderman's references are omitted.) In Sunderman's judgment, this constitutes evidence for the mutation theory of cancer.

RESUME OF EXPERIMENTAL OBSERVATIONS THAT PERTAIN TO MECHANISMS OF METAL CARCINOGENESIS

| Experimental system | Metals whose compounds have yielded positive experimental results in the system | | | | | | | | | |
| | Metals that are recognized as carcinogens in humans and/or animals | | | | | | | | | Other metals |
	As	Be	Cd	Co	Cr	Mn	Ni	Pb	Zn	
(1) Aberrations in base-pairing or conformation of nucleic acids in vitro			X	X		X	X		X	Ca, Cu, Mg
(2) Infidelity of DNA replication by DNA polymerase in vitro		X	X	X	X	X	X	X		Ag, Cu
(3) Stimulation of RNA chain initiation despite diminution of overall RNA synthesis			X	X		X			X	Cu
(4) Mutagenicity in E. coli	X		X		X					Hg, Mo, Se, Te, V
(5) "Rec-assay" in B. subtillis	X		X		X	X				Hg, Mo
(6) Mutagenicity in S. typhimurium					X				X	Fe, Pt, Rh, Ru, Se
(7) Chromosomal aberrations in tissue culture cells	X		X		X		X			Sb, Te
(8) Aberrant DNA synthesis or repair in tissue culture cells	X				X		X			
(9) In vitro transformation of tissue culture cells	X	X	X		X		X	X		
(10) Enhanced susceptibility to viral transformation or chromosomal damage in vitro	X	X	X		X		X	X		
(11) In vivo binding to nuclear macromolecules or organelles			X	X	X		X			
(12) In vivo inhibition of DNA or RNA synthesis.			X				X			

Ag (silver); As (arsenic); Be (beryllium); Ca (calcium); Cd (cadmium); Co (cobalt); Cr (chromium); Cu (copper); Fe (iron); Hg (mercury); Mg (magnesium); Mn (manganese); Mo (molybdenum); Ni (nickel); Pb (lead); Pt (platinum); Rh (rhodium); Ru (ruthenium); Sb (antimony); Sc (scandium); Se (selenium); Te (tellurium); V (vanadium); Zn (zinc).

Metals That Cause Birth Defects in Animals

Teratogenic substances—substances reported to have caused birth defects—have been surveyed by T. Shepard in *Catalog of Teratogens*, 1976. Although many types of natural and synthetic substances have been said to cause birth defects in animals and human beings, only one category will be reported in this survey—those which are metallic elements of the earth itself. Here are the metals in Shephard's review of the literature which have been reported to damage fetuses or to cause severe birth defects in animals:

Antimony	Cesium-137	Indium	Rhodium
Arsenic	Chromium	Lead	Selenium
Barium	Cobalt	Lithium	Tellurium
Bismuth	Fluorine	Mercury	Thallium
Cadmium	Iodine-131	Nickel	

Of some 600 substances and compounds tested for teratogenicity, says Shepard, "only about twenty of these are known to cause defects in the human." There is, he says, "a wide difference between our knowledge of experimental teratology and the role that external agents play in producing human malformations."

Minerals

Silicates

In 1976, NIOSH listed a group of naturally occurring minerals that had been reported to be carcinogenic. Several are relatively rare—e.g., *chlorite and tantalum.* But some are more commonplace variants of *crystalline silica: sand, pure quartz, rose quartz, agate, amethyst, chalcedony, onyx, and flint.* Of these, *sand* is the reportedly carcinogenic mineral to which human beings are the most regularly exposed and inhale with frequency.

Asbestos

Asbestos, considered to be a proved human carcinogen (see the industrial survey, Section V), is the generic name for a group of naturally occurring mineral silicate fibers of the serpentine and amphibole series. Many types of fibrous silicates are classified as "asbestos": the fibrous serpentine mineral *chrysotile* and the fibrous amphiboles *actinolite, amosite, anthophyllite, crocidolite, and tremolite* (IARC, Vol. 14, 1977).

Asbestos is radioactive (Harley et al., 1978).

Asbestos contains high concentrations of metals reported to be carcinogenic in man—*chromium, lead, and nickel*—and of *titanium and manganese,* reported above to be carcinogenic in animals (Schwartz, 1975). The presence in asbestos of nickel and other carcinogenic metals has also been reported by F. W. Sunderman, Jr., 1970. These authors suggest that the carcinogenic metals may either cause or intensify the carcinogenic effect of asbestos.

Asbestiform Silicates

Irving Selikoff noted in 1972 that much of the earth's crust is silicate and that a wide variety of silicates is known to be associated with human disease and cautioned that the "dissemination of silicate particles into the environment should be a matter for careful study."

Almost 8 percent of the earth's crust is composed of silicates of the amphibole series; all mining areas of the world represent potential sources of asbestos exposure and, consequently, of cancer. Asbestos is a common contaminant of talc deposits in the U.S. It is also a common contaminant of rocks containing minerals (IARC, Vol. 14, 1977).

The U.S. Bureau of Mines has reported that asbestiform minerals—by regulatory definition—are widespread in the bedrocks of almost half the United States.

Mines

Mines, which are holes dug deep into the earth's crust, are the source of the carcinogenic metals and minerals reported above. Mines are also the source of yet another reported carcinogen: *radon*. Radon, a natural radioactive gas, is emitted by rocks and remains trapped in closed areas; whenever men dig for metals and minerals, they are exposed to it.

When pure radon is breathed, it permeates the body and causes whole-body radiation. Radon daughters—the radionuclides *polonium-218, bismuth-214, lead-214, and polonium-214*—have a brief half-life and quickly attach themselves to dust particles. When these are inhaled, the radiation of these particles is delivered to the nose, pharynx, and tracheobronchial system (Archer et al., 1976; Wagoner et al., 1963).

Volcanoes

Volcanoes have been erupting throughout the earth's history. Approximately 80 percent of all active volcanoes today are found in the Pacific plate. In the United States, several volcanoes in the Cascade Range of the Pacific Northwest are active, as are several volcanoes in Hawaii, and about 25 in Alaska. The known products of volcanic eruptions in the American Cascade Range—lava flow, airborne rock debris, pyroclastic flow, and mud flow—last for 12,000 years (Keller, 1976).

Volcanic Aerosols

Particles from volcanic eruptions are always constituents of the atmosphere (Waldbott, 1978).

"Intense volcanic eruptions can directly inject particulate and gaseous materials into the stratosphere as well as the troposphere; as a consequence, these materials can be rapidly mixed throughout the atmosphere. Estimates of the mass yield of particles from volcanoes vary widely, but recent measurements suggest that yields could be quite large" (NAS, *Tropospheric*, 1978).

Volcanic Carcinogens

Many of the products of volcanic eruptions are substances which have been reported by scientists to be carcinogenic.

Heavy metals have been introduced into the atmosphere throughout the eons by volcanoes. Scientists who have analyzed the substances collected in the fumaroles and vents of active volcanoes report that copper, arsenic, zinc, antimony, lead, and mercury are found in volcanic particulate matter (NAS, *Tropospheric*, 1978). Volcanic gases are "probably significant sources" of mercury in the atmosphere (WHO, *Mercury*, 1976). Volcanic dusts are reported to contain lead (WHO, *Lead*, 1977; EPA, *Lead*, 1977). Volcanic action produces oxides of nitrogen (NO_x) (WHO, *Oxides*, 1977; NAS, *Nitrates*, 1978). And volcanoes eject enormous quantities of selenium; it has been estimated that throughout the history of the earth, volcanoes have released about 0.1 grams of selenium for every square centimeter of the earth's surface (Keller, 1976).

Copper, arsenic, zinc, antimony, mercury, lead, and selenium (see discussion of metals above) have been reported to be carcinogens; No_x has been reported to be a carcinogen promoter (Natusch, 1978). NO_x (which includes NO and NO_2) has been reported to be a mutagen promoter, and possibly a mutagen (Fishbein, 1978; Friberg et al., 1978; von Nieding, 1978).

Hawaiian lavas consist on an average of the following chemicals: oxides of silicon, aluminum, iron (ferric), iron (ferrous), magnesium, calcium, sodium, potassium, titanium, phosphorus, and manganese (MacDonald et al., 1970). *Iron oxide, titanium, and manganese* are reported to be carcinogens (see discussion of metals above).

Volcanoes also produce *sulfur dioxide* (MacDonald et al., 1970; Lave et al., 1977; Turk et al., 1978). Sulfur dioxide is reported to be a carcinogen promoter (Natusch, 1978; Brubaker et al., 1975).

Kilauea, which erupted in September 1977, was found to emit *methyl chloride.* This information appeared in the *New York Times*, on December 17, 1978, in an interview with R. Rasmussen at Volcanoes National Park, Hawaii. Methyl chloride is reported to be a carcinogen (NIOSH, 1976).

Volcanoes emit *benzo*(a)*pyrene* (Ilnitsky et al., USSR, 1976, 1977). Benzo(*a*) pyrene is reported to be a carcinogen (see the industrial survey, Section II, Energy: Fossil Fuels).

IV.   PRECONDITIONS FOR LIFE

Oxygen

Oxygen Appears

From the perspective of the living organisms on earth before the appearance of oxygen, oxygen was an appalling pollutant. Until then the life forms were anaerobic; they had evolved in the absence of air in a methane-rich atmosphere, and with oxygen they died or retreated to deep and airless crevices forever. According to contemporary theory, one of the most momentous events in Precambrian evolution was the development of mutants with systems that could metabolize oxygen, and later produce oxygen themselves by means of the process of photosynthesis. From such mutants did man ultimately emerge (Ward et al., 1972; Lovelock et al., 1975; Thomas, 1975; Schopf, 1978).

Oxygen: A Slow Poison

Scientists are becoming increasingly aware that oxygen is poisonous to man. Since man cannot live without oxygen, he must endure its destructive effects. Oxygen is a "sink" or receptor for the electrons in the body, and as it is metabolized, it causes severe toxic reactions: It produces the biologically dangerous superoxide radicals; it produces peroxide in the fat; it damages enzyme functions; it causes breaks in DNA. Despite the body's defense mechanisms, oxygen causes slow poisoning over the years and, ultimately, death. Man has only the choice to die immediately without oxygen, or to die of it eventually (Henderson et al., 1979, a review of the 1977 International Conference on Singlet Oxygen, in Canada; and Debrunner, 1980, a review of the 1978 Conference on the Biological and Chemical Aspects of Oxygen, in the U.S.).

Oxygen: A Carcinogen

Since the 1920s, oxygen has been thought by scientists to play a role in cancer. Oxygen has been reported to be a carcinogen in animal experiments (DiPaolo et al., 1966).

Malignant tumors are reported to produce superoxide radicals generated by anaerobic metabolism. Diminished enzyme activities combined with radical production appears to lead to many of the properties of cancer cells (Oberley et al., 1979).

Philip Handler, President of the National Academy of Sciences, considers it possible that "much of cancer is the simple result of the normal metabolic processes that generate superoxide" (Handler, 1979).

Oxygen: A Mutagen

A group of scientists at Oregon State University has reported that oxygen is a powerful mutagen in the Ames *Salmonella* test (cited by Handler, 1979).

Oxygen: A Teratogen

Many animal investigators have reported that too much oxygen—hyperoxia—produces birth defects in baby animals, i.e., mice, rabbits, hamsters (Shepard, *Catalog*, 1976).

Lightning

"The First Ancestor"

Some scientists believe that the existence of a common cellular ancestor must be posited to explain why all life forms share broadly similar physiological attributes. That common cellular ancestor, according to one theory, was fertilized by lightning. Lewis Thomas in *The Lives of a Cell*, 1975, writes: "The uniformity of the earth's life, more astonishing than its diversity, is accountable by the high probability that we derived, originally, from some single cell, fertilized in a bolt of lightning as the earth cooled."

Carcinogens Produced by Lightning

Lightning produces NO_x (which includes NO and NO_2) in the air that is breathed by man (WHO, *Oxides*, 1977). In 1977, Chameides et al. estimated that lightning can account for as much as 50 percent of the global production of NO_x (NAS, *Nitrates*, 1978). NO_x is reported to be a carcinogen promoter (Natusch, 1978).

Lightning is reported to produce *ozone* in the local air that is breathed by man (NAS, *Nitrates*, 1978). Ozone has been reported to be carcinogenic (NIOSH, 1976).

Mutagens Produced by Lightning

NO_x (which includes NO_2) is reported to be a mutagen promoter and possibly a mutagen (Fishbein, 1978; Friberg et al., 1978; von Nieding, 1978). NO_2 in aqueous solution is reported to be mutagenic (Fishbein, 1978).

Ozone is reported to be mutagenic (Fishbein, 1978; von Nieding, 1978; Henderson et al., 1979). Ozonated water is also reported to be mutagenic (Gruener, 1978).

Soil

Radioactive Soil

All soil is naturally radioactive. The radioactivity of any specific soil is that of the rock from which it was derived, diminished by the leaching action of outpouring water and increased by the absorption and precipitation of natural radionuclides from inflowing water (National Council on Radiation Protection and Measurements, 1975).

All soil contains *potassium-40, uranium-238, and thorium-232* (Beninson et al, 1977). The closer one is to the soil, the greater the exposure to its radioactivity—particularly from potassium-40, uranium-238, and thorium-232 (Eisenbud, 1973).

Carcinogenic Soil

Polynuclear aromatic hydrocarbons, including *3,4-benzpyrene* and its isomer *1,2-benz-pyrene,* reported to be strongly carcinogenic, are common natural constituents of soil, both on land and in the sea. They are produced by natural combustion and in the transformation of organic matter to peat and lignite. Man has been in contact with such carcinogenic hydrocarbons throughout his entire history (Blumer, 1961).

Almost every chemical element is present in all soils (Eisenbud, 1978). Thus, most if not all of the carcinogenic and mutagenic metals are present in any given soil.

Elements Required for Life

Lists of various chemicals required for the life of both plants and animals have been compiled. The following list is adapted from the lists of essential chemicals published by Furst, 1971; Schwartz, 1975; and Ehrlich et al., 1977:

Basic building blocks
Hydrogen
Carbon
Nitrogen
Oxygen

Macronutrients
Sodium
Magnesium
Phosphorus
Sulfur
Chlorine
Potassium
Calcium

Trace elements
Cobalt
Copper
Chromium
Fluorine
Iodine
Iron (for species
      requiring hemoglobin)
Manganese
Molybdenum
Nickel
Selenium
Silicon
Tin
Vanadium
Zinc

Of these substances, nine have been reported to be carcinogenic—*oxygen, cobalt, copper, chromium, iron, manganese, nickel, selenium, zinc.*

Elements of the Planet

Here is the complete periodic table of elements along with all the carcinogens and teratogens reported so far in this survey. The table lists the elements in alphabetical order. Those elements in parentheses are the most common isotopes of elements which occur only in unstable form, flickering in and out of existence—some lasting only a few seconds (Sorrell, 1973). Radioactive elements, already discussed in this survey, will not be discussed here.

Element	Reported carcino-gen	Reported terato-gen	Element	Reported carcino-gen	Reported terato-gen
(Actinium) (Ac)			Antimony (Sb)	X	X
Aluminum (Al)	X		Argon (Ar)		
(Americium) (Am)			Arsenic (As)	X	X

Element	Reported carcinogen	Reported teratogen	Element	Reported carcinogen	Reported teratogen
(Astatine) (At)			Neon (Ne)		
Barium (Ba)		X	(Neptunium) (Np)		
(Berkelium) (Bk)			Nickel (Ni)	X	X
Beryllium (Be)	X		Niobium (Nb)		
Bismuth (Bi)		X	Nitrogen (N)		
Boron (B)			(Nobelium) (No)		
Bromine (Br)			Osmium (Os)		
Cadmium (Cd)	X	X	Oxygen (O)	X	X
Calcium (Ca)			Palladium (Pd)		
(Californium) (Cf)			Phosphorous (P)		
Carbon (C)			Platinum (Pt)		
Cerium (Ce)			Carbon (C)		
Cesium (Cs)		X	(Plutonium) (Pu)		
Chlorine (Cl)			Polonium (Po)		
Chromium (Cr)	X	X	Potassium (K)		
Cobalt (Co)	X	X	Praseodymium (Pr)		
Copper (Cu)	X		(Promethium) (Pm)		
(Curium) (Cm)			(Protactinium) (Pa)		
Dysprosium (Dy)			(Radium) (Ra)		
(Einsteinium) (Es)			(Radon) (Rn)		
Erbium (Er)			Rhenium (Re)		
Europium (Eu)			Rhodium (Rh)	X	
(Fermium) (Fm)			Rubidium (Rb)		
Fluorine (F)		X	Ruthenium (Ru)		
(Francium) (Fr)		X	Samarium (Sm)		
Gaadolinium (Gd)			Scandium (Sc)		
Gallium (Ga)			Selenium (Se)	X	X
Germanium (Ge)			Silicon (Si)		
Gold (Au)	X		Silver (Ag)	X	
Hafnium (Hf)			Sodium (Na)		
Helium (He)			Strontium (Sr)		
Holmium (Ho)			Sulfur (S)		
Hydrogen (H)			(Tantalum) (Ta)		
Indium (In)		X	Technetium (Tc)		
Iodine (I)		X	Tellurium (Te)		X
Iridium (Ir)			Terbium (Tb)		
Iron (Fe)	X		Thallium *(Tl)		X
Krypton (Kr)			Thorium (Th)		
Lanthanum (La)			Thelium (Tm)		
(Lawrencium) (Lr)			Tin (Sn)		
Lead (Pb)	X	X	Titanium (Ti)	X	
Lithium (Li)		X	Tungsten (W)		
Lutetium (Lu)			Uranium (U)		
Magnesium (Mg)			Vanadium (V)		
Manganese (Mn)	X		Xenon (Xe)		
(Mendelevium) (Md)			Ytterbium (Yb)		
Mercury (Hg)	X	X	Yttrium (Y)	X	
Molybdenium (Mo)			Zinc (Zn)		
Neodymium (Nd)			Zirconium (Zr)		

In sum, when tested in their metallic form (or, repeatedly, in compounds):

—Almost 20 percent of all elements have been reported to be carcinogens.
—Almost 24 percent of all *stable* elements have been reported to be carcinogens.

—More than 19 percent of all elements have been reported to be teratogens.
—Almost 24 percent of all *stable* elements have been reported to be teratogens.

The radioactive effects of the elements are not discussed, as said earlier; but it must be remembered: *One cannot escape radioactivity.*

V.   VIRUSES, BACTERIA, FUNGI, PLANTS, TREES

Viruses

Many viruses are reported to cause cancer in animals, and some are suspected to cause cancer in man. These animal data are considered to be proved (F. Rapp et al., 1976): *Oncornaviruses* give leukemias and sarcoma to chickens, mice, rats, cats, cattle, and monkeys and give mammary cancers to mice. *Papovaviruses of the polyoma type* give a variety of tumors to mice, cause sarcomas in rhesus monkeys, occasionally cause cancer in rabbits, and cause benign papillomas in horses, cattle, dogs, and human beings. *The Lucké frog virus* gives kidney cancer to frogs. *The herpes virus saimiri* causes lymphoma and leukemia in several species of monkeys. *Marek's disease virus* causes lymphoid tumors of the gonads, kidney, lung, heart, spleen, liver, and skin in chickens. *Herpes virus of guinea pigs* gives those animals leukemia. *Cytomegalalovirus* infects both mice and man, and causes fibrosarcoma in hamsters.

More than 80 distinct adenoviruses have been isolated from a variety of animals, including 31 serotypes from humans. About two-thirds of the 13 human adenoviruses are reported to be cancer producers when injected into newborn hamsters (Green et al., 1977).

Bacteria

Nitrifying Bacteria

Various bacteria, fungi, and actinomycetes oxidize organic nitrogen and ammonia into a variety of nitrogen compounds, including NO_x (NO, NO_2) and N-nitroso compounds (NAS, *Nitrates*, 1978); WHO, *Oxides*, 1977).

Most N-nitroso compounds are reported to be carcinogens; NO_x is reported to be both a carcinogen promoter and a mutagen promoter, and possibly a mutagen (see Section IV, Lightning; Section VI, Vegetables and Cancer).

Antibiotic Bacteria

Bacteria found in the soil have been reported to have antibiotic qualities and have been cultured by man to produce drugs. A number of these cultures have been reported to be carcinogenic and mutagenic:

Streptozotocin, structurally related to an N-nitroso compound, is produced by *Streptomyces achromogenes.* It is reported to cause cancer and mutations (Freese, 1971; IARC, Vol. 17, 1978).

Actinomycin D is produced by various species of streptomyces, and is the principal component of the actinomycins produced by *Streptomyces parvullus.* They are reported to be carcinogenic in rats and mice (Kraybill, 1977; IARC, Vol. 10, 1976).

Azaserine is produced by *Streptomyces fragilis.* It is reported to be carcinogenic in rats (IARC, Vol. 10, 1976).

Chloramphenicol is produced by *Streptomyces venezuelae.* It is reported to cause aplastic anemia, associated with the subsequent development of leukemia in man (IARC, Vol. 10, 1976).

Mitomycin C is produced by *Streptomyces caespitosus.* It is reported to be carcinogenic in rats and mice (Kraybill, 1977; IARC, Vol. 10, 1976).

Daunomycin is produced by cultures of *Streptomyces caeruleorubidus* and *Streptomyces peucetius.* It is reported to be carcinogenic in rats and mice (IARC, Vol. 10, 1976; NIOSH, 1976).

Daunomycin, mitomycin C, and actinomycin D are reported to be mutagenic (Nagao, Sugimura et al., 1978).

Fungi

Some antibiotics have been discovered in fungi, and many of these, too, are reported to have provided carcinogenic substances.

Fungi, such as *Candida albicans,* have been found by Chinese scientists to have invaded the tissues of 30 percent of 155 Chinese patients with esophageal cancer. In studies at the Sloan-Kettering Institute in New York, it was found that the fungi generate epithelial growth and also act as catalysts in the formation of carcinogens from other substances, e.g., natural amines from grains and nitrites, producing the intensely carcinogenic nitrosamines (Buys, 1980).

Penicillic acid is produced by the following fungi: *Penicillium puberulum, P. cyclopium, P. thomii, P. suaveolens, P. baarnense, Aspergillus ochraceus,* and *A. melleus.* Penicillic acid is reported to produce sarcomas in mice and rats (IARC, Vol. 10, 1976).

Griseofulvin is a metabolic product of many species of *Penicillium.* It is reported to be carcinogenic in mice (Kraybill, 1977; IARC, Vol. 10, 1976).

A variety of forms of *penicillin,* the antibiotic produced by the *Penicillium* fungi, are reported to be carcinogenic in animals (Kraybill, 1977; NIOSH, 1976).

Plants and Trees

There is said to be a carcinogenic dimension in *all* plants and trees. Here are a few of the major carcinogenic chemicals reported in all, most, or many of the plants, shrubs, and trees that carpet the earth.

Phenolics

Phenol and many phenolic compounds have been reported to be carcinogenic (NIOSH, 1976). The phenolics are "the most widespread class of ecologically important plant secondary compounds." The group includes *flavonoids* and *polyphenols* such as tannins (McKey et al., 1978).

Tannin is found in practically all wood and vegetation. It is a component of leaves, twigs, bark, wood, or fruit. High tannin content is found in the bark of such trees as *oak, eucalyptus, mangrove, hemlock, pine, and willow;* in the wood of *chestnut and oak;* in the fruits of *tara, myrobalans, and divi-divi;* in the leaves of *sumac and gambier;* in the roots of *palmetto.* Many vegetable tannins and naturally occurring tannic acid are reported to be carcinogenic (IARC, Vol. 10, 1976).

Flavonoids are mainly found in the outer leaves of skin or peel of edible fruits, tubers, and roots. Of the flavonoids, *quercetin, kaempferol, rhamnetin, galangin, isorhamnetin, and fisetin* are reported to be the most strongly mutagenic—quercetin being the most potent (Nagao, Sugimura et al., 1978). Quercetin is one of the most common phenolic compounds in vascular plants and is found in many fruits, vegetables, and in tea (Bjeldanes, 1977).

Terpenes

Terpenes have been reported to be carcinogens and have been selected by the EPA as a top priority pollutant (NIOSH, 1976).

Terpenes are produced in leaf tissue and volatilize into the atmosphere surrounding shrubs and trees (Jones et al., 1975; Whittaker, 1970).

Terpenes emerging from vegetation and trees constitute one of the three major natural sources of aerosols in the atmosphere (NAS, *Particulate*, 1972).

Such terpenes as *isoprene, α-pinene, β-pinene, Δ-carene, myrcene, α-limonene, and paracymene* emerge from such vegetation as hardwood, junipers, aspen, pine, and their surrounding meadows and forests (Rasmussen et al., 1965).

Benzo(a)pyrene

One of the chemicals naturally synthesized by plants is benzo(*a*)pyrene, universally reported to be a carcinogen (see the industrial survey, Section II, Energy: Fossil Fuels; NOISH, 1976).

Benzo(*a*)pyrene is reported to have been synthesized by two types of bacteria, *Cl. putride and E. coli,* which were placed in sterilized soil and incubated at room temperature for six months (J. Miller, 1973).

"Evidence is now conclusive for the presence in vegetables of the potent carcinogens 3,4-benzo(*a*)pyrene, 1,2-benzanthracene and other polynuclear aromatic hydrocarbons (PAH), as normal products of plant biosynthesis, rather than from contamination" (Panel on Chemicals and Health of the President's Science Advisory Committee, 1973).

"The ubiquity of some polynuclear aromatic hydrocarbons in the environment suggests indigenous formation in plants and microorganisms . . ." (NAS, *Petroleum,* 1975).

Seven types of polynuclear aromatic hydrocarbons (PAH), one of which is benzo(*a*)pyrene, are believed to have been synthesized by phytoplankton. PAHs have also been found in algae "at levels much higher than environmental levels and in places remote from possible . . . pollution, indicating synthesis within the plants" (Grasso et al., 1976).

It has been reported that benzo(*a*)pyrene has been synthesized during the germination and growth of the soya bean and the lentil seed (Morton, 1977).

Polynuclear aromatic hydrocarbons (PAH) are generated by plants during germination (Shabad, USSR, 1979).

Many polynuclear aromatic hydrocarbons including benzo(*a*)pyrene are reported to be mutagenic, as well as carcinogenic (NIOSH, 1976; Fishbein, 1976). Also see the industrial survey, Section II, Energy: Coal; and Energy: Fossil Fuels.

Pyrrolizidine Alkaloids

Pyrrolizidine alkaloids are found in some 50 species of the families Compositae, Boraginaceae, and Leguminosae. More than 1,000 pyrrolizidine alkaloids have been isolated from plants (and from insects). The following pyrrolizidine alkaloids have been reported to be carcinogenic: *jacobine, monocrotaline, riddelliine, seneciphylline, and retrorsine* (Nagao, Sugimura et al., 1978; IARC, Vol. 10, 1976).

Many pyrrolizidine alkaloids are reported to be mutagenic: *heliotrine, echinatine, echimidine, lasciocarpine, senecionine, supinine, jacobine, platyphylline, monocrotaline, fulvine, and retrorsine* (Nagao, Sugimura et al., 1978; Vogel et al., 1976).

Diterpene Esters

Diterpene esters have been identified in these popular U.S. garden plants: *crown of thorns, pencil tree, caper spurge, candelabra cactus, coral plant, and machineel.* Diterpene esters are reported to be co-carcinogens in animal experiments (Hecker, 1979, 1978; Corbett, 1977).

Miscellaneous Carcinogenic Plants

Extracts from various parts of the following plants are reported to produce tumors in rats: *betel nut* (cured seed), *shining sumac* (root), *Jerusalem oak* (whole plant without root), *persimmon* (leaf), *and sassafras* (root, bark) (Kapadia et al., 1978).

The following plants or plant materials have also been reported to be carcinogenic: *amaranth, derris, Irish moss gelose, croton* (resin and oil), *raton, sali, sorsaka, watapama shimaron, and laraha* (NIOSH, 1976).

Thiourea, found in *laburnum shrubs,* is reported to be carcinogenic in rats (IARC, Vol. 7, 1974).

The latex of the plant *Euphorbia esula* is reported to contain the co-carcinogen *ingenol-3-dodecanoate* (Upadhyay et al., 1978).

The flower stalks of *Petasites japonicus maxim* produce cancers in mice and hamsters (Fushimi et al., 1978).

Vegetation and Soil: Radioactivity

Components of all living things and soils contain radioactive isotopes (see Section II).

Vegetation and Soil: Metals

As stated earlier, all living things, plants and animals as well as soil, contain trace amounts of most elemental metals. In order of abundance—from the most abundant to the least—some common elements in the soil are fluorine, barium, strontium, sulfur, vanadium, chlorine, chromium, rubidium, zinc, copper, cobalt, scandium, lithium, gallium, lead, boron, beryllium, uranium, tin, arsenic, molybdenum, iodine, thallium, cadmium, mercury, and selenium (Kubota et al., 1978). Reported carcinogenic: *arsenic, beryllium, cadmium, chromium, copper, lead, mercury, selenium, and zinc* (see Section III, Metals).

Fossilized Organisms

Throughout the billions of years of earth's existence, carcinogenic plants and other life forms have decayed and been fossilized. All forms of fossilized material contain carcinogens and are reported to cause cancer in animal and man.

Fossil carcinogens	Reference
Crude oil	NIOSH, 1976
Petroleum	Higginson, 1976; NIOSH, 1976
Shale oil	Kahn, 1979; WHO, *Health Hazards,* 1972
Anthracene oil	Higginson, 1976
Mineral and lignite oil	Lewis et al., 1977; Higginson, 1976
Naphthalene	NIOSH, 1976
Coal	Falk et al., 1979

Fossil fuels also contain radioactive substances and release the following radionuclides when burned: *lead-210, lead-212, radium-226, radon-222, thorium-228, thorium-230, thorium-232, uranium-234, and uranium-238* (Natusch, 1978).

Synthetic chemicals are generally made from the above substances. "Ninety-eight percent of synthetics are made from oil and natural gas (the rest are from coal)" (Holden, 1980).

VI. FOOD

Carcinogenic Plant Foods: Groups

The following eleven groups of plant foods have all been reported to contain chemicals that are carcinogens and/or mutagens:

Group 1: Caffeine in Beverages

Coffee beans, tea leaves, kola nuts, and cocoa trees contain caffeine (Greden, 1979). Caffeine is reported to have caused testicular atrophy and impaired spermatogenesis in rats (Weinberger et al., 1978). Caffeine has been reported to be mutagenic or to impair chromosomes (Nawar et al., 1978; Leonard, 1973; Kihlman, 1971; Kuhlmann et al., 1968; Sax et al., 1966).

Group 2: Other Chemicals in Coffee and Tea

Coffee, in addition, contains fructose (Kröplein, 1974). Fructose is reported to be a carcinogen (NIOSH, 1976). Coffee also contains acetaldehyde (Rhodes, 1979). Acetaldehyde is also reported to be a mutagen (EPA, *Potential Industrial,* 1977).

Teas (the teas commonly consumed in the United States, and various popular herbal teas) contain tannin, a plant phenolic. Tannin is reported to be a carcinogen (Der Marderosian, 1977; Singleton et al., 1973). Black tea also contains Ø-toluidine and aniline (Vizthum et al., 1975). Both substances are reported to be carcinogens (NIOSH, 1976). Teas brewed from Euphorbiaceae and Thymelaeaceae plants contain some diterpene esters which are reported to be co-carcinogens (Hecker, 1978).

Group 3: Safrole in Spices

Nutmeg, mace, ginger, star anise, cinnamon, and black pepper contain oils which contain safrole. Safrole is reported to be a carcinogen (J. Miller et al., 1979; Nagao, Sugimura et al., 1978; NIOSH, 1976; Wogan, 1974). Safrole is also reported to be a mutagen (Nagao, Sugimura et al., 1978; Dorange et al., 1977). Abraham et al., 1978, report a synergistic reaction between caffeine and certain condiments and spices.

Group 4: Other Carcinogenic Flavorings

Natural substances are used to flavor a wide variety of foods. The following are reported carcinogens or carcinogen promoters: *citral* (Seifter et al., 1979); *menthol* (NIOSH, 1976); *orange, lime, lemon, and grapefruit oils* (Homburger et al., 1968); *sesame oil* (Szepsenwol et al., 1979); *S. foetida oil* (Lee et al., 1968).

Group 5: Coumarin in Fruits and Wine

Dates, strawberries, blackberries, apricots, cherries, contain coumarin (Golberg, 1967); *woodruff,* used as a flavoring in May wine, oils from *tonka beans,* and *cassia* contain coumarin (IARC, Vol. 10, 1976). Coumarin is a reported carcinogen (NIOSH, 1976) and a mutagen (Grigg, 1978).

Group 6: Acetaldehyde in Vegetables, Fruits, and Alcoholic Beverages

Apples, grapefruit, oranges, peaches, Concord grapes, lemons, pears, pineapples, raspberries, and strawberries contain acetaldehyde (R. Winter, 1978). Acetaldehyde is found in all ripe fruits and may form in wine and other alcoholic beverages after exposure to air (EPA, *Potential Industrial,* 1977). Acetaldehyde is reported to be mutagenic (EPA, *Potential Industrial,* 1977).

Acetaldehyde is reported to be the major metabolite of *ethyl alcohol* (liquor) (NAS, *Drinking,* 1977).

Group 7: Flavonoids in Fruits and Vegetables

"Many fruits, vegetables and tea" contain quercetin, one of the most common phenolic compounds in higher plants (Bjeldanes et al., 1977). *". . . many edible plants, vegetables and fruits,"* e.g., *onions, the spice sumac, and bracken fern,* contain quercetin and another common plant flavonoid, kaempferol (Nagao, Sugimura et al., 1978). Both are reported to be highly mutagenic (Nagao, Sugimura et al., 1978; Seino et al., 1978; Macgregor et al., 1978; Hardigree et al., 1978; Bjeldanes et al., 1977).

Group 8: Fats in Grains and Cereals

Many plant oils are reported to be carcinogenic or to contain carcinogenic chemicals, e.g. *corn oil* or *Mazola oil* (NIOSH, 1976); *cottonseed oil* (Hendricks et al., 1980); *sunflower oil* (IARC, Vol. 11, 1976).

Auto-oxidizable *vegetable oils* are reported to be mutagenic (Ehrenberg, 1971). *Mustard oil* is reported to be weakly mutagenic (Auerbach, 1973).

Malonaldehyde is found in such plant foods as: *raisins, chopped walnuts,* and *peanut butter after exposure to air.* Malonaldehyde has been reported to be carcinogenic and mutagenic (Shamberger, 1977; Nagao, Sugimura et al., 1978).

Diets high in fats and oils are reported to be carcinogenic in animals. In experiments on animals kept on high-fat diets, the fat is said to enhance liver cancer (Hancock et al., 1969). In other animal experiments with high-fat diets, the fat is said to promote mammary cancer (Nishizuka, 1978).

Group 9: Estrogens in Cereals, Fruits, and Vegetables

Carrots, soybeans, wheat, rice, oats, barley, potatoes, apples, cherries, plums, wheat bran, wheat germ, rice bran, and the oils of cottonseed, safflower, wheat germ, corn, peanut, olive, soybean, coconut, and rice bran all contain compounds which produce estrogenic responses in experimental animals (Liener, 1969). Estrogens are also present in *damaged or diseased plants and vegetables,* e.g., *apple leaves, carrots, and potatoes* (Stob, 1973).

The estrogenic fungus *Zearalenone* produces effects on the vulva, uterus, ovary, cervix, and mammary glands of swine similar to those caused by the steroidal estrogen estradiol (Stob, 1973). Plant estrogens, such as those in carrots, are said to be comparable to the proved synthetic estrogen in DES (J. and E. Miller, 1979; Jukes, 1977; Ferrando et al., 1961).

Both natural estrogens in human beings and synthetic estrogens have been reported carcinogenic (IARC, Vol. 6, 1974). The possible carcinogenic effects of plant estrogens seem to be a function of "increased amounts . . . and continued exposure to the hormone"; plant breeders, accordingly, should produce strains low in estrogenic activity (Stob, 1973).

Group 10: Fungal Contaminants Potentially in All Foods, Plant or Animal

Carcinogenic mycotoxins—chemicals naturally produced by fungi—are ubiquitous contaminants of the world's food supply, and are found in America's food supply as well, home-grown and imported. Here are a few of the most important, and the foods in which they have been found to occur.

Patulin: *Commercial apple juice and rotting apples* (Rodricks, 1978); *homemade apple juices and apple jam* (Lindroth et al., 1978); and *apple juice and sweet apple cider* (Pool, 1977; IARC, Vol. 10, 1976) have been found to be contaminated with patulin. In one investigation, 37 percent of the samples of apple juice tested in the U.S. were contaminated with patulin (Rodricks, 1978). Patulin has been reported to be carcinogenic (Rodricks, 1978; NIOSH, 1976; IARC, Vol. 10, 1976) and mutagenic (Mayer et al., 1969).

Sterigmatocystin: *Country-cured ham, salami, green coffee beans, and wheat* have been found to be contaminated by sterigmatocystin, a reported carcinogen (IARC, Vol. 10, 1976) and a reported mutagen (Kuczuk et al., 1978).

Ergot: *Wheat, barley, rye, hybrids and a wide range of other grains and pasture grasses* (e.g., timothy) have been contaminated with ergot, which is reported to be carcinogenic (Weisburger, 1979; Wyllie et al., 1978; J. Miller, 1973).

Penicillium: *Yellow rice* has been contaminated by *Penicillium islandicum*, reported to produce carcinogens (Bamburg et al., 1969).

Aflatoxins: "... *virtually every food stuff or food product is potentially susceptible to contamination* [by aflatoxin] *which may occur at any stage of food production or subsequent processing. Samples of nearly every dietary staple have been found to contain some aflatoxin at one time or another"* (IARC, Vol. 10, 1976).

All over the world, aflatoxins have been found in food plants before they have been harvested, and at every step of processing: *ground nuts, peanuts, oil seed and oil seed products* (e.g., *cottonseed, soybean seed*), *copra, coconut, sesame cake, safflower meal, sunflower meal, sunflower seeds, edible nuts* (*hazelnuts, almonds, pistachios, brazil nuts*), *cereals* (*maize, wheat, wheat flour, sorghum, oats, barley, millet, rye*), *breakfast cereals, rice, spices* (*cayenne pepper, chili powder, dried chili peppers, black pepper, nutmeg*), *cocoa and cocoa products, wine, unrefined vegetable oils, haricot, mung beans, peas, and sweet potatoes* (Wyllie et al., 1977).

Recently in the United States, *brazil nuts, walnuts, almonds, pecans, pistachios, and cottonseed* have been found to be contaminated by aflatoxins (Campbell, 1977). Two million acres of *pre-harvest corn*, in Georgia, were found to be contaminated by aflatoxin in 1977; 90 percent of the field-collected samples were affected (McMillian et al., 1978).

Aflatoxin B_1 and aflatoxin G_1 are reported to be carcinogenic in four animal species—inducing tumors of the liver and other organs (Fishbein, 1978). Aflatoxin G_1, aflatoxin G_2, aflatoxin B, and aflatoxin B_1 and B_2 are reported to be carcinogenic (NIOSH, 1976). Aflatoxin B_{2a}, G_{2a}, M_1, and M_2 are also reported to be carcinogenic (Ford et al., 1978). Aflatoxin B_1 is reported to be mutagenic (Kuczuk et al., 1978). Aflatoxin B_1 is also reported to induce a high rate of chromosome breaks (El-Zawahri et al., 1977).

Group 11: Vitamins

Vitamin A is reported to enhance the process of carcinogenesis (Sugimura, 1976).
Vitamin B_{12}, found in many foods, is reported to be a carcinogen promoter (Temcharoen et al., 1978).

Miscellaneous Carcinogenic Plant Foods

The following individual foods of plant origin have been reported to contain chemicals that are carcinogenic:

Lemons: Citrus pectin has been reported to intensify the carcinogenic effect of certain chemicals in rats (Asp et al., 1979).

Honey: Honey produced from tansy ragwort, consumed in the United States, contains the hepatotoxic pyrrolizidine alkaloids found in that species. These alkaloids include *senecione, seneciphylline, jacoline, jaconine, jacobine, and jacozine,* and are reported to be carcinogenic, mutagenic, and teratogenic (Deinzer et al., 1977).

Mushrooms: Major edible mushroom species have been identified as potentially carcinogenic. They are *Gyromitra esculenta,* a commonly eaten mushroom in Europe; *Cortinellus shiitake,* a commonly eaten mushroom in Japan; and *Agaricus bisporus,* the most commonly eaten commercial mushroom in the United States. All either contain or produce, when metabolized, various types of hydrazines which are reported to be carcinogenic in mice and hamsters (Toth, 1979, 1977; Toth et al., 1978). Hydrazine and several of the hydrazine derivatives are mutagenic (Nagao, Sugimura et al., 1978).

Corn: Corn oil (Mazola) has been reported to be carcinogenic (NIOSH, 1976). Maize plants contain a mutagen, 4-hydroxy-1,4-benzoxazinone (Sugimura, 1979).

Red peppers: The red pepper *Capsicum frutescens,* also known as chili, is reported to cause tumors in rats (Bababunmi, 1978; Lewis et al., 1977).

Salad: Bracken or fiddlehead fern is used extensively as salad in Japan, Canada, England (Wales), and the United States. The fern has been linked to esophageal cancer in Japan and has produced bladder or intestinal cancer or both in cows, rats, mice, guinea pigs, and quail (Pamukcu, 1979; Yoshihira et al., 1978; Markus, 1978; NIOSH, 1976; Evans, 1976; Price et al., 1968). Extracts of bracken are reported to be mutagenic (Fukuoka et al., 1978). Milk from cows that have eaten bracken and urine of rats which have eaten bracken are also reported to be mutagenic (Nagao, Sugimura et al., 1978).

Potatoes: The sap from the green tops of potatoes is reported to have produced cancer in rats. Several *N*-nitroso compounds were identified in the sap (Ivankovic, 1978). *N*-nitroso compounds are reported to be potent carcinogens (see industrial survey, Sections VII and VIII; also see discussion of *N*-nitroso compounds in this survey, below).

Sweet potatoes: The toxic chemical 4-ipomeanol, a furan derivative, is found in moldy sweet potatoes. An analysis of the way this substance is metabolized has led to the warning that it may have carcinogenic implications for man (Boyd, 1979).

Soybeans: Soybeans are reported to contain several carcinogens (Arenaz et al., 1978). Soybeans are also reported to contain several mutagens (Kimura et al., 1979).

Cycads: A family of plants with 9 genera and about 100 species, cycads are found in all continents except Europe and Antarctica. In various parts of the world—e.g., the Philippines, Indonesia, the Malay peninsula—the leaves are eaten as vegetables, and the seeds, stems, and underground tubers are used for starch to thicken soups and to make tortillas, bread, and cakes and are cooked in combination with other foods (Yang et al., 1969). Cycasin, the toxic component of cycads, is reported to be a potent carcinogen and mutagen (Matsumoto, 1979; Burchfield et al., 1977; Laqueur, 1977; Laqueur et al., 1973, 1968; Yang et al., 1969). Cycasin is carcinogenic in mice, rats, hamsters, guinea pigs, rabbits, and fish (IARC, Vol. 10, 1976). Cycasin is activated by bacteria in the intestinal tract (Fishbein, 1978; Freese, 1971).

Cycasin is reported to be a transplacental carcinogen in rats; tumors appear in the offspring of mothers fed on cycasin (Laqueur et al., 1973).

Carageenan: Otherwise known as Irish moss gelose (a sulphated polysaccharide), carageenan is an extract of various red seaweeds. Carageenan forms gels and has been used in many foods all over the world. It is reported to have produced tumors in mice and rats (IARC, Vol. 10, 1976; NIOSH, 1976).

Vegetables and Cancer: *N*-Nitroso Compounds

There is a complex interaction between mammals, including man, and the nitrate-containing vegetables they consume, which is believed to be relevant to the formation of nitrosamines in the human body, and thus to cancer. To understand it, one must follow the process in stages:

Nitrates from Vegetables

Nitrates are found in vegetables, which supply almost 90 percent of our nitrate intake (NAS, *Nitrates,* 1978). The plant foods which contain varying amounts of nitrate are *spinach, leeks, purslane* (Kroes, 1977); *cucumbers, asparagus, lettuce, radishes, beets, celery, white potatoes* (NAS, *Nitrates,* 1978); *cabbage, broccoli* (Office of Consumer Inquiries, FDA, 1978); *peppers, corn, turnips and greens* (petioles), *kale, onions* (Lorenz et al., 1974); *celery juice* (NAS, *Drinking,* 1977); *carrot juice and beet juice* (Marshall, "Scotch," 1979).

Vegetable Nitrates Converted to Nitrite

In plants: Some 45 genera of bacteria and fungi naturally reduce the nitrate in plants to nitrite (NAS, *Nitrates,* 1978; WHO, *Nitrates,* 1978; Fishbein, 1978).

In the store and the kitchen: Bacterial reduction of nitrate to nitrite may also occur naturally during the storage of fresh vegetables, particularly at room temperature, when nitrite concentrations may rise to very high levels (WHO, *Nitrates,* 1978).

In saliva: Bacterial reduction of nitrate to nitrite occurs in human saliva (Tannenbaum, Archer et al., 1978; Tannenbaum et al., 1974; Klein et al., 1978). The concentration of the salivary nitrite seems to be related to the ingestion of dietary nitrate, which comes predominantly from vegetables (Stephany et al., 1978).

In the stomach: Bacterial reduction of nitrate to nitrite also occurs in the human stomach (Sander, 1973).

In the intestines: Bacterial reduction of nitrate to nitrite also occurs in human intestines (Tannenbaum, Fett et al., 1978).

Nitrite + Amines = *N*-Nitroso Compounds

While man is consuming vegetable nitrite, and producing nitrite by himself, he is also consuming both plant and animal foods containing amines, which may interact, in his body, with the nitrite. Such foods are ubiquitous in nature (IARC, Vol. 17, 1978; Magee et al., 1976). They include fish, vegetables, tea, wine, spirits, and beer (Magee et al., 1976). Cereals and the amino acids (e.g., proline from the breakdown of proteins) are also a source of amines (Berenblum, 1974).

The simultaneous ingestion of nitrite and amines produces *N*-nitroso compounds in the stomach (Endo et al., 1977; NAS, *Drinking,* 1977). The simultaneous ingestion of nitrite and amines produces *N*-nitroso compounds in the intestines (Wang et al., 1978). Intestinal bacteria that inhabit the intestines of most mammals, nitrosate amines and amides, produce carcinogenic and mutagenic compounds (Mandel et al., 1977; Grasso et al., 1976).

N-Nitroso Compounds: Carcinogenic and Mutagenic

About 100 N-nitroso compounds (nitrosamines and nitrosamides) have been tested in animals, and about three-quarters of them are reported carcinogens (Tannenbaum et al., 1977; P. N. Magee et al., 1976). N-nitroso compounds cause cancers in virtually every organ, and in every species tested. Many of these compounds are mutagenic (NAS, *Nitrates*, 1978; WHO, *Nitrates*, 1978; Freese, 1971; Endo, 1977). Many N-nitroso compounds are also transplacental carcinogens; if pregnant animals are fed on them, the offspring develop cancer (Magee et al., 1976, 1973; Ivankovic, 1973; Mohr, 1973).

Carcinogenic Animal Foods

Many animal foods have been reported to contain natural carcinogenic components, or may contain natural "additives" through contamination by carcinogenic fungi or by the animals' own diet of carcinogenic plants.

Meat and Fowl

The fatty acid peroxide malonaldehyde was found in a variety of *raw* animal foods: *sirloin steaks, ground sirloin, round steak, ground beef, rolled rump roast, veal, sirloin tip roast, ground round steak, pork chops, hot dogs (beef and pork mixture), turkey, and chicken*. The cuts of beef tested were all lean: "Fat contained little or no malonaldehyde" (Shamberger, 1977). Malonaldehyde is reported to be carcinogenic and mutagenic (Shamberger, 1977; Nagao, Sugimura et al., 1978).

Carcinogen-Contaminated Meats

Feed animals—the animals that are used as food, e.g., cattle—may feed on carcinogenic plants, e.g., bracken fern, and the resultant meat may be contaminated with plant carcinogens (Rodricks, 1978). Plants commonly consumed by range animals include the plant species that certain pyrrolizidine alkaloids, e.g., *Senecio, Crotalaria, and Heliotropium*. They are reported to be potential liver carcinogens (Rodricks, 1978; IARC, Vol. 10, 1976; Newberne, 1968; Schoental, 1968). Pyrrolizidine alkaloids are reported to be mutagenic (Sugimura, 1979; Hirono et al., 1979; Auerbach, 1973).

Meats can also be contaminated by potentially carcinogenic estrogenic plants and fungi (Rodricks, 1978).

Meats—e.g., country ham and salami—have also been reported to be contaminated by aflatoxins (see above, in Group 10).

Carcinogen-Contaminated Milk

Milk from cows that have fed on plants can be contaminated with plant residues reported above to be carcinogenic and/or mutagenic.

Milk may be contaminated by the bracken fern eaten by cattle (Rodricks, 1978).
Milk may be contaminated by plant and fungal estrogens (Rodricks, 1978).
Milk may be contaminated by pyrrolizidine alkaloids (Rodricks, 1978).
Milk may be contaminated by aflatoxins (Nabney et al., 1967, and Mickelsen et al., 1964, both cited by Golberg, 1967; Wyllie et al., 1977).

Carcinogens in Cheeses

Samples of American cheese, Swiss cheese, American diet cheese, mozzarella, and ricotta were reported to contain malonaldehyde, the fatty acid peroxide. Malonaldehyde is a reported carcinogen and mutagen (Shamberger, 1977; Nagao, Sugimura et al., 1978).

Carcinogens in Eggs

Hens' eggs—both yolks and whites—have been reported to produce cancer in rats (Szepsenwol, 1963).

Eggs have also been reported to be contaminated with aflatoxins (Nesheim et al., 1978; Wyllie et al., 1977).

Universal Carcinogens in Food

Certain reported cancer-causing agents are found in all living organisms—plant and/or animal—and are consequently found in all foods. Here are examples of some of these universal compounds as reported in literature reviews:

Proteins

Proteins are found in all plant and animal foods. High-protein diets may be linked to increased cancer incidence in man (Kroes, 1977). When protein intake is reduced, the incidence of cancers in laboratory animals is reported to be reduced (McLean, 1973; Cummings, 1978).

Cholesterol

Cholesterol occurs in all body tissues of higher animals, particularly in the brain and spinal cord, and in animal fats. Many animal studies report that cholesterol has acted both as a carcinogen and as a carcinogen promoter (Cruse et al., 1979, 1978; NIOSH, 1976; IARC, Vol. 10, 1976; Wogan, 1974).

Sugars

Sugars are found in all plants and many animal foods:

Sucrose is the sugar found in all plants, fruits, and vegetables (commercial sucrose is extracted from sugar cane and beets). Sucrose consumption is said to entail a potential risk of cancer, including the pancreatic cancer to which diabetics are susceptible (Cranmer, 1978; Kraybill,1975; Kessler, 1970; Yudkin, 1972).

Lactose is the sugar found in the milk of mammals, including human mothers' milk. Lactose is a reported carcinogen (NIOSH, 1976).

Fructose is the sugar found in all fruits. It is a reported carcinogen (NIOSH, 1976).

Maltose is a starch sugar, and a reported carcinogen (NIOSH, 1976).

Xylitol is a sugar alcohol synthesized by cells in plants. It is commercially extracted from birch trees and corn cobs as a sweetener. Xylitol has been reported to be a carcinogen (Shubik, 1979; Smith, 1978).

Salt

Salt (common salt, sea salt, rock salt, table salt) is found in virtually everything on earth, animate and inanimate. It is reported to be a carcinogen (NIOSH, 1976). It is reported to intensify the carcinogenicity of certain *N*-nitroso compounds in animal experiments (Sugimura, 1976).

Hydrocarbons

Hydrocarbons are found in all plants, some of the most ubiquitous being reported carcinogens:

Terpenes are found in all vegetation, hence in all plants and vegetables consumed by man and by feed animals. They are produced in leaf tissue, and are one of the major sources of hydrocarbon aerosols in the atmosphere. Terpenes are reported carcinogens

(NIOSH, 1976). Plant diterpenes and related phorbol esters are reported to be tumor promoters (Lee et al., 1978).

Benzo(a)*pyrene* is reported to be naturally synthesized by bacteria, algae, and phytoplankton and by all plants during germination. Benzo(*a*)pyrene and other polynuclear aromatic hydrocarbons are said to be formed indigenously in vegetables eaten by man (Shabad, USSR, 1979; Morton, 1977; Grasso et al., 1976; NAS, *Petroleum*, 1975; J. Miller, 1973; Panel on Chemicals and Health, President's Science Advisory Committee, 1973; for further information see Section V, Plants and Trees.

Many polyaromatic hydrocarbons, including benzo(*a*)pyrene, are reported to be carcinogenic and mutagenic (NIOSH, 1976; Fishbein, 1976); also see industrial survey, Section II, Energy: Coal; Energy: Fossil Fuels.

Metals and Minerals

All plants and animals contain metals and minerals in various combinations and amounts. Here are some examples of specific foods containing reportedly carcinogenic metals and minerals—all required for life (examples taken from Underwood, 1971, 1973).

Chromium occurs naturally in the *branny layers and germ of cereal grains*, and in *raw sugars*.

Cobalt occurs naturally in *green leafy vegetables* (*spinach, cabbage, and lettuce*), in *corn*, and in *dairy products*. It is a component of *Vitamin B₁₂*, also reported as a carcinogen (see Group 11, above).

Copper occurs naturally in *leafy plants and plant tissues*, in *whole cereal grains, nuts, dried legumes, dried vine fruits, pit-fruits, cocoa, crustacea and shellfish, organ meats (liver, kidney), milk, butter, cheese, white sugar, honey, and fresh fruits.*

Iron occurs naturally in plant and animal foods—e.g., *organ meats (liver, kidney, heart), egg yolks, dried legumes, cocoa, cane molasses, shellfish, milk, milk products, sugar, flour, bread, potatoes, and most fresh fruits.*

Lead occurs naturally in *plants, cow's milk, and muscle meats.*

Manganese occurs naturally in *nuts, cereals, fresh leafy vegetables, meats, fish, and dairy products. Tea and cloves* are exceptionally rich in manganese.

Mercury occurs naturally in *fruits, vegetables, cereal grains, meats, dairy products, and fish.*

Nickel occurs naturally in *fruits, tubers, grains, meats, eggs, dairy products, tea, oysters, and green leafy vegetables.*

Selenium occurs naturally in *wheat, milk, eggs, and muscle and organ meats.*

Zinc occurs naturally in *wheat germ, wheat bran, roots, tubers, white flour, bread, milk, leafy vegetables, meat, fish, eggs, whole cereals, nuts, and leguminous seeds. Oysters* are particularly rich in zinc.

Cobalt, nickel, iron, and zinc (Underwood, 1973) usually occur in higher concentrations in leguminous plants—i.e., *peas and beans.*

Radioactivity

Potassium-40: Although man ingests many natural radionuclides in some degree, the main naturally occurring source of *internal* radiation in man is said to be potassium-40. It is found in a great number of foods (Beninson et al., 1977; National Council on Radiation Protection and Measurements, 1975; NAS Committee on Food Protection, 1973).

Radium: All foods contain radium in different amounts. The radium content of brazil nuts is about 1,000 times higher than the radium concentration in the average U.S. diet. Here is a table showing the comparison of radium activity in various foodstuffs (table compiled by Mayneord, 1958; reproduced in Eisenbud, *Environmental Radioactivity*, 1973):

Foodstuffs containing radium	Maximum α activity observed per 100g (pCi)
Brazil nuts	1,400
Cereals	60
Teas	40
Liver and kidney	15
Flours	14
Peanuts, peanut butter	12
Chocolate	8
Biscuits	2
Milks (evaporated)	1–2
Fish	1–2
Cheeses and eggs	0.9
Vegetables	.7
Meats	.5
Fruits	.1

VII.   COOKING

Carcinogenic Cooking

The discovery of cooking with fire is viewed by some scientists as a major evolutionary step in human development, because it allowed man to eat a wide variety of dangerously toxic plants which cannot be eaten raw. Cooking appears to have occurred "only in the most recent 2 percent of the anthropological record" (Leopold et al., 1972).

In the last fifteen years, it has been reported by many scientists that every type of cooking—including every type of food preparation such as salting, smoking, and fermenting—is producing carcinogenic and mutagenic substances which are being ingested by man. Here are some of the reported discoveries:

Broiling, Roasting, Baking, and Boiling Foods Produces Carcinogenic PAH

Polyaromatic hydrocarbons have been identified in charcoal-broiled steaks: *benzo*(a)*pyrene, benz*(a)*anthracene, dibenz*(a,h)*anthracene, and chrysene* (Lijinsky et al., 1964). All are reported carcinogens: chrysene weakly so (and possibly uncertain), benz(*a*)anthracene moderately strong, dibenz(*a,h*)anthracene, and benzo(*a*)pyrene potent (NAS, *Particulate*, 1972).

Three of the above four PAH have also been reported in fish broiled over a gas flame: benzo*(a)*pyrene, benz(*a*)anthracene, and chrysene (Yamazaki et al., 1977).

Polycyclic aromatic hydrocarbons including benzo(*a*)pyrene have been produced in roasted coffee beans and extracts of tea leaves at high temperatures (Grimmer et al., 1966).

Benzo(*a*)pyrene has been found in the charred crusts of biscuits (Kuratsune, 1956, cited by J. W. Howard et al., 1969).

Starch heated in the absence of air and at atmospheric pressure produced benzo(a)pyrene; the higher the temperature, the greater the amount of benzo(a)pyrene in the distillates (Howard et al., 1969).

Carbohydrates, amino acids, and fatty acids were subjected to high heat. No polycyclic compounds were found at 300°, but 19 hydrocarbons including benzo(a)pyrene were isolated from the same materials at 500° and 700° C. At 500° more polycyclics were produced from carbohydrates; at 700° C. more were produced in the fatty acids. These temperatures are reached by baking bread and by cooking fats in boiling sauces (Howard et al., 1969).

When amino acids and amines—both widely found in foods—are heated at high temperatures, they produce the carcinogen benzo(a)pyrene (Patterson et al., 1978).

Smoking Foods Produces Carcinogenic PAH

Smoking foods (cheeses, meats, sausages, fish, ham) over wood or charcoal produces benzo(a)pyrene and benz(a)anthracene (Soos et al., 1978; Kroes, 1977; Howard et al., 1969; Lijinsky et al., 1965).

The benzo(a)pyrene content in smoked fish is five times higher than that of meats and sausages (Fritz, 1977).

Malting, Broiling, Frying, and Cooking Foods Produces Carcinogenic Nitrosamines

The nitrosamine N-nitrosodimethylamine (NDMA), reported to be a very potent carcinogen in animal tests, was discovered in 6 out of 7 brands of Scotch tested, and in 18 brands of beer. Both Scotch and beer producers use a similar process of barley malting. According to German scientists, the use of hot air drawn directly from fire has been producing NDMA in the malt (Marshall, 1979).

N-Nitroso pyrrolidine (NNP) is formed during the grilling or frying of bacon. NNP is not found in raw bacon; it is formed exclusively by the heat of frying or grilling (Tannenbaum, 1980; Bharucha et al., 1979; Coleman, 1978; Engel, 1977).

Frying bacon also produces N-nitrosodimethylamine (NDMA), the same nitrosamine found in beer and Scotch. Again, it is produced by heat alone (Mottram et al., 1977).

Braising, Broiling, and Baking Foods Produces Carcinogenic Malonaldehyde

Malonaldehyde, a product of the peroxidization of fat, is found in the lean flesh of meats and fowl. It is a reported carcinogen and mutagen (Shamberger, 1977; Nagao, Sugimura et al., 1978). Shamberger analyzed the amounts of malonaldehyde found before and after cooking and reports that while the pattern is not consistent, cooking some meats and fowl increases the amount of malonaldehyde. These data are taken from his table:

MALONALDEHYDE LEVELS IN DIFFERENT TYPES OF MEAT

Cut of meat	Treatment	$\mu g/g$
Round steak*	Uncooked	1.2 ± 0.4
	Cooked, braised**	5.8 ± 2.1
Sirloin tip roast*	Uncooked	9.4 ± 3.1
	Cooked 2 hr. at 325°	27.0 ± 6.3
Ground round steak*	Uncooked	3.8 ± 0.4
	Broiled at 450° for 15 min.	10.4 ± 2.1

Cut of meat	Treatment	μg/g
Pork chop*	Uncooked	1.3 ± 0.2
	Cooked at 425° for 1 hr. with crumb covering	8.1 ± 2.3
Pork chop*	Uncooked	4.1 ± 0.3
	Broiled at 425° for 1 hr. with crumb covering	11.1 ± 2.7
Chicken*	Uncooked	7.7 ± 2.1
	Cooked at 350° for 1½ hr.	39.0 ± 8.0
Chicken*	Uncooked	4.0 ± 0.8
	Cooked at 350° for 1 hr.	20.6 ± 5.2

* Mean value and Standard Error of 3 separate experiments.
** Fried in corn oil for 5 min., 1 cup of water added, simmered for 2 hr.

Leftovers: In some cases, the cooking temporarily reduces the amount of malonaldehyde, but it is produced again during the storage of leftovers in the refrigerator. Here are several examples from Shamberger's data:

MALONALDEHYDE LEVELS IN DIFFERENT TYPES OF MEAT

Cut of meat	Treatment	μg/g
Round steak*	Uncooked	7.2 ± 1.0
	Cooked at 325° for 1½ hr.	3.7 ± 0.2
	Cooked and refrigerated 1 day	5.4 ± 0.2
Rolled rump roast*	Uncooked	1.4 ± 0.2
	Cooked 4 hr. in water 250°	0.3 ± 0.1
	Cooked and refrigerated 2 days	0.8 ± 0.1
Turkey	Uncooked	10.8
	Cooked at 325° for 5 hr.	9.1
Turkey	Cooked at 350° for 3 hr. refrigerated 1 wk.	13.5

* Mean value and Standard Error of 3 separate experiments.

Fermenting Foods Produces Carcinogens and Mutagens

Fermented foods and beverages, such as beer, wine, bread, olives, and yogurt, contain ethyl carbamate or urethane, which is reported to be a carcinogen (Weisburger, 1979).

Wine that is overoxidized—exposed to air—can contain acetamide. Acetamide is a reported carcinogen (IARC, Vol. 7, 1974). It can also contain acetaldehyde, which is a reported mutagen (EPA, *Potential Industrial,* 1977).

Ethyl alcohol (ethanol, fermentation alcohol, grain alcohol, potato alcohol, molasses alcohol, spirits of wine) is a reported carcinogen (NIOSH, 1976). Alcohol (ethanol) consumption is reported to act as a procarcinogen or a carcinogen activator in rats (Seitz et al., 1978).

Potable spirits: According to David Pearson (1977) the chemicals that are found in significant amounts in the common liquors or potable spirits include *ethanol, 2-methylpropan-1-ol, 3-methylbutan-1-ol, 2-phenylethanol, acetone, and acetaldehyde.* The first five chemicals are listed as reported carcinogens by NIOSH, 1976. Acetaldehyde, the sixth, is a reported mutagen (see above); it is reported to be the major metabolite of ethyl alcohol (NAS, *Drinking,* 1977).

The fusel oils which are found in alcoholic beverages are carcinogens and mutagens (Gibel et al., 1974).

Salting Food Produces Carcinogenic Nitrosamines

Salted fish contains a variety of nitrosamines, which give rats nasal and nasopharyngeal cancers. Salted fish is also reportedly mutagenic (Ho et al., 1978).

Mutagenic Cooking

Broiled Beef and Fish Are Mutagenic

The charred external parts of broiled beef and broiled fish are reported to be mutagenic. The mutagenicity, according to the scientists, is too great to be accounted for by benzo(a)pyrene alone (Nagao, Sugimura et al., 1978; Sugimura, Nagao et al., 1977; Nagao, Honda et al., 1977).

Fried Hamburger and Beef Extract Are Mutagenic

Ground beef (hamburger) and concentrated beef stock (beef extract) are reported to contain mutagens, formed during the respective frying and boiling processes. No mutagenic activity was found in raw beef. The higher the temperature, the greater the production of mutagenic activity. The mutagens are said to be distinguished from benzo(a)pyrene and from mutagenic amino acid and pyrolysis products (Dolara et al., 1979; Commoner et al., 1978; Vithayathil et al., 1978).

Cooked Proteins and Amino Acids Are Mutagenic

The cooking of certain proteins at high temperatures is reported to be mutagenic (Nagao, Sugimura et al., 1978; Sugimura, Kawachi et al., 1977; Sugimura, Nagao et al., 1977). The tars from the following amino acids in protein are said to have most mutagenic activity: *tryptophan, serine, glutamic acid, creatinine* (Nagao, Yahagi et al., 1977).

Cooked Sugars Are Mutagenic

Sugars such as *glucose, arabinose, fructose, and sorbitol,* when cooked at high temperatures, are all reported to be mutagenic; *cooked glucosamine* is reported to be mutagenic with metabolic activation; *cooked glucose* contains two chemicals which are found to be mutagens—*acetaldehyde and glyoxal*—but, say the authors, the mutagenicity of the cooked glucose is too great to be solely explained by those two chemicals; *caramel* is reported to be mutagenic (Nagao, Sugimura et al., 1978).

Cooked Garlic and Onions Are Mutagenic

Both onion and garlic, when cooked at high temperatures, were reported to be strongly mutagenic. Garlic contains alliin and allicin, and onion contains allicin; the pyrolysates of both chemicals were also reported to be mutagenic (Nagao, Sugimura et al., 1978).

Some Vegetables Are Mutagenic

Some plants commonly eaten as vegetables (the names were not given) were also reported to be mutagenic when broiled (Nagao, Sugimura et al., 1978).

Exceptions to the "Rule"

In the series of experiments by Japanese scientists reported here, there were foods which did not prove to be mutagenic when cooked at high heat; namely, carbohydrates and vegetable oils (Nagao, Yahagi et al., 1978; Sugimura, Kawachi et al., 1977).

VIII.   AIR

The Myth of "Pure" Air

". . . some conservation groups advocate that all pollutants be removed from the air and that all emission of pollutants be prohibited. However, many pollutants are natural constituents of the air. . . . There is no possibility of removing all pollutants from the air" (Lave and Seskin, 1977).

Oxygen

Oxygen has been reported to be carcinogenic and mutagenic (see Section IV, Oxygen).

Radioactivity

All air is radioactive. Natural radioactivity is often measured by its presence in the air (Beninson et al., 1977; National Council on Radiation Protection and Measurements, 1975).

Radionuclides from the soil, the atmosphere, and the galaxy are inhaled by man (NAS, *Tropospheric,* 1978; NCRP, 1975).

Soil, Sand, Salt, Dust

The air contains soil particles which are inhaled and ingested by man (Turk et al., 1978; Hopps et al., 1978). All soil is radioactive (see Section IV, Soil).

The air contains crystalline silicates, the constituents of sand (Waldbott, 1978). Sand is reported to be carcinogenic (NIOSH, 1976).

The air contains salt from the evaporation of sea spray (Turk et al., 1978; Waldbott, 1978). Salt is reported to be carcinogenic (NIOSH, 1976).

The air contains dust from volcanic eruptions (Turk et al., 1978; Waldbott, 1978). (See Section III, Volcanoes.)

Metals

A variety of life processes release heavy metals into the air: Metals emerge from the continuous degassing of the earth's crust; metals emerge from the sea, where the sea salt flux is converted to a metal flux; metals emerge from land and marine plants. Among these metals are *arsenic, cadmium, copper, iron, lead, manganese, mercury, selenium, and zinc* (NAS, *Tropospheric,* 1978).

Plants, e.g., pea and broadbean plants, give off metal-rich airborne particulates; pine tree seedlings release *zinc and lead* into the air (NAS, *Tropospheric,* 1978; Beauford et al., 1977, 1975).

The air contains *lead* from silicate dusts, volcanic aerosols, forest fires, sea salt, meteoric particles and smoke, and lead derived from decaying radon (WHO, *Lead,* 1977; EPA, *Lead,* 1977).

Metals and their compounds are released into the air by meteoritic particles, which are constantly impinging upon the earth's atmosphere. Among these metals are *chromium, cobalt, iron, manganese, and nickel* (Waldbott, 1978).

All the metals named above are reported carcinogens (see Section III, Metals).

Forests

As reported above, terpenes are reported carcinogens and have been selected by the EPA as top-priority pollutants (NIOSH, 1976).

The air contains terpene hydrocarbons which emerge from the foliage of trees, plants, from "oleoresin blisters and bud resins, and the cell lysis and decay of leaf, bark and wood tissues" (Friberg, 1972).

Terpenes—specifically isoprene and a-pinene—have been identified as emerging, on an average, from 72 percent of the trees in U.S. forests. The following examples are from Rasmussen, 1972:

In eastern U.S. forests,
—a-*Pinene* is emitted by white pine, red pine, jack pine, longleaf pine, slash pine, shortleaf pine, loblolly pine, hemlock, white cedar, larch, spruce, fir, balsam fir, and cypress.
—*Isoprene* is emitted by oak, sweetgum, sycamore, willow, cottonwood, and balsam poplar.
—*Isoprene and* a-*pinene* are emitted by sweetgum, yellow poplar, balsam poplar, and spruce (softwood).

In western U.S. forests,
—a-*Pinene* is emitted by ponderosa pine, Jeffrey pine, sugar pine, lumber pine, western white pine, lodgepole pine, grand fir, white fir, alpine fir, western hemlock, western red cedar, Douglas fir, redwood, and larch.
—*Isoprene* is emitted by aspen and buckthorn.
—*Isoprene and* a-*pinene* are emitted by Sitka spruce, Engelmann spruce, and Colorado blue spruce.

Drying hay emits terpenes (Rasmussen et al., 1965).

Terpenes, and other organic volatiles, form the blue haze over forest canopies and constitute a natural photochemical smog. In October and November, when the numbers of dying cells reach their peak, there are high concentrations of terpenes and organic volatiles. In autumn, the leaf litter, especially if dampened by rain, is a major source of terpenes (Rasmussen et al., 1972, 1965; O'Sullivan, 1972; Went, 1960).

Fire and Smoke—Benzo(a)pyrene

Benzo(a)pyrene is a natural constituent of the air. As reported above, B(a)P is said to be produced by bacteria, algae, all green plants and vegetables, by forest fires, by burning wood and virtually anything else—and it is reported to emerge in cooking and in cooking vapors (see Sections VII and X).

Benzo(a)pyrene is a reported carcinogen (see Section X; and industrial survey, Section II, Energy: Fossil Fuels). In the laboratory, active mutagenic derivatives are "readily formed" from B(a)P in simulated atmospheric conditions. Directly active mutagens are formed from B(a)P in photochemical smog (Pitts et al., 1978).

Nitrogen Compounds

Nitric oxide (NO) in the air is produced:
—by lightning and by ionizing cosmic radiation (NAS, *Nitrates*, 1978);
—by the oxidation of natural ammonia, in photolysis and reactions with OH radicals, and by emissions from microbial flora in soils, leaf litter, and muds (Rasmussen, 1975).

Nitrous oxide in the air is produced by microorganisms in seawater which are released to the atmosphere (Waldbott, 1978).

NO_x (including NO and NO_2) in the air is produced:
—by bacteria (WHO, *Oxides* 1977);
—by volcanoes (NAS, *Nitrates*, 1978; WHO, *Oxides*, 1977; see Section III, Volcanoes);
—by lightning (NAS, *Nitrates*, 1978; Chameides et al., 1977);
—by an inflow from the stratosphere (NAS, *Nitrates*, 1978);
—by forest fires and by burning or incineration (NAS, *Nitrates*, 1978).

NO and NO_2 are always measured together as NO_x (NAS, *Nitrates*, 1978). NO_x is a reported mutagen promoter and possibly a mutagen (see Section III, Volcanoes; and Section IV, Lightning). NO_x is a potential nitrosating agent, which can form carcinogenic nitrosamines in the air (WHO, *Nitrates*, 1978). Carcinogenic nitrosamines can be formed, theoretically, in the human being by the reaction of inhaled NO_2, NO and H_2O (NAS, *Nitrates*, 1978).

Sulfur Compounds

The air contains various sulfur compounds from natural sources; e.g., SO_2 emerges from volcanoes. SO_2 is a reported mutagen (Fishbein, 1978).

Ozone

The air contains ozone from natural sources:
Lightning produces ozone (NAS, *Nitrates*, 1977).
Solar radiation, in the presence of both hydrocarbons and NO_x, produces ozone (Henderson et al., 1979).
Ozone is reported to be mutagenic (Fishbein, 1978; von Nieding, 1978; Henderson et al., 1979).

Carbon Tetrachloride

CCL_4—carbon tetrachloride—is formed in the air. It is produced by normal atmospheric processes (Ehrlich et al., 1977; Lovelock et al., 1975, 1973). CCL_4 is a reported carcinogen (NIOSH, 1976; E. Miller et al., 1971).

Polluting Nature vs. Polluting Man

Where human risk is concerned, local concentrations are crucial. In global terms, however, nature often "pollutes" the air on a far vaster scale than does man. Here are some illustrations of the total amounts of certain kinds of air pollution as contributed by nature and by man. *All substances named below have been reported in this survey as carcinogens or as mutagens, or as promoters or enhancers of carcinogenicity and mutagenicity.*

Salt and Sand: Nature the Sole Source

Salt: One billion tons of sea salt, ejected in the form of aerosols from the ocean, fall on the continents each year (Waldbott, 1978).
Sand: In 1952, silicates as constituents of sand constituted 42.5 percent of the particulates in rural air near London (Waldbott, 1978).

Hydrocarbons: Nature vs. Man

The annual global production of forest hydrocarbons alone is estimated to be 175×10^6 tons per year—175 million tons—or more than six times the hydrocarbon emission rate from all man-made sources (Rasmussen, 1972).

Nitrogen Oxides: Nature vs. Man

Lightning alone may produce about 30–40 megatons of NO_x per year, possibly accounting for as much as 50 percent of all the NO_x in the atmosphere (Chameides, 1977).

The quantities of NO and NO_2 produced by bacteria, volcanoes, *and* lightning "by far outweigh those generated by man's activities'" (WHO, *Oxides,* 1977).

"On a global scale, biological production of nitrogen oxides (NO_x) of 768×10^6 tons per year exceeds industrial emissions . . . by a factor of 15" (Fishbein, 1976).

Sulfur Oxides: Nature vs. Man

Man's contribution of SO_2 is about 35 to 45 percent of the total in the air (NAS, *Tropospheric,* 1978).

Radioactivity: Nature vs. Man

Natural radioactivity by far outweighs any man-made radioactivity (see Section II).

Metals: Nature vs. Man

Many of the metals found in the atmosphere come from the earth's crust and from sea salt. Here is the table offered by NAS (*Tropospheric,* 1978):

GLOBAL FLUX OF METALS TO THE ATMOSPHERE BASED ON TOTAL CRUSTAL MATERIAL FLUX AND TOTAL SEA-SALT FLUX

Element	Crustal material 10^9 g/yr	Bulk sea salt 10^9 g/yr	Fossil-fuel combustion products 10^9 g/yr
*Al	20,000	0.15	1,400
*Fe	14,000	0.5	1,400
Na	6,000	3×10^5	300
*Mn	200	0.005	7
Sc	6	0.000015	0.7
*Cu	14	0.04	2
V	30	0.05	12
*Se	0.013	0.003	0.5
*Pb	3	0.0008	150
*Cd	0.05	0.0008	—
*As	0.5	0.05	0.7
*Zn	18	0.08	0.5
*Sb	0.05	0.007	—
*Hg	0.02	0.0005	1.6

*Metals which have been reported in this survey to be carcinogenic.

According to these calculations, pollution by mercury, arsenic, lead, and selenium is greater from man-made sources—strikingly so in the case of lead.

Nature vs. Man: Overview

Both the following tables are taken from NAS, *Particulate,* 1972.

SOME SOURCES OF NATURAL AEROSOLS IN THE ATMOSPHERE

Source	Estimated aerosol production rate, tons/day
Primary	
Dust rise by wind	20,000–1,000,000
Sea spray	3,000,000
Forest fires (intermittent)	400,000
Volcanic dust (intermittent)	10,000
Extraterrestrial (meteoritic dust)	50–550
Secondary	
Vegetation: hydrocarbons	500,000–3,000,000
Sulfur cycle: $SO_4^=$	100,000–1,000,000
Nitrogen cycle: NO_3^-	1,000,000
NH_4^+	700,000
Volcanoes: volatile SO_2 and H_2S (intermittent)	1,000
Maximal total	~10,000,000

SOME IMPORTANT SOURCES OF ANTHROPOGENIC AEROSOLS IN THE ATMOSPHERE

Source	Estimated aerosol production rate, tons/day
Primary	
Combustion and industry (potentially containing traces of POM*)	100,000–300,000
Dust rise by cultivation (intermittent)**	100–1,000
Secondary	
Hydrocarbon vapors (incomplete combustion, etc.; may involve traces of POM*)	7,000
Sulfates (SO_2, $H_2S\rightarrow SO_4^=$)	300,000
Nitrates ($NO_x\rightarrow NO_3^-$)	60,000
Ammonia	3,000
Maximal total	~ 700,000

*POM = "polycyclic organic matter," e.g. benzo(a)pyrene.
**U.S. only

IX. WATER

Natural Carcinogenic "Pollutants" in the Ocean

Radioactivity, Metals

Relatively little is known about the ocean, but significant "pollutants" have been identified. The ocean contains all cosmic and terrestrial radioactive nuclides at varying concentrations. It also contains all the elements in varying concentrations (Joseph et al., 1971; Goldberg et al., 1971). Data on man's contribution to the metals in the ocean are generally inadequate (NAS, *Tropospheric*, 1978).

Oil

An unknown amount of oil seeps naturally into the ocean from submarine crevices in the earth. The southern California coastal area is one of the regions where seepage takes place (Kraybill, 1978).

Present technology cannot accurately assess the total amount of oil entering the sea from natural seeps. All previous estimates may be too low. Recently, in the Atlantic, a layer of oil 800 nautical miles long, 1 nautical mile wide, and 100 meters thick—one megaton—was identified. It was not refined oil and had emerged from a submarine seep. This one natural seep, found accidentally, "may have been greater than the total estimated oil entering the sea annually" (Harvey et al., 1979).

Crude oil contains all the classes of hydrocarbons found in refined petroleum, including carcinogenic polyaromatic hydrocarbons (PAH) (NAS, *Petroleum*, 1975).

Fossilized Plants

Marine sediments have been found to contain polycyclic aromatic hydrocarbons from layers of fossil minerals which are thought to have been originally formed by the pyrolysis of plants. These newly discovered PAH in the sea are likely to have a global distribution which "makes it necessary to investigate their importance as environmental carcinogens and mutagens" (Blumer et al., 1977).

Natural Carcinogenic "Pollutants" in Rivers, Lakes, Springs, and Drinking Water

Water is the third major source of exposure to toxic and carcinogenic substances—following air and food in its importance to man. The natural carcinogens in drinking water have scarcely been investigated, but here are a few of them.

Radioactivity

The natural radioactivity in various waters varies with the degree of radioactivity in the local rocks and soils. *Uranium-238, radium-226, and radon-222* are found, in varying amounts, in natural waters and springs all over the world (Comar et al., 1973).

Anomalously high rates of radioactivity are found in certain waters. In the U.S., one such area is the South Texas, U.S.A. Uranium District. It contains 5 percent of the U.S. proved uranium reserves. Several hundred wells used for public drinking water, as well as water used in bathtubs and showers, were analyzed, and high concentrations of radon were found (Gesell et al., 1977). Other such areas in the U.S. are northern Illinois and southern Iowa, where the drinking water has exceptionally high concentrations of radon-226 (Eisenbud, 1973). All over the world, and in the U.S., many mineral springs contain relatively high concentrations of radium and radon. Spas have attracted visitors who drink and bathe in radioactive waters, and sit in "emanatoria" where they can breathe the radon emanating from the rocks (Eisenbud, 1973).

The largest contribution to the radioactivity in drinking water comes from potassium-40 (NAS, *Drinking*, 1977).

Metals

The following metals have been identified in samplings of U.S. drinking water: *aluminum, arsenic, barium, beryllium, cadmium, chromium, cobalt, copper, iron, lead, manganese, mercury, nickel, selenium, silver, tin, vanadium, and zinc* (NAS, *Drinking*, 1977). All have been reported to be carcinogenic, save for barium, tin, and vanadium, which is a reported mutagen (see Section III, Metals).

Natural processes can affect the concentration of metals in water—e.g., the decaying of vegetation in which certain metals are concentrated, and the runoff of rainwater from the soil (NAS, *Drinking*, 1977). The most common natural cause of excess metallic concentration is erosion of the soil (EPA, *National Water Quality*, 1976).

Rivers that run through different parts of the country have different concentrations of metals that have been reported to be carcinogens. Rivers that drain glaciated parts of the continent have more *titanium, chromium, nickel, and manganese;* West Coast rivers are higher in *lead* (Cannon et al., 1971). In certain areas of Oregon, well waters can contain 30 to 40 times as much *arsenic* as is considered acceptable. The elevated arsenic levels are thought to be due to volcanic deposits (Whanger et al., 1977). High *arsenic* content is also found in the Yellowstone River in Wyoming and Montana from natural rock deposits (EPA, *National Water Quality*, 1976).

Asbestos

Natural concentrations of asbestos fibers in water are reported to range from 10,000 to 1,000,000 fibers per liter (NAS, *Drinking Water*, 1977).

X. FIRE

Fire: Unexplored Territory

Relatively little is known about the chemistry of fire and its effects. In 1978, Thomas F. Mancuso, writing about industrial substances exposed to heat, said: "Consequently, we have serious fundamental problems: the realization that the microchemical environment contains not only the many thousands of chemicals known to be introduced into the work environment, *but in addition, now we know that when these chemicals and products are subjected to heat, new chemicals are formed, which multiplies the range of the thousands of chemicals whose toxicological and cancer effects have not been studied, either alone or in combination with other chemicals."* (Emphasis added)

This observation applies not only to the 70,000 estimated industrial chemicals, but to the millions of chemicals that are estimated to exist in nature. In the section below, a few of the carcinogenic substances produced by fire will be reported.

Benzo(a)Pyrene

B (*a*)P is "a ubiquitous environmental contaminant which may be one of the most prevalent chemical carcinogens to which man is exposed" (W. Levin et al., 1977).

"[Benzo(*a*)pyrene] results from almost any fire, burning almost any material. It is universal, practically speaking" (E. Cuyler Hammond, *Hearings: Occupational Diseases,* 1978).

"Although no evidence exists to indicate that benzo(*a*)pyrene is either the most widespread or the most potent polynuclear carcinogen in the environment, it has been studied more than any other, and in many cases is the only one estimated" (WHO, *Health Hazards,* 1972).

B(a)P: An Evolutionary Hypothesis

As a means of estimating the natural levels of polyaromatic hydrocarbons, scientists in the USSR analyzed benzo(a)pyrene levels in permafrost soil. B(a)P was found in all the layers of permafrost and is attributed to natural sources throughout the history of the earth (Ill'nitskii et al., 1979).

Max Blumer, in "Polycyclic Aromatic Compounds in Nature," 1976, suggests that PAH may have played a significant role in the formation of the species: "Polycyclic aromatic hydrocarbons from pyrolysis have been present on the earth for a long time. Man has been in contact with combustion products throughout his history, and natural fires and reactions in sediments formed polycyclic aromatic hydrocarbons long before the advent of man. Moreover, we now know that the hydrocarbons in smoke, in fallout from the air, in sediments and in fossil fuels include, in addition to already recognized compounds that can give rise to cancer and mutations, new carcinogens and mutagens. That raises a new question: Have such materials contributed significantly to the role of mutation in the evolution of species? They might then rank among other natural mutagens such as ultraviolet radiation and background nuclear radiation."

Forest Fires

The role of forest fires as contributors of toxic chemicals to the atmosphere was considered minimal until recently. Although the exact quantities are unknown, that contribution is now being sharply revised upward, as data on the immensity of the areas burned are being acquired. Many of the forest fires are occurring in preindustrial and tropical areas of the world where statistics are unavailable or poor. In Brazil, as much as 3 percent of the forested areas in several large states is being burned each year (NAS, *Nitrates*, 1978). In Canada and the United States, preventive measures are improving, but natural forest fires are still consuming gigantic wooded areas. C. S. Wong, 1978, reports that in Canada more than half of the forest fires are caused by lightning, less than half caused by man.

Chemicals Produced by Burning Plants

Here are a few of the commonly identified chemicals produced by the burning of plants and other organic substances, both living and fossilized:

The burning of trees and wood produces NO_x (NAS, *Nitrates*, 1978); *nitrosamines and polynuclear arenes* (Burchfield et al., 1977); and *benzo*(a)*pyrene* (WHO, *Health Hazards,* 1972). As this survey indicates, NO_x, nitrosamines, and B(a)P have been reported to be carcinogenic and mutagenic.

The burning of plants, wood, and fossilized organic substances such as peat and lignite produces methyl chloride, reported to be mutagenic (Friberg et al., 1978).

The burning of fossilized vegetation and organic substances—the fossil fuels—is reported to produce many carcinogens and mutagens. For a more detailed list, see industrial survey, Section II, Energy: Coal; Energy: Fossil Fuels. Here, only the classes of substances produced are given: *cyclic hydrocarbons, unsaturated aliphatic hydrocarbons, halogenated hydrocarbons, aromatic amines, polycyclic hydrocarbons, aldehydes, nitrosamines or substances* (NO_x) *which form nitrosamines, nitroolefins, metals and metal compounds, radioactive materials, and O3, peroxides, and substances which form peroxides.* Carcinogens and mutagens are reported in each of these categories (Friberg et al., 1978). SO_2 is also released from burning fossil fuels (Carter, 1979). SO_2 is a reported mutagen (L. Fishbein, 1978).

The Most Notorious Burning Plant

The practice of "smoking"—namely, inhaling the smoke of burning tobacco leaves—is universally agreed to be a cause of cancer of the lung, and of other organs as well. Tobacco, accordingly, has been studied more thoroughly than almost any other natural substance. Here are some of the carcinogenic and mutagenic substances reported in the plant and the smoke of its burning leaves:

Radioactive Elements in Tobacco Plant and Smoke

These radioactive substances have been identified in tobacco and tobacco smoke: *potassium-40, isotopes of rubidium, strontium, and cesium,* and some radionuclides of the *radium and thorium* series (Stedman, 1968). *Radioactive polonium* has also been reported in and on tobacco leaves (Interagency Task Force on Ionizing Radiation, 1979; Ehrlich et al., 1977).

Carcinogenic Metals in Tobacco Plant and Smoke

Many metals that are reported to be carcinogens appear both in the leaf and the smoke of tobacco. They are *aluminum, arsenic, beryllium, chromium, cobalt, copper, iron, lead, manganese, mercury, nickel, selenium, silver, titanium, and zinc* (Stedman, 1968). *Cadmium* has also been identified in the plant and in the smoke (IARC, Vol. 11, 1976). F. W. Sunderman, Jr. (1973) suggests that nickel is one of the carcinogenic components of the plant. (For references on carcinogenicity, see Section III, Metals.)

Chemical Carcinogens and Mutagens in Tobacco Plant and Smoke

Among the many chemical compounds identified in tobacco smoke, the following reported carcinogens have been identified:

Carcinogenic polyaromatic hydrocarbons (PAH): In 1964, the Surgeon General's Report on Smoking and Health identified seven aromatic hydrocarbons in smoke as carcinogens: *benzo*(a)*pyrene, dibenz*(a,i)*pyrene, dibenz*(a,h)*anthracene, benzo*(c)*phenanthrene, dibenz*(a,j)*acridine, dibenz*(a,h)*acridine, and 7-H dibenzo*(c,g)*carbazole.* A later review also identified *chrysene, benz*(a)*anthracene, benzo*(e)*pyrene, benzo*(b)*fluoranthene, benzo*(j)*fluoranthene, and indeno*(1,2,3-cd) *pyrene;* some of these are carcinogen promoters, rather than direct carcinogens. (Both reviews cited by Van Duuren, 1968).

In 1977, Kakvan et al. reported that 10 of 18 hydrocarbons in cigarette smoke tar can induce cancer in animals.

Various carcinogenic *nitrosamines* have been reported in nicotine, tobacco plants, tobacco curing, and smoke (Hoffmann et al., 1979; WHO, *Nitrates,* 1978; Magee, 1978; Hecht et al., 1978; Fine et al., 1977).

Some scientists postulate that the mutagenicity of tobacco tar is produced mainly by the pyrolysis of proteins and amino acids (Nagao, Sugimura et al., 1978). The mutagenicity of cigarette smoke condensate is reported to correlate positively with the content of protein in tobacco shreds (Yoshida et al., 1978).

Various sugars have been identified in tobacco plants. They include *arabinose,* fructose,* galactose,* glucose,* maltose, sorbitol, and sucrose.* Those with asterisks are also found in tobacco smoke (Stedman, 1968). Of these sugars, *fructose* and *maltose* are reported carcinogens (NIOSH, 1976), and *sucrose* has been linked to cancer in human beings (see Section VI, Universal Carcinogens in Food). *Arabinose, fructose, glucose, and sorbitol* have been reported to be mutagenic when pyrolyzed (Nagao, Sugimura et al., 1978).

At least one carcinogenic aromatic amine has been identified in cigarette smoke: *2-naphthylamine.* It is reported to cause bladder cancer in animals and is strongly linked to bladder cancer in man (EPA, *Potential Industrial,* 1977).

Phenol, eugenol, and related compounds have been identified in cigarette smoke, most formed by pyrolysis of cellular constituents. They are reported to be co-carcinogens (Stedman, 1968). Phenol is also a reported carcinogen (NIOSH, 1976).

Other reported carcinogens or mutagens have also been identified in fresh leaf tobacco and cigarette smoke: *nicotine,* reported to be carcinogenic (NIOSH, 1976); *methyl chloride,* reported to be mutagenic (EPA, *Potential Industrial,* 1977); *hydrazine,* reported to be carcinogenic and mutagenic (Nagao, Sugimura et al., 1978), and a hydrazine compound, reported to be carcinogenic (Toth, 1977); *acetaldehyde,* reported to be mutagenic (EPA, *Potential Industrial,* 1977); and *2-nitropropane,* reported to be a carcinogen (NIOSH, cited by EPA, *Potential Industrial,* 1977).

Irony: Tobacco Gets Cancer

The tobacco plant develops crown gall teratomas, which are being studied in an attempt to learn more about the mechanisms of tumor development (Wood et al., 1978).

Two Other Burning Plants

Poppy: Burning opium produces mutagens. Smoking opium and sucking or chewing its tars may be linked to cancer (Hewer et al., 1978; Sadeghi et al., 1979).

Marijuana: The smoke of burning marijuana has a greater carcinogenic hydrocarbon content than that of tobacco (Karler, 1977). The condensates of marijuana smoke are reported to be mutagenic (Busch et al., 1979).

XI. MAN

Carcinogenic Chemicals Produced by the Human Body

Essential Chemicals

Cholesterol, found in the human brain, spinal cord, and fat, is reported to be both carcinogenic and a carcinogen promoter (Wogan, 1974; IARC, Vol. 10, 1976; NIOSH, 1976).

Urea is reported to be carcinogenic (NIOSH, 1976).

Blood

The digestion of sugars produces acetaldehyde in the blood; acetaldehyde is reported to be mutagenic (EPA, *Potential Industrial,* 1977).

Trace amounts of nitrosamines are normally present in human blood following consumption of conventional foodstuffs (Fine et al., 1977).

Metabolism

The metabolism of carbohydrates requires insulin, which is reported to be carcinogenic (NIOSH, 1976).

Digestion

Saliva contains bacteria which convert nitrate to nitrite, which may form carcinogenic nitrosamines (Tannenbaum, Archer et al., 1978; Tannenbaum et al., 1974).

The stomach contains bacteria which are reported to be able to convert foods into carcinogenic nitrosamines (Sander, 1973).

Intestinal bacteria are reported to produce carcinogenic nitrosamines (Tannenbaum, Fett et al., 1978); to metabolize sterols to carcinogens (Moore et al., 1978); and to form co-carcinogens from bile acid and cholesterol (B. Miller et al., 1979). The intestinal bacteria *E. coli* are reported to produce a carcinogenic metabolite, ethionine (Lewis et al., 1977). *E. coli* incubated in a sterile medium produced the reported carcinogen benzo(*a*)pyrene (J. Miller, 1973).

Mutagens, identified as *N*-nitroso compounds or volatile nitrosamines, have been found in the feces of healthy people (Bruce et al., 1977; Varghese et al., 1978; Wang, 1978).

Sex and Reproduction

Natural human sex hormones—estradiol, estrone, estriol, progesterone, and testosterone—are reported to be carcinogenic (Clement Associates, 1978; IARC, Vol. 6, 1974). Steroid hormones may precipitate or promote cancer; the synthetic steroids are reported to be metabolized in the human body by the same mechanisms as those of the natural hormones (IARC, Vol. 6, 1974).

Smegma is a reported carcinogen; horse smegma is carcinogenic in mice. It is recommended by some scientists that the carcinogenicity of smegma be studied further in connection with penis cancer (Muir et al., 1979).

Sperm may cause testicle and prostate cancer. In rats, the penetration of sperm into the cells and tissues of testicles and prostate caused cancer of those tissues (Stein-Werblowsky, 1978, 1978).

Mother's milk contains lactose—milk sugar. It is reported to be carcinogenic (NIOSH, 1976).

Radioactive Man

"Radioactive substances of natural origin are in the air we breathe and the food we eat. These radioactive elements become incorporated into our tissues to such an extent that, on average, the atoms of which our bodies consist are disintegrating at a rate of about 500,000 per minute, due to the presence of naturally radioactive species of carbon, potassium, and other elements" (Eisenbud, 1978).

·   ·   ·

That, then, is the survey on natural carcinogens—my own collection of findings in the literature. How valid they are, once again, the layman cannot know, but if they are valid in any significant measure, we are staring at yet another calamity. If we consider these same data with the same "official" assumptions—above all, with the no-threshold theory in mind, the theory that tells us that there is no safe dose of any carcinogen, that even the most minute amount can trigger a malignancy—we see that we are now confronting a second carcinogenic hell. The industrial data, which *included* natural data, suggest that by virtue of human action, there is nothing we can breathe, eat, or drink without encountering carcinogens. These data, exclusively natural, suggest that by virtue of the nature of reality itself, there is nothing we can breathe, eat, or drink without encountering carcinogens. In fact, of the two carcinogenic hells, there is something even more hellish about this one. However appalled one may be by the industrial data, one is always aware, subliminally, that there is an industrial spigot, so to speak, and that for substance after substance, the spigot could be turned off. Industrial carcinogens are susceptible to political action; one can ban products, one can close factories. Hypothetically, the whole Industrial Revolution could be turned off. But the carcinogens that have been reported here cannot be turned off; if the data or any significant portion of them are valid, they are expressions of laws of nature, and even Congress in its wisdom cannot repeal them. This carcinogenic hell, the scientists are telling us, is the planet earth itself, and we cannot escape it. It is, consequently, a more awesome picture.

It is also a picture of mind-boggling complexity. We see that carcinogens are reported to be every kind of thing: They are animate, inanimate; chemical, physical; animal, vegetable, and mineral; they are motionless crystals, flowing gases, liquids. They are everywhere: They rain down upon us from the skies, they radiate upward from crevices beneath the sea, from the rocks and soil, they flow through the veins of plants and trees, they gush out in torrents from forests. They are alive: They grow, they crawl, they bloom, they blossom. And they are inside us: They are part of our vital physiological processes; they course through our bloodstream, through our hormones; they are in our saliva, in our digestive tracts. We inhale them, we drink them, and we feed on them ceaselessly, and in the act of absorbing them, we renew the needed supply in our bodies, for we cannot live without them; we ourselves are carcinogenic and radioactive beings. And even the act of dying is carcinogenic, for putrefaction, whether of plant or of animal, breeds new carcinogens. Were we to perish on a fiery bier, our broiling tissues and the very ash to which we were reduced would be carcinogenic. If these extraordinary data are valid, they tell us that in some ungraspable way the entire universe is implicated in the disease that is known as cancer.

Clearly, the carcinogen as reported in the literature is a far more mysterious thing than we had ever supposed. Hueper's "germ" metaphor—still being relayed in 1980 by Marvin Schneiderman of the National Cancer Institute[40]—does not capture the complexity that is implied here. Although they are individually identifiable, carcinogens, it appears, are not just single entities; they are aspects of the earth, they are preconditions for birth, reproduction, and survival, they are augurs of life and death, they are an attribute of existence itself.

These data, reported by scientists in so many fields, also give us insight into one aspect of man's role on earth. They suggest that man has always been a producer of carcinogens, and that unless he reverts to a hunter-gatherer culture and ceases even the primitive "technology" of building a bonfire, he must always produce carcinogens. The problem, according to these data, lies in the nature of the planet itself, in that extraordinary carcinogenic dimension. According to these findings, one cannot thrust a pick into the crust of the earth, one cannot burrow into a deep hole, one cannot slice, chop, pulverize, recombine, or burn even the crudest and the most primary substances of earth, not to mention its layers of fossilized vegetation, without unleashing carcinogens. And the more imaginatively one manipulates the substances of earth, as in organic chemistry, the more carcinogens must one unleash. On a planet where almost one out of four of the stable elements has been reported to be a carcinogen, and where nature itself—still barely explored—is already said to be gushing millions of tons of reportedly carcinogenic material into the air each day, technological man cannot be other than a producer of carcinogens. Man has clearly added to the stock of carcinogens to which we are exposed, and added to it in great quantities—but it is quite apparent, if one can trust animal tests, and if mutagenicity is a cause of cancer, that the phenomenon of carcinogenicity cannot be exclusively attributed to the Faustian sin. If ultimate "guilt" there be—and in the face of data like this, moral terminology is senseless—it is nature's.

This is scarcely the perspective on carcinogens that Americans have been taught for twenty years. On the contrary, the natural data allow us, for the first time, to gain perspective on our teachers. In fact, we are actually engaged here in an experiment. We can now examine two kinds of carcinogens discovered by identical methodologies, and differentiated only by one variable: their source. One set of carcinogens has been created by man—the synthetic chemicals; the other set by nature. The purpose of the experiment is not to measure quantities of anything, but to test consistency and logic. If the key apocalyptic and governmental ideas that have been taught to the American public have any validity, they will be consistent with both the synthetic and the natural. That alone would not necessarily guarantee their truth—false statements may, within a given context, be consistent; but such consistency would surely forbid us to rule them out. If, however, the apocalyptic propositions are not consistent with the data, or if they apply only to one kind of carcinogen and not to the other, then we know that those propositions are invalid, for if a *something* causes cancer, it causes cancer; the identity of its creator is irrelevant. We shall, accordingly, examine the key apocalyptic ideas presented so far, and check them against the relevant data in both surveys. First, we shall examine the propositions pertaining to cancer causation, then the key governmental assumptions pertaining to cancer prevention:

Apocalyptic Proposition No. 1: Nature's role in cancer causation is insignificant because over the eons, man and animal have adapted to natural substances.

If the data given here have any validity, this evolutionary idea is false. Over and over again, it is reported that natural entities, forces, and substances create malignancies in animals and man.

Apocalyptic Proposition No. 2: Any substance not created by nature is a dangerous violation of evolutionary "balance," and we may assume that carcinogenicity is a preferential attribute of synthetic chemicals.

If the data in the *industrial* survey are valid, this second evolutionary idea is false. In the section of that survey called "Chemicals," the EPA reported in

1979 that only 20 percent of all chemicals tested proved to be carcinogenic in animal tests. According to Douglas Costle of the EPA, the chemicals with the most "suspect" structures were tested first.[41] While this chapter was being written in 1980, the EPA, acting in its official capacity, reprinted an article by science reporter Judith Randal, an article originally reprinted in the *Washington Post*, and made it available to the press. In it, Randal reported that she had been told—no source was identified—that about 7 percent of all chemicals tested had proved to be carcinogenic, and calculated that some 6,500 industrial chemicals out of 7,000 had been given "a clean bill of health."[42] It would appear from these statistics—if one can believe the EPA—that carcinogenicity is not, on the whole, a dominant attribute of man-made chemicals.

Apocalyptic Proposition No. 3: The vast majority—perhaps as much as 90 percent—of cancer deaths are attributable to the synthetic products of the chemical industry which developed after World War II.

We already know this proposition is baseless. The apocalyptic scientists have clearly announced that they have no such knowledge, and that most industries have not been studied (by epidemiologists) for their carcinogenic effects on man.

Apocalyptic Proposition No. 4: Our economic system, with its powerful corporations, its huge investments in technology, its profit motive, its manipulative advertising that induces artificial needs in consumers, is responsible for most of the cancer that is killing one out of every four.

This proposition is false. As both surveys tell us, scientists in a variety of economic systems—communist, socialist, social democratic, and capitalist— are now struggling with problems of carcinogenicity, from both synthetic and natural sources.

We now come to the governmental assumptions, ideas that were crystallized decades ago. Several of those assumptions have been tentatively accepted in the process of compiling the surveys—i.e., that the animal tests may be taken as evidence of potential cancer in man and that we can ignore negative data— and are not, for the moment, in question. The others are all variants of a single idea—the no-threshold or no-safe-dose theory of carcinogens and its one-molecule hazard, which is a critical regulatory principle and a key concept in cancer prevention. That idea is the one we shall consider.

Unsurprisingly, we can form no opinion on the biological truth of the no-threshold theory: Some of its advocates claim there is scientific evidence to support it, while some claim that *because* there is no scientific evidence to support it, it must be assumed in order to be "prudent." In the face of this contradiction, one can only wonder why they disagree, but as laymen, we can make no judgments. It is difficult to avoid the suspicion, however, that the no-threshold/one-molecule theory would never have been formulated had the natural data been discovered before the synthetic data. One cannot readily imagine a group of NCI scientists trooping before Congress to testify that one molecule of spinach is a threat to the Republic. But that suspicion, however culturally reasonable, does not constitute a refutation of the no-threshold/one-molecule theory.

We can only judge that theory with confidence when it is offered simply as an expression of "prudence." It may indeed be prudent when applied to carcinogens in factories, where some men are exposed to high doses of carcinogenic chemicals for many years, but it is not prudent when applied to most of the huge vista of natural carcinogens reported in the literature. As the survey shows, large numbers of natural substances which have been said to be carcinogens or which interact with other natural substances to promote or produce carcinogens are prerequisites for human life. Man cannot survive without air and water, which are said to be naturally "contaminated" by many carcinogens. Man cannot survive without oxygen, in particular, reported to be mutagenic and implicated in many types of malignancies. Man cannot eat without a variety of nutrients, many of which have been reported to contain chemicals that are carcinogenic, co-carcinogenic, or mutagenic, many of which are reportedly radioactive, and many of which contain reportedly carcinogenic metals. Man cannot digest those nutrients without saliva and digestive bacteria, both of which, according to the data, have been implicated as carcinogens, or as producers of carcinogens. Man cannot function as a sexual being or reproduce his own kind without sexual hormones, and they too have been reported to be carcinogenic. Finally, man cannot seek shelter from the elements or from predatory beasts, or cook many natural foods in order to detoxify them, without fire, but combustion is said to produce mutagens and carcinogens. If any significant portion of the data in this chapter are valid, and if the "prudence" of the no-threshold theory were to be invoked, crucial physiological functions might have to be medically prohibited. A theory which, according to the scientific literature, would kill off the human species cannot be accepted as prudent.

And with that last proposition, this little experiment terminates. It tells us that four of the four apocalyptic ideas we have examined in the light of the data are false or baseless (nature is essentially noncarcinogenic; synthetics tend to be carcinogenic; most cancer is industrial; and carcinogens are a free-market phenomenon). As for the key regulatory theory of cancer prevention, the no-threshold/one-molecule theory (which does or does not have scientific support), it is practically inapplicable to nature, and would apparently, if consistently applied, kill us all.

This is an absurd record. It tells us that the ideas which flooded the nation in 1976 were pure mythology. Unless the animal and mutagen testers lost *all* their competence as we moved from Chapter 3 to Chapter 4, we learn here that the ideological heritage of the apocalypse is a religious-political parable. The reported data on natural carcinogens contradict that parable so profoundly, so ludicrously, that one wonders what, exactly, was going on in the heads of all those apocalyptic scientists and governmental spokesmen when they were drilling it into the heads of Americans that they were being murdered en masse by synthetic chemicals and that, explicitly or by implication, nature was a Sunday-school version of the Garden of Eden.

Some scientists were quite aware that Americans were being taught nonsense. In a book published in 1977, edited by Herman Kraybill and Myron A. Mehlman of the National Institutes of Health, these editors wrote:

A widely held view is that modern technology is exclusively responsible for introducing into the environment a host of pyrolytic products and other chemical agents that are directly or indirectly responsible for all adverse effects on humans attributed to environmental insults. However, many of these insults and potential insults are the result of substances that are of natural origin.[43]

They further declared that there had been considerable underestimation of the complexity of the problem of environmental health hazards. They did not explain the genesis of the idea that "technology" was "exclusively responsible" for environmental assaults on human health, nor did they say how it came to be a "widely held view." At the very opening of their essay, however, almost disconnected syntactically from the analysis, they referred to the zeal of the "environmentalists" and "activist groups" who were seeking legal solutions to the problem; presumably, these were the people who had been engaging in the oversimplification that the two scientists proceeded to dismantle.[44] Nowhere, however, did Kraybill and Mehlman suggest that the fallacy had been systematically nourished by some of their colleagues at the NCI, nor that the American public was being given a false vision of the phenomenon of environmental cancer by the selective process of the cancer prevention establishment itself.

It is clear that this extraordinary misrepresentation rests, at root, on three interlocking errors, and one learns a good deal by identifying them:

The first error is the claim to nonexistent knowledge, and the reliance on a huge floating abstraction to justify that claim. For twenty years, apocalyptics have been announcing that there were only a few natural cancer-causing agents and rationalizing that statement with the theory of evolution. The most vivid illustration of the futility of the process can be found in Rachel Carson's conclusion that such "invented" chlorinated hydrocarbons as methyl chloride and carbon tetrachloride were "unnatural" evils, while the bracken fern standing proudly by the roadside represented the intrinsic goodness of nature. In fact, all three are creations of nature and all three are reported to be carcinogenic. Methyl chloride emerges from the ocean and from forest fires in quantities vastly greater than are produced by man.[45] Carbon tetrachloride, too, is reported to be produced in the atmosphere in quantities vastly greater than are produced by man.[46] As for the proud bracken fern, it is reported to be a destroyer of human lives.[47] The theory of evolution did not inform Carson of these facts. Nor did it inform Carson or anyone else that many other reported carcinogens presumed to be exclusively human inventions were actually natural products—that other chlorinated hydrocarbons are produced in great quantities in the soil by bacteria and fungi;[48] that isoprene emerges by the ton from forests;[49] that vinyl chloride is found in tobacco;[50] that phthalate esters, which leach out of polyvinyl chloride packaging and plastic bottles, are also found in plants.[51] These are just a few of the recent discoveries of "synthetics" first invented by nature, discoveries that could not be predicted by the theory of evolution. Darwinian theory—like the idea that "life is a unity" which emerges from that theory—is a wide descriptive abstraction. It is not a substitute for the scientific analysis of concrete entities and actions. Carson and Commoner did use it as a substitute for scientific knowledge, and their analysis was widely accepted. It was an ersatz analysis, however, and their "axiom" of nature's benevolence was spurious.

The second error is the failure to discover or acknowledge the existence of natural carcinogens that were already known. The carcinogenicity of tobacco was established in the 1950s; and carcinogenic metals, minerals, viruses, and fungi were reported in the 1930s and 1940s. Thus, long before Carson and Commoner established the spurious "axiom" of nature's benevolence and attributed carcinogenicity primarily to the synthetic, evidence existed that major aspects of earth—its elements, its crust, its living entities, its natural processes—were or might be carcinogenic. The information was in the scientific literature; that literature went unread, or was ignored.

The third error is the presence of a crude double standard. Scientists observed that the presence of some synthetic chemical carcinogens doubtless meant that others were yet to be discovered and concluded that an aggressive search for them was necessary. No comparable judgment was made by the apocalyptic scientists about the chemicals in nature. Irving Selikoff, speaking of the potential hazards of "untested chemicals," has observed:

The expression "there is no evidence" usually means nobody has looked for the evidence. Unfortunately it is too often used to support the notion that a particular substance is harmless because it has not been proved dangerous. The facts are so often to the contrary that I do not think this "no evidence" phrase or attitude is one with which we can be satisfied in the future.[52]

Selikoff was talking of the blindly reflexive defense of industrialists, but precisely the same point can be made of those apocalyptic scientists who blindly exonerated nature, saw no need to "look for the evidence," rushed to inform the nation that cancer was almost entirely attributable to our industrial and economic system, and substituted moral and political analyses for data.

It should be said that ignorance and error as such are not the problem. Science makes no claim to infallibility or omniscience. There is, however, something disconcerting about this pattern of error. Given the curious practice among some scientists of expressing public and unsubstantiated speculation, one might have expected the errors to be more varied, more imaginative, to take the form of different and intricate speculations. That, however, has not been the case. What is so striking about the pattern of error is its monotony. For almost twenty years, the error has always worked in one way: It has invariably promoted or reinforced the "axiomatic" belief that nature was deficient in cancer-causing agents, and it has invariably promoted or reinforced the corollary idea that science, technology, and industry, and, often, the American economic system, were the morally culpable agents. Inevitably, the result of the pattern of error has been the acute politicization of the cancer issue.

When each of the specific components of the pattern of error is identified—the claim to nonexistent knowledge, the substitution of vacant abstractions for scientific analysis, the preference for opinion over data, and the transmission of moral and political doctrines as though they were scientific statements—we find that we are looking at something very familiar. It is, once again, the "apocalyptic paradigm," the same pattern of error to be found in the mental processes of those apocalyptic scientists who brought us the urgent moral news that man, science, technology, etc., were about to destroy all life on earth. The congruence of the two patterns of thought should not be surprising. Both the "environmentalists" and many of the experts in "environmental" cancer emerged from the same world. Indeed, some of the most vocal and influential leaders were exactly the same people.

The discovery of this pattern of error must necessarily affect one's attitude to the entire field of carcinogenesis research, and it affected mine. While it is obvious from this survey on natural data that many scientists in the field are free from the conventional myths and dogmas—most of the natural data would not exist save for that independence—it is also obvious that the apocalyptic faction, which has a foothold in government, is intellectually influential and has played an important role for almost twenty years in shaping the science of chemical carcinogenesis. In view of what I had learned of the apocalyptics' capacity to improvise conclusions in a vacuum and to substitute moral and political notions for data, I was forced to wonder whether or not such habits had invaded the laboratory. It was clearly unwise to accept *any* of the assumptions, practices, and findings in this field without subjecting them to close scrutiny.

It was consequently time to confront the science of carcinogenesis itself in its theoretical and applied forms. While it is the applied science of cancer prevention that affects us most directly and that had influenced the investigation so far, if I was ever to judge that science and its animal and bacterial tests, its data, its extrapolations to man and its risk assessments, I realized that I had to have some idea of the basic science on which it depends for its theoretical validity. Thus, it was to basic science that I went with certain questions in mind: What had the basic researchers definitively learned about the causes of cancer that had led scientists to believe that cancer prevention was possible? Did cancer, in fact, start with a mutation, and might we assume that mutagenic substances cause cancer? What was the genesis and the precise scientific status of the no-threshold/one-molecule theory of cancer? And did regulatory theory accurately reflect the discoveries of basic research of the period? In the next three chapters, I will report on what I learned when I sought to answer those questions.

PART

III

BASIC SCIENCE

Chapter 5

The Mystery of the Malignant Cell

In many respects, the study of chemical carcinogenesis is akin to attempting to unravel a Gordian knot. As one traces a promising thread, it invariably leads to other mysteries and entanglements in daunting number. . . .[1]
—Frederick F. Becker, 1979

B asic science as such cannot be summarized. The most illuminating short description of the process can be found in this passage from Lewis Thomas:

There is nothing to touch the spectacle. In the midst of what seems a collective derangement of minds in total disorder, with bits of information being scattered about, torn to shreds, disintegrated, deconstituted, engulfed, in a kind of activity that seems as random and agitated as that of bees in a disturbed part of the hive, there suddenly emerges, with the purity of a slow phrase of music, a single new piece of truth about nature.[2]

There is no way to capture the flux of information as it is being created, torn to shreds, and recombined in new forms. In this chapter, I have confined myself only to the major discoveries that occurred just before, and for a few years after, a group of American scientists proposed a cancer prevention program to the Surgeon General.

Four stories of discovery will be told here. All the scientists named had important predecessors, collaborators, and successors, and almost all worked, at one time or another, on all the problems that will be described. Nonetheless, within the "beehive" of collective endeavor, certain individuals are known for particularly critical contributions, and in the stories that follow, only their names will be linked to the discoveries. Because this is a book by a lay author written for lay readers, the focus will be almost entirely on what was discovered and not on the explanatory biological mechanisms, which are invariably speculative and always appallingly technical.

Although almost all the discoveries to be discovered occurred within a very few years and were almost simultaneous, the stories will be told in a sequence which permits the reader to acquire a realization of the complexity of carcinogenesis in discrete stages. The growing complexity was intensely startling to the scientists. There was one basic reason for the general astonishment:

Most students of chemical carcinogenesis began by assuming, as Rachel Carson had reported, that cancer was caused by the properties of a chemical. What they learned, in the course of relatively few years, was that they were confronting not just a chemical mystery, but a biological mystery that was to grow ever more mysterious.

1. THE MILLERS

One discovery, above all, had led some scientists to believe, in 1970, that they knew enough to prevent cancer. It was the achievement of James and Elizabeth Miller of the University of Wisconsin. To understand its significance, one must know about a problem that had been plaguing cancer researchers since the 1950s. As Gary Flamm of the National Cancer Institute puts it, the workers in carcinogenesis had become "chagrined" by the fact that they were discovering carcinogens in a "bewildering array" of chemical classes,[3] e.g., polycyclic aromatic hydrocarbons, azo dyes, aromatic amines, carbamates, nitrosamines, nitrosamides, nitrofurans, hydrazines, halogenated hydrocarbons, halo ethers, epoxides, etc.[4] On the assumption that carcinogenicity was a property of the chemical, they had been struggling to predict carcinogenicity from molecular structure, but they had not succeeded. The structures of these different classes of chemicals were extremely different, and no common denominator had ever been found.

Then, within a few years, a solution appeared. It had occurred to some scientists that the chemical common denominator might be found not in the original chemicals but in the new compounds into which they were metabolized in the body. Two of those scientists, James and Elizabeth Miller, finally demonstrated, in a series of remarkable experiments done between 1966 and 1970, that this was indeed the answer. Carcinogenic chemicals, they reported, were usually not active in the forms in which they were actually ingested or inhaled. The original chemicals were, rather, "precarcinogens" which had to be metabolized by enzymes in the body into reactive forms which the Millers called "proximate" and "ultimate" carcinogens; it was the "ultimate" metabolized compounds which were the cancer-causing agents. A common denominator did exist for those "ultimate" carcinogens, said the Millers; all of them were electrophiles carrying a positive charge that enabled them to interact with nucleophilic sites in the cell. By such interactions normal cells were converted into cancerous cells.[5] The cellular conversion was apparently irreversible;[6] as the Millers put it, in discussing the various implications of their discovery, the change was "quasi-permanent."[7] Verifying evidence for the metabolization of carcinogens emerged from the laboratory in following years, the Millers' theory was universally accepted, and they won the celebrated Bertner Award for seminal research in cancer. The chemical mystery had been solved.

Like all seminal discoveries, this one had complex repercussions. In one case, it generated a new problem; in other cases, it precipitated new discoveries. The new problem will be described first. It pertained to species differences, and once again, one must know the background. Although mammalian physiology is generally similar in pattern and although the use of animals is crucial in all biological, medical, and pharmaceutical research, animals are not always reliable substitutes for man, and for that matter, they are not always reliable substitutes for each other. A considerable degree of variation exists in animal responses, whether the substances tested are toxic or carcinogenic. As Norbert Page of the National Cancer Institute observes, there are "great differences" in the response of different species to carcinogenic chemicals.[8] Researchers in pharmacology, who have the most experience in extrapolating animal findings to man, have always been aware of this dimension of uncertainty, and when they use animals as surrogates for man, they cross their fingers and hope for the best. A candid expression of this attitude comes from pharmacologist Stephen L. DeFelice. In describing the process of testing for lethal doses of toxic chemicals, he says:

Commonly, two rodent and one non-rodent species are used. . . . The dog, or, occasionally, the monkey is usually the choice for the non-rodent category. This is an arbitrary decision, based on economic, rather than scientific considerations; rats are cheap and gorillas are not. We hope that the rat, rather than the gorilla, is more like man in its response to drugs!"[9]

One understands the necessity for "hope" when one acquires a few examples of the diversity of species responses to toxic chemicals, some of which are so astonishing as to constitute a kind of professional folklore. There is the harrowing story of the investigators who had been studying the effects of LSD in the cat and wanted to study its effects in an elephant. They extrapolated the dose of LSD appropriate for the body size of the elephant, and administered it to the gigantic creature. The results were thus described by Knut Schmidt-Nielsen, a Duke University scientist: ". . . after the injection . . . the elephant immediately started trumpeting and running around, then he stopped and swayed, five minutes after the injection he collapsed, went into convulsions, defecated, and died."[10] The image of the convulsing, dying elephant, killed by an apparently reasonable act of extrapolation, is imprinted in the brains of a generation of animal researchers. Then there is the distressing story told by David P. Rall, Director of the NIEHS, of the tiger who was given a shot of phenobarbital, an anesthetic that had worked well on small animals: "The tiger fell asleep promptly but never woke."[11] One might conclude from this that larger animals are far more sensitive to chemicals than smaller ones—until one learns about the case of fluroxene, a drug that man has taken without toxic effects for more than a decade, but that is lethal to three much smaller species—the dog, the cat, and the rabbit.[12] And then there is the cautionary tale of penicillin, which has saved millions of human lives, but which is lethal to the guinea pig and the Syrian hamster.[13]

The same kind of diversity of species response is continually reported when one tests animals with carcinogenic chemicals. Here are examples of the kinds of species differences one finds scattered through the literature. Once again, their validity cannot be judged by laymen. These are the most common reports: Cats, dogs, rats, mice, and hamsters get cancer from 2-acetylamino-fluorene—but guinea pigs, lemmings, and the cotton rat do not.[14] Rats, mice, rabbits, and monkeys get cancer from beryllium—but guinea pigs, hamsters, chickens, dogs, cats, and goats do not.[15] Mice get cancer from dieldrin—but hamsters do not.[16] Mice get cancer from perchloroethylene—but rats, rabbits, guinea pigs, and monkeys do not.[17] Rats develop a high incidence of liver cancer from aflatoxin B_1—but mice and monkeys are "relatively resistant" to its effects[18] and Japanese quail are genetically resistant to it.[19] Man gets cancer from β-naphthylamine—but most strains of rats do not,[20] and hamsters are reported to be resistant to it.[21]

To complicate matters, the same carcinogens can affect entirely different organs in different mammalian species; for example, benzidine is reported to cause bladder tumors in man, liver tumors in the hamster, and acoustic tumors in the rat.[22] And estrogens are said to give breast tumors to mice, uterine and abdominal tumors to the guinea pig, and kidney tumors to the hamster.[23] What is more, some species get more of some kinds of tumors than they do of others; according to various scientists, the incidence of breast tumors varies from none at all in pigs and sheep to 100 percent in selected strains of mice.[24] Finally, the sex of an animal can affect the response to a carcinogen. As Benjamin van Duuren, a prominent cancer researcher, observes: "It is clear from the results of the chronic feeding experiments that there is a difference in tumor responses by sex and species. This can be ascribed to various factors, including differences in hormonal status of females and males and species differences in metabolic pathways."[25] Reptiles, says OSHA, have not been shown to react to carcinogens in ways comparable to mammals.[26]

In recent years, more has been learned about the reasons for the different responses in mammalian species, and one reason towers above them all. Here are the explanations given at various times by David Rall, who is an expert in animal testing for anticancer drugs and who worked at the National Cancer Institute in the 1960s before becoming the Director of the NIEHS—and before informing the nation in 1976 that mice and rats predict well for man.

[1968] I think there is quite good consistency between species if you can exclude the variability of microsomal drug metabolism.[27]

[1969] The metabolism of drugs is, however, far from comparable from species to species, as Dr. Williams and Dr. Burns documented. Not only are different metabolites formed, but, when the same metabolites are formed, they may form at different rates from one species to another. It is in this area that interspecies comparisons break down.[28]

[1973] It is, however, becoming increasingly apparent that in the hazardous process of attempting to extrapolate data for laboratory test systems to man, the major impediment is the different metabolic patterns in the various species of test organisms and man. These differences may be both qualitative in that different chemical metabolites may be produced and quantitative in that different rates of production may occur.[29]

[1974] The metabolic patterns are increasingly important because we are beginning to realize more and more clearly that very often the compound that was administered is not the ultimate carcinogen, and it takes metabolic processes within the body to create the active compound.[30]

Although Rall was considered to be particularly qualified to discuss this issue, these judgments were not his alone. In 1978 the British biochemist R. T. Williams also observed that there were "tremendous variations" within the metabolic patterns of different animal species, despite their broad similarities.[31] He reviewed the different ways in which man and a variety of animal species metabolized a group of different compounds. The species included Old World monkeys, New World monkeys, carnivores, and rodents, and the variations and inconsistencies were so striking, even within these classes, that at one point Williams remarked: "In fact, the more species one studies, the more complicated the picture tends to become."[32]

In an earlier American paper, Marcus M. Reidenberg of Cornell University Medical College had also reviewed comparative metabolic data in the same range of species, reporting the same kinds of inconsistencies; he had concluded his paper with the comment that "much about drugs can be learned in animals but 'the proper study of mankind is man.' "[33]

By now, the reader will have grasped the mischievous nature of the legacy left by James and Elizabeth Miller. In discovering that the carcinogenicity of chemicals was often the carcinogenicity of the compounds into which they were metabolized, the Millers had hurled the problem right into the one area in which researchers were least confident of mammalian similarity—that is, metabolism, the only area, as Rall put it, "where species comparisons break down." And to make matters worse, it is frequently said that there are few direct carcinogens and that the majority of carcinogens are metabolized[34]— which, if true, means that it is precisely the realm in which the majority of carcinogens do their deadly work that species-to-species extrapolation is most unreliable.

II. THE MILLERS AND BRUCE AMES

If James and Elizabeth Miller threw a spanner into the animal prediction process, they also inspired the solution to another problem that had long been distressing researchers. There was a very old theory in the field of genetics— dating back at least to 1928[35]—that cancer was actually caused by a mutation. The theory was cherished by many geneticists, but experimental evidence was unsatisfactory. Exactly how unsatisfactory it was is unclear, since conflicting statements have been made on the subject. According to H. Bartsch of IARC, data had been slowly emerging in the 1960s suggesting a relationship between mutagenesis and carcinogenesis;[36] but according to Charles Heidelberger of the USC Cancer Center in Los Angeles, experiments had shown an inverse correlation between the two phenomena.[37] In any event, the evidence in support of the theory was fragile.

After the Millers' discovery that metabolism was involved in carcinogenesis, however, some geneticists, most notably H. V. Malling,[38] saw a possible reason for the laboratory failure: The bacterial test systems in which mutagens were tested lacked mammalian metabolism. A molecular biologist named Bruce Ames brilliantly translated this theoretical insight into "technology": he introduced liver homogenate into his bacterial test system, thus creating a miniature metabolic system in a petri dish. He then tested eighteen carcinogens. The results were spectacular. In 1973, Ames announced them in a paper triumphantly entitled "Carcinogens Are Mutagens."[39] Convinced that he had discovered a rapid means of testing for carcinogenicity, Ames began a systematic testing program. In 1975, Joyce McCann, Bruce Ames, and their colleagues announced that they had tested 174 carcinogens and that 90 percent of them were mutagenic.[40] Influential publications immediately appeared—e.g., by P.N. Magee of Temple University,[41] and by Thomas H. Maugh II[42]—reporting that it was now common belief that "all" carcinogens were mutagens. "All" was an overstatement, but in the next few years, the Ames data were replicated with impressive results. Barry Commoner, using the Ames test, got even better results than Ames; he reported that the correlation between mutagens and carcinogens could be as high as 97 percent.[43] Takashi Sugimura, Director of the National Cancer Center Research Institute in Japan, announced that 400 chemicals had been tested and that 80–90 percent of the carcinogens had been mutagens, and that 70–80 percent of the noncarcinogens had been nonmutagens,[44] and he and several colleagues reported, although they were later to qualify that conclusion, "In spite of many arguments to the contrary, it is now generally concluded that most mutagens are carcinogens and vice versa."[45]

Imposing statistical support for the mutation theory of cancer now existed, but it required a causal explanation. To demonstrate that mutations actually caused cancer, biological, not just statistical, evidence was needed. By following various lines of reasoning, supporters of the mutation theory of cancer ferreted some biological evidence out of the literature. The logic of their search is clearly explained by J. E. Trosko and Chia-Cheng Chang, and the principal lines of deduction are summarized here. If a mutation caused cancer, scientists reasoned, then, since a mutation is a heritable and self-replicating phenomenon, all the cells in a given tumor should logically be descendants of a single cell. They scoured the literature for information that might support the idea of a single-cell origin of cancer, and found some: Several researchers had reported in earlier transplantation experiments that a malignancy could evolve from a single cell; and evidence for the single-cell theory was also deduced from the study of women with a rare medical condition. In addition, the scientists reasoned, since mutations are linked in bacteria to unrepaired damage to DNA, it should be possible to show that cancer in human beings was linked to unrepaired damage to DNA. They hunted for evidence for that idea too and found some: A few years earlier, J. E. Cleaver and J. E. Trosko (whose analysis is being summarized here) had discovered that the skin cells of people suffering from the rare disease called xeroderma pigmentosum lacked a certain enzyme needed to repair DNA damage from ultraviolet radiation and were, consequently, acutely susceptible to skin cancer; thus, in people as well as bacteria, concluded the scientists, there was a relationship between defective repair of damage to DNA and cancer.[46] Of the two types of supporting evidence, the second was considered by a number of prominent geneticists to be the more telling; Richard B. Setlow of Brookhaven Laboratories[47] and P. N. Magee of Temple University[48] considered xeroderma pigmentosum to be the principal evidence for the idea that DNA damage was a cause of cancer.

Thus, a new theory of cancer causation was launched. As the Japanese geneticists observed, it did not have universal support, and the arguments against it will be reviewed later. But the combination of the Millers' discovery and Ames' discovery thrilled many in the world of genetics and of carcinogenesis. As Gary Flamm of the National Cancer Institute put it, the somatic-cell mutation theory of cancer had merged with the electrophilic theory of chemical carcinogenesis.[49]

Another idea was also launched at that time which was to reverberate throughout the world of cancer research: the one-molecule theory. In 1971, Bruce Ames had published a paper which said:

It is worth emphasizing, however, that one molecule of a mutagen is enough to cause a mutation. . . . My general feeling is that if a compound is a mutagen in any organism then it should not be used on humans unless there is definitive evidence that it is neither mutagenic nor carcinogenic in animals, or unless the benefit outweighs the possible risk.[50] [Emphasis added]

Whether Ames was actually the first to attribute this power to one molecule of a mutagenic chemical is not clear, but after his endorsement of the idea, it was immediately integrated into the repertoire of those concerned with cancer prevention. By the mid-1970s, as we have seen, the notion that even one molecule of an industrial chemical could trigger deadly and irreversible cancer was being disseminated to Congress, the press, and the public by campaigners for the Toxic Substances Control Act.

III. ISAAC BERENBLUM (PART ONE)

In the excitement generated by the Miller and Ames discoveries which launched the regulatory and prevention program in the United States, little attention was paid to another discovery—this one made by Isaac Berenblum. Berenblum, who works at the Weizmann Institute of Science in Israel and whose career in carcinogenesis is almost as old as the field itself, had actually made several important contributions. In this section his earliest discovery, and those of the scientists who built on that discovery, will be described.

In 1929, Berenblum published a paper in which he reported that he had repeatedly painted mouse skin with a carcinogenic tar—an experiment which had always produced cancers—but when he also applied a chemical compound called dichloroethyl sulfide, no cancers appeared: The second compound had inhibited the carcinogenic process.[51] No one had previously been aware that chemical antagonists to the carcinogenic process existed: Berenblum had discovered the first anticarcinogen—the first chemical that *inhibited* the development of cancer.

At first, knowledge of the phenomenon grew slowly. Lee W. Wattenberg of the University of Minnesota, one of the foremost American specialists in the field, reports that for some thirty years, other anticarcinogens effective in mouse skin had been found in only four classes of chemical compounds.[52] But with the discovery that chemicals were metabolized into carcinogens, research leaped forward. By 1976, Wattenberg reported that many new anticarcinogens had been discovered, and that they were effective in many animal organs, not simply in mouse skin.[53] By 1978, he reported that anticarcinogens were being discovered in so many chemical classes that it was no longer possible to predict where they might next show up.[54] And by 1979, he reported that they were of a great many kinds: They were natural substances as well as synthetic, and they ranged from simple inorganic compounds to complex organic molecules.[55] It was that diversity, said Wattenberg, which "indicates that this capacity to inhibit does not reside in restricted chemical characteristics and suggests that a considerable number of other inhibitors not yet identified almost certainly exist."[56]

In this brief report little can be said about the complexities of the phenomenon of anticarcinogenesis, but one factor should be mentioned. That factor is time—in experimental terms, the time interval between the application to an animal of the carcinogen and of the inhibiting chemical. According to Hans Falk of the NCI, the maximal effectiveness of the inhibition is usually reached when the animal ingests the carcinogen and the anticarcinogen at the same time, and effectiveness diminishes as the interval grows greater. In other cases, however, the maximal effectiveness is reached when the anticarcinogen is administered during a period which can range from a week before to a month or more after the administration of the carcinogen. Depending on the substance and when the animal ingests it, the anticarcinogen can either delay the appearance of tumors, diminish their number slightly or drastically, or prevent tumor development completely.[57]

The anticarcinogen can also, at times, do one other thing which is of particular importance: It can *reverse* the early effects of carcinogenic chemicals. In a 1971 paper, Hans Falk included in the definition of anticarcinogenesis the power of a chemical to arrest the development of "initiated" cells.[58] Later reports, however, pertain to cells that have already undergone precancerous or cancerous changes. In 1974, the NCI sponsored a workshop on the possibilities of reversing early cellular changes;[59] in 1976, Wattenberg was discussing the "reversing of early stages of neoplasia";[60] and by 1978, Michael Sporn of the NCI was reporting a case of reversal of "precancerous lesions of epithelial cells" in organ culture.[61] This tells us something exceedingly curious: During the very years that some students of carcinogenesis and mutagenesis were informing the country that chemical cancer was an "irreversible" process, students of anticarcinogenesis (many of them the same people) were actually discovering that the early stages of the process could, at least temporarily, be arrested or reversed.

According to Wattenberg, the most intensively studied anticarcinogen with the capacity to produce such a reversal is Vitamin A and its synthetic analogs called retinoids.[62] Retinoids produced the reversal in cell culture reported by Michael Sporn,[63] and the NCI conference on reversal of early neoplasia concentrated heavily on Vitamin A and its analogs.[64] Vitamin A is the only anticarcinogen which is being considered for human use, not in its natural form, which is fiercely toxic in high doses, but rather in the form of the synthetics. In addition to its power to reverse the early cellular changes of cancer, the record of Vitamin A as an inhibitor of carcinogenesis is impressive. It has inhibited tumors of the forestomach and cervix in Syrian hamsters treated with carcinogenic polycyclic hydrocarbons;[65] it has inhibited prostate tumors in mice treated with the carcinogen methylcholanthrene;[66] and the synthetic analog 13-cis-retinoic acid has inhibited bladder cancer in rats treated with the carcinogen N-methyl-N-nitrosourea.[67] In addition, it has been reported that retinoids have inhibited precancerous tissue changes caused by asbestos,[68] and have inhibited malignant transformation of mouse fibroblasts caused both by radiation and by chemicals.[69] There is, finally, strong animal evidence that a deficiency of Vitamin A causes carcinogens to have a more intense effect.[70] In sum, Vitamin A, natural or synthetic, is an example of a potent and wide-ranging anticarcinogen.

Very little is known about the mechanisms of carcinogenesis inhibition, although some hypotheses exist. The first insight into a mechanism came in 1956 when scientists discovered how a carcinogenic azo dye had been inhibited by the carcinogen 3-methylcholanthrene. They found that one carcinogen induced enzymes which converted the other carcinogen to inactive or noncarcinogenic metabolites. This was, in fact, a pioneer study in the field of metabolism, and it opened up the entire realm of research into enzyme induction, which is critical to the understanding of both carcinogenesis and anticarcinogenesis.[71] By 1978, scientists had enough experimental evidence to suspect that carcinogen inhibitors might be working through a great variety of mechanisms. Wattenberg has thus summarized the possibilities: (1) Anticarcinogens may alter the metabolism of the carcinogen by decreasing its activation, by increasing the detoxification process, or by doing both; (2) they may scavenge the active molecular species of carcinogens and prevent them from reaching critical target sites in the cell; and (3) they may compete with each other, thus inhibiting the carcinogenic effect. There are also, he says, mechanisms "involving reversal of early phases of the carcinogenic process."[72]

To the layman, particularly if he has been taught to think in exclusively chemical terms, the existence of an antagonist to carcinogens may seem paradoxical, but to the scientist who thinks in biological terms, it is not paradoxical at all. As Berenblum wrote in 1978, addressing himself to fellow scientists:

We all know that biological processes in general can be influenced in two opposite ways—by being stimulated, augmented, or speeded up or by being inhibited, delayed, or actually blocked—and that either of these modifying influences may function naturally (i.e., through age, sex, hormonal and immunological status of the animal, etc.), they may be the consequence of environmental factors (diet, infection, occupation, etc.), or they can be artificially induced in planned experiments, to serve as analytical tools.[73]

This statement gives one a helpful perspective on both carcinogenesis and anticarcinogenesis. It allows one to see that researchers have actually been investigating two faces of the same coin: They have discovered that physiological processes can convert chemicals into carcinogens and they have also discovered that physiological processes can detoxify chemicals that are carcinogens.

The discovery of the existence of this biochemical point-counterpoint has created significant problems for those scientists who are trying to assess the precise effects of chemicals in man. Again, Vitamin A is a good example.

In 1980, even as powerful evidence of the anticarcinogenicity of Vitamin A was building up, Sanford A. Miller, Director of the Bureau of Foods for the FDA, was discussing that vitamin in the following way at an MIT conference: "At low levels, Vitamin A is an essential nutrient. At high levels it is a potent, toxic substance that is a teratogen, and under some circumstances may possibly be a carcinogen. Its effect at extremely low levels . . . is not known. If Vitamin A is indeed a carcinogen, how then should it be regulated?"[74] Is Vitamin A causing cancer or is it inhibiting cancer or is it doing both? It is a baffling question. And clearly, a similar question could be asked about other substances as well.

The problem is equally perplexing in the realm of mutagenesis, where antimutagens have also been reported—and in 1979 that perplexity was expressed by eleven of Japan's most prominent cancer researchers and coauthors of a paper on the relationship of mutagens and carcinogens: M. Nagao, et al., citing several experiments in which naturally occurring compounds had potentiated, reduced, or obliterated the mutagenic reactions of various chemicals, both natural and industrial, complained: "This balance between activation and detoxification of genotoxic-carcinogens makes the evaluation of environmental mutagens very difficult."[75]

It also makes it very difficult to envisage a fully successful cancer prevention plan. John Higginson, Founding Director of the IARC, observed that even if one day all mechanisms of cancer were understood, one still might not be able to reduce cancer to a minimum level because "it is possible that factors leading to one cancer may protect against another."[76]

The broadest implication of the fact that human beings are being simultaneously bombarded by both carcinogens and anticarcinogens was discussed at a 1979 cancer conference by Wattenberg. He put it in the form of a series of questions:

. . . what is the current impact of these compounds in man? . . . Is there, in fact, a significant balance between carcinogenesis and anticarcinogenesis? Or, to rephrase it another way: When epidemiological studies demonstrate different tumor incidence figures in population groups or different geographic areas, are these due always to differences in exposure to carcinogens or, in some instances, are these due to the fact that some groups are protected?

He then responded to his own questions in the following manner:

The answer to all three questions, no matter how we phrase it, is we simply don't know. The fact that there are a large number of inhibitors, that they are diverse in structure, obviously would support the probability that man is, in fact, being affected by these; but I think that solid, firm evidence that this occurs simply doesn't exist at the present time.[77]

Given the fluid contemporary use of the word "evidence," it is important to state here that by "solid, firm evidence," Wattenberg was referring to the highest epidemiological standards for such evidence—reliable findings in man supported by a thorough laboratory demonstration of a biological explanation for those findings. There are, he says, good, careful case studies and indirect laboratory studies which conclude that human beings are affected by one group of anticarcinogens (the indoles in cabbagey vegetables) in the same way as animals, but by the most rigorous scientific standards, the case is still unproved.

Even a few verified examples, however, still would not tell us how to assess the overall "balance" between carcinogenesis and anticarcinogenesis. To that, there is no answer. There is, however, a counterquestion. At an entirely different cancer conference in 1978, a few months before Wattenberg had declared that it was both obvious and probable, if unproved, that man was being protected by anticarcinogens, two other scientists were speculating about the other half of the problem, namely, about the carcinogenic barrage to which man has been subjected by both nature and industry. The scientists were Joseph Rodricks of the FDA and Gary Flamm of NCI. Rodricks pointed out that the common statement that there are "four million chemicals" is misleading. Most compounds studied, he said, "had their origins in nature," and "most chemical compounds occur in nature." He added, "My guess is that there are hundreds of millions of chemical compounds in nature."[78] Flamm, for his part, described some of the data on natural carcinogens, guessed that there are "tens, hundreds, thousands of natural substances that are carcinogenic," and, on considering the additional carcinogens that had been introduced into the environment by the petrochemical revolution, he exclaimed, "How did we survive? As a biologist, I'd have calculated that the human race would be extinct by now. But that didn't occur."[79] Why didn't it? That is the counterquestion. And why do three out of four Americans die of causes other than cancer? Part of the answer may lie in what both the Japanese scientists and Wattenberg call the "balance" between the activation and detoxification of both natural and industrial carcinogens.

IV. ISAAC BERENBLUM (PART TWO)

In addition to his discovery of anticarcinogenesis, Berenblum was one of a small group of scientists who made a set of discoveries that were to revolutionize the understanding of carcinogenesis. To understand the magnitude of the revolution one must know that until quite recently, the progression of chemical cancer, as understood by most researchers, consisted of three parts: initiation, preneoplasia, and transformation. As those terms were defined by Thomas Maugh II in *Science* in 1974: Initiation referred to the changes in cells right after they had been exposed to the carcinogen; preneoplasia was the long and mysterious "latency period," which could last twenty years or more in human beings; and transformation was the abrupt onset of a series of cellular changes that took place when that long waiting period was over and the exposed cells began the proliferation which terminated in a malignant tumor. Reflecting this understanding of the process, scientists had been approaching the problem both at its beginning and at its end: Some tried to destroy the malignant cells with chemotherapy after they had appeared, and others sought to prevent cellular contact with the carcinogen before the process could begin. But what was happening in that long latency period called preneoplasia, said Maugh, no one knew, and almost no effort had been made to find out.[80]

That last comment was not quite accurate. Some scientists had tried to find out, and they had uncovered a phenomenon thirty years earlier that bore directly on the mysterious latency period. That line of research, however, had come to appear to the consensus of scientific opinion to be of trivial value, which is why *Science* was unaware of it. In fact, the consensus was wrong and the results of that line of research were shortly to startle the world of carcinogenesis and generate a headline in *Science* saying: "Carcinogenesis Gets More Complicated"[81]—a masterly understatement.

The story of the "complication" of carcinogenesis began in the early 1940s, and it is a fascinating tale of the convergence of two lines of inquiry, compounded by an extraordinary number of confusions and controversies. The first line of inquiry was Berenblum's. Just as he was the first to discover anticarcinogenesis, the power of chemicals to *inhibit* the action of carcinogens, he was also the first to discover co-carcinogenesis, the power of chemicals to *potentiate* or *enhance* the action of carcinogens.[82] Specifically, he had discovered a peculiar natural substance, croton oil, which if applied simultaneously to mouse skin with low doses of the carcinogen benzo(*a*)pyrene produced many more tumors than did benzo(*a*)pyrene alone. This discovery that croton oil had this strange enhancing power led to a long series of other experiments by Berenblum alone and with his co-worker Philippe Shubik between 1941 and 1949, the purpose of which, says Berenblum, was to study the nature of the newly discovered co-carcinogenic action of croton oil and to study the nature of the changes in mouse skin during the long latency period of carcinogenesis.[83]

One of the results of this series of experiments on co-carcinogenesis was the discovery that croton oil had yet an additional power: Not only could it enhance carcinogenesis if applied *simultaneously* with the carcinogen, it could also enhance carcinogenesis if it was applied *after* the carcinogen.[84] Whether Berenblum and Shubik were the exclusive discoverers of this strange delayed power of croton oil is unclear. Jean Marx, in *Science*, identifies Berenblum as the discoverer of the general phenomenon;[85] but the National Cancer Advisory Board Subcommittee on Environmental Carcinogenesis, as cited by OSHA, says that the phenomenon was pioneered by J. C. Mottram, and was "markedly accelerated" by Berenblum and Shubik.[86] On the other hand, Benjamin van Duuren of NYU merely credits J. C. Mottram with developing Berenblum's discovery,[87] and Erich Hecker of Heidelberg says that Mottram contributed "an important modification" to "the Berenblum experiments."[88]

This historical uncertainty appears to reflect the uncertainty of Mottram's own data. A footnote in a Berenblum paper in the 1940s observes:

These published results by Mottram, carried out shortly before his death, are based on relatively small numbers of animals. His interesting conclusions must, therefore, be accepted provisionally, awaiting their confirmation by others on a more adequate scale.[89]

What is certain, despite the confusion, is that the new phenomenon of temporal enhancement was Berenblum's original theme. Ultimately, it was established that not only could croton oil operate both *simultaneously* and *belatedly* as a carcinogen enhancer, but that it had no effect whatever when applied *before-*

hand. These findings were interpreted to mean, says Berenblum, that the start of the carcinogenesis process and its completion involved separate mechanisms and stages of development.[90]

The second line of inquiry was that of Peyton Rous. And here once again there is some historical confusion. Rous is sometimes identified as the primary creative figure in these experiments,[91] but for some reason the NAS document as cited by OSHA omits his name entirely.[92] Berenblum himself, however, accords a major role to Rous.[93] Rous was working on a problem quite different from the one that concerned Berenblum. He was trying to understand why the benign papillomas induced in rabbit skin by a carcinogen tended to regress, and whether these unstable tumors were authentic precursors of cancer. Between 1941 and 1944, Rous and various co-workers conducted a series of experiments on rabbit skin and demonstrated that the benign papillomas that had apparently regressed completely could be made to reappear at the original site, if one subjected the skin to irritants—i.e., by punching holes in the rabbit's skin or by applying corrosive substances such as turpentine. Rous inferred from this that the initial tumor cells induced by the carcinogen had never vanished, but had remained in a latent or dormant state and had been "reawakened." He, too, concluded that the original induction process and the "reawakening" process involved separate mechanisms.[94]

Although the mouse skin and the rabbit skin experiments were quite different, the ultimate interpretations were the same: Both had produced the conclusion that initial exposure to the carcinogen created a latent cellular phenomenon which could be enhanced or "reawakened," and that both processes occurred in discrete steps.

After these historic experiments, there ensued a period of considerable chaos, for the various research groups had been using entirely different concepts to describe the same discovery. Berenblum's group had called the initial stage "precarcinogenesis" and the second stage "epicarcinogenesis" and had identified the later development of benign papillomas into malignant tumors as a third stage called "metacarcinogenesis." Rous, on the other hand, had called the first two stages "initiation" and "promotion." Mottram had used yet other terms. Under these circumstances, communication was impossible. Rous, accordingly, proposed that everyone use his clearer terms, and everyone agreed to do so.[95] Thus, in the midst of a terminological imbroglio which added to the confusion over authorship, the "initiation-promotion theory" or the "two-stage theory" of carcinogenesis was born.

In experimental terms, the most striking aspects of the "two-stage" theory of carcinogenesis were the roles played by dose and time. Here are some of the generalizations for the data that come from Berenblum and van Duuren:

- The actual number of tumors that appeared when a promoter was applied after a dose of the initiator carcinogen was quantitatively related to the initiating dose.[96]
- On the other hand, the time it took to produce the tumors by promotion was irrelevant to dose: Whether the initiating dose was very large or very small,

the tumors appeared inexorably in approximately thirty-five days. This suggested that a precise period of time was required to promote initiated cells into visible growths.[97]

- While there were insufficient data to calculate the exact time of initiating action, the time was thought to be a matter of "hours, rather than weeks or months."[98]
- The effects of initiators were extremely persistent. A single treatment with the initiator followed by repeated applications of a promoter would produce tumors whether the interval between the two applications was two weeks, thirty-six weeks, or fifty-six weeks. Only when the promoter was applied after intervals of fifty-eight weeks and sixty-two weeks did the tumor incidence decrease significantly.[99]

There were, in other words, clear quantitative patterns in the latency period: "Berenblum's experiments" had obviously produced a major new step in the investigation of carcinogenesis.

Oddly enough, instead of becoming increasingly important to the professionals in the field, the initiation and promotion experiments became increasingly unimportant to many. It is not difficult to see why it happened. There were a great many oddities in this field of research, and two were particularly odd. First, only one promoter had been discovered during a twenty-year period—Berenblum's croton oil. The chemical constituents of that oil, which were actually causing the promotion effects, were not known until the 1960s, after extraordinary analytic labors by scientists from many countries, most notably Benjamin van Duuren of NYU and Erich Hecker of Heidelberg; and only then were a few other promoting agents discovered.[100] Thus, to a whole generation of scientists, croton oil appeared to be the only promoter in existence, and many thought it an aberration. The second peculiarity of these experiments was the fact that the only species on which the promoting effect of croton oil could be demonstrated was the mouse. Indeed, croton oil was "species-specific": In 1950, Shubik discovered that it was effective in mouse skin but not in the skin of the rat, guinea pig, or rabbit.[101] This, too, led many to the conclusion that the entire phenomenon of two-stage carcinogenesis with its complex findings was a chemical-genetic curiosity having no significance wider than itself. In fact, between the early 1940s and the mid-1970s, two-stage carcinogenesis had only been discovered by means of studying the effects of croton oil on mouse skin. As late as 1976, van Duuren was still reporting that most work on co-carcinogenesis and all work on promotion had only been done with mouse skin.[102] And in 1977, too, Roy Albert of NYU and Chairman of the Carcinogen Assessment Group of the EPA said that while the phenomenon of promotion had been experimentally established beyond question, most of the work had been done on mouse skin.[103] It is thus unsurprising that many had come to see the phenomenon as inconsequential. As the *British Medical Journal* put it, speaking of Rous and Berenblum, "experimental work on the stages of carcinogenesis seemed little more than a laboratory game, relevant only to the skin of rabbits and mice."[104]

Not everyone, however, shared this view. Berenblum worked on the phenomenon systematically, and so did other scientists who did see wide implications in these apparently narrow discoveries. Then, in the late 1970s, to the astonishment of those who had minimized these experiments, evidence of promotion was reported in a variety of different biological systems: It had been identified, although with no great degree of certainty, in experiments on the thyroid, the liver, the lungs, the breast, and colon;[105] and, finally, in cell cultures.[106] Quite abruptly, the fact that carcinogenesis might occur in two distinct stages, a latent stage and a promoted stage, was no longer an oddity pertaining to mouse skin. The theory had suddenly become respectable. In 1978, one enthusiastic scientist observed that it was "universally accepted."[107]

In that same year (like the Millers before them) Isaac Berenblum, by then in his mid-seventies, and Philippe Shubik, his collaborator, received the Bertner Award for their achievements in the field of carcinogenesis.[108] The role of Berenblum had been particularly striking: He had discovered cancer inhibitors, he had discovered co-carcinogenesis, he had discovered the first chemical promoter, and he was one of the discoverers of the phenomenon of initiation and promotion. It was an astonishing record of achievement. In 1980, Berenblum and the Millers were awarded prizes of $100,000 for the fundamentality of their discoveries.[109] The old scientist working in Israel who had glimpsed a broad principle in his mouse skin experiments and who stubbornly stuck to his unfashionable quest had contributed to a revolution in the field. The result, as *Science* put it bemusedly, was that carcinogenesis suddenly became much more "complicated."

It was suddenly so complicated that scientists were uncertain how to use the terms "initiators," "promoters," and "co-carcinogens." Once again there was a whirlpool of terminological confusion. As van Duuren observed in 1976, the terms "co-carcinogens" and "promoters" are often used interchangeably.[110] And as recently as 1978, Berenblum was still patiently explaining to fellow scientists how to differentiate between the two. In essence, said Berenblum, a co-carcinogen was a "permissive" agent or physiological condition—and he illustrated "permissive" action with hormones, caloric intake, and dietary influence. By contrast, he said, promoters were actual "components" of the carcinogenic action.[111]

An extraordinary vision of chemical carcinogenesis had emerged from this research. Not only was man being bombarded by direct and "ultimate" carcinogens, but he was being bombarded by co-carcinogens, carcinogen promoters, and anticarcinogens, not to mention capricious chemicals which, depending on dose, timing, and the coexistence of other chemicals, performed one or more of these functions in more than one part of the body and in more than one temporal sequence. What is more, the bombardment was coming from within the body as well as from outside the body, from nature as well as from industry.

This incredible array of new interactions, however, did not put an end to the complexity. The implications of the "two-stage" theory of carcinogenesis were even more complicated than this. Over the years, in fact, evidence had accumulated indicating that the theory had been baptized too soon, and that there were considerably more than two stages. As early as 1949, Berenblum and Shubik were aware of this possibility; they had concluded from their experiments on promotion that "carcinogenesis is at least a two-stage process."[112] Shubik followed this up with a series of other experiments in the early 1950s and concluded that the transition from a benign papilloma to a malignant tumor involved at least one and perhaps several distinct steps.[113] Aware of these experiments, Sir Richard Doll, of Oxford University, Britain's foremost epidemiologist, used human data to test the multistage hypothesis; he analyzed human mortality rates for seventeen types of cancers and concluded that the resultant data might be explained by "a complex process of perhaps six or seven stages."[114] In the early 1960s, several scientists reached the conclusion that there was more than one stage in the initiating process itself.[115] In 1964, another researcher concluded that the promoting process was also made up of two separate stages.[116] In 1975, epidemiology studies by Irving Selikoff and E. Cuyler Hammond demonstrated that smoking was a promoter for asbestos, and that the two agents acted on two entirely different stages of the carcinogenic process;[117] and, according to Richard Peto of Oxford, the ultimate determining stage of lung carcinogenesis in smokers came just a few years before death.[118] By the time the "two-stage" theory of cancer was widely recognized in 1978, it was no longer a two-stage theory at all, but a multistage theory. In August of that year, the *British Medical Journal* informed British scientists that benign neoplasia apparently evolved into malignant neoplasia in three or more stages.[119] In the same month, *Science* informed American scientists: "Most investigators now think that it involves as many as five or six discrete events."[120] Obviously nobody knew exactly how many stages there were—but it appeared to be the universal belief that there were many, with many different mechanisms operating at each stage.

And even this does not capture the full complexity of the vision of carcinogenesis that had so abruptly emerged during this period. It had also become clear from both human and laboratory data that various stages of carcinogenesis could also retreat from malignancy as well as progress toward malignancy. There was no longer any question about it: The mysterious process could work backward. By the late 1970s, there was clinical evidence that developed cancers (neuroblastomas, choriocarcinomas, teratomas, and Burkitt's lymphomas) could occasionally regress.[121] There was clinical evidence that latent cancers existed in human beings (in the prostate, lung, kidney, and thyroid) that neither developed nor did any harm, but just remained there in an apparently arrested or dormant condition.[122] There was statistical evidence from human studies that the final virulent proliferation of cells in the lungs of smokers could be inhibited by the cessation of smoking.[123] There was laboratory evidence that the promotion of dormant tumor cells could be interrupted simply by stopping the application of the secondary substance.[124] There was laboratory evidence that anticarcinogen chemicals could arrest, inhibit, or reverse the early stages of neoplasia.

By 1978, eight years after the Surgeon General had been informed that cancer prevention was possible, and two years after the passage of the Toxic Substances Control Act, the modern picture of carcinogenesis had been changed beyond recognition. And natural physiological processes, and natural substances, were inextricably enmeshed in the weird complexity.

Chapter 6

The Mutating Theory of Cancer

"Carcinogens Are Mutagens."[1]
—Bruce Ames et al., 1973

While the suggestion is reasonable, there is no evidence that carcinogenesis involves mutation of the chromatin of a cell. . . .[2]
—William Lijinsky, 1978

The one major problem that continues to diminish the immediate importance of the results of every experiment in this field [carcinogenesis] and casts a shadow of uncertainty on the relevance of every observation is our inability to define the malignant cell. . . .[3]
—Frederick F. Becker, 1979

We have decided by definition that initiation is non-reversible. . . .[4]
—John Higginson, 1979

Of all the discoveries to emerge from basic research, the one with the most extraordinary implications for our lives is the mutation theory of cancer, and the technological application of that theory by Bruce Ames, in the form of a simple test. If the mutation theory of cancer is true, then, in principle, the geneticists are on their way to discovering the predominant mechanism of cancer; and if the mutagen tests can predict for carcinogenesis in animals (on the assumption that animals can predict cancer in man), then we have a bona fide "cancer test," one which works rapidly, and can identify the carcinogenic substances in the environment, so that we can act to get rid of them—or, if we cannot get rid of them, avoid them. The tests, in fact, could screen tens of thousands of industrial chemicals within a relatively short time and ascertain which were causes of cancer in man. The practical significance of Ames' discovery, then, appeared to have extraordinary significance both for control over exogenous carcinogens and for control over the economic system. That is why I have saved until now a full discussion of both the test, which seemed to have validated the mutation theory of cancer, and the theory itself.

The first question to be answered, as we pick up the story, is: Was the mutagen test valid—meaning, did it really predict carcinogenicity in animals, and did it predict cancer in man? And the second question is: Was the mutation theory of cancer itself valid, and did it have a sufficient biological base? These were the two realms of controversy, and I will discuss each in turn.

THE TEST

Within a few years of the test's dramatic arrival on the scene—that is, of the announcement, to the excitement of all cancer researchers, that there was an astoundingly high correlation between carcinogens and mutagens—trouble with the discovery began to emerge. It took the form of problems in the test results themselves, and problems pertaining to predictive capacity. As this array of vicissitudes is spread before the reader, *it is crucial for him to remember at all times* that Ames and other mutagen testers were correlating *bacterial* data with *animal* data. Thus, throughout the following discussion, every time the word "mutagen" is used, it means a chemical that has been reported to cause a permanent and heritable change in the DNA of a *cell* (e.g., of a bacterium such as *Salmonella* or *E. coli*), and every time the word "carcinogen" is used, it means a chemical that has been reported to cause cancer in one or more *animals*.

Mutagens and Carcinogens

The first problem to surface pertained to the 90 percent correlation between mutagens and carcinogens. Although several prestigious scientists—notably Iain Purchase of Britain and Takashi Sugimura of Japan—had confirmed that correlation, others found when they used the Ames test or when they reviewed the experiments of scientists who had used other mutagen tests that they were discovering very different kinds of correlations, correlations that caused some to doubt the reliability of the test itself. Most of the correlations reported between 1976 and 1979 were very high, about 85 percent, but the range—between 55 and 60 percent to 97 percent—was disconcerting.[5]

There were a number of reasons for the diversity of correlations between bacterial and animal data. For one thing, biology is rarely precise, and some variation was to be expected. For another, there was the tyranny of percentages. The number of chemicals in these different studies varied greatly, and thus the percentages are of varying significance. The diversity of correlations was also due in part to the problem identified by Marvin Legator of the University of Texas, who informed *Science* in 1978 that the results of short-term tests varied widely from laboratory to laboratory because different methods and systems were being used.[6] There may also have been errors in the data; the lowest correlation—55 percent—has been challenged by Ames' colleague, Kim Hooper, as a faulty calculation.[7] But not all of this variation was simply due to these factors. The most fundamental explanation is exemplified by an extensive study performed by Marvin Legator in which he tested 494 chemicals in forty-five structural classes and found that the correlation between mutagenicity and carcinogenicity existed only in certain classes.[8] As geneticist Gary Flamm of the National Cancer Institute explained it at a cancer conference: "The extent of correlation depends on what classes of chemical carcinogens we are looking at. Chances are that if we looked at just estrogens, we might find absolutely zero correlation, whereas if we were looking at nitrosamines the correlation might be 100%."[9] Takashi Sugimura also observed that the correlation might vary sharply as a function of chemical class.[10]

After his first exultant announcement—"Carcinogens Are Mutagens"— Ames acknowledged the conditional nature of the phenomenon. In *Science* in 1979, he reported again that "about 90% (158 out of 176)" of the chemical carcinogens tested by Joyce McCann, himself, and their colleagues were mutagenic, and stressed the fact that the test had been "independently validated" by others with similar results; of the three he cited as his most important validators, two were Iain Purchase and Takashi Sugimura. He then qualified that 90 percent, however, pointing out that the success rate was "markedly lower" for some classes of carcinogens, such as hydrazines and heavily chlorinated chemicals.[11] Similarly, his colleague Joyce McCann discussed its newly found limitations; she testified at the OSHA hearings that the test does "rather poorly" with some classes of carcinogens.[12]

Mutagens and Noncarcinogens

The second problem to surface pertained to the capacity of the mutagen tests to identify *non*carcinogens. To put it in the form of a question: Did the chemicals that showed nonmutagenic results in bacteria also show noncarcinogenic results in animals? This was a crucial issue, for if mutagen tests were to be used to predict for carcinogens, then the tests had to be able to differentiate carcinogens from noncarcinogens. As the IARC puts it, in defining the criteria for acceptable "short-term" tests, "the test should have been validated with respect to known animal carcinogens *and found to have a high capacity for discriminating between carcinogens and noncarcinogens*"[13] (emphasis added). Here, too, there was trouble. The Ames test and other mutagen tests had repeatedly reported mutagenic activity in chemicals that are reported in animal tests to be noncarcinogenic—a disparity known as the "false positive." And to appreciate the significance of a false positive, the layman need only consider the problems that would arise if pregnancy tests frequently signaled the existence of pregnancy in women who were *not* pregnant—or if blood sugar tests often showed high levels of blood sugar in people who did *not* have diabetes. Some false positives are inevitable in all biological tests, so the question really pertained to the frequency with which this was occurring. Between 1975 and 1979, rates of 24 to 35 percent of false positives were reported, with Ames himself reporting the lowest number of such false positives.[14]

In the realm of noncarcinogens, McCann and Ames were well aware of problems. They attributed the problems, however, to the animal tests themselves. In 1977, they expressed considerable consternation over the inadequacy of the noncarcinogenic findings in animal tests and declared that criteria for animal noncarcinogens were "vital," since mutagen tests could only be validated if they were shown to be able to differentiate successfully between carcinogens and noncarcinogens. They said of the animal noncarcinogens used in their own study:

The National Cancer Institute has recently [before 1975] published criteria for adequate carcinogenicity tests. . . . The application of such criteria in evaluating noncarcinogenicity would mean that virtually no chemicals classified as "noncarcinogens" in this study could be considered noncarcinogens with a high degree of certainty.[15]

Later, at the OSHA hearings, Joyce McCann similarly testified that the quality of the noncarcinogenic animal data was deficient and was causing "some so-called false positives." She said:

What in fact happened is that we did have some non-correlations. We had some false negatives in Salmonella, chemicals that were carcinogens in the animals, and we had some so-called false positives, chemicals that were positive in Salmonella but negative in the animal cancer tests.

So what we did in those cases is look at the data from both systems and what we found is that the animal cancer test data for the chemicals that showed some mutagenic activity in our tests but were negative in the animal cancer tests, was in general very limited. *The tests, most of them were clearly defective in that they would have very few animals or cover a very short duration.*[16] [Emphasis added]

That most of their animal data had been "clearly defective" had always been apparent to McCann and Ames. In their 1975 paper, they had recorded their struggle to acquire the most reliable data of the period, primarily through correspondence with individual scientists. They had also recorded the serious inadequacy of those data for the scientific world to see—provided the scientific world took the trouble to read the last page of densely packed footnotes which explained the coded symbols used in the tables of data. One footnote clearly warned that carcinogenicity testing in animals was difficult and that "noncarcinogens" were particularly difficult to identify. The codes indicated the nature of the problem in the classification of carcinogens. The authors were actually working with *three* kinds of carcinogens: (1) "carcinogens," (2) "weak carcinogens," and (3) "carcinogens" in "limited studies" where "further confirmatory work is required." And the condition of the noncarcinogens was much worse. McCann and Ames were working with *four* kinds of noncarcinogens: (1) "noncarcinogens," (2) "noncarcinogens" in "limited studies" with "further confirmatory work required," (3) *"noncarcinogens"* in *"most studies,"* but reported in others as having *"weak or marginal"* carcinogenic activity, (emphasis added), and (4) an additional batch of forty-six chemicals, described as "noncarcinogens or presumed noncarcinogens." On top of this, there was an additional classification of data which were so "inadequate" that it was impossible to tell whether the chemicals were carcinogens or noncarcinogens.[17]

Despite these classificatory problems, however, the Ames team had reported in 1975 that it had discovered "few" false positives, i.e., that the correlation between nonmutagens and noncarcinogens was high, and three years later, Joyce McCann testified to OSHA: ". . . for the chemicals that registered positive in our tests that were negative in the animal cancer tests, my personal feeling is that I do not believe there is a good example of a true false positive among those." In fact, McCann thought the problem of false positives insignificant, granting only that it was a possibility.[18]

It is understandable that geneticists are far more confident of their own discipline than they are of carcinogenesis, and one can see why Ames and

McCann may have felt intuitively that if the data in their mutagen tests clashed with the data in animal tests, the mutagen data were liable to be right. Nonetheless, if the animal data, particularly the noncarcinogenic data, were as bad as the McCann-Ames paper said, those data could not be used to produce highly reliable test correlations. By 1978, a portion of the scientific community was aware that the mutagen tests were skipping classes of carcinogens and were finding carcinogens where none should be. Inevitably, the Ames test became a focus of controversy.

"Validation"

During the OSHA policy hearings of 1978, scientists were in substantial disagreement on the validity of the Ames test—and on the validity of other mutagen tests as well. The disagreement was caused, according to OSHA, by widespread confusion over the meaning of a "validated" test, and the published material supported OSHA's observations:

From the arguments raised, it was apparent that what constituted a valid test to one scientist did not necessarily constitute a valid test to another. To some witnesses "validation" meant reproducibility, while to others the term meant standardization. To others, the term meant the establishment of a correlation between results in the test and positive results for carcinogenicity. Even the use of these terms was ambiguous. Reproducibility, for example, was used by some witnesses to describe results from other short term tests, while others used the term to indicate concordance with results in long term animal bioassays [the IARC definition, and that used by Ames]. Still others referred to reproducibility within the same test or laboratory. Standardization was used to refer to criteria for test protocols in most instances. Often, the same witnesses used the term in several of the contexts described above.[19]

OSHA found it "clear" from all this that much of the disagreement about the state of validation of the different tests reflected semantic confusion rather than different interpretations of the data. It was even clearer, however, that the confusion reflected the fact that no classical validation tests had ever been conducted. When scientists genuinely want to test tests, they do not hurl competing definitions and correlations at each other in a public forum or testify, as did McCann, about their "personal feelings"—they conduct orderly studies in which standardized substances are tested "blind" by teams of scientists who have no idea what they are testing and cannot, consciously or unconsciously, influence the outcome of the tests to conform to their opinions or emotions. According to H. V. Malling, the geneticist who wrote the first published work on the metabolic activation of mutagens, no completed blind study of the mutagen tests had been done as of 1977.[20]

But in 1978, even as the witnesses at the OSHA hearings were arguing, a blind study was being conducted by the International Program for the Evaluation of Short-Term Tests for Carcinogenicity. The program, referred to earlier, was "specifically designed to examine the ability of various test systems to distinguish between known chemical carcinogens and known noncarcinogens."[21] It was a classical blind trial: Twenty-five carcinogens and seventeen noncarcinogens, carefully chosen from animal data to represent different sets of closely related chemical structures in a wide range of chemical classes, had been distributed to laboratories in several countries and none of the participating scientists had known what chemicals he was studying until the test was over. The project had begun in England and had been extended to the United States and Japan with the support of the NIEHS, the EPA, and the National Cancer Research Institute of Japan.[22] The Coordinating Committee, accordingly, consisted of eminent scientists from the three countries. The Americans were Frederick J. de Serres and Michael D. Shelby of NIEHS. Japan was represented by Takashi Sugimura. Britain was represented by Bryn Bridges of the University of Sussex, Peter Brookes of the Institute of Cancer Research at the Royal Cancer Hospital, and John Ashby and Iain Purchase of Imperial Chemical Industries, Ltd. Significantly, Takashi Sugimura and Iain Purchase, two of the scientists whose confirmations had meant the most to McCann-Ames, were now participating in a real validation process.[23]

In December 1979, a meeting was held at NIEHS at which members of the Coordinating Committee—de Serres and Shelby of NIEHS, Ashby and Purchase of ICI—explained the project and reported on the first set of findings. Much of the report was technical, but some of the major conclusions were not, and many applied both to the animal tests and to the mutagen tests.

The discovery that there was substantial trouble in the realm of the animal tests was confirmed. There were severe problems in the classification of carcinogens and noncarcinogens. The committee reported that the identification of animal carcinogens had been inconsistent in prior tests; certain chemicals had been called carcinogens by some and noncarcinogens by others. The committee had convoked an "expert group" to provide an "independent opinion" on the carcinogenicity and noncarcinogenicity of the chemicals they proposed to use in the blind test. The experts convoked included Lorenzo Tomatis of the IARC in Lyon; R. Preussman of the German Cancer Research Center in Heidelberg; and D. B. Clayson of the Eppley Cancer Research Institute in Omaha. The definition of a carcinogen was established by the "expert group" despite contradictory assessments of specific chemicals in the literature. But the identification of a noncarcinogen proved to be very difficult. The "expert group" could not find any publication in existence which had ever defined noncarcinogenicity or established the criteria for such a finding. The expert committee consequently had a great deal of trouble in establishing what was and was not a noncarcinogen and ended up breaking the noncarcinogens down into three classes—those with the best evidence, those with the poorest evidence, and a category in between. The Coordinating Committee said: ". . . these limitations in terms of classification of carcinogenicity apply to all previous studies of the validation of short-term tests for carcinogenicity."[24]

The discovery that the mutagen tests, despite remarkably high correlations, were insensitive to certain classes of chemical carcinogens (false negatives) was also confirmed. John Ashby, a member of the Coordinating Committee, estimated that "between one-quarter and a third of most carcinogens are difficult to detect in the Salmonella assay."[25]

The discovery of the false positives—the tendency of the bacterial tests to produce correlations between mutagens and *non*carcinogens—was confirmed as well.

One class of short-term tests, the bacterial repair assays, posed "serious problems," the most important of which was their positive reaction to carcinogens requiring metabolism even when the equivalent of metabolism was lacking. These bacterial tests were signaling carcinogenicity for reasons no one could understand, and they caused great "concern" to the committee.[26]

Four bacterial point mutation tests, including Ames' *Salmonella* test, were found to be equally effective at predicting carcinogenicity, but the incidence of false positives was "sufficiently high" as to cause the committee to conclude that data from such tests could not stand alone, but needed backup from test systems utilizing the cells of higher organisms: "We cannot rely on the data with bacterial test systems used in isolation, they must be used as a part of a battery of tests." No explanation of the tendency to false positives was given.[27]

In the last analysis, the committee concluded that there were "short-term" tests that could be used to predict carcinogenic activity, but said that "no single assay or battery of assays was readily apparent as best suited for the purpose."[28] Nearly all tests, said the committee, produced false negatives as well as false positives,[29] and the more tests one used, the greater the number of errors of both types. To use a battery of such tests, said the committee, would require a "tradeoff" between the two types of error.[30]

This first blind study clearly confirmed certain hopes for the Ames test and clashed with others. It supported the predictive efficacy of the test, but also pointed to the limitations of all bacterial tests. While strongly confirming the utility of the mutagen tests, provided they were surrounded by other tests to check their margin of error, the blind study had damaged the early illusion that the tests were independently accurate.

By the time these storms settled, the Ames test was still a remarkable achievement, but there was a mysterious gap between mutagenesis and carcinogenesis. In addition, those geneticists who had been following the problem closely had also learned that the animal data in the field of chemical carcinogenesis were not the Rock of Gibraltar they had supposed them to be.

Prediction

Those problems, however, were almost insignificant as compared to another—the predictive capacity of the tests. The geneticists had certainly found evidence that many animal carcinogens were mutagens, but they did not know whether the carcinogen-mutagen correlation was true *in reverse*—that is to say, whether mutagens themselves were generally carcinogens. It is on that assumption, above all, that mutagenicity can be used to predict the carcinogenicity of chemicals that have *not yet* been tested in animals. Again, an analogy is needed for the layman. If one discovers a collection of known criminals with enzyme X, does that mean that every time in the future that one detects enzyme X in a person, the person may be identified with certainty as a criminal? Clearly, it is a different question, and equally clearly, without further studies, one does not know. Thus, while it was widely believed that most animal carcinogens were mutagens, it was quite a different matter to conclude that most mutagens were animal carcinogens.

In 1977, Frederick J. de Serres of NIEHS reported that there were two schools of thought on the subject. Many proponents of mutagen tests believed, he said, that "since at least 90 percent of chemical carcinogens are mutagens, the reverse correlation is also 90 percent if not higher." On the other hand, "there is an equally vocal group which feels that the actual correlation is much lower." De Serres dismissed both views: "In actual fact, we have too little data to determine the correlation between mutagenic and carcinogenic activity. Very few of the chemicals detected as mutagens have been tested for carcinogenic activity. . . ." He warned against the danger of relying on single mutagen tests like *Salmonella* which could produce "false indictment and premature banning of economically important chemicals."[31]

At the OSHA hearings in 1978, Joyce McCann discussed the identical issue: "The evidence is now quite strong that almost all human and animal carcinogens are mutagens. It is a somewhat different question, however, whether chemicals that are turned up by short-term tests will be found to be carcinogens [i.e., are mutagens carcinogens?]. Ultimately, in evaluating the usefulness of short-term tests as predictors of carcinogenicity this is the more relevant of the two questions." Such data, she said, took much longer to generate because they could only be produced by animal tests. Although she expressed the belief that false positives would be few and advocated that the mutagen tests play an immediate role in regulation, she recommended that a close watch be kept on the emerging correlations.[32]

There was yet another predictive problem confronting the geneticists. They could not say which mutations were actually linked to cancer. It had been postulated some years before that carcinogenesis was linked to a certain type of mutation ("frameshift"). But, reported Bryn Bridges, after enough experiments were conducted, the hypothesis fell apart. Some chemical classes of carcinogens produced the suspected type of mutation, but other chemical classes produced another type ("base-pair substitutions"), and yet other chemical classes produced both types. There was no consistency, no common denominator.[33] As of 1980, there was still no answer; as Bernard D. Davis of Harvard Medical School observed, progress has been made in relating carcinogenesis to mutagenesis, but most of the basic questions are unanswered—the first of those, he said, being the inability to identify the specific mutations that are linked to carcinogenic effects.[34]

Finally, it is rarely known what the effects of mutagenic chemicals might be on human beings. As Lawrence Fishbein put it in 1972: ". . . we have no way at present to evaluate the effects of chronic exposure to any type of mutagenic agent on man himself." Six years later, according to British scientists who were still quoting Fishbein, the situation was largely unchanged.[35] In this intellectual void, some geneticists were making educated guesses. In 1977, Ames and McCann said: "We believe that this damage [to DNA by environmental mutagens], accumulating during our lifetime, initiates most human cancers, as well as genetic effects, and is quite likely to be a major contributor to aging . . . and heart disease." It might also be, they said, the principal cause of "disability" and "death" in "advanced societies."[36]

These, however, were "beliefs," and on this issue, the genetics community has split into those who are anxious to regulate industry on the basis of such "beliefs" and those who are not. Many geneticists who are willing to speculate, and who are anxious to regulate on the basis of speculation, are actively cooperating with the regulatory agencies; and the limited means of assessing risks in human beings does not deter them from trying to make such assessments. In 1979, a Banbury Conference, supported in part by the EPA, was held at the Cold Spring Harbor Laboratory and was published as a volume entitled *Assessing Chemical Mutagens: The Risk to Humans*. During that conference, the participants struggled to figure out ways of extrapolating data from bacteria and the cells of *Drosophila* flies, via mice and marmosets, to man, and to make risk assessments for human beings so that the regulatory agencies might have numbers with which to ban mutagenic substances. The ardor in this group of geneticists both for additional research funds and for the banning of mutagenic chemicals was so great that Victor K. McElheny, Director of the Banbury Center, in a foreword to the published transcript, reports: "The Conference was reminded several times that prolonged research did not necessarily imply more and more onerous regulations."[37] After contemplating this combination of a zeal for regulation and a lack of scientific information, James V. Neel of the University of Michigan Medical School told his colleagues: "You have talked yourselves and the public into a kind of psychosis."[38] He said that the calculations they were undertaking were impossible in the absence of standards derived from human genetic data, that customary disciplines in genetics were being ignored, and that meaningless numbers should not be handed to regulatory agencies, and declared that he saw no reason to "prostitute my profession."[39] James D. Watson of Cold Spring Harbor Laboratory retorted that Neel was too "academic" and was really saying that "we shouldn't stick our necks out."[40] Moral indignation vibrated in the air, but even the most ardent advocates of banning failed to challenge Neel's fundamental observation; the crucial human data were missing.

Not all scientists consider it "academic" and cowardly to try to understand a problem before rushing to "solve" it by means of law. In the case of cancer, in particular, given slithering correlations between mutagens and carcinogens, an uncomfortable rate of false positives and false negatives, and the geneticists' ignorance of the mutations that might be linked to cancer, there are scientists who are unimpressed by the idea that mutagen tests should be used as screening agents for carcinogenicity. In 1976, one researcher commented: "To use this kind of test as a test for carcinogenicity is a bit like looking under the lamppost for a coin lost a block away because of the availability of light"; the criticism was quoted approvingly by H. P. Burchfield and Eleanor Storrs in 1977.[41] It can be translated as follows: The mutagen tests are there, they are rapid, and they are cheap—but that does not mean that they predict for cancer. According to Bernard Davis, the same thing could be said in 1980. The most crucial question could not yet be answered.

THE THEORY

Meantime, another problem was looming on the horizon. While the first group of problems to hit the mutation theory of cancer had left its enthusiasts in a state of uncertainty about their statistics and what they meant, the second consisted of a biological anomaly which could not rationally be ignored. Yet again, some background is needed. There had never been universal agreement over the mutation theory of cancer, but in the blinding glare of Ames' 90 percent correlation, it seemed unimportant. As the glare dimmed and people could see again, it turned out to be extremely important indeed. The basic controversy was between two different theories of cancer causation. One, the mutation theory, is called the "genetic" theory of cancer, which states that malignancy is caused by a mutated cell; the other is called the "epigenetic" theory of cancer, a theory that states that malignancy depends on altered regulation of the genes, rather than mutational alteration in their structure. Most of the views of the advocates of the mutation or genetic theory have already been mentioned, but for the purposes of illustrating the controversy, they will be recapitulated. Here, briefly, is how the argument goes; and for reasons which will become clear later, it is more important that the layman know that the argument exists than that he *understand* it completely. The information comes from P. N. Magee, a prominent researcher in carcinogenesis.[42]

- The advocates of the genetic theory of cancer believe that chromosomal aberrations are frequent in tumors; advocates of the epigenetic theory observe that many early tumors do not show chromosomal abnormality.
- Advocates of the genetic theory of cancer claim that most chemical carcinogens are mutagens; advocates of the epigenetic theory reply that not all mutagens are carcinogens.
- Advocates of the genetic theory state that chemical carcinogens and radiation are similar in that both interact with DNA; advocates of the epigenetic theory point out that chemical carcinogens and radiation also interact with RNA and proteins.
- Advocates of the genetic theory claim that evidence for a mutational origin of cancer can be found in diseases such as xeroderma pigmentosum and ataxia telangiectasis, where DNA repair is defective and high sensitivity to UV and X-ray carcinogenesis is found; advocates of epigenetic theory of cancer argue that the two diseases may be unique examples of the phenomenon.
- Advocates of the genetic theory of cancer declare that it is to be expected that tumors are clones of a single cell; advocates of the epigenetic theory declare that tumors are not necessarily clones of a single cell and may emerge from stable epigenetic change.
- Advocates of the genetic theory affirm that the malignant change on the cellular level is permanent and irreversible; advocates of the epigenetic theory of cancer affirm that the malignant change on the cellular level is not neces-

sarily permanent or irreversible; that spontaneous regression may occur; and that malignant cells can, in some cases, differentiate into normal tissue.

Each of these different ideas has been extensively discussed in the literature, but only two of the most important challenges will be considered here. The first was directed at the evidence for the mutation theory, taken from rare genetic disease. In the last chapter, in describing the biological evidence selected to support the genetic or mutation theory of cancer, one piece of evidence above all was stressed by certain scientists—the discovery by James Cleaver of UC, San Francisco with James Trosko that sufferers from xeroderma pigmentosum had defective DNA repair systems that made them acutely susceptible to ultraviolet radiation. This was considered by some to be the strongest available evidence for the mutation theory of cancer. In 1979, however, James Cleaver himself warned that the leap from that one disease to the general theory of mutation was an act of oversimplification. He pointed out that there were other genetic diseases characterized by defective DNA repair which did not conform to the same pattern; that some could be correlated with mutagenesis and some with malignancy, but that one could not make easy generalizations about all.[43] According to Cleaver, the famous example of xeroderma had been stretched beyond its capacity to "prove" the mutation theory of cancer.

The second challenge to the mutation theory of cancer was even more fundamental. It pertained to the idea that in cancer induction the change at the cellular level is irreversible. According to P. N. Magee, summing up the view of scientists on the issue, a mutation is a "heritable" change in the DNA of a germ or somatic cell;[44] "heritable" means a permanent and irreversible change. In the theory of cancer, it accounts for the self-replicating cell. Advocates of the mutation theory of cancer could accept the idea that established tumors could regress, that tumors or tumor cells could lie dormant in the body, and that even early neoplasia could be reversed. They drew the line at one thing, however—the *cell* with the presumably heritable change. That cell, according to the mutation theory of cancer, could not be restored to its normal state. For the mutation theorist, this was an absolute.

There was only one problem with this absolute: It wasn't absolute. Starting in the 1940s, exceptions had been reported, first one, then another, until by the late 1970s they were a few too many to ignore. Some of these reports had come from prominent figures and from major research institutions:

- Crown gall tumors in plants had been reported to revert to normal. This indicated, said F. Meins of the University of Illinois, that mutation did not account for plant cancers.[45]
- Malignant cells—neuroblastomas and human leukemia cells growing in culture—had been found to revert to normal. This meant, said A. C. Braun of Rockefeller University, that any explanation for cancer must recognize its potential reversibility.[46]
- Malignant embryonal cells were introduced into the peritoneal cavities of

mice, and instead of replicating themselves inexorably, the clones developed into fourteen well-differentiated benign tissues, as well as into embryonal carcinoma. This, said L. J. Kleinsmith and Q. B. Pierce, who conducted the experiments, supported neither the concept of the irreversibility of the malignant transformation nor the mutation theory of cancer.[47]

- Single malignant teratocarcinoma or embryonal cancer cells were injected into the blastocysts of mice, and these were then implanted in the uteri of females. Several of the tumors developed into healthy cancer-free baby mice with a wide variety of benign tissues derived from the tumor *cells*. In addition, cells from the tumors produced sperm which gave rise to many normal progeny. The phenomenon lasted for 200 transplant generations. This, said Beatrice Mintz and K. Illmensee, who conducted this experiment, was "an unequivocal example in animals of a non-mutational base for transformation to malignancy and reversal to normalcy."[48]

- The nuclei of malignant adenocarcinoma cells were injected into the eggs of a frog. The frog produced normal progeny. This, said R. McKinnell et al., who performed the experiment, meant that the transplanted tumor genes needed for normal growth had not been mutated.[49]

- Leukemia cells infused into a normal cellular environment were *not* found to induce leukemia, while normal cells infused into a leukemic cellular environment were capable of producing leukemic progeny. This, said A. Z. Bluming of the University of Southern California School of Medicine, contradicted the idea that a mutagenic event produced self-cloning cells.[50]

In addition to all this, it had been discovered that two types of carcinogenesis did not conform to the mutation theory of cancer. Hormonal imbalance and the nonchemical stimuli of metal or plastic film inserted under the skin both produced cancers. Neither phenomenon, said Isaac Berenblum[51] and John Cairns,[52] could be reasonably imputed to a mutational change in a cell.

Quite suddenly, at least for those scientists who were aware of the literature and who were concerned about theoretical consistency, there were too many anomalies. As Thomas S. Kuhn would put it, the mutation theory of cancer was in crisis. In fact, the prevailing theories of carcinogenesis were under challenge as well, for all theories until then had postulated that cellular initiation was irreversible.

In the field of carcinogenesis, in 1978, Isaac Berenblum published a paper on some of the data that contradicted current theory, including the theory of irreversibility, and recommended that more might be gained from trying to resolve the anomalies than from "building up plausible theories that fit some of the available facts but ignore exceptions."[53]

And in the field of mutation theory, in 1978, James Trosko, too, declared that the contradictions had to be faced. Speaking of the McKinnell and Mintz and Illmensee experiments, Trosko declared that they "force us either to reject the mutation theory of cancer or to modify the theory of cancer to include both mutational and epigenetic mechanisms for carcinogenesis."[54] Working with Chia-Cheng Chang at Michigan State University, he and Chang proposed such a modification. They combined both the genetic and epigenetic theories of cancer with the initiation-promotion theory of cancer and postulated that mutagenesis was responsible for initiation and epigenetic mechanisms were responsible for "the reversible phase of promotion."[55] It was a very engaging hypothesis, for it allowed theorists in both mutation theory and carcinogenesis to hold a tight grip on the initiation process while attributing all unnerving reversibility to promoters. Unfortunately, there was a vacuum at the heart of the Trosko-Chang theory, and one need merely remember the date of the theory to know why. In the year 1978, few promoters were known. The initiation-promotion theory had just barely emerged from its thirty-year-long restriction to experiments on mouse skin with croton oil and its fractions. Just the year before, in 1977, P. N. Magee was still reporting that the promoter most extensively used in laboratories was croton oil.[56] In 1978, Berenblum himself conceded that most of the data on the initiation-promotion theory still came from mouse skin.[57] To prove that all promoters were nonmutagenic, one needed more than an idea and a few examples; one needed validated studies showing a high correlation between promoters and nonmutagenicity. Such data did not exist. Trosko and Chang had confronted the contradictions and they had galloped bravely to the rescue of the imperiled theory that initiation is irreversible, but their hypothesis was just that—a hypothesis.

Many scientists, even when strongly sympathetic to the mutation theory of cancer, have been careful to indicate the limitations of the theory. John Cairns, former Director of the Cold Spring Harbor Laboratory of Quantitative Biology in New York and later Director of the Imperial Cancer Research Fund's Mill Hill Laboratory in London, said that the idea that initiation is mutational was "persuasive," but described it as "admittedly circumstantial" and also described the nature of promotion as "still very obscure."[58] Berenblum was also strongly persuaded by the theory, but wrote carefully that the initiating phase of carcinogenesis was "presumed to be mutational" and that the promoting phase was "presumably epigenetic," and in his analysis of theoretical contradictions, said that both of these concepts "still lack proof."[59]

Other scientists have pointed out that the presumption that initiation is a mutation may be fallacious. The reasons they give are essentially the same: The mechanism of carcinogenesis and the mechanism of mutation may be different. The Millers have warned that the correlations of mutagenic and carcinogenic chemicals "cannot be taken as evidence for the mutagenic nature of carcinogenesis," pointing out that such correlations might merely be "a reflection of the nucleophilicity of the targets for both carcinogenesis and mutagenesis."[60] Similarly, Sugimura and his colleagues observed: "The mechanisms of the induction of cancer and mutation may be different, so that carcinogenesis and mutagenesis must be considered separately even though carcinogens have been shown to overlap mutagens."[61] And in England, N. Bishun and his colleagues working at the Tissue Culture and Cytogenics Unit of the Marie Curie Memorial Foundation expressed similar reserves: ". . . it does not follow that a chemical which is mutagenic and produces chromosomal abnormalities is necessarily carcinogenic, although there might be similarities in those interactions with

DNA. . . ." In fact, these British scientists said that "far from finding a close correlation between mutagenesis and the development of cancer, one may conclude that almost any chemically reactive compound, if tested by a sufficiently wide range of methods, is likely to prove mutagenic in some systems."[62] If one pays close attention to all the "mights" and "mays," one sees that these are all ways of saying that the mechanisms of carcinogenesis are still shrouded in ignorance.

There are, finally, some scientists who have thought it necessary to make explicit the ignorance of the mechanisms underlying the complicated speculations in both genetics and carcinogenesis. At a New York cancer conference, in 1979, John Higginson, Director of the IARC, declared that the concept that the initiation of cancer was irreversible was entirely arbitrary: "We have decided, by definition, that initiation is non-reversible and because it is initiation, it can't be reversible." He observed that there was a tendency, in the face of ignorance, to "legislate your answers" or to "give a definition" and warned scientists that if "Congress or others" legislated this definition, it would then really become irreversible in a different way, one that was undesirable for science.[63]

At the very time that Higginson was speaking, such "legislating" was going on at the OSHA policy hearings, where all the issues discussed in the last two chapters were being considered as a basis for regulatory policy. William Lijinsky, a prominent cancer researcher, testified at those hearings, and he described the degree of ignorance that underlay all the theories, the speculations and assumptions about the mechanism of cancer:

Unfortunately, the mechanism of action of carcinogens at the biochemical level is understood in only a rudimentary way. Most of the hypotheses that have been advanced during the past 50 years have been discarded and the remainder are inadequate. While splendid work has been done in the area of metabolism ... by the Millers and of polynuclear compounds by a number of investigators and of N-nitroso compounds by Magee and others, we have no deep insight into the mechanism by which any chemical carcinogen induces neoplasia. . . .

While the suggestion is reasonable, there is no evidence that carcinogenesis involves mutation of the chromatin of a cell, and the action could be epigenetic, rather than genetic. The target in the cell of the carcinogen is not known, although DNA has been suggested. . . . While it can be maintained as an article of faith that reaction with DNA is involved in chemical carcinogenesis, the evidence supporting it is circumstantial rather than factual, and it provides no basis for the concept that one molecule of a carcinogen is sufficient to cause cancer. However, neither does the available evidence tell us how many molecules of a carcinogen are necessary to cause cancer; the number must be between 1 and infinity."[64]

Lijinsky did not merely identify the uncertainty underlying the mutation theory of cancer; he also dismissed the phenomenon of anticarcinogens in a few words and questioned the base of the initiation-promotion theory as well. He observed that the possibility of promoters is real "although we have very little idea of what they might be, or even of their nature"; then he summed up the initiation-promotion theory quickly and said: "While this model is interesting and philosophically satisfying, the evidence that it has relevance to types of cancer other than skin, in animals or in man, is very flimsy."[65]

Lijinsky's statement seems to wipe out almost all the content of the last two chapters, and in a way it does. He was saying that none of the theories was solidly grounded in biological explanations, and that is apparently the case. Every once in a while, a cancer conference opens with an analysis of the unsolved problems in the field. One of the most eloquent, and most revealing, was made by Frederick F. Becker at the University of Texas, System Cancer Center, at the conference which was honoring Berenblum and Shubik for their contributions to the initiation-promotion theory. Becker said this, and allows it to stand as his view of 1982:

In many respects, the study of chemical carcinogenesis is akin to attempting to unravel the Gordian knot. As one traces a promising thread, it invariably leads to other mysteries and entanglements in daunting number, for, although we accept that the chronic exposure of a number of mammalian tissues to a variety of chemical agents often results in the evolution of the exposed cells to malignancy, there is no phase nor facet of this process, from its primary cellular interaction to its terminus in the death of the host, that is fully understood. We cannot state with certainty that the process results solely from the interaction of the suspected chemical agent with target cells, now that we understand the impact of the action of cocarcinogens or promoting agents, alterations of the host's immunological and hormonal modulating capacities, and the nagging possibility that the final common pathway might be the release of a genetic component—an oncogene—that lurks in the host's genome as a result of some ancient "miscegenation" with a wayward virus, a kind of biological original sin made manifest by a forbidden chemical agent. . . .

The one major problem that continues to diminish the immediate importance of the results of every experiment in this field and casts a shadow of uncertainty on the relevance of every observation is our inability to define the malignant cell and, further, to define that macromolecular characteristic which is the basis of malignancy. A vast amount of information exists that describes what *this cell does and to a lesser extent* how *it does what it does . . . but the* why *evades us.*[66] [Emphasis added].

Ultimately, the *why* is everything. It is the *why* alone that allows science to explain and predict. Until the *why* is known there is a sense in which it may be said that nothing is known, or more precisely, that everything that seems to be known or appears to be plausible may be revised overnight. In cancer research, all the discoveries and hypotheses described so far might be altered by the discovery of a single biological mechanism that works in a way that no one has anticipated. Today the complex discoveries, the provocative correlations, the theoretical structures in the field of carcinogenesis are all different approaches to a central mystery. That mystery is the *why* of the malignant cell.

Basic research in biology is sometimes compared to basic research in physics for the purpose of stressing the immaturity of biology. Lewis Thomas has observed that it is commonly supposed that biology and medicine are far richer in coherent and applicable information than, in fact, they are. The biomedical sciences, including cancer research, he says, have not yet reached the stage where their knowledge is generally applicable to human disease. He compares basic research in biology and medicine to the physical sciences of the early twentieth century, "booming along into new territory, but without an equivalent for the engineering of that time": "We have to face, in whatever discomfort, the real possibility that the level of insight into the mechanisms of today's unsolved diseases—schizophrenia, for instance, or cancer, or stroke—is comparable to the situation for infectious disease in 1875. . . ."[67] Berenblum says precisely the same thing: Cancer research, he says, is not even as advanced as was basic physics during World War I, and any expectation of an applied science at this stage is, he says, "irrational."[68]

Still, in some fashion, basic research *is* being applied to man. In OSHA's policy document, it cites the NCI Ad Hoc Committee statement of 1970 which says, "An effective program to protect man from the mass of environmental cancer hazards is within reach"[69]—and that was a decade ago. Today, such regulatory agencies as the FDA, EPA, and OSHA describe their activities as "cancer prevention." Given the chaotic complexity of carcinogenesis and the ignorance of fundamental mechanisms, how do the regulators apply the theoretical insights of basic science? The answer to this question will be very brief—a postscript, in effect, to this section on basic science; but before we enter the government-dominated world of cancer prevention, we must have some idea of the relationship between the universe of basic science and the regulatory universe. Even a cursory glance at one agency's approach to basic science will prepare us for the next stage of this journey.

Chapter 7

The Bridge to the Regulatory World

> OSHA believes ... OSHA does not believe ...
> OSHA is persuaded ... OSHA rejects ...
> OSHA intends ... OSHA concludes ... OSHA
> will establish ... OSHA will require ...
> OSHA will impose ...[1]
> —OSHA policy document, 1980

Somewhere, between the remote silent world of basic science and the daily din of the headlines informing us of the latest carcinogenic threat to our lives, there is a passageway, an intellectual bridge that connects both worlds. In a general way, the layman knows that the bridge consists of the regulatory agencies, and if he reflects on the matter at all, he dimly assumes that their function is to apply the truths discovered by basic science. He is not altogether wrong, but he is just wrong enough to require that he be given at least a glimpse of the actual nature of that connecting bridge. This chapter will provide the reader with such a glimpse. The intellectual connection between the two worlds can best be illustrated by a document—the first complete policy statement on basic science ever to be prepared by a government agency. It is OSHA's policy document of 1980.

Book II of that document is one of the most interesting publications ever to come rolling off a government printing press. On the surface, it does not look interesting at all. It has no identified author. It is long; it is extremely technical; it is chaotically organized; it is printed in agonizingly small type; it is badly written; it is pedantic, pompous, and repetitious. It even succeeds, somehow, in being simultaneously polemical and boring. It is a wretched piece of literature, and there can be no more than a few thousand people in this republic of 280,000,000 who could endure to be exposed to its content for more than five minutes. And yet there is good reason to read this document, even to study it intensively, for it tells a remarkable story. It explains exactly how a regulatory agency reduces the beautiful, if precarious and unresolved, complexities of basic science to a set of "policies."

OSHA is not the only agency of government which has attempted to formulate a "cancer policy." In a discussion of such attempts, Richard Merrill, former general legal counsel for the FDA, has observed that each of the four federal agencies which carry the major burden of cancer prevention—the Environmental Protection Agency (EPA), the Food and Drug Agency (FDA), and the Consumer Product Safety Commission (CPSC), as well as OSHA—has sought to establish its views on the criteria by which it identified and regulated "potential" carcinogens—some in a more formal manner, others on an ad hoc basis, allowing the "policy" to emerge, by implication, from specific decisions. When it was realized in the late 1970s that no uniform criteria existed among these agencies, Merrill reported, yet other new institutions sought to integrate their various approaches to the problem: the National Toxicology Program within the Public Health Service, and the President's Office of Science and Technology (OSTP), each of which has formulated its own policy for identifying and assessing carcinogenic chemicals. And finally, as Merrill put it, "Concern about the consistency and rationality of federal regulation of chemical carcinogens has also surfaced in other quarters." Organizations like the Regulatory Analysis Review Group (RARG) at the Regulatory Council have been studying the lack of integration of the policies of the existing agencies.[2]

One might profitably choose any one of these institutions for a close-up view of the intellectual bridge that connects the world of basic science and the regulatory world of cancer prevention, and, in fact, certain policies of many of these agencies are mentioned at one time or another in this book. OSHA, however, is the most enlightening agency to study in this context, because, as Merrill observed, "OSHA has made the greatest investment in the establishment of an agency cancer policy. In October 1977, OSHA initiated a rulemaking proceeding *in which it proposed to resolve conclusively many of the scientific issues that recur in proceedings to regulate individual chemicals*—such as, for example, the relevance of animal data, high-to-low dose extrapolation, and the existence of thresholds. . . . Although the agency's final regulations are more flexible than those originally proposed, *they explicitly limit the right of participants in subsequent rule-makings to contest many of the scientific premises underlying OSHA's regulation of toxic chemicals.*"[3] (Emphasis added)

It is precisely because OSHA has sought "to resolve conclusively" many of the scientific issues that emerge from the young science of carcinogenesis and limits the right to "contest" many of its "scientific premises" that the views of that agency are particularly worthy of inspection. OSHA, in fact, has "processed" basic science for regulatory purposes and has produced the most detailed and elaborate expression of "official" science that exists at this time of writing.

OSHA's processing of the basic science of that period can be readily described, although it is doubtful that OSHA itself would relish the description. It is the intellectual equivalent of making applesauce. The process consists, essentially, of mashing basic science through a sieve and of picking out the portions that the agency finds useful for its purpose. OSHA's legally mandated purpose is to protect workers from the carcinogenic substances being manufactured by American industries. The only practical expression of this purpose, however, is to regulate the production of carcinogenic substances. Thus, the agency's processing methods can be described even more precisely: After mashing basic science through a sieve, OSHA picks out the parts that can best serve as a rationale for regulation; it then ignores, dismisses, or outlaws the remainder.

Among the various issues that OSHA processed—many more than have been mentioned so far—were the four aspects of basic science described in the last two chapters, namely, the discoveries of the Millers, of Berenblum, and of Bruce Ames and the geneticists, and the unresolved controversies surrounding the mutation theory of cancer. Which aspects of these discoveries and of these unresolved controversies did OSHA pick out as applicable and inapplicable to its regulatory goals? The answers, found in the 1980 policy document, give us an unexpected insight into the relationship between the regulator and the "science" on which he is presumed by the public to stand. We will take the discoveries one by one, and report on what OSHA chose to "believe," to "disbelieve," to find "persuasive," and to "reject" in each case.

Species Differences

As the reader will recall, the Millers' discovery that the active carcinogens were often the metabolic products of the tested substances threw the issue of carcinogenesis into the one realm where different mammalian species were least comparable. At the OSHA hearings, scientists debated extensively over whether metabolic information was needed to determine whether a substance that was carcinogenic in animals was also carcinogenic in man. OSHA's opinion was this:

Our present ability to use metabolic and pharmacokinetic information is greatly limited by the paucity of specific data available. . . . Indeed, the number of chemicals for which the ultimate carcinogenic metabolite in animals is known is quite small. . . . Information on metabolism and pharmacokinetics of carcinogens is generally deficient even for experimental animals and is especially deficient for humans. . . .

To rebut the qualitative presumption that a chemical found carcinogenic in animals poses a risk to exposed humans, it would at least be necessary to show: (a) that the metabolite identified as the ultimate carcinogen in animals is not produced in human tissues, and (b) that other metabolites of such a substance produced in human tissues are not carcinogenic. *OSHA does not believe that such information is available for any carcinogen, and indeed OSHA believes that such information is unlikely to become available* because of the wide variability in metabolic differences between different tissues and between individuals in the population. . . .

OSHA concludes . . . that . . . information on metabolism and pharmacokinetics is of extremely little practical value at the present time.[4] [Emphasis added]

In sum, said OSHA, the implication of the Millers' discovery as it pertained to interspecies differences was inapplicable to regulation.

Co-Carcinogens and Promoters

OSHA also heard extensive testimony on co-carcinogens and promoters and expressed its conclusion as follows:

It is reasonable to discuss all such agents [co-carcinogens, promoters, enhancers, etc.] under the same heading, if only because of the practical impossibility of distinguishing between them experimentally. . . .

. . . OSHA concludes that *it would not be practicable or justifiable to establish different criteria for the identification, classification, or regulation of initiating and promoting agents.* OSHA agrees . . . that "any factor or combination of factors which increases the risk of cancer in humans is of concern regardless of its mechanism of action."[5] [Emphasis added]

In sum, said OSHA, Berenblum's differentiated categories were inapplicable to regulation.

Anticarcinogens

OSHA had no "beliefs" on anticarcinogens. In the course of the hearings, the phenomenon of anticarcinogenesis was mentioned by witnesses, but its applicability was not considered.

Mutagen Tests

OSHA acknowledged that there was "substantial disagreement" among scientists on the "short-term" tests and on the capacity of such tests to predict cancer. But the agency concluded that only one side of the controversy merited its support:

OSHA intends to rely on results from more than one short-term test, combined with the results from at least one long-term animal bioassay, as the basis for instituting regulatory action. The probability of obtaining false positive results is greatly reduced by requiring a second corroborative test. The probability of obtaining false positive results in one animal bioassay *and* in more than one short-term test is vanishingly small.

There were a number of other witnesses who did not agree that there was a correlation between mutagenicity and carcinogenicity which could be used for predictive purposes. . . . However, these witnesses offered no specific data that would offset the reliability of the correlations reported by Purchase et al. (1976), Sugimura et al. (1976), McCann et al. (1975), and the other authors cited by Dr. Brusick. Thus, although OSHA recognizes that there is some divergence of opinion, OSHA concludes that there is in fact a better than 90 percent correlation between the results of certain short-term tests and animal bioassays for carcinogenicity.

Since there is little scientific argument against the conclusion that most carcinogens are also mutagens, protection of workers from the mutagenic effects of carcinogens that are also mutagenic would be an additional benefit from the regulation of carcinogens.[6]

In sum, said OSHA, Bruce Ames' 90 percent correlation made the "short-term" test applicable to regulation.

Irreversibility

OSHA heard testimony on both the reversibility and the irreversibility of malignancy and concluded:

However, there is no evidence . . . that the initial [cellular] transformations can be reversed: indeed they remain latent for most of or all of the animal's lifetime. The impor-

tance of these findings for regulation of carcinogens is that even brief exposures early in
life must be assumed to have irreversible effects which may be manifested as cancers
late in life.[7]

In sum, said OSHA, the concept that initiation was reversible was inapplicable
to regulation.

The Malignant Cell

OSHA heard extensive and speculative testimony on the origins of malignancy
and concluded:

There is evidence that the first stage in initiation of carcinogenesis may result from the
interaction of a molecule of the carcinogen with DNA or other genetic material in the
cell. . . . Hence it would follow from the fact that cancer develops from a single cell, that
cancer may be initiated by the interaction of a single molecule of a carcinogen with the
critical target site in a cell.[8]

In sum, said OSHA, the "single-cell theory" of cancer and the "one-molecule
theory" of cancer were applicable to regulation.

It should be clear from this group of opinions alone that OSHA does not
reflect the complexities of basic science, which had by then emerged. In fact, as
we see, OSHA dismissed as practically inapplicable many of the theories and
discoveries described in Chapter 5. According to OSHA, most of what Berenblum and his associates had discovered about the complex biochemical archi-
tecture of carcinogenesis could not be integrated into the animal tests; carcinogens, co-carcinogens, and promoters were distinctions of no significance, said
OSHA—all were the same to laboratory rats. And although their existence was
acknowledged, Berenblum's anticarcinogens were not deemed worthy of regulatory attention. As for species differences in metabolism, rendered so important by the Millers' discoveries, there was no way, said OSHA, to know
whether men metabolized carcinogens in the same way as did rats and mice;
what is more, said OSHA, it was unlikely that one would ever know. Thus, all
would continue unchanged: Rats and mice would still be used to predict cancer
in man.

OSHA's practical choices were those which could be integrated into conventional biological screening programs. Those conventional screening programs, apparently, could not deal with human biology and human action. If
men metabolized chemicals in ways other than did rodents, or if the human
body itself was implicated in carcinogenesis (e.g., hormones or genetic propen-
sities), or if human activities were implicated in carcinogenesis (e.g., diet), that
could not be dealt with by laboratory tests. In fact, those tests were good for
only one thing: to study specific chemicals, usually one at a time. If the bizarrely complicated nature of carcinogenesis could not be integrated into those
tests, said OSHA, in effect, the bizarrely complicated nature of carcinogenesis
was of only academic interest. For regulatory purposes, it did not exist.

There was actually nothing new about this attitude. So profoundly had the
vision of carcinogenesis been determined by the purposes and limitations of the
regulatory process that many scientists had not even known about certain phe-

nomena that had been in the literature for years. The most striking example was anticarcinogenesis. In 1976, Hans Falk of the NCI addressed himself to that problem. Speaking to a group of researchers in carcinogenesis at a conference on extrapolation from animal to man, he said:

... many of us think in terms of additive effects of all these small amounts of carcinogens that we don't even know yet how to identify that are present in water, in air, on food, or whatever else we do. We don't think about the others that are actually "inhibitory" at the same time. The question of inhibition of carcinogenesis is probably as old as carcinogenesis itself. It goes all the way back into the 1930s when it was described as a curiosity. Today hardly anyone is familiar with the fact that there are processes of inhibition of carcinogenesis. . . .[9]

Today, very little has changed. There are military secrets that are more widely known than the fact that a wide range of both synthetic and natural chemicals have been reported to have the capacity to delay, inhibit, prevent, or arrest the effects of carcinogens. "Additives" are widely discussed; almost no one knows about the "subtractives." What the regulators cannot deal with, citizens, including many scientists, tend not to know.

If OSHA's practical choices were obviously limited to available laboratory tests, its theoretical choices were also obvious. One must set out those choices in order to see what they achieved:

- OSHA heard testimony from scientists—e.g., Lijinsky—on the controversy between the "genetic" and "epigenetic" theories of cancer, and heard blunt statements that there was, as yet, no scientific proof of the mutation theory of cancer. OSHA then ignored the existence of such testimony, and declared that there was "little scientific argument" against the idea that "most" carcinogens were mutagens.[10]
- OSHA published data from Marvin Legator demonstrating that correlations between carcinogens and mutagens are functions of the chemical classes tested and that the Ames test skipped certain classes of chemicals. The reference to Legator's study in the last chapter came straight from OSHA's policy document. OSHA, however, ignored the significance of the Legator data on false negatives. The agency supported only those scientists who reported high correlations and expressed its official belief in Ames' 90 percent correlation between carcinogens and mutagens.
- OSHA published no survey data on false positives—the internationally reported tendency of the mutagen tests to identify noncarcinogens as carcinogenic. The agency did publish Joyce McCann's "personal feeling" that the issue of false positives was insignificant—the passage that appeared in the previous chapter.
- OSHA published some testimony which referred to the idea that carcinogenesis was a reversible process at certain stages,[11] but published no testimony from the scientists who considered that their experiments had demonstrated the reversibility of the initiating process. The agency, instead, announced that there was "no evidence" that the initiation process was reversible.
- OSHA published testimony declaring that a single malignant cell is the

source of cancer.[12] It published no testimony on the dramatic experiments showing that single malignant cells had also produced benign tissues, cancer-free organs, and cancer-free animals. OSHA then officially espoused the single-cell theory of cancer.

• Finally, OSHA said "it would follow" from single-cell origin that a cancer might be triggered by "a single molecule" because "a single molecule" might trigger cancer in a single cell, a curiously circular statement. OSHA was embracing the one-molecule theory, voiced in 1971 by Bruce Ames, and here, interestingly, the agency published only a footnote to support its position.[13]

The footnote cited a 1977 National Academy of Sciences study, and when one looks it up, one finds the following passage:

THRESHOLDS
Biological Considerations

Whether or not a particular effect follows a dose-response relationship that has a threshold depends entirely on the mechanism of the effect. Many effects have thresholds. For example, the gastrointestinal-radiation syndrome, acute drug toxicity, and radiation or drug control of some tumors all have dose-response curves that show thresholds. . . .

However, other effects may well *not* have threshold dose-effect relationships. *If an effect can be caused by a single hit, a single molecule, or a single unit of exposure, then the effect in question cannot have a threshold* in the dose-response relationship, no matter how unlikely it is that the single hit or event will produce the effect. *Mutations in prokaryotic and eukaryotic cells can be caused by a single cluster of ion pairs produced by a beam of ionizing radiation. We would expect that mutations can be caused by a single molecule or perhaps group of molecules in proximity to the DNA. The necessary conclusion from this result is that the dose-response relationship for radiation and chemical mutagenesis cannot have a threshold* and must be linear, at least at low doses. It is one step further to correlate mutagenesis with carcinogenesis. Nevertheless, the evidence is strong that there is a close relationship between the two (McCann et al., 1975; McCann and Ames, 1976; Ames, 1976; DHEW, 1977).

We therefore conclude that, if there is evidence that a particular carcinogen acts by directly causing a mutation in the DNA, it is likely that the dose-response curve for carcinogenesis will not show a threshold and will be linear with dose at low doses.[14] [Emphasis added]

Thus do we finally come face to face with at least one variant of the one-molecule theory. Since one of the goals we hoped to achieve was an understanding of the precise scientific status of that theory, we shall stop for a moment and consider it. We learn from this passage that the one-molecule theory is actually a hypothetical argument for a no-threshold theory. It postulates that *if a cancer comes from a mutation, one could "expect" that it was caused by one or a few molecules of a chemical—on the further assumption that radiation and chemicals work in the same fashion.*

Since these postulates and assumptions are part of the intellectual repertoire of risk assessment, I will not discuss them further in this chapter. Even this much, however, gives us considerable insight into OSHA. That agency had accomplished something astonishing in its little footnote to the single-cell origin of cancer. It had smuggled a version of the no-threshold argument—one intuited from *radiation-induced mutagenesis*—into its definition of the probable origin of carcinogenesis. The practical result for OSHA was a brand-new concept of malignancy wherein a cancer is born with a one-molecule/no-threshold theory derived from mutagenesis engraved in its originating cell. This is as striking an illustration of building a desired conclusion into the definition of a problem and "legislating" that definition as one is liable to find. When John Higginson of the IARC warned scientists that this was going on, he was entirely correct.

When one looks at the "beliefs" espoused by OSHA, along with the systematic discarding of data that contradicted those "beliefs," one sees that OSHA was systematically taking sides in the genetic vs. epigenetic controversy and was throwing its weight to the mutation theory of cancer. The agency duly noted that "several chemicals" which were considered to be well established as human carcinogens were not mutagenic, and offered three examples: asbestos, nickel, and diethylstilbestrol.[15] But OSHA officially declared the mutation theorists' single-cell theory—with its footnoted one-molecule theory and its absolute of irreversibility—to be among the "distinctive features of carcinogenesis."[16] OSHA had no obligation to adopt the mutation theory of cancer; the agency's legal responsibility would not differ if cancer were dependent on altered gene regulation, or on the release of an oncogene. What OSHA wanted was the concept that one molecule of a carcinogen could cause irreversible cancer. And what OSHA wanted, it took—even if it had to invent a theory of malignancy to do it.

Earlier, I said that OSHA's choices revealed that the "policy" espoused by that agency did not reflect the complexity of basic research. That was too restrained a statement. To judge by these examples alone, regulatory "policy" is an active manipulation of basic research, and an active violation of it. It is obvious from the OSHA hearings that unknown men in the nation's bureaucracies have been arbitrarily deciding what is and is not scientific truth, and under the bland title of "policymaking," have imposed personal opinions on a nation which innocently imagines those opinions to be the voice of science. The reader may find this exceedingly strange and ask why the achievement of so estimable a goal as protecting Americans from environmental cancer requires crudely arbitrary decisions by regulatory agencies, and why it requires the violation of science. It will take the rest of this book to provide a full explanation, but one reason for this element of falsification can be named right now, for it emerges from the nature of science itself. One of the most important dimensions of that collective intellectual enterprise is *time*. It is time, above all, that allows the disorderly question-asking, the random explorations, the piecing together of disparate findings, the replicating and refuting, the public criticism, the productive arguing, the exposure of error, illusion, and fraud. It is time that is required for the creation of a context from which "there suddenly emerges, with the purity of a slow phrase of music, a single new piece of truth about nature."

In the regulatory world, however, there is no time. Or, rather, time is measured by electoral periods, by the tenure of high officials, by the frequency of the choral laments in the press about real or imagined malfeasance, and by the intervals between congressional investigations. OSHA, like all regulatory agencies, has only the time for "beliefs," for a sensitivity to fashionable people and trends both in science and politics, and for patching together a rationale to justify a rigorous regulation of industry. It has no professional interest in the slow exquisite emergence of truth. Thus, the "policies" it emits are often half-truths or pseudo-truths—or, quite simply, myths.

With this, our survey of the purely theoretical aspect of carcinogenesis ends, providing the reader with the necessary background for the continuous evolution of the field. We shall move directly now to the realm of applied or "regulatory" science—to the world of "cancer prevention." In that world there is a set of entirely different issues to consider: the conduct of animal tests, the data that emerge from those tests, the extrapolation of those data to man, and the process of risk assessment. The broadest questions we must ask as laymen are these: Are these different procedures valid? And how can we as laymen know when or whether we are hearing the truth? In the next part of this book I will report on what one learns in an attempt to answer those questions. But, in one sense, the learning process has already begun. In this chapter the reader has been walking across a little bridge that leads him into the regulatory world. At the end of that bridge a warning sign is posted that he may already have read. In case, for some obscure reason, he hasn't noticed it, I will reproduce it here: *You are now leaving the realm of basic science and are entering the realm of "regulatory" science. Tread warily. The land is mined.*

"REGULATORY" SCIENCE

Chapter 8

The Unanswerable Question

There is no study published to date that cannot be taken apart if one wishes to critically evaluate everything.[1]

— Paul Newberne, MIT; cited by GAO, 1980

Even in the unlikely event of a successful challenge to the study, the outcome would not be clear: it would appear to the media and the public as such things inevitably appear—as rather arcane, confusing debates among the cognoscenti. Thus the possibility for real embarrassment even given the worst possible outcome of our evaluation is very slight, simply because outcomes are never that clear in a matter so complex.[2]

— Donald Kennedy, FDA Commissioner, in a letter to Joseph Califano, Secretary of HEW; cited by GAO, 1980

For the first time since we started this intellectual voyage, we find ourselves back in the world from which we originally fled—the world where great bureaucracies use animals to identify carcinogens, to predict their effects on man, and to prevent those effects by legal means. It is the world of unending lists of "potential" or "suspected" carcinogens; of national hysteria over specific industrial compounds; of corrosive battles over the validity of carcinogenic data and the degree of risk they pose for man. It is the world of the applied science of carcinogenesis, when transmuted into politics.

No distinction has ever been formally made to the layman between the science of carcinogenesis and the political form of that science but the distinction between the two is absolutely necessary, so I must invent the missing descriptive terms. In this book, I shall call the political form of the science either "the science which uses animals to prevent cancer in man" or, for want of a briefer term, "regulatory" science. "Regulatory" science is *not* to be confused with regulation, regulatory hearings, regulatory decision-making or regulatory assessments of specific chemicals, but the term is justified because it captures the unique aspect of this science: It is *only* applicable by government, which is to say, by law and by regulatory action, and it is *only* applied to industry. Above all, "regulatory" science is not to be confused with basic science. Although many basic scientists engage in the practical testing and screening of chemicals

231

for the government, they often do so in the course of basic research projects or even as a means of doing basic research—and in that sense, they too are "regulatory" scientists. But basic science and "regulatory" science are not the same thing; they are distinguished by their purposes. In principle, basic science is concerned to explain the biological mechanisms of cancer; its goal is understanding. In principle, "regulatory" science is concerned with the legal elimination of carcinogenic substances in the environment whether biological understanding exists or not. Since a science severed from a quest for understanding is not a *normal* science, throughout this book it will always have the qualifying term "regulatory" attached to it.

In a forceful essay, published in 1977, on the ethical standards that should be upheld by "environmental toxicologists"—i.e., "regulatory" scientists—Umberto Saffiotti compared such toxicologists to those who work in the crime laboratories of forensic medicine and said: "When we review the scientific evidence on a suspected environmental carcinogen, we are, in fact, testifying on the circumstances of a suspected mass murder case."[3] His language is strong and, given that the "suspect" is industry, clearly politicized—but the reader is advised to remember it for it does capture the essence of the difference between basic science and "regulatory" science. The basic scientist, whether he works for the government or at a university, is an intellectual explorer in search of truth, and coercion is no part of his repertoire. The "regulatory" scientist, whether he works for the government or at a university, is an intellectual policeman whose judgments, if accepted by regulators, are backed up by the guns of the state.

This chapter, and several that follow, are dedicated to an examination of the work of those policeman-scientists or "regulatory" scientists. We will be, as Saffiotti puts it, examining the quality of the unusual science that attests to the crime of "suspected mass murder."

There is, we already know, some reason to raise the question of the scientific validity of "regulatory" science. We have learned that there is a philosophical distortion in the field born of the erroneous assumption that carcinogens are essentially modern inventions like atomic weapons. We have also learned that there is a strain of scientific pathology in the field associated with that same philosophical distortion, a tendency in some scientists to make baseless assertions, and to rush into legal action against industrial compounds on the basis of poor data or even none at all. We have found evidence of this pathology in the regulatory interpretation of basic science. We thus begin this investigation with the hypothesis that scientific pathology is likely to be present in this world of "regulatory" science.

The idea does not remain hypothetical for long, since it is almost instantly confirmed. As one reads the literature of the field of cancer prediction and prevention, one's attention is immediately riveted by an internal controversy on that very subject, a controversy so odd, in some respects, that the attempt to explain it generates nothing but mysteries. Evaluations of the poor state of the science are to be found in profusion within the broad world of "regulatory" science, and they are essentially of two types. One type is sharply critical, charges that the quality of a great deal of "regulatory" science is bad, and calls for high standards. The other type does not deny the charges but rather offers justifications for the problem, which is described as unsolvable. It is informative to examine both viewpoints. Here, to begin with, are several examples of criticisms.

In 1978, the International Agency for Research in Cancer (IARC), the most prestigious carcinogen research institution in the world which evaluates the work of "regulatory" science, issued a warning to the professionals in the field. Observing that a debate about "social responsibility" existed in the biomedical sciences, and that the debate was "at its sharpest" in the field of carcinogenic hazards, the IARC defined its own responsibility in that debate. It was, said that agency, to make sure that its contributions to the debate were based on "a rational evaluation" of the data. What was going on in the world of "regulatory" science, however, the agency said, was significantly less than rational: "Today, unfortunately, emotional rather than scientific evaluation is widespread with a resulting loss of public confidence. . . ." Scientists, said the IARC, "may overemphasize hazards" in a way that seems to "the average man" to violate "common sense." And the IARC warned: "If the scientific community is to maintain the support and the confidence of the public, it must avoid 'crying wolf' too often and must limit pronouncements to those that can be supported by facts."[4]

In 1980, Herman Kraybill, of the Division of Cancer Cause and Prevention of the National Cancer Institute, yet another institution that guides the work of "regulatory" science, cited the IARC and issued an "admonition" to workers in the field. He pinpointed the area of animal experimentation as the one in which major problems were arising. It was an area of "emotionalism," he said, which "abounds with opinions . . . and certain interests and influences which may transcend science and scientific truths." He warned scientists to take great care in the design of studies so that the data and the conclusions reached on the basis of the data "have a high degree of scientific validity." Many studies, he said, raised more questions than answers in the determination of whether a chemical was a carcinogen. He also warned that the publicity given to "poor experimentation" and "the fact that a chemical may be falsely indicted as a carcinogen" causes damage that cannot be undone. Such publicity and the recording in the literature of such false indictments, he said, exaggerated the hazards of "isolated" and "questionable" carcinogenic findings and had "an adverse effect on the public."[5]

Finally, to cite a distinguished academic who functions both as a basic and as a "regulatory" scientist: In 1978, Charles Heidelberger of the University of Southern California Cancer Center in Los Angeles expressed to an audience at a cancer conference his concerns about the quality of "regulatory" science. Among his comments were these: "I think it is very incumbent upon us as scientists to be quite responsible about the way we dispense the data. . . . I think the public is tired of the carcinogen of the week. I think the public is tired of apparent cries of wolf. . . . I think it is incumbent upon us as scientists . . . to try to be balanced and factual in these presentations. . . . I feel very uncomfortable that adversary procedures in courts of law seem to be the forum in which scientific decisions are made. I would hope that if the scientists develop better data and better responsibility, that scientific decisions need not be made in courts of law."[6]

These are indeed serious criticisms. They say that a significant portion of the work in the field of cancer prevention is bad; that experimental designs are poor; that data are inadequate; that interpretations are not being based on fact; that hazards are being exaggerated; and, that scientists are being irresponsible, emotional, irrational. Taken together, these criticisms constitute a veritable proclamation of the existence of pathology in the science of cancer prevention.

Is there any direct answer to such harsh assessments? Apparently not. In the ten thousand-odd documents I read for this book, I found no praise of the quality or practice of "regulatory" science from any source. I did, however, find defenses of scientific public policy from government regulators and scientific advisory committees, defenses which make revealing estimates about the quality of the science they use. Here are some examples of those defenses which were published during the same period. In a 1980 Report to the President by the Toxic Substances Strategy Committee, chaired by Gus Speth, the existence of a demand that regulatory decision-making be more "scientific"—the quotation marks are the committee's—is acknowledged and discussed:

The need for expanded public participation is one criticism that is sometimes made of regulatory decisionmaking; another is that the process should be more "scientific." Proponents of the latter approach favor standardization of regulatory phases, the clear separation of facts from value judgments, and the organizational separation of scientists from the policymakers. Although theoretically neat, TSSC does not consider it realistic because of the inseparability of science and policy at every stage of decisionmaking. . . . Rather, flexibility in the decisionmaking process should be preserved without making artificial distinctions between science and policy.[7]

In sum, said Speth and the TSSC, it is impossible for public policy to be "scientific" because value judgments are conceptually inseparable from facts. This statement was instantly "balanced" by a recommendation that value judgments *should* be conceptually separated from facts: "The role of all facts, theories, uncertainties, and value judgments should be made explicit at every stage and open to public scrutiny and participation." The committee seemed unaware of any self-contradiction.

Again, in 1980, obviously concerned by criticism from some in the scientific community, Steven D. Jellinek, Assistant Administrator for Pesticides and Toxic Substances for the EPA, published an article in *Technology Review*. It was addressed to "scientists" and it was a moral justification of "regulators." Its title was "On the Inevitability of Being Wrong." Jellinek made a strong distinction between "scientists" and "regulators," the latter group including scientists like himself. The two groups, he said, approached chemical problems, including such problems as carcinogenesis, very differently and were obliged to do so. "Scientists," he said, tend to be "cautious" about accepting evidence as valid: "When confronted by a great deal of uncertainty, they avoid drawing conclusions, and instead call for additional careful study and research. There's always the chance that others may beat them to the result, but this risk is worth taking compared with being 'wrong' or misleading the scientific profession." Regulators, said Jellinek, have a very different problem. They are morally responsible for the health of the population and don't have the "luxury of putting off decisions until certainty arrives"—particularly in such realms as cancer, with its long latency period separating cause and effect; they must make such socially responsible decisions in the midst of "enormous scientific uncertainty." Therein, said Jellinek, lay the "inevitability" of error.[8]

One also finds "scientific" justifications in government documents for acting with great gaps in the data. In 1979, the staff scientists of the Office of Science and Technology, writing on the evaluation of data and assessment of carcinogenic risk, said: "Impartial scientific judgment is crucial for this function, since the uncertainties in the data—or at times the lack of data—require a high level of scientific competence."[9]

This is clearly an entrenched debate, but it is a debate of a peculiar kind. None of the critical scientists quoted above were directing their attacks at regulatory agencies or at the government, nor have I ever seen such an attack; they were clearly criticizing what the IARC calls the "widespread" irrationality and poor scientific work common in the field. But, to repeat, it is never the colleagues of such critics who respond; responses to charges of bad science always come from the government defending its scientific policy. And yet, these volleys from ships that pass in the night, volleys that pass over the bows and engage no one in direct battle, produce exactly the same picture of "regulatory" science:

- The critics charge that the science *as widely practiced by scientists* is riddled with subjective and value elements, is based on poor or even nonexistent data, and often reaches conclusions that are baseless and wrong—and state explicitly that this is outrageous.
- The government defenders agree that the science *they use in public policy* is riddled with subjective and value elements, is based on poor or even nonexistent data, and often reaches conclusions that are baseless and wrong—but state that this is inevitable.

When one examines the statements from government sources more closely, however, one sees that they are not just discussing public policy, they are also making statements about the quality of the science as such. Jellinek of the EPA says the science itself is inevitably poor or "wrong"—a word Jellinek also places within quotation marks—because the regulators must act in the face of "enormous scientific uncertainty"—which is to say that the current state of the science itself is inadequate. The Office of Science and Technology Policy also says that there are "uncertainties in the data" and often that judgments must be made where there are gaps in the data—also indicating that the current state of the science itself is inadequate. Only the Speth committee is less candid. It argues that at no stage of government "decisionmaking" can scientific fact be extricated from value judgments—but that same committee would never dream of making such a comment about such scientific fact as the life-saving value of penicillin or the second law of thermodynamics. Thus, by implication, this committee, too, is telling us that the science with which it begins is riddled with value judgments.

We are, therefore, left with a puzzling set of questions. Is it true, as the critics within the world of "regulatory" science charge, that the science of cancer prediction and prevention is being violated by scientists who, for reasons unexplained, are in the grip of mass subjectivity, incompetence, hysteria, and irrationality—a charge that implies that an objective, value-free science exists? Or is it true, as government sources indicate, that "regulatory" science in its present state is so full of "enormous uncertainties" and value judgments that to use it now is, inevitably, to be wrong? Is this, in other words, a quarrel over the state of the art? It appears to be that, and yet one cannot be sure. If it is a quarrel over the state of the art, one wonders why it must take the form of angry attacks on a huge epidemic of scientific incompetence and irrationality versus bland governmental defenses of public policy and regulatory decisionmaking which include a tiny epidemic of quotation marks around such concepts as "scientific" and "wrong." There is something perplexing about this controversy over the state of the art which needs explanation.

Yet another question is raised by this controversy. Why are the critics in the world of "regulatory" science so concerned about the public's judgments on their science? Physicists and chemists do not tremble in fear that the "average man" may be "tired" of their data, or find their quarks, black holes, and antimatter lacking in "common sense." Nor, when they discover that they have shamelessly misplaced neutrinos and that gravity is quite different from what they had supposed, do they shiver with fear that they will arouse the ire of the "average man." Why, then, are experts in cancer prevention trembling? And why, in particular, is it the *critics* who tremble? The more one examines this disjointed controversy within the world of "regulatory" science, the less one understands its scientific or political logic and the more opaque it becomes.

We cannot hope to disentangle the mystery until we answer the questions that have now made their appearance. What is the condition of the "regulatory" science? Is it a solidly developed science? And if it is not, what exactly *is* it? There is, accordingly, only one way to proceed. We must put the entire process of cancer prevention, from mouse tests to risk assessment, under our own microscope and examine it closely, as well as the data it produces, paying special attention to the separate controversies in the field, for they may eventually provide clues to this mysterious quarrel over the state of the art—if that, in fact, is what it is.

The first thing one learns on going to the literature is that the science of cancer prevention has never been adequately described to the public. In fact, the education of the layman has been so primitive as to be the equivalent of no education at all. If the layman has any impression at all of what goes on during an animal test, for example, it is probably captured fairly well by this description that has been transmitted in a little booklet by the NCI to the public:

In brief, groups of about 50 mice or rats of each sex are exposed to the test substance at different dosages for about two years. Other groups, known as controls, are treated identically, but are not exposed to the test substance. At the end of the experiment, the animals are carefully dissected and examined by pathologists (doctors who interpret the changes in body tissue caused by diseases), and the frequency of tumors in the test groups is compared with that of the controls. Carcinogens produce a tumor frequency higher in the exposed animals than in the unexposed control animals. Noncarcinogens, by contrast, do not produce tumors.[10]

This is a reasonable, short description of an animal experiment, but if this is essentially all one knows about the process, and if one's understanding of the other aspects of the science of cancer prediction and prevention is of a comparable simplicity, one is entirely unprepared to assess any of the events to which the layman has been exposed. Above all, one will be unable to separate political from scientific assessments.

This is a particularly critical problem to the layman, for whom the phenomenon of carcinogens has always been posed in a political context. In 1976, many laymen learned for the first time, and simultaneously, that animal tests for cancer existed, and that the data produced by industry were unreliable. The new scientific information, in fact, was embedded in political scandal. Industry, the public was told by horrified reporters who had been attending Senate hearings chaired by Edward M. Kennedy, had been conducting outrageously bad carcinogen tests, had, for years, been submitting invalid and even fraudulent data to the regulatory agencies, and had been ignoring toxicological data indicating their products were dangerous to workers and citizens.[11] Throughout 1976 and 1977 as well, television viewers listened appalled as a collection of EPA and FDA officials, consultants to agencies, environmental activists, and "whistle blowers" testified to the incompetence and bad faith of industry and of the commercial laboratories which worked for industry and to their willful violations of the stringent standards of the science of carcinogen testing.[12] At least one implication of the national furor was that the science of carcinogen testing actually had stringent standards. No one had been more outraged than Senator Kennedy or more confident in the existence of such standards. He declared passionately: "Inaccurate science, sloppy science, fraudulent science—these are the greatest threats to the health and safety of the American people."[13] Echoing attacks on industrial scientists reverberated through the nation. Unique only for the bluntness of his expression, not for his sentiments, Miles Lord, U.S. District Court Judge for Minnesota, as we have seen, thundered imprecations at the "kept scientists or the kept consultants, the hired guns of the scientific world," who, he said, were "hired to misconstrue, to skew, to overlook, and to fabricate."[14] Samuel Epstein was so overcome by this vision of the commercial corruption of his science that he built a second career on the denunciation of industrial data—that is a major theme of The Politics of Cancer. Equally distraught, Umberto Saffiotti called for the government licensing and control of commercial laboratories[15] and identified the unusual and historically unprecedented crime of "suspected mass murder." The message to the public rang out clearly: There was a developed science of carcinogen testing, and a venal industrial system was desecrating it.

There was no doubt that much, conceivably most, of industry's carcinogen tests had been bad, and that industrial data were unreliable. The categories of problems that had infested industry's tests were angrily listed by Epstein. Among them: Too few animals were used; animals had been tested at dosages so high it had killed them before cancer could emerge; tests had been terminated too early for cancer to emerge; animals had been poorly housed, fed, and cared for and had sickened and died prematurely, thus falsifying the experiments; dead animals had decomposed and cancers were missed in the autopsies; the autopsies themselves were inadequate; and records had been destroyed. Such deficiencies, said Epstein, were common and had been common for years.[16] And to judge by the information emerging from the regulatory agencies, Epstein was entirely accurate. On the basis of such shocking information the antagonism to industry among politicians, press, and public was understandable and justified.

It was also reported by government scientists that there had been cases of industrial fraud and that records of cancer tests had been falsified by major firms and commercial laboratories. According to R. Jeffrey Smith, in *Science*, three particularly lurid cases had been presented by the FDA and the EPA at the Kennedy hearings involving G. D. Searle and Co., Biometric Testing, Inc., and Industrial Biotest Laboratories, Inc.[17] In animal tests conducted by these companies and commercial laboratories, according to Ernest Brisson of the FDA, gross lesions had not been examined or reported and experiments had been deliberately designed to conceal toxic effects. Brisson said further: "We also encountered creative penmanship which causes test animals to appear and disappear throughout the course of a study. . . ."[18] Adrian Gross of the FDA reported that Searle, when advised of deficiencies in its data, had submitted a revamped version of the same deficient study to the FDA, and, said Gross, "Instead of changing the summary to more accurately reflect the data, however, the data had been changed to more accurately reflect the summary."[19] These various industries denied the allegations and, in one case—Industrial Biotest—the charges led to litigation. But there was no way for the layman then—or for the layman now—to make judgments on such matters. Laymen trusted the reports from the EPA and the FDA. On the basis of such information, and of generalizations indicating that such practices were not unique, there was once again ample reason for the widespread anger at industry.

There was only one problem with these revelations, however—a problem of which the horrified politicians, press, and public were unaware: The identical revelations might also have been made of carcinogen testing in the universities. The mass media had covered the Kennedy hearings of 1976, had transmitted what they had been told, and had gone on to cover other issues. But they had heard only part of the story. In 1977, *Science*, which never leaves its beat, reported on the deficiencies in toxicity and carcinogen testing in the universities, where a large part of the work on product testing is done, and revealed that the situation was even worse there than in industry. Carl Blozan, an FDA research analyst, had conducted a pilot monitoring and inspection program in 1977 at forty-two laboratories in different parts of the country, and his report had informed the FDA, as Smith of *Science* put it, that when measured against the standards the FDA was proposing, the "corporate laboratories came out on top, followed by contract labs, and at the bottom, labs at institutions of higher learning." Five universities had been included in the study "and none had better than a 50% compliance score." The worst areas were quality control, the use of standard procedures, the storage of data, and the keeping of records. Blozan concluded that universities were "the most lax in animal study control." On the basis of this study, the FDA decided that the same standards had to be imposed on universities as on industry.[20] Smith explored the reasons for these "seemingly incongruous" findings and made several additional discoveries. According to Adrian Gross of the FDA, many of the university faculty members were not doing the animal testing for which they had received contracts, but were dumping the work onto graduate students "who just want to get their degrees and get out."[21] In addition, FDA officials told Smith, universities tend to be "poorly disciplined"; while corporations and commercial laboratories, which had employees rather than junior colleagues, could prescribe rigorous procedures and enforce them, universities could not.[22] The profit motive, Smith discovered, actually worked for scientific probity, not against it. He cited Gerald Laubach, the president of Pfizer, who had explained why industrial labs were more scientifically responsible than university labs. The reason, said Smith, was this: Industry lost both time and money when testing was bad and had to be redone; universities lost nothing.[23] The fact that corporate testing was scientifically superior to the university testing "would surprise many consumer advocates," said Smith, who was visibly surprised himself.[24] It would also have surprised many citizens, had they ever learned it. These findings never made headlines, nor did the TV documentarians rush in throng to report on how academic scientists were betraying the science of carcinogen testing. It is likely that up to the moment of writing, most of the press has never learned of these "incongruous findings." On December 7, 1980, the *New York Times Magazine* was still presenting the problem as dominantly one of industrial fraud and of industry's corruption of academic consultants.[25]

Deficient animal experimentation has not been the only flaw to have turned up in the academic world. Fraud, too, has made its appearance, and the number of cases has increased with the years. Despite its ideals and disciplines, dishonesty has never been entirely absent from science, and all sciences have had their share. Ewan Whitaker of the Lunar and Planetary Laboratory in Arizona observed in 1980 that "most of us would admit to knowing of one or two scientists in our own field who have resorted to 'subterfuge, rhetoric, and propaganda. . . .' "[26] And fraud was to be found in toxicity and cancer research as well.

Some recent examples are these:

In 1974, William T. Summerlin won a prestigious job at the Memorial Sloan-Kettering Cancer Center on the basis of remarkable experiments in transplant immunity. Unfortunately no one, including Summerlin, could replicate his impressive findings. It was reported that he had fabricated data, i.e., that he had painted the skin of his mice; he denied the charges, but was later suspended from duty.[27] In 1979, a number of scientists, whose names were not made public, were reported by the FDA to have done fraudulent work. Based on an interview with Michael Hendsley of the Office of Scientific Investigation at the FDA, Constance Holden of *Science* reported that "prestigious academics" had "flouted test protocols, falsified data and submitted phony informed consent documents."[28] In 1980, Elias Alsabti of the University of Virginia was charged with plagiarizing the data in five of his sixty papers; he had published widely in American, European, and Japanese journals of cancer research; he denied the charges, but later resigned.[29] Also in 1980, John Long, in the Pathology Department of Harvard University and of Massachusetts General Hospital, resigned, according to the *New York Times*, "after conceding that he had faked the results of an experiment." Long had been studying the mechanisms of Hodgkin's disease. Among other complex problems, his cell lines had been contaminated and were spurious; they had not come from human beings with Hodgkin's disease, but from owl monkeys. As Nicholas Wade of *Science* summed up the catastrophe: "A $750,000 research project at Mass. General eventually collapsed, leaving a legacy of invented data and useless cell lines."[30] And again in 1980, Nicola Di Ferrante, a senior member of a group of researchers studying certain skin fibroblasts, discovered that certain data originally published by the group had been "manipulated." Ferrante wrote a letter to *Science* publicly identifying the fact and apologized for "reviewing the original data with excessive enthusiasm and with a criticism not suited to uncover a scientific fraud." It was, said Ferrante, a "possibility" that the data had been "fabricated."[31] Yet again in 1980, *Oncology Times* published a page-long letter from a cancer researcher, whose name was withheld, announcing that he was leaving the research field. One of his major reasons was that the ethics of research had deteriorated since the entry of massive government funding into the field. Grant pressures, he said, were generating "anxiety" in "the young scientist" which "tempt him to cheat a little."[32] In 1980, in fact, there was such an epidemic of fraud in biomedical research, both within and outside the field of cancer research, that Philip M. Boffey, science editor of the *New York Times*, felt constrained to reassure readers that scientific frauds are self-correcting— that when work is significant, scientists try to replicate it and the process "eventually exposes fraud as well as error." Fraud is rare, Boffey explained, but the scale of science had changed; as the number of scientists had increased, more cases of dishonesty were being found and reported.[33]

Fabrication of data, however, is not the sole cause of the circulation of misleading information. One of the most startling cases of misleading data in cancer research was the result not of invention but of the failure to publish certain information. According to William J. Broad of *Science*, radiobiologists Paul Todd and Paul S. Furcinitti of the University of Pennsylvania published a pioneering threshold experiment in *Science* in 1979 on the effects of radiation on human kidney cells, and reported that when such cells were exposed to radiation, cell death occurred at minute doses. The story, appearing at the height of the threshold controversy in the field of radiation carcinogenesis, made headlines in the scientific press; the *New Scientist* announced: "Low radiation doses do cause cancer." The experiment was widely cited by advocates of the no-threshold theory as proving their case. Unfortunately, they had rejoiced too soon, for there was one fact they did not know: The cells in this famous experiment had come from a woman with cancer; they had been malignant to start with. For a variety of complex reasons, says Broad, some pertaining to clashing technical perspectives between radiobiologists and cell researchers as to what was and was not crucially relevant to the experiment, the authors of the study did not include the information that the cells were originally malignant; and in later publications of this research, when they did refer to it as a suspect factor, the references were cut out by editors of scientific publications as irrelevant or as weakening the point of the paper. Thus, information which had been available since 1977 was not made public until 1980—by Walter Nelson-Rees, a cytogeneticist at the University of Naval Biosciences Laboratory in Oakland. Rees, who had read the original experimental report in *Science*, had suspected that the cells were not normal, tracked down the information, and published it in *Science*. Inevitably, it provoked consternation among cell researchers to whom the fact of the cells' malignancy is crucial. In his report on these developments, entitled "The Case of the Unmentioned Malignancy," Broad said that the malignancy of the test cells has "cast a cloud over the whole experiment and raised a chorus of accusations and retorts concerning scientific credibility and candor."

The authors of this particular paper defended themselves hotly, arguing (1) that they had sought to identify their cells as malignant; (2) that their studies on cell-killing were irrelevant to the malignancy of the cells; and (3) that cells from that identical maligant cell line—He-La cells—had been widely used in molecular biology and that many of the principles of DNA and RNA synthesis had been established in He-La cells. Furcinitti and Todd, in fact, were unfortunate in being singled out by *Science*, since it soon emerged that their use of the malignant He-La cells was just the tip of an international iceberg. For many years, Nelson-Rees had been pursuing He-La cells—named after a woman called Henrietta Lacks from whom they had originally come—because the malignant cells of the long-dead woman had been contaminating other cell lines in laboratories all over the world. In April 1981, *Science* published Rees' source list of reference papers describing the properties of the known strains of He-La and other human cell lines "indicted" as He-La contaminants, as well as yet other types of contaminated cell lines in wide use in research laboratories. In the same month, *Science 81* published a popularized version of the story entitled "The Cells That Would Not Die": "Strangely reincarnated, Henrietta Lacks haunts the world's biological laboratories, undoing years of research. . . ." In fact, one of the complex strands of the John Long story, referred to above, also involved He-La cells. How much cancer cell research has actually been "undone" by the malignant He-La cells is unknowable to the layman, and is probably unknown to science. What is significant, in the context of this chapter, is that fraud is scarcely the only problem that can produce misleading academic data in the realm of cancer research.[34]

It is important to know about such *causes célèbres* in the world of academic cancer research only because so much publicity has been accorded to industrial error and malfeasance. But such dramatic cases, whether in industry or in the academic world, are misleading in one sense: They deflect attention from the real problem in the field of cancer research—the fact that an enormous amount of the work is bad not from moral deficiencies in the experimenters but from deficiencies in their knowledge.

What the theatrical headlines and the *causes célèbres* do not reveal is the phenomenon that dominates the literature of carcinogen research in particular—the existence of an extraordinary number of unresolved problems and controversies. There are few, if any, aspects of the process of carcinogen identification, cancer prediction in man, and risk assessment over which academic scientists are not quarreling bitterly. There is no way to describe all the controversies in the field; there are too many of them. Libraries full of scientific papers, many the size of books, have been devoted to analyses of the various entrenched quarrels, each written from a slightly different viewpoint. The layman, however, needs no such detailed information; he merely needs to know that these disagreements exist and to have some idea of their content and range. One readily available roundup of controversies can be found in the OSHA policy document of 1980. It does not include all, but it is a sizable collection, and the layman can profit simply by reading a list of them. It is important to remember that OSHA's policy document was not a regulator-versus-industry hearing, but a hearing on the state of the art in "regulatory" science; one finds academic scientists on all sides of the controversies. Here is how OSHA listed what the agency considered to be among the most intransigent controversies as of 1978; it is OSHA that presented them in the form of questions:[35]

Can strains with a high spontaneous incidence of tumors be used in carcinogenicity testing?

Does the presence of tumor viruses invalidate results obtained in mouse tests?

Is the spontaneous incidence of tumors in certain mouse strains unstable, and if so, does this invalidate positive results obtained in them?

Can liver tumors in mice be diagnosed reliably and consistently?

Is the induction of tumors in mice predictive of carcinogenicity in other species?

Can reliable results be obtained in inbred strains of rodents?

Are there other characteristics of rodents which would invalidate their use in carcinogenicity testing?

Should "non-positive" results in human studies outweigh positive results in animal experiments?

Should "non-positive" results in animal experiments outweigh positive results in other animal experiments?

What precautions should be taken to avoid placing weight on "false positive" results?

How should OSHA deal with data of varying quality?

Do biological reasons make testing of EMTDs inappropriate? [OSHA here is questioning Estimated Maximum Tolerated Doses or high-dose testing.]

How much weight should be placed upon the induction of benign tumors in animals as an indication of potential carcinogenic hazards in humans?

How much weight should be placed on the induction of a type of tumor which occurs spontaneously in untreated animals?

Are most routes of administration appropriate?

How much confirmation of positive results is necessary?

Can "safe" or "no-effect" levels be set for exposure to carcinogens?

Do "bionutrients" necessarily display thresholds?

Are there theoretical reasons to expect that a threshold exists at the cellular level?

Have thresholds in fact been demonstrated for specific carcinogens?

Is there a consistent relationship between dose and latent period that would result in a practical threshold at low doses?

Would the interaction among carcinogens invalidate the concept of a threshold?

Should criteria or protocols be established for the conduct and interpretation of carcinogenesis bioassays?

Does OSHA need to review protocols of animal bioassays which yield evidence that a substance is carcinogenic?

Should OSHA prescribe protocols for design and execution of carcinogenesis bioassays?

Should OSHA prescribe standards for interpretation of bioassay data?

What factors need to be taken into account by OSHA in the interpretation and evaluation of animal carcinogenicity experiments?

How should OSHA determine whether positive bioassay reports meet scientific criteria for acceptability?

Should tumor "promoters" be distinguished from tumor "initiators" and regulated differently?

Should metabolic and pharmacokinetic information be used in the identification or regulation of potential carcinogens?

In what circumstances would metabolic and pharmacokinetic information serve to rebut a qualitative presumption of risk?

Is our present knowledge of metabolism and pharmacokinetics sufficient to be useful in practice?

Can specific procedures or criteria for the use of metabolic and pharmacokinetic information be laid down on the basis of our present knowledge?

The layman will understand some of these questions; some have already been discussed, and others will appear to be arcane mysteries, but the very existence of such a list of questions—pertaining to every aspect of "regulatory" science—offers valuable information in itself. It tells us that sixty years after the birth of the science of carcinogenesis, twenty years after the appearance of the Delaney Clause, eight years after the Ad Hoc Committee informed the Surgeon General that a program to protect Americans from "the mass" of environmental carcinogens was "within reach," and two years after the passage of the Toxic Substances Control Act, scientists were still quarreling about some of the most fundamental aspects of cancer testing, cancer prediction, and risk assessment. In the course of "normal" science, which exists in a state of perpetual creative muddle, this would have no particular significance. But we are not looking here at "normal" science—we are looking at "regulatory" science, at the quality of the science which is dedicated to the detection of "suspected mass murder" and to the legal prevention of cancer. Here the muddle has quite a different meaning, for its consequences are not just peaceful theoretical debates which go on for decades, but have immediate practical consequences that affect us all.

Nonetheless, a list of questions is still too abstract, and one needs a more concrete sense of what such quarrels are about. Here, in more detail, are four of the most important controversies. The purpose in illustrating them is not to report on OSHA's coverage, but to give the reader an impression of the wide range of views. The opinions that follow are taken from the literature, which includes OSHA's policy document, but is not limited to it.

Man vs. Animal

Scientists disagree over the relative sensitivity to carcinogens in men and laboratory animals—an issue of importance if animals are to be used as surrogates for man. Some scientists—e.g., John Cairns,[36] Richard Peto,[37] and Robert Butler of the National Institute of Aging[38]—observe that the cells of long-lived animals such as humans and elephants are far more numerous; Peto professes his ignorance on the question, but according to Cairns and Butler, the cells of mammals with long lifespans are far less active in converting chemicals into carcinogens than are the cells of short-lived animals. The implication here, if true, is that man is presumably far more resistant to the risk of carcinogenicity than mouse. Other scientists, however, cite metabolic data to demonstrate that the larger the animal, the greater the danger of exposure to carcinogens. Herman Kraybill, observing that humans and large animals metabolize and distribute substances much more slowly than do small animals, points out that this implies that a toxic substance would remain in the bloodstream and the organs of humans longer than it would in rodents.[39] Similarly, an NAS committee, pointing out that man excretes compounds more slowly than mice, says this means that man "with a very small daily intake, can develop a greater accumulation of a compound over many years."[40] Others believe that man's sensitivity to carcinogens must be quite diverse. William Lijinsky speculates, "Since there is such a large variation in susceptibility to carcinogens even among a group of experimental animals which, while not inbred, are closely related genetically, there is obviously a probability that a much greater variation in susceptibility to carcinogens is present in the human population."[41]

Finally, David Rall, the scientist who for years told conferences that it was in the realm of metabolism that species similarity broke down, has speculated that "man is among the most heterogeneous systems on earth" and asserted: "If sufficient effort were exerted, one could find that metabolically some man would exhibit a pattern like a rat, another man would exhibit characteristics of a dog and so forth."[42] It is obvious from both the different positions and from the ideas themselves that in the absence of information about metabolic differences, these views are all speculative.

Man = One, Two, or Three Species?

Scientists disagree as to how many species of animals must be tested before one may apply a carcinogenic finding to man. Isaac Berenblum says that to be "at all reliable" a carcinogenic finding must be made in "at least three different species."[43] Marvin Schneiderman of the NCI reports as a "pragmatic guideline" that a test be conducted in "at least two species."[44] Norbert Page of the NCI says that at least two species must be tested if one is to know whether the outcome is metabolically atypical.[45] The NCI officially requires two or more species,[46] as does a joint committee of the Food and Agricultural Organization and the World Health Organization.[47] Others make the related point that a single experiment—which, by definition, is a test in one species—means little or nothing. Kraybill of the NCI says that "reliance on one test in the rat or mouse without other supportive data is of questionable value."[48] The Office of Science and Technology Policy notes that if a sufficient number of tests are conducted, at least one of them will produce statistically significant results "simply as a result of random variation" and recommends that scientists "view the outcome of any single test as potentially the result of chance variation." In effect, says the OST, a single test should be regarded as potentially meaningless.[49]

Others, however, deny the necessity of multiple species and multiple experiments and claim that one good experiment—i.e., an experiment in one species—is sufficient. Among those who expressed this view at the OSHA hearings were Bo Holmberg of Sweden, the Environmental Defense Fund, Lorenzo Tomatis of IARC, the EPA, Dr. David Rall of NIEHS, Harold Stewart of NIH, Curtis Harris of NCI, Samuel Epstein of the University of Illinois, and Philippe Shubik of the Eppley Institute.[50] Additionally, the EDF and Tomatis argued that to wait for confirmatory results of a first carcinogen test would expose workers to an additional period of hazard.[51] OSHA sided with this latter group. The agency, citing Fears et al., who claimed that "statistically reliable conclusions can be drawn from the results of single experiments," took the position in its policy document: "OSHA rejects the argument that positive results should be required in two species before an inference is drawn about human hazard or risk." OSHA considers that "a substance may be classified as a Category I Potential Carcinogen on the basis of scientifically evaluated positive results . . . in a single mammalian species in an adequately conducted long-term bioassay. . . ."[52]

Are Mice Reliable?

Scientists disagree over the reliability of mice, the most commonly used laboratory species. Laboratory mice have a high spontaneous incidence of tumors. They frequently register substances (e.g., organochlorine pesticides) as carcinogenic which do not produce carcinogenic effects in the rat. The mouse tumors that have come under challenge are those in the liver and lungs, mammary tumors, and lymphomas. Many scientists have questioned the legitimacy of relying only on mouse data when such tumors appear. Among the most commonly mentioned critics are Paul Grasso and Reginald Crampton, representing the Chemical Industries Health Council,[53] but others, too, share this concern. Norbert Page of the NCI considers establishing the biological significance of liver tumors in the mouse to be one of "the most perplexing problems" in using animals to predict carcinogenic danger to man.[54] Philippe Shubik declared that "there can be no question" that the induction of liver tumors in the mouse with no similar reaction in the rat and hamster "needs explanation."[55] Others who question the significance of certain tumors in the mouse and testified to that effect at the OSHA hearings are Robert Olson of St. Louis University, James Jandl of Harvard University, and Johannes Clemmesen of Denmark's Cancer Registry.[56] In addition, major scientific agencies and committees have also expressed concern about the reliability of certain mouse tumors. The IARC, in 1978, declared that lung tumors and liver tumors occurred spontaneously in high incidence in mice "and their malignancy is often difficult to establish"; the IARC says that "rigid guidelines" cannot be established and leaves the responsibility of assessing those tumors in mice to the different working committees which prepare the IARC monographs.[57] Similar uncertainty has been expressed by the National Cancer Advisory Board.[58] And in one particular case, that of the pesticide dieldrin-aldrin, the WHO-FAO working groups concluded that the induction of cancer in mouse livers was not predictive of human risk.[59]

Other scientists, however, have denied that there is any reason to question the validity of mouse tumors as predictors of cancer in man. Among those who were cited by OSHA as taking that position were Lorenzo Tomatis of the IARC, the EPA, Umberto Saffiotti of NCI, Samuel Epstein of the University of Illinois, Melvin Reuber of NCI, Harold Stewart of NIH, Walter Heston of NIH, I. Nathan Dubin of the Medical College of Pennsylvania, and Robert Squire of Johns Hopkins.[60] OSHA itself came down on the side of the mouse. The agency stated that it was "aware that doubts about the validity of the mouse liver tumor system are fairly widely held, and that several reports of scientific committees issued in the past two years have reflected the controversy." Nonetheless, the agency said, "OSHA concludes from analysis of these statements and exhibits that the alleged difficulty in identifying and interpreting neoplasms in the mouse liver is grossly exaggerated. The biological behavior of mouse liver neoplasms is well-understood and can be identified objectively and reliably."[61]

Even stellar supporters of the mouse, however, are not precisely lyrical in their praise. Addressing a group of cancer researchers at a Cold Spring Harbor Conference, Tomatis of the IARC relayed the information that no correlations existed between liver tumors in mice and liver tumors in other rodents, but that there was a positive correlation between liver tumors in mice and tumors at *other* sites in rats and hamsters. He then defended the mouse glumly, saying, "We all agree that the mouse should be discarded as a testing tool if a better experimental model can be found," adding that the mouse was "no worse qualified" than any other mammal for the identification of chemical carcinogens and for the prediction of potential risk to man.[62]

Do High Doses Cause Cancer?

Scientists disagree about the biological "appropriateness" of the MTD—the maximum tolerated dose to which animals are commonly tested. In February 1976, the year that the Toxic Substances Control Act was passed, the NIEHS held a conference in Pinehurst, N.C., which was later reviewed by Wil Lepkowski of the Hastings Center. He reported: "There was a swirl of other commentary on the dubious advisability of 'swamping' test animals with high dosages of carcinogens. The modes of action may be different at high dosages than at low and can thus obscure not only the mechanism of carcinogenesis but also introduce factors that may be irrelevant to the natural conditions, where dosages are usually low."[63] In the year of the OSHA policy hearings, scientists were still quarreling about it; according to H. F. Kraybill of NCI, most of a three-day conference on toxicology held in Washington in 1978 was dedicated to discussion of the maximum tolerated dose.[64] According to Lorenzo Tomatis of the IARC, two approaches to testing are possible: One can test at doses that "mimic" those to which man is exposed, and one can test at high doses that exceed anything to which man is exposed; the latter, he says, may be one of the principal reasons for indifference to animal experiments.[65] According to Marvin Schneiderman of the NCI: "The most commonly expressed objection to regulatory decisions based on carcinogenesis observed in animal experiments is that the high dosages to which animals are exposed have no relevance to human risks."[66] Because this is one of the most vehement of all the controversies and because it has odd repercussions in other realms of the research, this particular quarrel will be described in more detail. The basic arguments on both sides of the controversy can be quickly given, for with only the slightest shadings of difference, the two conflicting groups make the same points in presenting their respective positions.

The argument in favor of the MTD, or high-dose testing, is given by Marvin Schneiderman of the National Cancer Institute, whose formulation is unusually concise:

In general, dosages that are high in relation to expected human exposures must be given because in model experimental systems, we have no choice but to use few animals in comparison with the number of humans exposed.

An incidence of cancer of about 10% in a group of experimental animals represents a lower limit of reproducibility; 10% of a human population is very high. For example, an incidence as low as 0.01% would represent 1000 people in a total population of 10 million and might be considered unacceptably high even in the face of sizable benefits. To detect such a low incidence in experimental animals directly would require hundreds of thousands of animals. For this reason, we have no choice but to give large doses to relatively small experimental groups and then use biologically reasonable models in extrapolating the results to estimate risk at low doses.[67]

The argument against the MTD, or high-dose testing, is given by Herman Kraybill, also of the National Cancer Institute. Its basis is biological, rather than statistical, and because it conflicts with official policy, the chances are good that the reader has never seen it as it appears in serious scientific literature, so it will be presented here. Kraybill says:

This exaggerated dose is imposed upon the rodent for 18–24 months to establish a carcinogenic response, if possible. Quite frequently, these endeavors are failures since overdosing produces overt toxicity, which invariably produces organ refractoriness, such as a swamping of the liver microsomal enzymes. In addition, metabolic overloading may either result in a chemical being metabolized by an alternate pathway, not necessarily comparable to metabolic stress in human exposure situations, or the chemical may be unmetabolized, stored in the body or excreted unchanged.

For most every chemical, pollutant, or nutrient, the mammalian system has a finite value for a threshold or tolerance level that the well-defined biochemical and metabolic pathways can accommodate . . . and any useful chemical, if taken in excess, will lead to untoward effects. . . .

This essential pharmacologic threshold principle appears to be forgotten when attempts are made to maximize the response, either carcinogenic or non-carcinogenic, by administering excessive doses of a chemical.[68]

The lay reader might profit by a little translation here. Kraybill is saying that all mammals have "thresholds" for chemicals, that there are doses which the metabolic process can generally detoxify, and that the practice of high-dose testing, by drenching the metabolic process with poison, violates this basic threshold principle of toxicology. According to Kraybill, high dosing may falsify the experiment in one of two ways: It can either poison the cells and tissues so severely as to *prevent* a carcinogenic response that might otherwise have been found, or it can so "overload" and change metabolic processes as to *cause* a carcinogenic response which would not normally occur and which is a laboratory "artifact."[69]

Kraybill is frankly appalled by the magnitude of the doses used in many experiments. In a study of one pesticide, he reported, "the amount in pounds required for a lifetime study (bioassay) in the rodent exceeded the amount available from a manufacturer in his total annual production."[70] In a review of various experiments, Kraybill described the disparity between the doses given to animals and the doses to which human beings are exposed. He pointed out, for example, that in one experiment on the sweetener cyclamate, the test animals were given the human equivalent of 552 bottles of soft drinks a day; that in two experiments on trichloroethylene, used in decaffeinated coffee, the test animals were given the human equivalent of 5×10^7 cups of coffee a day and 10×10^7 cups a day; that in an experiment on diethylstilbestrol, the test animals were given the human equivalent of 5×10^6 pounds of liver a day for fifty years.[71] Kraybill concludes that data drawn from such tests "are almost science fiction."[72]

Aware of the need for an objective standard for validating a cutoff point in the higher dose ranges, Kraybill proposes that studies be undertaken of the dose effects of chemicals which are necessary to survival, and which he presumes are noncarcinogenic. He suggests that chemicals found naturally in the body and in the metabolic process, some of which have been demonstrated at extremely high doses to be carcinogenic—e.g., chemicals such as xylitol and tryptophan, vitamins, and essential minerals—be used as a guide to setting dose levels.[73] In addition, he recommends studies in comparative metabolism and pharmacokinetic studies, immunological studies, and specific tests on organ function to provide supportive data.[74]

This, then, is the essential statement of the controversy. It has split scientists in the highest reaches of the research establishment. The position enunciated by Schneiderman is shared by such figures and organizations as Arthur Upton, Richard Griesemer, Umberto Saffiotti, William Lijinsky, and Harold Stewart, all of the NCI; Donald Millar, Acting Director of NIOSH; David Rall,

Director of NIEHS; Steven Jellinek and Roy Albert, representing the EPA; and several NAS committees and OSHA.[75] Indeed, Upton, Director of the NCI, says of high-dose testing: "This practice has been endorsed by almost all workers in the field including . . . expert international and national committees. . . ."[76]

Short of conducting an opinion poll, however, there is no way to know where the actual consensus lies. The quarrel over the issue at two major conferences suggests the existence of considerable dissension. And along with Kraybill of the NCI, one finds many other scientists of repute who have expressed similar or identical concerns that high doses may be falsifying the results of animal tests by either inhibiting carcinogenesis or causing cancers artificially to appear. Most of the critics, interestingly enough, have not repudiated high-dose testing, but issue warnings against the dangers of the practice. Among them are Norbert Page of the NCI,[77] and the Office of Science and Technology Policy.[78] In addition, similar warnings come from scientists in other countries. In Britain, Richard Peto of Oxford, discussing the complexity of animal testing, has said:

Also, any chemical which causes proliferation or necrosis in any organ that is subject to spontaneous cancers is likely to modify the onset rate of tumours in that organ, and since the aim of most animal experiments is to study a dose which is nearly, but not quite, sufficient to cause significant weight loss or mortality within three months, it is not surprising that so many chemicals at such doses can cause cancers in animals.[79]

Ian Munro of Canada's Bureau of Chemical Safety and one of that country's most prominent researchers has made a similar analysis.[80] And another comes from D. Schmähl of the Institute of Toxicology and Chemotherapy of the German Cancer Research Center in Heidelberg, who is one of Germany's most prominent cancer researchers.[81] In fact, David Rall of the NIEHS has touched ground on both sides of the controversy. Asked by Thomas Maugh of *Science* to comment on Leon Golberg's criticism that high-dose testing was "completely inappropriate" and on the view of many scientists that "the complete spectrum of absorption, distribution, biotransformation and excretion of the chemical should be considered before determining the maximum dose for bioassays," Rall responded, said Maugh, that "he cannot disagree," but noted that "such studies would probably limit the number of chemicals that could be assayed to four per year."[82]

While the layman can form no opinion on this issue, he can form an opinion about what he has been told about the scientific controversy by government sources: He has been told nothing. In fact, he has been systematically encouraged to believe that only the scientifically illiterate "public" distrusts high-dose testing. To wit (emphasis added):

• Arthur Upton of NCI: "Contrary to *widespread popular belief,* there is no evidence that a chemical which is carcinogenic at high doses would not also be carcinogenic in lower doses."[83]
• Eula Bingham of OSHA: "But a difficulty with animal testing is *public mis-*

perceptions about massive dose testing. It is not true that any substance will cause cancer if administered to test animals in massive doses."[84]
- The NCI, in a pamphlet entitled "Everything Doesn't Cause Cancer:" "The *public* often misunderstands the reasons for high dosage testing, and misinterprets the results. . . . High doses of many chemicals are toxic, but they will not cause tumors."[85]
- Thomas Maugh of *Science*, interviewing David Rall of the NIEHS on the subject: "There is a misconception among the *public* that at high enough levels, virtually any substance will be carcinogenic." Maugh paraphrased Rall as declaring that the idea is "completely fallacious."[86]
- Sidney Wolfe, medical director of Ralph Nader's organization, testified at a Senate hearing chaired by Edward Kennedy: "In self-protection, although fueled somewhat by industry, *many people* have come to believe that enough of any chemical fed to animals can cause cancer. . . ."[87]

No one, of course, knows how many members of "the public" are actually conscious of the practice of maximum tolerated dose testing and have drawn the conclusion that all chemicals tested at MTD cause cancer. Nor does anyone know to what degree this notion has been "fueled by industry." What is clear is that by vehemently and repeatedly "correcting" this position allegedly held by "the public," prominent spokesmen for "regulatory" science have effectively concealed the actual academic controversy that exists, one which has caused intellectual strife within the NCI itself.

These are only four of the unresolved issues in the field of cancer testing, and one could produce equivalent roundups of clashing academic opinion on each issue named on the whole OSHA list of controversies. Even these four, however, give one a vivid sense of the degree of uncertainty that exists at the very base of "regulatory" science. The fact that academic scientists are quarreling over such issues as mouse-man equivalence, the validity of the mouse itself as an experimental animal, the number of species and experiments required to establish the legitimacy of a carcinogen, and whether the dosing practices are falsifying the results in experiments tells us that "regulatory" science—the science that polices industry and prevents cancer—is still in a precarious state.

Unresolved controversies, however, are just one aspect of the problem. Equally significant is the inordinate difficulty of the basic process of identifying carcinogens in animal tests. The animal test, which sounded so attractively simple in the little NCI description quoted above, is actually a nightmare of complexity in which innumerable elements can go wrong at any moment. It should be immediately noted that things can only "go wrong" in situations where it is possible for them to "go right." And there is a body of scientific lore—a collection of observations, practices, dogma, rules, "guidelines"— which indicates very generally how cancer tests, specifically tests in which the data are ultimately extrapolated to man, *should* be conducted. This lore, as Arthur Upton, head of the NCI, put it, "cannot be reduced to a formula."[88] It is steadily evolving and cannot be described as a body of authentic scientific principles, although the word "principles" is sometimes loosely used. Indeed, were there such a body of authentic scientific principles, we would not see the large numbers of unresolved controversies that still exist. There is, rather, a rough set of criteria on which, says OSHA, there is "substantial" agreement among experts.[89] One of the best ways to get an insight into the attributes of what such experts consider to be a good animal test is to have some idea of the attributes of a bad one. Some of the difficulties that beset cancer tests are so technical that only scientists can understand and appreciate them, and they cannot be described here. But there are also difficulties that a layman can understand and appreciate, and ten categories of those will be described. They will provide the lay reader with some idea of the major factors that chronically cause erroneous, inconclusive, meaningless, or downright false data in cancer tests, as well as in the identification of animal carcinogens in the environment, factors which must be known if one is ever to assess "regulatory" science.

FACTORS THAT CAUSE ERRORS IN ANIMAL TESTS

1. Collections of Causes of Error

Various documents list long collections of errors that can occur in animal testing. The most enlightening example of such a document is the one that sets forth "guidelines" for conducting a carcinogen test. Such collections of guidelines are published by research agencies like the NCI, and for every single guideline—there are hundreds of them—there is a potential pitfall or source of possible error in the experiment. The guidelines are actually warnings to scientists of those potential errors. Norbert Page of the NCI has reviewed the sixty-three pages of NCI guidelines for a carcinogenesis test—guidelines of which J. Sontag, he, and Umberto Saffiotti are the authors. According to Page, many factors can have significant effects on the outcome of tests; for example, diseases caused by microbes and parasites; chemically polluted feed, water, air, and bedding; infestation by vermin; cannibalism; and diet.[90]

Any pet owner or housewife can tell from this list that it must require great effort to control such factors in an experiment that may be utilizing hundreds of mice over a two-year period. According to Page, inadequate care of animals has ruined many experiments in toxicity, and he says, for carcinogen testing, "competent animal husbandry is of the utmost importance."[91] At a minimum, animals can become diseased and die in such numbers as to destroy any statistical basis for the experiment; at a maximum, diseases may affect biological processes in such ways as to alter the physiological effects of the test chemical and falsify the meaning of the findings.

Other scientists have made lists of yet different factors in animal tests that can affect the outcome and produce dubious data. According to the National Cancer Advisory Board, whose committee of consultants includes some of the most distinguished scientists in the field of carcinogenesis, there are elements in experiments which may produce carcinogenic data that cannot always be taken at face value as an indicator of human risk. The NCAB, opining in 1977, said this:

Certain methods (listed below) are important pointers to potential carcinogenicity and cannot be ignored: however, they may require additional studies before extrapolation to particular conditions of human usage can be made. Examples of these methods are:

Bioassays employing inbred strains of animals which develop high incidences of particular tumors in the untreated state. In some of these studies the particular characteristics of the animals and the results obtained may require additional evaluation. . . .

Bioassays in which, in addition to the test agent, animals are treated with a known carcinogen, or some other foreign material which itself may be carcinogenic or co-carcinogenic.

Bioassays in which the test animals are subjected to grossly unphysiologic and inappropriate conditions, in addition to the administration of the test compound, and there is reason to believe that these unphysiologic conditions may in themselves enhance tumor induction.

Bioassays in which the test compound is given by unusual routes of administration (such as bladder implantation) and there is reason to believe that the tumors that occurred may not be due to a specific effect of the test compound.[92]

Herman Kraybill of the NCI has compiled yet another list of factors which can introduce uncertainties or error into animal tests. His list contains one or two elements already mentioned, but it is useful to see it intact. He names inappropriate routes of administration; enhancement of the susceptibility of the animals by deliberate suppression of immune mechanisms; contaminants in the compounds being tested; exposure to other uncontrolled compounds; and, as the reader will recall, exposure to high dosages of the chemical which may cause a "metabolic overload" and falsify carcinogenic responses.[93]

Page, in addition, stresses several of the factors on his own list as being the most significant—above all, the diet of the animals, as well as contaminants in the air, water, diet, and bedding, which can alter the carcinogenic reaction. These factors, he says, "have not been studied in sufficient detail."[94]

Finally, each of the collections of factors listed above is not just a compendium of possible sources of error in a single science; it is also a compendium of possible sources of error in a great number of sciences. So far, by implication, we have been talking of specialists in animal testing as though they belonged to only one scientific discipline; in fact, specialists in many scientific disciplines participate in carcinogen tests and, more particularly, in the analysis of the experiment and in the interpretation of the data. This produces an entirely new and complex source of confusion and errors. According to Kraybill, the animal experiments "should withstand the scrutiny of scientists in various disciplines such as pharmacology, biochemistry, toxicology, molecular biology, pathology, nutritional biochemistry, statistics, and other fields." Unfortunately, he adds, "uniform approbation" is nonexistent: ". . . invariably there are debates about protocols and/or experimental designs and ultimately the conclusions drawn in evaluation of the data."[95] In other words, conflicts can occur in at least seven different scientific disciplines, and challenges to the data can come from as many different sources. And what is more, says Kraybill, such challenges "invariably" occur.

2. Diet as a Source of Error

Certain specific factors have a greater potentiality for causing error in animal tests than others. Diet is one of them. Given the reportedly extensive carcinogenicity of natural foods, carcinogen testers, with knowledge of this literature, have occasionally feared that they might unwittingly be feeding their animals carcinogens or carcinogen promoters, in addition to the controlled test chemicals. In 1975, Mark Hegsted of the Department of Nutrition at the Harvard School of Public Health told a cancer conference: "It is rather frightening to contemplate the possibility that the results of the extensive testing programs may be erroneous because of unexplored dietary effects."[96] In 1977, to repeat, Page of the NCI said there was "ample evidence" that diet could affect the outcome of a carcinogenesis experiment. In 1979, J. R. Sabine of the University of Adelaide, reporting on the genetic, physiological, and metabolic factors that influence carcinogenesis, warned that each could be influenced by nutritional variables; he pointed out that every experiment with animals was also a nutritional experiment, and that it was no longer enough just to feed the animals—it was necessary to identify all the biological factors that the food might be influencing.[97] Again in 1980, Kraybill declared that it was "distressing" to note that diet is frequently "overlooked" by those conducting animal tests, and pointed out that both the quantity and types of nutrients fed the animal, e.g., fats, carbohydrates, protein, vitamins, minerals, and dietary contaminants, can influence the reaction—carcinogenic and noncarcinogenic—to a test chemical.[98] How many carcinogenic findings have emerged from experiments which have been falsified by nutritional factors, no one knows.

3. Carcinogenic Contaminants as a Source of Error

Several of the scientists cited above, including the NCAB, in 1977, warned of the danger that carcinogenic contaminants might be present in the experiment, thus conceivably falsifying results. This too is not a new concern. In 1971, an FDA panel asked: "What can be the significance of the incidence of . . . tumors in susceptible strains when one is not certain about the presence of carcinogenic contaminants in the diet on which animals have been maintained?"[99] The question is not speculative; carcinogenic contaminants have been identified— in the feed and elsewhere. Here are some examples:

• Specific carcinogenic contaminants, industrial and natural, have been identified in the diets of laboratory animals. In 1977, H. P. Burchfield et al. reported: "Most animal chows contain small but variable amounts of pesticides, PCBs, and fungal toxins."[100] In 1978, a joint group of industrial and academic scientists discovered that NIH-approved laboratory feed was contaminated by nitrosamines.[101] The finding was confirmed by Joseph J. Knapka of the NIH, who sampled various batches of the feed and found nitrosamines present in ranges from 1.1 ppb to 172 ppb in different types of feed.[102] Also in 1978, R. Schoental of the Royal Veterinary College in London reported that mycotoxin contamination of animal feed—specifically by the fusarium species alone or with the estrogenic zearalenone—might account for the variation in tumor incidence in the same animal species in different laboratories, or within the same laboratory at different times.[103]

- Specific carcinogenic contaminants have been identified in the bedding of animals. In one case, when a certain chemical was tested on certain strains of mice in Australia, they had a low incidence of liver and mammary tumors or none at all, depending on which paper one reads. When the same chemical was tested on the same strains of mice in the U.S., they had a high incidence of such tumors. The difference was traced to the bedding used in the U.S.—shavings from cedar trees, an unexpected natural carcinogenic contaminant.[104]

- Viral contamination of laboratory mice has been reported by scientists from prominent cancer research centers in the U.S., England, Sweden, and the Netherlands, who report that the contamination has affected interpretations of carcinogenesis experiments. The LDH virus, which is widely distributed in nature, is a common biological contaminant of laboratory mice, and may increase the incidence and growth rates of certain tumors.[105]

- Chemical contaminants, carcinogenic or otherwise, may be introduced into an experiment as scientists walk between the various rooms of a laboratory in which chemicals other than the test chemicals are present. A study of potential contamination conducted by E. B. Sansone of NCI in 1979 indicated that the two prime sources of contamination were the floors and researchers' gloves.[106]

- Similarly, contaminants of bacterial and cell tests have been reported. According to Barry Commoner and his colleagues, the bacterial nutrient broth containing beef extract on which bacteria are tested is mutagenic, and the mutagenic effects of chemicals on certain *Salmonella* strains fed on this broth "could be considerably amplified."[107]

The phenomenon of carcinogenic contamination of a carcinogen test is frequently dismissed by scientists on the grounds that in any given experiment, both the control animals and the test animals can be assumed to be equally contaminated, that the contaminant constitutes a shared "background," and that the test is still measuring the critical difference between the two groups, which is the test chemical. Thus, Matthew Meselson of Harvard University argued at the OSHA hearings that it did not matter that bacteria used in mutagen tests were themselves being fed on mutagens because "it just contributes to the background."[108] And Elizabeth Weisburger, head of the NCI Carcinogen Metabolism and Toxicology Branch, made the same point for animals consuming nitrosamine-contaminated NIH feed; presumably the test group and the control group were eating the same food. Thus, she told R. Jeffrey Smith of *Science:* "As long as the test group is compared with the control group, there is no cause for concern."[109] Smith, however, reported tellingly that unnamed NCI scientists "were quick to point out that the NIH feed has not been used in any of the NCI carcinogen bioassays now under way."[110] Possibly they were "quick" because they had remembered the one critical situation in which contamination does matter. It can account for inconsistency or contradiction in the findings of different tests—e.g., the dramatic difference in mouse data caused by the U.S. and Australian bedding. That is one of the reasons for demanding multiple experiments and replication in different laboratories; it is the only way to determine if a specific contaminant has or has not played a significant role in the findings. The alternative is to bicker speculatively in the pages of *Science* as to whether the contaminant might or might not be affecting the findings.[111] In a situation where regulatory agencies (e.g., EPA, OSHA) are insisting that one experiment is sufficient evidence of potential carcinogenicity—and that replication is not needed—no checking for contaminants can take place.

4. "Stress" as a Source of Error

One of the other diverse factors which may affect the outcome of carcinogen tests, according to some scientists, is stress. Housing conditions of various types, as well as viral contamination, are reported to engender "anxiety" and stress in mice, as measured by various hormonal, cellular, and organ alterations which occur when the animal is agitated. According to Vernon Riley of the Pacific Northwest Research Foundation and the Fred Hutchinson Research Center in Seattle, "striking changes of enhanced tumor growth" occur in stressed mice.[112] Happy mice, it seems, got far fewer tumors. (A relevant observation from another field of study was made in 1980 by Robert M. Nerem and his colleagues from the University of Houston and Ohio State, who announced in *Science* that "socio-psychological" factors could influence biological outcomes of animal tests. They reported that regularly petting, holding, talking to, and playing with test rabbits produced more than a 60 percent reduction in lesions of the surface of the aorta in animals fed on a high-serum-cholesterol diet. Such factors, these scientists said, might account for different results in different laboratories, i.e., laboratories with loving and playful scientists might get different results from laboratories with nonloving and nonplayful scientists.[113])

5. Autopsy as a Source of Error

The examination of the animals' tissues for signs of tumor development is perhaps the most important activity in the cancer tests, and is also fraught with possibilities of error. Qualitative problems are too technical for the layman to understand, but he can appreciate the quantitative problems. In a properly conducted experiment, according to the NCI, the scientist who is trying to discover whether a test chemical has produced tumors in excess of the tumors "spontaneously" generated in the control groups must examine every tissue and every organ in the body of every animal in both test and control groups. What is more, he must do this for preliminary sets of studies in toxicity and dose-setting, as well as for the final study. Thus, according to the NCI, he must do several sets of the following analyses: He must do gross necropsies of *"gross lesions; tissue masses or suspect tumors and regional lymph nodes; skin; mandibular lymph node; mammary gland; salivary gland; larynx; trachea; lungs and bronchi; heart; thyroids; parathyroids; esophagus; stomach; duodenum; jejunum; ileum; cecum; colon; rectum; mesenteric lymph node; liver; thigh muscle; sciatic nerve; sternebrae, vertebrae or femur (plus marrow); costochondral junction, rib; thymus; gallbladder; pancreas; spleen; kidneys; adrenals; bladder; seminal vesicles; prostate; testes; ovaries; uterus; nasal cavity; brain; pituitary; eyes; spinal cord.*"[114] He must dissect all these tissues and organs, prepare blood smears, fix slices of them in formalin, prepare cross sections and slides. Then he must do detailed histopathologic (tissue) analyses of most of these same organs. Then he must write out reports of his discoveries. And finally, he must preserve all histologic slides at suitable temperatures; and, if working on an NCI contract, he may discard no material "without prior permission of NCI."[115]

If the scientist does not perform all of these examinations several times, in the course of *one* animal test, he may be charged with overlooking something essential. If he does do all of them, he may end up with as many as 50,000 or more slides that no one can ever fully review. If he does not house the material permanently and under proper physical conditions, he may be charged with failing to keep records. And whatever he does, he may be certain that other scientists will disagree with some, or many of, his analyses. The entire job of studying the effect of *one* chemical in one animal experiment takes at least three and a half years[116] and as of 1980 cost about $500,000 per substance.[117] And almost every action taken during those years is a potential source of error or controversy.

6. Statistical Incompetence as a Source of Error

Since control as well as test animals are specially bred species with strong tendencies to develop cancers independently of testing procedures, the problem of differentiating between the cancers they would "normally" get, as opposed to the cancers caused by the test chemical, must be solved by statistical as well as biological analysis. Statistics is an immensely complex science in itself; as in all fields, there are superb practitioners of the discipline, there are the competent, there are the mediocre, and there are the dishonest. Thus, some statistical error is inevitable. The chances of error are even greater when the experimenter settles for a simple statistical explanation of his findings—i.e., simply counts "lumps" and calculates the statistically significant excess of those "lumps," as opposed to conducting a biologically coherent analysis. Although the practice is frowned on, many experimenters settle for simple "lump" counting. In 1977, a Select Committee of the Life Sciences Research Office of the Federation of American Societies for Experimental Biology, observed: "There is an intrinsic elasticity in statistical reasoning associated with toxicological testing even under the best of circumstances." But, said the committee, the circumstances were not always the best, and it issued the following warning: ". . . claims of causal connections between substance A and physiological condition B continue to appear in print based not only solely on statistics but also solely on statistics involving inadequate numbers and inappropriate analytical procedures."[118]

The government itself is a source of statistics in this and other fields, and government is an unreliable source. In 1971, a President's Commission on Federal Statistics issued a report on the quality of government statistics. One of the members of the commission, William Kruskal of the Statistics Department of the University of Chicago, observed of all government data, generally, "Much of that huge cloud of statistical thought and action, a cloud that suffuses all government activity, is not carried out by people called statisticians, or trained as statisticians."[119] Statistics on toxic and carcinogenic substances processed and developed by regulatory agencies are reported to be particularly imprecise. According to one set of studies by the NRC, most of the reported thefts and losses of nuclear material such as uranium and plutonium are actually the result of a series of theoretical statistical errors.[120] According to one contributor to a study prepared with the support of the National Science Foundation: "Regulatory agencies have shown themselves dilatory to the point of sloth and procrastination in taking steps to assure the accuracy of the information they process and provide. Scrutiny as to how the Food and Drug Administration, the Federal Trade Commission and the Environmental Protection Agency get their information, what they do with it, and whose purposes it serves uncovers example after example of error, miscalculation, and sometimes downright deceit."[121]

There is no way, even for statisticians, to calculate the percentage of error in the study of toxicity and carcinogenicity that is due to statistical defects alone.

7. False Positives and False Negatives as a Source of Error

There is, in addition, the error that may spring from pure chance. Even the best test will fail, at times, to identify chemicals that are carcinogens and will, at times, report others to be carcinogens when they are not. Kraybill of the NCI observes that experiments in "any living system" are liable to produce both false negatives and false positives.[122]

Since a false positive may result in a public that is needlessly terrified and in industries that are senselessly damaged or destroyed, some scientists are increasingly sensitive to the phenomenon of the spurious carcinogen. Frederick de Serres of NIEHS observes: "If you do a large enough number of tests, sometimes you will come up with positive test data for statistical reasons rather than biological reasons. I do not understand how this happens, but it does happen."[123] Similarly, as was reported earlier, the Office of Science and Technology Policy says: ". . . if a sufficient number of tests is performed, predictably a 'statistically significant' difference will be found in at least one test . . . simply as a result of random variation"—this being the reason for which the OSTP recommends to scientists: "View the outcome of any single test as potentially the result of chance variation."[124] And Thomas B. Fears et al. of the NCI, also say: "There is danger in relying solely upon the finding of statistical significance," and warn of false positive results.[125]

There is a good deal of speculation about the magnitude of this error. As usual, there are clashing opinions. OSHA has minimized the problem, claiming it is "fairly rare," and relied on Donald Kennedy, FDA Administrator, as an authority for this position. Kennedy testified that the possibility of false positives "cannot be denied," but announced that the "weight of scientific evidence" suggested "strongly" that such an experience "may only occur infrequently." He observed, "It just turns out that with most animal studies the results of [experimental] error are more likely to make a substance come clean than to show that it is carcinogenic."[126] On the other hand, in the same year as the OSHA hearings, Roy Albert of NYU, consultant to the EPA, also discussed the random behavior of statistics and said: "There is a serious chance on a random basis that you will get a positive result. It makes it tough when you have a marginal response in a bioassay. There's no way to beat the possibility that it's a false positive."[127] There is also no way to make any estimate of the magnitude of the error. In a scientific paper published by Albert the year before, he and his colleagues had written formally: "One can expect that the rodent bioassay systems will also produce false positive results, but no evidence has been found on which to base judgments of how frequently and with what classes of agents false positive results are likely to occur."[128]

The same ignorance prevails in the realm of the false negative. Marvin Schneiderman and Charles C. Brown of the NCI have said: "It is not clear what the operating characteristics are of most test systems. That is, we do not know how often the system will mislead by labelling a material as 'positive' when it is not a carcinogen, or by labelling it 'negative' when it really is a carcinogen."[129] In sum, due to the peculiarities of both statistics and animal tests, *some* percentage of the tests is failing to identify real carcinogens and *some* percentage of the carcinogenic findings is spurious—and no one knows what that percentage is.

8. Premature Publication of Data as a Source of Error

Certain professionals in the field of carcinogenesis feel so compelled to communicate their early suspicions that a chemical may be a carcinogen that they will not wait for peer review, publication, or replication of their findings. This position has been defended as "ethical" by Norbert Page and Umberto Saffiotti of the NCI. They observed: "A delicate ethical dilemma confronts scientists in selecting the proper timing and extent for the release of carcinogenesis test results. Early findings may not be confirmed and may cause technological and economic problems and unnecessary anxiety. On the other hand, delaying public notification of highly suspicious findings until a final, detailed report is published may delay preventive actions that could protect exposed populations from unnecessary risk."[130] The solution, they concluded, was to publish preliminary findings in the *Federal Register* and to send a press release to the media "when the evidence is such that it suggests a strong likelihood that the positive findings will be confirmed in a definitive review."[131] This solution has been adopted by some, and we are already seeing the strange result: Scientists are quarreling about technical issues of pathology in the letters column of the *New York Times,* in response to press releases from the NCI that announce unverified preliminary data.[132]

Not all NCI scientists are equally enthralled by the idea of publishing unverified data. Kraybill warns that it will result in baseless regulatory decisions and social reactions. He advocates substantially higher standards, namely, that the data be reviewed extensively and that they be "unequivocally accepted by all scientific reviewers, representing many disciplines."[133] Philip Abelson, the editor of *Science*, has given unusually blunt reasons for the necessity to wait for peer review and publication. In the course of discussing the functions of scientific journals, he said: "Of equal or greater importance is the function that journals perform in keeping the scientific enterprise honest. In private conversations and even in public lectures, scientists often are not rigorous. They tend to be careless about announcing the results of experiments that may not have been well-controlled, duplicated, or even performed. However, most of them are much more cautious about what they try to put into print. They fear that other scientists will examine their work and will be zealous in pointing out its defects, both at the time it is being reviewed and later when it appears in print. A scientist who publishes sloppy work can suffer destruction of reputation and, for a scientist, that is very serious. . . . It is this discipline more than any other factor that keeps the scientific enterprise relatively honest."[134]

Thus we see that the difference in viewpoints actually represents a conflict between two concepts of ethics—a "new ethics" which gives priority to the scientist's personal assessment of his own work and to his subjective emotions versus the classical ethics of science which trusts neither the scientist's emotions nor his honesty, and trusts only the discipline of peer review and replicated findings. The number of premature warnings of carcinogenic hazard that are emerging from the "new ethics" is unknown, but, as the criticism at the opening of this chapter indicates, that number is believed by some to be considerable.

9. Scientific Incompetence as a Source of Error

Unfortunately, even the fact of publication in a journal does not constitute a guarantee that a carcinogenic finding is valid. Were that the case, we could assume here and now that most of the carcinogens named in the two surveys published in this book are established findings, since most have appeared in scientific publications. Publication may be, as Abelson says, the major factor in keeping science "relatively honest"—but it is simply the best discipline available; it is scarcely foolproof. And the discipline has grown weaker over the years. With the explosion of the number of scientists as well as the number of people who wish to think of themselves as scientists, and the corresponding explosion of numbers of scientific papers, there is an increasing amount not only of published fraud, but of published junk. J. M. Ziman, of the University of Bristol, writes in *Science:* "Many leading scientists feel that there has been a serious deterioration in the quality of the scientific literature in recent years."[135] He observes that the research scientist "is often distressed" by the large quantity of literature of "marginal" value, literature characterized by "the triviality of the results" and "the incompetence of the experimental technique."[136] There has, accordingly, been what Derek J. de Solla Price, a historian of science at Yale University, calls "the debasement of the coinage of scientific publication."[137] In its place an "invisible college" of elite scientists has been forming, a self-selected network of specialists who circulate their papers among each other for criticism, and publish only in certain key journals which maintain the highest standards.[138] The work done by some of these invisible colleges is said to be the best in the field. Unfortunately, the layman has no way of identifying the work of the members of these invisible colleges, or of identifying the work that is trivial, incompetent, and worthless.

10. Sampling as a Source of Error

There is, finally, another set of problems of which the reader should be aware. They are problems not in the *conduct* of animal tests but in the *application* of the discoveries. The only application which will be considered here is the search for the animal carcinogen which has escaped into air, water, and soil in the form of "pollution," e.g., DDT, dioxin. That is frequently the only time the layman ever hears of a carcinogen, and he frequently confuses the discovery of its location, usually communicated by the EPA, with prior discovery made in the laboratory. Because this confusion is so widespread, this particular application will be discussed.

The search for the carcinogenic pollutant is as riddled with pitfalls as is the original animal test, but the pitfalls are quite different. The skills involve chemistry, physics, and engineering, and the problems take different forms. One emerges from the fact that scientists build on each other's work, and much modern science rests on a foundation of prior calculations that are to be found in a variety of reference works and handbooks. Because of the historically unprecedented pileup of unevaluated information, some of the most basic data in physics and chemistry, essential to *all* branches of science and technology, and to carcinogenesis as well, are now unreliable. Walter H. Stockmeyer of Dartmouth, professor of chemistry and chairman of the Committee on Data Needs of the National Research Council of the NAS which evaluated the problem in 1978, warned readers of *Science:* "A particularly pernicious aspect of this problem involves numerical data. . . . Unfortunately, the scientific literature contains many erroneous values. Few scientists or engineers seem to have given much thought to the magnitude of the problem, and some probably regard every numerical entry in a handbook as revealed truth."[139] To this, Charles S. Tidball of the Department of Physiology at the Medical Center of George Washington University responded in *Science* that "the need for evaluated data is just as great in biology and the health-related sciences."[140] The committee report itself, published in 1980, warned, "Unreliable data can be worse than no data at all" and leads, among many things, to "poorly conceived experiments."[141]

Basic data in the realm of environmental sciences have been particularly bad or absent, according to the Commission of National Resources of the National Research Council of the NAS. According to its executive director, Richard Carpenter, that commission reported in 1976: "On most environmental issues, the advisory committee finds the factual data base to be incomplete, inaccurate, difficult to interpret, and often suspect of bias." As compared with physics and chemistry, he said, "ecology is not a predictive science and there are few agreed-upon ecological principles."[142] The EPA in 1979—although in guarded terms—made identically the same observations.[143] And in 1979, a report on the gross incompetence and subjectivity of much of the allegedly scientific and statistical literature in the realm of environmental and ecological sciences appeared in *Science,* written by George S. Innis of the College of Natural Resources of Utah State University.[144]

In addition, the number of instruments and complex analytical techniques used in the analysis of carcinogenic and other toxic substances grows constantly, and with them grow new sources of error. According to Joseph Rodricks of the FDA, the failure to take representative samples and to prepare them properly for analysis is likely to be "the major source of error in the analytical result obtained."[145] Because of flaws in both instrument use and sampling, errors in analytical data are common. Kenneth W. Gardiner of the University of California at Riverside reports that "the analytical numbers often used in regulatory enforcement and in limit-setting are subject to errors of varying magnitude."[146] Similarly, Marvin W. Skougstad, of the U.S. Geological Survey, warns against sampling errors, and observes that "the risk of obtaining misleading data, or, at least, atypical or nonrepresentative data, is too great to overlook."[147] Often, the issues in court cases are actually debates over instrument use. In at least one case—*EPA* vs. *Anaconda*—evidence against an alleged industrial polluter was overruled because of flaws in basic data. One judge found: "The evidence in our trial conclusively demonstrates that the instrument readings on which the proposed rule is based are totally fallacious, and the evidence conclusively demonstrates that the testing instruments were not in proper operating condition and that they had not been calibrated."[148]

Yet again: Basic laboratory work is often grossly incompetent. In 1978, the EPA audited the performance of 61 laboratories testing for nitrate and 166 laboratories testing for SO_2. According to John Taylor, Chief of the Gas and Particulate Science Division of the National Bureau of Standards, the EPA's results showed that only about 10 percent of the laboratories "could be classified as good" by EPA standards; 15 percent showed a need for technical assistance; and the remaining 75 percent showed "mixed" results;[149] errors of 50 percent were not uncommon.[150] The laboratories were seriously inconsistent, and "only a few have the ability to analyze all samples within acceptable narrow limits"; and Taylor added a reminder that this pertained only to the final measurement step: "To the errors noted should be added any due to sample collection and related matters." The data, consequently, may be even less reliable, he says, than the percentages just cited.[151]

Finally, the basic data on toxic and carcinogenic chemicals are often in a state of chaos. According to a 1980 Report to the President by the Toxic Substances Strategy Committee, "an integrated data network does not yet exist." Over the years, the many research and regulatory agencies have created "more than 220 separate systems," some sophisticated computer systems, others simple manual files, all with different purposes. "Information," says the committee, "is often incompatibly described, categorized, and filed."[152] The identifications of chemical substances "vary in accuracy and information content from file to file." In addition, "mistakes occur in attempts to transfer information from one file to another."[153]

We stop here with this compendium of ten categories of potential error, simply because ten is a nice round number, and one must stop somewhere. However, these examples, combined with the list of unresolved controversies, give one a glimpse of the hidden face of "regulatory" science. It tells us that it is an immature science and a horrendously complex one as well. This vision of complexity and confusion, of an enterprise ceaselessly haunted by the possibility of error, is central to any understanding of the 'state of the art'—and yet it has never been communicated to the American layman in terms he could understand.

Obviously, such information is not secret. It is readily available in science libraries and in collections of government documents; it simply has not been popularized. Regulators and scientists have supposed, and no doubt correctly, that the layman would have little or no interest in such apparently technical matters, and certainly any such presentation, out of context, would be unspeakably dull. Nonetheless, combined with laws and regulations indicting industries as "suspected" mass murderers and guaranteeing the citizen a "cancer prevention" program, the failure to disseminate such information has been a serious error. The layman's ignorance, as well as his assumption that the government would not make such extraordinary condemnations and such extraordinary pledges without the capacity to substantiate them, has left him with the erroneous impression that "regulatory" science is far more precise than it is, and that impression itself has had many consequences, of which two are particularly unfortunate. There has been a high degree of credulity in a substantial portion of the educated public, including the press, which has assumed that because a substance has been reported to be a carcinogen by a scientist, a journal, or a regulatory agency, or because carcinogenic pollution is reported, that report is true. And along with that credulity there has been disbelief and shock whenever a vivid sign of the precariousness of the science has appeared. In fact, it has been widely assumed that there is one basic explanation for bad work and dissension in the field: It must be somebody's fault, it must emerge from bad motives, it must be due to bad faith. For years, instances of serious deficiencies in cancer-testing programs and in pollution studies have been interpreted in the United States as moral and political scandals requiring congressional hearings, investigation and reports by the GAO, front-page headlines, and the grilling of alleged villains by outraged reporters.

Thus, in 1976, as reported earlier, there were cries of horror and charges of scandal when the poor quality of many of the carcinogen tests conducted by industry became known. That moral explosion, led by Senator Kennedy, has already been reported above—and industry was anointed a national villain.

Thus, in 1977 and 1978, there were cries of horror and charges of scandal when it finally emerged that nowhere in the regulatory world was there a body of established principles for testing carcinogenicity and interpreting the data. A full-scale investigation of this apparently unaccountable phenomenon was held by Congress. Gregory Ahart of the General Accounting Office testified grimly to Congress in 1977 that there was a "lack of NIOSH or OSHA policies and guidelines on the evidence needed to support classifying a substance as a carcinogen for regulatory purposes."[154] Worse yet, he testified in 1978, there was "disagreement among the agencies as to what test methods are appropriate to identify carcinogens."[155] In this case, the diagnosis was that of unpardonable political and administrative misconduct on the part of the regulatory and research agencies.

Thus, in 1979, there were cries of horror and charges of scandal when it was discovered that the National Cancer Institute itself was responsible for a series of bad carcinogenesis tests performed by laboratories to which it had awarded contracts. Once again, there was an investigation. This time the General Accounting Office informed Congress and the press of what appeared to be a veritable series of atrocities: The GAO report said that "about 25 percent of the bioassays"[156] for which NCI had contracted "were deficient in either the design or execution";[157] that "no standard methodology existed for conducting the long-term phases of the bioassays, for performing the pathology analyses, or for reporting results";[158] that "the problems encountered in the pathology performed on the older bioassays were so severe that NCI initially rejected about 60 percent of the written pathology narratives";[159] that "many of the older bioassays used very small numbers of animals in their control groups";[160] that NCI had "not been adequately informed about the overall laboratory conditions that could affect the quality of the bioassays";[161] that there was "testing of more than one chemical in a room";[162] that "numerous deficiencies still existed at the laboratories that could affect the bioassays' quality."[163] Gripped by the illusion that a fully developed science existed, one Democratic Senator, Henry D. Waxman of California, was so appalled by the NCI's apparent malfeasance that he charged, at least by implication, that a "cover-up" was going on—that this nation's leading cancer research institution was actually concealing the existence of cancer-causing substances from the nation.[164] And among the many individuals around whom scandal swirled was Philippe Shubik, who was doing research for the NCI under contract. In fact, one year after Shubik was honored along with Isaac Berenblum as one of the seminal theoreticians of basic research, he found himself anonymously charged in Science magazine with having "resisted following NCI's guidelines,"[165] a mysterious crime which suggested that Shubik—who has since been welcomed by Oxford University—had suddenly and inexplicably become hostile to science.

And thus, almost throughout its entire history, there have been cries of horror and charges of scandal over the scientific performance of the EPA—so many they cannot be summarized. A few more examples of the 1970s will be given here, and others of the 1980s are referred to in the final chapter. In response to one series of hearings investigating reportedly fraudulent EPA research, Congress passed the Environmental Research, Development and Demonstration Authorization Act, which accorded to the Science Advisory Board the job of overseeing EPA's research and development.[166] In 1977, the board repeatedly clashed with the EPA's judgment[167] and Dr. James L. Whittenberger, chairman of the Department of Physiology of Harvard School of Public Health and chairman of the Science Advisory Board Subcommittee, said that EPA's "health risk assessments are largely speculative, incomplete, and heavily dependent on studies of questionable validity."[168] In 1978, John Walsh of *Science,* reporting on EPA's difficulties in "dealing with uncertainty," said that "the validity of its scientific information is the make or break factor for the agency. And EPA's scientific capabilities are seen by knowledgeable critics as chronically weak.... There are persistent complaints that many of [EPA's] labs have not kept pace scientifically or developed sufficient competencies...."[169]

By the late 1970s, as a consequence of these "scandals," millions of "enlightened" Americans had come to perceive the nation as permanently peopled with conscious enemies of human health. They were vicious industrialists; they were corrupt bureaucrats; they were heartless cancer research agencies; they were venal doctors; there were hundreds, thousands of other individuals, professions, and institutions who were believed to have the scientific knowledge to identify, predict, and protect people from cancer-causing agents and yet—apparently due to monstrous flaws in their characters or in the social system itself—were malevolently refusing to do so. One thing, however, was exempt from criticism as this bizarre social paranoia developed: It was "regulatory" science itself. That science of carcinogen identification, prediction, and prevention had, in fact, become the standard by which both industry and government were judged, and by that standard, the country itself had become a carcinogenic sewer, and both productive enterprises and those who regulated them had become widely perceived as criminally irresponsible.

By 1978, the regulators, finding the political pressure intolerable, agreed that it was essential to arrive at uniform policies for conducting cancer tests and interpreting the animal data despite the profound disagreements that divided the scientific world. One result was OSHA's great 1978 hearings during which OSHA made one arbitrary decision after another. Given the network of unresolved issues, OSHA could scarcely have been anything but arbitrary. But even that truth was not told. OSHA, too, felt compelled to attribute this sudden rush to manufacture "policies" to the existence of a villain. Assistant Secretary of Labor Eula Bingham held a press conference to account for the phenomenon, and said:

One of the major factors inhibiting the issuance of regulations to control workplace carcinogens has been the need to cover the same ground in each and every rule-making proceeding. We found ourselves debating the same questions of appropriate testing and interpretation for each carcinogen we investigated. So, one of the major purposes of the cancer policy is to avoid this reinvention of the wheel....[170]

OSHA's policy document offers the same explanation.[171] It was, unfortunately, a half-truth at best. It was indeed true that every industry charged with manufacturing a cancer-causing agent had frantically debated the full roster of unresolved issues—each imperiled manufacturer challenging each whisker of each laboratory mouse as his turn came up at bat. The tunnel vision was pathetic and the resultant hearings were tedious, but it was those manufacturers' right to challenge each whisker. As of 1978, as the GAO had revealed, NIOSH and OSHA and the other regulatory agencies had never had a common policy "on the evidence needed to support classifying a substance as a carcinogen for regulatory purposes." It was thus not true that OSHA was holding its policy hearings "to avoid the reinvention of the wheel." There had never been a "wheel." But that fact and its significance had been submerged in "scandals."

So far, the "scandals" that have been described here have involved the scientific performance of industrial and governmental institutions. But there is also another type of "scandal" of which the nation has become anxiously aware, and that is the "scandal" that often erupts over the legal classification of a specific substance as a carcinogen, e.g., Red Dye #2, cyclamate, saccharin, DDT, nitrite. For the reasons which have already been given, the controversies over specific substances have also been widely perceived as morality plays in which virtuous "science" takes up the lance against death-dispensing "industry," and they are usually accompanied by crusading lay groups, outraged journalistic commentary, and, in certain cases, congressional investigations and GAO reports as well. This moral vision, too, has been largely illusory. When one goes to the literature, one discovers that the fundamental battles are usually not between "science" and "industry" at all, but between "science" and "science" with industry, most of which does little independent carcinogenesis research, clutching belatedly at the academic findings which are most favorable to its interests. Because these underlying scientific conflicts are usually concealed by the moral-political furor—the only thing habitually covered by the press—three examples will be illustrated here: Red Dye #2, DDT, and nitrite. It is useful to take cases that have commanded intense press attention because they will allow the reader to compare his own impressions of a few notorious "scandals" with the complex scientific muddles that lay hidden beneath the surface. The three stories that follow are not complete case histories or literature reviews—they do not report on the hundreds of experiments performed on the controversial substances. *No attempt whatever is made, here, to reach any conclusion about the carcinogenicity of the substance.* These stories do, however, illustrate the bizarre complexity of these alleged contests between "science" and "industry," between virtue and vice.

THREE TANGLED TALES

Red Dye #2

The scientific story that lies below the political "scandal" that raged over the synthetic food coloring Red Dye #2 has been told in detail by Philip Boffey, both in *Science* and in the *New York Times*.[172] Since Red #2 was the object of a four-year-long crusade by Ralph Nader, and since Boffey was an early Nader ally, his report on the underlying problems is of unusual interest. Between 1970 and 1976, says Boffey, some thirty animal tests had been conducted on the synthetic food coloring Red Dye #2 by the government, by independent laboratories, and by industry—all with "wildly" differing conclusions.[173] In the early

1970s, the picture was further complicated by reports of several Russian studies of a "Red Dye #2" that may or may not have been the same chemical compound used in the United States. According to Boffey, the Russian studies "were so flawed that even the most dedicated Red #2 baiters considered them suspect." (Among the "baiters," he listed *Consumer Reports* and the Center for Science in the Public Interest.)[174] One of the Russian studies declared Red #2 to be a teratogen—a cause of birth defects—a charge that greatly agitated the FDA, which had not tested Red #2 for its effects on fetuses. Jacqueline Verrett of the FDA promptly injected Red #2 into a huge number of fertilized chicken eggs, and produced deaths and deformities.[175] Many scientists, however, were not convinced that findings in chicken eggs were relevant to pregnant women, so another FDA scientist, Thomas F. X. Collins, tackled the teratogen problem with pregnant rats; he poured Red #2 through tubes into the stomachs of those pregnant rats, and he, too, produced deaths and deformities. This was an interesting finding until it was discovered that Collins could not replicate his own data—at which point everyone was back at square one.[176]

The FDA then decided to do a definitive master study, this time with a huge number of rats, 500 in all. It was an ambitious enterprise. Unfortunately, the scientist in charge of the 500 rats left the agency, and the rats were left unsupervised for a long time. When, finally, some scientists picked up the experiment in midstream, their work was slovenly: An unknown number of control rats got mixed up with the test rats, and dead rats, instead of being dissected immediately, were left to rot in their cages. "As a result," reported Boffey, "virtually all of the rats that died during the course of the experiment were so badly decomposed as to be of little use for evaluation. Only those rats that survived to the end of the experiment and were killed—some 96 in all—were available for detailed histopathological examination. 'It was the lousiest experiment I have seen in my life,' commented one scientist who reviewed the data."[177] Essentially the same story is told in *The Politics of Cancer* by Samuel Epstein, who described the experiment as a "fiasco,"[178] and by the *Environmental Law Reporter,* which called the experiment a "botched" study.[179]

Botched or not, it is the conviction of many (e.g., FDA,[180] OSHA,[181] and Bernard Weinstein of Columbia University[182]) that even a bad or "deficient" study can provide meaningful carcinogenic data (although it cannot be used to prove safety), and an attempt was made to extract data from the experimental catastrophe. Certain FDA biostatisticians picked laboriously over piles of rat corpses and reached the conclusion, as Boffey said in the *New York Times,* that there were "two bits of evidence that Red #2 might cause cancer and four bits of evidence that it might not."[183] The "bits," which did not appear in the *Times,* are quite enlightening, even to the layman. The report submitted to the FDA Commissioner on January 16, 1976, read as follows:

The evidence from this experiment demonstrating that FD&C Red No. 2 is a carcinogen is twofold:
1. A statistically significant increase in malignant tumors in females in the high-dose group versus low dose ("controls").
2. A possible dose-response relationship in females using all dose groups.

The evidence from this experiment not supporting the carcinogenicity of FD&C Red No. 2 is fourfold:

1. No statistically significant increase in malignant tumors was demonstrated in male animals.
2. No statistically significant events are observed if one aggregates all tumor types.
3. No unusual or unique tumor types were observed in the test animals.
4. No single tumor type showed an increase over that observed in the control animals.

On this basis, Red #2 was banned. The botched experiment, said the FDA, had not proved the product's "safety."[184]

DDT

As the reader knows, DDT precipitated one of the earliest and most memorable "scandals," and still symbolizes for many the war between "science" and "industry." An early and major target of the environmental movement, it was the chief compound against which Rachel Carson had gone to war in 1962. She was informed by the late Wilhelm Hueper of the NCI that he considered DDT to be decisively classified as a carcinogen.[185] And it has been widely assumed ever since that the famous pesticide is a cancer-causing agent. What is not widely known is that fifteen years after the carcinogenicity of DDT was announced, the issue was still enmeshed in scientific controversies.

The first and most fundamental controversy pertains to the role of the mouse. DDT was also reported to be carcinogenic by Innes et al. in 1969, and his findings were confirmed in later experiments by Samuel Epstein in 1970 and 1972, and by Tomatis et al. in 1972; in all cases, DDT had produced liver tumors in mice alone.[186] According to Charles Wurster of SUNY and a leader of the Environmental Defense Fund's crusade against DDT, those mouse tumors were among the chief considerations that led to the banning of DDT by EPA Administrator William Ruckelshaus in 1972.[187] Three years after the ban, in 1975, Tomatis et al. of the IARC conducted another set of experiments, and still only the mouse was affected. Tomatis reported that DDT indubitably caused liver tumors in male mice at several dose levels and in female mice at high dose levels, and that the two main metabolites of DDT—DDE and DDD—caused, respectively, liver tumors and lung tumors, again in mice; the DDT-induced hepatomas, however, "rarely metastasize and in many instances do not show obvious signs of invasiveness. . . ." As for other species, said Tomatis, DDT had no effect whatever on hamsters, and there was a "borderline carcinogenic effect of DDT in rats, which has not been confirmed, however, by more recent studies. . . ."[188] As late as 1977, the evidence that DDT affected any mammals but mice was still ephemeral. In his 1977 book, Thomas Corbett was still relying for mammalian evidence on mouse data; he had to reach back thirty years to bring in an inconclusive reference to rats.[189]

Suddenly, in that same year, the picture changed—or appeared to change. NIOSH, the research arm of OSHA, announced that the question was closed; DDT gave *both* rats and mice cancer: "In two of three experiments involving rats, increased occurrences of liver tumors of varying degrees of malignancy have been reported." NIOSH concluded: "Based on the demonstrated potential of DDT for inducing tumors in both rats and mice, NIOSH recommends that DDT be controlled and handled in the workplace as a suspected occupational carcinogen. . . ."[190]

Unfortunately, however, the rat question was not closed. In fact, the mouse question wasn't closed either. Still in the same year, 1978—more than fifteen years after Wilhelm Hueper had assured Rachel Carson that DDT was a definite carcinogen, and six years after DDT was banned—the NCI published one of its technical report series, and its subject, too, was DDT. Or, more precisely, as the NCI's title put it, the subject was the "possible carcinogenicity of DDT." This time bioassays had been conducted on DDT; on TDE, a major contaminant of DDT; and on p,p'-DDE, the major metabolite of DDT. The experiments were conducted on different strains of mice and rats. The results were so peculiar that it is best to present them first in the precise words of the NCI's own summary, despite the NCI's compulsion to be boring:

Under the conditions of these bioassays there was no evidence for the carcinogenicity of DDT in Osborne-Mendel rats or B6C3F1 mice, of TDE in female Osborne-Mendel rats or B6C3F1 mice of either sex, or of p,p'-DDE in Osborne-Mendel rats, although p,p'-DDE was hepatotoxic in Osborne-Mendel rats. The findings suggest a possible carcinogenic effect of TDE in male Osborne-Mendel rats, based on the induction of combined follicular-cell carcinomas and follicular-cell adenomas of the thyroid. Because of the variation of these tumors in control male rats in this study, the evidence does not permit a more conclusive interpretation of these lesions. p,p'-DDE was carcinogenic in B6C3F1 mice, causing hepatocellular carcinomas in both sexes.[191]

The truth is, these findings were not boring at all. They were downright astonishing. If the reader pores over the NCI passage, he will discover that it gives him three different kinds of information:

A. In five situations, three involving rats, DDT, its contaminant, and its metabolite were *not* carcinogenic.
 1. DDT was *not* a carcinogen in Osborne-Mendel rats;
 2. p,p'-DDE was *not* a carcinogen in Osborne-Mendel rats;
 3. TDE was *not* a carcinogen in female Osborne-Mendel rats;
 4. DDT was *not* a carcinogen in B6C3F1 mice;
 5. TDE was *not* a carcinogen in B6C3F1 mice.
B. In one situation TDE was linked to a "possible carcinogenic effect" in rats in the *males* of the Osborne-Mendel strain.
C. In only one situation there was a consistent carcinogenic response: p,p'-DDE caused liver cancer in B6C3F1 mice.

The NCI had magnificently muddied the waters. What is more, the rat situation became increasingly puzzling. In 1979, T. Syrowatka and his colleagues in Poland reported on male rats of the Wistar strain. When DDT was given in this strain, in combination with the carcinogen dimethylnitrosamine (DMNA), DDT appeared to intensify the carcinogenic response of DMNA—thus it might be a promoter of that particular compound. But given alone, the scientists said, DDT left the male Wistar rats intact.[192] As for the female rats and hamsters who had so consistently refused to be afflicted by DDT, talk about them had ceased.

To further complicate the issue, the DDT case has always been interwoven with the high-dose controversy, since enormous doses of the test compound were given to induce liver tumors in the test mice. As the reader will recall, the high-dose controversy reached one of its peaks in the realm of pesticide testing. That was the area in which Herman Kraybill said, without using names, that a scientist testing one pesticide used more than one manufacturer's yearly supply of the chemical. In another paper, Kraybill wrote about the high doses used in DDT testing, this time using names. In the animal tests on DDT performed by Innes et al., one of the series of tests that had so theatrically established DDT as a carcinogen for the country and the world, Kraybill had calculated at the time, he said, that the doses used were equivalent to 853 times the average amount found in the human diet. Another scientist, Loomis, had made an even more extraordinary estimate at the time—that the doses of DDT fed by Innes to the mice were 160,000 times that of human dietary exposure. That estimate had not been confirmed, Kraybill said, but the Innes experiments illustrate the "exaggerated dose schedules" that have been used, which are in no way comparable to the human experience and render toxicological evaluations "difficult."[193]

To add, finally, to this spectacular unclarity, there is the great mutagen anticlimax. If DDT is a carcinogen it should, according to the geneticists, be a mutagen as well. Marvin Legator testified to that effect at the 1972 hearings at which DDT was banned. According to Wurster's report on those hearings, Legator warned that DDT was a potential genetic hazard for man and reported on experiments that he and his colleagues had performed in which dominant lethal mutations were increased in rats after the males had been exposed to DDT.[194] Within four years of Legator's testimony, the issue of the mutagenicity of DDT had become chaotic. According to H. P. Burchfield and Eleanor E. Storrs of the Gulf South Research Institute, who conducted some of the NCI's early bioassays on DDT, the correlation between the carcinogenicity and mutagenicity of chlorinated hydrocarbon pesticides is poor. In some test systems, DDT and its metabolites DDE, DDD, and DDA have been reported to be nonmutagenic; and other chlorinated hydrocarbons too (e.g., aldrin, dieldrin, lindane, and heptachlor) have been reported to be nonmutagenic. In the *Drosophila* test, however, DDT has been reported to be a weak mutagen; it has also been reported to cause chromosome aberrations in human lymphocytes, but it has produced unclear responses in dominant lethal tests with mice. Finally, in a few other test systems, metabolites of DDT have been reported to be weak mutagens. At most, according to Burchfield and Storrs, DDT is a weak mutagen.[195]

After reviewing the data, the authors raised these questions: Did mutagen tests predict for carcinogenicity in *all* classes of chemicals? (They didn't.) And do substances that induce liver tumors in mice predict for cancer in man?[196] Thus the authors ended up where we began—with the question of the validity of liver and other tumors in mice. In 1977, they had no answers to the questions they raised save to say that answers were necessary so that regulatory agencies might make scientific decisions. The same questions, to repeat, were still being discussed feverishly at the OSHA hearings one year later. As for DDT itself, the authors concluded that it was a "borderline" mutagen.[197] At the time of that very conclusion, Thomas Corbett informed the nation that DDT might be a "disaster to the human race."[198] It might be; its major metabolite, said the NCI in 1978, definitely causes liver cancer in B6C3F1 mice. We do not know, of course, whether the "human race" metabolizes DDT as do B6C3F1 mice. According to OSHA, the question is unanswerable.

There is an additional aspect to this unfinished story which should not be omitted. A few years ago a portion of the citizenry found itself in direct conflict with the DDT ban. A plague of gypsy moths and spruce budworms fell upon them, drove them indoors, devoured their bushes and trees, and ravaged huge timber stands in the United States. Unaccustomed to hand-to-hand combat with insects, these American citizens fought the EPA bitterly to allow them to use DDT to rid them of the plague and to save the forests; the EPA allowed it. Herman Kraybill of the NCI found the spectacle "ironic." While all this was going on, he observed, the World Health Organization had endorsed the continued use of DDT as a health measure for a large portion of the world's population.[199]

Nitrite

A recent "scandal"—it exploded as this book was being written—pertains to the case of nitrite, a chemical used as a preservative for bacon, ham, and other meats, and a substance that is definitely known to protect human beings from the botulinus bacterium. It is the most complex story of this group, because, in this case, it is impossible to relay without some reference to bureaucratic politics. Only a small part of the bureaucratic story will be conveyed, however— just enough to serve as the glue that holds the scientific story together.

The case of nitrite is particularly odd because within two years, the FDA declared it to be a carcinogen, and then retracted its declaration. In August 1978, the FDA announced that it was planning to ban nitrite on the basis of an FDA-sponsored study by Paul Newberne of MIT. FDA Commissioner Donald Kennedy, in a joint announcement with USDA Assistant Secretary Carol Foreman, informed the nation that nitrites had been found to pose a risk for human cancer and that the agency would move toward a legal ban.[200] Kennedy, apparently confident of his decision, sent a memorandum to the Secretary of HEW, Joseph Califano, on September 11, 1978, in which he said: "We know more than enough about the Newberne study to be convinced that it is well-done and strongly supports the hypothesis that nitrites are carcinogenic per se."[201] In August 1980, however, exactly two years later, the FDA declared that on the contrary, nitrite had *not* been shown to be carcinogenic, this decision coming in a statement issued jointly by the new Commissioner of the FDA, Gere Goyan, again acting in tandem with Carol Foreman of the Department of Agriculture. On this occasion, the official words were: "There is no basis for the FDA or USDA to initiate any action to remove nitrite from foods at this time."[202]

The events that led to this retraction are complex, and they are told in detail in a GAO "Report by the Comptroller General of the United States" titled *Does Nitrite Cause Cancer? Concerns About Validity of FDA-Sponsored Study Delay Answer.* The GAO report is essentially a study of the complex decision-making process at the FDA—or more precisely, of a complex non-decision-making process involving half-conducted and nonterminated investigations, warring cliques, and, in at least one case, a face-saving memo. It emerged, on investigation, that Commissioner Donald Kennedy had not been quite so confident of the quality of the Newberne study as it appeared. He had also explained to HEW Secretary Califano in the September 11 memorandum why, even if the judgment was wrong, neither Califano nor he would suffer "embarrassment." First, said Kennedy, the law was so loose that nothing had to be proved anyway. He put it a little differently, of course:

Because of the Congressionally-mandated emphasis on prevention of harm to the public health, regulators are required to act without waiting for "complete" scientific evidence to support their action. Regulators are, of course, not free to act on the basis of the slightest of evidence. It is clear, however, from the health regulatory laws and from judicial interpretation of those laws, that regulatory action to protect the public health from a perceived risk is appropriate, even when the perceived risk is based on a mixture of scientific fact, theory and supposition.[203]

Secondly, Kennedy continued, in case the Newberne study proved to be no good, the press and public would never know what the ensuing argument was about, anyway, so face could be saved. Again, he put it a little differently:

Even in the unlikely event of a successful challenge to the study, the outcome would not be clear: it would appear to the media and the public as such things inevitably appear—as rather arcane, confusing debates among the cognoscenti. Thus the possibility for real embarrassment even given the worst possible outcome of our evaluation is very slight, simply because outcomes are never that clear in a matter so complex.[204]

These passages are illuminating for a number of reasons, not the least of which is that they offer the layman the rare opportunity of seeing how he is viewed by at least one of the prominent humanitarians who has claimed to be protecting him from industrial cancer. But their principal significance lies in the fact that the FDA Commissioner who banned nitrite actually had not known whether the substance had or had not been shown to be a carcinogen, and was worried about it.

In fact, there were substantial reasons for worry. In 1977, one year before Kennedy announced to the nation that the Newberne study was "well-done," the FDA had conducted an investigation into the Newberne study and had serious doubts about its validity. On three separate occasions in that year, according to the GAO, a team of FDA inspectors had visited the MIT lab to observe the Newberne study in the light of the Good Laboratory Practices Code that had recently been enunciated. They had studied "animal care, handling, and facilities; diet preparation and feeding; and neocropsies for the on-going nitrite study."[205] In addition, they had "reviewed histological slides, necropsy records, and research notebooks for the nitrite study, and the completed nitrite/morpholine study."[206] The resultant FDA's Establishment Report announced that a series of "deficiencies" had been discovered "that raise important questions about the validity of the study results."[207] As summarized by the GAO, the list of deficiencies discovered in 1977 was as follows:

1. An animal caretaker was observed feeding the wrong diet to a group of rats. He was feeding a test diet containing nitrite to a control group that was to receive a nitrite-free diet.

2. A vitamin supplement was administered to test animals without apparent authorization.

3. Test and control diets were mixed in a common container without washing between mixes.

4. Animals were changed from one study group to another without justification or inclusion of that fact in the final report (nitrite/morpholine study).

5. For the nitrite/morpholine study, differences were noted between the final report summary and the raw data summary of the number of rats started on the experiment. In some instances the final report lists a larger number than the raw data.

6. MIT had no quality assurance unit. Such a unit is responsible for assuring conformance of the facilities, equipment, personnel, methods and controls to the GLP regulations; the quality and integrity of the data obtained from the laboratory; and adherence to protocols and standard operating procedures.

7. MIT had no written standard operating procedures for laboratory tests, data storage and retrieval, test system observations, and the receipt, handling, and administration of test control substances.

8. Handling of test and control substances did not conform to the regulations in that:

(a) Diets were prepared in a common preparation room that had no dust control system, and no measures were taken to prevent cross-contamination.
(b) The positive control substance, urethane (a potent, highly volatile carcinogen), was stored on top of a cabinet in one of the rooms housing test animals.

9. Study protocols were not observed in that:

(a) Not all tissues requiring examination were examined by a pathologist.
(b) Changes in protocols were not documented or signed by the study director.

10. The animal room environment was not monitored for air quality, and drinking water was not periodically analyzed for contaminants.

11. Test and control substances undergo decay—a change in chemical composition . . . over a period of time. Test and control substances were not tested for stability, either before beginning the study or before feeding the animals.[208]

This report was received in the Bureau of Foods of the FDA on March 23, 1977, where a Good Laboratory Practices Unit reviewed it. The monitoring unit concluded from this "that the studies observed are of questionable integrity."[209] One FDA committee wanted to terminate the study immediately because of doubts of its validity. The Director of the Division of Toxicology wanted to complete the study "since he thought that the pathology data from the study would be valuable."[210] The conflict was resolved by a compromise: The study would be continued for five months. A letter was sent to Newberne stating:

Until we are assured that corrections have been instituted to preclude deviations from acceptable scientific procedures we cannot rely upon data from other studies you may have underway or contemplate for the future.

In the case of the [nitrite study] the investigatory findings give us reason to question the data at this time. We will have to discuss the matter at some length in view of these discrepancies. If the study can be completed we will review the data ... to see what conclusions can be drawn.[211]

Newberne replied to the FDA, denied some charges, refuted others, and generally argued in favor of the adequacy of his study. There were further charges, arguments, and denials, further exchanges of letters—and then, inexplicably, the FDA's correspondence file stops dead. The FDA reviews of the Newberne study were never completed, and, officially, no one knows why. The GAO said only this: "The Acting Director, Bureau of Foods, who had the ultimate responsibility in this matter, told us that he did not recall why the normal reviews had not been completed. . . ."[212] After extensive review, an interagency group concluded that the most serious of the unanswered questions were these:

• Whether the feed for test and control animals had been contaminated by other toxicants mixed in the test area.
• Whether, in particular, urethane, a highly volatile carcinogen, had contaminated "everything in the surrounding area."
• Whether the control animals had been eating carcinogen-contaminated feed.
• Whether there was a "feeding mixup" in which chemically treated feed had been given to a control group.
• Whether the feed and water fed to the test animals had been analyzed for nitrite levels.[213]

Within the year, and in defiance of these unresolved problems, Commissioner Donald Kennedy reached his decision to endorse the Newberne study. He did so, he informed the GAO, on the basis of a "briefing" which he described as "an intense two-hour discussion of the study data." By the end of that discussion he was "convinced that nitrite causes cancer."[214] Kennedy then made several decisions which ultimately boomeranged and precipitated the GAO investigation. He eliminated most of the usual steps of scientific review at the FDA and restricted information to a small "task force."[215] The reasons he gave to the GAO for rushing the decision through in this fashion were that the problem was unusually sensitive since it involved the banning of a known life-protecting substance; that it involved a $12-billion-a-year industry; and that open discussion of the issue might have upset the "public" and caused "possible panic."[216] The most important reason of all, however, he said, was that an extensive review "would have taken more time than the apparent seriousness of the study's findings would permit."[217] In other words, the danger was so great, there was no time to establish the truth of the danger—or, as a headline in the GAO report put it: "FDA Concludes Nitrite Causes Cancer—Later Reviews Question MIT Study's Validity."[218] The limited "task force," accordingly, produced a "position paper," and, some members told the GAO, "precautions were used to keep their discussions and conclusions, the MIT study and the position paper secret."[219]

It was an unusual way to arrive at a scientific assessment. It antagonized the many scientists in several agencies whose judgments were being excluded, and above all, it antagonized those at the FDA who already had strong doubts about the validity of the Newberne study. The resultant angry gossip was immediately siphoned into congressional ears, and led seven members of the Congress to demand the GAO investigation.[220] Not only did the GAO investigation uncover the earlier 1977 investigation which had so mysteriously ended with major questions unresolved, but it reported on many more problems in the Newberne study. In fact, in the GAO report, the MIT experiment underwent a Jekyll and Hyde transformation. From being a vessel of truth so luminous that Donald Kennedy could perceive its excellence in only a "two-hour briefing" it turned into a candidate for the title of the most execrable carcinogenesis study ever performed by man.

Seventeen scientists outside the FDA were asked for peer review comments. They represented the following institutions: the Office of Science and Technology Policy, Executive Office of the President; the National Research Council; the President of the National Academy of Sciences; the Department of Health and Social Security, U.K.; Iowa State University; and the Eppley Institute for Research in Cancer, in addition to several research organizations supported by various industries (the American Health Foundation, the Council for Agricultural and Science Technology). Their criticisms took up more than a page of the GAO report, and included the following:

The study report lacked sufficient animal data and/or inadequately described the study procedure to permit full review (65 percent raised this issue).

The practice of combining all control and all nitrite-treated groups regardless of nitrite dose or diet in calculating statistical significance raised doubts about the scientific validity of the study (53 percent raised this issue). . . .

The statistical significance of the study was disputed (47 percent raised this issue). . . .

The control groups had an unusually high incidence of lymphomas (35 percent raised this issue). . . .

The fact that the number of tumors in the rats did not increase proportionally as the level of nitrite exposure increased was unlike test results for other carcinogens (35 percent raised this issue). . . .

Additional studies are needed (41 percent raised this issue). The senior principal medical officer, Department of Health and Social Security, United Kingdom, concluded that this study would need to be repeated in another strain of rat and another species before a definite answer could be forthcoming.

Nitrosamines may have caused some or all of the tumors (24 percent raised this issue). Iowa State University scientists commented that there is no evidence available to support the statement that nitrite-caused tumors are distinct from those caused by nitrosamines. The National Research Council said lymphomas have been strongly associated with nitrosamine exposure.

Animals in nitrite study group 1, shipped to the researcher on October 23, 1974, became the control animals for nitrite-exposed animals in groups 5, 6, and 7; however, those animals came from a different lot shipped on October 30 (12 percent raised this issue). . . .[221]

According to the GAO, many of the same issues raised by the seventeen outside reviewers had been anticipated by FDA scientists and the Interagency Working Group (IAWG). They, too, were concerned about the "litter effect," about "deficiencies in executing the experiment" and the "failure to comply with acceptable laboratory procedures," about the possibility that the tumors were caused by nitrosamines, and about "the high incidence of spontaneous lymphomas in the control groups."[222]

The most serious criticism of all came from the IAWG. Presumably the most scientifically prestigious group, it included representatives from the FDA, USDA, the National Cancer Institute, and the National Institute of Environmental Health Sciences who were experts in toxicology, pathology, chemistry, risk assessment, statistics, and residue evaluation.[223] The IAWG's greatest concern pertained to "the accuracy of the pathology diagnoses." Two IAWG pathologists had reviewed tissue slides diagnosed by Newberne and found that they "were in basic agreement with one another, but in substantial disagreement with the researcher's [Newberne's] diagnoses of lymphoma."[224] The effect, said the GAO, was to reduce the number of malignant tumors of any kind by 17 percent.[225] The result of this disagreement was the decision by the IAWG that there was a need for "a thorough and complete, impartial review by an independent group of expert pathologists recognized on a national and international basis."[226]

Thus, on April 27, 1979, the FDA sent out a press release to the nation which was entirely unaware of this invisible crisis. The press release announced that the FDA had signed a $469,000 contract with the Universities Associated for Research and Education in Pathology (UAREP) "to review the more than 50,000 animal tissue samples involved in the study." It was, said the FDA, to be a blind study in which the pathologists would not have knowledge of the group of animals from which the tissue slides had come or of prior diagnoses. The FDA also informed the country that on April 19, UAREP had "held a public meeting to help develop the criteria for reviewing the pathology findings of the study," was developing those criteria, and that a "pilot study will be conducted in May to evaluate the criteria." The "full-scale review of the slides," said the FDA, "should begin in June" and "preliminary data should be available to FDA in September, at which time the agency will begin a statistical analysis." The FDA concluded its press announcement with the comment: "It is likely that a final evaluation of the Newberne study will not be available until late in 1979 or early in 1980."[227]

This was an unusually revealing press release, although its significance was not detected by the press. It raised an astonishing question: If 50,000 pathology slides were yet to be reviewed, if criteria for the review of those slides were yet to be "developed," if a pilot study was yet to be conducted to assess those criteria—*what criteria for the judgment of pathology findings had the FDA been using until that date?* Clearly, it had not only been Newberne's pathology findings which had been judged in the absence of such criteria: There had never been any such criteria before. This may have been the first time that any scientist who had actually produced the 50,000-odd pathology slides required by the NCI was being subjected to the experience of having all those slides reviewed. In fact, the entire episode revealed not only real or alleged inadequacies in the Newberne experiment but an extraordinary vacuum in the realm of regulatory evaluation of cancer tests.

Given this vacuum, the GAO inevitably made two major recommendations at the end of its report. One was that the HEW Secretary direct the FDA Commissioner to "develop guidelines for design and data collection and reporting of long-term toxicity studies and establish standards and methods for statistically evaluating such studies."[228] The FDA's response, in a word, was that it could not do so. The agency argued that it had a number of other methods for the evaluation of studies, but its chief reason as summarized by the GAO was this:

FDA officials stated that the scientific community had struggled for years toward an amenable solution to the very difficult and complicated problems of study design and statistical evaluation and pointed out the difficulty in developing a single set of guidelines that would receive universal approval by the scientific community.[229]

The GAO also recommended to the Secretary of HEW that he "direct the FDA Commissioner to develop a system for ensuring the accuracy of pathological diagnoses for FDA-sponsored studies on which regulatory action is contemplated and to consider the need for verifying tissue slide diagnoses as part of that process."[230] Again, after agreeing in principle, the FDA said it couldn't. As the GAO summarized the agency's explanation:

FDA officials generally agreed with the need to require verification of pathological diagnoses for FDA-sponsored studies. According to them, the cost of uniformly requiring separate verification of all pathology slides from all studies would be prohibitive and probably not justified from the perspective of the taxpayer. For that reason they do not intend to adopt a policy of verifying all pathology slides, but will explore the merits of having samplings from each contract verified. They pointed out, however, that undertaking verification could reduce other work that can be done either by contract or in-house and that the extent of verification will be limited by the relatively small number of trained scientists qualified to evaluate the pathology of tissues prepared from small animal/rodent experiments.[231]

In sum, there was neither enough time, or money, or trained personnel to establish the validity of the pathology analyses for which they had contracted—not even enough to do *samplings*. What is more, no criteria which met with the approval of the entire scientific community existed for evaluating this most important aspect of cancer testing—the analysis of the cancerous tissues themselves. FDA officials argued, however, that "FDA currently does verify pathology results" on an ad hoc basis when faced with certain inconsistencies and anomalies.[232] On this, the GAO had no comment.

Paul Newberne, however, did. When charged with not having observed "scientifically acceptable procedures" according to the "good laboratory practices" document, he observed that those "good practices" had been defined only after he had started his study, that the issues with which they dealt were controversial,[233] and that the document did not "address the question of how to resolve differences in diagnostic interpretation by pathologists."[234] In another letter to the FDA, Newberne observed: "There is no study published to date that cannot be taken apart if one wishes to critically evaluate everything."[235] It was a defensive remark, but it bears the earmark of truth. Where no objective criteria exist, any study *can* be "taken apart."

Eventually, the great investigation ground to its end. In August 1980, two years after Commissioner Donald Kennedy had endorsed the Newberne study after a two-hour "briefing," a new commissioner, Gere Goyan, withdrew the endorsement. As of this moment of writing, nitrite has not been declared to be a direct carcinogen.

These three examples illustrate the kinds of scientific—and bureaucratic—problems and conflicts that underly the various "scandals" that have steadily erupted in our political life. When one has even this small amount of knowledge, one sees clearly that all revolve around many, and occasionally all, of the potential errors to which animal tests are subject. Whenever comparable "scandals" erupt, it is always because of such problems; when individuals or institutions quarrel over animal data, these are exactly the kinds of things they quarrel about.

It is only when the layman has some idea of the problems, both in abstract and concrete form, and it is only when he grasps the impressive shortage of objective criteria of judgment, that he is able to realize the pathetic silliness of the moral cartoon of the problem of cancer prevention in our society with which he has been presented for many years—the notion that the *essential* problem in "regulatory" science is a conflict between good and evil, between virtuous "science" and nonvirtuous "industry," between regulators who seek selflessly to protect our lives and businessmen who seek selfishly to kill us all. This is not to deny the existence of moral defectives among businessmen, regulators, and scientists, but as these cases reveal, the root problem in "regulatory" science clearly lies in the state of the art itself. Indeed, that science can be so easily corrupted and politicized only because the state of the art permits it. To a far greater degree than is commonly realized, the findings of cancer tests constitute gigantic Rorschach blots into which one can read exactly what one wants to read. To know even that much is to free oneself from being a mental prisoner of a moral cartoon. Virtue and vice are *not* guides to the truths of carcinogenesis.

Liberation from the moral-cartoon vision of the problem, however, can be disconcerting to the layman, for it leaves him vulnerable to the actual uncertainties of the situation. If he cannot believe in the truth of the findings of the latest experiments that pour out at him from scientists, from journals, from regulatory agencies, and from the headlines—what is he to believe? If he cannot believe that regulators constitute a dedicated priesthood intent only on dispensing solid science—what is he to believe? If, in 1980, the practitioners of the science of cancer prediction and prevention still could not agree on some of the most fundamental criteria for conducting and evaluating carcinogenesis tests, if the scientists themselves often do not know what to make of their own data—what is he to believe? The implication of everything that has appeared in this chapter so far seems to suggest that he can believe nothing at all—that he can know nothing at all, and that, as Donald Kennedy put it so candidly, he is doomed forever to stand by in a state of glazed incomprehension as the "cognoscenti" debate.

There is certainly some truth in that view. It should be entirely clear by now that the layman can never attempt to form an independent opinion on the carcinogenicity of a substance. He has no means of doing it. Indeed, the more diligently he investigates any single "suspected" carcinogen, the more technical the issues become until, finally, he is sucked into the very eye of the hurricane where the "cognoscenti" of a dozen different disciplines debate each other in a half-dozen different tongues in realms where there are few objective criteria of judgment or none at all. For the layman, a narrow-focus investigation is impossible; *for him, the question "Is substance X a carcinogen?" is permanently unanswerable.* But there is an alternative—a wide-angle approach to the problem—that the layman can take. If he is doomed to get lost as he wanders among the individual trees, there is nothing to prevent him from leaping into a helicopter and flying over the entire forest to get a picture of its shape. That he can do, and if he does, he can learn a remarkable amount.

To translate this metaphor into applicable terms, the layman can seek to assess the science of prediction and prevention by its own standards; he can seek to learn how well it is achieving *its own stated goals.* That is the objective of the next group of chapters. Not until that aerial tour has been completed can the layman make a final judgment on the state of the art and decipher the clashing views of the critics and defenders of "regulatory" science. And only then can he discover why he himself is a source of growing fear in the hearts of the most critical "regulatory" scientists.

Chapter 9

The Case of the Missing Noncarcinogens

It is now quite clear that the best model for human cancer is *Herringus rufus*. All known chemicals are carcinogenic in this animal—a happy finding since it is now possible to reconcile all the theories of carcinogenesis advanced in the last century. . . .

The histology of the tumours is identical to that in man, but, if necessary, it may be different. Although the red-herring lives only two years, correction factors can be applied such that a herring aged 18 months is equivalent to a human being aged 20 to 70 years: the incidence of tumours is then found to be the same as, or different from, that in man.

Work on tissue-culture of *Herringus* explants has yielded results of great value in spite of the fact that they are intrinsically worthless since there is an instantaneous transformation of all cells to fibroblasts.[1]

> —"Animal Models in Cancer Research," by Anonymous, first published in *Lancet*, 1974; read aloud at a cancer conference by D. Mark Hegsted, Department of Nutrition, Harvard School of Public Health, 1975

The goals of the science of cancer prevention are not many, they can be clearly stated, and all rest on the primary goal of the animal tests. As Lorenzo Tomatis of the IARC defines it, "The first goal of the animal tests is to indicate whether or not the chemical is carcinogenic and thus is a qualitative goal."[2] Similarly, William Lijinsky speaks of "the objective of sorting out those compounds which are carcinogenic from those which are not."[3] The distinguishing evidence, as the NCI puts it in its primer for laymen, is: "Carcinogens produce a tumor frequency higher in the exposed animals than in the unexposed control animals. Noncarcinogens, by contrast, do not produce tumors."[4] In principle, once the substance is demonstrated to be noncarcinogenic it is "safe" in that it does not cause cancer. The carcinogenic data are then extrapolated to man and serve as the basis of risk assessment.

These, then, are the standards by which we will try, in the next few chapters, to assess the efficacy of "regulatory" science based on animal testing: (1)

its capacity to identify and to discriminate between noncarcinogens and carcinogens; (2) its capacity to predict carcinogenicity in man; and (3) its capacity
to assess risk in man.

Can "regulatory" science use animal tests to discriminate between carcinogens and noncarcinogens? The short, accurate answer is: no. In fact, "regulatory" science cannot identify noncarcinogens at all. Some readers may find it
inconceivable that the science which claims to be preventing cancer cannot advise them when a substance does *not* cause cancer. Other readers may find it
inconceivable that the science which is serving as a base for the regulation of a
giant industrial system cannot advise industrialists as to which substances to
manufacture which do *not* cause cancer. And both may inquire how this spellbinding fact never emerged into the open. The answer to all such readers is that
both situations are true, even if inconceivable, and that the fact *is* out in the
open. It is obscured from vision by a barrage of self-contradictory "information," a way of presenting data which alters with the purpose of the communication.

In fact, the reader has *already* been subjected to this barrage of contradictions in this book, but he may have been too focused on the different contexts
to notice it. If he has not been too distracted, he will have noticed that there has
been a gradual pileup in this book of astonishing information about noncarcinogenic or "negative" data. To recapitulate:

- We learned that the geneticists had discovered a void in the area of "regulatory" science where noncarcinogenic data should be. In 1976, when an international committee of scientists sought to correlate negative findings in
  mutagen and other short-term tests with the noncarcinogenic data in animal
  tests, they hit a stone wall. Iain Purchase, one of the coordinators of the International Study, reported in 1979 that a scientific definition of a noncarcinogen was nowhere to be found: "To our knowledge, we could find no
  publications nor any thoughts which had been put down on paper on definitions of noncarcinogenicity."[5] The committee had been required to form a
  little board of international "experts" to work out its own criteria for noncarcinogenicity and to identify its own noncarcinogenic test chemicals.
- We learned that when Bruce Ames and his colleagues tried to correlate their
  nonmutagenic data with the noncarcinogenic data from animal tests in their
  famous 1975 study, they observed that many of the noncarcinogenic animal
  data were of bad quality and unreliable. But in 1977, Ames and Joyce
  McCann went a good deal further: They informed a Cold Spring Harbor
  Conference of the "inadequacy of animal tests," which, they said, was
  "especially apparent in the designation of a chemical as a noncarcinogen,"
  and they declared that it was "vital" for the validation of mutagen testing
  that mutagen tests be correlated not only positively with carcinogens, but
  negatively with noncarcinogens,[6] and proposed a few guiding principles for
  establishing the lacking criteria.[7]
- We learned that "regulatory" scientists, in principle, always give priority to
  positive findings and consider noncarcinogenic findings unreliable.

- We saw that policy in action: Substances have been banned on the basis of positive studies, even bad positive studies—indeed, even atrocious positive studies—while negative studies have been rejected.
- But we also learned from the Department of Health, Education, and Welfare that a low percentage of the chemicals tested has been reported to be carcinogenic. And we learned that the EPA had endorsed and circulated a news story throughout the country reporting that only 7 percent of all chemicals tested had been reported to be carcinogenic, and that most of the rest were noncarcinogens.

This collection of information is giving us a series of quite different messages: (1) that we can all sleep fearlessly in our beds because most of the tested chemicals do not cause cancer; (2) that most of the tests reporting the negative results are unreliable and bad; (3) that there isn't any way to know whether these negative results are really negative because there isn't even a definition of a noncarcinogen, not even a criterion by which anyone can identify or accept evidence of noncarcinogenicity; and (4) that the same government agencies which are informing us that few chemicals are carcinogenic and most are not are refusing to consider negative data in their evaluation, which is to say that they are not acknowledging their existence.

The layman need not know how to conduct an animal test or evaluate the results to know that he is staring, here, at a nest of contradictions. Or, perhaps, at a word game. How, simultaneously, can we be told that most of the noncarcinogenic findings are unreliable and bad *and* that we may rejoice in our safety since most findings are noncarcinogenic? And how, simultaneously, can we be told that most noncarcinogenic findings are unreliable and bad *and* that there are no criteria with which to judge noncarcinogenicity? One gets the impression here that noncarcinogens are popping in and out of existence like boojums in a disturbed physicist's dream.

Given statements from the NCI and the IARC that the explicit goal of animal testing is the differentiation between carcinogens and noncarcinogens, the issue is clear: Either substances that *don't* cause cancer exist and can be identified and differentiated from substances that *do* cause cancer—or they can't. Which is it? It takes a certain amount of time for the lay researcher to discover the contexts in which noncarcinogens are and are not acknowledged. Here is what one learns when one tracks down these two "positions":

POSITION I: "... MOST SUBSTANCES DO NOT CAUSE CANCER" (OSHA)

There are numerous statements in the literature reporting that most of the chemicals which have been tested have not been reported to be carcinogens. Here is William Lijinsky's report on the tests conducted by the NCI, presented in his statement at the OSHA hearings:

The aim of testing substances for carcinogenic risks is to demonstrate safety of the substance or reasonable assurance thereof. That some substances will fail the tests and provide evidence of carcinogenic potential is to be expected. However, these will be few, as demonstrated by the results so far of the National Cancer Institute's Bioassay Program. *The overwhelming majority of the substances tested at two dose levels in two species of experimental animals were considered to have provided no evidence of carcinogenicity. This has been the experience with all of the testing of chemicals in animals that has been carried out during the past several decades, with the objective of sorting out those compounds which are carcinogenic from those which are not.* Many of these tests were not carried out with the rigor now required, and some of them cannot be considered conclusive, yet a great majority of the substances were considered non-carcinogenic. Some of the substances tested have been components of the environment, or of food (as food additives, for example), or drugs and medicines, agricultural chemicals and industrial chemicals. However, most of the compounds tested were solely of interest to the investigator and relevant to studies of the mechanism of carcinogenesis by a particular type of compound. This is certainly true of the many hundreds of polynuclear compounds which have been tested, very few of which occur in nature or are formed in pyrolytic processes. *Nevertheless, the fact that so high a proportion of substances tested because of a suspicion of carcinogenic activity have proved to be non-carcinogenic should be of comfort to those who are told that under suitable conditions anything can be carcinogenic. This is simply untrue.*[8] [Emphasis added]

This statement reveals a strong desire to offer "comfort." In fact, there has been a veritable competition to "comfort" us, with smaller and smaller percentages of carcinogens. Here are the reports I have found, including those cited in the industrial survey in Chapter 3 and those published after it was compiled:

Only 17 percent carcinogenic: OSHA's policy document of 1980 includes a section formally entitled "Most Substances Do Not Appear to Be Carcinogenic." OSHA said that the "available evidence" indicated that *"most substances do not cause cancer."* Apart from a number of personal opinions to that effect, OSHA's "available evidence" consisted of two scientific studies. The first, described here, was an HEW publication called "Survey of Compounds Which Have Been Tested for Carcinogenic Activity," Volume I–VII (1974–1976)—a compilation, according to OSHA, of unevaluated data on the 7,000 substances tested as of that time. It indicated, said the agency, that "only about 17% of about 7,000 substances were reported as showing tumorigenic effects. . . ."[9] The second study OSHA cited is described below.

Only 10–15 percent carcinogenic: In a 1977 paper, Saffiotti said: "A large proportion of the chemicals so far tested showed no evidence of carcinogenic activity. The proportion of those found positive [is] 10–15%. . . ."[10]

Only 10 percent carcinogenic: This is the most popular percentage, the one that showed up most frequently in the documents I read, although the scientists and institutions which cited it had to reach all the way back to 1969 for their percentage. In that year, Innes and his colleagues screened a number of pesticides and industrial chemicals and only a small percentage were reported to be carcinogenic. According to Samuel Epstein,[11] to OSHA,[12] to Norbert Page of the NCI,[13] to Matthew Meselson of Harvard University,[14] to the NCI 1979 primer for laymen,[15] and to Judith Randal, sponsored by the EPA (see below),[16] the proportion of carcinogens was less than 10 percent.

Only 7 percent carcinogenic: In January 1980, the EPA outdid the competition. It reprinted and sent out under its official imprimatur a reprint of an article by Judith Randal, a science reporter in the Washington bureau of the *New York Daily News.* Her article had already been reprinted in the *Washington Post* on July 22, 1979.[17] Randal's story included Innes' 10 percent, but it led off with a dramatically low percentage of carcinogens. She wrote: "Indeed, of some 7,000 that have been tested (some admittedly more adequately than others), all but about 500 have gotten a clean bill of health." She described this as "a finding that about 7 percent of the compounds cause cancer in animals." She estimated those which had "gotten a clean bill of health" to be "all but about 500," or about 6,500.[18]

Only 2 percent carcinogenic: In March 1979, Dr. Sidney Wolfe, Director of Ralph Nader's Health Research Group, won the grand prize for the lowest percentage. Testifying before Senator Edward Kennedy at a congressional hearing, he explained that the percentage came from data from "an unpublished study by Dr. Bernard Altshuler of the New York University School of Medicine." The unpublished study, said Wolfe, was itself based on "a National Cancer Institute–sponsored survey by Tracor-Jitco" on "findings in the NCI-sponsored IARC monographs," and on "estimates by Dr. Altshuler based on studies not yet evaluated by IARC." The ultimate calculation, said Wolfe, was that "only slightly more than 2 percent, 220 out of the 10,000 chemicals tested for carcinogenicity, are definitely positive."[19]

The competitive eagerness to "comfort" us and Congress with tiny percentages of carcinogens has been so intense that there is apparently no end to the "comfort" that awaits us. At this rate, it will only take two more studies to reduce the Ralph Nader organization's 2 percent to 1 percent, and then to .5 percent. By the time this book is published, we may have returned to an estimate made by Umberto Saffiotti, in 1973, when Congress as well as industry became alarmed by a rapid progression of pesticide bans. Saffiotti testified reassuringly at the public hearings concerning the cancellation of the pesticide registration of aldrin and dieldrin:

Not all chemicals can cause cancer, contrary to some ill-informed belief; in fact, only a relatively small proportion of the chemical species that have been studied are capable of such activity. . . . It can be expected that, when thousands of new environmental chemicals will be tested, only a few hundred, *or maybe just a few dozen,* will be found to be carcinogenic, and it will be possible to concentrate our preventive measures on them.[20] [Emphasis added]

This touchingly tiny estimate was dredged up by OSHA and included in its "proposed rulemaking" of 1977 that served as the basis of the policy hearings and debates in 1978—and this same quotation, cited above, still sits there in the final policy document of 1980. That was one of the opinions that OSHA used to support its observation that available evidence indicated that "most substances did not cause cancer."

Now, this is a stellar collection of voices assuring us that most tested sub-

stances have never been found to be carcinogenic: NCI, HEW, EPA, and
OSHA, not to mention Umberto Saffiotti of the NCI, Samuel Epstein of the
University of Illinois, and Sidney Wolfe, the scientific spokesman for Ralph
Nader's organization. But as one contemplates this list, one realizes that there
is something exceedingly strange about it. What we have been looking at are
some of the foremost activist scientists, who have clamored for years that most
cancer is "corporate cancer," and a group of government, scientific, and regulatory institutions which are dedicated to the war against "corporate cancer"—all
assuring us, suddenly, that "corporate cancer" is growing vanishingly small.
This requires that one ask a few questions:

1. Why were these various institutions and individuals suddenly possessed of
   the urge to produce these marvelously reassuring percentages? What purpose were they serving?
2. Why were we given most of the data in terms of percentages of *carcinogens*,
   as opposed to percentages of *non*carcinogens, when the latter were the subject at issue? Some readers will have observed this peculiarity; others will
   have performed the mental arithmetic they were tacitly being asked to perform in order to arrive at the percentage or the numbers of noncarcinogens.
   But none of the scientists offered us percentages or numbers of noncarcinogens. The only one who gave us an actual number of the chemicals which
   had gotten "a clean bill of health" was the EPA-endorsed journalist Judith
   Randal. In fact, with only two exceptions, the sources did not even refer to
   "noncarcinogens" or to substances that "do not cause cancer"; *only* OSHA
   and William Lijinsky did so, and neither gave percentages or numbers.
   Those laymen who performed the calculations were trapped by an implication or by a floating generalization. *In fact, no scientist gave us any quantitative information about noncarcinogens at all. Where were the scientific
   percentages and totals of noncarcinogens?*

The first set of questions is readily answered. The context in which these
percentages emerged and the purpose they served were invariably the same, or
closely related. Either the informants were making the point that the percentage of carcinogens was "artificially high" (to quote Saffiotti) because the chemicals tested had been selected in advance as suspected carcinogens, *or they were
arguing that given such low percentages, experimental manipulation or testing at
high doses could not be creating carcinogenic artifacts in the laboratory.* Most
said both. The second argument, however—the defense of high-dose testing—
was the most frequent and the most important. It was the principal point of the
entire section of OSHA's policy document entitled "Most Substances Do Not
Appear to Be Carcinogenic." It was the principal point of the headline of Judith Randal's article circulated throughout the nation by the EPA, adorned
with a picture of a large dead rat. It was entitled: "This Rat Died in a Cancer
Lab to Save Lives: Animal Tests Find Most Chemicals Aren't Killers." It was
the principal point of the statement by William Lijinsky of the NCI. It was the
principal point of the relevant section of the NCI primer for laymen entitled
Everything Doesn't Cause Cancer. And it was the principal point of the tiny per-

centage cited by Sidney Wolfe of Ralph Nader's organization; it was in that context that Wolfe was rebutting, in the presence of Senator Edward Kennedy, the idea held by many people and "fueled" by industry that high-dose testing caused cancer. And it was a point made by most of the others as well.

In other words, the purpose of the barrage of information—information which declared or implied the existence of many noncarcinogens, usually by reference to small percentages of carcinogens—was to reassure Congress, to reassure the public, *and* to fight off attacks on high-dose testing. So powerful was the perceived need to demonstrate that most of the chemicals tested were noncarcinogens that the NCI primer, OSHA, Epstein, Norbert Page, and Matthew Meselson of Harvard reached all the way back to 1969 for a tiny study in which the number of chemicals tested was either 150, 140, or 120, depending on the scientist, to get the less-than-10-percent figure.[21] That was the lowest and most popular percentage until Judith Randal/EPA came along with their 7 percent, and Ralph Nader's scientific adviser came along with his 2 percent (offering, respectively, no documentation at all, and unpublished, unverified documentation). Interestingly, the source most commonly cited to refute the charges that high-dose testing might produce carcinogenic artifacts, the 1969 test, had been performed by Innes, the scientist said to have fed such legendary amounts of DDT to mice. More interesting yet, as the reader will recall, this "misunderstanding" of the high-dose-testing issue was all being blamed on the scientifically illiterate "public" when, in fact, it was a severe conflict within the scientific world—both within the United States and other countries.[22]

Why, the reader may wonder, are we plunging in, once again, to the high-dose issue? The answer is because that *was* the issue, whatever else it may have looked like. Like the no-threshold theory, which is constantly turning up in different contexts and which will turn up again and again, the high-dose-testing theory, too, is never laid to rest. Both constitute the most vulnerable conceptual outposts of the animal-testing empire. That is why the stalwarts of "regulatory" science were doing sentry duty. They had not changed their position on "corporate cancer"—they were fending off the congressional and scientific foes. Why, then, the reader may ask, did these dedicated scientists and government agencies rely on assertions and implications? Why didn't they produce some real noncarcinogenic data? The answer is: They couldn't. Not without jabbing a sharp pointed stick in the regulatory eye. The strange fact is that they had not been able to support their contention that high-dose testing usually produced noncarcinogenic data, *for officially speaking there are no noncarcinogenic data.* Every one of the negative findings that was invoked was illusory by the very edicts of "regulatory" science itself.

POSITION II: THERE ARE NO NONCARCINOGENS

All of which brings us now to the other half of the contradiction. What are those regulatory edicts? If the reader is impatient and simply wants to read them without knowing how they came about, he can skip right to the section a few pages hence headed "In the Opinion of the Regulatory Bodies of the United States, 'Scientific Judgment' Should Always Take the Form of Giving Positive Data Priority over Negative Data." But if one can transcend the dryness of the language, it is a rewarding experience to see how "regulatory" science talked itself—or more exactly, double-talked itself—into the astonishing position of protecting the citizenry and regulating a giant industrial civilization without any definition of, criteria for, or official recognition of a substance that did *not* cause cancer, and thus produced a void where noncarcinogenic data should be.

The existence of this weird void in carcinogenesis was shockingly new to geneticists, who could not validate their mutagen tests without negative, as well as positive, data, but it was scarcely a revelation to the researchers and regulators in the field. In 1969, Isaac Berenblum reported that negative findings were not often published and were even rejected by scientific journals.[23] A decade later, in 1977, Norbert Page of the NCI recapitulated Berenblum's criticisms and proposals for solutions and reported that this same situation still prevailed.[24] (Berenblum's warning is now enshrined in the OSHA policy document of 1980, although OSHA's sole use for it was as a means of speculating that because negative findings were rarely published, "the percentage of substances tested for carcinogenic activity and found positive may be even lower than present data indicate."[25]) In any event, it is not a new void. In fact, had the geneticists not grown so frantic about it, no biologist outside the field of chemical carcinogenesis would ever have suspected that such a void existed. Certainly the citizens of this country do not know it.

The notion of a biological test with no negative results will undoubtedly startle many readers. They commonly take dozens of biological tests and return from their doctors' offices or from hospitals with negative results—informed that they are *not* pregnant, that they do *not* have high blood pressure, that they do *not* have TB, syphilis, ulcers or a variety of other complex ailments. Such negative findings, however, are not absolute; in logic, one cannot prove a negative, and doctors cannot prove the absence of a condition. What is more, all tests have false positives and false negatives. Such negative test results are based on the results of tests in many people and they are actually *statements of probability* in the case of the individual patient. The better the test, the more people on whom it has been tested, and the more frequently an individual is tested, the higher the probability that the negative finding is meaningful. On some level, people understand that a negative finding is conditional, for they willingly accept the concept of follow-up tests and the yearly check-up. But they also understand the value, indeed the rational necessity, of a negative finding. The absence of negatives in our customary biological tests would mean that no human being could ever know that, at any given time, he showed no sign of disease.

By contrast, in animal tests for carcinogenicity, there are no comparable negative calculations. There is no such thing as a noncarcinogen in the cancer test: There is only . . . the void.

How did the void come about? It is clear from the literature that the regulators did not abandon the concept of a negative finding immediately. In fact, at some point or another, every conceivable idea has been expressed on the issue. Those ideas fall into certain clearly identifiable categories, and the categories themselves are informative. One could simply present them as a set of self-contradictory ideas, with some scientists and research institutions finding themselves on all sides of the debate. If, however, one presents the ideas as though they were a discussion of the problem—the "headlines" constituting a running argument—one understands far better how "regulatory" science moved, inch by inch, into this peculiar vacuum in which no tested substances may ever be declared noncarcinogenic.

"Negative findings in animal tests can be proved."

One finds statements by scientists that indicate quite clearly a belief that it is possible to prove a negative or a noncarcinogenic finding. According to Saffiotti, writing in 1973, "good negative data" exist;[26] and his later statement of 1976 (Chapter 2) that "a chemical should be considered guilty until proven innocent" clearly states that chemical "innocence" can be "proven."[27] Similarly, Robert Squire of Johns Hopkins University is quoted by OSHA as declaring: "We must judge whether the results [of an animal test] are negative, positive, or inconclusive"[28]—again a statement that clearly states that negative data exist. OSHA itself declares that a carcinogen "is to be treated as a scientific and a policy matter as posing a carcinogenic risk to humans, unless scientifically sound and convincing evidence demonstrates otherwise for the substance under consideration"[29]—this, too, indicating that it is possible to provide "scientifically sound and convincing evidence" that a substance is a noncarcinogen.

"Unfortunately, in logic, negatives can never be proved."

One also finds statements from scientists indicating their awareness that, in logic, one cannot prove a negative. Thus, A. L. Brown of the May Clinic speaks, in 1976, of "the logical impossibility of proving a negative."[30] Richard Carpenter, Executive Director of the Commission on Natural Resources of the National Research Council, says in 1976: "Science is never complete; not all imaginable questions can be answered; negatives cannot be proved...."[31] Richard Doll of Oxford University, speaking in 1977 of epidemiological studies, says: "Their disadvantage (like that of any other scientific observations) is that they cannot prove a negative."[32] Richard Peto of Oxford University, writing in 1978, speaks of "the common sense idea that animal experiments cannot demonstrate non-carcinogenicity even for animals."[33] David Rall of NIEHS is cited by OSHA in its policy document of 1980 as saying: "You cannot design a large enough experiment to exclude beyond all sorts of probability a negative."[34] Similarly, epidemiologist Robert Hoover of the NCI was cited by OSHA as saying: "It is kind of a general principle of science that you cannot prove a negative. You can only fail to identify the positive...."[35] Epidemiologist Brian MacMahon of Harvard speaks, in 1980, of "the statistical impossibility of 'proving' absence of an association."[36] And OSHA itself says: "In principle, it is impossible to prove a negative with any study of a finite size."[37]

"What is more, negatives only reflect the terms of any given experiment."

Some scientists point out that a noncarcinogenic finding is merely a finding under a specific and delimited set of circumstances. Joyce McCann says: "But it is very difficult to prove a negative. . . . A negative animal cancer test can only tell us that a chemical is less potent than a certain lower limit of detectability value, depending on the particular design of that test."[38] Saffiotti, too, when he defines what he means by chemical "innocence," says that "negative results are only valid within the conditions of the observation. . . ."[39]

"That means, of course, that a negative finding is really only a tentative finding."

The implication of the limited meaning of a noncarcinogenic finding is that, at any moment, another experiment might alter the results and produce cancer. As Peter Goldman of Harvard put it in oral testimony to OSHA: ". . . a positive if confirmed, is *there,* whereas a negative—it could always mean that something was not really quite right and change the conditions a little bit, one could get it."[40] There have been examples of precisely such changed conditions in which a substance originally found negative was later found to be a carcinogen in more extensive experiments, e.g., furyl furamide in Japan and DB(a,c)A.[41]

"Yes, all that is true, and certainly positives are more reliable than negatives, but still one can determine criteria for negatives."

Scientists frequently express the view that positive data are more reliable than negative data, but in the process, they also make statements, direct or indirect, indicating their belief that criteria do exist, nonetheless, for negative data. Thus, the Interagency Regulatory Liaison Group, representing the CPSC, EPA, FDA, and OSHA, observes that positive results under very limited conditions are acceptable as evidence of carcinogenicity, but states: "Negative results, on the other hand, are not considered evidence of lack of a carcinogenic effect, for operational purposes, unless minimum requirements have been met."[42] OSHA, independently, observes: "If a bioassay is conducted with too few animals, with too low a dose, or for too short a period, this will generally invalidate a negative result, although a clear positive result will nevertheless be valid and meaningful."[43] It is also stated that the criteria for negative findings must be much more rigorous than the criteria for positive findings. In 1976, Saffiotti, at an IARC workshop, said that "particularly extensive" data were required for a negative result,[44] and in 1980 OSHA said that "criteria for acceptability of positive results need be far less stringent than criteria for acceptability of negative results or evidence of safety,"[45] and cited Donald Kennedy of the FDA as making the same point.[46] In all these cases, it is stated or implied that despite the greater certainty of positive findings, criteria do exist for negatives.

"But there are no 'minimum,' 'extensive' or 'stringent' criteria for negatives—there are no explicit criteria for animal tests at all."

Scientists also state, as has already been reported, that there are no explicit, agreed-upon criteria for conducting and interpreting tests for noncarcinogenicity. OSHA, mentioning that several scientific groups had published various reports on the conduct of bioassays to determine "safety," says: "These groups were largely concerned with negative studies. Despite this concern with safety studies, however, in almost no case was any specific recommendation made on exactly how the general considerations should be embodied in particular experimental designs or interpretation."[47] In fact, says OSHA, the same thing is true for positives: "There is simply no way to standardize experimental bioassays, nor is there a way to standardize means of interpreting results from bioassays."[48] And, "OSHA finds that . . . it is neither advisable nor possible to set particular experimental protocols for all acceptable carcinogenicity bioassays. The test protocols of scientific institutions are constantly being changed as new knowledge is gained, which makes specification of protocols impractical."[49] The solution, says OSHA, supported by such prominent "regulatory" scientists as David Rall, Director of NIEHS, and Arthur Upton, Director of the NCI,[50] is to rely on the judgment of "competent scientific experts."[51] The unspecifiable criteria for judgment are, so to speak, inside the "competent experts' " heads. In fact, one NIOSH authority located the missing criteria in just that way. OSHA's 1980 policy document reported on a fragment of a cross-examination that took place during the hearings:[52]

Mr. Edward Baier (Deputy Director, NIOSH) explained the NIOSH position on experimental protocols and interpretation as follows:
Q: The NIOSH does not have criteria for the evaluation of animal studies?
A: Not a written policy as such.
Q: Does it have an unwritten policy?
A: Yes. I think as we discussed this morning, we could probably enumerate what a lot of the criteria are, unwritten.
Q: They exist, then, in the heads of the people that work at NIOSH?
A: Yes, as professional judgment.

"In the opinion of the regulatory bodies of the United States, 'scientific judgment' should always take the form of giving positive data priority over negative data."

Whether competent or incompetent, "experts" in a young science do tend to quarrel, and if official "policy" is to be set, the theoreticians of "regulatory" science must provide it. They have settled for requiring an automatic bias in favor of positive data, although provisos about studying all the relevant data are always made. Here are some of the institutional edicts and individual statements advising scientists to ignore data that indicate that a substance does *not* cause cancer.

When animal data contradict each other, say the theorists, the carcinogenic findings have priority over the noncarcinogenic findings. Thus, NCI's Ad Hoc Committee, chaired by Umberto Saffiotti, declared in 1970: "Evidence of negative results, under the conditions of the test used, should be considered superseded by positive findings in other tests."[53] The National Cancer Advisory Board (NCAB) said, in 1977, "Negative results obtained in one species do not, however, detract from the significance of clearly positive results obtained in another species."[54] The Office of Science and Technology Policy said in 1979: "Assuming that appropriate testing procedures are followed, however, it is generally sound to let positive results supersede negative results in tests involving different species, given the frequent occurrence of interspecies variation."[55] Arthur Upton, Director of the NCI, was cited by OSHA in 1980 as saying: "I believe that a reproducible carcinogenic response in *any* species of test animal must be considered sufficient to describe the test compound as a carcinogen. . . . Negative results in a second or even third species of test animal do not in my mind establish that the test agent is not a potential threat for human beings."[56] OSHA itself says that "in general, positive results should supersede non-positive or negative results" and reports "general support" for that position from the witnesses at the policy hearings.[57]

Contradictions of other types of carcinogenic findings may also be illusory, say the regulators. The Interagency Regulatory Liaison Group, consisting of representatives of EPA, OSHA, FDA, and CPSC, lists a series of situations, in addition to conflicting animal data, in which contradictory results or a lack of "concordance" in tests do not challenge carcinogenic findings:

Ordinarily, if a substance has produced positive results in a single adequately designed and conducted animal bioassay and no other data are available, the conclusion is that the substance is likely to pose a risk of cancer to humans. These results may be further confirmed by data on chemical structure, in vitro testing, or relevant biochemical studies that suggest a carcinogenic potential. *However, negative data from the latter three sources do not override adequate positive data from an animal bioassay.*[58] [Emphasis added]

Statistical considerations provide an estimate of the level of detectability of an effect and the consequent level of probability that the effect may be missed in a repetition of the test in a given number of animals. *Apparent contrary results in any two tests may be simply an effect of chance variation and may be fully compatible with an identical mechanism and level of activity of the test compound.*[59] [Emphasis added]

Concordance of results obtained under differing test conditions (e.g., different species, different routes of administration, or markedly different basal diets) provides greater confidence in the evaluation of both positive and negative studies. . . . *Lack of concordance from tests performed under different conditions does not, in itself, detract from the validity of the positive test.*[60] [Emphasis added]

The same bias in favor of carcinogenicity must prevail, say "regulatory" scientists, when different tests are used, whether animal tests, epidemiology studies, or in vitro tests: a carcinogenic finding in one should supersede negative findings in the others. Robert Hoover of the NCI, speaking of all three, says: "Because of the severe limitations of each of these methods of investigation, a good study showing positive evidence of carcinogenicity should take precedence over negative studies."[61] And OSHA "believes that, as a general matter, only little weight, if any," can be given to "epidemiologic studies which result in 'non-positive' determinations," and considers carcinogenic findings in an animal test superior to human studies which report no evidence of carcinogenicity.[62]

In the last analysis, say the "regulatory" scientists, noncarcinogenic results really "don't count." As the NCAB put it: "Because of the limitations inherent in animal bioassays, a negative result obtained in a particular animal bioassay does not exclude the potential carcinogenicity of a compound in humans."[63] And, as the Interagency Regulatory Liaison Group put it: "Failure to detect an increase of tumors in a bioassay may be due to an insufficient number of animals tested and does not unequivocally prove that a substance does not pose a risk of cancer."[64] Translation: The fact that a substance does *not* induce cancer is no guarantee that it is not a carcinogen.

This, then, is the rough "progression" of ideas that has terminated in the practical obliteration of noncarcinogenic data. Guided by "prudence" or "conservatism," the policymakers for "regulatory" science have provided unending reasons for eternally refusing to define or accept noncarcinogenic findings— and since regulatory decisions in this realm are backed by the law, it is now true, today, that American law has declared that there is no way to ascertain that a substance does *not* cause cancer.

It need hardly be said that there are critics of this institutionalized rejection of noncarcinogenic findings. In 1977, Irving Kessler, a prominent epidemiologist, wrote indignantly: "Should one positive study outweigh the negatives irrespective of quality? Should two (or five or ten) negative studies outweigh one positive? Present law tends to ignore such subtleties and to invoke regulatory action whenever any studies are positive, irrespective of the number or quality of negative studies."[65] And Johannes Clemmesen of Denmark, one of the epidemiological fathers of environmental cancer, informed OSHA that its proposal "to ignore negative epidemiology where there are positive animal data" was "unsound," and found it "difficult to conceive how one could even consider ignoring relevant human experience."[66] There are scientists in the field of chemical carcinogenesis (e.g., Herman Kraybill of the NCI[67]) who are struggling to define scientific criteria for identifying noncarcinogens, but, generally, the view that carcinogenic data alone are of value is the view of the theoreticians of "regulatory" science.

The result of this "prudent" or "conservative" refusal to define or accept noncarcinogenic data has had a number of strange consequences. Inevitably, if a scientist is unable to draw the line which divides carcinogens from noncarcinogens, or if for some other reason he is disinclined to establish criteria for "innocence" as well as criteria for "guilt," the goal of his work changes imperceptibly. He no longer seeks to differentiate between carcinogens and noncarcinogens, for he actually acknowledges only the existence of proved carcinogens and not-yet-proved carcinogens—and his real goal is to triumph over the latter. The result is the spirit of *Herringus rufus* described at the head of this chapter—the spirit of the cancer researcher who dreams of finding the ideal test animal in which *all* chemicals will be carcinogenic. In 1976, this alleged aspiration of the cancer researcher was satirized by "Anonymous" in *Lancet,* and the satire was read aloud at a cancer conference by a gleeful Mark Hegsted of Harvard. Anonymous was funny—vastly funnier to scientists than to laymen—because he had obviously touched that strange little nerve of fanaticism which lurks behind the sober face of carcinogenesis. In 1975, it was a clever joke, and after a good chuckle, Mark Hegsted and the conference got down to business. But it was not just a joke. One day, the fantasy of Anonymous came true. Although no "ideal" test animal has ever been found in which all chemicals can be shown to be carcinogenic, someone has found the next best thing. In its 1980 policy document, OSHA *outlawed* the noncarcinogenic finding. The agency declared it was not interested in "safety," it was interested only in danger—and issued the following statement:

It is important to emphasize that "negative" results in carcinogenicity bioassays simply define a limit beyond which carcinogenic activity would have been detected. Absolute safety can never be demonstrated; agencies concerned with establishing safety standards must balance the relative insensitivity of animal bioassays with the high cost of such tests and the increasing chances of experimental error as the experiment becomes larger and more elaborate. If the results of animal bioassays appear to support a conclusion of lack of carcinogenicity, OSHA's interest in reviewing experimental protocols is limited to the possibility that a more extensive examination of pathological or other criteria may possibly lead to the conclusion that the compound was in fact positive for carcinogenicity. *If the available evidence indicates that the chemical is not positive for carcinogenicity, OSHA's position on that particular chemical is the same as if the chemical had never been tested for carcinogenicity.*[68] [Emphasis added]

OSHA has declared, in effect, that that which is *not* a cancer-causing agent does not exist.

OSHA, no doubt, imagines that it is demonstrating the maximum possible idealism and concern for public health by legally abolishing noncarcinogenic findings from its universe and refusing to recognize their existence. But in so doing, the agency has ended up in a quagmire of contradictions. Quite apart from the fact that somewhere or other, as shown above, OSHA takes every conceivable position on the issue of negatives, there are four contradictions, above all, that are particularly grotesque:

Contradiction #1: The Toxic Substances Control Act requires that industry refrain from posing an "unreasonable risk to health or to the environment."[69] In the realm of cancer prevention, the manufacturer may wish to, or be obligated to, demonstrate that a substance is noncarcinogenic. But once he steps into OSHA's world, he has no means of doing so, for OSHA has declared that no negative finding will be acknowledged. In OSHA's universe there is now no "innocence" among American industrialists—there is only the "guilt" that has been proved and the "guilt" that has not yet been proved. Kafka could not improve on this situation.

Contradiction #2: OSHA makes a strenuous attempt to assure the public that "most substances do not cause cancer"—i.e., that most substances are noncarcinogens. But OSHA also rejects the existence of noncarcinogens. OSHA is thus asking the public to believe in a phenomenon the existence of which the agency refuses to acknowledge. This is not just crying wolf—it is assuring people that most creatures are not wolves, while declaring that *only* wolves exist.

Contradiction #3: OSHA supports the finding that mutagen tests are valid predictors of carcinogenicity and expresses its intention to use those tests. It publishes a statement from Joyce McCann, the colleague of Bruce Ames, who criticizes the inadequate state of the noncarcinogenic data which are needed for the validation of mutagen tests.[70] It also publishes a long sympathetic statement from Umberto Saffiotti who, in a moment of forgetfulness, recommended that, for the purpose of such validation, a great registry of both carcinogens and *noncarcinogens* be created and maintained.[71] But by barring noncarcinogens from its terrain, OSHA has also barred the means of validation of the mutagen tests—tests the agency itself wants to use. Bruce Ames has declared that "the [mutagen] test must not only positively respond to carcinogens, it is also vital that it give a *negative* response with non-carcinogens."[72] OSHA has told him, in the very act of embracing him, that what Ames deems so "vital" does not exist.

Contradiction #4: OSHA, finally, has informed the nation and the world that the animal test identifies only carcinogens, not noncarcinogens. It has thus outlawed the "first goal" of the animal test, which is to discriminate between carcinogens and noncarcinogens. That means that it has outlawed the very capacity for discrimination which makes the animal test practically applicable—and *that* is to say that OSHA has declared that there is no rational basis for OSHA's own regulation on the basis of those tests. OSHA has victimized industry, the public, and the geneticists—and has finally jammed a knife into its own brain.

If OSHA were an individual scientist, one would unhesitatingly pronounce that scientist a lunatic. But OSHA is a bureaucracy, and bureaucracies cannot be so diagnosed. It is clear, however, that no single rational mind is responsible for the 1980 policy document and that it has never been reviewed for internal logical consistency. To engage in such a review, depending on one's perspective, is to weep, to collapse in laughter, or to doff one's hat in respect to *Lancet*'s "Anonymous." If Anonymous is still alive and wants to see what happens when the mental processes he satirized are applied in reality, he need merely peruse the OSHA policy document of 1980. It is the spirit of *Herringus rufus* incarnate.

And that terminates the analysis of Position II. What do we learn, finally, when we put together the two positions—the argument that most substances tested are not carcinogens (*only* made in the context of reassuring Congress and citizens that "Everything Doesn't Cause Cancer" and of defending high-dose testing from scientific attack) and the argument that there is no such thing as a noncarcinogen (*only* made in the context of regulating industry)? The first conclusion we can reach is that "regulatory" science is devoid of elementary logic. The second conclusion we can reach is that "regulatory" science and its defenders will take any position that comes to hand to maintain political power over industry, whether those positions are rationally coherent or not.

That also terminates the first stage of the "helicopter trip" over the realm of "regulatory" science during which we are trying to assess that science in terms of its own stated goals. How, then, may we assess the capacity of the animal test to meet what Tomatis calls its "first goal"—the goal of discriminating between carcinogens and noncarcinogens? Given official policy statements to guide us, the answer is that the goal cannot be reached. In strict logic, there is no need to consider the other aspects of "regulatory" science that are on our list, because a test which is intended to discriminate between substances which do and do not cause cancer but which cannot achieve that goal is an invalid test. From this one can predict with certainty that there will be serious trouble in each of the remaining aspects of "regulatory" science—but it will be informative to learn the form that trouble takes, so we will continue on our trip.

Chapter 10

The Case of the Missing Carcinogens

Science and Society have not arrived at a final consensus on the definition of carcinogen either in human population or in experimental animals.[1]
—*First Annual Report on Carcinogens,*
Department of Health and Human
Services, 1980

The layman might suppose that the problem of identifying carcinogens is much less difficult than the problem of identifying noncarcinogens. A cancer, at least, is an existing entity, as opposed to an absence of an entity. The layman might also suppose that just as Paul Revere didn't go galloping through the countryside shouting "The British are coming!" without knowing what an example of "the British" was or how to spot one if it showed up, so "regulatory" scientists do not go galloping through the countryside shouting "Carcinogens are coming!" without knowing what a carcinogen is or how to spot one if *it* shows up. Unfortunately, the layman's suppositions are not reliable. And that, too, should not prove too much of a surprise to the reader of this book, for he has already learned that carcinogenicity is a more ephemeral and debatable concept than he had been led to believe.

In fact, once again, he has been told more about this phenomenon than he may realize. To recapitulate:

• We learned that the same geneticists who had had such difficulties with non-carcinogens also stumbled into trouble with carcinogens. In the footnotes and coded symbols of the celebrated McCann-Ames paper of 1975, announcing the 90 percent correlation between mutagens and carcinogens, the authors reported problems with carcinogens as well as with noncarcinogens. Here is my passage describing those problems (Chapter 6) with the statements relevant to *carcinogens* emphasized:

One footnote clearly warned that carcinogenicity testing in animals was difficult. . . . The codes indicated the nature of the problem in the classification of carcinogens. The authors

295

were actually working with three *kinds of carcinogens: (1) "carcinogens," (2) "weak carcinogens," and (3) "carcinogens" in "limited studies" where "further confirmatory work is required."* And the conditions for the noncarcinogens was much worse. McCann and Ames were working with *four* kinds of noncarcinogens: (1) "noncarcinogens," (2) "noncarcinogens" in "limited studies" with "further confirmatory work required," (3) *"noncarcinogens" in "most studies," but reported in others as having "weak or marginal" carcinogenic activity* and (4) an additional batch of forty-six chemicals, described as "noncarcinogens or presumed noncarcinogens." *On top of this, there was an additional classification of data which were so "inadequate" that it was impossible to tell whether the chemicals were carcinogens or noncarcinogens.*

It is clear from this that the authors, who had engaged in extensive correspondence with experts in carcinogenesis and had struggled to correlate their mutagens with reliable data, had had some unhappy surprises.

• We also learned that the International Committee which in 1976—the year of the passage of TSCA—had begun to conduct a blind validating study of the correlation of "short-term" tests with animal tests also had some difficulties with carcinogens. They had found that in prior tests, substances had been inconsistently identified—but, more important, as we were informed in 1979, they had convoked their little three-man committee of experts. If the reader is wondering why that little band of "experts" is showing up once again, he has simply forgotten something: That committee had been formed explicitly to have an "independent" opinion, said the coordinators of the International Program, meaning that there was the danger of appearing biased if the *committee* called a substance a carcinogen all by itself. The experts, in that case, we were told, had no difficulty in agreeing on how to *define* a carcinogen. But one wonders why it was so risky a matter, in the year of the passage of TSCA, to *call* a chemical a carcinogen and why it was necessary to convoke a committee at all. For that matter, why had Ames et al. been engaging in such voluminous correspondence on the identification of carcinogens with *individuals?* Everyone at work on these two projects had access, for example, to the National Cancer Institute, or its equivalent in every industrial nation. In fact, Lorenzo Tomatis of the IARC was a member of the expert committee, and Frederick de Serres and Michael Shelby, two of the coordinators, were officials of the NIEHS. Why didn't someone ring up the NCI, or the IARC, or the NIEHS—or OSHA or the EPA or the FDA, for that matter— and say, "Please ship over your list of reliably demonstrated animal carcinogens"? Why, one year before the passage of TSCA, was it so difficult to call a chemical an animal carcinogen?

• Finally, we learned the answer to these puzzling questions. As late as 1978, no two regulatory agencies agreed on how to conduct or interpret an animal test. As late as 1979, the FDA, under the pressure of the nitrite "scandal," convoked, for the first time, a committee to define criteria for pathology studies—the studies that actually identify cancerous tissue. And as late as 1980, no criteria existed to resolve technical disputes.

This at least suggests the reason why, in 1975 and in 1976, no one picked up the phone and called in for a list of reliable carcinogens. There was obviously nobody to call. Or, if one did call, the lines were all busy because the people one was calling were all frantically calling other people for exactly the same reason.

A dark question may now be formulating itself in the reader's mind: Is it possible that "regulatory" science did not know by the time of the passage of TSCA what an animal carcinogen was? The best answer to that question is: "Regulatory" science knew something, but it was not in very good shape. In fact, it was in very bad shape. The "regulatory" scientists who had committed themselves to preventing cancer by regulating the chemicals used in American industry faced two serious problems, which one must know if one is to understand their predicament.

Their first problem was confusion over numbers, and, as the reader will recall, there were three sets of numbers. One was the number of chemicals that existed, one was the number of chemicals in use, and one was the number of carcinogens. They were of quite different orders of magnitude, but as the industrial survey in Chapter 3 reveals, all expanded wildly for a number of years.

The estimates of numbers of chemicals that existed seemed to be undergoing an explosion of some kind. In 1976, Russell Train, Administrator of the EPA, put the number at 2,000,000. In 1977, the EPA document entitled *Potential Industrial Carcinogens and Mutagens* put the number at 3,500,000. In 1978, the Chemical Abstracts computer registry of chemical compounds put the number at more than 4,000,000 and reported that the number was growing at the rate of 6,000 compounds per week. And in 1978, Joseph E. Califano, then Secretary of the Department of Health, Education, and Welfare, put the number at 7,000,000.

The number of chemicals in commercial use were also increasing. In four years they had multiplied at a breathtaking rate. In 1975, David P. Rall, Director of NIEHS, put the figure at approximately 10,000 and said, in addition, that between 500 and 1,000 new chemicals entered the market each year. In 1977, the EPA, in *Potential Industrial Carcinogens and Mutagens*, put the number at 25,000 and said the number was increasing at the rate of about 700 a year. In 1978, Samuel Epstein, in *The Politics of Cancer*, reported that the Chemical Abstracts Service had submitted to the EPA a list of "some 33,000 chemicals" which it believed to be in common use. Also in 1978, David S. Sundin, Chief of the Hazard Section, Surveillance Branch, of the National Institute for Occupational Safety and Health (NIOSH), reported that NIOSH had "approximately 46,000 product formulations" on file. And in 1979, *Science* magazine quoted EPA Administrator Douglas Costle as putting the number of chemicals in use at 70,000.

Finally, the number of reported chemical carcinogens quintupled in a decade. In 1967, Isaac Berenblum, in *Cancer Research Today*, put the number of synthetic substances reported to cause cancer in laboratory animals at 500. In 1976, Thomas Maugh, author of *Seeds of Destruction*, the report by *Science* magazine on cancer research, put the number of cancer-causing substances at 1,000—adding, "and many times that number are suspect." And in 1976, the National Institute for Occupational Safety and Health (NIOSH), which is the research arm of the Occupational Safety and Health Agency (OSHA), published a volume entitled *Suspected Carcinogens* and put the combined number of chemicals that had been reported to be neoplastic (causing benign tumors) and carcinogenic (causing cancers) at 1,905 and listed another 510 that were suspected—2,415 in all.

While the three kinds of chemicals were exploding, the political repercussions were heard all over the country and were convincing millions that Americans were indeed, as Train had said, risking their lives every time they breathed, ate, drank, or touched. In the face of this infinitely expanding universe of danger, a few scientists were struggling to stuff the explosion back into the test tube from which it had come. In 1979, James Miller, who, with Elizabeth Miller, had made the critical discovery of the metabolic activation of carcinogens, dealt, thus, with the first two layers of chemicals—those in existence and those in commercial use. He said—in a scientific paper intended for the researchers in his own field—that there had been widespread failure to understand these numbers. There had indeed been an enormous growth in manmade chemicals, he said. Between the early 1800s when modern chemistry was born and the end of World War II in 1945, about one million new organic compounds had been reported. Then, in the next fourteen years, another million were reported. Nine years later, there were yet a third million, and nine years after that, a fourth. But, he stressed, speaking as "one who appreciates the beautiful intellectual and practical basis of organic chemistry," this was not just a pileup of chemicals as such. Many had emerged from "explosions of basic research in organic chemistry," in particular from a group of "sophisticated, rapid, and sensitive spectroscopic methods for characterization." There were indeed many more of these synthetic organic compounds than those organic chemicals that occurred naturally. Miller thought there were probably not many in nature: perhaps not more than 100,000. But, he pointed out, the majority of the synthetics were intellectual creations "prepared in only small amounts for research and remain in laboratories; thus, the great majority never reach the human environment." He questioned the frequent estimate that 63,000 such chemicals were in common use: ". . . I think there is good reason to doubt that all, or even a majority, of these compounds are really in 'common use,' even though they are certainly commonly available." And, he observed dryly: "It is of some interest that an EPA official has referred to this list of chemicals as the 'strawman list.' "[2]

Meantime, the number of carcinogens began to implode as well. In 1978, it was abruptly realized that the NCI carcinogenesis bioassay program, which, according to Norbert Page, was possibly the largest carcinogen screening program in the world,[3] had devoted a great deal of its attention to relatively rare chemicals. In 1978, Thomas Maugh of *Science* reported that many of the chemicals tested had been produced in small quantities and that neither industrial workers nor the general population were exposed to them in any significant way.[4] Thus, a substantial percentage of the carcinogens reported by the NCI had had little or no practical significance. In 1979, James Miller dealt with these too. He said that the numbers of carcinogens had been generally exaggerated, and that "most of these chemicals were tested as structural analogs of known carcinogens, and the large number of compounds synthesized primarily for analyses of structure-activity relationships has highly inflated the list of known chemical carcinogens."[5] The NCI's theoretical absorption with inventing new chemical variations of known carcinogens had obviously contributed to, if it had not directly initiated, the chemophobia that had gripped so many scientists.

Unfortunately, while Miller and others were beating down the fires caused by the inflated and inflammatory numbers of chemicals, the research grants had begun to flow like liquid gold into the university laboratories so scientists might study yet other chemicals. In 1980, Tamas E. Doszkocs, Chief of the Technical Services Division of the National Library of Medicine, writing with several colleagues, published an article in *Science* describing the proliferation of scientific literature, explaining how it had been computerized, and many of the computerized data bases he described pertained to cancer research. One data base was called CANCERLIT, and it had 183,433 entries between 1976 and 1979; another was called CANCERPROJ, with about "16,000 summaries of ongoing cancer research projects in many countries."[6] Not all of these were animal experiments, but many were, and all were relevant to the problems being explored by animal testers. There were also toxicological, pharmacological, and chemical data bases, which contained much information relevant to cancer research. The computer had become a marvelous tool of communication for workers in the field of carcinogenesis, but a few problems were yet to be worked out. As Doszkocs and his colleagues described them: "Despite the impressive speed and flexibility of interactive retrieval systems, their impact has been lessened by limited awareness of their existence, uneven quality of retrieval, inadequate linkages among data bases and reliance on specially trained intermediaries."[7] The article was an attempt to inform scientists that these computers stuffed with data bases existed and to explain how to use them. In sum, by 1980, the "knowledge explosion" had hit cancer research all over the world, and only the computers and possibly their "trained intermediaries" knew how many substances had been reported to be carcinogens; most scientists didn't.

The same thing, meantime, was happening to mutagen research. By 1969, the newly formed Environmental Mutagen Society found that "access to chemical mutagenesis information had exceeded individual capabilities."[8] Between 1969 and 1972, there were already 8,500 "data holdings"—and as of 1980, according to Robert S. Stafford of the Environmental Mutagen Information Center, giant computers were being stoked with the mutagen research that had emerged from 30,000 papers; what the overwhelming body of research added up to, he said, given the enormous diversity of assay systems and test conditions, no one yet knew.[9]

From this, one gets some sense of how "regulatory" science was confusing itself. As with its left hand (and with the assistance of one of the most important basic researchers in the world) it was beginning to grasp that its initial vision of Americans being pounded to death by millions of chemicals had been hallucinatory, with its right hand it was doling out grants to scientists all over the nation, and to some in other countries, who were now beginning to stoke the computers with their new data. The incredible expanding-shrinking carcinogens were apparently expanding again.

But numbers were just the first problem. The second—and far more crucial—was the problem of validity. Not all experiments reporting carcinogens were "good" or "valid" experiments, assuming that scientists could agree on what such assessments meant—and, as the reader already knows, that is an assumption that cannot be made. How many of the thousands of reported carcinogens, then, were actually valid findings? No one is in a position to say with certainty. As Roy Albert put it tactfully in 1978, "A very wide range of quality of bioassay data has been generated over the years."[10]

As the industrial survey reported, different attempts have been made to estimate the number of carcinogenic findings in various collections of data. In 1976, NIOSH listed 2,415 "suspected" carcinogens that had been reported in the literature. One year later, the Environmental Protection Agency (EPA) published *Potential Industrial Carcinogens and Mutagens*, reporting that 1,000 chemicals had been shown to be "tumorigenic" (causing benign tumors) and 100 had been "definitely" shown to cause cancers.

In 1977, OSHA hired the consulting firm of Clement Associates to review the NIOSH list of 2,415, looking only for the first two reports of positive findings on any substance tested, and taking no other data and no negatives into account.[11] By this mechanical standard, 269 were deemed by Clement to be "carcinogenic chemicals,"[12] and several hundred (the numbers vary with the sources)[13] were considered to be "suspect." Samuel Epstein observed that this list of what he called "unequivocal" carcinogens contained rare laboratory concoctions to which no one was exposed and variants of the same chemical, and estimated that more than 100 would require regulation.[14] From 2,415 suspected carcinogens to 269 "unequivocal" carcinogens to Epstein's distillation of 100 was quite a process of deflation.

Saffiotti, too, has made various estimates of the proportion of the carcinogen tests that are valid. In 1976, discussing the 6,000 substances that had been tested for carcinogenicity, he observed that many of the older tests were "conducted by protocols now considered quite inadequate, and include tests of highly impure substances, tests on very small groups of animals or without adequate controls, tests not continued long enough to allow for the appearance of tumors, and tests not supported by adequate pathology," and estimated that only half the number had been tested with adequacy. Of the total number, he estimated that 1,000 had been reported to be carcinogenic; and of that number, he said, about half, some 500, "have been reasonably well-demonstrated" to be carcinogenic.[15] But, he added, "The number of 'known carcinogens' will vary considerably depending on the degree of critical stringency" used in evaluating carcinogenicity.[16] These estimates were repeated by Epstein in 1977[17]—but by 1977, Saffiotti had arrived at some new estimates. There were, he said, "some 1,000–1,500 chemicals" that had been suspected of being carcinogens on the basis of experiments, and of those, he estimated that "substantial evidence exists for the carcinogenicity of about 600–800."[18] In 1978, Saffiotti gave

Thomas Maugh of *Science* another variant of the same estimate: Of 7,000 tested chemicals, he said, a few more than 1,500 had been reported to be carcinogenic; of those numbers, however, at least half of the list had been inadequate, so the actual number of carcinogens was around 750. Again, he told Maugh, the number of "known carcinogens" will vary, depending on the stringency of one's criteria.[19]

It is clear from this progression of calculations how Saffiotti estimated valid carcinogens: He tended to chop all totals of reported carcinogens in half. Such estimates, however, leave one in a state reminiscent of that of the bewildered Chinese in columnist George Will's story: "In 1978, a Peking wall poster announced that Mao had been only 70 percent right, and 800 million people wondered which 30 percent of his 'red book' to disregard."[20] When one looks at Saffiotti's series of 50 percent estimates, one wonders which half to disregard. And when one adds his warning that the number of "known carcinogens" depends on the "stringency" of the criteria used for judging carcinogenicity, one realizes that Saffiotti's 50 percent could be another man's 60 percent or 40 percent, or 30 percent or 70 percent . . . Or 17 percent or 10–15 percent or 10 percent or 7 percent or 2 percent or "maybe just a few dozen" of the future chemicals to be tested, if one happened to be trying to reassure Congress and the public while fending off scientific opponents of high-dose testing.

It was in 1979—a year after Saffiotti's estimate that there were about 750 established carcinogens—that Sidney Wolfe showed up at Senator Edward Kennedy's latest hearings on cancer, brandishing the unpublished estimate of Bernard Altshuler of NYU that only about 2 percent of 10,000 chemicals tested were carcinogenic—i.e., 220. How Saffiotti's 750 carcinogens had collapsed into Altshuler's 220 is both unclear and unimportant. What is important is that nobody knew how many valid or good carcinogen tests had been conducted—and nobody *could* know. It all depended on the "stringency" of the criteria—those criteria that were all in the "competent 'experts'" heads—and that, according to Kraybill of the NCI, "invariably" generated disputes. In a scientific community in which Isaac Berenblum at one pole considered no carcinogen "at all reliable" unless it had been demonstrated to be such in "at least three different species" and in which at the other pole David Rall, Director of NIEHS, and OSHA argued that one test in one species was sufficient—even this single criterion of how many species had to develop cancer from a substance before one called it a carcinogen could cause shifts in the number of carcinogens by many orders of magnitude. In sum, a carcinogen was almost—not entirely, but almost—what anyone wanted it to be.

Was there, then, no list of identified animal carcinogens that could be described as definitive? In 1978, Saffiotti analyzed the data bases for reported carcinogens as follows:

Documentation of chemical carcinogenicity data is provided by the following sources: (1) IARC Monographs on the Evaluation of Carcinogenic Risk of Chemicals to Man, published by the International Agency for Research on Cancer which are, at present, *the only extensive reference source of carcinogenicity data evaluated by a systematic process of critical review of the experimental conditions, bioassay protocols, standards of pa-*

thology and results; (2) "Survey of Compounds Which Have Been Tested for Carcinogenic Activity," published by the National Cancer Institute which constitutes a key documentation source, *but without critical evaluation of the literature data;* (3) Suspected Carcinogens, a Subfile of the NIOSH Toxic Substance List, published by the National Institute for Occupational Safety and Health which lists about 1,500 chemicals reported in the literature as having "neoplastic" or "carcinogenic" effects, *with no critical evaluation;* (4) other lists of carcinogens compiled by various individual authors or groups in several books on carcinogenesis.

I believe that it is very important that all these sources be used with great caution, particularly when they have not been assembled through a critical review process.[21] [Emphasis added]

Although advising that "all these sources" be used with "great caution," it was obvious that only one of them actually *evaluated* the data: the IARC.

During this time, a great many people (including this author) were still searching for a definitive list of "known" or proved animal carcinogens. And so was Rep. Andrew Maguire of New Jersey, whose state had been reported to have very high cancer rates attributable to the chemical industry. In November 1978, the Congress, under the goading of Maguire, amended the National Cancer Act, and required that the HEW issue a report each year "which contains a list of all substances (i) which either are known to be carcinogens or may reasonably be anticipated to be carcinogens and (ii) to which a significant number of persons residing in the United States are exposed."[22] In 1979, Luther J. Carter, in *Science*, hailed this yearly report as "a potent weapon in the war against cancer."[23] The report, said Carter, "could in fact generate powerful political pressures that would be felt by all of the parties caught up in the war on cancer. . . . Certainly Rep. Andrew Maguire (D-NJ), the principal sponsor of last year's cancer act amendments, means for the report to be a compelling document."[24]

In July 1980, the "compelling document" appeared. It was published by the Department of Health and Human Services. It was entitled *The First Annual Report on Carcinogens*, and it was more apologetic than compelling. Its Executive Summary explained in some detail why only a relative handful of carcinogens—twenty-six—was being listed in this document and why "a number of limitations impeded its full development."[25] There had been some problems, it appeared, in complying with the law. Some progress, said the NTP, had assuredly been made in the past two years; but human exposure data were hard to get, risk assessments were hard to make, and worst of all, nobody knew with any certainty what a carcinogen was:

Science and society have not arrived at a final consensus on the definition of carcinogen either in human population or in experimental animals. Scientific judgment plays an important role in the final decision on whether a substance is a carcinogen where test results are unclear. This judgment rests on a knowledge base that is fluid and evolving.[26]

The whimpering between the lines was almost tangible. Rep. Andrew Maguire and the law had commanded that a list of carcinogens materialize—

but the National Toxicology Program didn't know how to identify a carcinogen; everything depended on "scientific judgment," and scientific judgment, in a fetal state, was resting on a "base that is fluid and evolving." Thus, said the NTP, compiling such a list was really a venture into the unknown; its report was of a "pioneering nature."[27] Here is the list of twenty-six carcinogens published by that "pioneering" document:

1. Aflatoxins	10. Cadmium and cadmium	18. Melphalan
2. 4-Aminobiphenyl	compounds	19. Mustard gas
3. Arsenic and inorganic	11. Chloramphenicol	20. 2-Naphthylamine
arsenic compounds	12. Chloromethyl methyl	21. Nickel and nickel
4. Asbestos	ether	compounds
5. Auramine	13. Chromium	22. Oxymetholone
6. Benzene	14. Cyclophosphamide	23. Phenacetin
7. Benzidine	15. Diethylstilbestrol	24. Phenytoin and
8. N,N-Bis(2-chloroethyl)-	16. Hematite and iron	phenytoin sodium
2-naphthylamine	oxide	25. Soots, tars, and oils
9. Bis(chloromethyl)ether	17. Isopropyl oils	26. Vinyl chloride

It was a surprising list, for the "pioneering" NTP had not published a definitive list of *animal* carcinogens at all. It had published a list of *human* carcinogens— a list that had come *exclusively* from epidemiological studies,[28] from studies of man. What is more, the list of chemicals and their compounds had been taken straight from the IARC—specifically, from a 1978 paper by Lorenzo Tomatis et al.[29] Most of the substances were occupational carcinogens and a few were medicinal. Some (e.g., mustard gas) had been known for decades. And at least one (soot) had been known since the eighteenth century.[30] The National Toxicology Program also informed Congress that the IARC had done later research—obviously published too late to be discussed intensively in its report—and promised that in the future it would deal with carcinogens identified in animal studies.[31]

Thus, as of 1980—ten years after the Surgeon General had been told that cancer prevention with animal testing was "within reach," and four years after the passage of TSCA—the official world of "regulatory" science still had no list of established animal carcinogens. This seemed so incredible that just before writing this chapter, I asked my research assistant Pamela Blanpied to call the heads of major research and regulatory agencies to check on whether any of them had yet produced such a list. She was shunted from office to office by puzzled officials who could not answer her question. During October 1 and 2 of 1980, she inquired of a variety of people if they had or knew of a "universally recognized and noncontroversial" list of animal carcinogens. Here are some of the answers she received, taken from her notes:

NIEHS: David Rall's office transferred me to Steven d'Arazien, Public Information Officer for the National Toxicology Program. D'Arazien said: "There isn't any such list. We don't have one." He suggested the IARC report by L. Tomatis of 1978, which the

National Toxicology Program used as the basis of its *First Annual Report on Carcinogens.*

OSHA: Eula Bingham's office transferred me to Peter Infante. Spoke to Jolie Appel, Assistant to Infante. Appel said: "We just don't have any animal carcinogens list." She talked to Infante and called back. Infante, she said, suggested we consult the IARC and Tomatis, as "the most recent and the best." Appel added: "We don't know of any other generally recognized list. We base ours on IARC."

EPA: Douglas Costle's office transferred me to Bob McGaughy, Deputy Director of the Cancer Assessment Group. McGaughy said: "Most people accept the IARC monographs." The IARC, he said, is "generally recognized" as valid. He was "pretty sure it will stand up," and added that the FDA views it as "accurate."

Roy Albert, Consultant to the EPA: Answered his own phone. He said immediately: "The IARC. You will probably do well enough with Tomatis, 1978. Tomatis, 1978, is the best there is."

NCI: The Director's office transferred me to Richard Adamson, Director of the Division of Cancer Cause and Prevention. Spoke to Miss Quinn, his assistant. She said: "Call Kraybill. He works with WHO . . . and has contacts with IARC."

More than this number were interviewed, and in every case the answer was essentially the same: Our office doesn't have a universally recognized list of animal carcinogens, but you will find it at the IARC. And this, too, was odd. If Tomatis of IARC had such a list, why hadn't the National Toxicology Program published it? And why wasn't it available at these regulatory agencies? For that matter, why didn't *I* have that list? Tomatis' 1978 paper had been sitting in my files ever since it had been published. I had read it carefully; was there something I had missed?

The answer to all these questions is clear when one looks at the Tomatis 1978 paper. If one scans it at top speed, it *seems* to contain a list of established animal carcinogens. If, on the other hand, one studies it carefully, if one reads every word of the text, the footnotes, the table, the distinctions between substances-with-asterisks and substances-without-asterisks, *and above all, the title of the table,* one sees that the Tomatis paper does *not* contain a list of established animal carcinogens. Here (in addition to the separate list of human carcinogens already published by the NTP) is Tomatis' list of animal carcinogens:[32]

List of chemicals for which there is some evidence of carcinogenicity in experimental animals only or for which the data were inadequate for evaluation of the presence or absence of carcinogenicity (IARC monographs, Volumes 1 to 16)

Acetamide*α	10. o-Aminoazotoluene*	17. Apholate
Acridine orange	11. p-Aminobenzoic acid	18. Aramite*
Acriflavinium chloride	12. 2-Amino-5-(5-nitro-2-	19. Arsenic trioxide
Actinomycins*	furyl)-1,3,4-thiadia-	20. Aurothioglucose*
Adriamycin	zole*	21. Azaserine*
Aldrin	13. 4-Amino-2-nitrophenol	22. Aziridine*
Amaranth	14. Amitrole*	23. 2-(1-Aziridinyl)-eth-
5-Aminoacenaphthene	15. Aniline	anol*
p-Aminoazobenzene*	16. Anthranilic acid	24. Aziridyl benzoquinone

25. Azobenzene*
26. Barium chromate
27. Benz(*a*)acridine*
28. Benz(*c*)acridine*
29. Benzo(*b*)fluoranthene*
30. Benzo(*j*)fluoranthene*
31. Benzo(*a*)pyrene*
32. Benzo(*e*)pyrene*
33. Benzyl chloride*
34. Benzyl violet 4B*
35. Beryllium*
36. Beryllium oxide*
37. Beryllium phosphate*
38. Beryllium sulfate*
39. Beryl ore*
40. BHC (technical grades)*
41. Bis(1-aziridinyl)-mor-
    pholinosphosphine
    sulfide*
42. Bis(chloroethyl) ether*
43. 1,2-Bis(chloro-me-
    thoxy)ethane*
44. 1,4-Bis(chloro-me-
    thoxymethyl)-
    benzene*
45. Blue VRS*
46. Brilliant blue FCF*
47. 1,4-Butanediol dimeth-
    ane-sulfonate (My-
    leran)*
48. β-Butyrolactone*
49. γ-Butyrolactone
50. Cadmium acetate
51. Cadmium chloride*
52. Cadmium powder*
53. Cadmium sulfate*
54. Cadmium sulfide*
55. Calcium arsenate
56. Calcium chromate*
57. Cantharidin*
58. Carbaryl
59. Carbon tetrachloride*
60. Carmoisine
61. Catechol
62. Chlorambucil*
63. Chlorinated dibenzo-
    dioxins
64. Chlormadinone
    acetate*
65. Chlorobenzilate*
66. Chloroform
67. Chloropropham
68. Chloroquine

69. *p*-Chloro-*o*-toluidine
    (hydrochloride)
70. Cholesterol
71. Chromic chromate*
72. Chromium acetate
73. Chrysene*
74. Chrysoidine*
75. C.I. Disperse Yellow 3
76. Cinnamyl anthranilate
77. Citrus red No. 2*
78. Copper 8-hydroxyquin-
    oline
79. Coumarin*
80. Cycasin*
81. Cyclochlorotine*
82. 2,4-D and esters
83. Daunomycin*
84. D & C red No. 9
85. Dichlorodiphenyldich-
    loroethane (DDD)
86. 1,1-Dichloro-2,2-bis(*p*-
    chlorophenyl)ethy-
    lene (DDE)
87. DDT*
88. Diacetylaminoazo-
    toluene
89. *N,N*-Diacetyl-
    benzidine*
90. Diallate
91. 2,4-Diaminoanisole
    (sulfate)
92. 4,4'-Diaminodiphenyl
    ether*
93. 1,2-Diamino-4-nitro-
    benzene
94. 1,4-Diamino-2-nitro-
    benzene
95. 2,6-Diamino-3-(phenyl-
    azo)-pyridine (hy-
    drochloride)
96. 2,4-Diaminotoluene*
97. 2,5-Diaminotoluene
    (sulfate)
98. Diazepam
99. Diazomethane*
100. Dibenz(*a,h*)acridine*
101. Dibenz(*a,j*)acridine*
102. Dibenz(*a,h*)anthracene*
103. Dibenzo(*c,g*)carbazole*
104. Dibenzo(*h,rst*)penta-
    phene*
105. Dibenzo(*a,e*)pyrene*
106. Dibenzo(*a,h*)pyrene*

107. Dibenzo(*a,i*)pyrene*
108. Dibenzo(*a,l*)pyrene*
109. 1,2-Dibromo-3-chloro-
    propane*
110. Dibutylnitrosamine*
111. *o*-Dichlorobenzene
112. *p*-Dichlorobenze
113. 3,3'-Dichlorobenzidine
114. *trans*-Dichlorobutene
115. 3,3'-Dichloro-4,4'-dia-
    mino-diphenyl
    ether*
116. Dieldrin*
117. Diepoxybutane*
118. 1,2-Diethylhydrazine*
119. Diethylnitrosamine*
120. Diethyl sulfate*
121. Diglycidyl resorcinol
    ether
122. Dihydrosafrole*
123. Dimethisterone
124. Dimethoxane*
125. 3,3'-Dimethoxybenzi-
    dine*
126. *p*-Dimethylamino-
    azobenzene*
127. *p*-Dimethylamino-
    benzenediazo-sodiu
    sulfonate
128. *trans*-2-[(Dimethyl-
    amino)methylaminc
    5-[2-(5-nitro-2-
    furyl)vinyl]-1,3,4-
    oxadiazole*
129. 3,3'-Dimethyl-
    benzidine*
130. Dimethylcarbamoyl
    chloride*
131. 1,1-Dimethylhydra-
    zine*
132. 1,2-Dimethylhydra-
    zine*
133. Dimethylnitrosamine
134. Dimethyl sulfate*
135. Dinitrosopenta-
    methylenetetramine
136. 1,4-Dioxane*
137. 2,4'-Diphenyldiamine
138. Disulfiram
139. Dithranol*
140. Dulcin
141. Endrin
142. Eosin (disodium salt)

43. Epichlorohydrin*
44. 1-Epoxyethyl-3,4-epoxycyclohexane*
45. 3,4-Epoxy-6-methylcyclohexylmethyl-3,4-epoxy-6-methyl carboxylate*
46. cis-9,10-Epoxystearic acid
47. Estradiol mustard*
48. Ethinylestradiol*
49. Ethionamide*
50. Ethylene dibromide*
51. Ethylene oxide
52. Ethylene sulfide*
53. Ethylenethiourea*
54. Ethyl methanesulfonate*
55. Ethyl Selenac
56. Ethyl Tellurac
57. Ethynodiol diacetate*
58. Evans blue*
59. Fast green FCF*
60. Ferbam
61. 2-(2-Formylhydrazino)-4-(5-nitro-2-furyl)-thiazole*
62. Fusarenon-X
63. Glycidaldehyde*
64. Glycidyl oleate
65. Glycidyl stearate
66. Griseofulvin*
67. Guinea green B*
68. Heptachlor
69. Hexamethylphosphoramide*
70. Hycanthone (mesylate)*
71. Hydrazine*
72. Hydroquinone
73. 4-Hydroxyazobenzene
74. 8-Hydroxyquinoline
75. Hydroxysenkirkine
76. Indeno(1,2,3-cd)pyrene*
77. Iron dextran*
78. Iron dextrin*
79. Iron oxide
80. Iron-sorbitol-citric acid complex
81. Isatidine*
82. Isonicotinic acid hydrazide*
83. Isopropyl alcohol

184. Isosafrole*
185. Jacobine
186. Lasiocarpine*
187. Lead acetate*
188. Lead arsenate
189. Lead carbonate
190. Lead chromate
191. Lead phosphate*
192. Lead subacetate*
193. Ledate
194. Light green SF*
195. Lindane*
196. Luteoskyrin*
197. Magenta*
198. Maleic hydrazide*
199. Maneb
200. Mannomustine (dihydrochloride)*
201. Medphalan
202. Medroxyprogesterone acetate*
203. Merphalan*
204. Mestranol*
205. Methoxychlor
206. 2-Methylaziridine*
207. Methylazoxymethanol acetate*
208. Methyl carbamate
209. N-Methyl-N,4-dinitrosoaniline*
210. 4,4'-Methylenebis(2-chloroaniline)*
211. 4,4'-Methylenebis(2-methylaniline)*
212. 4,4'-Methylenedianiline
213. Methyl iodide*
214. Methyl methanesulfonate*
215. N-Methyl-N'-nitro-N-nitrosoguanidine*
216. Methyl red
217. Methyl Selenac
218. Methylthiouracil*
219. Metronidazole*
220. Mirex*
221. Mitomycin C*
222. Monocrotaline*
223. Monuron*
224. 5-(Morpholinomethyl)-3-[(5-nitrofurfurylidene)-amino]-2-oxazolidinone*
225. 1-Naphthylamine*

226. Native carrageenans*
227. Nickel carbonyl*
228. Nickelocene*
229. Nickel oxide*
230. Nickel powder*
231. Nickel subsulfide*
232. Niridazole*
233. 5-Nitroace-naphthene
234. 4-Nitrobiphenyl*
235. Nitrofuraldehyde sen carbazone
236. 1-[(5-Nitrofurfurylidene)amino]-2-imidazolidinone*
237. N-[4-(5-Nitro-2-furyl)-2-thiazolyl]-acetamide*
238. Nitrogen mustard (hydrochloride)*
239. Nitrogen mustard N-oxide (hydrochloride)*
240. Nitrosoethylurea*
241. Nitrosomethylurea*
242. N-Nitroso-N-methylurethan*
243. Norethisterone*
244. Norethisterone acetat
245. Norethynodrel*
246. Norgestrel
247. Ochratoxin A
248. 17β-Oestradiol*
249. Oestriol
250. Oestrone*
251. Oil orange SS*
252. Orange G
253. Orange I*
254. Oxazepam*
255. Oxyphenbutazone
256. Parasorbic acid*
257. Patulin*
258. Penicillic acid*
259. Phenicarbazide*
260. Phenobarbital sodium
261. Phenoxybenzamine*
262. Phenylbutazone
263. m-Phenylenediamine (hydrochloride)
264. p-Phenylenediamine (hydrochloride)
265. N-Phenyl-2-naphthylamine*
266. Polychlorinated biphenyls*

67. Ponceau MX*
68. Ponceau 3R*
69. Ponceau SX
70. Potassium arsenite
71. Potassium bis(2-hydroxyethyl)-dithiocarbamate*
72. Progesterone*
73. Pronetalol hydrochloride*
74. 1,3-Propanesultone*
75. Propham
76. β-Propiolactone*
77. n-Propyl carbamate*
78. Propylene oxide*
79. Propylthiouracil*
80. Pyrimethamine*
81. p-Quinone
82. Quintozene*
83. Reserpine
84. Resorcinol
85. Retrorsine*
86. Rhodamine B*
87. Rhodamine 6G*
88. Riddelliine
89. Saccharated iron*
90. Safrole*
91. Scarlet red
92. Selenium compounds
93. Semicarbazide (hydrochloride)*
94. Seneciphylline

295. Senkirkine
296. Sodium arsenate
297. Sodium arsenite
298. Sodium dichromate
299. Sodium diethyldithiocarbamate
300. Sterigmatocystin*
301. Streptozotocin*
302. Strontium chromate*
303. Styrene oxide
304. Succinic anhydride*
305. Sudan I*
306. Sudan II*
307. Sudan III
308. Sudan brown RR
309. Sudan red 7B
310. Sunset yellow FCF
311. 2,4,5-T and esters
312. Tannic acid*
313. Terpene polychlorinates*
314. Testosterone*
315. Tetraethyl & tetramethyl lead
316. Thioacetamide*
317. 4,4'-Thioaniline*
318. Thiouracil*
319. Thiourea*
320. Thiram
321. o-Toluidine (hydrochloride)
322. Trichloroethylene*

323. Trichlorotriethylamine hydrochloride
324. Triethylene glycol diglycidyl ether*
325. Tris(aziridinyl)-p-benzoquinone*
326. Tris(1-aziridinyl)-phosphine oxide
327. Tris(1-aziridinyl)-phosphine sulfide*
328. 2,4,6-Tris(1-aziridinyl)-s-triazine*
329. 1,2,3-Tris(chloromethoxy)-propane*
330. Tris(2-methyl-1-aziridinyl)phosphine oxide
331. Trypan blue*
332. Uracil mustard*
333. Urethan*
334. Vinyl cyclohexane
335. 2,4-Xylidine (hydrochloride)
336. 2,5-Xylidine (hydrochloride)
337. Yellow AB
338. Yellow OB*
339. Zectran
340. Zinc chromate hydroxide*
341. Zineb
342. Ziram

* Asterisk, chemicals for which there is some evidence of carcinogenicity in experimental animals only.

If the reader examines this table of 342 chemicals, he will see from the title and the presentation alone that Tomatis et al. were not presenting a list of solidly established findings. The data indicating 221 chemicals showing "some evidence of carcinogenicity in at least one species of experimental animals" (with asterisks)—almost 65 percent of the total[33]—and the remaining "data which were inadequate for evaluation of the presence or absence of carcinogenicity" (without asterisks) were lumped together in one list, and that tells one a good deal: If one has a pile of gold nuggets and a pile of pebbles, one does not dump them into one sack, one "pans" them. The implication was clear that although the animal data had been carefully evaluated by IARC's expert committees and the majority had been found to have "some evidence" of carcinogenicity in "at least one species," the conclusions were such that Tomatis et al. could not separate out the experimental findings with confidence.

And the Tomatis text confirmed the implication. An attempt had been made, he explained, to divide the chemicals in the first sixteen IARC volumes into those for which "some evidence of carcinogenicity in experimental animals" existed and those for which the data had been judged "inadequate for evaluation." He stressed—and "stressed" was his word—that no attempt had been made to differentiate between "weak" evidence of carcinogenicity or "strong" evidence of carcinogenicity, or to indicate those substances which required confirmatory studies.[34] There had obviously been considerable uncertainty about where "strong" evidence ended and "weak" evidence began, and where "weak" evidence ended and inadequate data began. Thus, this table, far from representing a list of "known" or "universally recognized" animal carcinogens, was actually a revelation that firm criteria for classifying the findings of animal tests were lacking even at the IARC—the only institution that systematically evaluated data. And this, in 1980, said Roy Albert, consultant to the EPA, was "the best there is."

From studying this paper, one understands fully why the National Toxicology Program, ordered by Congress to produce a yearly list of carcinogens threatening to man, clung to the epidemiological—human—data presented in 1978 by Tomatis as to a lifeline, and postponed consideration of the animal data. The NTP was obviously disinclined to wander into that thicket of asterisks where it would discover experiments on mice, rats, hamsters, guinea pigs, rabbits, fish, ducks, shrews, dogs, marmosets, and monkeys, but would *not* discover which chemicals had definitely been found to be carcinogens.

We can, therefore, stop here—somewhere between 1978 and 1980—to consider once again the first question I originally set out to answer in this "helicopter flight" over the realm of "regulatory" science: Has cancer testing in animals succeeded in establishing its "first goal"—that of distinguishing between carcinogens and noncarcinogens? To judge both by the condition of noncarcinogens and carcinogens, it can be firmly concluded that, as of that period, that "first goal" had not been achieved. The animal testers were unable to differentiate between a cancer-causing substance and a non-cancer-causing substance. In the U.S., the numbers of reported carcinogens had been exploding, then shrinking, and were, possibly, re-exploding, and no one knew or had ever known what percentage of them were valid. And in the only institution in the world where the results of animal tests were being systematically assessed for their scientific validity—the IARC, in France—"regulatory" science was still unable to arrive at firm criteria for carcinogenic animal data.

Those are the problems in the realm of carcinogenesis that the geneticists bumped into in 1975 and 1976. They were still the same problems in 1978–80. American citizens were unaware of them. The verbal crusade against chemical cancer was in full swing: Congress had guaranteed a "cancer prevention program" based on animal tests; substances declared to be carcinogens in animal tests were being regulated and banned; and few realized that this blaze of seeming progress had only been made possible by a law which sheltered "regulatory" scientists from having to prove any of their claims. That law, as Donald Kennedy put it, permitted them to regulate or ban substances on the grounds of "a perceived risk," even when the perceived risk "is based on a mixture of scientific fact, theory, and supposition." And, as that same "regulatory" scientist added so enlighteningly, nobody involved in the legal process need ever fear "embarrassment" since the nonscientific plebes (including Congress, the courts, and the press) could not understand the quarrels of the "cognoscenti," and since nobody could ever know whether the scientific decisions were correct or not "because outcomes are never that clear in a matter so complex." The law itself, which had abolished the need for authentic scientific standards, was the greatest camouflage of the bemuddled state of the "cognoscenti" of "regulatory" science.

Given this information, one can deduce that as of 1978–80, "regulatory" science was in no position to achieve its second goal—namely, to use animal data to predict what would and would not be carcinogenic in man. But once again, one cannot rely on deduction, for Congress, led by Rep. Andrew Maguire, was now nipping at the heels of the cancer preventers; Something had to be done, whether or not anyone knew how to do it; and "regulatory" science, legally freed of the bondage of proof, is full of surprises. It may hardly seem possible to find anything more surprising than a legally entrenched absence of non-cancer-causing substances compounded by chronic confusion over how to identify most carcinogenic substances, but there is something yet more surprising and one finds it in the realm of animal prediction.

Chapter 11

The Case of the Missing Predictions

Mice and rats predict very well for human cancer.[1]
> —David Rall, Director of NIEHS, CBS-TV, 1976

There is ... no rational biological method of extrapolating from animals to man....[2]
> —John Higginson, Founding Director of the IARC, 1977

The educated layman would consider it absurd if scientists declared that since twenty-six heroin addicts had once smoked marijuana, it could be said that "marijuana smoking predicts for heroin addiction." He would consider it far too tiny a sample from which to extract so great a predictive generalization, and he would be scornful of the evasion of the thousands of marijuana smokers who do not become heroin addicts and thus falsify the prediction. If, on the other hand, the layman learned that 90 percent of a very large group of marijuana smokers, e.g., 5,000, did become heroin addicts, and had reason to believe it was true, he would take such a high correlation very seriously and would want to know why this was the case. In both cases, he would be thinking scientifically, even if he did not know the principle of scientific prediction involved.

Scientific prediction rests on the laws of probability. If one tosses a coin in the air, it might come up heads twenty-six times in a row. Gamblers—usually legendary—are said to have had "winning streaks" in which the coin comes up heads fifty or a hundred times in a row. But if one tosses that coin hundreds of thousands of times the laws of probability tell one that the results would come out roughly 50-50. When a scientist performs a controlled experiment and when the hypothesis he is testing shows some sign of being true—meaning that the phenomenon he is testing appears more often in his test group than in his control group—he must calculate the statistical probability that this result did not occur by chance. In a single experiment—and particularly an experiment which uses very few examples, whether of a physical or biological nature—an

310

apparently significant difference between the test group and the control group may be a random occurrence, a meaningless little "winning streak," so to speak. If, however, the experiment is replicated many times not only by that scientist but by others, and if the divergence from the random continues, then the probability is that the relationship he has discovered is a real one. It might, however, be a small probability. The greater the number of times the hypothesis is tested and the larger the sample in which the correlation is demonstrated, the higher is the degree of probability that it is a real relationship. A physicist, a chemist, and some biologists, depending on their field of study, seek very high probability levels—e.g., 98 percent, meaning they will not accept a finding unless there is a 98 percent probability that that finding did *not* occur by chance.

The same principle applies to all scientific endeavors. It applies to the scientist who is trying out a drug on a test group of patients and a control group of patients who have the same disease; it applies to the toxicologist who is studying the effects of a particular chemical on a test group of laboratory animals and a control group. It also applies to scientists who are comparing responses between groups of findings, e.g., the geneticist who tries to discover whether mutagenic responses in bacteria to certain chemicals correlate with the carcinogenic responses in animals to those same chemicals. And, finally, it applies to the scientist who wants to discover whether rodent responses to certain chemicals correlate with human responses. In all these cases these activities are conducted in the hope of establishing predictive principles; science *is* the quest for prediction. And in all these cases, the scientist must analyze his findings in terms of the laws of probability; he must know the degree to which they diverge from randomness. A scientist in the field of public health might not choose to hold out for a 98 percent probability that his findings are not random; he might settle for a 95 percent level of probability. But whatever the percentage he holds out for, he will still have to go through the same process: He must present statistically significant correlations for his findings to ensure that they are not random. If science is the quest for prediction, prediction is the quest for correlation—and for a scientific explanation of that correlation.

In the field of animal testing, a certain broad principle is often mistaken for a statement of scientific correlation. The assumption that a relationship *may* exist between the responses of animals and humans to chemicals is a broad biological abstraction. It is so broad, however, that it is virtually vacant; it is like "Life is a unity" or "Man is mortal." The similarity in the physiological structure of all mammals which underlies this broad abstraction is the premise of all biological, medical, pharmacological, and toxicological research, including carcinogenesis research. But having made that broad assumption, *one must then do the research*. One cannot simply intone, for decade after decade, the assumption with which one began—that a substance which gives cancer to an animal *may* give it to a man. The assumption that such a relationship may exist is the beginning of the research process, not the end; it is not *itself* a predictive statement. Only correlations between animal responses to specific chemicals and human responses to those same chemicals, correlations which transcend the random, will produce predictive principles.

With this brief background, we can now begin with a question: Did "regulatory" science have enough human data to match with animal data in order to arrive at predictive correlations? Clearly not, according to the Tomatis paper of 1978, which was "the best there is." According to Tomatis, there were twenty-six chemicals that had been found carcinogenic in man. That was not enough of a data base with which to establish correlations. It was certainly not considered enough of a data base for geneticists. Joyce McCann explained at the OSHA hearings why mutagen tests could not be validated with human data: "There are so few chemicals that are known to cause cancer in people. There may be about 25, but that is not a long enough list. . . .what was needed was clearly a much bigger list."[3] That, she said, was why they were trying to validate the mutagen data with animal data. Ironically, the same problem existed for the animal data: There was "not a long enough list" of human data for correlations.

This, then, was on the minds of many of those in "regulatory" science—particularly those who were being hounded on the one side by certain Congressmen and "environmental" pressure groups to produce lists of animal carcinogens which posed a cancer risk to man, and on the other side by different Congressmen and economics-conscious pressure groups who increasingly questioned the sense of imposing costly burdens on a troubled economic system on the basis of a biological assumption about tumors in mice. The "regulatory" scientists had a desperate need to demonstrate—without the necessary human correlations—that animal cancer predicted cancer in man. And that was the equivalent of saying that they desperately needed an act of magic.

Then, quite suddenly, that need was fulfilled. At the very height of the floundering, it was announced that a way had been found to solve the problem. It was a remarkable solution, and since it was arrived at by the IARC, it is perhaps wise to start with a few words about that institution, why it was so profoundly respected, why, when an inquiry for definitive animal data was made at American research and regulatory agencies, the IARC's name was on all lips, and why the layman should be particularly aware of that institution.

As already reported, the IARC was the only institution exclusively dedicated to the evaluation of carcinogenic data—the scientific determination of which human and animal studies are valid and which are not. It had evaluated only a few hundred of the thousands that have been reported, but those evaluations were widely considered to be reliable. The IARC was an adviser to all the regulatory agencies of the world, it was heavily financed by the NCI, and it was so thoroughly established at the intellectual pinnacle of the world of carcinogenesis that the institution could permit itself to say, in 1978:

The *IARC Monographs* are recognized as an authoritative source of information on the carcinogenicity of environmental chemicals. The first users' survey, made in 1976, indicates that the monographs are consulted routinely by various agencies in 24 countries.[4]

Unfortunately, throughout the 1970s, this celebrated institution had not been of much use to the American world of "regulatory" science, which is one of the reasons few Americans had ever heard about it. In fact, in one crucial respect, the IARC had become a severe irritant to that world, for the IARC did not support the claims that many "regulatory" scientists were making to each other, to Congress, and to the American people. In 1976, for example, David Rall, Director of the NIEHS, was assuring CBS audiences that "mice and rats predict very well for human cancer."[5] And, for another example, in 1977, a National Academy of Sciences Committee informed the scientific community that "there are large bodies of experimental data that indicate that exposures that are carcinogenic to animals are likely to be carcinogenic to man and vice versa."[6] But as of that time, no language comparable to Rall's had ever emerged from the IARC, and the IARC had produced no "large bodies" of impressive animal-man correlations such as those that the NAS committee declared to exist. In fact, the IARC had systematically refused, in the presentation of its data, to report on *any* human risk from animal carcinogens. At its very birth, in 1971, that institution had declared explicitly that no such calculations could be made: "In the case of some of the substances under consideration, the Group was faced with the problem of interpreting animal data, in the absence of human data, in terms of possible human risk. Since there are no objective criteria for doing so, the Group did not express any opinion on the significance of such data to man. . . ."[7] And from Vol. 1 in 1971 to Vol. 16 in 1978, every one of the IARC monographs had contained a standard preface entitled "Background and Purpose of the IARC Program on the Evaluation of the Carcinogenic Risk of Chemicals to Man." And in that standard preface, these words were always included, alone or along with other information:

At the present time no attempt can be made to interpret the animal data directly in terms of human risk, since no objective criteria are available to do so.[8]

The IARC, accordingly, had gone about its business of collecting and evaluating data in a systematic way. It studied various groups of chemicals, almost invariably industrial; it convoked expert committees to assess the validity of epidemiological evidence; it convoked expert committees to assess the validity of animal data; it reported in lucid detail on the findings from both scientific disciplines; and, increasingly, it reported, as well, on the findings of mutagen and other indirect tests. But at the very end of each analysis, the IARC monographs terminated with two short summaries, one called "Animal Data," the other "Human Data"—*and no link between them was ever established.* The IARC was actually collecting data from which, ultimately, an animal-man correlation could be made that might allow scientific prediction—but, said that institution, no such prediction could now be made, for no "objective criteria" existed with which to make it.

Thus, despite its theoretical acceptance of the broad biological concept that substances which were carcinogenic to animals might be carcinogenic to man—an acceptance reflected in the title of its monographs—the IARC was acting, *for practical purposes,* as though the only proof of a carcinogenic threat to man could be established by the study of man, and not by the study of animals. And since man's susceptibility to cancer can be studied only *after* he has gotten cancer and not before, these IARC monographs were tacitly denying the present possibility of a scientific method of preventing cancer, except on the basis of human experience.

Had the IARC been an institution of no significance, or had it been financed by industry rather than the NCI, its rigorous refusal to link carcinogenicity in animals to carcinogenic risks in human beings would have been dismissed as ignorant or denounced as yet another illustration of industry's malevolence. But no such condemnations could be leveled against the IARC. It was a highly respected institution; its expert committees were allowed to publish as much as they believed the data to show—and not one word more; that, in fact, is *why* the IARC was so highly respected. Precisely because of its scrupulously high standards, and the priority it accorded to knowledge over slovenly combinations of "fact, theory and supposition," the IARC could neither be ignored nor denigrated. That is why it mattered intensely to the world of "regulatory" science in the United States that the IARC in Lyon was presenting its carcinogenic animal and human data separately, and stubbornly insisting that "no objective criteria" existed to permit a scientific linkage. American "regulatory" science and the IARC were actually in profound conflict.

That clash was discussed in the famous Tomatis et al. paper of 1978. In it, Tomatis observed that while the evaluations of IARC's expert committees were widely accepted, there was also displeasure over the IARC's mutism in the realm of the human implications of the animal data. And Tomatis further announced, in that same paper, that the IARC, in response to this displeasure, was revising its criteria to allow for the assessment of risk to human beings. For the IARC, this was a drastic alteration of policy. Here is how Tomatis explained it:

The growing success and overall acceptance of this program have certainly not prevented suggestions and criticisms. Criticisms mostly refer to the fact that, except for the few instances in which an association between exposure to a chemical and occurrence of cancer in humans has been clearly confirmed, the monographs do not give a clear indication as to whether exposure to a chemical does or does not represent a hazard to humans because no attempt was made to evaluate the potential human risk. In most cases, in fact, the monographs only evaluate the carcinogenic risk of chemicals to experimental animals without making any attempt to interpret the results in terms of a possible risk for humans.

It was for these reasons that an *ad hoc* working group, jointly called by IARC/WHO, was convened in October 1977 in Lyon to update and revise the criteria on which the carcinogenicity of chemicals to humans and/or experimental animals is assessed and on which the evaluation of the possible carcinogenic risk that they may represent for humans is made.

The report resulting from this meeting will appear as the "Preamble" of Volume 17 of the IARC monograph series which is presently in preparation and will replace the introductory section called "Background and Purpose of the IARC Program on the Evaluation of the Carcinogenic Risk of Chemicals to Man," which appeared since 1971 with only minor modifications in all the 16 published monograph volumes.[9]

To sum up: (1) In 1977—a year after the passage of the Toxic Substances Control Act in the U.S.—criticisms had been made by unidentified people or institutions of the refusal of the IARC monographs to draw conclusions about human risk from animal data. (2) In response to these criticisms, the IARC had agreed to revise the criteria by which its judgments of animal carcinogenicity were made in order to permit calculation of risk to humans. And (3) *The IARC's standard preface with its long-reiterated statement that "objective criteria" for that very process did not exist would be modified in some significant fashion.*

Although it was doubtless not the intention of Tomatis et al. in 1978 to do so, they had made it entirely clear that the IARC's change of views was not a response to new scientific knowledge. Had Tomatis reported that a new scientific discovery had been made which now allowed the IARC to reject its prior statement (still in print in Vol. 16, 1978) that no "objective criteria" existed for interpreting human risk from animal data, and to declare that such calculations could now be performed scientifically, that would have been a thrilling announcement. It would have been presented with pride in the very first paragraph—doubtless by the future Nobel laureate who had made the discovery, for such an announcement would have meant that, quite literally, overnight, cancer prevention had become a predictive science, and that cancer would be obliterated from the roster of human diseases. That, obviously, was not the case. Indeed, Tomatis et al. made it clear that in scientific terms, nothing had changed at all. They wrote:

By applying the new criteria for the evaluation of the carcinogenicity of chemicals as they are described in the new preamble to the monographs, as well as acquiring further carcinogenicity and related data on chemicals and new knowledge on the mechanisms of carcinogenicity as it may become available, *we hope that in the absence of epidemiological data a more clear distinction can be made between chemicals for which there is or is not evidence of a possible carcinogenic effect in humans.*

We hope that in this way the critical analysis of the experimental and human data and the ensuing evaluations of environmental chemicals *will make future IARC monographs more useful in assisting national and international authorities in formulating decisions concerning preventive measures.*[10] [Emphasis added]

The sad truth, as Tomatis conceded here, was that neither the IARC nor anyone else really knew how to make that predictive leap from animals. Without knowledge of the mechanisms of cancer induction, and without epidemiological data, nobody knew in advance what would or would not be carcinogenic in man. And that is to say that in scientific terms—not the slithering language of the law—no one knew how to use animals to predict or prevent cancer. And yet, Tomatis was simultaneously announcing that the IARC was about to use animal data for just that purpose—that it had defined new criteria for the classification of animal data that would allow such a use of animals. In fact, said Tomatis, the IARC had already reached a new conclusion:

In the presence of appropriate experimental carcinogenicity data and in the absence of adequate human data, it is reasonable to regard chemicals for which there is "strong evidence" of carcinogenicity *as if* they were carcinogenic to humans.[11] [Emphasis added]

And in Vol. 17 of the IARC series—1978—the new preface contained that very conclusion, formulated in the following way:

For many of the chemicals evaluated in the first 17 volumes of the IARC Monographs for which there is *sufficient evidence* of carcinogenicity in animals, data relating to carcinogenicity for humans are either insufficient or nonexistent. In the absence of adequate data on humans, it is reasonable to regard for practical purposes such chemicals *as if* they were carcinogenic to humans.[12] [Emphasis added]

These were the words that would now replace the old simple denial of "objective criteria" for predicting human risk from animal data. They were just a few words, but they constituted a striking alteration in the thinking of the IARC, which had been steadily denying for seven years that there were any scientific grounds for making such predictions. There were no reasons given for this change in policy except the avowed desire to be "more useful" to "national and international authorities." The IARC, the citadel of scientific purity, had capitulated to the regulators' need for magic.

Scientific magic is done by several means. One was described by John Higginson and cited earlier in this book: The scientist builds the desired finding into his definitions. Another way is to present the data quite openly, in the form of unspeakably boring charts and tables, but in such a manner that only the most zealous will analyze their contents to discover findings the magicians prefer to ignore. And the third is to provide the necessary concessions in the text or in the footnotes so that, simultaneously, integrity can be preserved. We have already seen examples of most of these forms of scientific magic in this book, and all are present in the IARC's new gift to the regulators. If the reader wants to see scientific magic performed close-up, he will read what follows carefully, because if he doesn't, he will not understand the IARC's explanation of what it had done—for the IARC, however desirous of assisting regulatory bodies, had no intention of destroying its international reputation for scientific integrity— and it *did* explain. This is why a lay analyst can tell this story, and why a lay reader can readily assess it. Decisions at the IARC are made by international stellar committees—and the scientists were quite aware that nonscientific decisions were being made, and were determined to get it on the record. Thus, the stellar committee members did their unusual favor for the regulators—and then told us clearly that they had done it. The scientific conscience is a wondrous thing to behold, and we will now behold it.

We start, then, with the laying of the groundwork for the ersatz predictions—the definitions. And the reader should pay close attention to the definitions of *"sufficient evidence,"* for, in themselves, they constituted high scientific criteria for *evaluating* scientific data—far higher than those used by U.S. regulatory agencies and spelled out in detail to boot. These demanding criteria actually produced lists of industrial chemicals that are animal carcinogens and human carcinogens that are the best lists that exist in the world. *The unusual aspect of the process lay in what has already been quoted—the IARC's announcement that "in the absence of adequate data on humans, it is reasonable to regard such chemicals [those with "sufficient evidence"] as if they were carcinogenic to humans."* The criteria were actually playing a *double* role: They were serious evaluative criteria *and* they were also to be used "as if" they were scientific predictions.

Here, then, are the IARC's new criteria. They and all the rest of the material to be presented come from IARC Monographs, Supplement 1, by Ralph Althouse et al., in September 1979.[13] (They can also be found in an article in *Cancer Research* by Althouse et al. in January 1980,[14] in which the same material was reproduced and discussed.) The information on the new criteria, in this chapter, comes directly from Supplement 1, and permission has been granted by the IARC to publish it in condensed and tabular form.

IARC Criteria* for Animal Carcinogens[15]

"Sufficient evidence" of carcinogenicity:** "there is an increased incidence of malignant tumors: (a) in multiple species or strains, or (b) in multiple experiments (preferably with different routes of administrations or using different dose levels), or (c) to an unusual degree with regard to incidence, site, or type of tumor, or age at onset. Additional evidence may be provided by data concerning dose-response effects as well as information on mutagenicity or chemical structure."

"Limited evidence" of carcinogenicity:** "data suggest a carcinogenic effect but are limited because: (a) the studies involve a single species, strain, or experiment; or (b) the experiments are restricted by inadequate dosage levels, inadequate duration of exposure to the agent, inadequate period of follow-up, poor survival, too few animals, or inadequate reporting; or (c) the neoplasms produced often occur spontaneously or are difficult to classify as malignant by histological criteria alone (e.g., lung and liver tumors in mice)."

"Inadequate evidence" of carcinogenicity: "because of major qualitative or quantitative limitations, the studies cannot be interpreted as showing either the presence or the absence of a carcinogenic effect."

* *Author's footnote:*
"Negative" data and "No data" were also formally listed as criteria but were almost never used; they have therefore been cut from this list.
** *IARC's observation:*
"The categories 'sufficient evidence' and 'limited evidence' refer only to the strength of the experimental evidence that these chemicals are (or are not) carcinogenic and not to the extent of their carcinogenic activity. The classification for any chemical may change as new information becomes available."

IARC Criteria* for Human Carcinogens[16]

"Sufficient evidence of carcinogenicity indicates a causal association between exposure and human cancer."
"Limited evidence of carcinogenicity indicates a possible carcinogenic effect in humans, although the data are not sufficient to demonstrate a causal association."
"Inadequate evidence of carcinogenicity indicates that the data are qualitatively or quantitatively insufficient to allow any conclusion regarding carcinogenicity for humans."

Author's footnote:
An analysis of types of epidemiological data preceded these criteria; they, too, have been cut. They will be discussed later.

Tomatis' paper, published in 1978, had been a report on only the first sixteen volumes of IARC monographs—and his list had included chemicals in which "some evidence" of carcinogenicity existed in "at least one species," resulting in a finding that 65 percent of the total might be carcinogenic. By the end of 1978, however, the IARC had used far more stringent criteria to evaluate the 442 chemicals and industrial processes considered in twenty volumes and the IARC's expert committees had concluded that there was "sufficient evidence" of carcinogenicity in experimental animals in 142 cases—32 percent of the total.[17] This was a substantial shrinkage and an instructive example of how animal carcinogens vanish as the "stringency" of the criteria increase. Here, then, are the 142 chemicals which the IARC described as definitely carcinogenic in animals, and as *"reasonable to regard for practical purposes . . . as if they were carcinogenic to humans."*[18] The list also includes chemicals for which human data exist, but they will be discussed separately:

IARC: ANIMAL DATA

Acrylonitrile
Actinomycins
Aflatoxins
ortho-Aminoazotoluene
4-Aminobiphenyl
2-Amino-5-(5-nitro-2-furyl)-1,3,4-thiadiazole
Amitrole
Aramite
Asbestos
Azaserine

Benz(a)anthracene
Benzidine
Benzo(b)fluoranthene
Benzo(a)pyrene
Benzyl violet 4B
Beryllium
Beryllium oxide
Beryllium phosphate
Beryllium sulphate
Bis(chloromethyl)ether
β-Butyrolactone

Cadmium
Cadmium chloride
Cadmium oxide
Cadmium sulphate
Cadmium sulphide
Calcium chromate

Carbon tetrachloride
Chlorambucil
Chlordecone (Kepone)
Chloroform
Chromium
Citrus red No. 2
Cycasin
Cyclophosphamide

Daunomycin
N,N'-Diacetylbenzidine
4,4'-Diaminodiphenyl ether
2,4-Diaminotoluene
Dibenz(a,h)acridine
Dibenz(a,j)acridine
Dibenz(a,h)anthracene
7H-Dibenzo(c,g)carbazole
Dibenzo(a,e)pyrene
Dibenzo(a,h)pyrene
Dibenzo(a,i)pyrene
1,2-Dibromo-3-chloropropane
3,3'-Dichlorobenzidine
3,3'-Dichloro-4,4'-diaminodiphenyl ether
1,2-Dichloroethane
Diepoxybutane
1,2-Diethylhydrazine

Diethylstilboestrol
Diethyl sulphate
Dihydrosafrole
3,3'-Dimethoxybenzidine (ortho-Dianisidine)
para-Dimethylaminoazo-benzene
trans-2[(Dimethylamino)-methyl imino[-5-[2-(5-nitro-2-furyl)vinyl]-1,3,4-oxadiazole
3,3'-Dimethylbenzidine (ortho-toluidine)
Dimethylcarbamoyl chloride
1,1-Dimethylhydrazine
1,2-Dimethylhydrazine
Dimethyl sulphate
1,4-Dioxane

Ethinyloestradiol
Ethylene dibromide
Ethylenethiourea
Ethyl methanesulphonate

2-(2-Formylhydrazino)-4-(5-nitro-2-furyl)-thiazole

Glycidaldehyde

Hexachlorobenzene

Hexamethylphosphora-
mide

Hydrazine

Indeno(1,2,3-cd)pyrene

Iron dextran

Isosafrole

Lasiocarpine

Lead acetate

Lead phosphate

Lead subacetate

Melphalan

Merphalan

Mestranol

2-Methylaziridine

Methylazoxymethanol
acetate

4,4'-Methylene bis(2-
chloroaniline)

4,4'-Methylene bis(2-
methylaniline)

Methyl iodide

Methyl methanesul-
phonate

N-Methyl-N'-nitro-N-ni-
trosoguanidine

Methylthiouracil

Mirex

Mitomycin C

Monocrotaline

5-(morpholinomethyl)-3-
[(5-nitrofurfuryli-

dene)-amino]-2-ox-
azolidinone

2-Naphthylamine

Nickel

Nickel subsulphide

Niridazole

5-Nitroacenaphthene

1-[(5-Nitrofurfuryl-
idene)amino]-2-
imidazolidinone

N-[4-(5-Nitro-2-furyl)-2-
thiazolyl]acetamide

Nitrogen mustard and
its hydrochloride

Nitrogen mustard N-
oxide and its hy-
drochloride

N-Nitrosodi-N-butyl-
amine

N-Nitrosodiethanol-
amine

N-Nitrosodiethylamine

N-Nitrosodimethyl-
amine

N-Nitrosodi-N-propyl-
amine

N-Nitroso-N-ethylurea

N-Nitrosomethylethyl-
amine

N-Nitroso-N-methylurea

N-Nitroso-N-methyl-
urethane

N-Nitrosomethylvinyl-
amine

N-Nitrosomorpholine

N-Nitrosonornicotine

N-Nitrosopiperidine

N-Nitrosopyrrolidine

N-Nitrososarcosine

Oestradiol-17B

Oestrone

Oil orange SS

Polychlorinated bi-
phenyls

Ponceau MX

Ponceau 3R

1,3-Propane sultone

β-Propiolactone

Propylthiouracil

Safrole

Soots, tars, and oils

Sterigmatocystin

Streptozotocin

Testosterone

Thioacetamide

Thiourea

Toxaphene

Tris (aziridinyl)phos-
phine sulphide
(thiotepa)

Tris(2,3-dibromopro-
pyl)phosphate

Trypan blue (commer-
cial grade)

Uracil mustard

Urethane

Vinyl chloride

This, then, was the best available list of industrial chemicals that are carcinogenic in animals in the world in 1979–1980, as evaluated by demanding
scientific criteria. It was about half the size of Tomatis' list of animal carcinogens for which "some evidence" had been found in "at least one species." And
if Berenblum's even more stringent demand for carcinogenicity in *three* species
had been used, it would have been far shorter again. In fact, given the estimated cost of one animal test in 1980, $500,000, one suspects that a list of ani-
mal carcinogens that conformed to Berenblum's criteria could be printed on a

calling card. How many of these, then, were "real" animal carcinogens? In America, the sorrowful National Toxicology Program could only answer, in 1980: "Science and society have not arrived at a final consensus on the definition of carcinogen either in human population or in experimental animals." What has "society" got to do with scientific definition of cancer-causing substances? "Society," in that sentence, means the Congress, regulatory agencies, and courts. Are *any* of these substances, then, "real" animal carcinogens? Unquestionably. This was the best available list in the world of industrial chemicals that are carcinogenic in animals as evaluated by demanding scientific criteria. Am I not being circular here? I am. Why? I can't help it. "Science and society have not yet arrived . . ." and so forth. In order to stop chasing my tail like a maddened hound, I will, henceforth, refer to this list as the IARC's 1980 list of "established" animal carcinogens. Later in this chapter, the IARC itself will explain why "regulatory" science is in this dilemma. Meantime, we return to the story.

The IARC's expert committees had also assessed the available *human* evidence by the new criteria. Of the total of 442 chemicals in the twenty volumes, case reports or epidemiological studies had been published for only 60—and for various reasons, including time, only 54 of those 60 were evaluated.[19] The data were again divided into degrees of evidence—and again, the reader would be well advised to keep his eye on the category defined as "sufficient," because *that* was the IARC's best available list of "established" human carcinogens, except, of course, for the IARC's qualifications, which indicated that a few of them were not quite "established" yet.

IARC: HUMAN DATA[20]

"Sufficient"
In 18 cases, the committee decided that there was "sufficient evidence to support a causal association between the exposure and cancer": "The chemical, group of chemicals, or industrial process is carcinogenic for humans."

> *4-Aminobiphenyl; arsenic and certain arsenic compounds; asbestos; manufacture of auramine;* benzidine;N,N-bis(2-chloroethyl)-2-naphthylamine(chlornaphazine);BCME and technical grade CMME; chromium and certain chromium compounds;* diethylstilboestrol; underground hematite mining;* manufacture of isopropyl alcohol by the strong acid process;* melphalan; mustard gas; 2-naphthylamine; nickel refining;* soots, tars, and mineral oils;* vinyl chloride.*

> * *IARC qualification:*
> "The specific cancer-causing compound or compounds in these industries cannot be identified because there is also exposure to other substances; thus, the "responsible" carcinogen may not be listed here."

Probable
There was another group of chemicals which was described as "probably carcinogenic for humans." It includes "chemicals for which the evidence of human carcinogenicity is almost 'sufficient' as well as chemicals for which it is only suggestive." In both, the data were considered "not sufficient to establish a causal association." The group is divided into two degrees of "limited" evidence—the higher called subgroup A, and the lower called subgroup B. They are listed as follows:

Subgroup A (better evidence):
Aflatoxins; cadmium and certain cadmium compounds; chlorambucil; cyclophosphamide; nickel and certain nickel compounds;* tris (1-aziri-dinyl)phosphine sulfide (thiotepa).*

Subgroup B (worse evidence):
Acrylonitrile; amitrole (aminotriazole); auramine; beryllium and certain beryllium compounds; carbon tetrachloride; dimethylcarbamoyl chloride; dimethyl sulfate; ethylene oxide; iron dextran; oxymetholone; phenacetin; polychlorinated biphenyls.*

* IARC qualification:
The specific cancer-causing compound or compounds in these industries cannot be identified because there is also exposure to other substances; thus, the "responsible" carcinogen may not be listed here.

Unclassifiable
Of all the chemicals with some human data, 18 chemicals or groups of chemicals "could not be classified as to their carcinogenicity for humans":

Chloramphenicol; chlordane-heptachlor; chloroprene; DDT; dieldrin; epichlorohydrin; hematite; HCH (technical grade HCH-lindane); isoniazid; isopropyl oils; lead and certain lead compounds; phenobarbitone; N-phenyl-2-naphthylamine; phenytoin; reserpine; styrene; trichloroethylene; tris (aziridinyl)-p-benzoquinone (triaziquone).*

*IARC qualification:
The specific cancer-causing compound or compounds in this industry cannot be identified because there is also exposure to other substances; thus, the "responsible" carcinogen may not be listed here.

This, too, is a worrisome chart, although the IARC committee did its best to calibrate our degrees of worry, which, presumably, should be correlated with the degrees of evidence. On those grounds, we will concentrate on the group of eighteen chemicals with "'sufficient" evidence which, says the IARC, "are carcinogenic for humans" except for the ones that may not be, but where the *industries themselves* are definitely implicated. As for the "probables," the reader must consult later IARC data.

We come now to the most interesting table of all which, necessarily, was the dullest. It compared the "degrees of evidence" of those chemicals for which *both* human and animal data exist.[21] We are now approaching a very delicate point, for this was where we should have discovered the best correlations between human and animal data, if any indeed existed. Logically, one would suppose that, here, the good human-animal matches would be separated out from the poor or nonexistent human-animal matches. Such, however, was not the case. At this point, the IARC committee became totally dedicated to the *alphabet* as a means of organizing the most crucial scientific information. That is a warning sign—and the reader is invited to examine this table much as he would examine one of those puzzles for children which consist of a picture in which are hidden ten different animals that one can discover if one stares at the picture long enough. Often, such puzzles are accompanied by instructions such as: "It should take you ten minutes to solve this puzzle." I will give the reader thirty seconds, for I intend to tell him what the hidden "animals" are immediately and put him out of his misery. Here, then, is the extraordinarily boring-because-alphabetized table. Set your watch.

CLASSIFICATION OF THE DEGREE OF EVIDENCE OF CARCINOGENICITY FOR HUMANS OF CHEMICALS OR INDUSTRIAL PROCESSES FROM IARC MONOGRAPHS.
VOLS. 1 TO 20

	Degree of evidence	
Chemical or process	In humans	In experimental animals
1. Acrylonitrile	Limited	Sufficient
2. Aflatoxins	Limited	Sufficient
3. 4-Aminobiphenyl	Sufficient	Sufficient
4. Amitrole (aminotriazole)	Inadequate	Sufficient
5. Arsenic and certain arsenic compounds	Sufficient	Inadequate
6. Asbestos	Sufficient	Sufficient
7. Auramine	Limited	Limited
8. Manufacture of auramine	Sufficient	Not applicable*
9. Benzene	Sufficient	Inadequate
10. Benzidine	Sufficient	Sufficient
11. Beryllium and certain beryllium compounds	Limited	Sufficient
12. N,N-Bis(2-chloroethyl)-2-naphthylamine (chlornaphazine)	Sufficient	Limited
13. BCME and technical grade CMME	Sufficient	Sufficient
	Sufficient	Limited
14. Cadmium and certain cadmium compounds	Limited	Sufficient
15. Carbon tetrachloride	Inadequate	Sufficient
16. Chlorambucil	Limited	Sufficient
17. Chloramphenicol	Inadequate	No data
18. Chlordane and heptachlor	Inadequate	Limited
19. Chloroprene	Inadequate	Inadequate
20. Chromium and certain chromium compounds	Sufficient	Sufficient
21. Cyclophosphamide	Limited	Sufficient
22. DDT	Inadequate	Limited
23. Dieldrin	Inadequate	Limited
24. Diethylstilbestrol	Sufficient	Sufficient
25. Dimethylcarbamoyl chloride	Inadequate	Sufficient
26. Dimethyl sulfate	Inadequate	Sufficient
27. Epichlorohydrin	Inadequate	Limited
28. Ethylene oxide	Limited	Inadequate
29. Hematite	Inadequate	Negative
30. Underground hematite mining	Sufficient	Not applicable*
31. HCH (technical HCH and lindane)	Inadequate	Limited

| | Degree of evidence | |
Chemical or process	In humans	In experimental animals
32. Iron dextran	Inadequate	Sufficient
33. Isoniazid	Inadequate	Limited
34. Isopropyl oils	Inadequate	Inadequate
35. Manufacture of isopropyl alcohol (strong acid process)	Sufficient	Not applicable*
36. Lead and certain lead compounds	Inadequate	Sufficient (for some soluble salts)
37. Melphalan	Sufficient	Sufficient
38. Mustard gas	Sufficient	Limited
39. 2-Naphthylamine	Sufficient	Sufficient
40. Nickel and certain nickel compounds	Limited	Sufficient
41. Nickel refining	Sufficient	Not applicable*
42. Oxymetholone	Limited	No data
43. Phenacetin	Limited	Limited
44. Phenobarbitone	Limited	Limited
45. N-Phenyl-2-naphthyla- mine	Inadequate	Inadequate
46. Phenytoin	Limited	Limited
47. Polychlorinated bi- phenyls	Inadequate	Sufficient
48. Reserpine	Inadequate	Inadequate
49. Soots, tars, and mineral oils	Sufficient	Sufficient
50. Styrene	Inadequate	Limited
51. Trichloroethylene	Inadequate	Limited
52. Tris(aziridinyl)-p-benzo- quinone (triaziquone)	Inadequate	Limited
53. Tris(l-aziridinyl)phos- phine sulfide (thio- tepa)	Limited	Sufficient
54. Vinyl chloride	Sufficient	Sufficient

*It is difficult to expose experimental animals to the same conditions to which workers are exposed; therefore, no animal data are available.

The following table, one sees, after staring at it for thirty seconds, is set up as a "correlational" table, one inspects it for "correlations," and one finds that most of the "degrees of evidence" do not match well, if at all. But when one investigates the table carefully, one sees that there are ten perfect cases of mutually confirming findings—findings declared to be valid by the IARC's highest criteria, "sufficient" evidence.

As of 1980, this was the best illustration available of the hypothesis that what gives cancer to an animal may give it to a human being. And according to the new criteria of the IARC, in these ten cases the hypothesis had been proved

Chemical or process	In humans	In experimental animals
4-Aminobiphenyl	Sufficient	Sufficient
Asbestos	Sufficient	Sufficient
Benzidine	Sufficient	Sufficient
BCME and technical grade CMME	Sufficient	Sufficient
Chromium and certain chromium compounds	Sufficient	Sufficient
Diethylstilbestrol	Sufficient	Sufficient
Melphalan	Sufficient	Sufficient
2-Naphthylamine	Sufficient	Sufficient
Soots, tars, and mineral oils	Sufficient	Sufficient
Vinyl chloride	Sufficient	Sufficient

to be true. These ten examples were extremely valuable to the field of carcinogenesis, for they rendered it impossible for anyone to argue against the concept of a potentially shared animal-man susceptibility to carcinogens. And yet, one was forced to pry those precious examples out of the table by oneself. In a manner of speaking, the IARC had hidden them. This presentation in the mode of the purloined letter tells us clearly that the IARC had no desire to brandish the dramatic little set of matching animal-man findings. Why? One reason immediately came to mind on making this discovery. Perhaps the IARC feared that if it stressed those few matching animal-man findings, that act would undermine the significance of the large number of animal data which did *not* match with human data—although they were now to be viewed *"as if* they presented a carcinogenic risk for humans."* Was it possible that the IARC did not believe its own "as if"? What *was* the IARC's scientific assessment of its own new criteria and data? For the answer to that question, one could only go to Althouse et al., the ad hoc committee which made those judgments. *And they told us.*

One thing they told us, with extraordinary candor, is that if one wants *scientific* information, one has no reason whatever to accept that huge table of "sufficient" animal data as predictive of human cancer. Here is how Althouse et al. reported on the meaning of the IARC's new language:

An *ad hoc* Working Group met in October 1977 to review the criteria for the assessment of the carcinogenic risk of chemicals to humans. The group drafted guidelines for subsequent Working Groups which standardize the evaluations of carcinogenicity studies both in humans and in animals. More importantly, they recommend that in the absence of adequate data in humans it is reasonable, for practical purposes, to regard chemicals for which there is *sufficient evidence* of carcinogenicity (i.e., a causal association) in animals *as if they presented a carcinogenic risk for humans. The use of the expressions "for practical purposes" and "as if they presented a carcinogenic risk" indicates that at the present time a correlation between carcinogenicity in animals and possible human risk cannot be made on a scientific basis, but rather only pragmatically, with the intent of helping regulatory agencies in making decisions related to the primary prevention of cancer.*[22] [Emphasis added]

What this meant, quite plainly, was that when the IARC's Ad Hoc Committee thought scientifically, it *still* affirmed that there was no scientific way to predict a carcinogenic danger to man from carcinogenicity in animals. When that committee thought "pragmatically," it recommended the use of animal data in order to "help" the regulatory agencies "prevent" cancer, i.e., to predict the very human danger which the IARC declared to be unpredictable. The IARC, in other words, had not changed its mind about science, it had changed its mind about politics.

Althouse et al. gave us further startling information about the scientific status of these new criteria—if one struggled to understand it. They had created one new category of analysis—the evaluation of carcinogenic risk to humans where "sufficient" evidence for human beings was lacking, but which was "based on consideration of both the epidemiological and experimental evidence." In discussing this new category, they commented on "the breadth of the categories for human and animal evidence" (sufficient, limited, inadequate) and observed that it "allows substantial variation within each." As for the conclusions themselves, "the decisions reached by the group regarding overall risk incorporated these differences. . . ."[23] This murky section, indicating that the categories were extremely elastic and that many different opinions might be reached about classifying data within them, was prefaced by the stern reminder: *"Presently, no objective criteria exist to interpret the animal data directly in terms of human risk."* [24] Once again, the IARC took away with its left hand what it had bestowed with its right.

This section, however, raised a new question. If the categories for human and animal data had such "breadth," and if the "variation" within each was "substantial," and if "differences" were "incorporated" into the "decisions reached by the group"—how exactly did the group go about "incorporating" these "differences"? And that question, too, was answered by Althouse et al. They said:

Dividing lines were by no means firmly drawn between sufficient evidence and limited evidence for animal studies and between inadequate evidence and limited evidence for both human and animal studies. *When differences of opinion occurred among the members of the Working Group, the classification was made by majority vote.*[25] [Emphasis added]

You have read this correctly: They *voted.* To say that scientists have been voting destroys our capacity to take the resultant conclusions seriously. Even a profound commitment to democracy cannot blind one to the fact that when scientists take to voting they are not engaging in a scientific activity. In science, discoveries are not determined by majority vote. Scientists resort to the ballot only when for some institutional or political reason they feel compelled to produce a unified public answer to a question on which they profoundly disagree. The same little paragraph gave us some insight into the precise areas in which the conflicts and voting occurred. To spell it out more clearly:

• The scientists could not always agree whether animal data were "sufficient" or "limited," and thus voted in this area—*a fact that undermines the great list of "predictive" animal data.*
• The scientists could not always agree whether the data in both animal and

human studies, considered separately or together, were "limited" or "inadequate," and thus voted in this area—*a fact that undermines both the "predictive" human-and-animal-data-combined.*

If the reader has been counting on his fingers, he will realize that there was
only one thing left to disagree and to vote about: "sufficient" or first-rate epidemiological studies—and those alone were not mentioned in this little paragraph. We may thus speculate, given the privacy of the ballot booth, that *at a
minimum,* the scientists all agreed on the eighteen "chemicals, groups of chemicals, and industrial processes," and above all, on the precious "hidden" ten.

Thanks to these extraordinary clarifications by Althouse et al., we are left
with the conclusion that the capacity of the IARC to predict human danger
from animal carcinogens had not changed by an iota since pressure from unidentified "critics" had precipitated that institution into defining new criteria.
In the bad old days of 1971–1978, the IARC's working committees appeared to
be certain only about danger to human beings that had been identified by
first-rate human data; in the good new days of 1979 and 1980, the IARC's
committee still appeared to be certain only about danger to human beings that
had been identified by first-rate human data. In the bad old days, the IARC's
committees had been indecisive about how to classify most animal carcinogens;
the same indecision persisted in the good new days. And now, in addition, the
IARC's committees were indecisive about how to classify most combinations of
human and animal data. A stream of impressive "predictive" data had resulted
from the new criteria because the indecisions and clashes had been papered
over by majority vote. But no genuinely new knowledge of how to use animal
data to predict carcinogenic hazard in man had been produced by the new criteria. It could not have been produced in this way. Scientific prediction cannot
be *defined* or *voted* into existence. The IARC committees had not been engaging in prediction from animals, as Althouse et al. so candidly admitted. They
had been engaging in a process that might be called "prediction by metaphor":
"as if." Or, as the IARC preferred to describe the process, it was "pragmatic,"
not scientific.

In fact, only one thing had been definitely accomplished by this sad attempt, on the part of an institution with a reputation for unbreachable scientific purity, to define animal prediction into existence. The language of the
IARC, which appeared just in time for the OSHA hearings, was now in harmony with the language of American "regulatory" science. And even that harmony was illusory, because the IARC's criteria of "sufficient" evidence, which
require multiple species and strains or multiple experiments, are rejected by
OSHA and the EPA (as the OSHA policy document reveals) as too demanding
and time-consuming, and although no one said so, as far too costly. The
American regulatory agencies wanted the IARC's "predictive" *language,* but
not its *standards.* And, in fact, in its description of the IARC monographs,
OSHA published one, but not the other. In the course of a discussion of the capacity of animal tests to predict for man, OSHA's policy document of 1980
quoted this following passage to illustrate the IARC's views on the subject:

For many of the chemicals evaluated in the first 17 volumes of the IARC Monographs for which there is *sufficient evidence* of carcinogenicity in animals, data relating to carcinogenicity for humans are either insufficient or nonexistent. In the absence of adequate data on humans, it is reasonable to regard for practical purposes such chemicals as if they were carcinogenic to humans. (IARC 1978, Vol. 17, p. 20.)[26] [Emphasis in original]

Here is what immediately followed that passage in Vol. 17, p. 20:

Sufficient evidence of carcinogenicity is provided by experimental studies that show an increased incidence of malignant tumors: (a) in multiple species or strains, and/or (b) in multiple experiments (routes and/or doses), and/or (c) to an unusual degree (with regard to incidence, site, type and/or precocity of onset). Additional evidence may be provided by data concerning dose-response, mutagenicity or structure.[27] [Emphasis in original]

OSHA had cited the first paragraph containing the "predictive" *language,* and had chopped off the experimental requirements that gave the language its only meaning, "pragmatic" as that meaning might be. Instead, OSHA had supported its own limited standards with statements of "regulatory" scientists such as that of David Rall, Director of the NIEHS, who had said: "The point really is that the evidence is overwhelming that compounds which are carcinogenic in laboratory animals—and this may well be only in one species in a good test— have a *very high probability* of being carcinogenic for man."[28] (Emphasis added)

On the basis of the totality of the information presented in this section, it is unclear why Dr. Rall was so "overwhelmed" by animal-man correlations, or why he used such scientific language as "high probability"; but since he had already found reasons to inform the country on CBS in 1976 and a group of environmentalists in 1977 that rodent data "predict very well for human cancer," one must conclude that Rall is easily "overwhelmed" and has forgotten the scientific meaning of "high probability." The only correlational data from *evaluated* studies comes to us from the IARC; they can scarcely be described as "overwhelming," and they have no scientifically calculated "probability" at all—the only statistical calculation made to establish a "probability" for man was the majority vote!

Even in its "pragmatic" mode, the IARC was a more reliable informant. It explained (in Vol. 17) why it was so difficult to establish degrees of evidence: "They may change if and when new data on the chemicals become available. The main drawback to any rigid classification of chemicals with regard to their carcinogenic capacity is the as yet incomplete knowledge of the mechanism(s) of carcinogenesis."[29] In the last analysis, as long as the mechanism or mechanisms of cancer were not understood, the identification of evidence of the process of carcinogenesis was on chronically shaky ground, save for strikingly powerful carcinogens. That is the fundamental explanation of why no final word on so many animal carcinogens can ever be said. That was why the scientists had to vote, and that is why we were offered ersatz prediction by an institution which felt compelled, to preserve its good name as a scientific organization, to warn us that it was ersatz even as it felt compelled to "help" the regulatory agencies by providing them with lists of a mixture of demonstrated perils from epidemiology and undemonstrated perils from animal tests.

"Undemonstrated perils," of course, is not the language of our American "regulatory" scientists, who have always preferred to describe the limitations of their predictive powers more obliquely. In 1977, the NCI was quoted as conceding the "lack of *absolute certainty*" in identifying an agent as a human carcinogen from animal data.[30] Similarly, in 1978, Arthur Upton, Director of the NCI, granted that "when the data come solely from animal studies ... they cannot provide *conclusive* or quantitative indications of the risks for human beings"[31] (emphasis added). Such "concessions," which I have italicized here—both made when no two regulatory agencies agreed on the definition of a carcinogen and possessed no universally acknowledged list of demonstrated animal carcinogens—implied to the public that "regulatory" science was teetering on the brink of predictive perfection but was confessing sorrowfully that it had not quite reached that state. Given the fact that in the very year of Upton's statement the IARC's arm had been twisted by unknown institutions into conducting majority votes and relying on a metaphor, the NCI's official language may politely be called obfuscation.

Behind this "brink of perfection" language, there was complete awareness that the animal tests had never been validated. It was perfectly well understood among the theoreticians at the NCI, for example, who were actually seeking some means of validating the animal tests. In 1978, Curtis C. Harris and Umberto Saffiotti of the NCI, working with Benjamin Trump of the Department of Pathology of the University of Maryland, reported as follows:

Carcinogenesis researchers have striven for decades to interpret data obtained from animal studies in terms of their applicability to humans. . . . An experimental approach to the direct study of carcinogenesis in human tissues and cells was recently developed *to assess the:* (a) mechanisms of carcinogenesis in human cells, (b) variation of carcinogenic susceptibility among individuals, and (c) *validity of the extrapolation of carcinogenesis data from experimental animals to the human situation.*[32] [Emphasis added]

Saffiotti described the goal as follows: "The new culture methods make it possible to establish closely comparable conditions of exposure to carcinogens between animal and human target tissues *and open the way toward a precise step-by-step objective approach to the old problem of 'extrapolating from mouse to man'* "[33] (emphasis added). Thomas Maugh of *Science* also described the goal of this project as that of "trying to confirm animal results."[34] The complex attempt to use human cells for the validation of animal findings was still in an early stage, according, respectively, to Roy Albert et al., and Maugh in *Science.*[35] According to Albert, the NCI, while enthusiastic for "future possibilities," had reported that "such tests do not now provide an adequate basis for characterizing an agent as carcinogenic for humans or animals."[36] Whether this direct use of human cells—as opposed to the study of whole human organisms with their complex activation, detoxification, repair, and immune systems—will ever solve the problem, the layman cannot know. What he can know is that at the NCI, scientists have been trying to "assess" the "validity" of animal tests and to establish an "objective" approach to animal-man extrapolation. This means, quite simply, that the "validity" of animal tests has *not* been "assessed," and that the use of animal carcinogens to predict human cancer is *not* "objective." For seven years, the IARC had been saying this, until "criticism" forced the chemical carcinogen division of that institution to eat its own words, which it did, while simultaneously refusing to do so.

This particular piece of information—that the animal tests have not been validated and cannot yet predict for man—is a striking example of necessary information that has not been communicated to the public. What we have heard, rather, is highly publicized opinion from a group of scientists who have insisted that animal data *do* predict cancer in man. Since this is the position that has been heard to saturation point, it is important to understand not only *that* it is erroneous, but *why* scientists have made such claims. They are expressions of a logical fallacy, *specifically the fallacy of selecting data that support the theory in which one believes, and ignoring the data that don't.*

Sir Peter Medawar has identified this as a fallacy characteristic of the "superstitious" or of others who believe in unproved doctrines. Medawar, a Nobel laureate in medicine and physiology in 1960 who, ironically, had himself been vulnerable to the ecological apocalypse, wrote a book called *Advice to a Young Scientist,* and among his various counsels was the strong recommendation to avoid disputes with people engaging in that fallacy. He offered an example of it that is particularly helpful to laymen. He said:

Another way in which a scientist loses friends is to call attention to the tricks that selective memory can play upon judgment. "Three times, no less, I dreamed of Cousin Winifred and on the very next day, she rang me up. If that doesn't prove that dreams can foretell the future, then I'm sure I don't know what does." But, the young scientist expostulates, on how many occasions did you dream of Cousin Winifred without a subsequent telephone call?—and is it not a fact that she rings up almost every day?[37]

Medawar was aware that scientists themselves might commit this fallacy of selecting only the data that support their beliefs and warned "any scientist of any age": "The intensity of the conviction that a hypothesis is true has no bearing on whether it is true."[38] In a portion of the world of "regulatory" science, the use of the Cousin Winifred fallacy to bolster the intense belief that animals predict for man is epidemic. The Cousin Winifred argument can be paraphrased as follows: "Three (four, five, six) times, no less, we have found a substance that was a carcinogen in man as well as in animals (or vice versa), and if that doesn't prove that animals can foretell cancer in man, then I'm sure I don't know what does." One finds this precise fallacy, explicit and implicit, in the writings of OSHA,[39] Samuel Epstein,[40] Arthur Upton of the NCI,[41] William Lijinsky of the Fredericks Cancer Research Center,[42] David Rall of the NIEHS,[43] the National Cancer Advisory Board,[44] Gus Speth, Chairman of the Toxic Substances Strategy Committee under President Jimmy Carter,[45] the Toxic Substances Strategy Committee itself,[46] Lorenzo Tomatis of the IARC,[47] Renate Kimbrough of the Atlanta Center for Disease Control,[48] John H. Weisburger of Naylor Dana Institute for Disease Prevention,[49] and Cesare Maltoni, the Italian toxicologist who first identified vinyl chloride as an animal carcinogen[50]—all stellar representives of "regulatory" science.

The Cousin Winifred demonstration that animals predict cancer in man appears in three distinct forms: (1) the scientist brandishes a tiny collection of animal carcinogens that were later shown by epidemiology to be carcinogenic in man; (2) vice versa, he brandishes a tiny collection of human carcinogens that have also been shown to be carcinogenic in animals (usually conceding a few exceptions); and (3) he brandishes both. *And in no case is the "evidence" placed in the context of the tiny human data base or the huge number of reported animal carcinogens in which no confirming human data exists.* One rapid illustration of each will be given here:

Version 1: In 1977, William Lijinsky of the NCI observed that "several compounds"—he cited vinyl chloride and diethylstilbestrol—"were first shown to be carcinogenic in experimental animals, and these results later turned out to be accurately predictive of the compounds' carcinogenic effects in people exposed to them."[51] Lijinsky then asserted that *"animal tests are predictive of carcinogenicity in man,* who is not an exceptional species in this regard"[52] (emphasis added).

Version 2: In the 1980 policy document, OSHA presented the argument in reverse:

All substances or mixtures of substances that have been proven carcinogenic by direct observation in humans have also been known to be carcinogenic in animals (with the exception of arsenic and perhaps benzene, still under experimental study).[53]

Both versions combined: In 1976, Samuel Epstein used both arguments:

All chemicals known to produce cancer in man, with the possible exception of trivalent inorganic arsenic, also produce cancer in experimental animals, generally in rodents. Recent experience with carcinogens such as bis-chloromethyl ether, diethylstilbestrol, and vinyl chloride monomer, moreover, *amply confirms the predictive value of animal carcinogenicity data to humans.*[54] [Emphasis added]

Subtle variations of this fallacy can be seen in these three examples. Like David Rall in 1976 and 1977, Lijinsky and Epstein stated explicitly that animal data predict for man, while OSHA preferred to cling to reality by a shred of brink-of-perfection language: Such prediction, OSHA confessed, was not "absolutely definitive."

There is also a variant of the Cousin Winifred fallacy which claims a high probability for animal-man prediction, but cites no examples at all. Thus, in 1977, a National Academy of Sciences Committee, cited earlier in this chapter, wrote authoritatively:

. . . there are *large bodies* of experimental data that indicate that exposures that are carcinogenic to animals are likely to be carcinogenic to man, and vice versa.[55] [Emphasis added]

In this case, the NAS committee was dreaming of Cousin Winifred in color, and was too excited even to count the number of dreams; in fact, that committee actually hallucinated "large bodies" of data into existence.

Whatever the variations, however, the fallacy is always the same. It is the fascinating *obverse* of the IARC's "concealment" of the precious ten animal-man matches. What is in common is the *severing* of the small number of matches from the huge number of animal carcinogens that match with nothing; they are not perceived simultaneously.

In the face of a widely shared fallacy, one does not ask "Why?"—one asks "What is there to lose by abandoning it?" One finds the answer in a paper by Herman Kraybill of the NCI, one of the earliest leaders of the cancer prevention movement. In 1980, Kraybill circled cautiously around the Cousin Winifred fallacy without baptizing it by that name; he observed the pattern of selection and evasion. Some scientists, he said, cited such carcinogens as 4-amino-biphenyl, mustard gas, vinyl chloride, and aflatoxins as evidence that is helping to resolve the controversy over the validity of animal-to-man extrapolations. But, he added, *"no mention is made of the wide spectrum of suspect or weak carcinogens where the difficulties of proving out associations are well-recognized."* And he reached the conclusion one must reach when one allows oneself to perceive all the data at once: "Despite these optimistic claims on animal-to-man associations, we need a far more comprehensive data base before we can make any extensive claim in this area."[56] What Kraybill makes clear is that the very act of abandoning the Cousin Winifred fallacy forces one to lose the illusion that animals predict for man. It does not overwhelm one with surprise that that fallacy should be so widespread in the one field which has the greatest vested interest in animal tests.

If animals do not predict for man, what *do* they do? The most helpful answer comes from the Office of Science and Technology Policy in 1979: "The various testing methods discussed above [cancer and mutagen tests] cannot provide a simple yes or no answer regarding the potential for human carcinogenesis. Rather, test results *offer a probability that such a potential exists*"[57] (emphasis added). Why do "regulatory" scientists bombard Americans into stupefaction by "probabilities of potentials"—above all, by "probabilities of potentials" which usually come from *single* experiments which the OSTP itself declares should be viewed as statistical flukes? OSHA states the official reason most clearly. Using the characteristic brink-of-perfection language, the agency said:

OSHA recognized that there may be no data which provide absolutely definitive evidence—*one way or another*—as to whether cancer is caused in humans by a substance that has been shown to be carcinogenic in test animals.

OSHA stated, however, that *the failure to assume that such a substance does pose some level of carcinogenic threat to humans seemed imprudent and could lead to a public health disaster.*[58] [Emphasis added]

In sum, the stated reason for the deluge of pseudo-predictions is not scientific but *moral*—that special "Donald Kennedy morality" which states that the peril is so great there is no time to discover whether there is any peril, or to establish its extent and nature.

In an attempt to endow this "morality" with scientific content, "regulatory" scientists have violated the deepest ethics of science itself. They have tried to *select* and *evade* animal prediction into existence. They have tried to *assert* and *imply* animal prediction into existence. They have, on at least one occasion, *fantasied* animal prediction into existence. They have tried to *define* animal prediction into existence. They have tried to *vote* animal prediction into existence. And they have tried to *legislate* and *regulate* animal prediction into existence. They have not, however, done the only thing that matters from a scientific point of view: They have not *correlated* animal prediction into existence.

One gains final perspective on this convulsive embrace of pseudo-prediction when one learns that for some years it was a relatively parochial phenomenon in industrial nations. In 1977, Tomatis and Ruggero Montesano reported on a survey of occupational cancer legislation in thirteen industrialized countries, in addition to the United States: Australia, Belgium, Federal Republic of Germany, France, German Democratic Republic, Ireland, Italy, Japan, the Netherlands, Sweden, Switzerland, the United Kingdom, and the USSR.[59] In only eight industrialized nations were scientists attempting to prevent cancer by such "prediction." In only four countries were there laws forbidding the production and import of known or potential carcinogens; the carcinogens covered by those laws varied from country to country, and the criteria determining animal carcinogens in those countries were inconsistent. Six industrialized nations were unimpressed by pseudo-prediction. Tomatis concluded at that time not only that consensus was missing on the extrapolation from animal to man, but that "there is also no consensus on the extrapolation from one human population group to another."[60]

How much the situation has changed since 1977 is unknown; as of 1981, according to the Tomatis office at the IARC, no follow-up study had been published,[61] but in 1981, John Weisburger, Head of the Naylor Dana Institute for Disease Prevention and former Head of the Carcinogen Screening Section and Director of the Bioassay Segment of the Carcinogenesis Program of the NCI, was still calling for internation uniformity.[62] Apparently, there still wasn't any. And so much for "prediction."

We will now move to the last of the goals of "regulatory" science, the one known as "risk assessment." Risk assessment is a process by which scientists try to quantify the risks of carcinogens in man by extrapolation from animal data. And by now, the reader should be able to anticipate that this is a hopeless enterprise. It seems unlikely that a biological test is going to be able to make *quantitative* measurements of risk if that test has not been validated; has no objective or universally established criteria; is testing for the presence of a phenomenon whose mechanism is unknown; can only classify the evidence of carcinogenicity by negotiated debate; reaches different conclusions about the same substance depending on the committee, the agency, and the country; cannot identify a noncarcinogen at all; and has insufficient correlational data to predict human risk.

Nonetheless, we will examine the theory and practice of risk assessment with care, because it is the final goal of the entire body of activities known as "regulatory science." It is by this means that the hazards of carcinogens are calculated so that the American public can be protected in advance from cancer-causing substances. Risk assessment, in other words, is the ultimate practical expression of cancer prevention. There are actually two kinds of risk assessment, and they are arrived at in different ways. Each will be described in a separate chapter. The first is the no-threshold theory.

Chapter 12

The Case of the Missing Thresholds

A prudent policy of cancer prevention requires protection of the most sensitive individuals in the population.[1]

—Umberto Saffiotti, NCI, 1978

For scientific or regulatory purposes, *threshold* would be a dosage level below which an effect (cancer) *could not* and *never would* occur. . . .[2]

—OSHA, Policy document, 1980

In August 1979, students of oddities in the culture may have noted an article in the science section of the *New York Times* entitled "How Tiny Chemical Traces Are Found." It quoted Lawrence Garfinkle, Vice-President and epidemiologist of the American Cancer Society, as saying: ". . . one part per *billion* of anything seems just too small to worry about. Some of us think all instruments capable of detecting chemicals and concentrations lower than one part per million ought to be smashed before we drive ourselves crazy."[3] Had some new form of Luddism made its appearance in the heart of cancer research? Why was talk of instrument-smashing coming out of the mouths of prominent students of cancer—and at the very time when technology was doing the precise bidding of the theoreticians of cancer prevention who were committed to ridding the continent of every last trace of a carcinogenic molecule? Without such marvelously sensitive instruments, the job could not be done. Why, then, were fantasies of instrument-smashing being ventilated in the science section of the *New York Times*?

What the student of oddities in the culture may not have known is that that hostility to the very instruments on which the new science of cancer prevention relied was not new. It had simply become more intense among those who saw where the instruments were taking them. In 1976, when Alexander Schmidt was the FDA Commissioner, he complained that "we will be chasing a 'receding zero,' and some idiot in some lab will come up with something sensitive to parts per quintillion, and our policy says we will adopt it."[4] Obviously, such scientists felt trapped, and Schmidt's irritable little prophecy tells us clearly that it was not the technology itself that was tormenting them, but "our policy."

That policy was the no-threshold or the no-safe-dose theory, which, to repeat, holds that the most minute amount of a carcinogen, even a single molecule, might give someone cancer and, consequently, that the only safe dose or exposure is zero. But zero was an increasingly unattainable goal. For years some scientists, at least, such as Herman Kraybill and Gary Flamm, had understood that "zero exposure" was simply a function of the lowest amount of a carcinogen that contemporary instruments could measure. As the instruments had rapidly increased in sensitivity, the detectable amount of a carcinogen was rapidly growing more and more minute, with the result that both the concepts of "threshold" and the location of "zero," thus of safety, were growing ever more remote.[5] "Regulatory" scientists were, in fact, chasing a "receding zero" and official policy did say they would adopt it. Such outbursts were rare, however, and they were rarely followed by a full-scale analysis of the problem. What is more, some of the critics vastly preferred to denounce the technology rather than the policy.

To understand why sophisticated scientists would prefer to portray themselves as Luddites and denounce technology, rather than the values served by that technology, one must understand more about the no-threshold theory than has yet been explained in this book. The no-threshold theory is the premise of the process by which American citizens are sheltered from carcinogenic risk by American "regulatory" science. It is so remarkable a premise, however, that it merits a chapter on its own. That may come as a relief to the reader who, by now, may feel that it is time to take the no-threshold theory firmly in hand and keep it from wandering all over the book. I confess that it has indeed wandered. It first showed up in Chapter 2, and I warned the reader then that it would show up again. It did so, in Chapter 3, Chapter 4, and Chapter 7. It made a fleeting appearance in Chapter 8. And now that we are surveying the goals of "regulatory" science, it is showing up again. I pledge to deal with it firmly in this chapter, but, unfortunately, I cannot pledge to keep it from continuing to wander all over the book, because it will. It will show up in the next chapter, and the next, and again until the very end. There is no way to pen it up. It is a direct form of risk assessment, it is a major premise of quantitative risk assessment, it is a major premise of cancer prevention, it is a major premise of cancer regulation, it is a major premise of "regulatory" science, and it will turn out to be a major premise of the universe—or at least, as the reader will later discover, that is a claim that the FDA has made for it in court. In sum, this is a premise for which one must have some respect. It is the rock on which the temple of cancer prevention has been built.

There is only one thing wrong with this premise: Nobody has any idea if it is true. As Marvin Schneiderman of the NCI put it at the OSHA hearings:

Another problem *and one which unfortunately is not amenable to scientific solution,* is the existence of a threshold. Is there a lower limit of exposure below which normal repair and recuperative processes will prevent cancer? This is perhaps one of the most pernicious questions that confront the regulatory agencies. It is the refuge of the apologist for industry and has support from traditional toxicology.[6] [Emphasis added]

A premise that "is not amenable to scientific solution" is a problem in a scientific endeavor, and it does generate hostility to regulators who impose it coercively. The reader is doubtless aware that "apologists for industry" are hostile to the no-threshold theory. He may not be aware, however, that "traditional toxicology" is also hostile to it, which is to say that a substantial number of "regulatory" scientists are as antagonized by the no-threshold theory as others are devoted to it. In fact, because regulators are loathe to inform citizens that anyone but industrialists condemns their policies, the reader may be unaware that this is by far the most intense battle within the world of "regulatory" science itself.

The academic conflict over the no-threshold theory is so profound that it has caused certain institutions and people to adopt a position of cautious neutrality. In 1978, the Office of Science and Technology Policy circulated an early draft of its guidelines for the control of carcinogens. The draft was "widely" circulated among scientists, and responses were received from several dozen, including Roy Albert of NYU, Douglas Costle of EPA, Joseph Fraumeni of NCI, Philip Handler of NAS, D. Mark Hegsted of the USDA, Norton Nelson of NYU, David Rall of NIEHS, Joseph Rodricks of the FDA, and Arthur Upton of the NCI and the NCI staff.[7] On the basis of the responses from these scientists, the OSTP decided to leave the subject of thresholds out of its policy report:

Most comments made reference to lack of consensus among scientists regarding this issue. Since a full presentation of the debate is beyond the scope of this paper, we have elected to omit explicit reference to thresholds from the paper.[8]

In the same year, Thomas Maugh of *Science* magazine, who did try to review the debate, also preferred to remain neutral. Acknowledging the intensity of the conflict in the scientific world, Maugh, who is not normally given to hyperbole, said: "Debate between those who think carcinogens can be detoxified and those who do not has raged for years with all the intensity of a jihad. The analogy to religion is not inappropriate, moreover, since there is little hard scientific evidence to support either point of view. . . . Arguments on both sides of the question often seem to be little more than articles of faith, and it is exceptionally difficult for an impartial observer to decide which faith is more deserving of support."[9]

In this book, however, the reader is not being asked to support or reject any of the "articles of faith" of "regulatory" science, but rather to recognize an "article of faith" when he sees one, and to discover why one set of baseless beliefs achieves dominance over another. In this case the discovery can be made by the layman, but only under one condition: The threshold controversy must *not* be ripped out of context. If one examines the no-threshold/one-molecule debate by itself, one must inevitably end up perched on the fence, for "it is not amenable to scientific solution." If, however, one examines it within the context of the goal of cancer prevention, it becomes luminously clear that the "articles of faith" of one camp—the no-threshold camp—have necessarily been triumphant and that the dissenters against this position have necessarily been defeated in the battle. When it is properly understood, the goal of cancer prevention permits only one of the two sets of "articles of faith" to prosper.

The stated goal of the cancer prevention program in the United States is, quite simply, to protect—in advance—every one of the 280,000,000 citizens from the real or potential effects of carcinogens. The goal is stated in slightly different terms by different scientists, although they all mean the same thing. According to one group of NCI scientists, including Charles C. Brown, Thomas R. Fears, and Marvin A. Schneiderman, "all members of a heterogeneous population must be protected at all times," and thus a regulatory agency "must consider the lowest threshold for an individual over his exposure period, as well as the lowest thresholds in the entire population."[10] And Umberto Saffiotti of the NCI expresses the same idea more economically: "A prudent policy of cancer prevention requires protection of the most sensitive individuals in the population."[11] This goal is resonant with good intentions, but it poses very peculiar problems. On the face of it, it is obvious that no one can possibly know the identity of all the individuals in a nation of 222,000,000 or any random portion thereof who will be "most sensitive" to a disease that has not yet occurred and that is not understood. All that can be known is that individual reactions are very different. Many scientists (e.g., Harold Stewart, NIH; William Lijinsky, NCI; Donald Kennedy, Commissioner of the FDA; and Saffiotti himself[12]) have testified to OSHA that, as OSHA puts it, there is a "wide variability in susceptibility to cancer within a population."[13] Science is not presently capable of identifying the degree of "susceptibility" of every individual in the nation, particularly in a "heterogeneous" population.

In fact, the "heterogeneity" of the population may be the biggest obstacle of all to the identification of the "most sensitive individuals." A "heterogeneous" population is an "outbred" population, a population which has accumulated a reservoir of genetic diversity. The simplest way for the layman to understand the problem of varied susceptibility to cancer of a "heterogeneous" population is to remember the observation of David Rall of NIEHS. After years of informing scientific conferences that it was in the realm of metabolism that species similarities broke down, he solved the embarrassing problem by observing that "man is among the most heterogeneous systems on earth" and asserting: "If sufficient effort were exerted, one could find that metabolically some man would exhibit a pattern like a rat, another man would exhibit a characteristic of a dog, and so forth." The "and so forth," however, is more important than the rest because Rall only mentioned laboratory animals, but his statement, at a minimum, means that any given man may metabolize a carcinogen like any given *mammal*, i.e., that somewhere a citizen of the United States may be metabolizing carcinogens like a gorilla, a leopard, a zebra, or an aardvark. The ultimate goal of cancer prevention in a heterogeneous species, then, is to protect that unknown susceptible citizen living somewhere on this gigantic continent who may, unknown to him or anyone else, metabolize carcinogens like an aardvark; and the aardvark, for all we know—since "sufficient effort" has not been exerted—may be helplessly vulnerable to carcinogens.

For the sheer pleasure of naming things, we will call this the Aardvark ·Principle. This "principle" is merely a symbolic restatement of the goal of cancer prevention as defined with greater solemnity by the above-quoted scientists at the NCI. Once one understands the Aardvark Principle, one also understands that there is no way on earth, now or ever, of identifying, in advance, a safe dose of a carcinogen that will hold for the entire population, or for a random slice of the population, or, in fact, for anybody at all. OSHA, accordingly, defines a threshold in the manner most appropriate to the Aardvark Principle.

For scientific or regulatory purposes, *threshold* would be a dosage level below which an effect (cancer) *could not* and *never would* occur, not merely a point below which an effect would be infrequent, no matter how very infrequent.[14] [Emphasis in original]

It must now be observed that the Aardvark Principle, all the more formal definitions of the goal of cancer prevention by NCI scientists, and OSHA's definition of a threshold as a dose that *"could not"* and *"never would"* cause a carcinogenic response in a single citizen have one unusual thing in common: To establish a threshold dose, all require the proof of a negative, which is impossible in logic. There is no way of demonstrating that an unknown individual in a population of 222,000,000 is *not* unusually susceptible to a disease whose mechanism is unknown; there is no way of demonstrating that an unknown individual does *not* metabolize carcinogens like an aardvark; there is no way to identify any metabolic response that *"could not"* and *"never would"* occur. The goal of cancer prevention may be resonant with good intentions, but a student of Logic I who presented a comparable proposition would receive a resonant F. Assuming, however, that one accepts a public health goal that sets forth the need for a set of logically impossible calculations, one must thereafter conclude that one cannot perform those calculations—which is to say that one cannot calculate a threshold dose for man from any carcinogen—which is to say that even one molecule of a carcinogen may cause cancer in someone, somewhere, sometime. One could hardly conclude anything else: The noble-irrational goal of preventing, in advance, a disease that is not understood in the most sensitive individual in a heterogeneous population of 222,000,000 people actually *contains* the answer to the much-debated question of thresholds.

Under these circumstances, a great many scientists have understood perfectly well that there is no way on earth to calculate a threshold dose for a population. Again, their statements take slightly different forms, although all mean the same thing. Some scientists simply say forthrightly that the calculations cannot be performed and short of challenging the logic of the goal, explain why. For example, Richard Bates of the NIEHS and FDA testified to OSHA as follows:

At the present time, we are still in a position of being unable to unequivocally decide whether or not thresholds exist, as defined at the molecular or population level, or to determine which individuals in the population may or may not be able to tolerate additional exposure from carcinogenic chemicals.[15]

Similarly, Harold Stewart of the National Institutes of Health, Chairman of the Ad Hoc Committee on Testing for Environmental Carcinogens, was quoted by OSHA as describing the search for a safe dose as "unrealistic:"

In the case of the human population, with the completely unknown variations in sensitivity to any chemical carcinogen and with the impossibility of knowledge of other variables that may affect responsiveness to these agents, attempts to establish threshold levels for carcinogenicity are unrealistic.[16]

And William Nicholson of the Mt. Sinai School of Medicine was quoted by OSHA as saying the attempt to establish a threshold was almost "impossible":

Despite considerable research on the effects of carcinogenic substances . . . no data exist that would define a threshold for any carcinogen. The task confronting one who would define a level below which no carcinogenic risk exists for human populations is virtually an impossible one.[17]

Other scientists, including representatives of regulatory agencies, prefer to make it sound as though the inability to determine threshold doses for a population are, rather, a function of a missing consensus which might one day make its appearance. Thus, in 1979, the Interagency Regulatory Liaison Group, Work Group of Risk Assessment, representing CPSC, EPA, FDA, and OSHA, said:

There is no *presently acceptable way* to determine reliably a threshold for a carcinogen for an entire population.[18] [Emphasis added]

And occasionally a scientist tries to make the impossibility of performing irrational calculations sound like a creative scientific discovery. Thus, in 1979, Samuel Epstein informed his readers that the statisticians of NIEHS had played a notable role in confirming the "scientific base" of the Delaney Clause—the "inability" of science to determine thresholds.[19]

However they choose to formulate the problem, these scientists are simply expressing self-evident truth: No one can conceivably calculate the dose of a carcinogen that will be "safe" for the most sensitive individual in a population of 222,000,000 people. The Aardvark Principle—the moral goal of cancer prevention—allows no such calculation.

In logic, this is actually all one needs to know about the threshold controversy: As long as one is determined to protect every human being in the Republic from a disease without having much human data and without knowing the mechanisms of the disease, no one can calculate safe or threshold doses in advance and there is nothing to argue about.

This leaves us with yet another of the puzzles that are always springing up in "regulatory" science: If there is nothing to argue about, what *are* the scientists arguing about—and why is the argument raging with the force of a "jihad"? Maugh, in *Science*, was satisfied to declare that neither side had enough information to support its position and that the conflicting positions were "articles of faith." There is surely a profound truth in that comment, but something else is unquestionably involved, for there is a weird aspect of this battle that cannot be explained by clashing faiths. The curious fact is that none of the arguments purportedly offered in support of, or in repudiation of, thresholds are *relevant* to the concept of a threshold as it is defined by the goal of cancer prevention, i.e., a *dose* of a carcinogen which *"could not"* and *"never would"* give anyone cancer. A rapid review of those arguments will illustrate the point.

The main arguments offered in support of the no-threshold theory are merely listed here because the reader has heard all of them already. Some of the sources for these ideas, however, may be new:

1. *Cancer may start with the transformation (possibly mutagenic) of a single cell.*
    R. Truhaut, Université René Descartes, 1979; David Hoel of NIEHS, Richard Peto of Oxford University and Lorenzo Tomatis of IARC, 1980; Edward P. Radford, University of Pittsburgh, 1980; OSHA, 1980.[20]

2. *One molecule of a carcinogen or a mutagen may trigger cancer.*
    Bruce Ames, 1971; "Researchers from the National Cancer Institute," cited by Jacqueline Verrett, FDA, 1975; The Safe Drinking Water Committee, 1977; Eula Bingham, Assistant Secretary of Labor, 1977; OSHA, 1980.[21]

3. *Cancerous cells are self-replicating, multiplying, proliferating entities.*
    Umberto Saffiotti, 1977; R. Truhaut, Université René Descartes, 1979; Harold Stewart, NIH, 1980; I. Nathan Dubin, Medical College of Pennsylvania, 1980; Emmanuel Farber, University of Toronto, 1980, OSHA, 1980.[22]

4. *The initiation of the process of carcinogenesis is irreversible.*
    Arthur Upton, Director, NCI, 1980; OSHA, 1980; Robert Squire, Johns Hopkins University, 1980; Marvin Schneiderman, NCI, 1980; Emmanuel Farber, University of Toronto, 1980.[23]

5. *Carcinogens interact with each other synergistically;*
    Samuel Epstein, 1978; William Lijinsky, 1980; Irving Selikoff, Mt. Sinai School of Medicine, 1980; Richard Griesemer, NCI, 1980; Robert Squire, Johns Hopkins University, 1980.[24]
    and "additively" or "incrementally" or "cumulatively";
    Arthur Upton, Director, NCI, 1978; Matthew Meselson, Harvard University, 1980; Donald Kennedy, FDA, 1980; William Lijinsky, NCI, 1980; David Kaufman, University of North Carolina, 1980; David Rall, Director, NIEHS, 1980; OSHA, 1980.[25]
    thus, every minute dose of a carcinogen is added to a "background dose" which increases the risk of cancer.
    Umberto Saffiotti, NCI, 1977; Richard Peto of Oxford University, 1980; OSHA, 1980.[26]

These, as the reader will have recognized, are the major ideas endorsed by OSHA's policy document of 1980 (and that OSHA declared to represent the scientific consensus);[27] and each of these ideas is mentioned in literature reviews of the controversy, e.g., OSHA, Truhaut, as an argument for the probable nonexistence of thresholds.[28] But these ideas are descriptions of a hypothetical process of carcinogenesis. They do *not* demonstrate that there is no *dose* of a carcinogen that "could not" and "never would" give anyone cancer; one can neither prove nor disprove such a proposition. These ideas are simply a collection of the most intimidating aspects of the various theories of carcinogenesis which are being brandished *as if* they were proof of the nonexistence of a safe or threshold dose.

And precisely the same thing is true, in reverse, of the critics of the no-threshold theory who may not, as OSHA claims, represent the "consensus," but whose numbers are sufficient to have generated a "jihad." The alleged rebuttals to the no-threshold theory are exactly as irrelevant to the moral goal of cancer prevention as are the defenses. Although most scientists do not make all of these arguments at once, taken collectively, they constitute the mirror opposites of the positions cited above, and are listed in reviews of the literature (e.g., Truhaut) as arguments against the no-threshold theory.

1. *Exposure to very low levels of carcinogens—or to a single molecule of a mutagen or a carcinogen—may not necessarily be a significant threat, given the existence of a series of repair, recuperation, deactivation, and detoxification systems and other biological defense mechanisms in the total organism.*

    P. N. Magee, Courtauld Institute of Biochemistry, 1977; Hans Falk, NIEHS, 1978; Philip Handler, President of NAS, 1979; Herman Kraybill, NCI, 1980; Gio Batta Gori, NCI, 1980.[29]

2. *A minimum number of molecules in a cell must be affected before any biological reaction, including carcinogenesis, can take place.*

    D. Henschler, 1974; Hans Falk, NCI, 1980; Robert Olson, St. Louis University, 1980.[30]

3. *Human beings are being pounded so consistently by so many carcinogens that nothing much happens at the target-cell level; the cells die and no carcinogenesis occurs.*

    Isaac Berenblum, Weizmann Institute of Medicine, cited by John Higginson, founding director, IARC, 1979.[31]

    In addition, human cells are far more resistant both to radiation and chemical carcinogenesis than are the cells of mice.

    H. B. Jones and A. Grendon, University of California at Berkeley, 1975; John Cairns, Director, Mill Hill Laboratory, London, 1978.[32]

4. *The process of carcinogenesis is not necessarily an irreversible no-threshold phenomenon, for a great many metabolic variables (including high-dose testing itself) may inhibit or potentiate the carcinogenic response.*

    Herman Kraybill, NCI, 1977; Norbert Page, NCI, 1978.[33]

5. *While examples of synergism do exist, there is no scientific evidence to support the idea that there are cumulative or incremental effects of carcinogens, i.e., that minute doses of different combinations of carcinogens add up together to produce a cancer.*

K. Kay, 1974; Herman Kraybill, NCI, 1977–1980; Jerome Cornfield, 1977; Nathan Mantel, George Washington University, 1978; John Higginson, 1979.[34]

In fact, certain combinations of carcinogens are less *carcinogenic than the same carcinogens ingested individually.*

R. Kroes et al., National Institute of Public Health, the Netherlands, 1973; Hans Falk, NCI, 1976; D. Schmähl, German Cancer Research Center, 1978.[35]

And, finally, there are anticarcinogens which act to prevent or inhibit carcinogenesis.

Raymond Shamberger, Cleveland Clinic Foundation, 1978; Herman Kraybill, 1980;[36] and, of course, Isaac Berenblum and Lee Wattenberg (chapter 5).

Even on the assumption that all these arguments are true, they too add up to a description of a hypothetical process of *resistance* to carcinogenesis. They do *not* constitute evidence that a dose of a carcinogen exists which *"could not"* and *"never would"* cause cancer in a single human being. Here, arguments are being brandished as if they constituted disproof of a population threshold, which is as impossible as a proof. The scientists who use several or all of these arguments have made a collection of reassuring data; but apart from demonstrating that the opposite camp has a preference for terrifying data, these arguments are as guilty of irrelevance to the moral goal of cancer prevention as are their mirror opposites.

Even more curious, critics of the no-threshold theory are often arguing with a strawman, for many, if not most, of the defenders of the no-threshold theory are in full agreement that the second set of phenomena exist; they just argue that they cannot be measured—a proposition with which their opponents generally agree! Many of the defenders of the no-threshold theory also think, as do the critics, that the one-molecule theory of cancer is insignificant. David Rall, for example, says: "Most scientists would agree that a highly potent carcinogen such as an aflatoxin, nitrosamine or a chloromethyl ether is probably perfectly safe at an exposure level of one molecule, ten molecules, a hundred molecules, or maybe even a thousand molecules per mouse or rat or dog or man; but we all believe that it is totally unsafe to be exposed to 10^{20}, 10^{21}, 10^{22} or 10^{23} molecules of the same compound. In an isolated situation in a clean laboratory experiment, it is perfectly reasonable to expect that very low concentrations have such a low probability of causing a deleterious effect as to be essentially zero. In point of fact, we can never determine this."[37] Similarly, Lijinsky says: "While most would agree that exposure to a single molecule of a carcinogen is unlikely to present a risk to man, no one knows how many molecules do represent a risk. Accepting that there must be a threshold of action for a carcinogen, as there is for all toxic phenomena, it is not possible to determine what that threshold is."[38]

In addition, many of the defenders of the no-threshold theory are in full agreement that there may be individual thresholds. OSHA, for example, says:

". . . observation of the marked individual differences in the response of humans to carcinogens shows that some individuals obviously do not develop cancer in their lifetime, whereas others develop it rapidly after the same exposure to the same carcinogen." But OSHA adds: "Although these observations may be compatible with the existence of different 'thresholds' for individual humans in certain conditions, they are not a basis for predicting a 'no-effect,' 'threshold,' or 'safe' level of a carcinogen in other individuals exposed in the same or different conditions."[39]

There is also full agreement that repair and other detoxification systems exist in the human body which protect it from a variety of toxic and carcinogenic effects, but here too the point is made that no one can calculate the point at which these mechanisms fail to function. Thus Schneiderman of the NCI says that "these reactions are not likely to be perfect, complete";[40] Arthur Upton of the NCI says, "We know of repair mechanisms . . . but we know that they do not operate with 100% efficiency";[41] and OSHA too says "that DNA repair is not normally 100% efficient, and indeed that it would be unreasonable to expect it to be so. Accordingly, our knowledge of DNA repair cannot be used to justify the assumption of population thresholds for carcinogens either in general or in specific cases."[42] And to be sure, no one who brings up the question of detoxification and repair systems would dream of suggesting that they are invariably "perfect."

Finally, just as no critic of the no-threshold theory ever denies the phenomenon of synergism, no informed defender of the no-threshold theory denies the existence of anticarcinogens and inhibitory reactions; e.g., Robert Squire of Johns Hopkins University says: "Numerous experiments involving co-carcinogenesis indicate that different carcinogens may have additive, synergistic or *antagonistic* effects in organisms exposed to them" (emphasis added). But, he adds: "It is unlikely that we can predict which, if any, of the above effects will occur in the case of specific chemicals. . . ."[43] And again, no one who invokes the existence of anticarcinogens or inhibitory responses suggests that he can make such predictions.

When one examines this controversy carefully, one sees that this is not quite the "jihad" over thresholds that it is said to be. It is a complex, angry battle in which scientists tend to polarize around the most terrifying versus the most reassuring components of the various theories of carcinogenesis. In fact, there is no war over *population* thresholds at all, and there cannot be one. No opponent of the threshold theory has ever claimed to have set a safe dose of a carcinogen for the total population, including its most sensitive individuals. The scientists engaged in this "jihad" are clearly angry at each other about an unnamed something, but it cannot be about a set of ideas with which most of them agree.

It is so unreasonable for professionals in "regulatory" science who *share* the moral goal of cancer prevention—namely, the Aardvark Principle, which forbids any calculation of thresholds—to fight in perpetuity about an unprovable issue which is forbidden by their goal that one must try to account for it.

One explanation for this peculiar conduct has already been given, although only in a phrase. Marvin Schneiderman declared that opposition to the no-threshold theory has won support from "traditional toxicology." It is clear that there is, then, a nontraditional toxicology and that the two kinds of toxicology are at war, in some fashion. And so, we must find out what that conflict is, where the traditionalists and the nontraditionalists diverge, and why those divergences so antagonize the "traditionalists" that they are engaging in a futile war over thresholds which is irrelevant to and, in fact, contradictory of their own moral goal of cancer prevention.

Toxicology is an old and complex science, and one cannot provide a compact summary of its contents. But one can give a bit of its history and one or two of its cardinal principles, and that, for our purposes, will suffice. The history of toxicology is, in effect, the history of man. Man was not born into a toxic-radioactive world with a copy of *Consumer Reports* in his hand. To preserve his own life, and perhaps because the Faustian "sin" is ever present in the species, even primitive man became a toxicologist of sorts. Over the millennia, as he saw his fellow man die in agony after eating certain plants, berries, or fish, he learned to call those entities "poisons," and avoided them. In later stages of human development, when a vast lore on poisons had already been collected, men learned to kill others with natural toxic substances—e.g., Socrates was killed with a cup of poison brewed from hemlock; and kings had human "tasters" who ate and drank first what was put before the king; if the tasters did not die in agony, the meal was deemed safe and the king ate and drank without fear.

This crude experimentation, however, protected man only from the most virulent, fast-acting poisons where cause and effect could be quickly identified. By the sixteenth century, a far more subtle discovery was made by a German physician named Theophrastus Bombastus von Hohenheim, known as Paracelsus. He had learned that every substance could be toxic, depending on the dose. His famous proposition, originally stated in German, was: "What is it that is not poison? All things are poison and none without poison. Only the dose determines that a thing is not poison."[44] A Latin translation later reduced the idea to *Dosis sola facit venenum*[45]—"Only the dose makes the poison." And on the frontispiece of a current text, *Toxicology: The Basic Science of Poisons*, edited by Louis J. Casarett and John Doull, yet another translation stands: "All substances are poisons; there is none which is not a poison. The right dose differentiates a poison and a remedy."[46] The idea of Paracelsus is endlessly retranslated and reformulated because it is the fundamental principle of modern toxicology, the science of which Paracelsus is the recognized father. Libraries are stuffed, today, with studies of the toxicity of natural substances, and the knowledge is constantly growing. In 1979, the German toxicologist Schmähl reported: "Paracelsus' idea was recently confirmed by a case when a man in Germany died because he had drunk 17 liters of water within a very short time. He died from a cerebral edema and electrolyte disturbance. In this special case, even water acted as a fatal poison."[47]

From this remarkable discovery that all substances at some dose could be poisons and that poisons were dose-related it was just a step—a long step—to the systematic use of laboratory animals as "tasters" for men. In a contemporary toxicology laboratory, animals are tested at different doses of a drug or an industrial substance, and their responses to each dose level are recorded.[48] The lethal dose—LD50—is that dose at which 50 percent of the animals die; and the responses to a graded succession of doses are recorded to identify the "dose-response" curve.[49] Traditionally, the safe or threshold dose for man has been calculated at a minute percentage of the dose which has no effect whatever on the animal.[50] Although today toxicology grows ever more complex as responses are identified down to the molecular level, the principle of Paracelsus' dose-response relationships remain unchanged. For example, one finds this chart in Casarett's textbook, which gives one a simple idea of how one classifies the relative potencies, and therefore risks, of toxicants or poisons:[51]

SUMMARY OF CLASSIFICATION PLACING TOXICANTS INTO CATEGORIES RELATED TO THEIR RELATIVE TOXICITIES*

Toxicity rating	Commonly used term	Probable human lethal dose 70-kg (150-lb) man	
6	Supertoxic	<5 mg/kg	A taste; <7 drops
5	Extremely toxic	5–50 mg/kg	7 drops-1 teaspoonful
4	Very toxic	50–500 mg/kg	1 tsp-1 ounce
3	Moderately toxic	0.5–5 g/kg	1 oz-1 pint or pound
2	Slightly toxic	5–15 g/kg	1 pint-1 quart
1	Practically nontoxic	>15 g/kg	>1 quart

*Data from Hodge and Sterner, 1949; Gleason et al., 1969.

Thus does the laboratory mouse serve as a taster for man in the fields of pharmacology and industrial toxicity. If, today, most human beings are not poisoned in a highly toxic world, compounded by the highly toxic industrial revolution, one may conclude that the animal has served as a fairly efficient taster.

This does not imply, however, that the laboratory animal has rendered it unnecessary to study man directly. Errors have always been made, animals have not always predicted well for man, men have died from doses of drugs and toxicants which had been thought to be safe, and further knowledge was gained from these accidents. In the last analysis, however helpful the animal tasters, one still only knows with certainty what is dangerous to man by studying man. Conversely, one only knows what benefits man by studying man; penicillin, to cite the classic case, kills hamsters and guinea pigs, but it is a lifesaver for most men. In Casarett's toxicology text he explains that the empirical study of man must continue even after animal predictions are made. The standards set on the basis of animal dose-response curves, he says, are "provisional":

[They] are usually modified as more experience is gained with human exposure under conditions of use. Community standards are likewise developed and modified on the basis of current knowledge. Thus the "standards" set for safety in all circumstances are not firm, fixed, immutable figures. Rather, they represent the best judgment, at any given time, of the safety of a toxicant based on the sum total of all toxicologic information.[52]

Direct human experimentation has been reduced to a minimum with the use of animal "tasters," but it is still necessary to engage in empirical studies of man himself. Man remains his own most reliable experimental animal.

So far, of course, we have just been discussing chemical toxicity. But carcinogenesis is a form of chemical toxicity, and Paracelsus is the father of this science as well. Indeed, the same toxicologists study both toxicity and carcinogenesis. And the fundamental discovery of Paracelsus, *Dosis sola facit venenum*—"Only the dose makes the poison"—and the modern study of dose-response curves are also applicable to carcinogenesis. Indeed, if any firm principle of carcinogenesis is known at all—a principle that applies both to animal and man—it is Paracelsus' principle of dose-relatedness. Here is an explanation of the phenomenon as offered by William Lijinsky at the OSHA hearings, and fortunately for the layman, it begins with an example of human data:

In the case of cigarette smoking there is a clear-cut dose-response relationship; that is, the incidence of lung cancer is greater, the larger the number of cigarettes smoked per day and the longer the period for which they are smoked. Thus we can say that the higher the dose rate, or the longer the period of exposure, the higher is the risk of developing lung cancer. . . .

Exactly the same experience pertains to tests of chemical carcinogens in experimental animals. Those receiving higher dose rates, or the same dose rates for a longer period, have the highest risk of developing cancer. . . .

From the animal tests another aspect of dose-response can be deduced, namely that the higher the dose of carcinogen administered, the earlier the tumors appear. . . . Furthermore, only at the highest doses do all of a group of animals die of the tumors induced, and at lower doses the animals often live out their natural lifespan and die without any induced tumor.

When considering dose-response we have the two measures, time to death with induced tumors . . . and proportion of animals with induced tumors; the former decreases and the latter increases as the dose of carcinogen is increased.[53]

Similarly, Jerzy Neyman, Director of the Statistical Laboratories at the University of California at Berkeley, working with the carcinogen urethane, describes "a striking difference between crops of lung tumors in mice depending on the high or low dose-rate. With the high dose-rate, there are many more tumors."[54] Finally, carcinogenesis is dose-related in radiation carcinogenesis as well as in chemical carcinogenesis.

As Henry Pitot of the University of Wisconsin sums it up: *"As in the case of most agents producing effects in biological systems, the evidence is overwhelming that chemical and physical [radiation] induction of the neoplastic transformation is dependent on the dose of the carcinogenic agent."*[55] This is pure Paracelsus.

Where, then, is the conflict between "traditional" toxicology and "nontraditional" toxicology? We learn its essentials from Umberto Saffiotti, who, in 1977, announced the birth of a "new toxicology." There was one primary difference in this "new toxicology" which led, in turn, to other differences. The primary difference was a rejection of what Saffiotti called the "traditional empirical approach" to man.[56] One would use animal research in carcinogenesis just as one did in pharmacology and industrial toxicology—but, said Saffiotti, when it came to setting provisional safe doses, based on that animal research and then assessing the effects of those doses in man, that "empirical approach" would not do for carcinogenic chemicals. The reason, he said, lay in the mechanisms of carcinogenesis, which were uniquely different from the mechanisms of toxic substances in that they were characterized by "a trigger change in the target cell's regulatory mechanism, which determines a self-replicating cell lesion." That initial molecular damage, produced by exposure to a carcinogen, might be very restricted—"even to a few cells." Depending on the condition of the individual, it would then manifest itself in "the proliferation of the altered cell population." Such carcinogenic effects, he said, were different by nature from the effects of terminal toxicity. He called them "self-replicating toxic effects," and he observed that a "new toxicology" was evolving to control the carcinogens which induced such "self-replicating" toxic effects. That "new toxicology" was interdisciplinary, he said, and needed the participation of professions "ranging from chemistry and physics to biology and pathology, and from environmental sciences and sociology to law and economics."[57]

Two aspects of that explanation are of particular interest. First, since no one, in 1977, knew the mechanisms of cancer, Saffiotti was not actually describing those mechanisms. He was simply using a good many words, including the postulate of the "single-cell" or "few-cell" theory, to describe what everyone already knew about cancer—that something unknown, whether inside or outside the individual or both, made cells proliferate. The conference title itself had described cancer more economically; it was a conference on "cell proliferation." Saffiotti was actually enunciating a new *moral* edict for toxicology: that while the "empirical approach" to man might be permissible for drugs and other toxic substances, it was impermissible for chemicals that might be "potential" carcinogens. Carcinogens in man must henceforth be studied without reference to man.

The second innovation of the "new toxicology," as Saffiotti explained it, was the invitation into the ranks of toxicology of a group of unusual new specialists who knew nothing whatever about biology, toxicity, or carcinogenicity: sociologists, lawyers, and economists. It is not difficult to see why sociologists, lawyers, and economists moved into the "new toxicology" just as empiricism was being evicted. In the very year that Saffiotti defined the "new toxicology" for his colleagues, he had also defined the professional ethics of animal testers in carcinogenesis as that of bearing witness to "suspected mass murder." With such a view of the function of the "new toxicology," the empirical approach to man was of little use—in fact, it was an obstacle; "suspicion" could not flourish in the atmosphere of empiricism. The "new toxicology," in sum, was a demand for a new moral-political approach to toxicology which would, with the aid of sociologists, lawyers and economists, rationalize the pursuit of "suspected" industrial "mass murder" without any need for the empirical evidence of harm to man traditionally demanded by both science and the law.

Although Saffiotti alone is quoted here, for he is invariably the most explicit philosopher of "regulatory" science, the reader will recognize that this is a description of the contemporary American approach to the risks of carcinogens, which are determined, ultimately, by lawyers and the courts.

The "new toxicology" was morally and politically triumphant, a triumph which was profoundly satisfactory to all those who imagined, as did Saffiotti's Ad Hoc Committee in 1970, that "the mass" of environmental cancer came from industry and that the disease could be virtually obliterated by law. But a strange price had been paid for that triumph. The study of carcinogenesis was still in its infancy, but the "new toxicology" had committed itself to cancer prevention—to the identification of "potential" carcinogens and to the assessment of carcinogenic risks to man—with only a sparse handful of human data available, and a taboo against the "empirical approach." However one may applaud its morality, the "new toxicology" had actually paralyzed itself scientifically. Without the "traditional" empirical method in a disease that no one understood, it was left immobilized in a posture of moral probity—and was unable to learn anything that it did not already know about the exogenous causes of cancer in man. Above all, it could never begin to discover what chemicals or what *doses* of chemicals did or did not have effects, save in mice and rats. But the purpose of cancer prevention was not to protect mice and rats, but to protect people. Thus, the "new toxicologists" could only declare, on *moral* grounds, that even the tiniest dose of an animal carcinogen, even a single molecule, had to be considered perilous for man. *The no-threshold theory was born of the abandonment of empiricism.*

That is why that theory "is not amenable to scientific solution." It was never a scientific theory at all. It was what was left in the hole created in toxicology after empiricism had been gouged out of that science: It was a moral theory and a political theory. And, unsurprisingly, it required sociologists, lawyers, and economists to interpret it. There was, in fact, nothing a scientist could say about a theory that "is not amenable to scientific solution"—and there still is not.

The problem was compounded when the moral goal of cancer prevention was identified as that of protecting the most vulnerable individual in a heterogeneous population who might, for reasons unknown, unimaginable, and evolutionary, be felled by a single molecule of a carcinogen. That bred the no-threshold theory for the *nation*—for the entire population of 222,000,000 or any portion thereof—and with the appearance of the unchallengeably moral Aardvark Principle, the trap closed on "regulatory" science. It became a church that worshiped the Aardvark man, and it bred religious wars. Ultimately, and inevitably, "articles of faith" replaced empiricism.

The strangest thing about those wars, however, has still gone unexplained. The scientists who defend the no-threshold theory—the "new toxicologists"—understand perfectly, as their testimony before OSHA reveals, that the Aardvark Principle forbids calculations. They are given to rationalizing their theory in scientific terms to clothe its bare moral bones, but the point of their language is always the same: that population thresholds cannot be calculated. The traditional toxicologists, however brilliant they may be and whatever impressive positions they may hold at the NCI or in the university, cannot seem to grasp that with a "new toxicology" which morally forbids empirical studies of dose-response effects in man and with a moral goal of cancer prevention which forbids any calculations at all, there is no scientific argument to be made. They keep repeating the classical concepts of toxicology as if that science had not been eviscerated, and they stubbornly keep adapting its tenets to carcinogenesis—above all to the idea that there *must* be a threshold dose. But when they are challenged by the "new toxicologists" to prove a negative—to set a threshold for a given group of people which will *never, ever* give any one of them cancer; to set a threshold for the total population which will *never, ever* give anyone cancer . . . they fall still.

It is from that eerie stillness that emerge such angry prophecies as that of Alexander Schmidt: "We will be chasing a 'receding zero' and some idiot in some lab will come up with something sensitive to parts per quintillion, and our policy says we will adopt it." In the late 1970s, a fulfillment of Schmidt's prophecy occurred in a far more dramatic form than he could ever have dreamed. It involves a particular court case, and if the reader wants to understand the ultimate implications of the no-threshold theory, he must know the story.

In 1973, it was found that acrylonitrile—a chemical that now stands on the IARC's list of "established" carcinogens—could migrate from plastic bottles and containers into the food and drink they contained, and the FDA instituted proceedings to ban the use of acrylonitrile in the manufacturing of such containers. The manufacturer, the Monsanto Chemical Company, reported, however, that its technology had improved during this period, and that with its new bottles no evidence of molecular migration could be detected. The company, consequently, demanded a new hearing and, with some difficulty, got one. The legal stages of the process are of no significance to us here; what we are concerned with is one of the major issues that turned out to be at stake in the ensuing proceedings: It was the law of diffusion. Both the FDA and Richard Wilson of Harvard University, who had been asked to serve as consultant to the industry, found themselves discussing that law of physics, which governs the movement of all molecules of liquids, gases, and solids as they intermingle in nature.[58]

This may not strike the layman trained in the humanities as odd, for he may know as little about physics and its law of diffusion as he does about carcinogenesis. But it is very odd indeed, and to appreciate it one must know something about the law of diffusion. Here is a simple explanation of its meaning which has a reassuringly literary context. A 1977 paper by George B. Koelle of the Department of Phamacology of the University of Pennsylvania began with this passage:

In a memorable scene from Samuel Butler's *The Way of All Flesh*, old George Pontifex drops and breaks a pint bottle of Jordan water that he has been saving for many years for his first grandson's christening. The quick-thinking butler averts an impending crisis ... by snatching up a sponge, recovering half the treasured liquid from the floor, and filtering it through a bit of blotting paper. On reflection, the same purpose would have been served by the simpler expedient of turning an adjacent tap and drawing a fresh pint from the local English water supply.

Koelle explained that the Jordan poured 6.5×10^6 tons of water into the Dead Sea every day and, when the outpouring of one day had intermingled with all the waters of the world—an amount of water estimated at 1.5×10^{18} tons—an intermingling which could be expected to occur over a huge expanse of time, "a pint of water sampled from any source will contain 3.7×10^{12} molecules of Jordan water."

He then distilled the calculation into its simplest terms:

... if a pint of water is poured into the sea and allowed to mix completely with all the water on the surface of the earth, over 5,000 molecules of the original sample will be present in any pint taken subsequently. The general conclusion to be drawn from these calculations is that nothing is completely uncontaminated by anything else.[59]

This "general conclusion," without the technical reasons, is the law of diffusion, and with that prefatory explanation, we shall return to the case of the migrating acrylonitrile molecules.

The reason for which the FDA and Richard Wilson, for Monsanto, were discussing the law of diffusion was quite simple. The FDA had declared that it didn't matter whether one could no longer measure the migrating molecules in Monsanto's new bottles—that according to diffusion theory, molecules of acrylonitrile *were* migrating and could be so legally described. Richard Wilson responded that application of the theory of diffusion indicated that the migration was so infinitely small (a few parts per billion) as to be toxicologically insignificant.[60] To this, the FDA replied, consistent with the Delaney Clause and the no-threshold theory, that no amount of a carcinogen was toxicologically insignificant.[61] Monsanto appealed the case, and it was heard by Judges David Bazelon, Spottswood Robinson, and Harold Leventhal of the District of Columbia Circuit Court. A summary of the court's findings was published by Peter Barton Hutt, former legal counsel to the FDA and later a partner in the law firm involved in the case. A number of different issues were involved, and Hutt speculated on their implications, but we restrict ourselves here exclusively to what the court had to say on the subject of diffusion theory. The legal opinion, cited in the footnotes, is long and technical, but Hutt's summary of that opinion, written for the legal profession, is an adequate substitute; it is accurate, succinct, and has the additional merit of being funny. Here is the essence of it:

... the court remanded to FDA its decision that any use of acrylonitrile, at any level and under any circumstances, could potentially result in migration. To the extent that FDA's "diffusion principle" amounted to nothing more than a restatement of the second law of thermodynamics, the court explicitly rejected it. . . .

... the court held that Congress did not intend that reasonable expectation of migration would be satisfied merely by a . . . simple recitation of the diffusion principle. In short, the court agreed with the industry contention that Congress did not enact, as part of the definition of "food additive," the second law of thermodynamics.[62]

There was no implication here that the court found limitless migration of molecules of acrylonitrile tolerable. In fact, the first bottle, which did have detectable amounts of acrylonitrile leaching into the food, was found unacceptable by the court—the improved bottle was found acceptable. As Hutt put it, "this is one of those rare cases where both sides won."[63] The layman, of course, can make no assessment either of the safety of Monsanto's bottle or of the carcinogenicity of acrylonitrile. What he can assess is the linkage of the no-threshold theory with the law of diffusion. Although the judges in this case did not say so—it was doubtless irrelevant to the legal-administrative considerations they are required to consider—they had actually come face to face with the true significance of the no-threshold/one-molecule theory: the fact that that theory, with the number of increasingly sensitive measuring instruments, inexorably skids into the dimension of reality governed by the law of diffusion—and that there is no way to arrest that skid.

It has always been clear to many scientists that this was the inevitable destination of the no-threshold theory. But it was not obvious, apparently, to those who had been educated by the "new toxicologists." This extraordinary case caused no visible stir in the world of "regulatory" science, or in the country, which was simply shocked by the danger that molecules of a carcinogen— above all, a carcinogen manufactured by the plastics industry—might be migrating into the food supply. No other aspect of the case appeared to be of interest to either the government, the press, or the public. Or, at least, if there was concern behind the scenes of "regulatory" science, it was shrouded in silence. The public, including most of the educated public, was still unaware of the problem of the "receding zero."

But in 1979, once again, the strange Luddite phenomenon appeared when Garfinkle, an eminently civilized scientist at the American Cancer Society, ventilated his fantasies and those of other cancer researchers about smashing the new instruments before they all drove themselves "crazy." We can now appreciate more fully what this cultural oddity means. It is not Luddism at all, of course. It is an expression of violent frustration by scientists who have found themselves in an obviously bizarre trap and cannot think their way out of it. In a situation like this, a layman who has no professional vested interests, no professional responsibility, and no concern for peer judgment—who, in a word, has nothing to lose—may be able to see the nature of the trap more clearly, and in this case, he can. It is, in fact, a rather simple trap, but it must be set forth in five steps:

1. If, *on moral grounds,* one expels the "empirical approach" from toxicology and one is left with an infant science that lacks both theory and human dose data;
2. If, *on moral grounds,* one establishes a goal of cancer prevention based on a logical fallacy which requires that one prove a negative—namely, the iden-

tification of a dose of a carcinogen which could not *now* or *ever* give cancer to the most susceptible individual of a population of 222,000,000;

3. If, *on moral grounds,* one tolerates that logical fallacy which leaves one with no calculation for thresholds other than the calculation that no calculation can be made, and that the only safe exposure is a zero exposure;

4. And if the instruments keep growing so much more sensitive that the zero goal keeps receding at a breathtaking rate;

5. Then one finds oneself in an extraordinary trap in which one realizes that one is driving oneself and others "crazy" and starts having fantasies about smashing instruments.

Such a fantasy, however, simply means that one has only thought oneself back from Step 5 to Step 4, but has not pursued the reasoning further. What would keep intelligent scientists from thinking themselves back to Steps 3, 2, and 1? The answer stands out clearly, particularly since I have obligingly italicized it three times. To think back one step further than Step 4, where the mischief can be blamed on instruments, the scientist would have to challenge the core of the "new toxicology"—the prevailing concept of morality, of goodness, that is held by his colleagues and by the regulatory agencies and that has now been taught to the Congress, the press, and the public and is enshrined in the law. For reasons that pertain to cultural matters outside the realm of this book, one of the last things on earth that most respectable people—scientists and nonscientists alike—will do is challenge the conventional moral beliefs of their peers, however irrational they may be. It is psychologically easier for such men, even when highly educated, to express the fantasies of primitives—knowing that they are the fantasies of primitives—than to stand up and say aloud: "What is really 'driving us crazy' is our notion of morality." And that may well be at least one of the unnamed—or unnamable—*somethings* that all these men are really fighting about.

The plain truth is that there *is* something "crazy" about the moral standards of the "new toxicology" and "regulatory" science which have culminated in the Aardvark Principle and the law of diffusion, not to mention the identical moral standards which have ruled out the very existence of non-cancer-causing substances (although in the latter case one may *not* prove a negative, and in the former case, one *must*). This mixture of morality and logical fallacy as a substitute for data is unmistakable folly, and it has caught both the scientists and their science in a trap. Nothing demonstrates it more vividly than the sight of the "new toxicology" falling like a stone into a bottomless abyss—falling into that invisible dimension of nature in which single molecules of every substance on earth endlessly intermingle, falling with *no scientific concepts at all* to break its fall because they have been *morally* disallowed. Whatever else may be said about the no-threshold/one-molecule theory, it is its suicidal inability to differentiate itself from the law of diffusion that tells us it is intellectually bankrupt.

It is on this bankrupt premise that the entire regulatory process, that cancer prevention, and that quantitative risk assessment is based. And we will now have the curious experience of discovering how scientists quantify the risks of a disease they do not understand, a disease that may be caused by "potential" carcinogens the identification of which is often uncertain, through toxicological procedures from which the acquisition of human data is barred. It will come as a surprise to no reader, at this point, that the goal of quantitative risk assessment—the ultimate goal of "regulatory" science—cannot be achieved. But the way of *not* achieving it is very imaginative, and it will be discussed in the next chapter.

Chapter 13

The Case of the Missing Risk Assessments

To the Editor: As with most of the hard sciences, there can be a substantial gap between theory and the real world even in a discipline as exact as ghost demographics.

In his Aug. 11 letter to the editor regarding an infinite sequence of ghosts, Ethan Taub is guilty of a conceptual error. At some point in his infinite series, actually fairly early on, Mr. Taub is going to reach a mass equivalent to some smallest particle that can be considered an element of mass. This will define the lower limit to the series which, therefore, can no longer be considered infinite. This removes Mr. Taub's upper limit of total mass, as it no longer is two times the mass of the largest ghost.

Even at this smallest mass, Adrian Berry is correct in his assumption of ghost overpopulation, given an infinite number of ghosts.[1]

> —Robert Bensetler, Cambridge, Mass., letter to the *New York Times*, published August 18, 1980.

Probable-Possible, my black hen,
She lays eggs in the Relative When.
She doesn't lay eggs in the Positive Now,
Because she's unable to postulate How.[2]

> —F. Winsor and M. Parry, quoted by Jeff Masten in "Epistemic Ambiguity and the Calculus of Risk: Ethyl Corporation vs. Environmental Protection Agency," *South Dakota Law Review*, 1976.

On May 16, 1980, a curious lament appeared in *Science* magazine. It was written by a disconcerted layman who had found himself in the position of having to decide on the danger posed to public health by carcinogenic substances when he was incapable of doing so. The layman's name was David L. Bazelon, he was a Senior Circuit Court Judge of the U.S. Court of Appeals for the District of Columbia Circuit in Washington, D.C., and for years he had been required to assess the disputes between scientists over the health risks of a variety of carcinogens. He wrote:

When it comes to the effect of chemical exposure on hormones, chromosomes, and the like, the experts acknowledge how little they agree and how little they know. They disagree about acceptable measurement techniques and about the reliability of raw data. They disagree even more about the inferences to be drawn from the facts. Often, they can tell us only of "the risk of risk." . . . Courts must not be expected to resolve such questions. What judge knows enough to understand issues on the frontiers of nuclear physics, toxicology, and other specialties informing health and safety regulations?[3]

Bazelon, for all his confusion, was still in a better position than most lay-men because he, at least, knew the meaning of the "risk of risk" (or the "probability of a potential" risk), and had learned over the years how extraordinarily precarious was its scientific base. The layman, generally, knew neither what this mysterious type of risk meant nor the void in which it hung. To understand the mystery of the "risk of risk," it is best to heed the advice of John Higginson, Director of the IARC, who declares: "I think we must always distinguish between a potential and a real risk." Higginson defines a "calculable real risk" as one to "which we can give numerical terms in the sense of epidemiological data," and he defines a "potential or theoretical risk" as one "based on an in vivo or in vitro model, and for which . . . we can only extrapolate within limitations."[4] To translate, a "real" risk, says Higginson, is a risk in which the calculations come from human data, and the "non-real" or potential risk—the "risk of risk" or the "probability of a potential" risk—is one in which the data are extrapolated to man from laboratory animals or bacteria.

We will now examine the difference between "real" and "non-real" risk. Here, for example, are some "real" risks of physical accidents, offered by Herman Kraybill of the NCI, in terms of the risk of death per million persons a year from various causes. The risk, according to Kraybill, is 0.1 for lightning as compared to 20,000 for motorcycling; 1.7 for earthquakes in California as compared to 12 for accidents in the home; 9 for traveling in airplanes as compared to 20–30 for traveling in automobiles, 70–90 from falls, and 400 from canoeing.[5] It is obvious that without human data on such accidents one could not calculate such risks. It is also obvious, although it would occur to no sane person to attempt it, that no such data could be acquired by a study of the source of the danger alone; a lifetime devoted exclusively to the study of lightning, canoes, or slippery bathtubs could not tell one how many people were endangered by them.

Similarly, we need human data to calculate the risk of disease; one cannot derive the statistics by studying the "germs" themselves. There are tens of thousands of bacteria, or viruses, or "germs," in the world, but if we had no human data, we would not have the faintest idea which of these germs were deadly to man, which caused mild discomfort, and which were just spending their lives in the ear of a mongoose, quietly doing whatever it is that bacteria like to do. For example, if one went out chasing germs directly, one might readily find a rod-shaped bacillus between 3 and 4 microns long, but unless one had human data, one would never know that it was the chief cause of death in a great part of the world, striking 15,000,000 annually, but that it is now *not* a significant risk to most Americans: It is *Mycobacterium tuberculosis.*[6] Again, if one simply went out hunting germs in our Western states, one might readily discover a rod-shaped bacillus linked end to end in chains, but unless one had human data, one would never know that it had killed an estimated 100,000,000 in the year 540, another 25,000,000 in the fourteenth century, and 13,000,000 more between 1896 and 1917—but that it kills almost no one today: It is *Pasteurella pestis,* the bacillus that causes the plague.[7] To find a germ and to have no idea of its effects on people is an entirely useless activity if one is concerned with risk assessment. It is the data on human disease and death that give the germ its medical significance and allow one to make the "real" calculations of its danger.

Finally, for a third example, we need human data to calculate the risks of toxic and carcinogenic substances. In the last chapter, we learned that there are a great many human data for toxic substances, accumulated throughout the history of man; and, in more modern eras, data of increasing precision on human responses to chemicals, in the form of drugs and toxic industrial substances. In toxicology all substances are tested in animals until the safest doses that can be projected are arrived at, and later, they are tested in man. As knowledge of human responses is gradually gained, the capacity to estimate toxic risk in man grows increasingly refined. We have also learned, however, that in the realm of carcinogenesis, a "new toxicology" arose which broke with the empirical tradition of toxicology on moral grounds. The result, as already reported, was a triumph for the moral and political values of the "new toxicology," but a collapse of toxicology, in the field of carcinogenesis, as a study of man. There is, thus, no human data from toxicology itself with which to calculate "real" carcinogenic risks for real human beings.

It is obvious that there is substantial ambiguity in scientists' views when they discuss the phenomenon of human data. Since such data can only be acquired either by waiting until after men have gotten cancer or by studying man in the process of being exposed to carcinogens, human data have acquired an aura of immorality. And yet without them, the scientists can learn nothing about the disease and cannot calculate risks. Thus, one finds a curious emotional tension on the subject in many scientific papers. Repeatedly, one finds concessions that the lack of human data is strangling the process of risk assessment. In 1978, David Hoel, calling for such quantitative assessment, observed: "Epidemiological studies in carcinogenesis are naturally more appropriate for assessing human risk. Unfortunately, they require long-term prior exposures to man which do not exist with relatively new compounds. For older compounds, laboratory and epidemiological studies hopefully interact in a creative manner."[8] In that same year, Lijinsky testified to OSHA on the "baffling" nature of the attempts to study human cancer through animal models: "We have no idea where man is placed in the scale of susceptibility to chemical carcinogens except in the few unfortunate cases in which we have been able to count the number of people who developed cancer after known exposure to industrial chemicals."[9] In 1979, David Rall of the NIEHS, in discussing risk assessment—"the quantitative relationship between the amounts of a carcinogen that cause cancer in laboratory animals and in the human population"—declared:

"This problem is particularly difficult to resolve. Dose-response data can be easily, if expensively, obtained in laboratory animals. Similar data are almost non-existent in human populations."[10] And in 1979, Lorenzo Tomatis, too, wrote: "A difficult and major problem is the evaluation of the possible carcinogenic effect of chemicals on humans in the absence of epidemiological studies or case reports: it is in this context that the question of the quantitative validity of the experimental results is the most difficult to answer, since there are no adequate data presently available to interpret experimental carcinogenicity results directly in terms of carcinogenic potential for humans."[11]

Thus, in 1977, 1978, and 1979, major regulatory scientists were simultaneously denouncing the morality of the empirical study of man, deploring the tragic examples of human data that did exist, "hoping" that the tragic human data would be of help, and lamenting the "unfortunate" shortage of such tragic data. Scientists who abandon empiricism in an infant science devoid of theory tend, understandably, to be confused, since it is by no means clear on what facts that infant science should build, particularly if it intends to calculate risks. Indeed, the "new toxicology," crippled by its high moral determination to study carcinogenesis in man without studying carcinogenesis in man, had done something worse than confuse itself. It could only thereafter rely on animals, and as the Office of Science and Technology Policy conceded in 1979, "Extrapolation from the animal mode to the human represents something of a leap of faith."[12]

That, then, is the background one needs in order to gain perspective on "regulatory" science which does not compute "real" risks. Like those who calculate the risk of human beings being hit by lightning, "regulatory" science, too, is trying to calculate the risk of human beings' being struck down by a carcinogen; but there is one critical difference: *"Regulatory" science seeks to make this calculation without prior knowledge of human experience.* "Regulatory" science, too, has its "germ theory." As Wilhelm Hueper originally formulated it in 1964: ". . . it should be emphasized that the dogma still holds that *there is no cancer without a carcinogen,* just as there is no infectious disease without a specific microorganism."[13] Hueper's idea is still very much alive; as the reader knows, it was presented by Rachel Carson in 1962, it was cited with respect by Eula Bingham et al. in 1976,[14] and it was recommunicated to reporter Judith Randal by Marvin Schneiderman of the NCI in 1980.[15] But the germ theory of "regulatory" science is unlike the germ theory of bacteriology in one critical respect: *"Regulatory" science seeks to identify the risks of its carcinogenic "germs" without knowledge of their effects in man.* Finally, and most important, "regulatory" science, which studies chemical carcinogens, is a branch of toxicology, and it too uses animal "tasters" to predict for man. But yet again there is a crucial difference: *"Regulatory" science does so without being able to check the animals' predictions in man.* That is why "regulatory" science cannot calculate "real" risks. The ultimate goal of "regulatory" science, its most fundamental reason for being, is the calculation of the risk of cancer and its prevention in man; but the new toxicology had made itself incapable of assessing "real" carcinogenic risk—it could only assess "probabilities of potential" risks—or, as Judge Bazelon put it, "the risk of risk." "Real" risk can be established *only* by human data.

It is inevitable that when scientists are calculating "probabilities of potential" risks in a field already riddled with controversy, a battle rages in the field of quantitative risk assessment as well. In each of the battles we have examined in this field, there is always something peculiar and unique, and this one is possibly the most peculiar and unique of all. A veritable tempest of controversy rages incessantly, but it is almost impossible to identify the conflict; everyone angrily says essentially the same thing. The reader might suppose that because these are statisticians' debates, they are too arcane for a layman to comprehend. It is certainly true that the professionals in this field speak in an alien tongue, and I will give an example of it here, just to provide the flavor of that world:[16]

If the polynomials (7) and (12) are substituted in (1) to (4) and the factors not depending on α,β omitted the logarithm of the likelihood, L, of an animal experiment (i) and/or (ii) had additive terms of the form

$$\log p(t_{id'} \times_d; \alpha,\beta) = \log\{ \sum_{r=1}^{b} r\beta_r\, t_{id}^{r-1} \} + \log\{ \sum_{s=0}^{a} \alpha_s \times_d^s\} - \{ \sum_{r=1}^{b} \beta_r t_{id}^r\} \{ \sum_{s=0}^{a} \alpha_s \times_d^s\}$$

and

$$\log P (t_{jd}, \times_d; \alpha,\beta) = \log (1 - \exp\{ -(\sum_{r=1}^{b} \beta_r t_{jd}^r) (\sum_{s=0}^{a} \alpha_s \times_d^s) \})$$

and

$$\log Q(t_{kd}, \times_d; \alpha,\beta) = (- \sum_{r=1}^{b} \beta_r t_{kd}^r) (\sum_{s=0}^{a} \alpha_s \times_d^s)$$

where x_d denotes the dth dose level ($d = 1, \ldots, D$) and the t_{id}, t_{jd} and t_{kd} denote times to tumor t, death t or sacrifice T as explained in the above tables (i) and (ii), etc., etc., etc.

This, however, is not the disadvantage it seems, because statisticians also use their mother tongue constantly. Because of the importance of this issue, on which the practical utility of regulatory science ultimately rests, it is important for us to hear the voices of the scientists themselves, and in this section we will hear a greater number of them than usual.

The first set of voices we must listen to are those of the critics of quantitative risk assessment. The group is particularly interesting, since it includes representatives of "regulatory" science who in most conflicts are rarely or never to be found on the same side. Their views are presented in the form of a chart, and they are collectively described as "foes" of the process of risk quantification, which means that they consider the process unscientific or impossible and which also means—although this is not necessarily the case—that they actually refuse to engage in it.

CRITICISM OF RISK QUANTIFICATION BY "FOES"
(All emphasis added.)

1971: Hans L. Falk, NCI: "The difficulties of such [animal] experiments are over-whelming. Even with the experiments completed, *no assurance can be obtained that extrapolation of these data from animal to man or from one type of carcinogen to another is correct.*"[17]

1973: The eight-man Ad Hoc Committee on Testing for Environmental Carcinogens formed by the NCI: "In view of the wide differences in susceptibility to potent chemical carcinogens of different species, strains, and even individuals of the same species, *the extent of hazard for man cannot possibly be judged on the basis of dosage requirements for carcinogenicity in any other species.*"[18]

1976: R. H. Adamson of the NCI expressed views which were summarized by Sydney Weinhouse of Temple University, in the course of a report on a conference on extrapolation from animal to man. Adamson, he said, "dwelt on the many difficulties of evaluating species differences.... *He felt that we are not yet ready to extrapolate animal tests to man....*"[19]

1977: Umberto Saffiotti of the NCI (in the same paper in which he described the "new toxicology"): *No existing method allows us to predict precisely and reliably the level of carcinogenic response in humans to chemicals which are known to be carcinogenic only from experimental studies....*"[20]

1976–77: John Higginson, Director of the IARC, writing with C. S. Muir of the IARC (1976): "*Unfortunately, extrapolation from animal results to man remains largely problematical and no amount of mathematical sophistication can render such extrapolation more certain or permit extrapolation of a dose response.*"[21] Higginson, addressing the Urban Environment Conference (1977), also said: "*There is . . . no rational biological method of extrapolating from animals to man, either in terms of carcinogenic activity or dose effects....*"[22]

1977: The Pesticide Information Review and Evaluation Committee (NAS): "*The existence of large species differences in responses to chemical carcinogens is a fundamental uncertainty in the extrapolation of carcinogenicity data from laboratory animals to humans.... Unfortunately, any such assessment must rely to a large degree on subjective judgment about the magnitude of certain important numerical quantities because of the lack of specific knowledge about the nature of the dose-response curves for the tested animal species beyond the fixed experimental range* (i.e., within the range normally encountered in the environment). *Furthermore, assumptions must also be made about the unknown effects of potential species differences with respect to physiological, metabolic, and/or carcinogenic processes involved. Clearly this assessment process is not entirely objective.* Since the committee was charged with answering questions based on scientific facts, it considers it inappropriate to adopt such a judgmental procedure."[23]

1978: William Lijinsky, NCI: "*There is no way at present in which the risk can be quantified even imprecisely and no way in which the target organ or target cell in man can be predicted from the animal data.*" Also: "*I do not extrapolate risk.... I do not think it is possible to extrapolate risk at all at the moment,* except to say that any compound which induces tumors in experimental animals in a well-conducted test poses a risk to man if man is exposed to it. That is all you can say. *You cannot measure the risk.*"[24]

1978: Arthur Upton, Director of NCI: "The problem [of public "skepticism" and "resistance"] is particularly complicated when the data come solely from animal studies, *since they cannot provide conclusive or quantitative indications of the risks for human beings.*"[25]

1978: Samuel Epstein, University of Illinois (oral testimony): *"However, when you try to extrapolate and develop risk estimates from one species to another, this is a frightfully difficult game. In other words, going from the mouse to the rat is a frightfully difficult game. When you go from the mouse to the human . . . it becomes a terribly difficult matter to say I am taking dose-response data from animals to go to humans."* [26]

1978: Richard Griesemer, NCI: *"And where [the general principles of toxicology] do not apply, in my opinion, is when one tries to extrapolate to lower dose levels. In my opinion, as I have said, I do not believe that can be done, even for the animal. . . . But my belief then is that we should not attempt to extrapolate dose data . . . from animals to man; I do not think it is possible."* [27]

1978: Harold Stewart of NIH: *"In view of the enormous and largely unpredictable differences in susceptibility of different species and different individuals to most carcinogens,* and the fact that the significant factor is the totality of lifetime exposure (which can never be estimated accurately) to a large number and variety of carcinogenic agents and cocarcinogens, some known and many unknown, *little if any useful practical purpose can be served by attempts to assess the hazard for man of a particular environmental carcinogen on the basis of quantitative data obtained in laboratory animals. Emphasis on this point not only is misguided but is misleading and may be harmful."* [28]

1979: Curtis C. Harris of the NCI, writing with Umberto Saffiotti: *"No reliable procedure has yet been found for a direct quantitative extrapolation of the results of carcinogenic studies from one or more experimental species to another species (particularly the human). . . .* While much attention has been given to this problem in the last decade, *no methodology has been established to provide an adequate and reliable quantitative assessment of human risk simply on the basis of experimental animal findings."* [29]

1980: OSHA's policy document: "*. . .* OSHA draws the following conclusions. . . . (#8) *The uncertainties involved in extrapolating from high-dose animal experiments to predict low-dose risks to humans are far too large at present to justify using the estimates as the basis for quantitative risk/benefit analysis."* [30]

After hearing this chorus of objections, one is curious to learn what the risk quantifiers do which, according to this extraordinary spectrum of critics, cannot be done. The literature on the subject gives us a vast amount of information. It can be reduced, however, to five major points:

1. The scientists tell us that they make two sets of extrapolations.

As Charles Brown of NCI explained it: "The procedure for estimating this risk consists of basically two steps: 1) extrapolation of the experimental results at high dose levels to low dose levels for the animal species and 2) extrapolation of the estimated low dose results for animals to low dose levels for man." [31] In more detail, they do the following: To be "prudent" or "conservative" they choose the species, strain, or sex that is most sensitive to the carcinogen, [32] and graph the dose-response points to produce a curve that sweeps from the highest recorded dose at which the animals get cancer down to the lowest. They then consider everything else they believe or know about the biological effects of the tested carcinogen and introduce "species-conversion" factors (or "scaling" factors) and plunge into yet another extrapolation—this time to man.

Here, from the Interagency Regulatory Liaison Group, representing CPSC, FDA, EPA, and OSHA, is a detailed description of the second extrapolation process. It must be read in toto to understand why so many scientists simply say that it cannot be done. This second extrapolation is the aspect of the process about which the layman hears virtually nothing, and there is good reason for it, for this is the part of the process where the scientists take a flying leap into the unknown, and even possibly the unknowable. Here is how one "converts" the data from mouse to man—and again a warning is in order: It is *ineffably* boring, which means one should read it with strict attention, because the less "regulatory" science knows, the more impressive its prose:

Animal to Human Correlations
. . . Several species conversion factors should be considered in estimating risk levels for humans from data obtained in another species. *Many variables affect such species conversion factors, such as body surface, body weight, metabolic pathways, nutritional conditions, genetic variability, bacterial flora, as well as tissue distribution, retention and fate of the chemical, etc. In evaluating exposures to the general population, one should consider all ages, transplacental exposures, concurrent disease conditions and special susceptibility states.*

Other conversion factors should also be considered when observations were obtained from exposure conditions in test species that are markedly different from those in the population (e.g., different routes or modes of exposures, vehicles, modifying factors, variations in age, sex, perinatal exposures, disease states, single versus multiple exposures, etc.). The limits of uncertainty should be stated whenever possible.

Different carcinogens tested under comparative experimental conditions show a wide range of response; if extreme cases are included, the range of variation is more than one million fold. . . . On the other side of the correlation, the human response to carcinogens as well as to many other chemicals and drugs may also show great quantitative variations among individuals. Studies on the metabolic activation and chemical interaction of carcinogens in human tissues *in vitro* have shown inter-individual quantitative variations of about one hundred fold in relatively small population samples. . . .

A number of variables is relevant to the correlation of animal and human conditions. Some problems inherent in the use of animals must be kept in mind when one is using animal studies in the process of estimating the quantitative carcinogenic potential of a substance for humans. A concise statement of some of these factors is contained in the document "Drinking Water and Health," prepared by the Safe Drinking Water Committee, Advisory Center on Toxicology, National Research Council, National Academy of Sciences. *Factors discussed in this document include the rate of chemical absorption, distribution within the body, metabolic differences among exposed animals, the effect of bacteria in the intestinal tract, rates of excretion and reabsorption, differences in molecular receptor sites for the carcinogen, environmental and genetic differences and the number of exposed animals and susceptible cells.*

Metabolism and pharmacokinetics account for major differences in sensitivity to chemical carcinogens between species. In principle, this information could be used in estimating the relative sensitivity of humans compared to experimental animals. In practice, detailed metabolic pathways in humans are not known for many carcinogens and, moreover, the marked variation in metabolism and sensitivity among individuals of different ages, states of health, and other biological conditions require more information on the heterogeneity of human metabolic and pharmacokinetic responses than is usually available. It is hoped that future research will clarify these important correlations in much greater depth.[33] [Emphasis added]

Now, if the reader has had the courage to read this passage, he will have observed that it is nothing but a list; in fact, a list in which some factors have been mentioned more than once. It is a list of every category of information that anyone can conceive to be even remotely relevant to the countless variables in carcinogenesis. All this information is then presumably added to the mouse data by a risk assessor *even as he acknowledges that much or most of it is not available.* He then quantifies it (somehow) and the results of his endeavors are then extrapolated to the human race. Depending on the numbers of animals tested according, respectively, to David Rall of NIEHS and Herman Kraybill of NCI, one mouse may stand for about one million or two million human beings.[34]

This is actually enough to explain why risk assessment is in trouble—but for the layman who fears that there are profundities here which he might somehow be missing, here is a criticism of this process by a scientist, Richard Bates of the NIEHS and FDA, who testified on the subject to OSHA. It is particularly interesting because Bates is saying candidly that toxicologists do not know how to perform the miracle described above—and precisely because he is conceding ignorance, his language is clear, to the point, and intelligible:

The science of toxicology will have made immense strides when it becomes able to use the results of animal experiments to precisely predict the toxic risk of a chemical to any individual or group of humans. Unfortunately we are not there yet. The problem is terribly complicated. Absorption, rate of metabolism, and excretion of environmental chemicals may differ among species. Species may differ in the types of relative ratios of metabolites formed from any chemical and in the sensitivity of various organ systems to the toxic effects of these chemicals. Individuals within each of these species may show wide differences among these parameters depending upon their genetics and on modifying environmental circumstances. Susceptibility in the same individual may fluctuate during the phases of various biological cycles. Although we know these variables exist, we do not have enough knowledge to weigh each of the factors in any particular case and come up with a reliable multiplier for converting results of animal experiments to risk for any individual human under his or her conditions of life. . . .[35]

Most interesting of all, both passages actually offer the identical information—but the first is claiming to describe a reasonable extrapolation process while granting that it is full of unknowns, and the second simply says it can't be done, that there are too many unknowns. The difference between the two statements is reducible to one factor: candor. And so much for the two sets of extrapolations from animal to man, which constitute Point 1.

2. The scientists tell us about the assumptions of their competing theories of extrapolating from high to low doses in animal tests.

There are about five dominant theories. According to Henry Pitot of the University of Wisconsin, "the most commonly employed models" are called the one-hit (linear) model, the multi-hit (K-hit) model, the multi-stage model, the extreme value model, and the log-probit model.[36] These names are offered for the record; there is no need to explain them in detail save to say that they constitute different mathematical methods of calculating the degree of probability that an exposed population will get cancer, and of how fast the percentage will increase as the dose level increases. The layman must know, however, that all these theories must make certain assumptions.[37] According to an NAS study cited by OSHA, "All theories have one concept in common: that there is no known uniform threshold dose below which any carcinogenic response is impossible for all individuals at risk."[38] Some theories, in addition, assume some of the other "arguments" against thresholds, e.g., the irreversibility of the induction of cancer, and the additive-cumulative pileup of a carcinogenic "background."[39] These theories may or may not imply the mutation theory of cancer—but all *assume* the non-arguable, non-demonstrable no-threshold theory, which is to say the one-molecule theory—and *that* is to say that the major premise of "quantitative" risk assessment is a *moral* concept.

3. The scientists tell us about the shortage of human dose data for chemical carcinogenesis.

There is almost no human dose-response data to compare with the animal dose-response data, which is how toxicological dose-setting is customarily done. In 1975, a committee of the NAS including Matthew Meselson—often called the Meselson committee—examined the only existing examples, six in all, of reported carcinogens where some dose data for both animals and humans were available: benzidine, chlornaphazine, cigarette smoking, aflatoxin, vinyl chloride, and DES. Meselson et al. were attempting to find a way to predict cancer incidence in human beings from animals. They postulated that if one used the data from the most sensitive animal responses and based one's calculations on dose per body weight, one could predict lifetime incidence in human beings. Of the six sets of calculations, three of the predictions were strikingly exaggerated: Animals dosed with aflatoxin predicted ten times higher cancer incidence than was reported to occur in humans; baby female mice given a single dose of DES predicted fifty times higher cancer incidence than occurred in human DES daughters; and animals exposed to vinyl chloride predicted 500 times higher cancer incidence than occurred in human beings. On the other hand, said the Meselson committee, the predictions for benzidine, chlornaphazine and cigarette smoking seemed "approximately correct." Meselson et al. concluded from this:

Thus, as a working hypothesis, in the absence of countervailing evidence for the specific agent in question, it appears reasonable to assume that the lifetime cancer incidence induced by chronic exposure in man can be approximated by the lifetime incidence induced by similar exposure in laboratory animals at the same total dose per body weight.[40] [Emphasis added]

The layman may blame himself for failing to see how the Meselson committee reached its "working hypothesis" on the basis of three out of six examples. He need not do so. Those who choose to believe this "working hypothesis" do so; those who do not so choose reject it. Depending on who is writing about this little study, it is said to demonstrate that animal and human sensitivity are quite similar;[41] it is said to be unreliable because the data are few and inaccurate and include poorly controlled studies;[42] and it is said that it is hard to judge because there are great "complexities" and "uncertainties" in making such comparisons.[43] It is entirely apparent, however, that the fact that a

1975 examination of six animal-man comparisons has been earnestly discussed
and argued about for years signifies a virtual absence of the necessary carcinogenic dose data required for human risk assessment.

(For the reader with a long memory, these are the six chemicals that, according to David Rall, speaking at the Urban Environment Conference of
1977, showed "a definite relationship between the amount that caused cancer
in laboratory animals and the amount that caused cancer in man." This was,
for Rall, yet another "piece of compelling evidence that animals do predict for
man."[44] As previously noted, Rall is readily overwhelmed. By 1979, however,
he had recovered enough to grant—as reported a few pages back—that the
shortage of human dose data was a serious problem.)

4. The scientists tell us that the nuclear explosions of World War II are the
primary sources of human dose data.

The aristocrats of the extrapolation world are the statisticians who use radiation data and who usually accept the mutation theory. Their aristocracy rests
on the fact that radioactivity is universally said to be both mutagenic and carcinogenic,[45] and that there are a great many data on the Japanese who survived
the nuclear explosions over Hiroshima and Nagasaki.[46] The "linear" theory of
these statisticians is said, at the time of writing, to have the greatest prestige in
the world of "regulatory" science. The linear theory postulates that there is a
constant increase of probability that greater doses of radiation or of carcinogens will produce a greater probability of cancer, *and that at no dose, however
minute, is some degree of risk absent, i.e., the one-molecule theory of cancer.* As
the Interagency Regulatory Liaison Group (CPSC, FDA, EPA, OSHA) put it
in 1979:

The linear nonthreshold dose-response model is most commonly used at the present
time. Of the various models, it appears to have the soundest scientific basis and is less
likely to understate risk than other plausible models. It has, for many of the same reasons, a long history of use in protection against radiation.[47]

Similarly, Thomas Maugh, writing in *Science*, reported that the argument
from scientists he had most often heard for the one-hit or one-molecule linear
dose-response curve came from radiation data, e.g., "the induction of leukemia
by ionizing radiation from nuclear explosions."[48] (It is that one-hit or one-molecule risk assessment theory derived from radiation data that OSHA built, by
means of a footnote, into its hypothetical description of the birth of a malignant cell.[49])

Since the risks implied in such concepts as the one-hit or one-molecule
linear theory have little or no meaning to laymen, one must be grateful to Gary
Flamm for spelling out their implications in terms that are related to reality. In
1976, when he was Assistant Director of Cancer Cause and Prevention at the
NCI, he wrote:

Nevertheless—whether it can be proven or not—proponents of certain biostatistical
and theoretical tenets claim that less than one-tenth of one puff from one cigarette in an

entire lifetime can be responsible for the development of lung cancer. Indeed, application of the one-hit biomathematical hypothesis asserts that if a hundred million people were each to inhale that one-tenth of one puff in their lifetime, one individual from that population would acquire lung cancer as a consequence of the exposure. Whether this is true or not we may never know for certain, but it does point out the extraordinary nature of the problem presented by chemical carcinogens when viewed from the perspective of the one-hit hypothesis.[50]

In 1980, Herman Kraybill of the NCI recapitulated Flamm's analysis and added: "In the real world, one may never know whether such mathematical assumptions are indeed valid."[51]

5. The scientists tell us that there is incessant internal warfare in their field.

Every dominant school of statistical thought is the object of intense criticism, and so are the less dominant theories. The latter are the theories that have proposed "practical thresholds." One was the Mantel-Bryan theory, which attempted to establish a "virtually safe dose," a dose that would only give cancer to one in 100 million people; the second was the Druckrey theory, which calculated a dose that would not cause a cancer until the life span was over. These theories were highly criticized as insufficiently "conservative." As Marvin Schneiderman explained in 1978, speaking on the "virtually safe dose" theory: "Practically nothing happened to that procedure because people were not trying to extrapolate. The Delaney Clause said: 'No Safe Dose.'"[52] Readers who are particularly interested in the evaluations of and controversies over the different theories will find some references in the notes.[53]

Of the many controversies in the field, only two aspects of one controversy will be mentioned here. Both are challenges of the dominant (and simplest) theory used by the government—the linear no-threshold/one-molecule theory. Jerome Cornfield, a prominent statistician with an ironic cast of mind, observes of this preferred governmental theory:

The low dose linearity assumption . . . is justified in two different ways. (i) Because carcinogenesis is poorly understood, "conservative" assumptions are required to protect the public safety. (ii) Carcinogenesis is well enough understood to make the low dose linearity assumption a scientifically reasonable one.[54]

Cornfield is both funny and right. It does not seem to occur to the theorists of "regulatory" science that these two commonplace arguments (Chapter 3) for the use of the linear no-threshold/one-molecule theory—the argument from ignorance and the argument from knowledge—logically cancel each other out.

The second criticism pertains to the widespread use of radiation data to rationalize the linear no-threshold theory and to the assumption that the dose-response curve of ionizing radiation can be compared to that of chemical carcinogenesis. There is strong opposition to this comparison by such scientists as Herman Kraybill of the NCI and Edward E. Pochin of the National Radiological Protection Board in Britain. According to both scientists, radiation, which is ruled by physical and predictive laws, may score a direct hit on a target cell, while a chemical carcinogen must go through a series of biochemical stages and is metabolized. The equation of dose-response curves in these two realms, say these scientists, is unwarranted.[55] John Cairns makes a similar point about mutagenicity when caused by radiation as opposed to chemicals.[56]

And that terminates the description of the five aspects of risk assessment that arouse such disapproval in so many scientists with different viewpoints. It is clear from this information that the state of the art leaves much to be desired, and many, if not all, of the major figures in the field concede this. Why then do they do it? The essential answer is that there is a desperate need for it and because in some areas, the law requires it. The alternatives to risk assessment are grim. They are: (1) to frighten every American to death by failing to differentiate major from minor and negligible risks or "risks of risks" and (2) to ban every "suspected" carcinogen in sight or to impose protective technological burdens on the American industrial system that could only be afforded by the richest corporations and would wipe out the smaller and marginal companies. The clear need for risk assessment, however, does not compensate for the deficiencies of the process, and the criticisms of the state of the art by its practitioners and supporters are vastly more revealing than their pragmatic defenses, for they tell us in no uncertain terms that the differences between the views of the "friends" and "foes" of risk assessment are negligible. Here is a chart which will convey some criticisms by supporters and practitioners of risk assessment. Except for the fact that all quoted here are, or appear to be, advocates of this process, one can barely differentiate them from the opposition.

CRITICISM OF RISK QUANTIFICATION BY "FRIENDS"
(All emphasis added.)

1974: Daniel G. Greathouse, EPA: *"The state-of-the-art for extrapolation of animal experimental results to man does not nearly satisfy the requirements of a regulatory agency which is charged with the responsibility of setting standards for environmental contaminants. Due to severe inadequacies of present methods, it would seem that a major effort should be undertaken to develop better techniques as soon as possible."*[57]

1974: Leo Friedman, FDA: *"I do not know, of course, whether these calculated probabilities of tumour occurrence are real risks, either for men or for mice. I doubt whether it will ever be possible to ascertain this with the desired certainty."*[58]

1974: World Health Organization: *". . . the toxicologist must assess the risks associated with different levels of exposure. Proposed approaches for such evaluation [have been made]. All the proposals suffer from lack of sufficient data to establish their validity and/or from arbitrary assumptions that lead to unrealistic estimates."*[59]

1975: David Hoel et al., NCI: *"The extrapolation of the results from laboratory animal studies to man is probably the most difficult and least understood aspect of the total extrapolation problem. The difficulty arises in attempting to predict quantitatively from animal data to man."*[60]

1976: R. L. Dixon, NIEHS: "There appears to be worldwide agreement concerning the fact that extrapolating laboratory animal toxicity data to man remains a major unsolved problem in toxicology. . . . *The lack of understanding in this area makes the building of mathematical models for extrapolation unreliable at the present time. . . . The usefulness of animal studies in predicting irreversible toxicity such as mutagenesis and carcinogenesis and the extrapolation of exposure levels to estimate human risk are especially difficult problems. . . ."*[61]

1976: L. Tomatis of the IARC recognized that *"it is impossible to extrapolate from experimental data to man,"* but rejected that impossibility as an argument for inaction: "There is really no justification to wait for the proof that a chemical causes cancer in man before measures to avoid exposure are taken."[62]

1978: Norton Nelson, Institute of Environmental Medicine, NYU: "The forms of the curves relating cancer response to dose have received much attention and *one can find in the literature examples to support almost any postulated pattern. . . . The practical application of such models at this time is very restricted, since the basic data are rarely available."*[63]

1978: Marvin A. Schneiderman and Charles C. Brown of NCI: *"The current mathematical models that relate exposure to attributable risk are, at best, extremely crude tools."*[64]

1978: Gary Flamm, NCI, condemned what he perceived as a trend toward *"blind or mindless application of mathematical models."*[65]

1978: IARC, Vol. 17 (now embarked on the policy of recommending "pragmatic" prediction while declaring it unscientific): "Data that provide 'sufficient evidence' of carcinogenicity in test animals may therefore be used in an approximate quantitative evaluation of the human risk at some exposure level, provided that the chemical concerned and the physiological, pharmacological and toxicological differences between the test animals and humans are taken into account. *However, no acceptable methods are currently available for quantifying the possible errors in such a procedure, whether it is used to generalize between species or to extrapolate from high to low doses."*[66]

1978: Thomas Maugh of *Science* reported that "results from animal carcinogenesis studies must usually be obtained with high doses of carcinogens in relatively small numbers of animals. Inferences from these results must then be extrapolated to predict what will happen when large numbers of humans are exposed to much smaller amounts. *David B. Clayson of the Eppley Cancer Institute reflects the views of many investigators when he argues that this extrapolation is now so inexact as to be valueless in the predictive sense."*[67] In a 1979 paper, D. B. Clayson also said: *"Let us not pretend at this time that efforts at dose-response extrapolation for carcinogens is any better than pragmatic level-setting."*[68]

1979: Philip Handler, President of the NAS: *"What is painful to recognize is that there is no chemical carcinogen for which the medium dose, much less the very low dose end of the dose-response curve has been reliably examined."*[69] "For pollutants, as for food additives and other materials, it is time we acquired credible dose-response curves, down to more realistic low doses. *Surely, we should not quarrel indefinitely about the probable shape of a curve that no one has seen."*[70]

1979: Henry Pitot, University of Wisconsin: "None of [the more commonly employed mathematical models] can prove or disprove the existence of a threshold of response *and none can be verified on the basis of biological argument. . . . Thus the reader must note that the quantitative determination of human risk based on bioassay data is an extremely difficult process which, at the present time, rests on extremely flimsy scientific grounds."*[71]

1979: Office of Science and Technology Policy: "There are two major obstacles to the quantification of human carcinogenic potency or activity. *First, potentially carcinogenic chemicals act through a variety of mechanisms and with dose-response curves that may not necessarily be parallel. Thus, direct comparison among chemicals over wide dose ranges is difficult. . . . Second, most available data relating dose and tumor incidence are derived from animal experiments. Extrapolation from the animal mode to humans represents something of a leap of faith."[72]*

1980: Gio Batta Gori, NCI: "These statistical exercises would be justified if the animal data used in their elaboration reflected generalized human risk conditions, but they do not; nor is there a basis for deciding in which direction their results should be adjusted.... The conclusion is that past and current testing practices do not unequivocally identify human carcinogens *and do not yield quantitative information about conditions of human risk, and that biometric sophistication does not overcome the limitations of these data."[73]*

1980: Joseph Rodricks, FDA, while defending the FDA's choice of the linear no-threshold model as a prudent measure: *"We do not pretend that this form of extrapolation predicts actual risk. There is at present no way to ascertain whether any such extrapolation predicts actual risk...."[74]*

When one reads these statements by real or apparent friends of risk assessment, one is reminded of the old saw: "With such friends, who needs enemies?" Despite their conviction that risk assessment is a social, political, economic, and legal necessity, it is entirely clear that many of the advocates and practitioners of this art are as aware as the critics that the quantitative calculation of risk for man from animal data is either an impossible procedure or a procedure so riddled with subjective estimates and guesswork that it amounts to being impossible. The most candid members of the group say without qualification that they haven't the faintest idea whether the risk estimates they produce have a relationship with reality.

The ultimate evidence of failure, however, is nonverbal. It is the actual spectacle of the clashing numbers that emerge from the various statistical theories. To illustrate precisely that point, OSHA, in its 1980 policy document, presented a group of risk assessments on two carcinogens as performed by representatives of various schools of statistical thought. The two tables follow, and they tell us vividly that quantitative risk assessment depends entirely on what any given statistician chooses to assume.[75]

As OSHA reported in presenting these two tables, carefully citing its sources:

For comparative purposes, all the risk estimates presented in the record are converted here to lifetime risks at an exposure level of 1 ppm [one part per million]. Seventeen such estimates are presented in the first table ... [vinyl chloride] ... these estimates span an enormous range; even if the "threshold" postulated by Claus is discounted, estimates of risk at 1 ppm range from 10^{-8} to less than 10^{-2}—more than a *million-fold variation....*

The second table ... [saccharin] ... *shows a range of variation of more than five million-fold in estimates of human risk, although all the estimates were derived from the same set of experimental data on rats....*

For each of these two chemicals, estimates of possible risks at exposure levels which are currently permitted vary over ranges of 1–10 million or even more.[76] [Emphasis added]

OSHA's calculations may be entirely accurate, but even were that agency exaggerating the problem, this is quite sufficient to inform the reader that a science of carcinogenic risk quantification is nonexistent. It also makes it clear

ESTIMATES OF LIFETIME RISK FROM EXPOSURE TO 1 PPM VINYL CHLORIDE

Source	Estimate of lifetime risks	Method of extrapolation	Source of data
Wilson (S. 53)	25×10^{-4}	Linear	Epidemiological unspecified source
Wilson (Exh 251 B)	5×10^{-4}	Linear	Epidemiological and Maltoni (unspecified)
Crump and Guess (1977), exhibit to Hoel statement	2×10^{-4}	Multi-stage, upper confidence limit	Maltoni (1975)
Guess et al. (1977), exhibit to Hoel statement	2×10^{-4}	Multi-stage, upper confidence limit	Maltoni (1975)
	1×10^{-4}	Mantel-Bryan, upper confidence limit.	Maltoni (1975)
Claus (S 38)	0	Assumption of threshold at 10^4 molecules per cell, calculated to occur at exposure level of 4.9 ppm.	
Nisbet (post-hearing comment, p. 8)	4×10^{-3} to 1×10^{-2}	Linear	Maltoni (1977), Table 12.
Gehring et al. (1978), p. 590	10^{-8}	Log-probit, extrapolation of observed dose-response curve.	Gehring et al. (1978), dose-response curve based on unmetabolized VC
Hooper and Ames (1979)	Greater than 10^{-3} (rats)	Linear	Maltoni (1977), liver angiosarcomas.
	Greater than 10^{-2} (rats)	Linear	Maltoni (1977), mammary tumors.
	10^{-1} to 10^{-2} (humans)	Linear, extrapolated to humans.	Maltoni (1977)
Food Safety Council (1978)	10^{-2}	Multi-hit	Maltoni (1975).
Do	2×10^{-2}	Multi-hit, upper confidence limit.	Maltoni (1975).
Do	5×10^{-3}	Multi-stage	Maltoni (1975).
Do	8×10^{-3}	Multi-stage, upper confidence limit.	Maltoni (1975).
NAS (1977), exhibit to Hoel and Rall statements, p. 794	2×10^{-2a}	Multi-stage, upper confidence limit.	Maltoni (1975).

* Assuming breathing rate of 15 m³/day to convert from oral intake to inhalation exposure.

ESTIMATED HUMAN RISKS FROM SACCHARIN INGESTION OF 0.12g/DAY (FROM NAS 1978, pp. 3–72)

	Lifetime cases/million exposed	Cases per 50 million/yr
Rat dose adjusted to human dose by surface area rule:		
Method of high- to low-dose extrapolation:		
Single-hit model (Hoel, 1977)	1,200	840
Multi-stage model (with quadratic term (Hoel, 1977)	5	3.5
Multi-hit model (Scientific Committee of the Food Safety Council, 1978)	.001	0.0007
Mantel-Bryan probit model (Brown, 1978) .	450	315
Rat dose adjusted to human dose by mg/kg/day equivalence:		
Method of high- to low-dose extrapolation:		
Single-hit model (Saccharin and Its Salts, 1977)	210	147
Multi-hit model (Scientific Committee of the Food Safety Council, 1978)	.001	0.0007
Mantel-Bryan probit model (Brown, 1978) .	21	14.7
Rat dose adjusted to human dose by mg/kg/lifetime equivalence:		
Method of high- to low-dose extrapolation:		
Single-hit model (Brown, 1977)	5,200	3.640
Multi-hit model (Scientific Committee of the Food Safety Council, 1978)	.001	0.0007
Mantel-Bryan probit model (Brown, 1978) .	4,200	2,940

why scientists, customarily on different sides of the controversies that rend the field of chemical carcinogenesis, so often stand arm in arm on this particular issue. It finally explains why, in the last analysis, so many statisticians in the field concede most or all of the criticisms of the opposing camp, and why they are in a state of perpetual warfare.

Their conflicts are among the most intense in "regulatory" science. They are bad enough when only animal carcinogens are at stake, but when risk calculations are applied to known human carcinogens, the antagonism between the conflicting schools of statistical thought reaches its peak. The nation has witnessed this for years in the realm of radiation from nuclear power plants; the professional conflicts are fully explained in the BEIR report of 1980 in which the NAS participants split into three irreconcilable positions.[77] As in all such public wrangling, the underlying problem is the science of carcinogenesis itself. Statistics is an established science, but, assuming competence and honesty, it is only as good as the data with which it has to work. The data, it need hardly be said by now, are paralyzingly bad.

At the head of Chapter 9, in which we started our aerial voyage over the realm of "regulatory" science in order to assess it in terms of its own goals, and at the head of this chapter, 13, in which we conclude that voyage, there stand three quotations. Each is amusing and none was published in a spirit of frivolity.

The first quotation was the tale of *Herringus rufus,* satirizing the dream of finding a test animal in which all substances would be carcinogenic; as we have seen, that satire contained a harsh core of truth: In "regulatory" science, despite caveats and self-contradictions, there *are* no non-cancer-causing substances.

The second quotation, at the head of this chapter, is a rhyme about a hen which I discovered in a legal paper discussing various key court decisions on carcinogenic and toxic pollution. The rhyme tells us that the hen "doesn't lay eggs in the Positive Now, because she's unable to postulate How." This is a simple explanation of the most fundamental reason for which the identification of noncarcinogens and carcinogens, the prediction from animals, the identification of threshold or safe doses, and quantitative risk assessment are afloat in such oceanic ignorance. Until the mechanisms of cancer are known, until the hen can postulate How—and above all *Why,* although it does not rhyme—there will be trouble in all of these realms.

The third quotation, also at the head of this chapter, is a portion of a published controversy among playful statisticians about the mass of the population of ghosts in the universe. That passage, too, carries a serious message. There is far less difference than one might suppose between the spectacle of statisticians applying their skills to carcinogens and the spectacle of statisticians applying their skills to imaginary entities. In fact, it is a delicate question whether the gigantic double extrapolation from one mouse to one or two million men is more or less of a flight from reality than the calculation of the mass of an infinity of ghosts.

Taken together, the three quotations are sophisticated metaphors that capture, in an uncanny way, cerain aspects of the intelligent madness of "regulatory" science. And with this act of translation, we have completed the last stage of our aerial survey of the realm of "regulatory" science—the science that uses animal tests to predict and prevent cancer in man.

We can now sum up our discoveries in one sentence: "Regulatory" science can do *none* of the things it claims to do.

Chapter 14

Paradigm Found

... at the time that the issue of environmental cancer was deposited on the layman's agenda, in 1975, one year before the passage of the Toxic Substances Control Act, the apocalyptic typhoon was still blowing through the brains of the press and the "elite." The sources quoted in this chapter tell us clearly that the apocalypse provided the intellectual framework for the interpretation of the deluge of "suspected" carcinogens descending upon us and that, once again, it was scientists both in and out of government who were legitimizing the interpretation. The essential message of that entire educational process had been economically summed up by Ralph Nader in his re-baptism of cancer as "corporate cancer."

—Chapter 2, this book

The scientific method depends on two essential things—a thesis or idea, and a means of testing that idea. . . .[1]

—Leon Rosenberg, geneticist, Yale University, testimony before the U.S. Senate, 1981

After voyaging through the American empire of "regulatory" science, we discover that we know several things with certainty:

We know, because the *toxicologists* have demonstrated it repeatedly, that cancers can be induced in *animals* by means of chemicals, both industrial and natural.

We know, because the *epidemiologists* have demonstrated it—according to the IARC in at least eighteen cases—that cancers can be induced in *man* by means of chemicals, both industrial and natural.

We know, because the scientists in *pharmaceutical* and *toxicity* research have demonstrated it, that toxic substances which cause a biological effect in an animal *might* cause it in man; that the same broad biological principle is applicable to cancer, which is a form of toxicity; and that as of 1980, there were ten examples of this phenomenon.

On the subject of "regulatory" science, however, we are certain about quite different matters. We know that as of 1980, "regulatory" science could not achieve any of its goals. And we know that for the full decade that followed

372

Saffiotti's Ad Hoc Committee's announcement to the Surgeon General, in 1970, that prevention of the "mass" of environmental cancer by means of animal-man extrapolation was "within reach," that it was an official illusion. Of all the concessions of the impotence of "regulatory" science that I have encountered in the literature, the most incisive brief analyses come from four sources: John Higginson, Founding Director of the IARC; Umberto Saffiotti of the NCI; David Clayson of the Eppley Institute for Research on Cancer; and from the IARC itself. They are exceptionally lucid charges or avowals of the scientific void that has existed behind the regulatory facade:

- In 1977, seven years after cancer "prevention" was launched, John Higginson of the IARC flatly dismissed the predictive value of animal tests. He declared: "There is no rational biological method of extrapolating from animals to man either in terms of carcinogenic activity or dose effects. . . ."
- In 1977, Umberto Saffiotti himself avowed, at a cancer conference, that animal tests and short-term tests had never been validated as predictors for man. He issued a call for extensive correlational studies of the results of animal tests, short-term tests, and epidemiological research *"in order for us to assess their validity and predictive value."* After a discussion of the new short-term tests utilizing human cells, he ended his paper by expressing his hope of what such tests might one day achieve: *". . . we hope to contribute to replacing fiction with facts in the extrapolation from 'animals to man.' "*[2] (Emphasis added)
- In 1978, eight years after cancer "prevention" was launched, David B. Clayson of the Eppley Institute analyzed what he described as "the core mythology of chemical carcinogenesis":

The present viewpoint is that a compound demonstrated to be carcinogenic to animals must be assumed carcinogenic in man. This assumption contains three implicit ideas:
1. That extrapolation from rodents to man is always possible and represents the best, the safest assumption;
2. That extrapolation from high doses, represented by the maximum tolerated dose administered to animals, to the low doses to which man is environmentally exposed, is valid;
3. That our present definition of a carcinogen as something which significantly increases the incidence of malignancies in a population is adequate.

Combine these basic precepts with one further assumption;
4. That there is no threshold dose for a carcinogen;

and we have a series of poorly validated statements which represent the core mythology of chemical carcinogenesis. Mythology concerns belief and faith, and should be foreign to the scientific method.[3]

- In 1979 and 1980, one decade after cancer "prevention" was launched, the IARC in its scientific, non-"pragmatic" mode, stated on the subject of animal-man extrapolation:

. . . at the present time a correlation between carcinogenicity in animals and possible human risk cannot be made on a scientific basis. . . . [Chapter 11]

And on the attempt to quantify risk:

... no acceptable methods are currently available for quantifying the possible errors in such a procedure, whether it is used to generalize between species or to extrapolate from high to low doses. [Chapter 13]

In all cases, although different ideas were stressed, these scientific sources were making or conceding identical points: (1) that it has never been shown scientifically that animal tests can be used to establish qualitative or quantitative carcinogenic risk in man, and (2) that "regulatory" science is operating on the basis of "irrationality," "mythology," and "fiction."

It should not be supposed, however, that these were the only scientists who were aware that "regulatory" science was unprepared for the claims it has made and for the political power it wields. In 1977, Lorenzo Tomatis of the IARC indicated that many and conceivably most scientists in the field of chemical carcinogenesis were not confident of their own procedures. Tomatis reported gloomily on what he perceived to be the general attitude of his colleagues. He observed that "prevailing" opinion was warning scientists "not to extrapolate unduly" from animals to man. In addition, he said that it was "clear" that there was "no general consensus" on the use of animal experiments for prediction of carcinogenic risk in man, and he reported a "diffuse discontent and distrust" of animal tests.[4] There is reason to accept Tomatis' observations on the prevalence of such attitudes. Here are a few examples of "discontent and distrust" which have surfaced in scientifically sophisticated places.

- In 1977, Philip Abelson, the editor of *Science*, devoted an astonishing editorial to what he considered the inadequacy of the scientific base underlying the banning of TRIS, the fire retardant used to fireproof children's pajamas. The editorial was astonishing because, although Abelson supported the ban on moral, i.e., "prudent," grounds, in the course of this analysis he tacitly challenged most of the crucial tenets of "regulatory" science: The regulators, he said, had not offered "proof" that TRIS gave humans cancer; they had relied on inconsistent animal tests; there was no way to know which animals predicted for man; and almost no attempt had been made to study the actual effects of TRIS in human beings.[5] Ostensibly, Abelson was criticizing only one ban; in fact, he was challenging the very assumptions of "regulatory" science—a fact that Robert Harris of the Environmental Defense Fund was quick to perceive. In a responding letter, Harris recited the relevant positions of the NCI, the regulatory agencies, and the courts on these matters.[6]
- In 1978, Ian Munro, a prominent Canadian scientist, speaking at a cancer conference, reviewed the major problems in animal testing and in the interpretation of data. His analysis was so critical that he felt obliged to conclude: "I don't want to leave you with the impression that animal studies are useless, but there are a great many hurdles.... [g]uidelines have been formulated for conducting studies; now guidelines are needed for interpretation...."[7]
- In 1979, Irving Selikoff, Director of the Environmental Sciences Laboratory at Mt. Sinai and a major figure in the epidemiological demonstration of the

carcinogenicity of asbestos, was reported in the *New York Times* (by William Burrows, a former *Times* reporter and assistant professor at the Columbia School of Journalism) as supporting animal tests in principle, but simultaneously as having little faith in them in practice: "There is no reason to believe that what causes cancer in animals will do it in human beings. . . . If you can't extrapolate from a mouse to a rat, how can you do it from a mouse to a man?"[8] Selikoff had already expressed his "insecurity" about animal-man extrapolation in a private letter published, in 1977, by Thomas Corbett.[9]

- In 1980, Richard Peto of Oxford expressed doubts about the public health benefits of much regulation based on animal testing. He observed that "for most toxic chemicals we have both qualitative and vast quantitative uncertainty about the health benefits of restriction. . . . The results of animal tests simply are not an uncomplicated key to human hazard identification." And he followed that with his criticism of high-dose testing in animals with organs "subject to spontaneous cancers": ". . . it is not surprising that so many chemicals at such doses can cause cancer in animals."[10]

- In 1980, Gio Batta Gori, Deputy Director, Division of Cancer Cause and Prevention of the NCI, also warned that a methodology calculated by basic researchers to produce high crops of cancer in strains of animals bred to be cancer-prone—a procedure which was entirely appropriate for the study of cancer mechanisms—had been transferred, despite warnings, to the animal tests where the findings were presumed to be applicable to human conditions. The result, said Gori, was an "introduction of deliberate bias" into animal testing procedures, from the experimental design to the interpretation—a "bias" that consistently produced exaggerated numbers of carcinogens and exaggerated risks.[11]

In addition, there have been criticisms of the irrationality of criteria which appear to be infinitely elastic. One was made by Jerome Cornfield, who has already been identified as a statistician of great prominence, given to mockery. He was first quoted as pointing out the absurd self-contradiction in "regulatory" science which simultaneously defends the no-threshold theory on the grounds of its scientific ignorance *and* on the grounds of its scientific knowledge. Cornfield had a wider target, however—the revered "conservative" approach to risk assessment. After describing "conservative" choices in the selection of one statistical theory over another and of one "species conversion factor" over another, Cornfield asked rhetorically where "conservatism" stopped, and said that the problem was that it could stop nowhere:

Similarly, why stop at using the most sensitive species, the most sensitive strain within species, and the more sensitive sex? *Why not use only the most sensitive individual animals thus obtaining 100% incidence at each dose level?* Or why stop at the upper 95 or 99% confidence limits when an uncountable infinity of more "conservative" choices remain? In practice, of course, people do stop, but then it becomes difficult to understand what they mean by being conservative.[12] [Emphasis added]

It was so "difficult to understand" that Cornfield never did explain it or what to do about it, except to attempt to assassinate it with humor; he then merely went on to discuss other matters that fascinate the statisticians of "regulatory" science, leaving "conservatism" expiring on the ground.

Again, Gary Flamm of the NCI made a similar observation, in two different realms. In the course of a conference on both carcinogens and mutagens, he offered a description of what is usually called the "evolving" protocols in biological tests. There is "constant modification of protocol," he said. "If you don't like the test you keep modifying the protocol until you get the results you want." The problem was compounded, he said, by the rapidly increasing sensitivity of the new instruments. "Analytical chemists," he said, "can find small amounts of dangerous substances in *everything.*" And, he said, "at those levels, you find whatever you want to find."[13]

It is clear from these statements by major figures in the field, as well as from the material in preceding chapters, that there has been a substantial amount of what Tomatis called "diffuse discontent and distrust" of the entire approach to "cancer prevention" as well as of every aspect of animal testing and animal-man extrapolation. There has been something less diffuse as well: an active distrust of data produced by indefinable, nonobjective, and elastic criteria, and a bitter skepticism in the face of the *Herringus rufus* mentality which permeates a field where one is *only* rewarded—where one is only published, and where one is only hailed as a savior of public health—by finding something to "suspect."

Such criticisms, however, as the layman well knows, are scarcely the only views on the state of animal-man extrapolation. In fact, if he gleans his knowledge of "regulatory" science from the daily or weekly press, which relies almost exclusively on government handouts or on handouts from scientists eager to publicize their real or imagined discoveries before the lengthy process of peer review and replication, he may never have heard any such criticisms at all. What the layman has generally heard is an insistent defense of animal-man extrapolations by official spokesmen for government science and the view, explicit or implicit, that only "industry" challenges the animal test. What is normally not conveyed in popular presentations of such defenses is the intellectual context in which they are embedded. The defending scientists, invariably, are critics too, and, at least in papers intended for the eyes of scientists, they always grant the inadequacy, uncertainties, and unsolved problems in the field. But they are particularly interested in one argument—that one must *act* in the absence of knowledge. Some of these defenders are scientists like Steven Jellinek of the EPA, who, as we have seen, has candidly renounced the title of "scientist" and now calls himself a "regulator," distinguishing between the two roles by explaining that the regulator, on moral grounds, acts quickly in the face of ignorance, whether or not he is wrong. And it is worth remembering (Chapter 8) that in his original statement, he put quotation marks around the word "wrong" as if to imply that such concepts as "right" and "wrong"—translation: confirmation and falsification—were scientific myths. Other defenders call themselves scientists, but hold precisely the same views and similarly refuse to be deterred from action by the limits on their knowledge. Some, in fact, go further than using quotation marks to hint at their resentment of scientific disciplines, but express their antagonism overtly. The prototype of such a defender is Tomatis. In 1977, he used the Cousin Winifred fallacy, implying that five cases of matching animal-man carcinogens demonstrate that animals predict for man, and declared that far more might have been accomplished "if the sacred monster of absolute objectivity had not so often played the role of the devil's advocate."[14] Prefacing "objectivity" with the word "absolute," of course, is a bit of rhetorical camouflage; not even physicists speak in terms of absolutes. But certainly objectivity is the ideal of science, and to describe it as a "sacred monster" that plays the role of "devil's advocate" is a repudiation of that ideal. It is rare that one hears so clear an expression by a scientist of hostility to objectivity.

The usual rationalization for the "regulatory" scientist who defends action without knowledge is moral. Customarily, he uses the words "prudent" and "conservative" to communicate that moral idea. These moral concepts, so attractive to the layman who wants to feel that "science" is keeping him safe, are, in fact, used as a substitute for data and a camouflage for arbitrary procedures in the field of animal testing and animal-man extrapolation where no aspect of the work is free of brutal or subtle assaults on reason. There is not one branch of "regulatory" science where we have not stumbled across crude logical fallacies invoked as justification for the methodology and epistemology of the field, fallacies which, in some respects, are sufficiently absurd to make a certain type of critic, e.g., Cornfield and *Lancet*'s Anonymous, attack with scathing humor. This actually should not surprise the reader. He, no more than the scientists, can eat his facts, logic, and science, and have them too. To act in advance of knowledge and to justify it as scientific requires the rejection of all three. That is the context of the professional defenders that is never given to the layman.

We must now ask a question of considerable importance. To what degree do the critics or defenders within the world of "regulatory" science represent the consensus? If, in 1977, as Tomatis reported, the prevailing view was one of "diffuse discontent and distrust" of the animal tests, then one may conclude that the scientists who were claiming, in 1970, that cancer prevention was "within reach" did not represent the consensus. If, in 1978, as OSHA reported, its views often represented the consensus, then within one year there had been a miraculous alteration in that consensus—assuming that Tomatis was correct to start with. It is a little difficult to trust OSHA's estimates on this particular matter, however, because the agency crudely packed its hearings with the heads of government research and regulatory agencies who are professional "spokesmen" for and defenders of "regulatory" science and who never inform the public of scientific conflicts within and among their own institutions. I have found only one other report on the consensus, and it, too, came from a professional defender, namely David Rall, Director of the NIEHS. It was published in 1979—and it was as joyous as Tomatis' report had been pessimistic. Rall, also brandishing the Cousin Winifred fallacy and citing a few animal-man matches, declared:

These examples convince me that, *like it or not,* we are in the midst of a revolution in the way that the scientific community identifies carcinogens. In 1775, Sir Percival Pott used epidemiological tools to identify carcinogens. In the 1960s and '70s such scientists as Nelson, Van Duuren, Maltoni and many others used laboratory animal studies to identify chemicals later shown to be carcinogens in man. We have learned a lot in 200 years.

The scientific community—and the downstream lawyers and politicians—are beginning to believe that the results of animal tests can and do predict carcinogenicity in man.[15] [Emphasis added]

In one significant respect, Rall's joy confirmed Tomatis' gloom: If, in 1979, the "scientific community" was just *"beginning* to believe" that animal tests predicted "carcinogenicity in man," that meant that "the scientific community" had *not* believed it before—and that it had not believed it for a full nine years after Saffiotti's Ad Hoc Committee told the Surgeon General that cancer could be prevented. But the statement was interesting in yet another way—Rall himself had backslid, so to speak. If one reads Rall's statement with care, one sees that nowhere did he himself state that "the results of animal tests can and do predict carcinogenicity in man"; he only implied it, and said that "the scientific community" and the "downstream lawyers and politicians" are "beginning to believe" that that is the case. The switch, conscious or unconscious, from "I imply" to "They are beginning to believe" is all Rall could allow himself— along with a subtle threat addressed to no one: "like it or not." In 1976 and 1977, Rall could—and did—inform CBS and the Urban Environment Conference that rodents predicted well for man, and that the evidence for it was "compelling." But by 1979, Rall could not say it to an audience of scientists— and did not say it anywhere else in his paper—not while scientists at the NCI were struggling to find a way to establish correlations that might one day validate animal tests.

There is yet another reason to believe that "the scientific community" is substantially distrustful of animal tests. And that is the mysterious internecine controversy over the state of the art. There isn't any. That, too, turns out to be one of the deceptive controversies that seem to abound in "regulatory" science. No person and no official, whatever he may say to Congress, the press, or the public to camouflage the sad story, ever acclaims the state of the art *in a paper intended for scientists* or denies that it is riddled with vast uncertainty, subjective beliefs, and value judgments. What is more, even those addicted to the Cousin Winifred fallacy cannot deny it. The field, as we have seen, is almost explosive with conflict; there are clashing theories, there are clashing speculations, there are clashing versions of the data, there are clashing criteria for analysis of the data, there are clashing interpretations of the data, and there are clashing approaches to solutions. And that means to scientists exactly what it means to laymen: It means *ignorance.*

By the end of the decade, there were only shades of difference between those who thought that the state of the art was riddled with "uncertainties" and subjective values, that it was bad, unspeakably bad, "mythology," or "fiction." There were shades of difference in the degree of hope that the problems would be solved and that the "revolution" was approaching when it might finally be learned how to predict human cancer from animals. Even the truest believers in animal-man extrapolation were permanently impaled on the concept "sus-

pected." The most ardent international defender of the mouse, Lorenzo Tomatis, could defend it only in lugubrious terms. The most ardent American
propagandist for animal prediction, David Rall, was reduced to a fallacy, a
hint, and a threat.

What then gives rise to so strong an impression that there is a quarrel over
the state of the art between "defenders" and "critics" of "regulatory" science?
Once again, the answer seems to be: These are really quarrels about something
else—something those in conflict prefer not to name. There *is* a bitter battle in
that world, a battle that exists, for the most part, on a subterranean level and
permeates every one of the specific and interlocking controversies in the field.
While one cannot put people into rigid boxes, there do tend to be opposing
factions that show up on one side or the other of the controversies—and the
sides are usually determined by whether the position favors or diminishes the
stringency of regulatory action. There is every reason to believe that the root of
this profound and nameless war is politics—specifically, warring attitudes toward the American industrial system.

Unquestionably, since the phenomenon of carcinogenicity itself is not in
doubt, the principal battlefront is the no-threshold theory, which, as the reader
has seen, encompasses or is related to all the most important and embittered
sub-battles in the field. The no-threshold theory, which is "not amenable to scientific solution" because it is a *moral* theory, is the rock on which the cancer
prevention program rests. It is also a devastating and undiscriminating attack
on industrial production and growth. The various scientific "arguments" for
and against that unprovable theory are, by now, familiar to the reader of this
book, but here are three characteristic examples of *political* assessments of the
threshold problem:

- Lewis Thomas of the Sloan-Kettering Institute described the conflict over
  thresholds as "a kind of ideological argument, like an expression of belief,"
  and observed that "the dilemma" it created for "our regulatory agencies"
  and "almost all our major industries," above all the chemical industry, was
  "almost unsolvable"; he suspected that it would inhibit industrial innovation,
  for "if there isn't any such thing as a threshold, then there is no such thing as
  a safe compound."[16]
- In her Presidential Address to the American Association for Cancer Research, Elizabeth Miller, who, with her husband, James, made the major discovery in basic science that carcinogens were often the products of metabolic
  activation, discussed the needs of "highly industrialized societies." She endorsed the philosophy of benefit/risk, and declared: "The single fact that *at
  very high doses* a chemical causes some cancers in experimental animals or
  some mutations may not be an adequate reason for removing it from uses
  beneficial to the public."[17] (Emphasis added)
- An entirely opposing position on the same problem was offered by Samuel
  Epstein. He testified to OSHA that only the "Delaney zero tolerance concept" was scientifically acceptable, i.e., that no safe doses exist; that all who
  criticized the concept of zero exposure for all carcinogens "are clearly identi-

fied with protection of industrial interest"; and that they were characterized by "their lack of expertise and national recognition in the field of chemical carcinogenesis."[18]

These three positions on the no-threshold theory—the theory that states that even one molecule of a carcinogen might, somehow, somewhere, give some citizen cancer and that *morality* requires that the theory be accepted—may seem to be the standard argument about *regulation* to which every layman is by now accustomed. That is what is so misleading about a public "education," which consists almost solely of arguments about regulation. These three positions, *when seen in the context of the entire set of controversies that rage behind the scenes,* constitute a great deal more than an argument about regulation. Taken together, they constitute a formal indictment of the pathology of a pseudoscience which has only one practical result: the irrational undermining of industrial civilization in the name of ignorance and an "ideological belief." And, taken together, they also tell one why ignorance and "ideology" have triumphed.

One act of imagination—admittedly a powerful imagination—is required to understand this. One must imagine that these three scientists made these statements at the same time, in the same place, looking into each other's eyes as they spoke, and that Jerome Cornfield was present as a moderator. Within a millisecond, Samuel Epstein would become mute. His "position" consists simply of an insult: He says that anyone who takes a position on the one-molecule theory other than his own is a corrupt industrial hack and an unknown ignoramus in chemical carcinogenesis. If he uttered such words to Lewis Thomas and Elizabeth Miller, even Ralph Nader would blanch. Epstein would have to scramble for the only fall-back position that exists. It is the first contradiction one stumbles across in this book: It consists of *simultaneously* arguing that the no-threshold theory must be accepted because of one's profound ignorance, while rapidly offering "scientific" arguments for it. At that point, Jerome Cornfield would fall off his chair in laughter and would cease to be a functioning moderator. And Lewis Thomas and Elizabeth Miller would turn aside and continue the conversation together. It would consist only of this:

Elizabeth Miller: I advocate a benefit-risk approach.
Lewis Thomas: How?

And Elizabeth Miller would become mute, because there is no answer: One cannot calculate benefits and risks if one cannot calculate risks. And as Thomas and Miller sat in silence, contemplating the "ideological belief" that is threatening the industrial civilization they both cherish, that they cherish *not* because they are "bought" ignoramuses but because they are civilized . . . and while Jerome Cornfield laughed uncontrollably because that is his personal response to illogic . . . Samuel Epstein, smiling grimly, would walk out of the room. The scientist who came equipped with an insult and an "ideological belief" would win the argument by default. There is only one answer to that position. It is a question: "How *dare* you presume to attack industrial civilization on the basis of an undemonstrable belief?" And not one person in that room would say it . . . on the record.

Do scientists say it off the record? Many do. But precisely because it is off the record, I cannot document it. We will rely only on the statements that are on the record. This book, and this chapter, is full of them. They indicate that there are many scientists who think—who, according to Lorenzo Tomatis and David Rall, have *always* thought—that cancer "prevention" by means of animal-man extrapolation alone is an unscientific procedure which is not compensated for by its unverifiable benefits. In terms of the industrialized *world,* the skeptics and antagonists may constitute the majority. Certainly, there is no country save ours in which this pseudoscience has been embraced with such civic passion: It is not irrelevant that the apocalypse and its hatred of industrial civilization is an *American* cultural pathology. Almost every controversy in this book is a covert quarrel between scientists who are committed to a blind assault on industrial civilization and scientists who are committed to a blind attempt to defend it. The critical word, here, is *blind.* From the very first step of the process of animal-man extrapolation to the last, the process is sightless, for the hypothesis can never be tested by the science that produces it. For the last seven chapters, we have been looking at bitter and sightless quarrels. Those seven chapters can be summarized as follows—and I quote a passage from the first chapter of this book:

> There are scientists in existence today who are deeply distrustful of, or even hostile to, science as well as technology. They are guided by the belief that Western industrial civilization will, if not arrested and reversed, destroy life on earth.
> The idea of the apocalypse has greater power over such scientists than any attachment to the disciplines of science, and in the name of that idea they are entirely willing to reject those disciplines. Even when they are fully aware that the known data do not support that idea, they do not tolerate rational limits on their knowledge. They aggressively convert not-knowing into a kind of knowing, a pseudo-knowing that Myrdal in one instance called "quasi-learnedness" and Nagel in another describes as an "unenlightening" substitute for "genuine knowledge." The spurious knowledge is always used to rationalize their expectation of catastrophe. The characteristics of the spurious knowledge—vacant abstractions, arbitrary extrapolations, conclusions based on inadequate or nonexistent data; the rejection of logic; and the incorporation of moral attitudes into the very core of their "scientific" thought—are so standardized that they constitute a pseudo-"paradigm." It will be called, henceforth, the "apocalyptic paradigm."
> From the moment that this "apocalyptic paradigm" appeared, "traditional" scientists have been clashing with the apocalyptic scientists—actually clashing over the "apocalyptic paradigm" itself.

We have been finding traces of that mock-scientific paradigm everywhere that we have wandered in this journey. But we can now identify its precise location. *It is embedded in the official cancer prevention program.* The "apocalyptic paradigm" is a description of the mental processes of "regulatory" science when it bases itself solely on animal data, and it accounts most fully for the battle it generates. In fact, the entire conceptual structure of "cancer prevention" by animal testing alone, which has been crudely superimposed on the authentic work being done in basic research, *is* the "apocalyptic paradigm." It serves the same function in the world of cancer that it served in the "environmental" movement: Without being able to generate applicable data, without predictive power for man and in a void of scientific ignorance, it declares frightful catastrophe to be imminent, so imminent that there is no time for facts, logic, or the slow, serious development of an authentic predictive science—*if* such a predictive science is possible.

Once adopted, the "apocalyptic paradigm" acquires a pathological life of its own. It only leaves time for hysteria, for "suspicion," for scientific "fiction" and "mythology," for demagogy—and for the use of political force to impose moral and political substitutes for science on industry, on the nation—*and most crucial of all on the academic opposition.* It is an overt assault on innovation, production, and the marketplace; it takes little insight to discover this, since apocalyptic scientists are entirely candid about it. What is covert, and far more fundamental, is its antagonism to the marketplace of ideas. It is a profoundly anti-intellectual phenomenon, which, in the realm of science, is to say that it is profoundly antiscientific.

Characteristically, within the confines of its ruling models, the practice of science is one vast argumentative muddle. Debate and controversy are its hallmarks. It has taken a whole book to transmit only a sampling of the major academic controversies over animal-man extrapolation to the reader. Clearly, the controversies exist—the literature is full of them. Equally clearly, they have not reached the press and the public. In a situation where press and public have received pronouncements from government "spokesmen" for science, the press and public have not heard the voice of science in its normal combative state, but have heard the voice of "official" science—which is to say, the voice of state-imposed science. When the voice of state-imposed science is heard in *any* land, the voice of the scientific opposition—an opposition which is unusually dependent on the state for its very survival—invariably falls still, and is not heard in the public forum. And it has not been heard in our public forum, the press. The ultimate effect of the "apocalyptic paradigm" has been to inaugurate a mitigated Lysenkoism in the United States of America—mitigated because those scientists who dissent are free to publish in arcane journals rarely or never seen by the press or the public. They are simply not free to argue with the state where the citizens and the press will hear them. The only opposition to the state that we, as laymen, have heard is the voice of industrial science, which is, necessarily, discredited, since fortunes ride on the outcome of industrial experiments. Thus the public has not only been kept from encountering scientific dissent, but has been educated to believe that scientific "truths" imposed by the state are morally and intellectually proper, while dissent from the state in this realm is evidence of intellectual and moral corruption. Whatever other roles it may play, this particular result of the "apocalyptic paradigm" is culturally deadly.

It is important to understand that on the core issue—the biological relationship between animal and man—the government has not overtly misinformed us. In fact, official spokesmen are customarily uncommunicative and use a kind of baby talk to Congress, the press, and the public. All we have usually been told, as laymen, is that what causes cancer in an animal *might* cause it in man, that it is a "potential" cause of cancer. It must be repeated over and over again that *this is true*. It is also true that Man Is Mortal, that Life Is a Unity, that the Planet Is Finite. But such truths are vacancies waiting to be tenanted by science. We have been devastatingly misinformed, but principally by *omission*. What has not been described to the American press or public is the enormity of the vacancy.

Because of a decade of incessant reiteration of a true, but vacant, abstraction and the failure to explain this vacancy, we end with the very situation with which we began—with a baffled public, and a heavily ideologized pseudo-science, in which even the scientists today are often unable to differentiate between a scientific and a political position. Now, however, we know something we did not know when we began: that this cultural horror is embedded in "regulatory" science itself.

And we also know *why* this cultural horror has occurred. At the head of this chapter stand two quotations. The first is a simple reminder, from Chapter 2, of the historical source of this corruption: the apocalyptic movement which swept through the educated classes of this country. The second is a brief but useful definition of science that comes from Leon Rosenberg, a geneticist at Yale University, who said: "The scientific method depends on two essential things—a thesis or idea, and a means of testing that idea." As the IARC explains when it is not being "pragmatic," and as the National Toxicology Program explains when it is being "pioneering," toxicology is just barely capable of testing the thesis that a specific substance is causing cancer in a given animal strain. And as "regulatory" science itself explains over and over again, without human data—i.e., without the science of epidemiology—it is incapable of testing the thesis that the contradictory and incoherent animal data can predict cancer in man. Cancer prevention, by means of animal data alone, is a *science that is still unborn*. It is a moral illusion created by the "apocalyptic paradigm," by a "new toxicology" which has removed empiricism from toxicology, by the invention of ersatz forms of prediction, and by laws and regulations which have declared the ruthless disciplines of science dispensable. Behind that moral illusion is a void—and a huge group of silent scientists who, apparently, if Lorenzo Tomatis of the IARC is to be believed, never thought that one could extrapolate from animal to man to begin with.

When, as a result of ideological frenzy, a bureaucratic "science" is launched on so mythic and irrational a base, makes pledges to the nation that it cannot honor, is largely regulating a giant industrial civilization by means of arbitrary edict, and clings to power by failing to acknowledge the magnitude of its ignorance to the nation, one can be certain that it will be increasingly racked by internal crises and that some of its most far-seeing members will be aware of its peril. That is, in fact, the case. In the last chapter of this book, I will describe two of these crises which point to the eventual dissolution of the "apocalyptic paradigm." In the process, I will also answer the last question that is yet unanswered: Why are some "regulatory" scientists afraid of laymen?

PART

V

THE PLANET APPEARS

Chapter 15

Paradigm in Crisis

If nobody knows but somebody must pretend to know, then the governing of an institution becomes theatrical. It follows that the people employed by the institution should become preoccupied with the appearance of things, with the way things look and sound rather than with whatever it is they supposedly mean.[1]

—Lewis Lapham, editor, *Harper's*, 1978

How extraordinary!... The richest, longest-lived, best protected, most resourceful civilization, with the highest degree of insight into its own technology, is on its way to becoming the most frightened.[2]

—Aaron Wildavsky, political scientist,
University of California,
New York Times, 1979

"Carcinogenicity in Mice of Mutagenic Compounds from a Tryptophan Pyrolyzate"[3]

—Norio Matsukura, Takashi Kawachi,
Kazuhide Morino, Hiroko Ohgaki,
Takashi Sugimura, and Shozo Takayama, *Science*, 1981

If one erects a building on the base of a profound error in one's calculations, that building will ultimately crack, buckle, and collapse. The same thing is true for a conceptual-bureaucratic structure, although the process is far slower—for it can be maintained by faith, politics, and vested interests for decades. The legal-conceptual house built by "regulatory" science is now showing signs of cracking and buckling in the form of two crises. The first is a practical crisis—the paralysis of the cancer prevention system—the sole definition of which is a chase after the carcinogenic *industrial* "germs" that infest the continent so that they may be regulated or banned. The second is a philosophical crisis—the emergence of data on *nature's* carcinogenicity which challenges the very apocalyptic premises of "regulatory" science.

THE PRACTICAL CRISIS

To understand the practical crisis one must take a step backward and look at the order of the discoveries of the science of chemical carcinogenesis. The order was illogical, and that illogic was explained, illuminatingly, in 1974, by Isaac Berenblum:

The order in which discoveries are made is not always predetermined by logical reasoning. Instead of basic principles being discovered first and modifying or ancillary factors later on, the opposite is usually the case. For instance, in the field of carcinogenesis, it would have been more helpful if the sequence of discoveries had been: (a) of naturally-occurring carcinogens; (b) of artificially-produced carcinogens which find their way in man's environment; and (c) of "exotic" carcinogens (ranging from simple models to complex structures) synthesized in the laboratory. In fact, the historical sequence has been (b)-(c)-(a).

Yet the historical approach cannot be altogether ignored. The very choice of experiments usually rests on working hypotheses derived from accumulated knowledge, and the interpretation of results cannot be divorced from the historical evolution of the subject.[4]

Berenblum confined himself in 1974 simply to saying that "it would have been more helpful" if the progression of discoveries had been logical; but five years later, John Higginson flatly described the illogical progression as a cause of trouble: ". . . the whole problem of carcinogenesis in the environment has been bemuddled by the fact that we started off first by identifying occupational hazards and this has been the thinking ever since. . . ."[5] The "whole problem of carcinogenesis" comes not from the random order of the original discoveries, which is inevitable in both life and science, but from the fact that long after the logical relationship among the discoveries was obvious, the mental processes of the field were set in stone, and worse yet, in legal stone, and could not change.

One can understand the problem best if one imagines what would have occurred had the cancer researchers, fortuitously, made their discoveries in the ideal order. They would have started, of course, with (a) nature—with a vision of a radioactive-carcinogenic-mutagenic planet that had burst out of a vast nuclear explosion in the heart of the sun. They would then after a period—decades, surely—of intense study of nature itself have progressed to the examination of (b), how, by the simple fact of manipulating the substances and molecules of the planet, man had added to the natural dimension of radioactivity, carcinogenicity, and mutagenicity. While one cannot project exactly what they would have done then, (c) one can be sure that those cancer researchers would have spent a long time pondering on the relationship of cancer in human beings to the earth and to the universe itself. And one can be absolutely positive, as I observed in Chapter 3, that they would not have gone rushing off in a body to the Surgeon General and to Congress to opine "authoritatively" that even one molecule of spinach might cause cancer, and to demand a law to allow them to go chasing after every carcinogenic "germ" on the continent.

The sequence of discoveries, however, was not made in logical order. Given the sequence that actually occurred, it was entirely reasonable that scientists, on learning that man-made substances were carcinogens, should seek to investigate the whole realm of synthetic chemicals. But it was entirely *unreasonable,* as we have already seen, to accept the conclusion that nature was a

Garden of Eden from which cancer had been largely banned by "evolution," that carcinogens were, for the most part, "sinister" artifacts of the science, technology, and industry of post–World War II, and that one could prevent most cancer by identifying and catching the carcinogenic industrial "germs," then regulating or, ideally, banning them. It would have been vastly more sensible to realize that everything man makes ultimately emerges from the earth itself and, in effect, to work backward—to investigate industry all the way back to the beginning of the Industrial Revolution and, since all paths would have inevitably led to nature, to study nature as well. As we know, some scientists did exactly that—which is, of course, how we know that the discoveries were not made in logical order.

The official embrace of the industrial "germ" theory of cancer cannot be explained by the logic of science, for it was an outright rejection of logic. It can only be explained by the *zeitgeist* of the period.

While it is not the function of this book to present a portrait of that period, the reader must, even for an instant, be reminded once again of that strange cultural outbreak which so profoundly shaped the history of chemical carcinogenesis and froze it in its present form. Two illustrations of events that took place during that era—one from the humanist world, one from the scientific— will suffice. It was an era when apocalyptic humanists engaged in symbolic ecological rites. Paul Seabury, a prominent political scientist, has described how two Episcopal cathedrals, St. John the Divine in New York and Grace Cathedral in San Francisco, became centers for the activities of the chic apocalyptic neoprimitives. Seabury describes one scene in Grace Cathedral as follows:

In 1971, during one nature ceremony in the cathedral, a decidedly ecumenical audience watched reverently as the poet Allen Ginsberg, wearing a deer mask, joined others similarly garbed to ordain Senators Alan Cranston and John Tunney as godfathers of animals (Cranston of the Tule elk and Tunney of the California brown bear). The cathedral dean was dimly seen through marijuana smoke, wrestling atop the high altar to remove a cameraman, while movie projectors simultaneously cast images of buffalo herds and other endangered species on the walls and ceilings to the accompaniment of rock music.[6]

And it was an era in which apocalyptic scientists called for the cessation of all technological development. In 1976, Ross Hume Hall, a biochemist, was discussing the hazards of chemical food additives in an NBC documentary and declared:

You've come up against the limitation of the science. And of course, as we are learning, many of the tests are not carried out competently. But that isn't what I'm concerned about. I'm concerned about the limitation of science itself, which is much more serious. The analytical techniques are very good and very sophisticated, yes. But that's analytical science, and what we're looking at is the other side of the coin. What are the biological effects? And they cannot say what the biological effects are going to be. . . you could put every biologist in the United States to work on this problem, and there still would be no solution. *The solution is to stop. To stop the technology. To hold it in abeyance until such time as we have an idea what is going on.*[7] (Emphasis added)

If one had to select two incidents from this era to put into a time capsule, these would be reasonably representative of the trends which had the greatest impact on "regulatory" science. It is that apocalyptic frenzy led and legitimized by scientists in the field of ecology—i.e., the "environmental movement"— which encouraged susceptible scientists in the realm of "environmental cancer" to make the irrational leap to the conclusion that cancer was primarily the product of modern science and technology and that the key to cancer prevention was to chase industrial "germs" across the length and breadth of the continent.

One may understand the cultural context of that irrational leap, but there is no question that it was at that moment that a fatal error was made. The goal of identifying and chasing the modern "germs" was frozen into the law and immediately triggered a nonstop series of crises because no one actually knew how to do it. One of the documents of the period immediately preceding the passage of the TSCA gives one a glimpse of the pressure coming from the NCI (where the artificial laboratory curiosities were being studied) on other cancer researchers who had no idea whether the animal tests used by basic research to study mechanisms could be applied directly to man. Only one year before the passage of the Toxic Substances Control Act—in 1975—Frank J. Rauscher, Director of the National Cancer Program, wrote a letter to Philippe Shubik, Berenblum's collaborator for years, and then the Director of the Eppley Institute for Research in Cancer. It said in part:

As you know, current program activities supported largely by the National Cancer Institute have and will continue to produce data on the subject of environmental carcinogenesis and on chemical carcinogenesis in particular.... The pressures upon us and regulatory agencies are mounting due largely to program efforts of this Institute and therefore we must be certain that we are prepared to respond to the inevitable questions and to render responsible advice. *To this end, I ask that you as chairman of the National Cancer Advisory Board Subcommittee on Environmental Carcinogenesis undertake, with your members and consultants and whatever additional consultants you find necessary, to determine whether the current state of the art will permit the development of definitive and interpretive guidelines, the latter to include such issues as dosage, risk-benefit, etc.*[8] [Emphasis added]

The reader may suppose that, for some unexplained reason, the Director of the National Cancer program was unusually ignorant of the vast progress made by the science of toxicology. It is an unlikely supposition. That same year, during a hearing on the act, David Rall, Director of the NIEHS, testified to a Senator that legislation was necessary in order to prevent damage by hazardous chemicals including carcinogens, compared the law to "preventive medicine," endorsed it strongly, then dropped in this remark:

I should point out, however, that there are very serious lacks in the science base in toxicology, not only in the United States, but in the world. This science simply is not far enough advanced in relation to the problems which it confronts.[9]

Rall also informed the Senator that "we are concerned about the lack of the number of competent toxicologists," and put the total number in the U.S. at

900, "a very small cadre to look at the very large numbers of compounds." The Senator was deeply appreciative; he expressed his interest in the training of toxicologists and said to Rall: "I want to thank you for giving us that added insight into the problems of regulation."[10] It did not occur to the Senator to ask Rall one simple question: If the science of toxicology was "simply not far enough advanced in relation to the problems which it confronts," and if there were only 900 toxicologists as of 1975, how did Rall expect to "prevent" anything significant in a society with 50,000 or 60,000 industrial compounds to be tested, not to mention the new compounds that appeared every year? He might also have asked if there were actually enough laboratories, enough mice, and enough money to do the job. No questions of that kind were asked. The Senator apparently needed no such information; he was collecting "insights." His deepest "insight" had doubtless come from the days when he was parading around St. Grace Cathedral, surrounded by worshipers in deer masks, participating in a totemic ceremony that had pronounced him godfather of the bear. It was John Tunney, and he was now an eminent participant in a new totemic ceremony—the chase after the post–World War II industrial "germs" that were allegedly causing most of the cancer in man.

No sooner had the ink dried on the paper on which the law was printed than "regulatory" science found itself stricken by a practical as well as by an intellectual paralysis. The questions that Senator Tunney had failed to ask David Rall turned out to be very important questions indeed. And just as it had been known that no scientific means of using animal tests to predict cancer in man had yet been established—as it still has not—so in every case the practical problems were known in advance and each of the crises had been both predictable and predicted.

The first predictable crisis was the problem posed by the sheer numbers of the "suspected" carcinogens that had been reported. There were many thousands of them in the literature already, and the industrial system had scarcely been investigated—a fact known and published by Thomas Maugh and Jean Marx of Science in their book, Seeds of Destruction, one year before the passage of TSCA.[11] Those thousands, however, came as a shock to the Chemical Selection Subgroup of the Clearinghouse on Environmental Carcinogens of the NIH at its first meeting in 1976, the year of the passage of TSCA. Gary Flamm, a member of the group, declared: "There are more carcinogens than we ever really thought existed and they are more ubiquitous and they are more difficult to control than we ever thought."[12] Two years later, John Walsh reported in Science that the EPA's "most obvious problem" was the fact that some 63,000 chemicals were in the marketplace and an estimated 1,000 new chemicals were appearing every year; thus, "at the end of the second year since the passage of TSCA, questions are being raised as to whether the law is enforceable...."[13] Three years after the passage of the law, Isaac Berenblum declared without qualification that adequate animal testing was "impossible" with approximately 1,000 new compounds or products being invented annually.[14] And four years after the passage of TSCA, the Toxic Substance Strategy Committee, chaired by Gus Speth, informed President Carter in a tone of solemn astonishment: "Until recently, nearly everyone—legislators, regulators, scientists, and

industry officials—seems to have underestimated the magnitude of the research, data, regulatory and enforcement tasks involved. . . ."[15] The committee
also said: "Obtaining all the data and information needed to understand toxic
substances and to select effective methods of reducing or eliminating hazardous
effects is a herculean task. It is not yet known how many of the tens of thousands of chemicals in commercial use pose hazards, much les the amounts and
the circumstances."[16] Why the Speth Committee was still so astonished, in
1980, by the magnitude of the task of subjecting every substance in a gigantic
industrial civilization to an animal test and then calculating the risks of each
substance for 222,000,000 people, it is impossible to say—since it had been obvious for years that it could not be done.

In addition to being engulfed by the sheer numbers of chemicals and reported carcinogens, "regulatory" science was engulfed, again predictably, by
(1) the economic and temporal limitations of animal tests and by (2) the shortage of laboratories. In 1975, the year before the passage of the law, Maugh and
Marx had also reported that each animal test was expensive—$70,000 at the
time—and took three years to execute.[17] The cost could have been expected to
rise, since the NCI had piled on more and more complex requirements for animal tests, e.g., 50,000 slides, in an inflationary period; the cost in 1980, as the
reader will recall, could be as much as $500,000 for one unreplicated test.

In 1975, Maugh and Marx also knew that laboratories in which animals
could be tested existed in finite numbers: "Even if all the screening facilities in
the country were mobilized, by one estimate, it would still be possible to screen
only about 700 chemicals per year." Thus, they concluded before the law was
passed, it would take "many years" to test all the new chemicals being introduced in any single year and "a much longer time" to test all the chemicals that
had already been introduced into the environment.[18] Two years after the passage of TSCA, the estimates of what could be accomplished by the existing
number of laboratories had dropped sharply. Saffiotti informed Maugh, who
reported it in *Science* that tests on no more than 500 chemicals could be started
each year, and that even if all the 1,000 new substances that were invented each
year were to be tested, there would be no way to test those that had already
been introduced into the environment.[19] In the same article, the complete
practical predicament of "regulatory" science was summed up in one sentence:
*"There are simply not enough toxicologists, pathologists, animal suppliers and
laboratory facilities to test all chemicals."*[20]

For some reason, the shortage of toxicologists was particularly shocking to
some, although Rall had declared such a shortage to exist during the hearings
on the Toxic Substances Control Act. Three years after the passage of the act,
in 1979, the General Accounting Office of the United States reported the lack
of trained personnel as if it were news hot off the presses: "The shortage of toxicologists is also caused by the newness of the field of toxicology—there is no
consensus about the characteristics of a training program in this field. Often . . .
they are not qualified in the areas needed by the [NCI] program. For example,
in attempting to fill toxicologist positions, NCI staff interviewed 16 people
working as toxicologists; 8 of the 16 were not qualified in the areas of expertise

needed." The disturbed GAO repeated again that "no job standards for toxicology exist." Who, then, were the "experts" performing the animal tests from which the barrage of terrifying data was emerging? "Often," said the GAO, they were learning on the job.[21]

In sum: Since the passage of the law for which its "activist" leaders had so ardently campaigned, the world of "regulatory" science has received a series of terrible "shocks," all of which add up to its inability to detect and chase all the carcinogenic "germs" in America, and thus prevent cancer. And not one of those "shocks" need have occurred, since they were well known before the passage of the law. As conceived, the cancer "prevention" program had, in fact, been a complex scientific-legal fantasy, an expression of symbolic anger at the industrial system which had been charged with causing "the mass" of that ravaging disease. Less practical thought had been invested in the project than a small-town grocer invests before ordering a sack of potatoes. It had not taken genius and prophetic talent to know that the project as presented to Congress was a fantasy. It had merely required some contact with reality. That quality was exhibited by at least one NCI scientist. In 1971, at the outset of the National Cancer Program, Hans Falk wrote in terms of the knowledge then available:

To safeguard 200 million people for a major portion of their lifespan against each of the potential environmental carcinogens appears to be a staggering and hopeless task, unless a complete ban on some economically essential, but also hazardous, chemicals be imposed. This action will still leave naturally-occurring carcinogens without control. The outlook is bleak for achieving complete absence of carcinogenic hazards from man's environment.[22]

It does not detract from Falk's intelligence to say that this calculation was relatively simple. He stands as evidence that as early as 1971, it was possible to know that the chase after individual carcinogenic "germs" would be a "staggering and hopeless task."

Until the passage of the Toxic Substances Control Act, in 1976, the impotence of the cancer prevention establishment was not particularly visible. After the frenetic campaign to pass TSCA, however, during which Americans were informed by Russell Train that they were being assaulted by 2,000,000 toxic chemicals, few of which had yet been tested for carcinogenicity, and that if they breathed, ate, drank, or touched, they were risking their lives, vigorous action was necessary. The orgiastic screaming was over, the Congress, the press, and the public were suitably appalled, and "regulatory" science, which only one year before did not know whether animal tests could be used to prevent cancer, now had to honor its word. It could not do so.

By 1978, as we know, the cancer prevention establishment was fully aware of its own chaos. No two regulatory agencies agreed on the definition of a carcinogen, on how to conduct an animal test, or on how to fulfill the promises that scientists like David Rall had made to Congress. It was not too difficult to find a solution, for there was a handy scapegoat: "industry." In that year, the year of the OSHA hearings, Eula Bingham told the press that "industry" was

forcing the regulatory agencies to reinvent the "wheel." And in that year, unknown bureaucrats put words in the mouth of a lay political appointee, Joseph
Califano, then Secretary of HEW, words which one would call "lies," were one
not aware of the magnitude of the ignorance and confusion behind the scenes.
Whatever the reasons, a set of extraordinary untruths emerged from that political layman's mouth, just as they had emerged from the mouth of Russell Train
two years before. Califano delivered a speech announcing the existence of a
peril without precedent—7,000,000 chemicals to which, he said, the American
public was "exposed"—and he announced the creation of an entirely new layer
of bureaucracy to cope with that peril, a bureaucracy which would address itself to a solution. The key points of that speech were summarized and quoted
in an HEW press release and it was sent out all over the nation. Both the peril
and the solution were nonexistent. Here is one section of the release:

HEW Secretary Joseph A. Califano, Jr., today announced the establishment of a major
federal program to help combat the growing public health threat of chemical hazards in
the environment. . . .
   "The phenomenal technological advances in this country have brought with them
unfortunate and unforeseen byproducts creating serious health hazards, as in the case
of *asbestos,"* the Secretary said.
   "We must act quickly and with all available resources to identify and control *the
many toxic substances to which our citizens are exposed."*
   He said, *"A relatively few of the more than seven million chemicals have been tested
for carcinogenicity.* There have been published reports of various animal testing of only
about 15,000 chemicals."
   Production and use of chemicals in the United States has increased dramatically
since World War II. As many as 60,000 are now believed to be in or had commercial
use. An estimated 600 to 700 new chemicals are introduced into commerce each year.[23]
[Emphasis added]

   This document was siphoned into the communications arteries of the
United States and was understood to say exactly what it *did* say; namely, that
Americans were "exposed" to 7,000,000 chemicals. I heard that 7,000,000
coming out of the mouth of Tom Brokaw of NBC, in a little introduction to an
interview with Samuel Epstein on the occasion of Epstein's new book on carcinogenesis.
   The Califano statement was a masterpiece of misinformation. As basic scientist James Miller explained, one year later, Americans were *not* exposed to
millions of hazardous chemicals, tested or untested. Worse yet, the sole illustration of the alleged 7,000,000 perils was *asbestos*—a known human carcinogen. Finally, the statement that "relatively few had been tested for
carcinogenicity" implied that they *should* have been tested for carcinogenicity
(presumably by their producers), that this had not been done, and that the failure to do so had left citizens "exposed" to 7,000,000 possibly *carcinogenic*
perils. Finally, as the last paragraph in that sequence indicates, it was quite
clear that the anonymous authors of this document were aware of the difference between the number of *laboratory* chemicals known to organic chemistry
and the number of chemicals in *commercial production.* Two sets of numbers

were given. It was quite impossible for laymen to understand the difference; the speech and the release *said* that the public was "exposed" to those 7,000,000 possibly carcinogenic perils. It was only two years since Train, another lay administrator, had uttered his equally untrue warning. Between one administration and the next, the number of chemical hazards had more than *tripled;* and in both cases the implication was that the American industrial system had subjected an innocent citizenry to a monstrous catastrophe.

That was not all. This incredible danger, said Califano, had necessitated the creation of a new integrated bureaucratic superstructure to solve the problem. That superstructure, he said, would henceforth be headed by David Rall—this, the only artistically attractive aspect of the document. The specific details of the problem and the name of the solution were presented as follows, and note once again, that they applied only to *carcinogenesis* testing:

Limits in laboratory facilities and trained personnel restrict the nation's capacity for testing. Present resources for *carcinogenesis testing* in the United States by government and industry combined will permit testing no more than 500 chemicals a year. It is estimated that each animal experiment takes from three to six years and costs at least $300,000. Califano said, "The limited resources and high costs point up the need for this program *for establishing priorities in chemical testing* and using government resources as efficiently as possible."[24] [Emphasis added]

In the context established by that extraordinary press release, that paragraph meant that the beleaguered "regulatory" science establishment had, somehow, to test 7,000,000 chemicals for carcinogenicity and that the purpose of the program was to use animal testing to establish priorities. But mice could not establish priorities. Mice could not even determine *if* a substance caused cancer in man, much less determine which substances were more or less dangerous to man. The only accurate concepts in that speech and press release were the figures about the lack of laboratories, the length of time, and the cost of animal testing. *Only the facts pertaining to the paralysis of "regulatory" science were true.*

The reader may entertain himself by seeking a benign interpretation of this phenomenon. In objective terms, it was a savage misrepresentation. It was a profoundly apocalyptic document, unquestionably written by staffers who viewed "industry," i.e., science, technology, production, and, above all, organic chemistry, as a metaphysical evil. Had there been the slightest impulse in the world of "regulatory" science to tell the public the truth, the bureacracy would have put quite different words into its administrator's mouth. Califano would have found himself saying: "We have known for five years that we could not possibly test all chemicals; a 'priority' system devised by the NCI has turned out to be a hypothetical construct; and we now don't know what to do." That, in fact, was the case, and the information which allowed this judgment to be made had been published one year before Califano's speech by Norbert Page of the NCI.

According to Page, it had been realized as early as 1973—three years after a little group of men had rushed to the Surgeon General to announce that

cancer prevention was "within reach"—that there were insufficient resources to
test all chemicals, and that a process of "judicious selection" was required, one
which systematically considered "a multitude of factors." That "multitude,"
said Page, had been identified by the NCI. This first "priority" system had
eleven criteria, of which the most important, called "Human Exposure," had
six subcriteria. Unfortunately, said Page, there were a few problems: Not all
the criteria could be evaluated "due to lack of data for many compounds."[25] In
fact, as the reader knows, almost no human exposure or dose data exists to this
day. As of 1975, Matthew Meselson of Harvard had found only three out of six
examples of animal and human dose-response data that could be compared; on
that minute number, he and his committee built a resplendent theory of
matching rodent-man sensitivity to carcinogens based on body weight. The
NCI criteria that Page was recapitulating in 1977 were doubtless theoretically
superb, but in practice, they were useless because the most critical data by
which the "priority" system could be tested—data about chemicals that were
"worst first" in human beings—were largely nonexistent.

One year after Califano's false announcement, in 1979, "priorities" were
again called for in the field of all environmental hazards by a National Research Council report, prepared by the Committee on Environmental Research
and Development. This time the criteria had shrunk considerably. In fact, there
were only three, and they were so muffled in the jargon of ignorance posing as
knowledge that translation will be needed. Here is the original: "One must determine the importance or severity of the environmental problem under consideration, assess the extent to which research and development can eliminate
uncertainties and clarify issues, and evaluate the extent to which the results of
research and development will have a significant effect on environmental decisions."[26] In English, this means, roughly: Figure out what is believed to be most
dangerous, figure out if anybody really knows anything about it, and figure out
what difference it will make to anybody if one allots time, personnel, and
money to study it.

These two "priority" systems have gone nowhere with great speed. But
there is one that now dominates the scene—the short-term or *in vitro* test, most
notably the Ames test—and, in the eyes of many, it is the only solution for the
self-created crises of a "regulatory" science that could have known before it
campaigned for TSCA that there was no way to pursue every carcinogenic
"germ" in the continent, The Ames test—a test of the response of the *Salmonella* bacteria to chemicals that are popped into a petri dish—is cheap, and it
can chase carcinogenic "germs" with incredible speed, assuming, of course,
that mutagen tests *do* predict for carcinogenicity. As Gary Flamm, speaking of
short-term tests, put it at a conference in 1978: "It's the only possible way to
test tens of thousands of chemicals. The results could be used for setting priorities."[27]

The original idea was, simply, that the mutagen tests would serve as "pre-
screens"—i.e., would screen out the chemicals that required investigation by
the more costly and time-consuming animal tests. The most articulate spokesman for this school of thought has been Bruce Ames. He and his associate,

Joyce McCann, and their collaborators have been advocating this use of their test as a pre-screen for animal tests ever since they announced their famous 90 percent correlation between carcinogens and mutagens in 1975.[28] They advocated it again in 1977.[29] In 1979, however, Ames had something new to say about "priorities" that launched an enormous controversy, one that is still unresolved as I write. Since it is the only new idea for breaking the paralytic trance of "regulatory" science, it will be described more fully.

Publishing in *Science*, Ames mentioned some of the major quantitative problems facing cancer "prevention"—some natural carcinogens and "50,000 synthetic chemicals" which, he said, were "used in significant quantities" of which only a small number had ever been tested for carcinogenicity or mutagenicity. For reasons of costs and time, he said, animal tests and human epidemiology were both inadequate to the task. He proposed that a battery of "short-term" tests, including mutagen tests, be used and declared that mutagens should be taken seriously for many reasons, including "their probable carcinogenicity" (by 1979, Ames was no longer saying that "Carcinogens Are Mutagens").[30] His most exciting announcement, however, was that he was building on the base of a study by Matthew Meselson of Harvard and was using mutagenic potency to measure the relative potencies of carcinogens. His group had already discovered, he said, that the potencies of carcinogens "can vary by well over a millionfold." What is more, he said, he was also solving the unsolved problem of the nonexistent noncarcinogen. He and his colleagues, he said, were now measuring *negative* results "by assigning the chemical a maximum potency value," thus establishing the long-missing parameters required for a negative finding in a biological test. Ames, he said, was no longer using "the quantitatively meaningless term 'non-carcinogen.' "[31]

The implication was clear—if mutagenic potency predicted for carcinogenic potency, then Ames, building on Meselson's base, had indeed solved the priorities problems. What, then, was Meselson's base? Meselson, writing with Kenneth Russell, had presented that base in a paper at the Cold Spring Harbor Conference in 1977, and a word should be said about that paper, because Meselson is a scientist who pulls gigantic conceptual rabbits out of very tiny factual hats. Had he done it again?

He had. This time, however, his "data base" was enormous, as compared to his "data base" for postulating the similarity of rodent and human sensitivity—it was not just six examples—it was fourteen. And this time, the theory was not based on body weight, but on life span. To do Meselson justice, he had hedged this hypothesis around with several fortified layers of qualification. After a long technical analysis, he and his co-author, Kenneth Russell, reported that there were *"major uncontrolled variables"* that might be altering the relationship between carcinogenic potency and mutagenic potency and they cautiously *"suggested"* that, with proper adjustments for the life span of the respective species, there was a *"possibility"* that the carcinogenic potency of mutagens *tends* to be *roughly* equal in rodents and man . . ." (emphasis added). They further expressed the view that "it would be valuable to have additional cases" in which one could test that *"possibility."*[32]

That was the hypothesis Ames was seeking to confirm. His own description of Meselson's accomplishments was more enthusiastic than Meselson's. One year later, Ames published the statement that although Meselson's study was "only exploratory," his study of fourteen chemicals showed a "good, but not perfect, correlation." He intimated that he expected the project to be successful, and said that there was a "good correlation" for most of the chemicals that had been studied as of that date as indicated by the work of Meselson et al., by his own work, and by other studies. In addition, he reported that other "short-term" tests show potency responses similar to those found by his *Salmonella* test; potency measures in a short-term test using human cells, he said, had just been obtained for sixteen chemicals, and they too showed a millionfold range, as well as a "remarkably good" agreement with the Salmonella results.[33]

Even before Ames had finished his study, however, the inevitable polarization took place. The issue had been raised at the OSHA hearings, and cudgels were taken up for and against the concept of establishing priorities of risk by using mutagen tests to determine carcinogenic potency. Some of the principals, notably Joyce McCann (Ames' colleague) and Matthew Meselson, supported the project.[34] Meselson said, enthusiastically, that "if we could even reliably divide chemicals into, say, four categories of carcinogenic chemicals— very strong, strong, medium and weak . . . we would be a big step beyond where we are today. If we could divide them into 10 shades, 10 categories, that would be tremendous."[35] Others, too, felt it would be tremendous. David Hoel of NIEHS, citing the Meselson-Russell paper, recommended that such measures of potency be used "in order to have a rational standard setting and methodology."[36] Philippe Shubik declared: "Some attempt to divide carcinogens into strong and weak actors is essential."[37]

Others—at the OSHA hearings and elswhere at later dates—were unenthusiastic, for a variety of reasons. Gary Flamm of the NCI observed that "human exposure and potency are totally different issues," and that while a range of potency of one to one millionfold was "impressive," "a high potency positive in an *in vitro* test means that either everyone will get cancer or that one in a million will get cancer, or one in a million over geologic time. We can be wrong by thousands of fold in our decision making."[38] Maugh, in *Science*, reproduced some of Ames' potency data showing, for example, that the natural mold aflatoxin was a million times as potent as the synthetic compound saccharin, but warned that "great caution" be used in making potency calculations because of varying test conditions and species differences. Aflatoxin, he said, is very potent in rats, but is not carcinogenic at all in adult mice; fluorenylacetamide is a very potent carcinogen in one strain of rat, but not in another; and 2-naphthylamine is a potent proved human carcinogen, but does not cause cancer in rats.[39] And similar points were made by Saffiotti[40] and Berenblum.[41] (The reader will observe that the concept of noncarcinogenicity had suddenly reappeared in the debates along with a passionate desire to discuss species differences.) Robert Hoover of the NCI, too, made the same point about species differences, but applied it to all of mankind; to attempt to rank carcinogens by potency, he said, would be to ignore the great variability among people.[42] Isaac

Berenblum denied again, as he had denied for years, that carcinogenic potency could be quantified, since it varied with the test conditions.[43] And Saffiotti presented a long technical argument at the OSHA hearings,[44] but made a short, clear argument at a conference which summed up the essential biological and logical objections:

The concept of potency is an attempt to measure an interaction, the effect of an agent on a biological system. Any definition of potency cannot pertain to the agent alone. Some carcinogens appear to have high levels of effect in some individuals, species or tissues, but low [levels of effect] in others. It isn't the potency that changes, it is the effects on [different] host tissues.[45]

Finally, some perceived limitations in the concept of potency but tended to favor it, e.g., Donald Lassiter of Stanford University and Herman Kraybill,[46] saying that while *absolute* potency could not be determined, perhaps *relative* potency could: and the Office of Science and Technology Policy actively favored the incorporation of potency estimates into risk assessment.[47]

This may sound exactly like a dozen other controversies to which the reader has been subjected, but it has its own unique aspect. There was something exquisitely circular about the whole argument. The explanation of its circularity was actually given at the very conference in 1977, at which Meselson presented the original hypothesis. Lorenzo Tomatis, suddenly possessed by the law of noncontradiction, observed to the attending scientists that there was "little logic" in fleeing from their "distrust" of animal tests and their lack of consensus on the predictive value of those tests into an "acritical enthusiasm" for mutagen and other short-term tests, *when these tests, themselves, are usually judged by their ability to "match the results" of animal tests.* He further observed: "What is badly needed is agreement on the validity of experimental results, be these obtained through long-term or short-term tests."[48]

One year later, both NIOSH[49] and OSHA repudiated the very concept of "priorities." Here is OSHA's policy document of 1980 on the subject—a remarkable statement in its own right, above all the joke which constitutes its climax, for it may be the most forthright admission of regulatory ignorance on record:

The proposals concerning the setting of priorities presented in the Record had three major limitations:
(i) Most priority-setting systems that were proposed were far too elaborate, many of them requiring full scientific review of all data on all candidate substances, together with elaborate risk estimation schemes and in some cases cost-benefit analyses for all substances, before any ranking could be undertaken;
(ii) *Most proponents of priority-setting apparently assumed that extensive data were available on human exposure and risks, and were unaware of the extremely limited data actually available on most substances;*
(iii) *Several proposed schemes included numerical systems for estimating risks, involving the assumption that quantitative risk estimation could be conducted reliably and consistently for all substances.*
The essence of a good priority setting system is that it should improve the efficiency of a regulatory system by enabling the regulatory agency to treat the "worst

first." If the system is too elaborate, it will actually reduce the efficiency of the regulatory system by absorbing the resources of the agency in the priority-setting exercise, to the point where actual regulation is postponed.

OSHA regards proposals that its priority-setting system should be based on "systematic review of all the scientific evidence" as disingenuous, both because most of the scientific evidence required for systematic review is lacking, and because consideration of all the scientific evidence available is more appropriately done in the final stage of classification and regulation. *To adopt such proposals would achieve little except to delay—if not postpone forever—the initiation of regulation. This approach, which OSHA rejects, has been characterized by some as "Paralysis by Analysis."*[50] [Emphasis added]

After this spellbinding candor, the agency then presented its own system—a series of "Candidate Lists," "which, based upon OSHA's brief review of available data, appear to be candidates for further scientific review or for regulation as potential occupational carcinogens."[51] This does *not,* however, mean "worst first." In fact, it doesn't even mean that the substances have been determined, by OSHA's standards, to be carcinogenic at all. OSHA laid great stress on this point: "OSHA emphasizes that the Candidate List is not a final scientific determination that any listed substance is a potential occupational carcinogen nor is it intended as even a pre-classification warning."[52] What kind of a priority system is this then? The answer is: It isn't. It represents OSHA's determination to continue chasing carcinogenic "germs" for the purpose of chasing carcinogenic "germs," regardless of scientific validity, in the absence of any reason to pounce on "germ" A rather than "germ" B and in splendid indifference to the fact that the process of testing every industrial substance might require 1,000 years—or 10,000. It would be an error, however, to criticize OSHA for being arbitrary in its choices. Since, indeed, "most of the scientific evidence required for systematic review is lacking," there is nothing to do but be arbitrary. It is those who imagine that such evidence exists who are in the grip of illusion. OSHA is not. Ultimately, OSHA's joke—"Paralysis by Analysis"—is the most revealing sentence in the agency's statement. It means, as OSHA clearly explains, that any demand for full, authentic scientific evidence on carcinogenicity and, above all, on human risk would bring regulation to an end.

Others, however, above all the EPA, which is the guardian of the skies, the waters, and the soils of the continent, are aware that "paralysis" has occurred even without "analysis"—and that the cheap and fast-acting mutagen tests are the only known means of preventing a total breakdown in the system. In 1980, it was announced that a Committee on Environmental Mutagens of the National Research Council, supported by a "consortium of federal agencies" through a contract with the EPA, was studying the whole realm of mutagen testing. A report on the activities of the committee appeared in the monthly register of the activities of the NAS, the National Research Council, and other research institutions. It said in part:

Although it is clear that mutagenic substances in the human environment pose hazards, the extent and kind of hazards and exposures to them are not understood satisfactorily. Human exposure to an array of synthesized compounds suspected or known to be mutagenic prompts public-health concerns. Yet questions persist concerning mutagenic substances themselves, the mutation process, carcinogenicity, and mutations that cause heritable diseases. Dose-response relationships aren't understood for mutagens. A National Research Council committee is examining scientific problems raised in trying to assess the likelihood that exposure to mutagens will lead to cancer or to genetically transmissible diseases perhaps including cancer.

As a first step the committee is examining various means available—including laboratory-animal and microorganism tests and evaluation criteria—for judging potency of evidently mutagenic compounds. . . .

The second phase of the committee's work will study possible relationships between compounds' potency as mutagens and their potency as carcinogens. The committee will study the feasibility of using mutagenicity tests in the detection and regulation of carcinogens.[53]

To translate: (1) Mutagens are dangerous. (2) We don't know, in general, what mutagens do to man. (3) We don't understand the dose-response effects of mutagens. (4) We don't know if mutagens cause cancer. (5) We don't know whether mutagenic potency predicts for carcinogenic potency. (6) So the EPA has given us a contract to study all these unknowns and decide whether it is "feasible" to use mutagen tests in regulation to identify industrial carcinogens and predict their potency.

Lest the reader suppose that the Committee on Environmental Mutagens was lacking in information, he might find it enlightening to know that a National Research Council Committee studying pesticides reported that empirical data on the mutagenic effects on man are rare and that "the basis for inferring those effects from laboratory experiments with animals is generally lacking."[54] He might find it even more enlightening to know that at the Banbury Conference on the role that geneticists might play in regulation, as summed up by an editor of the published conference transcript, Victor K. McElheny, the geneticists made no secret of the limits of the state of their art. Those attending the conference, he said, "inclined to the view" that genetic research could assist in the protection of workers and the general population from chemicals and genetic risks while "emphasizing areas of ignorance and repeatedly counseling great caution in quantifying mutagenic risks of chemicals. . . ."[55] These statements, all published in 1980—seven years after Bruce Ames had excitedly informed the world that "Carcinogens Are Mutagens"—told us something achingly familiar. There was little understanding of the effects on man of mutagens. There was no knowledge yet of whether mutagens cause cancer. There was little empirical data on man himself. And, after one had swallowed down all the qualifications about "areas of ignorance" and counsels of "great caution," one knew that geneticists were no more capable than researchers in carcinogenesis of quantifying the risks of a chemical mutagen for man.

The EPA, however, was required to police the "germs" of the continent, and it could not afford to be critical. The agency had been enmired, since its inception, in scandals over both its data and its risk assessments. In 1980, a committee of the Environmental Studies Board of the National Research Council of the NAS had politely devastated the EPA after an investigation of both. Although routine warnings that risk assessments might be in error always accompanied the EPA's estimates, said the committee, it "did not encounter any document that conveyed the impression that the risk estimates could well be in error by as much as 1,000–10,000 percent." There was nothing wrong with the EPA's methods of extrapolation, said the committee—it was simply that the state of the art was inadequate, and those methods themselves are subject to "uncertainties" of that magnitude.[56] The committee criticized the EPA's attempts to quantify cancer incidence in man from animal data, saying the process was sometimes "misused" and that "our present understanding of the mechanisms of cancer development does not permit us to draw reliable numerical inferences from the kind of laboratory data normally available. . . ."[57] Incessantly chastised for incompetence and exaggeration, paralyzed by the state of the art of "regulatory" science, the EPA was in feverish pursuit of a solution, and the solution seemed to lie in the mutagen tests.

Between 1980 and 1982, the quest for speed continued. The EPA's Gene-Tox program was evaluating twenty-three types of short-term tests for the power to predict for carcinogenicity. As of 1982, however, the mutagen tests were still enmired, themselves, in the unknown relationship between mutagenesis and carcinogenesis. The tests were still talented and capricious. They were even more precise by then in their power to identify "genotoxic" substances—i.e., substances with the capacity to interact with or damage genetic material in bacteria and in cells.[58] But they were still incapable of identifying various types of carcinogens such as DDT and other chlorinated hydrocarbons; natural hormones and synthetic hormones such as diethylstilbestrol; drugs such as phenobarbital; solid-state carcinogens (e.g., asbestos); and generally, immunosuppressors, co-carcinogens, and promoters.[59] All of these were now being lumped by many scientists under the category of "epigenetic."[60] In fact, the complex concepts of the "epigenetic" theory of cancer had simply been redefined by some scientists into whatever it was that the mutagen tests did *not* predict. Available tests were once again creating biological theory.

It was predictable that some "regulatory" scientists would eventually argue that whatever carcinogens the mutagens tests *could* predict would be the carcinogens which required the most urgent regulation—and in 1982 it happened. Roy Albert of NYU, head of an EPA advisory group, circulated a document among scientists asking whether "genotoxic" carcinogens should be considered more dangerous than the "epigenetic" and should receive more stringent regulation.[61] That priority system would permit the EPA to chase "germs" in the U.S. waters and regulate them with far greater speed; and the proposal was being considered by the new EPA administration. It was also predictable that prominent animal advocates, particularly those given to "brink of perfection" language, would suddenly remember that nobody really understood the "genetic-epigenetic" dichotomy, or understood the mechanisms of cancer, and would oppose such a solution. Arthur Upton did oppose it for precisely those reasons.[62] It was equally predictable that when that happened, public participants in the controversy would suddenly forget that the EPA's animal data and risk assessments had always been scandal-ridden—and that the frantic groping for the mutagen tests would be construed as a resolve by "industry" interests to commit "suspected mass murder." And that too happened.

In December 1982, Democratic Congressman Albert Gore, Jr., informed *Science* reporter Eliot Marshall that he had acquired "disturbing" knowledge. Said Gore:

The upper echelon science policy-makers have made a crass, calculated, cynical change in the *traditional policy* of seeking to prevent cancer.[63] [Emphasis added]

Such alteration in regulatory methods, prophesied Gore, "will probably result in hundreds of thousands of additional deaths attributable to cancer." And Gore charged dramatically that the Republican Administration

had reached way down into the process of government to control the science. They think that if you control the science you can control the conclusions about whether to control this or that substance. What they're doing is not supportable.[64]

Like Edward Kennedy before him, Gore had supposed that there was a "science" and that animal extrapolators could calculate numbers of human deaths. He clearly assumed that this was the first occasion on which these calculations were being "controlled," and that the new administration was abandoning the "traditional" way of preventing cancer in order to allow American industrialists to kill with greater license. Perhaps Gore thought that control of a nonscience by Democrats was in some way more scientific than control of a nonscience by Republicans. Even Eliot Marshall had forgotten that John Walsh of his own publication had reported only two years after the passage of TSCA that "questions are being raised as to whether the law is enforceable." It never had been enforceable and it still was not enforceable. That is why, whatever the quarrels, the mutagens tests exercised so magnetic a fascination on such "regulatory" scientists as Roy Albert, who can scarcely be conceived as "pro-industry." Whatever exceptions there might be to the predictive capacities of those tests, they were the principal hope for liberating "regulatory" science from its paralysis.

By 1982, that paralysis had become almost grotesque. According to John Weisburger, both the disciplines of veterinary medicine and *pathology* were still "scarce specialty skills":[65] *The science that actually analyzed the cancerous tissues produced by the animal tests was still a rarity.* To compound the problem, "environmentalists" had made the horrifying discovery that "regulatory" science was itself engaging in "mass murder"—of mice. In 1981, a bill (HR 556) was again introduced in Congress for the purpose of establishing a National Center for Alternative Research to discover methods of research and testing that did not require the use of live animals, an "ethics" embraced by some "regulatory" scientists, such as Weisburger.[66]

Weisburger, who now views animal tests as the last resort, suggests that all scientists build their initial test batteries on the base of the Ames bacterial mutagenesis test, the Hsie et al. mammalian mutagenesis test, and the William DNA repair test, and says:

In particular, because of their complementary nature, positive results in the test system of Ames and Williams provide strong and *possibly certain* evidence of carcinogenicity.[67] [Emphasis added]

The desire for those tests for genotoxic chemicals is dominant in the minds of many "regulatory" scientists today. The short-term tests alone can break the twelve-year-long paralytic trance that has never been avowed to the nation, and is always compulsively attributed to "industry"—or, temporarily, to Republicans.

The "genotoxic" tests have been in wide use ever since the 90 percent correlation between mutagens and carcinogens was announced, and it is a reasonable guess that one day there will be an official proclamation—at least by the EPA—that cancer is being "prevented" by a battery of short-term tests, with the mutagen tests heading the list. The guess is reasonable because it is the only way known to chase industrial "germs" across the land and to inject some semblance of rationality into the process. It would certainly *look* like progress, whether or not mutagen tests predict for all or even for most carcinogens, and whether or not they predict for human cancer, for they can chase the "germs" faster and faster. It would *look* even more like progress if mutagenic potency were used in risk assessment, for that would produce impressive "priority" lists of "worst first," even though no one on earth would know whether, in fact, they were "worst first" for man. Above all, it would *look* like progress, for it would give the geneticists a front-stage role in the regulatory control of industry for which a group of geneticists, despite their avowed ignorance, has been clamoring for years.

At this point, the reader, now entirely familiar with the pattern of a group of scientists rushing into political action without adequate knowledge, may shrug and ask the equivalent of "What else is new?" And the answer is this: Something *fantastic* is new. Fortunately, it is easy to understand. To invite the geneticists to spearhead the regulatory process is to legitimize an activist legion of would-be regulators who are now stamping in the wings with utopian plans for protecting the nation from industrial mutagens—which is to say, with utopian plans for protecting the nation from they-do-not-know-what. The chemical carcinogen experts have at least been kind enough to tell us that the hazard at issue was cancer. But what is the hazard the geneticists are concerned with? Or, more accurately, what *isn't* the hazard they are concerned with? Their speculations start with the degeneration of the species; move to death, aging, heart disease, and cancer; encompass rare and nonrare diseases; and culminate with the baby born with a hammertoe.

The most serious of the genetic activists are the ones who firmly believe that human data are necessary before they can presume to make calculations. Some, e.g., James Neel of the University of Michigan, want to monitor the mutation rate of the entire population by a variety of means including the examining of newborn babies, in order to be able to tell whether that rate is rising. In 1973, Neel is reported to have estimated that one could eventually detect a 50 percent rise in the human mutation rate within a year,[68] and he consistently calls for human population monitoring.[69] One must admire Neel's insistence on human data—but the proposal is criticized by other geneticists who have considered the implication of population monitoring, e.g., James

Crow of the University of Wisconsin, in 1971,[70] and John L. Drake of the University of Illinois, in 1978. To quote Drake, monitoring the population for mutation rates *"would be likely only to identify a crisis without providing the data to resolve it. . . ."*[71] In other words, the headlines might blare out one day: "NATION'S MUTATION RATE UP BY 50%"—and would convert the entire United States into a hysterical Love Canal overnight, a population gripped by terror while it waits for years as epidemiologists rush to the rescue in an attempt to track the catastrophe to its source—which may or may not be possible. However daunting this possibility, the solution offered by the critics of population monitoring is even more daunting. The critics have, they say, a far better idea. They will prevent they-do-not-know-what *before* it happens. In 1975, Committee 17 of the Environmental Mutagen Society recommended a *"mutagenic budget"* for U.S. industry: *". . . no single mutagenic agent should be allowed to exceed 10% of the total mutagenic budget."* The report was published in 1978 by Drake, who clearly thought it a valuable recommendation that merited serious consideration by the genetics community.[72] It is fortunate that the proposal was not submitted to economists; whatever their persuasion, all would have perished simultaneously of heart attacks. Committee 17 had actually proposed an economic dictatorship by bacteria.

The reader may imagine, on reading this, that such ideas and events could not prevail. He is quite mistaken. The mystique of "preventing" diseases that are not understood by means that do not exist is upon us, and the laws on the books today not only permit such events to occur, they invite them. Today any biologist who feels driven to preserve the genetic purity of the species by means of regulating industry may indulge that desire, knowing that he need never prove any of his hypotheses; he need merely acquire a group of allies and a beachhead in a regulatory agency and postulate the "risk of risk." A portion of the world of genetics is hungry for power over industry; many have not concealed their passion to be scientific policemen. As the reader will recall, at the Banbury Conference, supported in part by the EPA, the participants had to be reminded "several times," according to McElheny, "that prolonged research did not necessarily imply more and more onerous regulations." Neel, be it noted, was one of the more sober heads at that conference, and was charged with being a timid "academic" by James Watson for wanting to have human data before plunging into a *triple extrapolation* from bacteria or cells through animals to man. These *are* the kinds of thoughts that the "activist" geneticists are expressing, and since they are the most assertive and the most vocal, self-selection guarantees that these are the types who will command the headlines on the day that genetics is used to spearhead the regulatory process. And that day may come.

Political pressure is increasing on the regulatory agencies to honor the pledges of cancer "prevention" as they are presently conceived. The industrial "germs" must be frantically chased, even if no one knows what they mean to man. In one form or another, Lapham's law of governing bodies—that "if nobody knows, but somebody must pretend to know," only the way things *look* will be considered—will take over. Lapham's law is already operating as a solution to the crisis of ignorance in animal testing, prediction, and risk assessment. It may well be invoked as a solution to the practical crisis as well.

THE PHILOSOPHICAL CRISIS

That, then, is the first crisis born of the apocalyptic perspective and of a set of discoveries made in illogical order. We can now consider the second crisis—the emerging perception of the logical order, specifically, the recognition of data reporting the carcinogenicity of nature, which strikes at the philosophical root of the apocalyptic ideology itself.

As the reader knows, since he has read the nature survey in Chapter 4, a great many natural carcinogenic and mutagenic findings from animal tests have been reported in the literature. As he also knows, most of these findings have not been relayed to the nation, as have the reports on "suspected" industrial carcinogens. This absence of information cannot be attributed to the fact that the natural carcinogens have not yet been evaluated by a stellar committee; most of the reports on industrial carcinogens that have shown up in the press for a decade have not been evaluated by stellar committees either. The IARC in France is the only institution that engages in systematic evaluation by high standards in the field, and its first list of "established" carcinogens appeared only in 1979–1980. What proportion of the natural data is valid, by those standards, there is no way to know. There is not even a Saffiotti of nature who is making rough guesses that 50 percent of the reported carcinogenic results are probably legitimate scientific findings.

The absence of most of this information about nature in the press does not imply that such data have been kept secret. The papers and books have been freely published and are to be found in libraries, and findings are discussed at specialized cancer conferences. They are readily available to anyone who cares to hunt for them. They might legitimately be called, however, an *institutional* secret. There is no regulatory agency in charge of investigating nature. There are no Senators seeking to enhance their careers by subjecting nature to grillings under hot television lights. There is no ardent political constituency demanding that nature's chemical innovations be arrested. There are no dramatic legal contests in which nature is the defendant. And thus, there are no Xerox machines endlessly churning out government bulletins about nature's latest toxic, carcinogenic, and mutagenic derelictions and mailing them to the press. Nature's carcinogens and mutagens are a philosophical irrelevancy to the institutions created by the apocalyptic movement. The apocalyptic assumption that nature was almost entirely noncarcinogenic and that most human cancer had emerged from post–World War II test tubes forbade the very concept of a research agency, let alone a regulatory agency, dedicated to the study of and the dissemination of information about the carcinogenicity and mutagenicity of the earth. Just as most of the scientists are still frozen in the position determined by the history of the field, so are our institutions.

And yet, as the survey of natural carcinogens in Chapter 4 reveals, investigation of nature goes on and discoveries have been filtering through the ideological curtain. Most are still unknown, but a few have finally been discovered by the heirs of Rachel Carson. Three have been particularly shocking to them:

Vinyl chloride is the very symbol of synthetic evil, but in a paper entitled "Carcinogenic Natural Products," E. K. Weisburger of the NCI reported that vinyl chloride is found in tobacco. It is a natural constituent of at least one plant.[73] If this is true, *all* Americans, who live in a society of smokers, have thus been inhaling and ingesting molecules of vinyl chloride all their lives. The law of diffusion guarantees it.

Benzo(a)pyrene is an established animal carcinogen usually linked to the energy and automotive industries. But many scientists—listed in the natural survey—have reported benzo(a)pyrene as a natural substance which emerges from bacteria, growing plants, and above all from pyrolysis. It is present whenever one cooks one's food, whenever one burns wood, coal, or petroleum, whenever there is a wiener roast, a backyard barbecue, a bonfire, a prairie fire, or a forest fire. Here there is not even a question: *All* Americans have definitely been inhaling, eating, and drinking molecules of benzo(a)pyrene all their lives.

Asbestos is an established occupational carcinogen, and in 1976, Russell Peterson, Chairman of the Council of Environmental Quality, informed Congress during the hearings on TSCA: "No level of asbestos fibers in tissues are regarded as safe—a single fiber may initiate a response."[74] But asbestos is a natural substance, its fibers can be microscopically small, and they are probably part of the natural carcinogenic "background" in which we live. In 1977, an NAS committee in a work called *Drinking Water and Health*, a document frequently cited as authoritative by OSHA, estimated the "background" amounts of asbestos in the air and water. The committee said that "natural" air (air sampled in areas remote from industrial civilization) might contain about .01 fiber per cubic centimeter, and that "natural" water might contain about 10^4 to 10^6 fibers per liter.[75] Again, if this even approaches accuracy, *all* Americans have been inhaling, drinking, eating, and washing themselves with asbestos fibers all their lives.

Such data obviously clash violently with the apocalyptic assumptions about nature. And, to further confuse the heirs of Carson, it was finally "discovered" in 1980—and published as "news" in the *New York Times*—that it was not just nuclear plants that might be leaking radioactivity into the surrounding areas, but that radioactivity was emerging from people's homes from certain natural construction materials—e.g., granite—and from the rocks and soil in people's backyard gardens.[76]

But the discoveries that appear to be most shocking to "regulatory" scientists—at least the ones they have fought over in both the literature and at the OSHA hearings—are the findings on naturally carcinogenic components of man himself. Three of them, described as "established" carcinogens by the IARC, have preoccupied a great many scientists:

Nickel and chromium industries are reported to have high cancer rates—but nickel and chromium are essential nutrients for human growth.[77]

DES, an estrogen, causes vaginal cancer in some of the daughters of the women who take the drug—but, according to IARC Monograph Vol. 6, natural estrogens and other sex hormones are carcinogens (see the nature survey in Chapter 4). Yet again, sex hormones are essential to human physiology.

Nitrite used to cure bacon is a chemical which, combined with the amines in industrial substances and a great range of natural foods, e.g., proteins, cereals, vegetables, produces *N*-nitroso compounds in the body—and *N*-nitroso compounds are reported to cause cancer in a *dozen and a half animal species*. But, according to the IARC in 1978, 70 percent of the nitrite that enters the stomach is naturally formed in saliva;[78] and according to Steven Tannenbaum, Professor of Food Chemistry at MIT, in 1980, "probably thousands of times more nitrite is formed in the intestine than is contributed to the intestine from pre-formed nitrite in the diet."[79] In this case, too, the human body is a natural nitrite and nitrosamine factory.

Inevitably, on learning of such findings, scientists again have taken up the lance. Within the NCI itself, Hans Falk[80] and Herman Kraybill[81] consider carcinogens which are required for human life to constitute major evidence that at low levels, such substances do *not* cause cancer. The NCI opposition, represented at OSHA's hearings, argued that the fact of man's need for such substances did not constitute proof that the substances were *not* carcinogenic in low doses. (As always, the theoreticians invoke or reject the fallacy of proving a negative as it suits them.) Arthur Upton of the NCI stated: "I do not see that the existence of evidence for essentiality of a material as a trace nutrient is incompatible with the concept that that same material may be carcinogenic in trace amounts."[82] Umberto Saffiotti of the NCI argued similarly that it was a "logical non-sequitur" to argue that because selenium, chromium, and nickel were essential to the body that they could not be carcinogens.[83] Marvin Schneiderman of the NCI made the same general point about estrogenic hormones to Thomas Maugh in *Science* magazine.[84] And David Rall of the NIEHS, also speaking of carcinogenic sex hormones, argued that there was no reason to assume that there were safe or threshold doses within the body: "I know of no biochemical or physiological principle that indicates there is any reason to believe that. I find it much more comfortable scientifically to believe that they are indeed carcinogens, even at that concentration which is a biological necessity."[85]

The nature and level of the argument was summarized by OSHA by means of yet another joke. OSHA described the position of those who argue that chemicals required for survival cannot be carcinogenic at low doses as a "hypothesis" which "is apparently based upon an assumption that 'Nature wouldn't do it to us.' "[86] This particular joke is genuinely funny, although not in the sense OSHA intended. The potentates of "regulatory" science would not be in their present position were it not for the hardcore apocalyptic belief that "Nature wouldn't do it to us." They rode to power on exactly that belief.

The "Nature would-or-wouldn't do it to us" controversy is, of course, the controversy over the no-threshold theory. The quarrel over the natural carcinogens has grafted itself onto the most dramatic battle in the field. But there are two distinct audiences who are watching this drama, one in the world of chemical carcinogenesis, one in the world of radiation studies, and both have a special perspective on it. Some of the more theoretical minds in the world of chemical carcinogenesis appear to be baffled by the incessant focus on the perils of ineffably low doses, whether natural or industrial. They appear, although their dignified language camouflages it, to be asking helplessly: Where did the known danger of high doses go? As Elizabeth Miller put it in her presidential address in 1978 to the American Association of Cancer Research: "Much data have clearly established that chemical carcinogenesis is a strongly dose-dependent phenomenon. . . . The strong dose dependence is too often slighted in public discussions of possible human hazards from mutagenic and/or carcinogenic chemicals."[87] And Kraybill of the NCI made the same point in 1980, stating that the issue of dose dependency is never brought up in public argument over the potential threats to human beings from chemical carcinogens and mutagens.[88] Where *did* the high dose danger go? While some of the basic researchers and theoreticians of carcinogenesis weren't looking, it was obliterated by the twenty-year-old incremental-additive-cumulative-background theory advanced as an "argument" for the nonarguable no-threshold/one-molecule theory which is the moral absolute of regulation and of risk assessment. One cannot teach people that their greatest peril is high doses of a carcinogen while simultaneously teaching them that their greatest peril is an accumulation of submicroscopic specks of all-the-carcinogens-in-the-environment—*and* while defining the ultimate moral goal of cancer prevention as that of protecting the Aardvark man who might, somewhere, sometime, be struck down by a single molecule of a carcinogen to which he is peculiarly sensitive. In the process of justifying regulatory practices and training Americans to rear, like frightened horses, at the very idea of one molecule of an industrial carcinogen or mutagen, the spokesmen for "regulatory" science have expunged the strong dose dependency of carcinogenesis from the public dialogue.

While some in the scientific audience attending the unending drama over thresholds, or its new "Nature would-or-wouldn't do it to us" spinoff, perceive it as a baffling mystery about a vanishing high dose danger, others in the audience perceive it as a farce about the scarecrow-terror of small doses. The issue, of course, is the same. The most vocal mockers in the gallery are those scientists in the field of radiation who did not learn their lesson backward, who have always known that nature *would* do it to us, that, in fact, nature *has* done it to us, and who never forget for an instant that the earth was hurled out of a nuclear explosion in the heart of the sun and that every living being is simmering in his own, and the planet's, low-level radioactivity. The laughter of a portion of this audience is so full of contempt that it has an almost savage quality. Thus: Rosalyn S. Yalow, Nobel laureate, testified to Congress in 1979: "As an adult, living human being, my body contains natural radioactivity; 0.1 microcuries of potassium-40 and 0.1 microcuries of carbon-14. According to the current rules of the NRC, if I were a laboratory animal who had received this amount of radioactivity as 'by-product material' and died with the radioactivity still in my body, I could not be buried, burned, or disposed of in the garbage."[89] Thus: R. H. Mole of the Radiobiology Unit of Harwell, in Britain, has written that "every time someone throws a cabbage leaf on his compost heap he is discarding into the environment in an uncontrolled manner radioactive material with a half-life 50,000 times of plutonium."[90] Thus: Petr Beckmann, publisher of *Access to Energy*, has issued bumper stickers bearing the legend "Ralph Nader

Is Radioactive"; has declared: "There simply is no waste that is *not* radioactive: No water must go down the drain, for even distilled water may contain tritium (radioactive hydrogen)"; and has proposed that various Senators be arrested as "felons" for urinating in states that forbid the storage of radioactive waste. He has also cried out in mock passion: "If the Washington, D.C., air should get too dirty, remember the Declaration of Independence, whose paper pollutes the environment with several picocuries of radioactivity. . . . Shred it, mash it, pulverize it, and bury it deep in the ground!"[91]

To sum up, with the belated discovery that exposure to carcinogens is inescapable, both externally and internally, philosophical revisionism is now occurring in the world of "regulatory" science. When OSHA takes to mocking people for believing that "Nature wouldn't do it to us," we know we are looking at a serious corrosion of the apocalyptic premises which have shaped the profession of chemical carcinogenesis, the ideology of "regulatory" science, and the views of the culture itself. If Rachel Carson had been able to hear the testimony of the NCI experts at the OSHA hearings testifying in chorus to nature's malignant intentions, she would have whirled furiously in her grave. There is little question that nature's carcinogenicity and mutagenicity, which has, so far, been barely explored, is forcing "regulatory" scientists into a direction for which they are unprepared. The regulatory agencies are certainly not stopping to reconsider their intellectual evolution and the fact that their basic premises emerged from discoveries made in an illogical order. They are backing into the logical perspective inch by inch like a group of nervous crabs—while still clinging to Hueper's ancient belief that their mission is to chase every man-made carcinogenic "germ" on the continent. Since they are backing into it, they will soon crash into the most appalling shock of all—that, given the radioactive-carcinogenic-mutagenic dimension of the earth, given the law of diffusion, and given the one-molecule theory of cancer, they must, to be consistent, chase after every carcinogenic "germ" on the planet, including those within man himself. Because they cannot see with the backs of their heads, they do not know it, but they are in full philosophical crisis.

This philosophical crisis brings us to our last unanswered question: Why are some of the most critical "regulatory" scientists afraid of "the public"? The reader will recall some of the criticisms themselves that appeared in Chapter 8. There were charges from within the world of "regulatory" science itself of epidemic irrationality, of repeated publication of unsubstantiated findings, of frantic cries of wolf, of the abandonment of scientific disciplines and standards, and of the politicization of science. These were, clearly, protests against manifestations of the "apocalyptic paradigm." Although fear of a public reaction was revealed, the reason for that fear, other than that the public might be bored with or irritated by bad science, was not stated explicitly. The implication was clear that some scientists were afraid of a layman's rebellion of some kind, but it is difficult to imagine the American public, or even a significant portion of it, identifying and rebelling against bad science, since most have no standards for good science. One need scarcely fear an epistemological rebellion from a population in which mysticism, astrology, and telepathy are thriving expressions of the "educated" culture, and in which the National Science Foundation and the Department of Education are reporting "a current trend toward virtual scientific and technological illiteracy."[92] The fears expressed by those scientists quoted earlier were somewhat subjective; they were expressed in the scientists' own terms, not in terms applicable to laymen. There is one scientist, however, who has stated explicitly of what aspects of the public reaction he is afraid— and in terms that *are* applicable to laymen. He is Joseph Rodricks of the FDA, and he has apparently been aware for some years of a particular threat to "regulatory" science that will, he believes, emerge from the public. His analysis is interesting and important, and since the reader *is* "the public," he can evaluate it himself. Rodricks' ideas must actually be read in two stages, for he had an early perspective on a scientific problem and a later perspective on the public reaction to that problem. The connection between his two analyses is revealing, both for what he did say and for what he might have said but didn't.

Rodricks, precisely because he was at the FDA and was a student of the chemistry of foods, had a broader perspective on the phenomenon of carcinogenicity than did most of his colleagues in chemical carcinogenesis who were still frozen in the historical posture of the birth of the field, and whose experimental work was concentrated on synthetic chemicals. Rodricks was aware of nature's role in the problem—at least insofar as it touched on his own field, food. In fact, this particular scientist, who was clearly aware of the illogical order of the discoveries of carcinogenesis, produced his own imaginative version of what might have happened had the discoveries started with natural carcinogens, rather than with man-made carcinogens. In 1978, in a paper entitled "Food Hazards of Natural Origin," he opened with these words:

Let us assume for a moment that the 19th Century revolution in the science of synthetic organic chemistry never took place and that our society is not inhabited by any of those forms of technology that depend on the achievements of this science. And then let us make a second assumption, admittedly incompatible with the first, that our health scientists are blessed with up-to-the-minute knowledge of the role of chemicals in human disease and, moreover, have access to all the techniques of modern chemistry and toxicology. An environmental scientist seeking a life-long supply of funds in such a fancied society would be well-advised to take a close look at the food consumed by its inhabitants.[93]

He then gave his reasons for recommending a focus on food—it exposed the people continuously to the most chemically complex compounds; those compounds had, on the whole, never been identified; the toxic effects of the foods, singly or together, had never been studied; and exposures to these chemicals were largely unknown. In other words, said Rodricks, there was no reason whatever for the widespread assumption that the natural food supply was "safe." He then "emphatically" stressed that he was not suggesting that one abandon the investigation of chemical additives—but, he said, public health would be better served if scientists acknowledged the existence of chemical risks in natural foods and sought to reduce or eliminate them. Hazard, said

Rodricks, is hazard, and "whether a chemical in food is natural or synthetic, or is an intentional additive, natural constituent, or accidental contaminant is entirely irrelevant to whether it represents a human health risk." Any other view, he said, was "simplistic." Finally, he called for "priorities" in establishing such risks, whatever their source. The rest of the paper was dedicated to a discussion of several examples of naturally toxic foods and of naturally carcinogenic molds and estrogenic substances in plant foods—all of which appear in the nature survey in Chapter 4.

In fact, Rodricks' 1978 paper had been cautious and his documentation limited. As the nature survey indicates, by that date an astonishing number of carcinogens and mutagens had been reported in the food supply. The year before, Takashi Sugimura, reporting on his work with eleven collaborators, all prominent figures in Japanese cancer research, had informed a scientific audience of some of the latest findings of "mutagen-carcinogens" in foods and cooking methods.[94] (Those findings as well as yet later ones are in the nature survey.) No reflection of such data had appeared in the Rodricks' 1978 paper. In the same year, however, Peter Hutt, already identified in this book as former legal counsel for the FDA and now a member of a law firm that has represented corporate clients, was far more loquacious on the subject. In a keynote address to a conference on the Delaney Clause, sponsored by the International Academy of Environmental Safety, Hutt declared: "Virtually every food product on the market today contains some constituent that has been shown to be carcinogenic in at least one animal test. . . . It would be difficult to plan a diet for even one day that would be entirely free of animal carcinogens. It would surely be impossible to live for any significant time on such a diet, in light of the utter ubiquity of such substances."[95] And Hutt reeled off a list of reported carcinogens in various foods and their components—essential vitamins and minerals, lactose, maltose, charcoal-broiled steaks, etc., all of which have, in fact, been reported in the literature and can be found in the nature survey. By 1979, Jane Brody of the *New York Times* was interviewing James and Elizabeth Miller on the subject of naturally carcinogenic foods. According to the Millers, she said, "Evidence gathered thus far indicates that there may be as many naturally occurring carcinogens as there are carcinogens conjured up in industrial laboratories." James Miller also cited a few of the thirty examples of which he was aware: "Every day we eat far more estrogenic substances from plant foods than we do of DES contaminants in meat." He also mentioned aflatoxin in the nitrate-rich vegetables which, when mixed with amines in other natural foods, may form carcinogenic nitrosamines in the human digestive system.[96]

Almost none of this rapidly growing body of information about naturally carcinogenic foods, however, was being announced to the public by the FDA, which had brought the law of diffusion into court to argue that even one molecule of a synthetic carcinogen is a hazard to the public. But two of the FDA's former legal counsels, Peter Hutt and Richard Merrill, both writing with quite different perspectives for the legal profession[97]—Merrill being substantially more sympathetic to regulation than Hutt—explained the agency's mysterious silence on the subject. Both cited the FDA's policy on natural carcinogens and naturally carcinogenic contaminants in foods which had been published in the *Federal Register* in 1979 as follows:

Indeed, a requirement for warnings on all foods that may contain an inherent carcinogenic ingredient or a carcinogenic contaminant (in contrast to a deliberately added carcinogenic substance) would apply to many, perhaps most, foods in a supermarket. Such warnings would be so numerous they would confuse the public, would not promote informed consumer decisionmaking, and would not advance the public health."[98]

This statement, tucked into the middle of a long opinion on reportedly carcinogenic hair dyes, had been overlooked by all but specialists in FDA regulation. The plain but astonishing fact was that by 1979, twenty years after the passage of the famous Delaney Clause which forbids the inclusion of carcinogens in foods, the FDA, as a matter of policy, was refusing to warn the American people, so as not to "confuse" them, that much if not most of their food supply was contaminated with natural carcinogens or was intrinsically carcinogenic itself. The reason, said Merrill, was obvious: "The number of carcinogenic substances that naturally occur in foods would ultimately require so many warnings as to be deafening."[99] Thus, the agency would only warn the public of "deliberately added" carcinogens, and an enormous and growing literature of experiments reporting carcinogens and mutagens in natural foods was being officially ignored. Ironically, a 1977 paper by Sugimura and his colleagues had ended with these words:

Studies on the relation of diet and nutrition to cancer should be fully supported academically and multidisciplinarily. These studies will provide clues to ways of preventing *most of the common types of human carcinogenesis* resulting from exposure to mutagen-carcinogens in normal everyday life. *Finally, we must say that it really seems peculiar that the importance of mutagen-carcinogens in foods has not been the main subject throughout the long history of cancer research.*[100] [Emphasis added]

It was indeed "peculiar." Yet more "peculiar" was the fact that even when a veritable torrent of data on the carcinogenicity and mutagenicity of natural foods and on every process of cooking had finally emerged, the FDA's lips were apparently glued together: Government science was silent on the subject.

It was in 1980 that Joseph Rodricks, then Acting Associate Commissioner for Health Affairs of the FDA, stood up one day before an audience of scientists and explained why he was worried about the public. Again, he was cautious. None of this background—and certainly no hint of a conscious FDA policy of withholding such "confusing" information—was mentioned. But in a lecture at the New York Academy of Sciences on risk assessment for carcinogens, Rodricks ended with these words:

It seems clear to me that as we begin to apply our current methods for detecting risks to some of the myriad natural components of food, it is highly probable that we shall uncover an uncomfortably large number of chronically hazardous substances. Although this should not shock anyone who understands the chemical nature of food, it will surely come as a surprise to the public. I suspect that at least two monumental dilemmas will surface:

(1) The public's skepticism about the adequacy of current methods to measure risk will rise, perhaps, to unmanageable proportions.

(2) If we have high confidence in the methods we now use to measure risks from synthetic chemicals, and if on the basis of such measurements, we vigorously pursue the management of such risks, how can we justify not applying the equal vigor to the management of risks from the natural components of foods?

I hope my projection about uncovering numerous and hitherto unrecognized risks among the natural components of food are incorrect so that we shall not have to face these dilemmas. But I fear I am right.[101]

It is of minor historical interest, but of major bureaucratic interest, that the research in this book on natural carcinogens and mutagens in foods and in food preparation was completed almost two years before Rodricks issued this warning that it was "highly probable" that "an uncomfortably large number of chronically hazardous" components of food could be "projected" for the future. On the assumption that Rodricks knew at least as much about the experimental literature as I did, he did not "fear" he was right, he *knew* he was right.

In the same year that this "projection" was being made, 1980, a short article appeared in a scientific journal entitled: "Formation of Mutagens in Cooked Foods. III. Isolation of a Potent Mutagen from Beef." The authors were numerous and were of some interest; they included Takashi Sugimura, Director of the Japanese National Cancer Center Research Institute, and John H. Weisburger of Naylor Dana and former Head of the Carcinogen Screening Section and Director of the Bioassay Segment of the Carcinogenesis Program at the National Cancer Institute. The work had been supported in part by the NCI's U.S.–Japan Cooperative Cancer Program and the U.S. Public Health Services, as well as a group of Japanese institutions. The summary was terse:

The major mutagenic component of fried beef has been isolated using a series of chromatographic steps. The pure compound has been analyzed. . . . The results indicate that the molecular weight of this extremely mutagenic compound is 198, with an elemental composition of $C_{11} H_{10} N_4$. The compound is different from the known mutagenic pyrolysis products of amino acids or proteins.[102]

The powerful mutagen had been isolated from two sources, fried beef and beef extract—the essence of boiled beef.

This was a highly technical paper describing the methods by which the chemical had been isolated, and from the layman's point of view, the footnotes were more interesting than the details of the paper. Here are some of them, considerably shortened:

Commoner, B., et al., 1978, "Formation of Mutagens in Beef and Beef Extract in Cooking"

Matsumoto, T., et al., 1977, "Mutagenic Activity of Amino Acid Pyrolysates in *Salmonella typhimurium* TA98"

Nagao, et al., 1977, "Mutagenicity of Protein Pyrolysates"

Nagao, et al., 1977, "Mutagenicities of Smoke Condensates and the Charred Surfaces of Fish and Meat"

Spingarn, N. E., et al., 1979, "Formation of Mutagens in Sugar-Ammonia Model Systems"

Spingarn, N. E., et al., 1980, "Formation of Mutagens in Cooked Foods, *II. Starchy Foods*"

Spingarn, N. E., et al., 1979, "Formation of Mutagens in Cooked Foods. *I. Beef*"

Sugimura, T., et al., 1977, "Mutagen-Carcinogens in Food with Special Reference to Highly Mutagenic Pyrolytic Products in Broiled Foods"

Yamaizumi, Z., et al., 1980, "Detection of Potent Mutagens, Trp-P-1 and Trp-P-2 in Broiled Fish"[103]

Many of the co-authors were the top scientists at the Japanese cancer institute, including Takashi Sugimura, the Director, and Takashi Kawachi, the Vice-Director. They, in conjunction with Weisburger's laboratories, were engaged in an ongoing series of experiments in the mutagenicity of the cooking process. Since a high proportion of carcinogens were already known to be mutagens, but it yet remained to be established that a high proportion of mutagens were carcinogens, this systematic study of mutagens in the cooking process implied that at some point, these workers in genetics were going to run those potent mutagens through animal tests to see if they were carcinogens. One could tell from those footnotes and the series I, II, III that both geneticists and scientists studying the relationship of nutrition to cancer were holding their breaths. It is an educated guess that Rodricks was holding *his* breath, even as he was addressing his fellow scientists.

The next year, in 1981, two papers appeared, which were part of this sequence of studies, and so did a news story which few laymen noticed. One paper was written by a group of scientists at the Japanese cancer institute, including Takashi Sugimura. It was entitled "Structure of a Potent Mutagen Isolated from Fried Beef." And again, there was the dry, technical little summary:

A new potent mutagen was isolated from fried beef. The molecular formula was determined as $C_{11} H_{11} N_5$ by exact mass measurement. The chemical structure of this mutagen was [etc. etc.].[104]

The paper informed readers that two potent mutagens had been previously isolated from broiled fish, and named them in chemical terms. One of those same mutagens had now been identified and isolated from *"heated beef extract and fried-beef, suggesting that it is present in a variety of cooked foods."*[105]

The second paper was a short article in *Science* entitled "Carcinogenicity in Mice of Mutagenic Compounds from a Tryptophan Pyrolyzate," written once again by a group of scientists from the Japanese cancer institute, including the Director, Sugimura, and the Vice-Director, Kawachi. This paper reported on two mutagenic chemicals which had been found in broiled fish. One of those mutagens, said the authors, was more potent than aflatoxin B_1, *which is to say that it was the most potent mutagen ever discovered.* The authors reported that they had tested these chemicals in mice. At 200 parts per million, they said, they had caused liver cancers in the mice. The chemicals had not been poured into the mice in great amounts and they had not been operated on so that experimenters might implant the carcinogen directly into internal organs. The mice had simply eaten minute amounts of those chemicals in their food pellets. And, particularly important, only *one* control mouse got liver cancer. These were not ambiguous findings. Although the intensely potent chemical was more mutagenic than aflatoxin B_1, said the authors, "its carcinogenicity is similar to that of 2-acetylamino-fluorene";[106] it had matched with carcinogenicity, but less well with potency. Their conclusion contained one short and memorable sentence:

Thus, we report evidence of the carcinogenicity on oral administration of mutagenic compounds produced by cooking.[107]

The first mutagens discovered in the cooking process had produced cancers.

That year, Takashi Sugimura, like the Millers and Berenblum before him, won the Ernst W. Bertner Memorial Award for his research on "naturally occurring mutagens and carcinogens in food"[108] and was awarded a $100,000 prize, according to the *New York Times*, for "excellence in cancer research."[109] Almost no American knew why, or had been given any reason to care.

In that same year, 1981, I wrote to Dr. Sugimura to ask if he would be good enough to review, or to ask someone to review, my survey of natural carcinogens, and to answer several questions. He wrote back and said, generously, that he would be pleased to do so and that he had asked the Vice-Director, Takashi Kawachi, to review the survey. In 1982, I heard from Dr. Kawachi, who wrote me a three-page letter about the survey of natural carcinogens in Chapter 4, answering my questions and telling me about the latest work that had been going on at the Japanese cancer institute on dietary mutagens and carcinogens. *I must stress here, because of the diplomatic implications of the FDA's "policy," that Dr. Kawachi, like Dr. Sugimura, knew nothing of the context of this book; only the survey and my questions were sent to Japan.* Since Dr. Kawachi's letter discussed a number of interwoven issues, I shall break down his comments in terms of my questions—and then will report on their work.

I asked if he could estimate the percentage of the reported natural carcinogens in my nature survey that were valid, and requested a general assessment of the survey. He replied that he believed that there are that many "kinds," i.e., categories, of natural carcinogens in our environment, but did not know their implications for human cancer.

I asked if he could confirm that there were carcinogens in the human diet. He replied that "carcinogens certainly exist in our diet."

I then asked an epidemiological question: I asked if the scientists at the Japanese cancer institute still believed, as they did in 1977, that natural carcinogens in the diet were the causes "of most common types of human carcinogenesis." He discussed the recent "complication" of carcinogenesis by the phenomenon of promoters, and said: ". . . we still believe that diet is *likely* to be linked to 'most of the common types of human carcinogenesis' but the evidence is still circumstantial."

In sum, Dr. Kawachi confirmed both the carcinogenic dimension of nature and the present inability to predict human cancer from animal carcinogens alone.

Dr. Kawachi then told me about the ongoing work in Japan:

In 1977, we found various mutagens in the diet. At that time [we knew] that almost all carcinogens (80 to 90%) were mutagenic; of course mutagens were not necessarily carcinogens. However, the mutagens which we identified in pyrolyzates of amino acids, proteins, and foods were very potent mutagens, and so far we have identified fourteen compounds of pyrolysis products. We have carried out long-term carcinogenesis experiments on seven [of those] compounds. We have found that six of the seven are *hepatocarcinogens*. On the other hand, quercetin, which is found ubiquitously in plants is mutagenic, but it is not carcinogenic.[110]

Once again, what these mutagens and carcinogens might mean for man he could not say; but far more significant: While the U.S. FDA was refusing to inform Americans of natural carcinogens in foods, the Japanese cancer institute was reporting that fourteen extremely potent mutagens—one of them the most potent known—had been identified in the cooking process itself, in broiling, frying, and boiling (at least the boiling which produces beef stock) and that six out of the seven already tested had produced liver cancers in mice.

In the same year in which I received Kawachi's letter, 1982, Shoichi Katayama et al. (a group which included John H. Weisburger) reported that they had found a chemical which induced prostate cancer, as well as colon and breast cancer, in rats. It was DMAB, a synthetic chemical "with a close chemical similarity" to the mutagens isolated from "cooked meat or fish."[111] (Synthetic versions of a natural chemical are often used in experiments, e.g., the research on the anticarcinogen Vitamin A.) The triad of colon, breast, and prostate is biologically interesting: In human beings, these particular cancers are linked in genetic syndromes.[112] They are also relevant to the epidemiological theory of diet-induced cancer. Katayama wrote: "... there is an association, in turn, between the incidence of cancer of the colon, breast and prostate gland in meat eating populations."[113] It is Weisburger's hypothesis that the mutagens in fried or broiled meats or fish "may be the genotoxic carcinogens in colon carcinogenesis."[114] That is one variant of the theory that some epidemiologists and laboratory scientists are studying, and that is "circumstantial" and unproved. But Weisburger's laboratory experiment was of considerable interest. A chemical of the structural type produced in cooking had also caused cancers in rats.

In that same year, Americans found dietary warnings falling from the skies. A National Research Council committee had sent out a press release telling them to avoid fatty meats and dairy products, to eat fresh fruits and green vegetables, and to eat cereals.[115] This, they were told, might prevent colon, breast, and prostate cancer. They were not told—although Sugimura was a consultant to that committee—about the laboratory findings. In other

words, an unproved and presently unprovable dietary hypothesis from epidemiology was suddenly transmitted to the citizens, but the reports of carcinogenic chemicals in cooked foods were not communicated to the press or
public.

Such data are neither more nor less significant than the data used in regulating industry. No one, including their Japanese discoverers, can say in advance what those chemicals are doing (if anything) to man, because no one can
say in advance what any chemical is doing (if anything) to man. Nonetheless,
as Rodricks said, the double standard is "simplistic." A chemical which produces cancers in laboratory animals is a chemical which produces cancers in
laboratory animals, and if one molecule of such a chemical or one "exposure"
to such a chemical must be assumed to be a cause of human cancer, then one
must assume that cooking is a cause of human cancer. Unless the FDA plans to
break off relations with Japan, or to hide all natural carcinogens in a vault, at
some point these interesting data will become known to the broad public.

These, then, are the two earthquake faults that lie beneath the house of
"regulatory" science. Between 1980 and 1982, the two faults were moving rapidly to join each other in a paradoxical fashion. A premature "regulatory" science, swept into power by the apocalyptic typhoon—bankrupt, paralyzed,
brandishing false numbers of man-made chemicals, hiding natural chemicals—was testing the predictive power of the remarkable but inconsistent mutagen tests and was praying that those tests might save it from practical
disaster. Meanwhile, in nonapocalyptic Japan, the predictive power of those
tests were also being tested. Japan was not hiding nature, natural chemicals
were being studied as well as industrial, and the results were exposing the philosophical bankruptcy of U.S. "regulatory" science. There was hope for a real
or apparent solution to the practical crisis; however great the margin of error of
the mutagen tests and other short-term tests, however great the number of industries missed or falsely indicted, there was a way of escaping the paralysis.
There was no escape from the philosophical crisis.

Most "regulatory" scientists were unaware of the danger. Few thought
about the practical or philosophical implications of their actions. Some did,
and Rodricks was one of them. He was understandably nervous; his own FDA
had been refusing to inform Americans about the natural carcinogens in the
food supply. But reports were coming out of the East, one following swiftly on
the heels of another, from a laboratory too important to ignore. The reports
could not be hidden forever.

And they won't be.

One year after Dr. Kawachi reviewed the survey of natural carcinogens in
this book, the skies opened once again and a cluster of dietary carcinogens and
mutagens in that survey fell into the front pages. They had been reported, in-
congruously, by an apocalyptic hero—Bruce Ames, the archetypal "regulatory" scientist and one-molecule theorist.

In the process of trying to create a priority system for the regulation of industrial chemicals, Ames had been correlating mutagenic and carcinogenic

potency. And in the course of doing that, he had broken through the ideological-regulatory barrier and had crash-landed on the planet.

In a literature review in *Science,* Ames informed the world that Nature was not benign, that the natural food supply was full of an extraordinary number of complex and toxic chemicals, that there were so many carcinogens and mutagens and genotoxic substances in the natural diet that one could eat no meal without consuming them; indeed that there were so many that he could discuss only a few examples. The ones he named were those he considered most important by virtue of their potency and the quantity consumed.

Inevitably, his list included the Japanese discoveries that cooked, browned and burned proteins, amino acids and sugars were mutagenic and carcinogenic. He also reported that oxidized fats and cooking oils were mutagenic and carcinogenic, that their potency increased in the cooking process, and that they might be metabolized into the dangerous oxygen radicals that Philip Handler and others had long believed to be linked to much of cancer. (Ames dedicated his paper to Handler.) He suggested that natural anti-carcinogens in foods such as carrots might be functioning as protective anti-oxidants. In addition he reported that carcinogenic nitroso-compounds could be formed by eating a host of nitrate-rich vegetables; that such spices as black pepper and such foods as mushrooms contained powerful carcinogens; that commonplace vegetables and fruits and generally plant foods contained carcinogens and mutagens, e.g., pyrollizidine aklaloids, phenols, and flavonoids; that various natural molds, e.g., aflatoxin, added their potent carcinogenicity to a great variety of plant and animal foods; that the mutagen and the co-carcinogen acetaldehyde was produced by the human body in the course of metabolizing liquor; that coffee was mutagenic; that coffee, tea and chocolate were genotoxic. On the basis of these and other discoveries, as well as the epidemiological data which revealed, he said, that the American life span was steadily increasing and that the rise in America's cancer rates could plausibly be attributed to tobacco, Ames was investigating both nature and culture as the most significant factors in cancer causation. The tobacco plant alone, he said, was already causing 30 percent of cancer deaths and its grim toll had not yet peaked in women. The natural diet, he thought, was also likely to be a major factor in cancer. How did Ames calculate the risks for so great an array of natural carcinogens, mutagens, and genotoxic substances? He didn't. Risk assessment would, he said, constitute a major challenge. The noted one-molecule theorist did not utter the word "molecule."[116]

For the reader of this book, who has already read about these natural findings, and for a great many scientists who were already aware of them, the "news" about nature and the natural diet is less astonishing than the fact that Ames transmitted them. He had not ceased to be concerned with industrially caused cancer, he had not ceased to counsel prudence, but he had decisively ceased to be an archetypal "regulatory" scientist. The first great apocalyptic defector had made his public appearance.

And precisely because he had apocalyptic "credentials," the American press found him "credible"—and listened. For a day or two stories appeared in the national press in which its foremost science editors solemnly relayed the "new" discoveries about natural carcinogens in foods. Some readers undoubtedly grasped that environmental cancer was more complicated than they had previously thought. Some readers undoubtedly resolved to give up eating, or, perhaps, to live like rabbits on carrots. Some natural food addicts were undoubtedly consulting their psychiatrists since their novel form of self-esteem was turning out to be carcinogenic. But most people never read or heard the news at all. One literature review, one news story were not enough to penetrate the consciousness of the inhabitants of a major city, let alone the continental land mass of the United States. And one major apocalyptic defector was not enough to alter any consciousness that had been soaked in apocalyptic bromides for a generation. The skies had opened briefly, a few natural carcinogens had tumbled out of nowhere . . . and the skies had closed again.

But something decisive had happened, nonetheless. The ideological wall of silence that surrounded nature had been breached. For an instant, some unknown number of scientists and laymen got a glimpse of that radioactive-toxic, carcinogenic, mutagenic fire ball, still cooling from that primeval explosion that give it birth—got a glimpse of that astonishing phenomenon in the universe that Man calls home. For an instant, the trailing shrouds of apocalyptic dogma parted, and planet earth appeared. Where the influential Ames had trod, others would follow. The knowledge of the awesome carcinogenicity and mutagenicity of the natural food supply and of cooking had begun its slow leak into the culture. Rodricks' "projection" was coming true.

One day—date unknown—a critical mass of literate Americans will wake up to discover "chemical" demons dancing in their "natural" Garden of Eden. Of all the demons that could most alarm a population trained to tremble at a single carcinogenic molecule, those in the natural food supply and produced by the most common forms of cooking will be the most frightening. Food is of enormous symbolic significance in every culture; it is the crucial necessity for life known to all. A portion of the public will discount such findings as yet another cry of wolf. But those who have taken "regulatory" science most seriously will be afraid. Many will be afraid for themselves; all will want to know if they are giving their children cancer.

No one will be able to tell them, because no one has the faintest idea. No one can say whether a substance that mutates a bacterium or causes cancer in an animal is causing cancer in man. No one can predict from such data. No one can quantify the "probability of a potential" of risk, let alone quantify the risk. All that can be said is that if those chemicals had been added to the food supply by "industry," they would be banned in accordance with the Delaney Clause as "potentially" deadly, and the FDA would seek to prevent a single molecule from entering the mouth of a human being.

Not only will those Americans be suddenly struck with the realization that they are breakfasting, lunching, and dining on animal carcinogens, but they will discover that they, too, are responsible for "suspected mass murder." If such an indictment is valid for "industry," it is valid for them. "Industry," in fact, is not known for feeding its workers potent mutagens and carcinogens from the moment of birth. But that is what millions of American adults will learn they are doing to American children.

At that moment, it is certain that the questions Rodricks so dreads will be asked.

As he predicts, they will pertain to two broad issues—the two broad issues with which this book is concerned. One set of questions will be directed to the actual meaning of the animal and bacterial data for man. Americans will discover that they are eating and feeding their children some of the most potent mutagens discovered by science. They will discover that they are eating and feeding their children perfect data, by contemporary standards, substances that induce mutations in bacteria *and* that produce cancers in animals. The public will discover that unusually powerful genotoxic "germs" exist in their normal diet but that no one on earth can say what their implications are for man. The public will discover the abyss between the laboratory mouse and the one or two million Americans it represents in the minds of some statisticians. The public will discover that risk assessment, as Rodricks himself said, may have no relationship whatever to biological reality. The public will discover that the Sinister Molecule it has been taught to dread is a moral fiction devised to permit regulatory action in the absence of epidemiological knowledge—action based on a hypothesis that cannot be tested. The public will discover that it is now engaging in "suspected mass murder" because of that terrifying moral fiction alone—and it will not think that fiction "moral" at all. The public will get a glimpse of what it feels like to be an American industrialist.

As Rodricks also predicts, questions will be raised on another issue as well, the hypocritical double standard for industry and for nature. The public will discover that the story that cancer was invented in post–World War II test tubes is false. The public will learn that it has been taught myths about the planet. The public will discover that the cancer "preventers" have been brandishing industrial perils at them while declining to inform them of the natural. The public will realize that by virtue of this selective process, it has been systematically pitted against its own economic system. The public will discover why "The richest, longest lived, best protected, most resourceful civilization, with the highest degree of insight into its own technology, is on its way to becoming the most frightened."[117]

It will not be a minor crisis.

It is the crisis toward which this country has been heading ever since the day, twenty years ago, that Rachel Carson taught the citizens of an advanced industrial civilization a fairy tale she had learned from an old man at the NCI, who had made up his mind decades before that nature was a Garden of Eden and that cancer was a novelty on earth, the result of a new kind of "germ" invented by organic chemists in collusion with wicked capitalists—a "germ" so powerful that it might destroy all life on earth.

Rachel Carson and the citizens who embraced this fairy tale are, of course, symptoms of a far deeper cultural crisis. It is a complex crisis, and since we are enmired in it, its history has not yet been written. But some of its cultural components, as they apply to this situation, can be named:

- Humanists who have learned nothing new about the Industrial Revolution and capitalism since William Blake denounced "Reason," "Science," and "satanic mills" and want to have their capitalist cake while eating their capitalists.
- A science of biology so immature that it soaks up religious, cultural, and political trends like a sponge—soaked them up under Hitler, soaked them up under Stalin, and, in contemporary America, soaked up the new left and counterculture ideology of the 1960s.
- A generation of Americans possessed of a belief in legal psychokinesis—a population convinced that all problems can be solved, that all evils can be corrected, that the laws of nature themselves can be abrogated, by the Congress and the courts.
- A "mass elite," including biologists, which, when modern physics transported man into outer space, broke into two mystical segments: one which watched television and fell on its belly to worship the planet, another which peered into microscopes and denied the existence of the planet—both united by their belief that metaphysical catastrophe was imminent and was directly attributable to the American economic system.
- A mass of scientists who do not share this psychopolitical pathology, but feed lustily off the grants that the pathology has made possible and do not expose the scientific and cultural malpractice of their colleagues.
- And, finally, millions of producers and salesmen across this land who receive neither sympathy nor intelligent guidance from the nation's intellectuals, and are thus rendered incapable either of accepting moral responsibility for their long-range actions or of protecting themselves from irrational assault.

This is not a crisis that can be easily untangled. But when one sees even these few components of it, one realizes that the pattern is in no way different from the pattern of a dozen other crises we have seen. That pattern characterizes our society. This is contemporary American cultural folly, and it has invaded biology. It did not occur spontaneously in other countries, although some Americans have tried desperately and with some success to export it. It did not happen in Japan. It is interesting to note that it never occurred to Japan's most highly placed students of genetics and carcinogenesis that "the mass" of a disease, which is branded in the bones of dinosaurs, had been invented by their "corporations." That is the "discovery" that Saffiotti's Ad Hoc Committee brought to the Surgeon General, and that is the "news" that "the NCI" disseminated to the American press.

This cultural folly is *not* intrinsic in "germ" chasing. There must, apparently, be a period of "germ" chasing. The early science of bacteriology chased germs fervently until it finally occurred to the scientists to study the people afflicted by the germs, and eventually they studied the people's interaction with the germs, which is now modern medicine (and is also modern cancer research in the *empirical* sciences which test their hypotheses). There is no aspect of this collection and study of carcinogenic "germs," however, which is malevolent in itself; it will produce knowledge that is beneficial to man. The malevolence of the cancer "prevention" establishment—and it is malevolent, despite the generous intentions of many—emerges from the primitive "germ" chasing rendered maniacal and destructive by American cultural pathology.

Complex as it may be, the essentials of this situation will be understood by many Americans. Just as the public grasped the apocalyptic abstraction that "chemicals" were evil and that "nature" was benign, so will it grasp that the scientists who hid nature and pitted them against their own economic system are not to be trusted. A bomb has been dropped on the Carsonian religious-political parable which is the only meaning Americans have ever been given for "environmental cancer." When that parable explodes, as it must, and the public understands the magnitude of the ideological delusion in which the entire country was enmeshed, a few other, and more sophisticated, questions will be asked. For example: While the Biologist State was concocting a pseudo-science and regulating industry on the basis of a fairy tale, while it was manipulating theory and data the way a cardsharp shuffles cards, while it was suffocating American minds with myth . . . *where were the critical scientists who knew that this was happening . . . and where was the watchdog press?*

Those are the questions I asked after finishing this book. In the Epilogue, I report on the answers.

Epilogue

... it's now generally accepted that about 60 to 90 percent of all human cancer is caused by manmade toxic chemicals of various sorts.[1]
—James Bishop, Jr., National Energy and Environmental Correspondent of *Newsweek*, 1976

It's been said that we are suffering a cancer epidemic in slow motion.[2]
—Dan Rather, CBS-TV News, "The American Way of Death," 1975

In truth what we are witnessing is the unmistakable emergence of a national cancer epidemic. An epidemic of frightful proportions. A cancer pox. The numbers and the trends point clearly to the calamity that is already upon us.[3]
—Larry Agran, journalist, *The Cancer Connection*, 1977

Says the NCI's Dr. Umberto Saffiotti: "Cancer *in the last quarter of the 20th century* can be considered a social disease, a disease whose causation and control are rooted in the technology and economy of our society."[4] [Emphasis added]
—"The Disease of the Century," *Time*, 1975

The news tonight is that the United States is number one in cancer. The National Cancer Institute estimates that if you're living in America your chances of getting cancer are higher than anywhere else in the world.[5]
—Dan Rather, CBS-TV News, "The American Way of Death," 1975

The U.S. has one of the world's highest incidences of cancers associated with environmental pollution.[6]
—"The Disease of the Century," *Time*, 1975

Where *were* the critical scientists while America was being embalmed in a fable? And where *was* the watchdog press? These questions, of course, are simply ways of asking how this nation could be blanketed in scientific mythology with no apparent protest. On the face of it, this could not have been achieved without the press, so that was the place to begin. I decided to investigate the "axioms" of the apocalyptics—the particular group of false or baseless ideas about environmental cancer which had invaded the press and are now deeply entrenched beliefs in our culture. All those "axioms"—quoted at the head of this chapter—were actually claims to knowledge of *human* data in one or all countries, knowledge which could only have come from the science of epidemiology. I therefore studied the history of cancer epidemiology to find out what epidemiologists had actually reported on those subjects. In the process, I hoped to evaluate the responsibility of the press as a purveyor of mythology. In this Epilogue, I set forth what I learned from the epidemiological literature "axiom" by "axiom"—after which I shall say a few words about the American press and the scientists who have educated that press, as well as those who have remained silent.

THE GARDEN OF EDEN/POST-WORLD WAR II THEORY OF ENVIRONMENTAL CANCER

The first "axiom" is the apocalyptics' environmental theory of cancer—namely, the theory that Wilhelm Hueper of the National Cancer Institute transmitted to Rachel Carson, that nature is a virtually cancer-free Garden of Eden rendered carcinogenic primarily by post–World War II organic chemists. We already know that this theory was false, since at the time that it was promulgated, there was a great body of literature reporting on natural carcinogens. One learns from epidemiology, however, that the theory was false for entirely different reasons. Since the 1930s—three decades before the cancer apocalypse surged out of the NCI—it had been obvious to trained cancer epidemiologists that the Garden of Eden/post–World War II theory of environmental cancer was a myth.

Its mythological status is most simply illustrated by the very subject of a particular cancer conference in Israel held in 1968. It was a conference which could never have existed if the post–World War II synthetic theory were true. It had been dedicated to a detailed examination of the problem of cancer in the preindustrial world. After listening to a paper by John Higginson, which will shortly be discussed, Isaac Berenblum, the basic scientist who had discovered anticarcinogenesis and co-carcinogenesis, and who was one of the fathers of the initiation-promotion theory, delivered a little talk. The enormous body of literature on human cancer in preindustrial nations, he said, had altered the prevailing understanding of the disease. Many of the "cherished beliefs" about cancer, he said, now required "drastic revision." Among those he named were "the old belief that cancer is predominantly a disease of economically advanced countries." Another was "the impression that environmental causes of human cancer are necessarily industrial in type."[7] Those ideas which, according to Berenblum, required "drastic revision" were precisely the ideas that were coursing feverishly through the arteries of the American culture at that very time.

A striking series of discoveries about cancer in the preindustrial world had decisively damaged those "old beliefs." When Higginson, at that 1968 conference in Israel, sought to describe the global epidemiological discoveries that had been piling up since the late 1930s, he did so by means of a sampling of the data. He described the incidence of eleven types of cancers which appeared all over the world, breaking them down into high-incidence areas, medium-incidence areas, and low-incidence areas. Here are some of the examples he gave:[8]

• *High* incidence of nasopharyngeal cancer (in males) was found in Singapore (Chinese) and in southern China; *medium* incidence was found in Malaya, Thailand, Indonesia, and Kenya; *low* incidence was found in Europe, most areas of Africa, and India.
• *High* incidence of mouth cancer (excluding the lip) was found in Ceylon and India; *medium* incidence was found in France; *low* incidence was found in "most countries."
• *High* incidence of esophageal cancer was found in Japan, China, southern Africa, Jamaica, Iran, southern USSR, and the Caribbean area; *medium* incidence was found in France, Switzerland, Singapore, India, and Chile; *low* incidence was found in North America, "most European countries," and Israel.
• *High* incidence of stomach cancer was found in Japan, Chile, Iceland, Colombia, Finland, Newfoundland, and the USSR; *medium* incidence was found in "most European countries," Canada, and the Caribbean area; *low* incidence was found in Africa, the U.S., and India.
• *High* incidence of liver cancer (in males) was found in Mozambique and southern Africa; *medium* incidence was found in Japan, Singapore (Chinese), Nigeria, and Uganda; *low* incidence was found in North America, Europe, Jamaica, South America, and India.
• *High* incidence of cervix cancer (in females) was found in Colombia, Puerto Rico, southern Africa, Jamaica, and among the nonwhite population of the U.S.; *medium* incidence was found in West and East Africa, Japan, Singapore (Chinese), India, and Europe; *low* incidence was found in the United Kingdom, in whites of the U.S., and in New Zealand, and in Israel it was "very rare."

That was the kind of information which had long since shattered the "cherished beliefs" that cancer was "predominantly" a disease of advanced industrialization and that cancers were "necessarily" industrial in type. Those cherished beliefs were, quite simply, false.

This was just a small selection of the data which had been collected by epidemiologists all over the globe; one can find these data in any good medical library. Among the most important compendia—the veritable bibles of international epidemiology—are several sets of studies. They include the seminal series of volumes entitled *Cancer Incidence in Five Continents,* edited by Richard Doll and associates; *Cancer Mortality for Selected Sites in 24 Countries,* edited by Mitsui Segi and associates; and a group of international committee reports published by the World Health Organization.[9] These compilations include not only incidence and mortality data, but an enormous amount of technical material on the biological characteristics of the different types of cancers found all over the world. It was from this vast body of data collected over decades that Higginson had plucked his examples.

This was "environmental cancer," as discovered and defined by epidemiologists. It was a global concept derived from the varying rates of cancers all over the world, and the concept encompassed the least industrialized as well as the most industrialized nations on earth. Not only had the epidemiologists discovered that preindustrial peoples who lived in a "balanced" relationship with nature were dying of a variety of cancers, but they had discovered that in some cases their cancers occurred at far higher rates than did those of industrial peoples; what is more, they had discovered that there was great inconsistency among the industrial nations themselves. Higginson had also informed the audience at the 1968 conference that Singapore Chinese got about 20 times as much nasopharyngeal cancer as did people in "most countries"; that people in Mozambique had about 100 times as much liver cancer as did people in North America and Europe; that Canadians had about 10 times as much breast cancer as did Japanese; that Denmark and the United States had as much as 7 or 8 times as much rectum cancer as did Japanese and Colombians; and that the range of stomach cancer in high-incidence countries—Japan, Iceland, and Chile—varied from about 27 to 45 times as much as that in the low-incidence countries—Uganda, Mozambique, and the United States. Indeed, within the United States itself, one found some of the highest incidence rates in the world of certain types of cancer (e.g., colon) and some of the lowest in the world (e.g., stomach and liver).[10] By the 1960s, "environmental cancer," as discovered by the epidemiologists, was an unfathomably complex phenomenon.

One of the reasons for which it was unfathomably complex pertained to the scrupulous mental processes of the leading epidemiologists of the world, who had launched this quest for the understanding of human cancer. They did not begin with a ready-made causal theory; they began with the knowledge of their own ignorance. Accordingly, they had not selected data to conform to any prior beliefs; they had collected every bit of information they could find about human cancer rates and had excluded nothing. Their environmental theory did not exclude the industrial-chemical theory of cancer; all epidemiologists knew that some human cancer had indeed come from industrial chemicals, since it was epidemiologists who had made those discoveries in man. Their theory did not exclude the phenomenon of occupational cancer or drug-induced cancer or radiation-induced cancer, since it was epidemiologists who had made those discoveries in man. Nor did their theory exclude the fact that industrialized nations (e.g., America) tended in the aggregate to have much more cancer than did preindustrialized nations (e.g., Thailand), or that Americans rarely died of infectious diseases and tended to live until their seventies while (as late as 1974) the Thais were being decimated by infectious diseases and their median age was sixteen,[11] approximately the life span of a cherished American house cat. They knew that cancer rates had risen precipitately in those nations where a variety of factors, including plumbing, an abundant food supply and control of infectious diseases, had increased the human life span. They recorded the cancer rates of man who lived in jungles and of man who lived in skyscrapers. They had ruled out nothing, and had collected all the information they could find about every type of cancer in every type of country, society and region. And precisely because they had ruled out nothing, their resulting data conformed to no preexisting "cherished beliefs" about the nature of cancer and was chaotically complex.

There had been an important by-product of this scrupulous global search: The epidemiologists had destroyed the rational possibility of any kind of simpleminded reductionism in the analysis of the causes of human cancer. And they had destroyed that rational possibility decades *before* Wilhelm Hueper of the NCI and his intellectual heirs had told one of the most advanced industrial civilizations on earth their fairy tale. From epidemiology, one learns why the cancer apocalypse, of necessity, arrived in America in the form of a fable. It could not have emerged from fact. The epidemiologist fathers of the theory of environmental cancer had made the first "axiom" of the apocalypse a scientific impossibility.

90 PERCENT OF CANCER COMES FROM INDUSTRIAL CHEMICALS

The second "axiom" of the cancer apocalypse was the famous report (cited in Chapter 2) attributed by journalists and politicians to anonymous sources at the "National Cancer Institute" in the middle and late 1970s that as much as 90 percent of cancer was "environmental"—and by "environmental" the anonymous informant(s) meant the "man-made" or *industrial* environment. We have no way of knowing who Anonymous is unless reporters decide to tell us. It is obvious, however, that some scientists at the NCI were espousing a similar concept. Hueper's doctrine certainly meant the same thing, and so did Saffiotti's 1976 statement in which he expressed the belief that cancer "largely" emerged from "external agents" in our industrial system. It is less important to know the identity of "anonymous" at the NCI than to know that major NCI scientists were disseminating such views, and it tells us clearly that journalists did not misunderstand the meaning of what they were being told; they understood that meaning perfectly.

That 90 percent estimate, so cherished by the apocalyptics, did emerge from science—but it emerged from the science of epidemiology. And it did *not* mean what "the NCI" said it meant. The full explanation of that 90 percent had also been in existence for many years. In fact, at that same 1968 cancer conference in Israel, John Higginson had reported the following conclusion about the United States:

While we do not know the etiological factors for many cancers, we are in a position to estimate on theoretical grounds the proportion of all cancers which may be of environmental origin. Calculations would indicate that in the United States approximately 80 percent of all malignant tumors are likely to be environmentally conditioned and thus theoretically preventable.[12]

And in another much more extensive 1968 paper, Higginson estimated that 90 percent of all cancers were theoretically preventable.[13]

Again, to understand the significance of that 90 percent, one must know how the calculations had been made. One must reach back in time to tell the story, for without prior knowledge of the varying global incidence rates it would be unintelligible. The epidemiologists had discovered that when they mapped the extraordinary variations in cancer rates all over the globe, they were looking at a phenomenon that resembled patches of epidemic disease. This raised an urgent question: Did these patches represent some hereditary tendency in certain groups of people to develop certain types of cancer, or were they regional outbreaks caused or influenced by external factors; i.e., were they "environmental"? The first serious attempt to answer the question had been made twenty-four years before Higginson's lecture in Israel—in 1944, by Sir Ernest Kennaway, one of Britain's most brilliant scientists. Kennaway, who in 1932 had been the first scientist to synthesize a pure chemical carcinogen in the laboratory,[14] realized that the forcible transplantation of huge numbers of blacks to the Americas had created a natural experiment that could be used to examine the question of heredity versus environment as it pertained to cancer. He conducted a comparative study of primary liver cancer in the Bantu population of South Africa and in the blacks of the United States. He found that while the Bantu suffered from extraordinarily high rates of that cancer, the American blacks did not. He concluded that liver cancer "was not of purely racial character" and that the problem in African blacks "may be due to some extrinsic factor which should be studied."[15] This was the seminal study that suggested for the first time that cancer in an entire population could be a function of geography, of place—of the environment.

The implications of this single study were staggering, and, clearly, the question required more extensive investigation. From 1953 to 1955, John Higginson, then in the Department of Pathology and Oncology at the University of Kansas Medical Center, working conjointly with A. G. Oettlé, conducted a far more complex study. They compared the rates of a whole range of cancers in the Bantu in Johannesburg with the rates of the same cancers in American blacks. The cancers examined were gastrointestinal, including the esophagus and the liver; genitourinary, including cancers of the testis, penis, uterus, and breast; soft-tissue cancers; leukemia; and children's cancers, such as retinoblastoma and nephroblastoma. Apart from cancer in children, where "the frequency is not significantly different from that observed in the United States," the rates of each one of this array of cancer types were strikingly different in the Bantu and the American blacks. In some cases, the Bantu had much more of a certain type of cancer than American blacks; in others, much less—and it was evident that cultural practices were relevant to some of the differences, e.g., circumcision, sexual and reproductive customs, and diet.[16]

In the 1960 paper reporting on these extraordinary disparities, Higginson concluded that almost none of this large range of cancers was hereditary, that most were "environmental"—a concept which clearly and explicitly included the concepts of natural factors and cultural patterns. And in the conclusion of that paper, he wrote these words:

If a cancer incidence is calculated for a hypothetical population using the lowest rate available from the American or Bantu figures, it would appear probable that in Western communities at least two-thirds of all cancers (excluding skin) are environmental in origin and therefore hypothetically preventable.[17]

Some years later, C. S. Muir of the Epidemiology Unit of the IARC and co-editor with Richard Doll of *Cancer Incidence in Five Continents* explained Higginson's reasoning to a scientific audience in New York. Higginson, said Muir, had compared the differences in the incidence of specific cancers as they were recorded in Vol. I of *Cancer Incidence in Five Continents* and had performed the following calculations:

Assuming [said Muir] that the smallest rate represented a level which should be considered as due to genetic factors, he [Higginson] postulated that the difference between this rate and the highest observed rate probably represented those cancers due to exogenous factors.[18]

That is how Higginson arrived at his progressive estimates of 65, 80, and, finally, 90 percent.

Although a specific percentage was not universally accepted, the revolutionary idea that "most" cancers are environmental, thus theoretically preventable, had traveled swiftly throughout the world of cancer epidemiology. The 1950s and 1960s were a period of intense ferment and activity in that science generally, and Higginson's study had contributed greatly to the intellectual excitement. Between 1962 and 1969, Segi, Kurihara, and others had studied cancer mortality in forty-eight countries and fifteen Soviet Republics.[19] By the early and mid-1960s, several World Health Organization committees had agreed that environmental factors accounted directly or indirectly for the majority of human cancers, and thus that the majority of cancers were theoretically preventable.[20] And by the late 1960s, the first great integrative summaries and interpretations of the epidemiologists' findings were in print in the form of two books—one by Johannes Clemmesen of Denmark (1965)[21] and one by Richard Doll (1967),[22] both classic works in the study of environmental cancer.

And still the story is not over. The epidemiologists kept examining their own revolutionary conclusion, and it bred yet another hypothesis to be tested. If it was true that most human cancers were environmentally influenced and had, as in the case of the blacks, changed in type and pattern after they had been brought to America, then one should be able to track the patterns of cancer in a migrant population *in the process of changing*. W. Haenszel and M. Kurihara (who had also with Segi been instrumental in collecting and integrating global data) undertook to test this hypothesis. They traced the mortality records of several of the cancer types of Japanese migrants to the United States, and found that the Japanese and their offspring lost the high rates of stomach cancer that prevail in Japan and instead acquired the low rates of stomach cancers that prevail in the United States; conversely, they lost the low colon-cancer rates of Japan and acquired the high colon-cancer rates of the U.S.-born.[23] The process had been captured in motion! That seminal paper was published in 1968, and once again, the revolutionary hypothesis had been dramatically replicated.

Over the years, other similar studies of migrants changing their cancer patterns from those of the mother country to those of the new country—Indians who had moved to Fiji and Natal; Europeans who had moved to North America, Australia and to the tropics[24]—repeatedly reinforced the discovery that cancer patterns in man shifted with geography and culture. Thus was the modern theory of environmental cancer actually born. It was a global theory that embraced natural carcinogens as well as industrial carcinogens, and it had arrived on the scene with an extraordinarily dramatic estimate of the proportion of human cancer believed to be "environmental"—namely, John Higginson's 90 percent.

It cannot be stressed too strongly that both the phenomenon of nature and the concept of culture—i.e., sexual and reproductive practices, dietary patterns, habits such as drinking, smoking, and sunbathing, etc.—were explicitly included in the broader term "environmental," not only by Higginson, but by all the seminal literature. The epidemiologists' theory of environmental cancer had been derived from studies of the preindustrial as well as the industrial nations, and that global theory had never equated "environmental" with "synthetic chemicals" or with "industrial chemicals," which is to say that the 90 percent had never been restricted to the "man-made." That, however, was the interpretation of the 90 percent transmitted to the American public.

Attempts were eventually made to correct this falsification of history. In 1978, when Elizabeth Miller delivered her presidential address to the American Association of Cancer Research, she took pains to explain the origin of the famous 90 percent and attributed it to John Higginson.[25] In 1979, John Higginson himself granted interviews to *Science* and to the *Washington Post* in which he explained that his theory of environmental cancer had been misinterpreted by the "ecologists," the "chemical carcinogenesis people," and the "occupational people,"[26] and bluntly described the erroneous beliefs about environmental cancer that were coursing through this society as "societal, political and quasi-scientific dogmas."[27]

A few corrections, however, could not erase the "misinterpretation." The famous 90 percent had been lifted from John Higginson's work and had been grafted onto the post–World War II industrial theory of cancer, to produce a nakedly political doctrine. That political doctrine had saturated the entire country. This second apocalyptic "axiom" was disseminated by many sources; some scientists, as we know, have built their careers upon that "axiom." But by far the most significant source, because it was most trusted by the press, was "the NCI."

A GREAT CANCER EPIDEMIC IS ARRIVING/WILL ARRIVE

These two "axioms" bred yet another. Those who believed the post–World War II synthetic/industrial theory of environmental cancer also believed, necessarily, that the cancer rates would shortly explode. Given the latency period of cancer, which might be five to thirty years or more, the logic was impeccable. A great epidemic was actually an ideological necessity for the apocalyptics, for that alone could validate their beliefs. A sudden sharp rise in the cancer rates in the middle and late 1970s would prove that the post–World War II industrial theory was true.

Predictions of a great cancer epidemic emerged from a great many sources, of which the most influential, once again, was the National Cancer Institute. In 1975, Umberto Saffiotti of the NCI informed *Time* magazine that cancer in "the last quarter of the 20th century" would emerge from the industrial system;[28] and, in the same year, "the National Cancer Institute" informed CBS-TV News that an epidemic was already on its way.

"The National Cancer Institute" was of two minds, it seems. According to the only source of information available—the mortality rates of the past forty years and three National Cancer Surveys which had sampled the incidence or new-case rates between 1930 and 1971—there was no "epidemic." The total number of cancer deaths had increased immensely over the past forty years, but so had the American population. According to an analysis of those mortality data by NCI biostatisticians Susan Devesa and Marvin Schneiderman, "most" of the increase had been due to: (1) the growth in population; (2) the increasingly aging population; and (3) the "joint effect" of both factors. The "real" increase in risk, they reported, was approximately 0.24 percent per year, a large part of that increase occurring between 1930 and 1940.[29] According to another analysis of the same body of data by Devesa and Debra Silverman of the NCI, there had been fluctuations upward in some cancers in various population groups (male, female, white, nonwhite); and there had been fluctuations downward in other cancers; and as the NCI's statistics revealed, those increases and decreases were generally slight. In forty years, only lung cancer had risen dramatically and only stomach cancer had dropped dramatically.[30]

Here is how the trends in U.S. cancer were reported in the years following those 1975 predictions:

- In 1977, the World Health Organization reported that in many countries, death rates were "either stationary or declining," in both males and females, for cancers other than that of the lung. The United States was one of those countries. The others were Australia, Austria, Canada, Chile, Costa Rica, Denmark, Egypt, Israel, Japan, Mexico, New Zealand, Norway, Sweden, Switzerland, and Venezuela.[31]
- In 1978, the Division of Vital Statistics of the National Center for Health Statistics reported that death rates from "all causes" had decreased during the years 1940 to 1976; that life expectancy at birth and at age forty-five had risen; and that when respiratory cancers were subtracted, all other cancers in the aggregate had declined—from 117 per 100,000 in 1940 to 98 per 100,000 in 1976.[32]
- In 1979, the American Cancer Society reported that the "overall incidence of cancer has decreased slightly in the past 25 years"; that there was an increased death rate in men which was "mainly the result of lung cancer"; and that for women "since 1950 the death rate has declined by 8 percent for blacks and 10 percent for whites."[33]
- In 1980, the United States Department of Health and Human Services pub-

lished *Health, U.S.: 1980,* showing that cancer rates had risen slightly between 1950 and 1977, but that the rise was primarily attributable to respiratory cancers.[34]

- In 1982, *The Nation's Health,* the official newspaper of the American Public
Health Association, cited the latest American Cancer Society figures, reporting: "Lung cancer rates are indeed the monster of cancer statistics, causing
the overall cancer death rate to increase over 18 years from 157.0 to 169.0 per
100,000 people when it would have decreased from 144.0 to 128.7 had it not
been for lung cancer."[35]

- And in 1982, a National Research Council Committee informed the press
that the "overall age-adjusted cancer rates have remained fairly stable over
the last 30 to 40 years, although the total number of cancer cases has risen
due to population increases. Exceptions to this are increases in respiratory
tract cancer related to cigarette smoking and decreases in stomach and uterine cancer."[36]

For seven years after those 1975 predictions of a great cancer epidemic,
the reports had been essentially the same. There was cause for elation in the
downward fluctuations, there was cause for concern in the upward fluctuations,
but U.S. cancer rates were reported to be fairly steady between 1930 and 1982.
More than forty years had passed since World War II and there still was no
great epidemic.

Despite the constancy of those reports from the major record-keepers of
the country and the world, announcements of the arrival of the great epidemic
were continuous between 1976 and 1980. In 1976, the press—e.g., CBS
News—suddenly reported, mentioning no sources, that cancer rates in the population at large were "soaring";[37] and as recently as 1980, the *New York Times*
reported that a monstrous epidemic of occupational cancer was occurring, citing "the Federal Government's own estimates" as the source.[38] "The Federal
Government" was indeed the source of those reports, and since they have left
much of the press and millions of Americans under the impression that cancer
rates have indeed exploded—an apparent confirmation of the prior apocalyptic
"axioms"—those reports will be explained. "The Federal Government" actually announced two distinct and different "epidemics"—a great general population epidemic in 1976 and a great workers' epidemic in 1978. The stories
overlap in time, but will be told in succession and in some detail, for in both
cases, the announcements were baseless.

The great general population "epidemic" suddenly materialized in 1976. It
came from the National Cancer Institute's Surveillance, Epidemiology, and
End Results Program (SEER), which was updating the three prior National
Cancer surveys on the United States and had produced new data for 1973 to
1976. The first report was made public before the data had been published in a
scientific journal and subjected to peer review—by Marvin Schneiderman of
the NCI, testifying before OSHA. The new data indicated, he said, that cancer
incidence had suddenly increased at an awesome rate in both whites and nonwhites and in both sexes. Even if lung cancer was subtracted from the data, he

said, white male cancer rates had risen by .9 percent between 1970 and 1975, nonwhite male cancer rates had risen by 2.7 percent; white female cancer rates had risen by 1.8 percent; and non-white female cancer rates had risen by 5.7 percent.[39] The formal publication of a scientific paper summarizing the SEER data did not occur until 1980. The data were published in the *Journal of the National Cancer Institute* by Earl S. Pollack and John W. Horm of the Biometry Branch of the National Cancer Institute. Comparing cancer incidence rates from 1969 to 1971 with the new SEER rates of 1973 to 1976, they reported an average annual increase of 1.3 percent per 100,000 cancers in white males and 2.0 percent for white females.[40] This was indeed an "epidemic." It had arrived just in time to validate the post–World War II theory and provided dramatic confirmation of the apocalyptic predictions.

On the publication of this paper, some scientists immediately performed frantic extrapolations. Brian E. Henderson of the University of Southern California, Los Angeles, explained at a cancer conference how those extrapolations were made. The SEER data, he said, indicated that within one decade, even excluding lung cancer, "cancer rates would increase by about 25 percent," and that by 1990, "the total cancer mortality among men and women will have risen 17 percent and 18 percent respectively." He then systematically took apart the data and declared the "epidemic" to be "artifactual."[41]

In fact, the catastrophe was illusory. Few had seen the first printout of the data produced by SEER (DHEW publication [NIH] 78-1837). In it, SEER had issued a warning: ". . . the SEER areas were not selected as a representative sample of the U.S. population. . . ." The SEER group explained:

Participants in the SEER Program were selected on the basis of their demonstrated ability to operate and maintain a population-based cancer reporting system and for the unique population subgroups which each of them offered. Thus, participants were selected with forethought to subgroups within the defined populations which were epidemiologically interesting rather than on the basis of being representative with respect to various demographic characteristics of the U.S. population.[42]

They observed that this "epidemiologically interesting" selection did represent more than 10 percent of the total population and was "fairly representative" with respect to age. But they said:

Blacks are somewhat underrepresented while other nonwhite populations (Chinese, Japanese, Hawaiians, and American Indians) are somewhat overrepresented. Rural populations (especially rural blacks) are also underrepresented.[43]

The NCI, in the process of setting up a new reporting system, one which included a variety of minority groups, had not set out to get a representative or continuous sampling of the U.S. population, and it had not gotten one.

Although they struggled to rationalize the data, Pollack and Horm conceded that the prior NCI cancer surveys, which covered forty years, and the SEER survey, which covered three years, were discontinuous, represented two different samplings of the U.S. population and that a question might arise as to whether they were comparable. The question did arise.

Other government agencies danced nervously around SEER's "epidemic." In 1978, the Department of Health, Education and Welfare in *Health, United States: 1978* repeated some of the SEER data, but felt obliged to publish a justification for accepting them.[44] And in 1980, the Toxic Substances Strategy Committee, chaired by Gus Speth, indicated that it wished to believe in the existence of an epidemic but couldn't. The committee solved the problem in its characteristic fashion: It contradicted itself. It declared that cancer rates were increasing, after justifying that conclusion for seven and a half pages.[45] In its last *sentence,* however, the committee ate its own words for the record: It said that the noncomparability between SEER's data and the prior data bases, as well as other uncertainties, "militate against drawing firm conclusions at this time."[46] It was widely reported in the U.S. press that the Speth committee had accepted SEER's epidemic, and *Science* reported in turn that the press had not read the committee's caveat.[47] The committee's caveat, of course, was virtually buried.

In 1980 and 1981, the American Cancer Society, which produces yearly reports on cancer trends in America, was faced with a curious problem. It had to use SEER's incidence data, for there were no other, but the ACS disavowed SEER's epidemic. The new yearly reports were prefaced with the following warnings:

Beginning with the 1979 edition of *Facts and Figures* SEER incidence information from the years 1973 to 1976 has been used. Each time a new data base is introduced to estimate incidence there may be sharp changes in figures due to the more accurate data. They do not indicate a cancer epidemic or new cure.[48]

Since comparisons of figures from different data bases are not valid, one can compare the 1978 *Facts and Figures* only with previous editions and the 1979 *Facts and Figures* only with later editions.[49]

The ACS, too, although in a different way, was trying to eat its cake and have it. It had declared the existence of an irreparable break in the U.S. record of cancer incidence, but it did not decline to publish the noncomparable data; the ACS simply denied their meaning, declared there was no epidemic, and informed its readers that they might have to wait for some years before they knew what was happening to U.S. incidence rates.

In 1981, the SEER data came under violent attack by Richard Doll and Richard Peto of Oxford University. In a detailed study of environmental cancer in the U.S. published in the *Journal of the National Cancer Institute* and republished as a book entitled *The Causes of Cancer,* they flatly dismissed the SEER data. Those data, they said, could not be compared with the prior rates recorded in the National Cancer Surveys that had preceded them: ". . . this particular comparison yields estimates of trends in real disease onset rates that are grossly discrepant with more reliable data."[50] U.S. cancer rates, they said, indicated that the currently common cancer types were not "peculiarly modern." They concluded that "there is no evidence of any generalized increase other than that due to tobacco."[51]

And in 1981, Marvin Schneiderman, who had launched the news of SEER's general population epidemic at the OSHA hearings, decided it was time to recant. He had by then left the NCI. He informed the *New York Times* that there was no epidemic, and the *New York Times* so informed its readers.[52] "The Federal Government's" general population epidemic, based on a discontinuous and nonrepresentative sampling of the U.S. population, had burst like the Great Mississippi Bubble.

In its wake, several technical quarrels are left. One is the conflict between those (e.g., John Berg) who have been willing to use SEER's incidence data independently of mortality data[53] and those (e.g., Richard Doll) who declare that they cannot be used independently until SEER has produced sufficiently "long and uniform" information.[54] Another and somewhat ironic conflict is the technical quarrel precipitated by SEER's *next* report, in 1981, that the mortality rates of certain cancers were *declining:* namely, stomach, breast, colon, cervix, leukemia, Hodgkin's disease. Some (e.g., Emil Frei III of the Dana-Farber Cancer Institute) argue that the primary cause of the decline is chemotherapy; others (e.g., John Cairns and Peter Boyle of the Harvard School of Public Health) argue that the primary cause is more likely to be the decline in incidence rates in younger age groups.[55] There is no way for a layman to form an opinion on this issue. He can only observe that this quarrel is about *declining* mortality rates and *declining* incidence rates—not about an "epidemic."

The second "epidemic" to emerge from the government was a great workers' epidemic. And the story is even stranger. Unlike the first, which emerged from the discontinuity of U.S. vital statistics, the second emerged from the feverish imaginations of apocalyptics in the health agencies. It was immediately shrouded in scandal.

The great workers' epidemic first materialized in 1978 in the form of a mimeographed paper, a "draft-summary" with a release date for the press, entitled "Estimates of the Fraction of Cancer Incidence in the United States Attributable to Occupational Factors."[56] Its listed "authors" were the National Cancer Institute and the National Institute of Environmental Health Sciences—which is to say that it had no authors. It named nine examples of occupational carcinogens—asbestos, arsenic, benzene, coal tar pitch and coke oven emissions, vinyl chloride, chromium, iron oxide, nickel, and petroleum distillates[57]—and said that the projections suggested that occupational cancers caused by those nine carcinogens alone might be anywhere from 20 to 38 percent or more of the total cancer incidence "in forthcoming decades."[58] The single most shocking extrapolation was that of asbestos deaths. Past exposure to asbestos, said this authorless document, "is expected to result in over 2 million premature cancer deaths in the next three decades" or "roughly 17 percent of the total cancer incidence experienced in that period."[59] The asbestos death rates previously projected had been disastrous enough—approximately 2,000 lung cancer deaths were then being recorded among asbestos insulators, *most of whom had also been heavy smokers.*[60] Never before had estimates of 2,000,-000 asbestos deaths been made.

On the same day that this "draft-summary" was released to the press, on September 11, 1978, Joseph Califano, Secretary of Health, Education and Welfare, funneled that 2,000,000 figure into the world of organized labor. Califano, who that same year had warned the press of the nonexistent peril of 7,000,000 possibly carcinogenic chemicals, electrified an AFL-CIO national conference on occupational safety and health with "alarming facts" taken from the authorless study.[61] He informed the American labor movement that occupational hazards were "constantly growing" and linked them immediately to synthetic chemicals: "In the chemical industry alone, production has skyrocketed from 1 billion pounds of synthetic organic chemicals in 1940 to more than 300 billion pounds last year, many of them new and untested substances."[62] He cited "a new study by scientists at the National Cancer Institute and the National Institute of Environmental Health Sciences" which was scheduled to be delivered to OSHA later that week, and presented a selection of its data. One was an estimate that "5 million American men and women . . . breathe significant amounts of asbestos fibers each day." Another was the extrapolation that "17 percent of all cancer deaths in the United States each year will be associated with previous exposure to asbestos."[63] Thus did Califano start a flash fire that still burns bright in the American labor movement and in the labor movements of the world.

Four days later, on September 15, 1978, a more detailed version of the same paper, this time thirty-nine pages long with an eleven-page appendix, was released to the press and the scientific community. It was different in several respects from the "draft-summary." The title had changed somewhat. It was now called "Estimates of the Fractions of Cancer in the United States Related to Occupational Factors"; the causal "attributable to" had been changed to "related to." The number of occupational carcinogens which were expected to produce as much as 38 percent of American cancer had abruptly shrunk; this time that awesome effect was not attributed to nine but to six carcinogens—asbestos, arsenic, benzene, chromium, nickel oxides, and petroleum fractions.[64] And the period in which the occupational catastrophe was to take place had become extraordinarily vague; it would now occur in "the near term and the future";[65] the precise "three decades" was absent. The scientific institutions which were said to have prepared the study had suddenly proliferated; this time the National Institute for Occupational Safety and Health (NIOSH) had retroactively joined the NCI and the NIEHS as authors. Finally, within four days, the study had suddenly acquired a stellar list of "contributors." Their names were listed in "alphabetical order"—a point explicitly made on the first page of the paper itself. The "contributors," who included two heads of health agencies, were these:

Kenneth Bridbord, NIOSH
Pierre Decoufle, NCI
Joseph F. Fraumeni, Jr., NCI
David G. Hoel, NIEHS
Robert N. Hoover, NCI

David P. Rall, NIEHS (Director)
Umberto Saffiotti, NCI
Marvin A. Schneiderman, NCI
Arthur C. Upton, NCI (Director)

There was also a "Contributor to the Appendix," Nicholas Day, NCI. The paper still had no responsible author, since, by scientific convention, the alphabetized list of names meant that no individual among them was taking responsibility for the data in the paper. Where these pseudo-authors had come from, and why their names had not been on the "draft-summary" four days earlier, was not explained. The "draft-summary" had simply metamorphosed into an imposing study adorned with the names of some of the most important scientists in America's health agencies.

The study was strange in one other respect. It had never been published in a scientific journal or reviewed by other scientists. It had simply rolled off a government mimeograph machine right into the labor movement after being "publicized" by Califano—the word "publicized" used unself-consciously by the Chief of OSHA's Media News Service in letters written to inquiring citizens.[66] It was altogether a most unusual way to inform America and the world that six occupational carcinogens were going to cause as much as 38 to 40 percent or more of the cancer in the United States—and unquestionably, according to this study, the percentage was far higher than 40 percent, since a list of other industrial carcinogens, which had not been included in the calculations, had been appended.

There was, finally, another striking aspect of this study. Not only did it predict the unheard-of number of 2,000,000 asbestos deaths, but it clashed violently with all prior estimates that had been made of the fraction of cancer that could be attributed to occupation. In fact, the challenge of those prior estimates was the stated intention of the paper.[67] Throughout the preceding decade, that fraction had been consistently estimated to be small by some of the most famous cancer scientists in the world—e.g., Johannes Clemmesen of Denmark,[68] Richard Doll of Britain,[69] and John Higginson of the IARC,[70] all of them fathers of the theory of environmental cancer. In addition, the occupational fraction of cancer had been described as small by L. M. Shabad in the USSR[71] and by scientists in the NCI itself. In 1974, Levin, Devesa, Godwin, and Silverman of the NCI's Biometry Branch, then headed by Haenszel, yet another father of the theory of environmental cancer, had said of occupational cancer: ". . . only a small proportion of the population are directly exposed and these exposures can often be controlled or eliminated when the hazard is recognized."[72] Commonly, the occupational proportion of the total cancer burden had been estimated at 1 to 5 percent and occasionally had risen to 10 or 15 percent. The new estimate of 40 percent or more made by the famous nonauthors at three health agencies was staggeringly higher.

The 40-percent-or-more estimate also clashed with estimates commonly made of the proportion of cancer associated with other factors. Tobacco had been said to account for 30 or 40 percent of all cancers in males, by such scientists as Guy Newell of the NCI[73] and Richard Doll in England.[74] Tobacco, and tobacco-interacting-with-alcohol, had been said by such scientists as Robert Flamant of INSERM in France to account for 50 percent of male cancers.[75] Nutritional factors had been said by such scientists as Ernst Wynder of the American Health Foundation[76] and Paul Newberne of MIT[77] to account for 30 percent of all cancers in men and possibly more in women. In addition, sexual practices and reproductive habits had accounted for yet another proportion of the cancer rate, e.g., infection, possibly herpes, was hypothesized to be a risk factor for cervix cancer;[78] low pregnancy rates had been correlated with high breast cancer rates;[79] and diet possibly combined with inflammation was also said to be associated with prostate cancer.[80] Clearly, if the new estimate that 40 percent or more of all cancer was linked to factory exposures was accepted, the other factors would have to shrink in significance. The implications of the NCI-NIEHS-NIOSH study—henceforth to be called the HEW study—were stunning to many epidemiologists.

In fact, the HEW study caused an explosion. The first protest—and perhaps the only one of which laymen were aware—was that of the American Industrial Health Council (AIHC), which released a thunderous critique of the study. One of the "authors," David Rall, head of the NIEHS, dismissed the critique with an ad hominem attack; it was, he said, "what might be expected of industry."[81] "Industry," however, was not alone in its shock. Thomas Maugh of *Science* analyzed both the HEW study and the industrial critique and declared that "the AIHC report appears to demonstrate some rather serious errors in the HEW report."[82] Maugh explained the central "error":

In each case, the investigators have taken the highest risk ratio available—ratios obtained for workers exposed to massive concentrations of carcinogens—and multiplied that by the total number of workers who might have been exposed to the carcinogen, *even though most or all of the workers have never been exposed to the concentrations upon which the risk ratios are based.* . . . [The] investigators have also rather sloppily equated deaths with incidence, even though the number of deaths resulting from a tumor is clearly only some fraction of the incidence, depending on the tumor. In short, the HEW projections are clearly exaggerated.[83] [Emphasis added]

The analysis of the HEW study, said Maugh, "necessitates the conclusion that its predictions are invalid."[84]

Within a few days of the appearance of the altered and embellished HEW study, academics, too, moved to protest it. Some of the most eminent epidemiologists in America, joined by molecular biologist John Cairns, descended on the NCI to query the "contributors." The meeting was held at the Sheraton International Conference Center in Reston, Virginia. Only one "contributor" was present—Umberto Saffiotti of the NCI, who was not an epidemiologist. He served both as spokesman for the HEW study and as chairman of the meeting. A transcript was made of the ensuing discussion,[85] and here are some of the scientists' criticisms—criticisms which were never transmitted to the public:

• Peter Greenwald, an epidemiologist in the New York State Health Department, observed politely that "there are no authors, there is a list of nine contributors in alphabetical order but there is not one that really takes the credit for it," and said he had hoped for an explanation of this phenomenon.[86]

- Cuyler Hammond, who, with Irving Selikoff, had done the most definitive studies on asbestos insulators—the workers with the highest exposures—professed himself "slightly puzzled" as to how the projections of 2,000,000 asbestos deaths had been made. He observed that "the only guess I can make is that we're going to see an increase for a short time in the number of asbestos related deaths and then a decline." He observed that the study used "rather tricky arithmetic."[87]

- Richard Peto of Oxford mocked the study's asbestos estimates. Observing that they were "possibly 1000" times higher than the 2,000 deaths indicated by the Hammond and Selikoff data, he said that the 4,000,000 men said to be employed in the asbestos industry were "all being treated as though they had been asbestos insulators for years. It's comical."[88]

- John Berg observed that "the report reads as if we're going to suddenly see this vast, drastic increase in the number of lung cancer deaths that are going to occur over the next 20 years" and that "there's no way to substantiate [it]." The document, he said, was "open to severe criticisms."[89]

- John Weisburger, disturbed by the exposure data, observed that "this document, if it ever sees the light of day, should be reassessed very critically and the numbers involved carefully inspected."[90]

- Michael Shimkin, observing that the estimates are "a good deal higher than might be legitimately based on scientific knowledge we now have," said: "I am somewhat surprised [that] scientists at the national level would themselves allow such a document to come out and be public and appear in the newspapers before it had adequate time for peer review." He considered the public release of the unreviewed study "a tragic mistake."[91]

Others spoke at this meeting, but these comments convey its tone. All scientists were critical, some were caustic, and some were depressed. The role played by Saffiotti as spokesman for the study was particularly revealing. At the opening of the meeting, he tried to defend the study. He was worried, he said, that the low estimates of occupational cancer were being made without sufficient data. He conceded that the study had not been published in a scientific journal, said it was a record prepared for the OSHA hearing, and assured the attending scientists that it was "the intention of the group of people who have worked towards this document to now go back to it and try and work on it further to prepare it for publication in the scientific literature."[92] The future intention to prepare a scientific document was a concession that the document was not scientific, and was ignored. Throughout the barrage of criticism, Saffiotti was silent, but one comment, not previously quoted here, affected him strongly. John Cairns, at the time the head of the Mill Hill Laboratory in London, had been particularly contemptuous. He had said of the document that "there are several parts of it which seem to be manifestly silly" and that anyone who could perform calculations "could see how stupid it is."[93] At the end of the meeting, Saffiotti indicated that he was offended by Cairns' expression "manifestly silly"; it was "a strong term," he said—and then he did his best, once again, to convert a disaster into a source of inspiration:

And this I emphasize again is just an early stage of this analysis and because of curious circumstances became much more of a public document than it was originally planned to be. I hope that this [meeting] at least will stimulate those whose names are listed in this document and many others to try and face the issue with facts, with data. . . .[94]

Saffiotti did not explain what "curious circumstances" had led a document without authors, "facts" and "data" to be funneled through the mouth of the Secretary of HEW to the American labor unions and directly into the press without peer review.

Equally curiously, no one asked Saffiotti for an explanation of those "curious circumstances." In strictly scientific terms, the government study was murdered at this private meeting, but it was a singularly bloodless murder, for the critics were mute about the obvious political dimension of that study. According to the transcript, not one scientist even hinted that he was criticizing a political phenomenon, and not one expressed concern that the country had been aggressively misinformed or that the labor movement had been gratuitously terrorized. The only effect of the study which was deplored at the meeting was the possibility of harm to the scientific community itself. Speaking with statesmanlike sorrow, Norton Nelson of NYU said he was "deeply concerned" that "a statement which is going to fall apart and cannot be adequately supported" would "damage the enterprise which so many of us are concerned with."[95] Others, too, shared this statesmanlike sorrow, but it extended neither to the political purposes of the study nor to the damaged polity.

News of the condemnation of the study sped like lightning from that closed conference throughout the scientific community. It generated a series of explosive rumors, and the rumors themselves shed considerable light on the mysterious mutism about the political nature of the document. The first rumor was never published, but it was widely repeated. One author, the story went, had sought to remove his name from the study, but had been threatened by the head of one agency that if he did so, his career in cancer research would end. A far more dramatic variant of that rumor appeared in print. It was eventually reported that the study had been repudiated by "several,"[96] "seven,"[97] and "all"[98] of its "contributors," a story which implied that there had been a revolt by scientific slaves against political masters. In fact, there was no genuine revolt at all; no scientist on the payroll of a federal agency *publicly* repudiated the study. The rumors, however, revealed that there was a widespread perception of the cancer prevention establishment as a political institution which used intellectual intimidation to achieve its goals. The political dimension of the study about which scientists had been abnormally mute when an NCI tape-recorder was running was the dominant content of the rumors.

Generally, the response of American epidemiologists to this astonishing study was secretive gossip. Those who criticized the document publicly were rare indeed. One who did so was Irving Kessler. At a toxicology conference, he expressed his conviction that information about occupational cancer would come only from serious epidemiological studies of human beings, not from analyses of old death certificates or from feeding rodents massive doses of chemicals.[99] He warned that epidemiology would never become an important medical discipline "if it degenerates into mindless statistical manipulation." He was particularly scornful of the HEW study:

I'm very much concerned by the political implications of enunciating cancer risks based on speculation, with pitifully little empirical evidence.[100]

At the same conference, Philippe Shubik observed that the HEW study had been thoroughly discredited and informed the audience that several of the "contributors" had been invited to attend that meeting to explain their work but had failed to respond to the invitations. He did not name the "contributors."[101]

Although the HEW study was enveloped in scandal from the moment of its appearance, the general public did not know it. That ignorance was exploited by certain advocates of the study. In October 1978, OSHA held a "seminar" for the press on occupational disease and repeated the data in the study. David Rall, who attended that seminar, also defended the study's estimates.[102] Then another protest was heard. Four days after the official media brainwashing, Philip Abelson, the editor of *Science,* attacked the study in an editorial. Abelson denounced the "opportunists" and publicity seekers who were alleging the existence of a cancer epidemic caused by chemicals. He criticized the scientists from the NCI, NIEHS, and NIOSH who, he said, had given Califano the "alarmist" estimates of cancer deaths used in Califano's speech. He also informed the readers of *Science* that the NCI-NIEHS-NIOSH report had been widely condemned by epidemiologists, that Richard Doll of Oxford had called it "scientific nonsense," and that the British journal *Lancet* had deplored the appearance of so inadequate a study "under such distinguished names."[103]

Significantly, Abelson mentioned only the names of a lay administrator and of foreign critics. The "opportunists" in the three health agencies were not identified. The "distinguished names," including those of the two agency heads, were still publicly protected, as were their American critics. But Abelson's column contained a warning signal: epidemiologists abroad were also angry.

In September 1979, Professor Rene Truhaut of the University of Paris denounced the HEW study as a *"scandale."* Speaking at the International Conference on Chemical Toxicology in Munich, he supported the British Royal Society's estimate that only 1 percent of all cancers were of occupational origin.[104]

In 1980, other more formal reactions from abroad were heard. Three were particularly noteworthy. The first was a paper in *Nature* headlined "Distorting the Epidemiology of Cancer," signed by Richard Peto of Oxford. An associate of Richard Doll, who had attended the first private protest meeting at the NCI, Peto discussed the political as well as the scientific aspects of the study. He criticized Califano's "absurd" 1978 speech to labor union leaders,[105] and discussed the "curious but extremely influential document which has been circulated privately for the past year or more."[106] He observed that it was prepared by "a working group of nine well known scientists, including Arthur Upton and David Rall," both of whom, he said, "still seem more ready to defend than repudiate it."[107] The study, he said, showed how "a group of reasonable men can collectively generate an unreasonable report."[108] And he challenged the fallacious estimates in some detail, again identifying the most commonly observed fallacy—that of applying the risk calculations derived from the highest exposures to people who had not experienced those exposures. The resultant estimates of occupational deaths, he said, were "utterly without foundation," although they were now being quoted repeatedly in the lay and scientific press.[109] Those estimates, he reported, had now penetrated the international labor organization in Geneva and a labor organization in the United Kingdom. In the United Kingdom, he said, the Association of Scientific, Technical and Managerial Staffs (ASTMS) had released a document to its members which had appropriated the NCI-NIEHS-NIOSH figures and had converted them into British figures; that union was now asserting that "20 to 40 percent of current United Kingdom cancer deaths are caused by occupational carcinogens."[110] According to Peto, the major causal factors in human cancer were tobacco and diet.[111]

Although Peto invested considerable effort in portraying himself as a neutral in the political controversies over environmental cancer, he was clearly angry. For good measure, he attacked Samuel Epstein, whose book *The Politics of Cancer* was a popular transmission belt for the HEW's occupational epidemic and had become the bible of the English-speaking labor unions.[112] There was a striking contrast between Peto's assault on Epstein—a private citizen whose work is read by choice—and his courtesy to the "reasonable" scientists at the head of U.S. agencies who, he said, had actually produced the data he was damning. It was a remarkable case of killing the messenger who had brought the bad news, probably attributable to the fact that *Nature* is a publication that is also read by laymen (for it should already be apparent that senior scientists rarely attack senior scientists where laymen can hear them).

The second response from abroad was austere and overtly nonpolitical—but given the source, it was a powerful counterattack. It was a paper called "Proportion of Cancer Due to Occupation," published in *Preventive Medicine*. It was written by one of the fathers of the theory of environmental cancer: John Higginson of the IARC.[113] The names of a "review committee"—scientists who had reviewed and approved the published manuscript—appeared at the head of the article. The committee included some prominent American scientists: Lawrence Garfinkel of the ACS, David Schottenfield of the Epidemiology Department of Sloane Memorial Hospital, and John C. Bailar of the *Journal of the National Cancer Institute*. But perhaps more important, that committee also included Johannes Clemmesen of Denmark's Institute for Cancer Epidemiology, the first historian of environmental cancer and possibly the most august father of the theory of environmental cancer; and it included Takeshi Hirayama of the Japanese National Cancer Center Research Institute, one of

Japan's most prominent epidemiologists. In this paper, Higginson estimated the probable upper limit of occupational cancers, putting it at 6 percent; 88 percent, he estimated, was due to "other life style factors."[114] He was quite aware, he said of the problem of the promotion of one carcinogen by another and of the multifactorial nature of cancer, but rough estimates based on known data, he said, could be made. His estimates of the proportional significance of various environmental factors were based on data from the highly industrialized city of Birmingham in the United Kingdom: Tobacco, he said, might account for 30 percent of male cancers; tobacco/alcohol for 5 percent; sunlight for 10 percent; diet, sexual behavior, etc., for 30 percent; radiation for 1 percent; medical for 1 percent; congenital for 2 percent; and unknown for 15 percent.[115] Speaking of the review committee, Higginson wrote that "the group" had concluded that there were no presently known data "which would seriously challenge" the estimate of 6 percent for occupational cancers.[116] In other words, the founding director of the IARC and two of the most prominent cancer epidemiologists in Europe and Asia had informed David Rall of NIEHS and Arthur Upton of the NCI, as well as the NCI epidemiologists whose names had appeared on the authorless study, that its feverish extrapolations were baseless.

Finally, in 1981, the most detailed attack of all appeared in print. It was the extensive Doll-Peto study which has already been mentioned. It was an extraordinary review of the known data by yet another of the epidemiological fathers of environmental cancer. Since it has been published in book form, the interested reader can consult it for technical details. In that study, written for the eyes of the world's scientists, the courtesy extended by Peto to American government scientists was abandoned. The HEW study was treated with withering scorn and language was used of a type that had never before been publicly directed at the U.S. health agencies. Because the study had been prepared for the OSHA hearings of 1978, and because OSHA was using its estimates, Doll and Peto deliberately called it "the OSHA paper." The estimates, they said, "were so grossly in error that no arguments based even loosely on them should be taken seriously."[117] They repeated the basic charge that the risks for all workers, whatever their exposure and however long it had been, had been established by criteria derived from the relatively few who had been most heavily exposed for many years,[118] and they said: "This disregard of both dose and duration of exposure is indefensible and produces risk estimates which are more than 10 times too large."[119] Of one particular estimate pertaining to nickel exposure, they wrote: "This calculation however might fairly be described as a confidence trick."[120] They finally declared:

It seems likely that whoever wrote the OSHA paper (it has a list of contributors, but no listed authors) did so for political rather than for scientific purposes, and it will undoubtedly continue in the future as in the past to be used for political purposes by those who wish to emphasize the importance of occupational factors, including the Toxic Substances Strategy Committee in their 1980 report to the U.S. President, as well as many newspaper articles and much scientific journalism. However, although its conclusions continue to be widely cited the crucial parts of the argument for these conclusions have, perhaps advisedly, never been published in a scientific journal nor in any of the regular series of government publications. Unless they are, with proper attribution of responsible authorship, we would suggest that the OSHA paper should not be regarded as a serious contribution to scientific thought and should not be cited or used as if it were. Furthermore any suggestions which derive directly or indirectly from it that 20, 23, 38 or 40 percent of cancer deaths are, or will be, due to occupational factors should be dismissed.[121]

In this analysis, prepared for the international world of cancer epidemiology, the U.S. health agencies had been charged with fabricating a politically motivated document and with using the devices of "confidence men"; and scientists all over the world had been warned that "the OSHA paper" should be treated as a contaminant of the scientific literature.

Doll and Peto also declared that despite the overlaps and uncertainties, one could make certain estimates of the proportions of cancer that were attributable to various environmental factors. They estimated that 30 percent of U.S. cancer was associated with tobacco, 35 percent with nutritional factors, 3 percent with alcohol, 7 percent with reproductive and sexual behavior, 3 percent with "geophysical factors," i.e., UV radiation, and possibly 10 percent with infection. As for industrial factors in cancer, they estimated that roughly 1 percent might be linked with food additives, 2 percent with pollution, around 1 percent with "industrial products," 1 percent with medicines and medical procedures—and 4 percent with occupation.[122]

In sum, the epidemiological fathers of the environmental theory of cancer had stood by, explained, and justified their low estimates of occupational cancer, which had been the target of "the OSHA paper."

The principal defender of that "paper" has been David Rall. Two of Rall's criticisms of scientists who have made low estimates of occupational cancer are worth noting. Both are recorded in OSHA's policy document of 1980. Here is the first:

In the first place the estimates of the fractions of cancers caused by occupational factors are based only upon the *known* examples of occupational carcinogens. . . . only a limited number of occupational exposures have ever been investigated for carcinogenic risk.[123]

And here is the second:

Recognizing that carcinogenesis is a multi-phased process whose progression is influenced by a number of factors, it makes little sense to assert that "only" 1 to 5 percent of cancers are attributable to a single factor. It would be consistent with our present knowledge to assert that *all* cancers are associated in one way or another with occupational factors, just as they are probably all associated with dietary factors, with genetic factors, and with hormonal factors.[124]

What one learns from the first criticism is that Rall is unself-consciously critical of epidemiologists who "only" base their analyses on knowledge. One learns from the second criticism that Rall had actually ended up by denying the validity of "the OSHA paper" itself. His criticism cited above actually means that there is no way to differentiate analytically among any of the major determinants of human cancer. If this "holistic" description of cancer is true, then no scientific analysis of the causal factors of environmental cancer was possible or will ever be possible. To be consistent, Rall should have retitled "the OSHA paper": "Estimates of the Fraction of Cancer Which Is Due to an Interaction between Occupational, Dietary, Genetic and Hormonal Factors"—and put it in a shredder. He should then have walked to the nearest blackboard and written a hundred times: "People who live in glass houses should not throw stones." Those actions did not occur to the Director of NIEHS. He apparently did not realize he was criticizing himself.

It is common in a polarized controversy to assume that if one side takes a fallacy-ridden position, the other side is right. There is no such implication here. No layman can permit himself to form an opinion on the estimated fraction of cancer associated with any particular environmental factor. The layman can probably do no better than to consider a question Kessler raised in 1979. He asked: "What would be the value of knowing what percentage of cancers are due to unidentifiable unspecified factors?"[125] The value is clearly political, and it is a value for both sides in this controversy. Epidemiologists, like animal and bacterial extrapolators, are deeply politicized; all are perfectly well aware of the practical implications of their various estimates, and all are perfectly aware that what they are fighting over is the body of industrial civilization.

On the subject of occupational cancer, the difference between U.S. government scientists and their critics is that the U.S. government scientists, with little human data and with the aid of crude logical fallacies, extrapolated a catastrophic epidemic into the unknown; their critics stubbornly challenged those extrapolations into the unknown with estimates based on the few data that are known. Since, in fact, epidemiological studies of occupational cancer have barely begun, since the dietary theory of cancer is highly suggestive but unproved, and since no firm causal explanations have yet emerged for most of the major cancers in the United States, let alone for most of the minor cancers, one suspects that this entire battle could have been avoided if all of its participants had been willing to say: "I don't know." In fact, the only value of having percentage estimates of industrially linked cancers based on *confirmed* human carcinogens is that it serves as a brake on the unbridled fantasies of apocalyptic scientists. That may be the real reason for which nonapocalyptic epidemiologists persist in making such estimates. Certainly they have no predictive value.

An illuminating interpretation of the battle of percentages is on the record. At the end of a 1980 conference on cancer prevention, Guy Newell of the NCI made four interesting observations of which the layman should be aware. In the face of the "array of percentages," he counseled "caution" and said the following:

I have no problem measuring the excess cancers among cigarette smokers because it can be done—it can be done with quantitation.... I am very confident that the figure of 35% or so of all cancers in men is related to cigarette smoking. The danger is in the temptation to extrapolate this methodology to areas where I think it is impossible, based on current knowledge, to quantitate. The tendency is to extrapolate to the areas where the science is infinitely soft at this time. . . . This temptation to extrapolate into soft areas leads to the term Dr. Rothman used—an "illogical deduction"—and I think that this illogical deduction has been put forth by some in the area of occupation, and by virtually all in the area of diet.[126]

Newell's second observation pertained to the fact that a given cancer might have more than one cause (e.g., both asbestos and tobacco cause lung cancer) and that causes could interact (as they do in the case of asbestos and tobacco). That, he said, made the use of percentages questionable. Third, he said, the use of percentages was being politicized and was creating "inflated expectations" in Congress and the public. Finally, he noted that percentages tended to be equated with money, specifically with shares of the NCI budget.

Whether the sole purpose of the war of percentages has been to "create inflated expectations" and to reallocate the NCI research budget may be doubted. Too many foreign scientists participated in it and the ideological dimension of the war is too crude. But Newell's explanation of the invalidity of "extrapolating into soft areas" is informative—and it applies to both sides in the controversy.

If the first great epidemic produced by "the Federal Government" ended in ruptured incidence records and in controversy, the second ended in an appalling international scandal, and in a shame, anger, and bitterness which is only expressed behind the scenes. The third "axiom" of the apocalyptics—the monstrous epidemic that must infallibly follow from the assumption that 90 percent of cancer is caused by post–World War II organic chemistry—has not occurred. Lung cancer apart, there have been rises—but there have also been declines. We owe the almost universal belief that a great epidemic has already arrived to a few intensely political men in "the Federal Government."

THE UNITED STATES IS "NUMBER ONE" IN CANCER

There was, finally, a last "axiom," and it, too, was derived from the apocalyptics' deepest assumptions. Where the apocalyptic was concerned, cancer was fundamentally a modern political disease caused by human innovation and productivity; 90 percent of it, he said, had come from "the Faustian sin"; from man's "conquest of nature"; from science, technology, economic growth, affluence; from the primary values of the Industrial Revolution, of Western civilization; and, not infrequently, from capitalism, the market, and profits. From that, it was just one step to the idea that the country which most dramatically embodied those attributes was America. Inevitably, the United States was transmuted by the apocalyptic mind into the carcinogenic sewer of the world.

Quite abruptly, in 1975, the press announced that it had been "discovered" that this country had the highest cancer rates in the world, that the U.S. had among the highest cancer rates in the world associated with industrial pollution, and that the majority of American cancers were caused by pollution. All three "discoveries" had apparently emerged from the science of epidemiology, since the report pertained to humans, not to animals—and all three "discoveries" were baseless. Since they meant quite different things and one must convey different types of epidemiological data to explain why they were baseless, the three ideas will be discussed separately.

In 1975, Dan Rather of CBS-TV News opened a documentary with these ominous words: "The news tonight is that the United States is number one in cancer. The National Cancer Institute estimates that if you're living in America your chances of getting cancer are higher than anywhere else in the world." The documentary was entitled "The American Way of Death."

This riveting "news" was nonsense. If by "getting cancer" Rather meant dying of cancer, and the show's title indicated that he did, the calculation was impossible. Changes in comparative global mortality rates are not calculated overnight; and according to the available data at the time—those of 1973—the United States was not "number one" in world cancer rates. Had a shift in the U.S. ranking suddenly occurred and had it been possible to collect global data in so brief a period, that catastrophe would have been reported in the scientific literature; it would not have been whispered by Anonymous into the ears of CBS-TV News.

Here is what one finds in the epidemiological literature of that period. Just two years before that televised "estimate" from "the National Cancer Institute," Mitsui Segi, one of the fathers of the theory of environmental cancer, had calculated the age-adjusted death rates for cancers in fifty-two countries. The data permitted an orderly ranking of cancer mortality rates among nations, both for specific cancer types and for overall cancer rates taken collectively. All such data are crude, but these were among the best available in 1975, and indeed were still among the best available as late as 1979 when the American Cancer Society published them in a document prepared for American blacks. The mortality rates of nine types of cancers considered by Segi—buccal, esophagus, colon and rectum, lung, stomach, breast, prostate, uterus, and leukemia—were selected by the American Cancer Society for reproduction. They included the major cancer killers in the United States. Here are the total age-adjusted death rates per 100,000 people from the above-named cancers in all the industrialized nations on the list:[127]

The industrialized country with the highest collective mortality rates from all nine cancers was Luxembourg, 219.48. There then followed, in order:

Czechoslovakia	213.63	Italy	182.79
Scotland	210.37	Switzerland	182.74
Belgium	204.07	Hong Kong	173.67
Netherlands	199.03	Denmark	171.65
Uruguay	197.86	New Zealand	168.97
Austria	197.35	Northern Ireland	168.45
France	196.55	Poland	168.24
U.S. (*Blacks*)	193.51	Australia	161.48
England and Wales	191.19	Chile	160.55
Hungary	189.28	Canada	160.39
Germany, F.R.	188.33	Ireland	160.08
Finland	187.12	U.S. (*Whites*)	155.90

Japan	149.37	Bulgaria	134.32
Sweden	146.47	Romania	132.81
Spain	141.43	Portugal	131.33
Cuba	137.83	Israel	126.69
Norway	137.78	Yugoslavia	124.76
Greece	137.69		

Yugoslavia was followed by such semi-industrial countries as Iceland, Costa Rica, and Puerto Rico; the nations listed above were industrialized. Given the rapid sharing of scientific, technological, and industrial discoveries by all industrial nations, and the rough comparability of medical treatment in all, these disparities in cancer mortality rates were striking. In some cases, where the ranking orders diverge by a percentage of a point, or a point or two, it may be less significant. But it is clear that the range between the extremes was astonishingly great. Luxembourg had almost *twice* the cancer mortality rate of Yugoslavia. The mortality rates of Denmark were much higher than those of the neighboring nations of Norway, Sweden, and Finland. And Czechoslovakia, Scotland, Belgium, France, England, and Wales had cancer mortality rates much higher than those of Canada, Japan, and Israel.

As for the United States: U.S. whites had cancer mortality rates in the *lowest* third of the set of industrial nations, while U.S. blacks had cancer mortality rates in the *highest* third. And at that, the U.S. black rates were lower than those of eight industrial nations: Luxembourg, Czechoslovakia, Scotland, Belgium, Netherlands, Uruguay, Austria, and France. Finally, the people of those eight nations *plus* the people of fifteen others—England and Wales, Hungary, Germany, Finland, Italy, Switzerland, Hong Kong, Denmark, New Zealand, Northern Ireland, Poland, Australia, Chile, Canada, and Ireland— had higher mortality rates from those same nine cancers than did the whites in the United States of America. The United States, whether black or white, was decisively not "number one."

In 1975, most of the citizens of this country never learned about the actual U.S. ranking of the period, nor did most become aware in 1977 of later World Health Organization data which ranked the United States as eighteenth out of forty-four nations.[128] Nor did most learn in 1979 of yet later WHO data, which ranked the United States as twenty-second of a slightly different set of forty-four nations.[129] Millions were left with the "news" disseminated by "the National Cancer Institute" to CBS that, as CBS had put it, cancer was the unique "American Way of Death."

It is possible, however, that by "getting cancer," Rather's NCI informant had not meant dying of cancer but had *really* meant "getting cancer," which is to say that he had told Rather that the U.S. had the highest *incidence* rates in the world. But that, too, was misleading. Ten months before the CBS documentary, in 1974, C. S. Muir, one of the leading epidemiologists at the International Agency for Research on Cancer, had given a lecture at an NCI-sponsored conference, in which he had presented a selection of the international incidence rates. Those global incidence comparisons—to select the cancers named above—indicated where the highest incidence rates in the world had been found.[130]

Mouth and throat: The highest incidence rates of tongue cancer were found in males in Bombay; the highest rates of lip cancer were found in males in Newfoundland; the highest incidence rates of larynx and pharynx cancers were found in males in Bombay. (No such cancers were listed for females.)

Esophagus: The highest incidence rates of esophageal cancer were found in males in Bulawayo and in female Bantus in South Africa.

Colon: The highest incidence rates of colon cancer were found in male Chinese in Hawaii and in females in Saskatchewan.

Rectum: The highest incidence rates of rectum cancer were found in males and females in Saskatchewan.

Lung: The highest incidence rates of lung cancer were found in males in Liverpool, England, and in female Maoris in New Zealand.

Stomach: The highest incidence rates of stomach cancer were found in males in Miyagi, Japan, and in female Indians in Natal.

Breast: The highest incidence rates of breast cancer were found in white females in Hawaii.

Prostate: The highest incidence rates of prostate cancer were found in U.S. blacks in Alameda, California.

Uterus: The highest incidence rates of uterine cancer were found in Maoris in New Zealand.

Leukemia: Not reported by Muir.

In addition, there were other strange findings. The highest incidence rates of brain cancer had been found in European-born Jews in Israel, male and female. The highest incidence rates of bladder cancer were found in U.S. males in Connecticut, with the highest female incidence rates found in Rhodesia. And the lowest incidence rates in the world of stomach cancer were found in U.S. females in Nevada.

These were among the best samplings of incidence rates all over the world at that time. Cancer is a long-latency disease; the global status of these cancers could not have been revolutionized between the last word of Muir's lecture and the first word of Rather's documentary.

Apparently, Rather's NCI informant had not told him that in 1970 Richard Doll had made the strange discovery that in almost all populations, approximately half the total amount of cancer is caused by only four or five cancer types.[131] Nor had the NCI informant told him that there are, to cite John Berg's phrase, cancers of affluence and cancers of poverty.[132] One comparison dramatically illustrates both observations: In the U.S. (and generally in the West), the dominant cancers were lung, colon, and hormonally linked cancers, e.g., breast, ovary, and prostate.[133] By contrast, in Uganda, an impoverished and preindustrial nation, the dominant cancers were penis, cervix, and eyeball cancers and ulcerating skin cancers on arms and legs.[134] Had the NCI informant given CBS the global data of that period, whether mortality data or incidence data, the network could have produced a dramatic documentary on the *real* meaning of environmental cancer, namely, the fantastic global variations of the disease which had led to the extraordinary discovery that patterns of cancer changed with patterns of culture.

There may of course have been an entirely different reason for that "number one" which was to resound so terrifyingly throughout the country. It is possible that Dan Rather had gotten a scoop on SEER's spurious general population epidemic. If that is the reason, then Rather was either briefed by someone who did not know the SEER operation, or he was deceived. SEER, which was trying to incorporate many racial minorities into the NCI's incidence sampling project, knew and said from the beginning that the sampling areas were nonrepresentative and discontinuous in relation to former sampling areas. This was widely known at the NCI by 1974; almost a year before the CBS documentary, Marvin Schneiderman talked about it at a cancer conference.[134a] For reasons unknown, this fact was not leaked to CBS.

We can now consider the two remaining variants of the idea that the United States was the most carcinogenic place on earth. They were the reports also attributed to the NCI that the United States had one of the world's highest rates of pollution-linked cancers and that the majority of American cancers were caused by pollution.

There was a veritable explosion of such reports in 1975, precipitated by the publication of the first cancer maps in America. Two years later, the event was jovially recalled to an audience of environmentalists by Robert Hoover, head of the Environmental Studies Division of the NCI's Environmental Epidemiology Branch. He said:

Several years ago we developed data on rates of cancer by specific site- and age-adjusted rates by sex and race for the 20 years between 1950 and 1970, in 3,056 U.S. counties. But the information hit the research community and the general public with a resounding thud until we developed it into a series of maps illustrating the incidence of various types of cancer by age, race, and sex in 3,056 counties.[135]

In addition to the first encyclopedic compilation of county-by-county mortality data published in 1974, the one that landed with a "resounding thud," the NCI epidemiologists had produced a second volume in 1975 containing a series of cancer maps—mortality rates plotted out geographically on the map of the United States. Glossy photographs of the maps had been prepared for reproduction in publications, including the press, and for transmission to those who requested them. There was a map for major cancers in males and females and there were maps for several of the minor cancers. They showed the areas of the country where one found the highest rates of each particular cancer. Awestruck reporters found themselves staring at a series of hideous black blotches which they learned to call cancer "hot spots" and the report circulated that according to NCI, most of those "hot spots," or more specifically, the "hot spots" in the Northeast, had been caused by industrial pollution. This time, the NCI data did not land on "the general public" with a "resounding thud"; they generated hysteria.

The layman's version of the NCI epidemiologists' work is on the record.

That record is extensive, and it is crucial to see several examples of it, and to see them in chronological order.

In February 1975, the *Washington Post* appears to have broken the story. Reporter Peter Bernstein wrote with awe:

Painstaking detective work by medical researchers is producing mounting evidence that environmental impurities in man's habitat are the *primary causes of most cancer.*

... researchers at the National Cancer Institute estimate that *60 to 90 percent* of all human cancers are caused by environmental factors from ultraviolet rays to plastics and pesticides. ...

Using computers to analyze mortality data, NCI researchers have pinpointed "hot spots" in industrial areas of the Northeast from Boston to Washington and certain riverfront cities in the Midwest and South from Chicago to New Orleans. They are pressing the Environmental Protection Agency to place tight limits on the use of chemicals thought to cause cancer.

Most of the discoveries center on human exposure to these chemicals. Tests in different parts of the country reveal that man-made carcinogens escape into the air Americans breathe, the water they drink and the food they eat. Last year an estimated 355,000 Americans died of some form of cancer, compared to 350,000 in 1973.

Researchers at NCI headquarters in Bethesda increasingly are turning to modern technology to unlock the secrets of cancer. *Analyzing death certificates for a 20-year period from 1950 to 1969 with computers, they found that the most prevalent forms of cancer tend to occur in regions of the country where carcinogenic chemicals seem most pervasive—the so-called "hot spots."*

Computed according to age, race and sex, cancer rates turned out to be highest among adult white males. ...[136] [Emphasis added]

This story was read by Senator John Tunney into the record of a February hearing on the Toxic Substances Control Act.

In October 1975, Tunney opened a hearing on the act with these words:

During the last 4-year period, while this legislation waited on the sidelines, over 1 million people in this country have died of cancer. And Americans are getting cancer at an ever-increasing rate. In fact, the rate of cancer mortality in this country has increased over 20 percent in the past 25 years.

It is clear from the National Cancer Institute studies that cancer is, indeed, a byproduct of an industrialized society. Up to 90 percent are caused by contaminants placed in the environment by man. NCI studies have also shown a high correlation between cancer and industrial centers around the country.[137] [Emphasis added]

Tunney then read a current *Time* story into the record. Here is one paragraph from that story published on October 20, 1975, and entitled "The Disease of the Century." It was packed with impressive facts:

The U.S. has one of the world's highest incidences of cancers associated with environmental pollution. A recent National Cancer Institute study shows that the highly industrialized and highly polluted Northeast has a particularly high incidence of lung cancer as do areas where rubber and lead smelters are located. The highest rates of bladder and liver cancers are found in counties with plants producing rubber and chemicals, perfumes and cosmetics, soaps and printing ink. ...[138] [Emphasis added]

In the same month, October 1975, CBS aired the NCI announcement that the U.S. was "number one" in world cancer, which appears to be a simplified variant of the same story.

Two months later, in December 1975, Carl A. Craft of the Associated Press and Bill Richards of the *Washington Post* informed their colleagues across the nation and newspaper readers across the country that Ralph Nader was educating American Congressmen on the basics of environmental cancer, that Nader had announced the arrival of "the carcinogenic century" and had rebaptized cancer "corporate cancer," attributing it to carcinogenic pollutants in the environment. According to Richards, the Congressmen had been told by Samuel Epstein that "the majority" of the cancer cases "reported last year" were attributable to "industrial polluters."[139]

In April 1976, James Bishop, the National Energy and Environmental Correspondent of *Newsweek,* appeared as an expert interviewer on CBS's "Face the Nation" and declared to the vast mass audience that ". . . it is now generally accepted that about 60 to 90 percent of all human cancer is caused by man-made toxic chemicals of various sorts."[140]

And by 1977, Journalist Larry Agran's *The Cancer Connection* appeared, attributing the man-made "up to 90 percent" to the National Cancer Institute.[141]

When one puts these laymen's statements together, one finds oneself in the presence of the full roster of apocalyptic beliefs: the famous "up to 90 percent"; the concept that cancer is essentially "man-made"; the arrival of the great epidemic; the awesome carcinogenicity of the United States. And all these epidemiological ideas had been tied to the National Cancer Institute, specifically, to studies of counties with high rates of cancer and industries within them.

In trying to discover the origin of the reports that the U.S. was riddled with pollution-linked cancers, one falls headlong over the birth of the apocalypse itself. It was born in 1975, and according to the press, it had surged out of the NCI.

It also surged into the work of some scientists. By 1977, Thomas Corbett, whose authority was enhanced by his award from the EPA, wrote in *Cancer and Chemicals*: "Statistics now show that the United States has one of the world's highest incidences of cancer associated with environmental pollution."[142] And by 1979, Samuel Epstein had updated *The Politics of Cancer* and, citing the NCI cancer maps and correlational studies, informed his readers that 30 to 40 percent of cancer in America might be caused by industrial pollution; Epstein's authority, too, was enhanced by the high official status of some of the reviewers of his book: Arthur Upton, Director of the NCI, David Rall, Director of the NIEHS, Umberto Saffiotti and Marvin Schneiderman of the NCI, Kenneth Bridbord of NIOSH, and Donald Kennedy of the FDA.[143] This apparently official information about America's pollution-linked cancers influenced people within and outside the United States.

Meantime, informed by high government officials of 2,300 suspected carcinogens, of two kinds of epidemics, of the pollution crisis, and of 7,000,000 chemical perils, the American public also gave voice. By 1978, the majority of the American people, according to polltakers Yankelovich, Skelly, and White,

believed the two greatest threats to their health—more significant than tobacco—were "industrial waste" (59 percent) and "pollution" (58 percent).[144]
"Industrial waste" meant soil and water pollution, and "pollution" was short-
hand for air pollution. Both categories of hazard, in fact, were "pollution." The
apocalypse had saturated the population.

It is clear from all these developments, which followed swiftly on the heels
of the NCI epidemiologists' maps and data, that those data were of astonishing
historical significance, as were the anonymous NCI reports that the U.S. had
one of the world's highest rankings in pollution-linked cancers and that the
majority of American cancers were caused by pollution. Even more astonishing
is the fact that neither of these reports was true. Something about the NCI's
maps and data had driven the press and Americans into hallucinatory hysteria.

How did *Time,* or anybody else, become convinced that the U.S. had one
of the highest incidences of pollution-linked cancers in the world? How did the
Washington Post, Tunney, and others become convinced that the NCI had
proved or was proving that the majority of American cancers were emerging
from the smokestacks of the land? And did that information emerge from the
county data and maps? We will take these questions one by one.

The best place to start the explanation is with the high U.S. ranking in the
realm of pollution-linked cancer. It was not only false—it was impossible. Such
a calculation implied that the calculator had identified the proportion of cancer
that is associated with low-level pollution of air, water, soil, and food all over
the globe and that he had added up all the pollution-linked cancers and discovered that the U.S. had more of them than did most countries. No such data existed in 1975, nor do they exist today, and the reason is plain enough. If it is
impossible to estimate the percentage in fractions of occupational cancers even
when men can be exposed to intensely high doses of a carcinogen for long periods and even when adequate control groups can be found, it is even more impossible to estimate the fraction of cancers caused by "pollution," which is to
say by widespread or universal exposure to microscopic amounts of carcinogens in the air, water, and soil. No one knows what impact those microscopic
amounts may have, if any.

The state of the art did not permit such calculations—an assessment made
thoroughly explicit in the literature of the period, and for many years after.
Here are some examples of the way in which epidemiologists discussed the
subject at the very time of the NCI's studies. At a 1974 cancer conference,
Malcolm C. Pike et al., who had done an air pollution study, said that they
thought it was "reasonable" to "assume" that carcinogens in the air caused
some lung cancer;[145] it may indeed have been reasonable, but it was an assumption. At that same cancer conference, John Berg said that "it is probably
epidemiologically hopeless to link specific cancer risks to a specific contaminant," although he hoped that in the future it might be possible to correlate
high general pollution levels with high cancer rates.[146] In 1977, in the course of
discussing water pollution studies, epidemiologist C. R. Buncher and his colleagues observed that "research into the relationship of cancer to drinking
water is still in its infancy."[147]

And as recently as 1980, Brian MacMahon of Harvard, in a National Research Council study entitled "Epidemiology's Strengths, Weaknesses in Environmental Health Issues," explained clearly why epidemiology could not readily start with chemical pollutants, i.e., with carcinogenic "germs," in the environment and figure out their effects on human beings. The logic of his explanation applies to animate as well as inanimate "germs" and can be briefly summarized. Normally in the study of a disease, he said, one asks the question: What is causing it? This might be a difficult question to answer, but he said: *"When the focus of investigation is a disease, one knows at least that the disease exists and that it must have causes."* When, however, one begins with a "germ"—as is the case in pollution studies—the question is reversed and one finds oneself asking: What is that "germ" doing, if anything, to human beings? This, said MacMahon, is a vastly more difficult question to answer, for *"when investigating an exposure, one does not know whether or not a problem exists."* What is more, said this Harvard epidemiologist, to pose that question requires that one be able to prove that no disease is being caused, which is to prove a negative—which is logically impossible. Finally, MacMahon explained, even the certainty or the suspicion that a particular substance causes illness at some exposure does not readily tell one "what its effects are, if any, at the *lowest* levels to which humans are being or may be exposed."[148] (Emphasis added)

That is why the pollution literature for forty years has been a ceaseless imbroglio of warring estimates. That is why it was flatly impossible that anyone at the NCI or anywhere else had ever proved the existence of any human cancers caused by pollution—and that is why no one had ever added them up, all over the world, to discover that the U.S. had most of them. The report that America had among the highest rates in the world of pollution-linked cancers was an absurdity.

The report that the NCI epidemiologists had discovered or were discovering that the majority of American cancers had come or were coming from pollution was even more absurd, if possible. This is most parsimoniously demonstrated by one study which was taking place when the pollution apocalypse broke out—and whether the study's finding is correct or not is entirely irrelevant. In 1980, Cuyler Hammond and Lawrence Garfinkel of the American Cancer Society published a paper entitled "General Air Pollution and Cancer in the United States." They had studied a half million men who had had at least ten years of exposure to the amount and type of air pollution occurring in their neighborhoods. They standardized the lung cancer rates by age and by smoking habits. When smoking was eliminated as a factor, only occupational exposures remained: Workers exposed to dusts, fumes, and fibers in factories had 14 percent more lung cancer than did others. The authors wrote: "We conclude that general air pollution at present has very little effect, if any, on the lung cancer rate."[149] The authors had a review committee. One of its members was Joseph F. Fraumeni, Jr., one of the NCI authors of the county maps and data. By 1980, he had endorsed a study which said quite plainly that pollution wasn't doing much of anything to anyone. One may be certain that he would not have been endorsing this paper if he and his colleagues had *proved,* five years earlier, that the majority of cancers were being caused by pollution.

The reader will observe that the conceptual content of the last apocalyptic "axiom's" two pollution variants has vanished as of this instant; both variants were baseless.

What then? Did the cancer maps themselves contain this devastating information? That, too, is impossible. Cancer maps are called geographic correlations. They correlate high rates of cancer with *place*. In a paper later published in 1978, Johannes Clemmesen, the Danish father of the epidemiologists' theory of environmental cancer, who had spent a good portion of his life pondering over global mortality figures plotted out geographically, observed:

As usual in cancer we mostly use the description geographic as long as we are ignorant of causes, and the same applies to socioeconomic high risk groups.[150]

To express it with primitive simplicity, a cancer map is a regular map on which blotches of high rates of specific cancers have been placed. It allows the cancer epidemiologist to study a map of Asia, let us say—or of the United States—and to scratch his head while he mutters to his colleague: "Why the hell is there so much liver cancer *here* when there isn't any *there?*" To which his colleague responds wearily: "Search me." A geographic correlation—a cancer map—has no *causal* content. It correlates high rates of cancer with *here* and *there*. There is no way, from looking at a cancer map, to conclude that the majority of anything causes cancer or that the minority of anything causes cancer, because a map does not convey cause at all.

That leaves us, finally, with the county data. Did *they* show that the majority of cancers came from anything? *Time* gives an adequate description of some of the county data emerging from the NCI; and I reproduce it so that the reader can examine it again:

A recent National Cancer Institute study shows that the highly industrialized and highly polluted Northeast has a particularly high incidence of lung cancer as do areas where rubber and lead smelters are located. The highest rates of bladder and liver cancers are found in counties with plants producing rubber and chemicals, perfumes and cosmetics, soaps and printing ink. . . .

There is one error here; these were not incidence data and the present tense is inappropriate. The county data were mortality data, studies using death certificates. But that is certainly what the NCI epidemiologists were doing. They were generating county-industry correlations. Does a correlation have a causal content? Again, no. Even when it is statistically significant? No. Even when it is highly statistically significant? No. There is a dramatically high correlation between the rise of television and the rise of lung cancer, but that does not prove that television causes lung cancer. There is an equally dramatic correlation between the increase in affluence and the *decrease* in stomach cancer. That does not prove that affluence is a cancer inhibitor. A statistical correlation, even a very high statistical correlation, simply says: There may be some relationship between these things . . . and there may not. It is the *connection* between them that is the cause, if any; it must be biological; and it must be identified in studies of matched test and control groups of human beings. The

NCI epidemiologists were, indeed, ferreting out counties with above-average rates of deaths from specific cancers and were correlating those deaths with the industries in those counties, but as the county data themselves reveal, they had not yet begun to conduct controlled studies of human beings.

On the face of it, we have explored all possibilities and there is no element of this story which accounts for the apocalyptic explosion in the press. And yet it did occur, and the reporters, Tunney, and others were referring to the NCI data and maps. One does not know who said what to the press, for that is off the record. But one document is on the record that points directly to the government's role in the apocalypse.

It should not surprise the reader by now to learn that when the government plays a role in cancer science, something complicated is liable to happen. In this case, it was more complicated than usual and takes a bit of patience to untangle. One begins the untangling process by turning to Appendix C. There the reader will find a document entitled "Fact Sheet: Atlas of Cancer Mortality for U.S. Counties: 1950–1969." The sources were identified as the United States Department of Health, Education and Welfare, the National Institutes of Health, and the National Cancer Institute. The document is undated, but it is an announcement of the publication of the book *Atlas of Cancer Mortality for U.S. Counties: 1950–1969,* which was published in 1975. Authored by T. J. Mason, F. W. McKay, R. Hoover, W. J. Blot, and J. F. Fraumeni, Jr., the *Atlas* followed the original encyclopedic publication of county-by-county tabulations of mortality data, the data which had landed with a "resounding thud" until they had been plotted onto maps of the U.S. showing the locations of the highest rates of many cancers. The *Atlas* contained those maps. It also included a minimal amount of mortality data. The explanatory fact sheet which accompanied the *Atlas* recommended the book to "health professionals" across the country and advised them to consult the original tabulations of county-by-county data along with the maps. The fact sheet was also sent to those who requested the maps and the original county data. That is how I received the document. Since I was working at a university on a book on cancer, I was treated as a "health professional."

The fact sheet, however, was something more than a neutral announcement of publication of a neutral presentation of geographic data. It called the reader's attention to high mortality rates in certain areas, and it transmitted some information which suggested causal interpretations, namely, some of the NCI epidemiologists' findings and their beliefs about the meaning of those findings. This may not seem odd to the lay reader, so an analogy might be useful. It was as if the Fed had released data about the GNP or unemployment statistics or the latest census—numbers which always evoke controversial interpretations by economists, sociologists, and political theorists—and had incorporated into its announcement of those numbers interpretations from a few economists or sociologists or political theorists within government agencies. On the face of it, the HEW-NIH-NCI fact sheet was an unorthodox announcement of the publication of a neutral data resource.

The reader is requested to turn to Appendix C and to read the government fact sheet carefully, and to read it *now* because if he does not, he will never again be able to perceive it with the same eyes.

On the assumption that the reader has read Appendix C, I continue. In one sense, it may have been an anticlimactic experience. Certainly, if the reader was expecting to find apocalyptic allegations, he has been disappointed. Clearly, some of its material appeared in the press, but the document does not say that the U.S. had the highest cancer rates in the world; it does not say that the majority of cancers were caused by pollution; it does not say that the U.S. had one of the highest incidences of pollution-linked cancers in the world.

In fact, it does not even use the word "pollution."

And that is not its only omission. The single most important thing about the HEW-NIH-NCI fact sheet is what it did *not* say and the impression it left because of what was unsaid. It did not say so many things it might have said about American cancer that the most efficient way to communicate what was missing is with a different fact sheet summarizing the views of prominent scientists of the period.

That alternative fact sheet is presented below, and it is based on the information available at the time of the pollution apocalypse. Along with some other papers, the basic document on which it relies was the 1974 conference organized by the NCI in cooperation with the American Cancer Society. That conference was an ambitious attempt to amass the best information on cancer causation acquired by the science of epidemiology throughout the decades; it was heavily attended by NCI scientists, and the authors of the county data and maps were among those who presented papers. In fact, the information gathered at that conference was considered to be so all-encompassing and important that at its completion, it was edited by one of the NCI epidemiologists, Joseph F. Fraumeni, Jr., and was published in book form in 1975 under the title *Persons at High Risk of Cancer: An Approach to Cancer Etiology and Control.*[151] In 1974, another overview of the epidemiological findings was prepared by David L. Levin, Susan S. Devesa, J. David Godwin II, and Debra T. Silverman of the NCI's Biometry Branch, then headed by William Haenszel. It was called *Cancer Rates and Risks*[152] and was offered to American health professionals. That volume was compressed into a small pamphlet called *Cancer Questions and Answers about Rates and Risks,*[153] published in 1975 by the Biometry Branch of the NCI. I use it in the fact sheet below. I also use material from another NCI-ACS-sponsored conference called *Nutrition in the Causation of Cancer,* all the papers of which were published together in *Cancer Research,* Vol. 35, in 1975.[154]

Here, from various epidemiologists, including the authors of the cancer maps and county data, is some of the information that could have been transmitted by the HEW-NIH-NCI with the cancer maps of the U.S.—and was not.

ALTERNATIVE FACT SHEET
1974-1975

UNITED STATES

Death, U.S.A.

In America, where death by infectious disease has virtually been wiped out, the greatest number of deaths are caused by accidents, homicide, and suicide (Shimkin, 1974).[155] Cancer is rare in young people and is a disease of middle and old age. The highest number of cases are found in people aged about seventy (NCI Q&A, 1975).[156]

In 1975, approximately 1 percent of the total population died, and among those who died of cancer, the dominant groups of cancers of which they died were: respiratory cancers, above all lung; digestive cancers, above all colon; and the hormonal cancers, above all breast, uterus, and ovaries in females and prostate in males.[157] They are the dominant cancers in affluent Western countries (Doll, 1975; Henderson, 1974).[158]

U.S.: Nonwhite

Within the U.S., nonwhites have had the cancers of poverty. Blacks: lung, esophagus, stomach, and cervix (Cutler and Young, 1974).[159] Puerto Ricans: mouth, pharynx, esophagus, stomach, cervix, vulva, and penis (Martinez et al., 1975).[160] Mexican-Americans born in Mexico: nasal passage, gall bladder, liver, male genital organs, cervix (Wakefield, 1974; Menck, 1975).[161]

U.S.: White lower-class cancers

The rural lower classes in the Southeastern U.S. have mouth and throat cancer, melanoma, skin cancer, and cervix cancer (Hoover et al., 1974).[162] Cancers of the esophagus and stomach are also linked to low socioeconomic status (NCI Q&A, 1975).[163]

A FEW PRINCIPLES

Contrast

Epidemiology does not study individuals, it studies selected groups. The classic epidemiological approach, as Cedric Davern puts it, is "the principle of looking for oddity." The science is born of the fact, he says, that people arrange themselves spontaneously into distinctive groups which differ strikingly from each other in behavior.[164] Thus, epidemiologists study males and females, rich and poor, fat and thin, black and white, smokers and nonsmokers, people who are exposed to substance X and people who are not exposed to substance X, etc.—always looking for extreme cases which may point to causal factors.

Controls

As in every other science, says Irving Kessler, only controlled studies of carefully matched groups are scientifically valid. A statistical correlation based on routinely collected data is simply a hypothesis to be tested.[165] C. S. Muir says that correlations are "a very blunt instrument" and that "their results should never be accepted without further testing."[166]

Replication

Many studies must be done to test a hypothesis, says Kessler. He observes: "The truth in medicine is reached asymptotically—by a multiplicity of studies, by a multiplicity of observations."[167] Brian MacMahon, too, says that correlational studies must be repeated over and over again until so much information is available that it makes alternative explanations unlikely.[168]

Exception to the rule

According to Richard Doll, there is one kind of problem that epidemiologists can solve rapidly. This science can track an unusual cancer type to its source: e.g., angiosarcoma of the liver to vinyl chloride and mesothelioma of the lung to asbestos.[169]

A FEW PROBLEMS

Time warp

When correlation studies are based on mortality rates, one is actually looking into the past. As Schneiderman of the NCI put it in 1974: "Today's cancers reflect conditions 20 or 30 years ago."[170] Or, 30 or 40 years ago (Selikoff, Hammond, 1974).[171] Or, 5 to 50 years ago (Higginson, 1974).[172]

"Social creep"
There is also the problem that Schneiderman calls "social creep." Occupational data, he says, may be unreliable because "the clerk is reported as an executive; the railway fireman is reported as an engineer; the janitor becomes a maintenance supervisor."[173] When death data are thus glamorized, they provide distorted information.

Medical reporting
Faulty diagnoses or faulty autopsies may be misleading, according to Higginson (1974), if one wishes to identify a causal factor.[174] The inconsistency of diagnoses, not to mention the selective process in autopsy (Schneiderman, 1974),[175] is a considerable problem for the epidemiologist.

CANCERS

Skin and melanoma: Caused by exposure to the ultraviolet rays of the sun (Jablon, 1974).[176]

Congenital and genetic: According to John Mulvihill (1974) "even the commonest types of cancer—colon, breast, skin—can be part of genetic syndromes."[177]

Familial susceptibility: There is a high risk for many cancers; e.g., breast, colon, lung, in first-degree relatives of people with those cancers. Almost all cancers exist in both a heritable and nonheritable form (Anderson, 1974).[178]

Multiple primary cancers: People with primary cancers in one location are likely to develop a primary cancer in the same or another location. An association has been reported between breast, uterine, ovary, and colon cancer in women. Nuns are at a higher risk of breast, colon, uterine, and ovarian cancer than the general population (Schoenberg, 1974).[179] In 1975, the NCI also reported similar associations, e.g., colon and breast, colon and endometrium (NCI *Q&A*, 1975).[180]

Disease-linked: In 1974, A. C. Templeton published a list of diseases which may result in an increased risk of cancer. Examples: herpes virus type 2 is linked to cervix cancer; hepatitis B to liver cancer; gastritis to stomach cancer; ulcerative colitis to colon cancer; diabetes to pancreatic cancer; and pernicious anemia to stomach cancer. Traumas—e.g., scars, burns, bites—are linked to skin cancer.[181]

Tobacco-linked: By 1974, an awesome number of cancers had been linked to tobacco smoking: mouth, lip, and tongue; larynx; pharynx; esophagus; pancreas; kidney; bladder (Hammond, Hoover, Muir, Shimkin, Schneiderman, Selikoff, Wynder, MacMahon, 1974).[182]

Alcohol-linked: Alcohol had been established as a strong risk factor for cancers of the mouth, pharynx, larynx, esophagus, and liver (Rothman, 1974; Templeton, 1974; Hammond, 1974; Vitale, 1975).[183]

Diet-linked: In 1967, Wynder et al. found a positive correlation for cancers of the breast and colon in women in twenty-one countries, and hypothesized that dietary habits were involved.[184] In 1974, Schneiderman of the NCI accounted for breast, colon, and rectum cancer by diet.[185] In 1974–1975, obesity, overnutrition, and a high-fat/beef diet were linked to breast, ovary, uterus and prostate cancers (Henderson, 1974; Berg, 1974, 1975).[186] These cancers and colon and rectum cancer had been strongly correlated with per capita meat and fat consumption in thirty-two countries (Armstrong & Doll, 1975).[187] Stomach cancer is linked to dietary deficiencies, (e.g., fresh vegetables); it has been rapidly falling in the United States (Haenszel, 1974).[188]

Sex-linked: Early menstruation was reported to be a risk factor for breast cancer (Henderson, 1974),[189] and early pregnancy had repeatedly been demonstrated to have a protective effect against breast cancer (MacMahon et al., 1970, 1973).[190] Uterine (endometrial) cancer had been repeatedly linked to obesity (Henderson, Berg, Templeton, 1974).[191] Cervix cancer had been associated all over the world with sexual promiscuity and was believed to be influenced by infections; possibly by herpes virus type 2 (Heath, Henderson, Shimkin, 1974).[192] Penis cancer had been associated all over the world with lack of hygiene and lack of circumcision (Henderson, 1974).[193] Testicular cancer is linked to the hormonal group; it is more frequent in higher socioeconomic groups (Henderson, 1974; Berg, 1975).[194] Populations with a high risk of breast, colon, and uterus (endometrial) cancer are also at a high risk of prostate cancer (Berg, 1975; Armstrong and Doll, 1975).[195]

Drug-linked: In 1974, Hoover and Fraumeni of the NCI reported that a variety of cancers (e.g., leukemia, sinus, liver, skin, bladder, vaginal, cervical, endometrial and breast) had been related to drug exposures in man. Examples: radioisotopes (radium, Thorotrast); cytotoxic drugs (e.g., Cyclophosphamide and Melphalan), synthetic estrogens and steroids.[196]

Occupation-linked: In 1974 Selikoff and Hammond reported that lung cancer is caused by chromates, nickel, asbestos, hematite mining, and bis (chloromethyl) ether.[197] In 1974 Cole and Goldman presented a table of carcinogenic agents which might be affecting workers in various occupations. He presented a list of carcinogenic agents, e.g., products of coal combustion, petroleum, benzene, aromatic amines, mustard gas, isopropyl oil, vinyl chloride, bis (chloromethyl) ether, arsenic, chromium, iron oxide, nickel, asbestos, wood, leather, ultraviolet rays, x-rays. Many cancers had been associated with these agents: skin, brain, nasal cavity, sinuses, larynx, lung, mesothelioma, liver (angiosarcoma), urinary bladder.[198] In 1974, Hoover et al. investigated high rates of bladder cancer among males in industrial counties. They calculated the percentage of workers employed in forty-one separate industries, compared the bladder cancer rates with the rates of the entire nation, discounting for smoking (which also causes bladder cancer), and only found statistically significant differences for six industrial categories out of the forty-one. For three categories of industry, the percentage of bladder cancer was lower than that of the nation.[199]

Pollution-linked: In 1974, Pike et al. made a variety of calculations based on benzo (a) pyrene concentrations in the air and concluded that there was "a small but not negligible" effect of air pollution on lung cancer. They observed that the effect must be small because even in heavily polluted areas, lung cancer rates had always been low in nonsmokers and women.[200] In 1974, Knudson noted that there were many uncertainties in pollution studies, citing the movement of people between urban and rural areas, changes in industrial practices, the enormous growth of automobile use in cities, and the long latency periods for cancer as factors which impeded the analysis of the role pollution might play in cancer. The strongest evidence of a carcinogen in polluted air, he said, was in areas where coal was used. He considered the question unresolved.[201]

At this point, the reader has reviewed the alternative fact sheet—a brief summary-outline of the mountains of findings and hypotheses about major and minor cancers that existed at the time of the pollution apocalypse. He has, I hope, gotten a strong impression of the complexity of the problem of environmental cancer. Genetic factors, disease, physical agents, chemical agents, biological entities, natural substances, and cultural practices had all been implicated in human cancer. The reader has also by now faced the full mystery of "multifactorial" cancer—meaning that any given cancer may be caused by more than one agent. Skin cancer is caused by the sun, but it is also caused by scars, genetic conditions, and occupational exposures. Tobacco is plainly the most dramatic killer—no known substance causes more cancers in man—but occupational agents, too, cause lung cancer and bladder cancer. Given these overlapping causes of cancer, one can easily see how the world of epidemiology was polarized and ended up in a war of percentages, with one faction struggling to interpret the major cancers of the West in terms of a hormonal-dietary theory and another faction struggling to interpret the major cancers of the West in terms of industrial agents via occupational exposures and pollution.

This was the type of material in the literature of the period. If the health agencies wished to present mortality data and cancer maps of the United States to Americans, providing unbiased interpretations and findings on cancer, these were the major interpretations and findings to transmit. But as we have seen in the government fact sheet in Appendix C, most of these interpretations and findings were missing.

With this background, the reader can now take a second and more informed look at the government fact sheet. If he examines it carefully in light of its omissions, the reader discovers quite rapidly how the dominant ideas of the pollution apocalypse—ideas which appeared in the press—may have come into being. Here is an analysis of the government fact sheet broken down into categories of cancers and their known and possible causes:

Sun: The government fact sheet told the reader accurately that the sun was a major cause of skin cancer and melanoma.

Tobacco and alcohol cancers: The government fact sheet offered a guiding principle with which to look at the U.S. cancer maps:

Similar geographic patterns for both males and females for a particular cancer suggest that common environmental factors may contribute to causation; *markedly different patterns for the sexes suggest effects of occupational factors.* [Emphasis added]

The second half of this "principle" was incomplete. Occupational factors did indeed differentiate the sexes, but so did tobacco cancers and alcohol cancers. The government fact sheet had offered readers a principle of epidemiology to guide them, *and in the process had left out tobacco and alcohol.*

The government fact sheet said:

High rates in the Northeast for cancers of the esophagus, larynx, mouth and throat, and bladder were limited to males, suggesting the influence of occupational factors.

Again, tobacco and alcohol were not there.

The government fact sheet said: "It is nearly certain, the NCI scientists believe, that industrial exposures have produced the striking geographic concentrations of bladder cancer deaths in males in the East." *Again, tobacco was not there.*

The government fact sheet said that there was an "unexpected concentration of above-average rates for cancers of the lip and mouth/throat among women in the South." This constellation is found in tobacco cancers and alcohol cancers. *Once again, they were not there.*

The government fact sheet mentioned smoking, as an aside: ". . . environmental factors, in addition to cigarette smoking, may be contributing to lung cancer deaths. . . ." The environmental factors were found along the Gulf Coast from Texas to the Florida Panhandle. They existed in thirty-eight of Louisiana's counties; they had hurled thirteen of Louisiana's counties into the top 1 percent of lung cancer deaths; and these environmental factors had also been causing high lung cancer deaths in seven other counties along the Gulf Coast and along the Atlantic Coast from northern Florida to Charleston, South Carolina. This was a huge geographic territory and it implied that some mysterious factor(s) in this region were giving men in Louisiana, and apparently both

sexes elsewhere, cancer. Tobacco (between commas) seemed almost an inci-
dental factor in the vast geographic sweep of death. There was no indication of
what these factors might be. *This was the only reference to tobacco in the government fact sheet.*

"Diet": The government fact sheet said that something related to "diet"
was causing higher rates of colon cancer and rectum cancer in five states in the
Northeast and in five cities along the Great Lakes. Whatever it was that was
relevant to "diet" was not present or less active in the Southern and Central
parts of the United States. What is more, this thing relevant to "diet" was also
playing a similar role in breast cancer, suggesting that—to the surprise of the
author(s) of the fact sheet—there was an environmental factor common to both
large intestine cancer and breast cancer. No mention was made of the beef/fat
theory of cancers of the hormone-dependent organs and of the colon. No mention was made of the fact that breast cancer had been linked to low pregnancy
rates, which were more common in cosmopolitan areas. No mention was made
of the fact that for almost a decade, the combination of breast and colon
cancers had repeatedly shown up in the literature. The implication was left that
some frightful carcinogen in the "diet"—a food additive or a pollutant—was
wreaking this havoc.

The government fact sheet said that high rates of stomach cancer were
found in the Dakotas, Minnesota, Wisconsin, and upper Michigan. NCI scientists believed that ethnic factors were responsible. They occurred in both sexes
in Austrians, Russians, and Scandinavians. No mention was made of the fact
that high stomach cancer rates exist in countries where few fresh fruits and vegetables are eaten. No mention was made of the fact that United States stomach
cancer rates had fallen rapidly for three decades and that something in the
"environment" was protecting Americans from stomach cancer. The implication was left that these people were eating some "ethnic" carcinogen.

Sex: The government fact sheet mentioned no sex-linked cancers. The
only sex difference named was occupation.

Occupation: The government fact sheet said that additional studies were
needed to clarify any occupational risks in counties with significant employment in the chemical industry. High rates of cancers of the lung, liver, and
bladder had been found in those counties. It was not clear why additional occupational studies were needed. If entire counties were being given lung, liver,
and bladder cancers by the chemical industry, surely the workers locked inside
the factories were getting them, too. On the basis of the information given, no
reader needed to wait to learn about further occupational risks. No mention
was made of Hoover et al.'s report that "the percentage of workers" employed
in forty-one industries had been calculated for the purpose of studying bladder
cancer, that of the forty-one industrial categories studied, three were below and
only six were above the national average. Had they forgotten to study the
workers in the chemical industry?

The government fact sheet said that in the Northeast, high rates of esophagus, larynx, mouth and throat, and bladder cancers were limited to males and
that this suggested the influence of occupational factors.

Pollution: The government fact sheet said, suggested, or implied that the presence of industries was decimating human beings in huge portions of the United States. Some kind of contaminant in the diet appeared to be causing higher rates of breast, colon, and rectum cancer in New Jersey, southern New York, Connecticut, Rhode Island, and Massachusetts, and in Buffalo, Cleveland, Detroit, Chicago, and Milwaukee. A monstrous pollutant appeared to have invaded the Gulf Coast from Texas to the Florida Panhandle, concentrating its power on thirty-eight of Louisiana's sixty-four counties and on an additional seven counties along the Gulf Coast and along the Atlantic Coast from southern Florida to Charleston, South Carolina. Human beings in unnamed counties in unknown numbers where chemical industries were located were being given high rates of cancers of the lung, liver, and bladder. Human beings in unknown counties which contained industries that engaged in the smelting and refining of copper, lead, and zinc ores were suffering from higher lung cancer rates, apparently because arsenic, a known human carcinogen, was polluting the air. Some kind of carcinogenic factor was attacking the lips, mouths, and throats of women in the South. A tremendous portion of the United States appeared to be getting cancers from pollution.

Principles of epidemiology: The government fact sheet said that markedly different patterns for the sexes suggest effects of "occupational factors," and that similar geographical patterns suggest "environmental factors." "Occupational" clearly referred to carcinogens *inside* factories. "Environmental," in a country which had been taught to believe that "environmental" meant "synthetic" or "industrial," could only mean industrial carcinogens *outside* factories, i.e., pollutants.

The government fact sheet failed to give its readers the following principles: (1) that correlations are hypotheses to be tested; (2) that they could only be tested with matched test and control groups of living human beings; (3) that when one looks at mortality data plotted geographically onto maps, one is peering blindly into the past.

Finally, at the very end of its report, the government fact sheet cautioned that deaths in one place might reflect "population movements, such as retirement." Apparently, the deaths signified by the black shroud over the tip of Florida were not to be attributed to pollution.

This was an extraordinary document to have been released in 1975 to health professionals and laymen, most of whom were not cancer epidemiologists. It had masked the dietary theory of cancers of the hormone-dependent organs and of the colon, it had eliminated the genital cancers, it had (with the exception between commas) absorbed the tobacco and alcohol cancers into the occupational category, and it had deprived the reader of many, if not most, of the current explanations of more than twenty cancers. By the time the health agencies who authored this document had finished their work, one explanation above all dominated the entire fact sheet. "Occupational" carcinogens were apparently flowing out of factory smokestacks and turning into "environmental" cancers—enormous numbers, apparently of "environmental" cancers, affecting huge geographic areas of the United States. For any lay reader or any health professional who did not know the epidemiological literature, the HEW-NIH-NCI fact sheet was a little pollution apocalypse unto itself.

If the reader was among those who received the *Atlas* itself, he was able immediately to consult the mortality data provided to get some sense of the relative significance of any given cancer. If he received the maps and the original encyclopedic volume of county-by-county tabulations with only the government fact sheet to guide him, he was required to go to some other source to get the information. If, for example, he had looked up the total estimated deaths for 1975 from cancers of various sites, he would have found numbers like these:[202]

Mouth and Throat	8,200	Stomach	14,400	
Larynx	3,250	Colon	38,600	
Esophagus	6,500	Rectum	10,600	
Lung	81,100	Bladder	9,400	
Breast	32,600	Liver	9,800	Total: 214,450

Whatever the source he consulted, however, he would have made the same discovery about the proportional significance of the various cancers named in the government fact sheet: *It included most of the cancer giants,* namely, lung, breast, and colon and rectum (the large intestine). He would have made one other discovery: That fact sheet had named *a majority of U.S. cancers.* And it had offered only industrial explanations, explicit or implicit, apart from a reference to sun and Finns. The failure to include the natural, life-style, and other categories of explanations of human cancer left one interpretation open to the layman who was unaware of the omissions and saw the biggest cancer killers on the list—above all lung, breast, and colon-rectum. He would *properly* conclude that the NCI was discovering or had discovered that the majority of American cancers was "linked to pollution," including, as the *Washington Post* had put it, cancer in "its most prevalent forms."

It is quite apparent that this fact sheet, which was prepared to accompany the county *Atlas,* and press briefings remarkably like it, ignited spontaneously with Higginson's famous 60 to 90 percent and the numbers were attached to pollution. HEW-NIH-NCI had invited readers to make the interpretation that we see in the press . . . without using the *causal* word "pollution."

We cannot leave the fact sheet, however, with mysteries hanging in the air when a few of them at least can be clarified. In 1977, two years after the maps appeared, William Blot, T. J. Mason, Robert Hoover, and Joseph Fraumeni, Jr., delivered a lecture before one of the largest cancer conferences that has ever been held. The paper was called *Cancer by County: Etiologic Implications.* Here is some of the information in it.

—The concentration of cancers of the lip and mouth/throat among women in the South were almost surely, they said, the result of the habit in rural Southern women of chewing tobacco and snuff. According to the footnotes in their paper, these cancers had been repeatedly identified by epidemiologists in the 1960's.[203]

—The Louisiana counties with high rates of lung cancer had been centers of the petrochemical industry.[204]

—The Southeast Atlantic Coastal counties with extremely high rates of lung cancer had been centers of the paper industry.[205]

—In that long trajectory of high lung cancer rates which had swept along the Coastal counties, ships had been built during World War II and the workers who built those ships had been exposed to asbestos.[206] The asbestos, said Blot et al., may have caused "part" of the excessive lung cancer. The word "part" faithfully reflects the relationship between asbestos and tobacco, discovered by Selikoff and Hammond:[207] *Tobacco* had been the "environmental factor" which turned asbestos into a virulent killer. *It* had been the great geographic monster crawling along coastal America, not the other way around.

—The high colon cancer rates in the Northeast were also discussed by Blot et al. Colon cancer, they said, was a rare cancer in preindustrial or semiindustrial nations and was characteristic of Western industrial societies. They reported on the meat/fat dietary theory and they suggested, on the basis of their geographic correlations, that there might be a carcinogen promoter of colon cancer in the Northeast or a carcinogen inhibitor in the lower-risk areas.[208] There was no reference in this paper to a Northeastern promoter for the breast or rectum, nor was there any reference to the authors' earlier report that if one controlled for social-class differences, breast cancer became higher for upper-class women and colon rates became uniform throughout the country.[209] And in a talk the same year, Hoover did not mention the breast, colon, or rectum at all, while Blot, Fraumeni, and Stone were busily studying the relationship between tobacco and pancreas cancer.[210]

So much for the major mysteries. By 1977, the cancer giants other than lung were gradually vanishing or had vanished altogether from the NCI epidemiologists' public discussions of the cancer maps. The great Northeastern promoter which popped out of a computer or popped back in, depending on the statistical analysis, was or was not affecting the giant cancers.

This still leaves a nagging curiosity about the lack of occupational data in the chemical industry. And it inspires a lively interest in the reasons for which the HEW-NIH-NCI fact sheet refused to use the word "pollution." In fact, we are now unclear about something else. Since it appears from the fact sheet that in 1975 the NCI epidemiologists did not know about tobacco in the case of the rural Southern women or in the case of the asbestos workers in the coastal counties, and since tobacco was mentioned only once, between commas, in the entire fact sheet . . . was something wrong with their tobacco research? These questions do not remain unanswered for long, for when one goes to the papers of the NCI epidemiologists the answers leap out at one from the pages.

Here is what one finds as one reads. Starting in 1974, Hoover, Blot, Fraumeni, Mason, and McKay with one or another of their colleagues had, in different combinations, been publishing papers correlating high rates of cancer to industries located in specific areas. But they repeatedly explained to their colleagues that "it may be dangerous to single out a particular county or even a small group of counties for special attention"; that they were engaged in "hypothesis formulation," i.e., that those correlational data were actually hypotheses yet to be investigated; and that their correlational studies were merely the first part of a "step-wise" process.[211]

These were not the only warnings they offered, however. As they repeatedly pointed out, in the papers they published in scientific journals, they did not have *tobacco* data.

Geographic analysis of U.S. cancer mortality, 1950–1969, revealed excess rates of bladder, lung, liver, and certain other cancers among males in 139 counties where the chemical industry is most highly concentrated. . . . Another limitation of this type of study is that the geographic correlation may be due to a mutual association with another variable. . . . *Of particular concern is cigarette smoking, which is associated with cancers of the lung, bladder, and other sites.*[212]

Counties in the United States have been identified with chemical establishments whose primary manufacturing processes use vinyl chloride. . . . This investigation of the possible health hazard to residents of counties in the United States with chemical establishments using vinyl chloride has several limitations. . . . *the effect of cigarette smoking which is associated with cancers of the lung and bladder could not be controlled for. The finding of excess mortality for lung cancer among men and women in counties with synthetic rubber manufacture could be due to differences in smoking habits, and not be directly related to the manufacturing process.*[213]

A survey of lung cancer mortality by county in the United States, 1950–1969, revealed excessive rates among males in counties where paper, chemicals, petroleum, and transportation industries are located. . . . *any attempt to attribute risk to specific environmental or demographic variables, however, is hampered by the absence of county data on the most important risk factor in lung cancer, smoking.*[214]

Industrial factors may account for the excess lung cancer rates in southern coastal counties. The petrochemical industry was the largest manufacturing process in the high-risk Louisiana counties, and the paper industry predominated in the Southeastern Atlantic Coast counties with extremely high rates. . . . *These findings should be interpreted cautiously because of the absence of county data on cigarette smoking, the single most important etiological factor for lung cancer.*[215] [Emphasis added]

In addition, the NCI epidemiologists did not have data on the *occupations* of those who had died and were uncertain about the consistency of diagnoses and autopsies across the country. In a New York Academy of Sciences document on occupational cancer, reviewed by Saffiotti and others, the cancer maps were discussed and the following warning was appended:

The Cancer Institute cautions that there are several limitations to these findings: the researchers did not know the occupations of the people who died from cancer; there was no way to consider the impact of smoking; and there may have been regional variations in the diagnosis of disease.[216]

Finally, the NCI epidemiologists did not have data telling them where those who had been factory workers had lived, how old they were, and how long they had worked in the industries in those counties. In one paper, they warned that there were "limitations in the data": *"No information on age, duration of employment, or actual county of residence of the workers was available."*[217] (Emphasis added)

These various advisories and warnings to their colleagues were both candid and astonishing. The NCI epidemiologists had not done occupational studies at all. What is more, they had not done pollution studies either! They could not have done pollution studies without smoking data and occupational data. To know why, one must understand one thing about pollution studies. At the 1974 conference, Pike et al. explained the problem lucidly:

The essential problem in evaluating the possible effect of air pollution on lung cancer is that it must be investigated in the presence of a powerful, known, lung carcinogen—*cigarette smoking.* . . . The other confounding factor is *occupational* exposure to lung carcinogens.[218] [Emphasis added]

Without smoking data and without occupational data, one cannot untangle the competing variables in a pollution study. And when, in addition, one does not know the age of workers, how long they worked in any local factory, or where those workers had lived, one cannot disentangle workers' cancers from nonworkers' cancers. These were neither occupational studies *nor* pollution studies. They were . . .

What exactly had the NCI epidemiologists been doing? As they said in 1974 and were to say repeatedly, in hunting for counties with a higher than average mortality rate of any given cancer and for industries within those counties, they were looking for "clues." As Fraumeni explained it in one paper: *"These analyses were designed to raise etiological questions, not resolve them, and have to be used cautiously with an understanding of their limitations."*[219] (Emphasis added) The NCI epidemiologists had not been reporting on the *findings* they had made about the above-average cancer rates in the county aggregates they had correlated with industries—they had been asking *"questions."*

And with that, one understands the cancer apocalypse and its mythic attributes. If the reader takes one last look at the press coverage and the government fact sheet, he will understand the phenomenon even better. In 1975, reporters from the *Washington Post* and *Time* walked out of the NCI with batches of "questions" in their briefcases and with off-the-record interpretations of those "questions." And in 1975, on the record, the HEW-NIH-NCI sent some of the NCI epidemiologists' "questions" to health professionals throughout the land as interpretations of the cancer maps of the United States. In both cases, it was a transmission of premature and untested hypotheses, supported by deficient data, according to the NCI epidemiologists themselves. As we know, the government's publicity release about the *Atlas* communicated *implicitly* what reporters said they had been told *explicitly*—namely that the majority of American cancers, including three major cancers, had been linked to pollution. But they had *not* been linked to pollution, and the government document did not use the word.

The pollution crisis was a myth born of scientific abnormality. It was abnormal, if original, to begin epidemiological studies with higher-than-average cancer rates in entire counties, including all the towns within them, and to correlate those higher county averages with industries situated in some of those towns. It was simply abnormal, with no redeeming originality, to disseminate to the public untested and precarious or untestable hypotheses about cancers in entire counties—let alone about cancers that may have been initiated twenty, thirty, or forty years ago in places unknown in the most mobile country on earth. In fact, it was so abnormal to disseminate such hypotheses that one can safely conclude that it was a high-level policy decision to do so. For only in the realm of cancer "policy," as this books reveals, are such niceties as testable hypotheses, testing, replication, and refutation dispensable. Only in the realm of cancer "policy" is crucial information, which would permit a rational perspective, withheld from laymen when it is freely given to scientists. And only in the realm of cancer "policy" is ersatz knowledge officially substituted for knowledge. It is quite clear that by disseminating untested correlations between industries and entire counties *and* by failing to disseminate the major nonindustrial findings and hypotheses about American cancers, anonymous policymakers at the HEW-NIH-NCI created the pollution hysteria.

And anonymous policymakers at the EPA reinforced that hysteria. As we know (Chapter 1), the pollution crisis was endowed with the dignity of numbers by the layman Russell Train, head of the EPA, who, in the course of the campaign to pass the Toxic Substances Control Act, summoned the Washington press corps to utter the words placed in his mouth: he warned Americans that they were exposed to 2,000,000 chemicals and that it was now dangerous to breathe, eat, drink, and touch. The 2,000,000 was false—just as Califano's later 7,000,000 was false—and it nailed the pollution crisis into place.

That is how the cancer apocalypse was born. It was a mythic drama about cancers caused by pollution derived from bits and pieces of nonpollution studies. It was a mythic drama in which "questions" were transmitted as though they were answers, by means of anonymous leaks and an anonymous publicity document. Above all, it was a mythic drama in which no known government scientists participated—and in which only the bewildered lay actors had names.

It was not only laymen who were confused by the NCI epidemiologists' correlations. Many scientists had not grasped that industries in specific towns had been correlated with counties containing many towns and had not known that the NCI epidemiologists did not have occupational data in general and worker residence data in particular with which to pry factory workers apart from other people in the towns within those counties. Many scientists had not read the original papers. By 1979, however, many had read them, the grapevine was working, and a critical mass had learned that the NCI epidemiologists had been publishing papers postulating that industries might be a source of cancer in workers and in local communities, without having the necessary data to resolve their broad county correlations. In that year, William Blot found himself facing a group of seventy scientists who wanted to hear his explanations of the county correlations, and while he was about it, his explanations of the great workers' cancer epidemic, which had immediately followed the industry-county correlations. It was at that meeting, which actually concerned both studies in which the NCI had participated, that Irving Kessler declared that "mindless statistical manipulation" and data derived from old death certificates were not a substitute for real epidemiological studies. In a discussion of a correlation with refineries, Kessler declared:

Not one of the people who were reported as cancer deaths in a county that had a refinery might even have lived in the town where the refinery was. This is the most serious indictment of this kind of information.[220]

William Blot conceded that the county data were "crude" but once again justified them as valuable for the generation of hypotheses to test, and informed the listening scientists that they had already begun studies which would allow the NCI to acquire medical data, occupational data, and smoking data. There was no argument among scientists over the value of acquiring data, formulating hypotheses, and testing them. They discussed only the validity of the methodology—in the presence of the senior scientist from the NCI.

But outside the walls, the apocalypse was howling and howling: 2,300 suspected carcinogens (NIOSH, 1976) . . . 2,000,000 chemical perils (EPA, 1976) . . . the Great Pollution Epidemic (HEW-NIH-NCI, 1976) . . . the General Population Epidemic (NCI, 1978) . . . 7,000,000 chemical perils (HEW, 1978) . . . the Great Worker Epidemic (NIC-NIEHS-NIOSH, 1978) . . . 90 percent of cancer comes from industry . . . the U.S. is number one number one number one. . . .

Many scientists were profoundly upset by the cancer apocalypse, and a few of them mentioned it in public. John Higginson, speaking of "dedicated" occupational scientists, said that it was no longer required that they be adversarial and pleaded for an "atmosphere of objectivity."[221] Weisburger, Cohen, and Wynder opened a paper in 1977 with a discussion of how the concept "environmental" had become the equivalent of "chemical," meaning industrial chemicals, in the consciousness of many scientists and laymen, and attributed it to the fact that they had primarily been hearing about industrial carcinogens.[222] Such discussions have continued throughout the years. The only thing that is *never* publicly discussed is the political dimension of the problem. Or rather it was never discussed until 1979, when Higginson declared that the "occupational people" and the "chemical carcinogenesis people" had misinterpreted the theory of environmental cancer, and denounced the prevailing ideas—above all the ideas about pollution—as "societal, political and quasi-scientific dogmas"; and until 1980 and 1981 when Richard Doll and Richard Peto of Oxford, whose own country was being invaded by the American apocalypse, had had enough and charged several U.S. health agencies, including the NCI, with fabricating data about occupational cancer for political reasons.

The torrential gush of industrial interpretations of cancer from the inner recesses of the Biologist State had one far-reaching—and political—result. The

information about the natural and cultural life-style cancers went into eclipse
and so did some of the most famous cancer scientists in the world. This had the
same effect on Americans as did the FDA's decision to keep them in a state of
imbecile innocence by failing to teach them about the carcinogenicity of their
own food. The blackout of both nature- and culture-linked cancers and of natural carcinogens pitted Americans, by default, against their own productive
system.

The "chemical" apocalypse occurred so swiftly that it caught one NCI scientist off-guard. At the 1974 cancer conference, the tobacco cancers, the alcohol cancers, the sex-linked cancers, the hormonal cancers were intensively
discussed and occupation and pollution studies were merely two specialized
fields among many. Umberto Saffiotti was so impressed by what he had
learned about the life-style cancers that, according to a scientific rapporteur,
Vincent Guinee:

Dr. Saffiotti urged creating and publicizing a concise slogan for personal avoidance of
carcinogens such as the American Cancer Society did with the seven danger signs of
cancer. For example, "protect yourself from cancer: do not smoke, do not drink hard
alcoholic beverages, adopt a prudent diet, avoid excessive sun (if you're fair skinned),
learn the cancer risks of the substances you work with."[223]

Along with occupation risks, which he had put last, Saffiotti had actually
listed some of the major natural and cultural life-style risk factors for cancer
which had emerged from forty years of epidemiological investigations. But
even as his proposal for a slogan campaign to educate the public was rolling off
the presses, Saffiotti had swiveled on a dime. In 1975, *Time* reported him as
saying that cancer was a disease of the American economic system.[224] And by
1976, Saffiotti was standing on the platform of an international cancer conference informing the world that American cancer was "largely" caused by modern technology and "conditioned by our societal *lifestyle*"—this one italicized
word apparently the only oblique reference to his former concerns.[225] If it was
such a reference, it was unintelligible. In that famous 1976 paper, there was not
one mention of any of the natural and cultural risk factors for cancer which
had so profoundly impressed him the year before.

The eclipse that occurred so dramatically in one man's mind reflects, in
microcosm, what happened to the entire culture. Save for an isolated natural
curiosity that occasionally trickled into the press, American citizens thereafter—for seven long years—inhabited a dark universe in which the only allow-
able causes of cancer were food additives, drugs, factory work, pollution—*and*
asbestos and tobacco provided that one grimly focused on death and profits
and forgot they were a mineral and a plant. Only with a sudden opening of the
skies, in 1982 and 1983, when the dietary theory and some natural dietary carcinogens fell upon the country from noplace, did a flash of intelligible light
penetrate that universe.

And that is the story of the last "axiom" of the apocalyptics—that America
was the carcinogenic sewer of the world. Depending on the variant of the idea,
it was as false or as baseless as all the other "axioms." Indeed, it appears to
have been the spawning ground for all the other "axioms." It is of interest that

the cancer apocalypse actually emerged from a cognitive black hole, pollution, a subject about which scientists are almost entirely ignorant.

. . .

One conclusion emerges strongly from this examination of the epidemiological base of the four "axioms" of the cancer apocalypse. All emerged from the U.S. cancer agencies and, when they took material form, all, save SEER's epidemic, were veiled in one or another form of anonymity. Their timing was uncanny: They erupted magically during the campaign to pass the Toxic Substances Control Act in 1976 and at the time of the OSHA policy hearings of 1978. And, always, bad or premature science was funneled by unknown persons, using scientifically unorthodox means, directly into the press, as well as into the labor movement and the public health world, before the scientific community—national and international—had a chance to exercise its normal process of challenge, confirmation, or refutation.

I originally investigated these mysterious "axioms" in order to assess the responsibility of the press in transmitting them. By the time I had finished, I had reached the conclusion that to blame the press under the circumstances described in this epilogue and elsewhere in this book is absurd. The American press covers events, not ideas, and does not see past the policymakers. It has been nourished on bad science since the inception of the cancer prevention program. It was trained, as one trains a circus dog, to view apocalyptics in and out of government as fountainheads of scientific truth; it has shown a consummate credulity in the face of arbitrary edicts brandished by the policymakers as the voice of science; it has been taught by scientists to treat secretive or baseless assertions from scientific sources like political scoops. No one has taught the press that science does not operate by assertions, by leaks, by off-the-record briefings, by mimeograph machines spitting out documents with release dates geared to the evening news, or by documents with no names at all. No one has taught the press that the very appearance of such phenomena means that what one is hearing is not science.

Undoubtedly, some journalists have been ideologically receptive to the apocalyptic "axioms"; some may have enjoyed the excitement of a new kind of war between Good and Evil; some have unquestionably seen themselves as righteous adjuncts of the regulatory process; and many, possibly most, have never known the meaning of the scientific words they were transmitting so excitedly to the public. But one cannot—I cannot—indict the lay press for failing to understand what it takes years to understand. To write this book, I had to read about 10,000 papers in carcinogenesis and genetics and about 500 books; and to write this Epilogue, I had to read two histories of cancer epidemiology, several epidemiology textbooks, and some 5,000 additional papers in that field. Reporters must write swiftly; they cover the *daily* news. They could not take off several years to do their "homework." Indeed, as laymen, they have never realized how much "homework" there was to do. In the context of this book, it would be absurd to waste time criticizing the press. The inadequacy of the coverage is the inadequacy of the informants.

The press coverage is, above all, a visible symptom of a far deeper problem. It is the problem of the scientist who rushes into political action as a substitute for scientific endeavor; the scientist who seeks to use the coercive power of the state to impose his unproved opinions. It is the problem of the irrational trends in biology which exploded in the 1960s. It is the problem of laws and regulations which have "liberated" scientists from the onerous burden of being scientists and have created a vacuum into which incompetents, opportunists, gurus, witch doctors, and ideologues have rushed. It is the problem of a cultural degeneration which manifests itself in an arrogant hostility to reason, to logic, to objectivity; in clamorous claims to nonexistent knowledge; in an unabashed pursuit of ideological goals in the guise of a quest for truth.

It is also the problem of the critical scientific witnesses for whom we have been searching. Clearly hundreds, thousands of scientists have known that the United States was being misinformed about environmental cancer, that it was being told fairy tales, that government agencies were generating pseudo-information to conform to those fairy tales. There have been witnesses to all the events described in this chapter. The quality of those witnesses varies, as does their own objectivity, but there are clearly many who knew that this country was being systematically enmeshed in an ideological delusion. They whispered, they gossiped, they complained—with great courtesy—but American scientists, for the most part, did not fight. When the U.S. agencies engaged in actions which scandalized cancer scientists all over the world, most American scientists hunkered down nervously and waited to be saved by an international expeditionary force. That is the nature of our Lysenkoism. Even in a "quasi" form, it generates degrading fear.

In the Preface to this book, I mentioned that in 1980, Philip Handler, then President of the National Academy of Sciences, called upon scientists to combat those very antireason, antiscience trends in the general culture and within the scientific culture itself. Those problems were particularly acute, he said, in the environmental sciences. He asked scientists to avow their ignorance, to make no claims to knowledge they did not possess—and to confront the "charlatans" in their midst. It was time, he said, for them to resist the "intimidation" to which they had been subjected for so many years; it was time to return to "the ethics and norms of science."[226]

That was desperately needed advice in 1980; it is still desperately needed advice today. In fact, it is the most fundamental conclusion I can reach in this book. I would add one thing: It is not only for the sake of the scientific culture that rational scientists should confront their own irrationalists; it is also for the sake of the humanist culture. It is a harsh fact that millions of American citizens have been so thoroughly besieged by myths, errors, and falsehoods about environmental cancer that they have been plunged into neoprimitive pathology. It may be difficult for cancer biologists to believe, but cancer in a culture is a far more devastating and dangerous disease, and possibly more incurable, than cancer in an individual. When a scientific endeavor becomes the means by which a nation is told grotesque untruths about itself, and when most serious scientists remain silent while such untruths are told to the public for a decade, that is cultural cancer. And if, as Handler said, those serious scientists are too intellectually intimidated by the irrationalists to speak out, either on behalf of science or of their countrymen, it may be terminal cultural cancer.

Many, however, may be less intimidated than unable to think effectively about a new cultural problem. The very best scientists are often indifferent to the very worst, for they have been taught by repeated experience that science has its own self-cleansing mechanisms, that superb science is never threatened by mediocre science, that one authentic discovery has the power to wipe out decades of intellectual trash. That is entirely true—for a closed scientific community. It is not true, however, for a nation. Countries do not have automatic self-cleansing mechanisms. The intellectual trash invades the law and the press. The intellectual trash piles up. The intellectual trash *becomes* the culture.

If the scientists in the field of cancer prevention really consider it reasonable to drag politicians, lawyers, journalists, and the public into the midst of the early thinking processes of half-born sciences, they no longer have the right to assume that the by-products of error will have the normal, healthy destiny of oblivion. In "normal" science, error and misrepresentation simply turn into old piles of paper. In the science of the "suspected," whether in carcinogenesis or epidemiology, error and misrepresentation are ceaselessly dumped by ignoramuses and manipulative cynics into the political and legal system, and the communications arteries of society. It is time for cancer preventers to recognize that by agreeing to ventilate untested or untestable hypotheses and "suspicions" to laymen, they are now using society as a dumping ground for their own toxic wastes. They have, accordingly, acquired the responsibility to create institutions to control the dumping.

This is not an unorthodox demand, despite the unorthodox metaphor. It was not only made by Handler in discussing the environmental sciences, but it has been made by others in different branches of biology and medicine as well. In 1975, ethicist Joseph Fletcher counseled scientists who were doing research with human subjects that they were "morally obligated . . . to accept monitoring by their peers," but not by scientific illiterates nor by "yellow journalism."[227] In 1978, Bernard Davis, writing in the field of genetics, published a powerful and important analysis of the problem of premature ventilation by individual scientists of their personal and ideological hypotheses about "conjectural dangers" and recommended that the scientific community have the opportunity to reach its best collective judgment before "gratuitous nightmares" were inflicted on laymen and magnified by the press.[228] No scholarly scientist would dream of calling these proposals prohibitions on "dumping," but that is precisely what they are.

More fundamentally, these are all calls for a return to "the ethics and norms of science": they are *moral* demands. The critical scientists are in a struggle with the "new ethics." It is the "ethics" of those who righteously proclaim that a threat to public health is so appalling that there is no time to discover if there *is* a threat to public health. The "gratuitous nightmares" are always justified on moral grounds. Rarely, however, do the scientific critics of such apocalyptic "dumping" recognize that they are in conflict with a "new ethics," or that it is that very "ethics" which must be identified and judged.

As a philosophy of public health, it is simple enough to judge, *if one does not overlook the public.* One need only observe that in the realm of environmental cancer, the "new ethics" has failed in its primary task to educate the citizens, specifically to teach them the *authentic* discoveries of cancer causation in man as they are made so that they can take *informed* action in their own self-interest. It would not have been difficult:

By 1975, the year of the apocalypse, every man, woman, and child in this country could have and should have known the details of the most extraordinary discovery that has ever been made in the history of environmental cancer. They could have known *all* the cancers which had been strongly associated with smoking and drinking.

By 1980, the year in which so many scientists had quietly mobilized to challenge baseless U.S. government data, every man, woman, and child in this country could and should have known the names of the proved carcinogenic drugs and occupational carcinogens—and the most thoroughly demonstrated nonindustrial factors in human cancer.

No such official information has ever been given to this country. In fact, there is no institution in this country whose function it is to evaluate all studies and to dispense such information; the only such institution is the IARC. Its data of 1979–1980 are published in this book, and a slightly expanded list appears in the IARC Annual Report of 1981. The IARC, however, has been primarily focused on industrial carcinogens, and only in 1981 did that institution begin to report on cultural factors in cancer causation, e.g., smoking and alcohol. Here is an updating and elaboration of IARC data published by Richard Doll in 1981, which did consider cultural as well as industrial factors. He considered the following to be "firmly established causes":[229]

RICHARD DOLL'S LIST OF "ESTABLISHED" CAUSES OF HUMAN CANCER

Occupational Exposure

Agent or Circumstance	Site of Cancer
Aromatic amines:	
4-Aminodiphenyl	Bladder
Benzidine	Bladder
2-Naphthylamine	Bladder
Arsenic	Skin, lung
Asbestos	Lung, pleura, peritoneum
Benzene	Marrow
Bis (chloromethyl) ether	Lung
Cadmium	Prostate
Chromium	Lung
Furniture manufacture (hardwood)	Nasal sinuses
Ionizing radiations	Marrow and probably all other sites
Isopropyl alcohol manufacture	Nasal sinuses
Leather goods manufacture	Nasal sinuses
Mustard gas	Larynx, lung
Nickel	Nasal sinuses, lung
Polycyclic hydrocarbons	Skin, scrotum, lung
UV light	Skin, lip
Vinyl chloride	Liver (angiosarcoma)

Medical Exposure

Agent or Circumstance	Site of Cancer
Alkylating agents:	
Cyclophosphamide	Bladder
Melphalan	Marrow
Arsenic	Skin, lung
Busulphan	Marrow
Chlornaphazine	Bladder
Immunosuppressive drugs	Reticuloendothelial system
Ionizing radiations	Marrow and probably all other sites
Estrogens:	
Unopposed	Endometrium
Transplacental (DES)	Vagina
Phenacetin	Kidney (pelvis)
Polycyclic hydrocarbons	Skin, scrotum, lung
Steroids:	
Anabolic (oxymetholone)	Liver
Contraceptives	Liver (hamartoma)

Social Exposure

Agent or Circumstance	Site of Cancer
Aflatoxin	Liver
Alcoholic drinks	Mouth, pharynx, larynx, esophagus, liver
Chewing (betel, tobacco, lime)	Mouth
Overnutrition (causing obesity)	Endometrium, gallbladder
Reproductive history:	
Late age at 1st pregnancy	Breast
Zero or low parity	Ovary
Parasites:	
Schistosoma haematobium	Bladder
Chlonorchis sinensis	Liver (cholangioma)
Sexual promiscuity	Cervix uteri
Tobacco smoking	Mouth, pharynx, larynx, lung, esophagus, bladder
UV light	Skin, lip
Virus (hepatitis B)	Liver (hepatoma)

This, according to Doll, is what cancer epidemiologists authentically *knew* about environmental causes or contributing causes of human cancer by 1981. By that year, this Doll-IARC list of industrial, natural, and cultural causes of human cancer was "the best there was." To what degree any one of these findings might yet be debated no layman can know, but it is certain that were an international list of "established" causes of cancer to be presented to the American public, it would contain most, if not all, of the listed factors.

How many Americans were aware of these reports by 1981, no one knows because no one has cared to find out. In my own group of friends and acquaintances, university graduates and many of them scholars, no one is aware of most of these reports *today*. I have even, quite accidentally, discovered a group of asbestos *insulators* who smoke and do not know that by smoking they are vastly magnifying their risk of cancer. I will be glad to inform a labor union or a public health agency of their identities, but it is unlikely that I have, by some miracle, bumped into the only ignorant asbestos insulators in the United States. The knowledge those men needed to protect their lives was available in 1976—at the peak of the apocalypse. Such ignorance, whether in scholars or in workers, is inevitable, for no one is teaching the public.

To judge by the press, the thirty-year-old tobacco–lung cancer connection is finally known; it was vehemently stressed in 1980. But most reporters—thus, presumably, most Americans—appear to know little else. They "know" the apocalyptic "axioms" or variants of them. They "know" the latest carcinogen in the headlines, whether the data are valid or not—until they forget it. They "know" that they are being massacred by "pollution." *They "know" primarily what is false or unknown—and they rarely know how to identify the actual threats to their lives.* That, too, is the result of the "dumping," of the ventilation of "gratuitous nightmares," of the cries of wolf by the "moralists" who are breaching the "ethics and norms of science." They have rendered most citizens incapable of differentiating between known and unknown hazards. And that, too, is the meaning of the fable of the boy who cried wolf: The ostensible protector of the community actually *disarmed* the community.

To quote his remarkable study once again, Bernard Davis, in discussing a parallel problem in genetics which he, too, called "crying wolf," said:

Just as a responsible physician would not tell a patient that the diagnostic possibilities in his case ranged from neuritis to cancer, so the scientific community has a responsibility . . . to proceed with care in transmitting conjectural information to an easily alarmed public.[230]

The point can be made even more powerfully when one considers the realm of cancer:

Were a physician to treat a patient for ten years by terrorizing him incessantly with hypothetical or false warnings of threats to his life, while failing to inform him of, and to treat, the known diseases from which the patient actually suffers, that physician would be recognized as a sadistic incompetent.

That is actually how the cancer prevention establishment has been "treating" this whole nation. And that is the actual effect of the "new ethics" of the apocalyptic scientists. By *humanist* as well as by scientific standards, the "new ethics" is flagrantly unethical.

The judgment is simple enough to make, provided that one uses the education of the public as the standard. If the scientific critics of the apocalyptics—within the government and without—do not use that standard, and do not seek humanist allies in their battle, they will continue to lose it. Until they stop coaxing the apocalyptics to return to the "ethics and norms of science," which is roughly the equivalent of coaxing the hungry fox out of the chickenhouse; until they explicitly challenge the moral philosophy of these "moralists" whose power to inflict damage is directly proportional to their victims' belief that they are ethical beings; and until they issue that challenge loudly in the hearing of those victims, the "new ethics," which is now lodged in the state, will continue to corrupt science and the culture, and to disarm the citizenry.

APPENDICES

Appendix A

Survey of Industrial Carcinogens

REFERENCES

Abelson, Philip H. "Methyl Mercury." Originally published in *Science 169* (1970). Reprinted in *Our Chemical Environment,* edited by J. Calvin Giddings, Manus B. Monroe. San Francisco: Canfield Press, 1972. *Mercury reported to cause chromosomal aberrations and birth defects, pp. 146–147.*

Adamson, Richard. "Administration of Therapeutic Agents." In *Cancer Symposium: An Academic Review of the Environmental Determinants of Cancer Relevant to Prevention.* In cooperation with the American Cancer Society. February 28, March 1, March 2, 1979. New York City. *Manuscript. My copy unpaginated; see Table 9.*

Adamson, R. H., Sieber, S. M. "Antineoplastic Agents as Potential Carcinogens." In *Origins of Human Cancer,* edited by H. H. Hiatt, J. D. Watson, J. A. Winsten. Book A, *Incidence of Cancer in Humans.* New York: Cold Spring Harbor Laboratory, 1977. *Potentially carcinogenic drugs: busulfan, cytoxan, melphalan, nitrogen mustard, thio-TEPA, triethylinemelamine (TEM), Table 1, p. 430; imuran, 6-mercaptopurine, Table 2, p. 431; actinomycin D, daunomycin, Table 3, p. 433.*

Allen, J. R., Norback, D. H. "Carcinogenic Potential of the Polychlorinated Biphenyls." In *Origins of Human Cancer,* edited by H. H. Hiatt, J. D. Watson, J. A. Winsten. Book A, *Incidence of Cancer in Humans.* New York: Cold Spring Harbor Laboratory, 1977. *PCBs potential carcinogens, pp. 173–180.*

Althoff, J.; Grandjean, C.; Gold, B. "Diallylnitrosamine: A Potent Respiratory Carcinogen in Syrian Golden Hamsters: Brief Communication." *Journal of the National Cancer Institute 59* (1977), *p. 1569.*

Anderson, Henry A.; Lilis, Ruth; Daum, Susan M.; Fischbein, Alf S.; Selikoff, Irving J. "Household-Contact Asbestos Neoplastic Risk." In *Occupational Carcinogenesis,* edited by Umberto Saffiotti, Joseph K. Wagoner. *Annals of The New York Academy of Sciences.* Vol. 271. New York: New York Academy of Sciences, 1976. *Asbestos causes mesothelioma, gastrointestinal and lung cancer in workers and in family members exposed to asbestos pollution, pp. 311–312.*

Battelle Memorial Institute, Dartmouth Medical School. Data cited by Staff of *Chemical & Engineering News.* "Trace Metals: Unknown, Unseen Pollution Threat." *Chemical & Engineering News 49* (1971): 29–33. Reprinted in *Our Chemical Environment,* edited by J. Calvin Giddings, Manus B. Monroe. San Francisco: Canfield Press, 1972. *Yttrium carcinogenic in mice, p. 132.*

Batzinger, Robert P.; Ou, Suh-Yun L.; Bueding, Ernest. "Saccharin and Other Sweeteners: Mutagenic Properties." *Science 198* (1977). *Saccharin reported mutagenic, pp. 944–946.*

Bencko, Vladimir. "Carcinogenic, Teratogenic, and Mutagenic Effects of Arsenic." *Environmental Health Perspectives 19* (1977). *Arsenic reported to be carcinogenic, mutagenic, teratogenic, pp. 179–180.*

Berenblum, I. *Cancer Research Today.* London: Pergamon, 1967. *About 500 synthetic substances carcinogenic in animals, p. 45.*

Bridbord, Kenneth. "New Horizons in Occupational Medicine." National Institute for Occupational Safety and Health, Center for Disease Control. May 1, 1978. *Manuscript. Vinyl chloride causes angiosarcoma of the liver and brain cancer, Table 1, Section A3.*

Bridbord, Kenneth, French, Jean G. "Carcinogenic and Mutagenic Risks Associated with Fossil Fuels." In *Carcinogenesis: A Comprehensive Survey.* Vol. 3, *Polynuclear Aromatic Hydrocarbons.* Edited by Peter W. Jones, Ralph I. Freudenthal. New York: Raven, 1978. *Gasified and liquefied coal: carcinogens found in the "process streams," effluents may interact with chemicals in air to form nitrosamines, Table 2, p. 457.*

Brubaker, Paul E.; Moran, John P.; Bridbord, Kenneth; Hueter, F. Gordon. "Noble Metals: A Toxicological Appraisal of Potential New Environmental Contaminants." *Environmental Health Perspectives 10* (1975). *Palladium compound, used in catalytic converters in automobiles and found in the air, is carcinogenic to mice; sulfur dioxide promotes the carcinogenic effects of polycyclic aromatic hydrocarbons, including the ubiquitous carcinogen benzo(a)pyrene, p. 50.*

Califano, Joseph E. Secretary of Health, Education, and Welfare, *HEW News,* November 13, 1978. *7,000,000 chemicals in existence, p. 2.*

Carter, Luther J. "Yearly Report on Carcinogens Could Be a Potent Weapon in the War on Cancer." *Science 203* (1979). *Ethylene dibromide, used in leaded gasoline, carcinogenic, p. 527.*

Chambers, Robert: see (GAO), General Accounting Office, 1978. (Hearings.)

Chemical Abstracts Computer Registry: see Samuel S. Epstein, 1978.

Chiazze, L., Jr.; Nichols, W. E.; Wong. O. "Mortality Among Employees of PVC Fabricators." *Journal of Occupational Medicine 19* (1977). *White women workers in vinyl chloride polymerization plants have excess breast and urinary organ cancer, p. 623.*

Chrisp, C. E.; Fisher, G. L.; Lammert, J. E. "Mutagenicity of Filtrates from Respirable Coal Fly Ash." *Science 199* (1978). *Inhalable particles of coal fly ash possibly mutagenic, p. 73.*

Cleary, Stephen F. "Biological Effects of Microwave and Radiofrequency Radiation." *CRC Critical Reviews in Environmental Control 7* (1977). *Radar, radio and TV operate in electromagnetic radiation reported to damage fetal growth, p. 142.*

Cohen, Bernard L. "The Disposal of Radioactive Wastes from Fission Reactors." *Scientific American 236* (1977). *Burning coal releases uranium, p. 12.*

———. "High-level Radioactive Waste from Light-Water Reactors." *Review of Modern Physics 49* (1977). *Table II, long-lived fission products, p. 3.*

(CPSC) Consumer Product Safety Commission. August 16, 1974. "CPSC Issues Ban on Vinyl Chloride in Aerosols." News Release, *pp. 1–2.*

———. April 7, 1977. "CPSC Bans Tris-Treated Children's Garments." News Release. *Tris (2,3-dibromopropyl) phosphate (TRIS), a flame retardant for children's clothing, is carcinogenic, p. 1.*

Costle, Douglas M.: on PCBs, see EPA, May 22, 1977; on pesticides, see R. Jeffrey Smith.

Cuddeback, John E.; Donovan, James R.; Burg, William R. "Occupational Aspects of Passive Smoking." *American Industrial Hygiene Association Journal 37* (1976). *Carcinogenic particulate matter released into indoor air by cigarette smoking, pp. 263, 264.*

Davis, Devra Lee, Magee, Brian. "Cancer and Industrial Chemical Production." *Sci-*

ence 206 (1979). *More than 20 percent of 7,000 chemicals tested reported carcinogenic, p. 1358.*

Dutra, Frank R., Largent, Edward J. "Osteosarcoma Induced by Beryllium Oxide." *American Journal of Pathology 26* (1950). *Metallic carcinogens: arsenic "proved," beryllium potential, p. 197.*

Eisenbud, Merril. *Environment, Technology and Health: Human Ecology in Historical Perspective.* New York: New York University Press, 1978. *Condensers, fluorescent lights, transformers leaking PCBs into environment, pp. 236–237.*

———. *Environmental Radioactivity.* New York: Academic Press, 1973. *High uranium content in commercial phosphate fertilizers, p. 166.*

Eisenbud, Merril, Kneip, Theodore J. *Trace Metals in the Atmosphere.* New York State Department of Environmental Conservation, Environmental Quality, Research and Development Unit. Technical paper 16. July 1971. *Manuscript. In petroleum and coal: chromium, lead, nickel, Table I, p. 5; beryllium, mercury at lower levels, pp. 4, 6, and Table VI.*

Eisenbud, Merril, Petrow, Henry G. "Radioactivity in the Atmospheric Effluents of Power Plants That Use Fossil Fuels." *Science 144* (1964). *Effluents released by coal-burning plants more radioactive than those of oil-burning plants, p. 288.*

(EPA) Environmental Protection Agency. *Reports to the Press:*

March 29, 1974. "EPA Seeks Immediate End to Reserve Mining Discharge into Lake Superior." *Environmental News. EPA warned that dumping by Reserve Mining Co. of taconite wastes containing asbestos fibers into Lake Superior constituted health hazard, pp. 1–2.*

May 24, 1974. "EPA Releases Additional Brand Names of Pesticides Containing Vinyl Chloride." *Environmental News. Vinyl chloride used in pesticide aerosols; suspended from sale, p. 1.*

September 16, 1974. "EPA to Set Vinyl Chloride Emissions Standard." *Environmental News. Vinyl chloride, a human carcinogen, is found in the air, p. 1.*

April 18, 1975. "EPA Releases Results of National Drinking Water Survey." *Environmental News. Carcinogenic chemicals (bromoform, bromodichloromethane, chloroform, dibromochloromethane) formed by the chlorination of water, pp. 1–2.*

February 26, 1976. "Train Urges Preventive Medicine to Curb Chemical Threat." *Environmental News. 2,000,000 chemicals in existence, p. 1.*

May 22, 1977. "EPA Proposed Regulations for Labeling, Disposal of PCB's." *Environmental News. PCBs suspected carcinogens, p. 1.*

June 17, 1977. "EPA Reports Finding of PBB Residues in Northern New Jersey, Staten Island." *Environmental News. PBBs contaminating water supplies, p. 1.*

July 15, 1977. "EPA, FDA, CPSC Form Task Force to Investigate Safety of Glasses Decorated with Lead-Containing Glazes." *Environmental News. Glasses decorated with lead-containing glazes may leach into food or liquid inside glasses, p. 1.*

September 13, 1977. "Confirmatory Tests Show Only Trace Levels of PBB's in Ohio River Catfish." *Environmental News. PBBs, suspected carcinogens, p. 2.*

November 20, 1977. "EPA Investigates Potential Asbestos Hazards from Crushed Stone." *Environmental News. Crushed serpentinite rock used in roadway construction contains carcinogenic asbestos, p. 1.*

November 21, 1978. "Statement by Environmental Protection Agency Administrator, Douglas M. Costle, on the Regional Survey of Hazardous Waste Dump Sites." *Environmental News. EPA estimates 30 to 40 million tons hazardous waste per year, p. 1.*

(EPA) Environmental Protection Agency. *Other Publications:*

Memo from Acting Assistant Administrator for Research and Development, Stephen J. Gage. "Precautionary Notice on Laboratory Handling of Exhaust Products from Diesel Engines." My copy stamped November 4, 1977. *Diesel particulates reported carcinogenic, mutagenic. My copy unpaginated; see first page.*

Office of Energy, Minerals and Industry. "Potential Environmental Impacts of Solar Heating and Cooling Systems." Interagency, Energy-Environment, Research and Development Program Report. EPA 600/7-76-014. October 1976. *Diphenyl, diphenyl oxide, see Table 4, section 2: Solar System Heat Storage Materials; sodium chromate, see Table 4, section 3: Absorption Refrigeration Fluids.*

Office of Solid Waste Management Programs. "Report to Congress—Disposal of Hazardous Wastes." U.S. EPA Report SW-115, 1974. In *Handbook of Solid Waste Management*, edited by David Gordon Wilson. New York: Van Nostrand, Reinhold, 1977. *Table 3.14: Representative Hazardous Substances Within Industrial Waste Stream, p. 77.*

Office of Water Supply. *Statement of Basis and Purpose for an Amendment to the National Interim Primary Drinking Water Regulations on Trihalomethanes.* January 1978. *Manuscript. Chloroform, a carcinogen, has been reported to be an air pollutant, p. 12.*

Potential Industrial Carcinogens and Mutagens. Prepared for the Office of Toxic Substances by Lawrence Fishbein. EPA 560/5-77-005. Washington, D.C. May 5, 1977.

Chemicals that are used in the processing and manufacture of books, magazines, newspapers, paper and paper products: Acetaldehyde, used as a solvent in paper treating, is mutagenic, pp. 113–114; acrolein, used in paper treating, is mutagenic, pp. 112–113; aziridines, used in paper production, are carcinogenic and mutagenic, pp. 61–63; azo dyes, used in color photography, dyeing paper, and printing inks, are possibly carcinogenic, and are mutagenic, pp. 263–265; chloroform, used in photographic processing, is carcinogenic, p. 164; epichlorohydrin, used to prepare resins for paper sizing agents, is mutagenic, p. 45; hydrogen peroxide, used to sterilize paper, is mutagenic, p. 125; hydroxylamine, used in paper pulp, and as a photographic color developer, is mutagenic, p. 212; PCBs, used in carbonless duplicating paper and in printing inks, are carcinogenic in rodents, pp. 174, 178–179.

Chemicals that are used in the processing, coating, coloring; fungus-, water-, and flameproofing; and dry-cleaning of fibers and textiles are carcinogens or possible carcinogens: 2-(1-aziridinyl)-ethanol, p. 63; 2-methylaziridine, pp. 62, 63; azo dyes, p. 263; benzidine dyes, pp. 245, 246; bis(chloromethyl)ether (BCME), p. 97; chloroform, p. 164; copper 8-hydroxyquinoline, pp. 270, 272; epichlorohydrin, p. 45; lactones, e.g., β-propiolactone, p. 56; perchloroethylene, pp. 148, 149; trichloroethylene, pp. 145, 146; urethan, p. 220.

Chemicals that are used in the processing, coating, coloring; fungus-, water-, and flameproofing; and dry-cleaning of fibers and textiles are mutagens, possible mutagens, or causes of chromosomal aberrations: acetaldehyde, pp. 113–114; acrolein, pp. 112, 113; anthraquinones and nitroanthraquinones, pp. 286, 287; aziridine, pp. 61–63; azobenzene azo dyes, p. 263; benzidine dyes, pp. 245, 246; bis(chloromethyl)ether (BCME), pp. 96, 97, 99; chloroprene, pp. 151, 152; diethyl and dimethyl sulfate, pp. 66, 67; epichlorohydrin, p. 45; ethylene dichloride, p. 87; ethylene oxide, pp. 43–44; formaldehyde, p. 107; glycidol, p. 47; hydrazine, p. 198; hydrogen peroxide, p. 125; hydroxylamine, p. 212; lactones, e.g., β-propiolactone, p. 56; peracetic acid, pp. 123, 124; semi-carbazide, p. 200; styrene oxide, p. 48; trichloroethylene, pp. 145, 147; urethan, p. 220.

Other reported carcinogens: 100 chemicals "definitely carcinogenic," p. 3; 1,000 chemicals "tumorigenic," 3,500,000 known chemicals, 25,000 chemicals in commercial use, chemicals increasing by 700 a year, p. 1; industrial carcinogens and mutagens—types, classes, p. 315; quotation: carcinogenic/mutagenic industrial agents, pp. 315–316; chloroform, used in drugs, carcinogenic, p. 164; sodium azide, used in protective air bags, mutagenic, quotation, p. 313; vinyl chloride monomes cause angiosarcoma of the liver, lung adenomas, brain neuroblastoma lymphomas in animals, may cause cancer of lymphatic and hematopoietic system in man, and is carcinogenic and mutagenic, and causes chromosomal breaks, pp. 134–135; vinyl chloride reported migrating from PVC water pipes, p. 133.

Epler, J. L.; Larimer, F. W.; Rao T. K.; Nix, C. E.; Ho, T. "Energy-Related Pollutants in the Environment: Use of Short-Term Tests for Mutagenicity in the Isolation and Identification of Biohazards." *Environmental Health Perspectives 27* (1978). *Coal gasification and liquefication processes release mutagens and potential mutagens, p. 16.*

Epstein, S. S. "The Carcinogenicity of Organochlorine Pesticides." In *Origins of Human Cancer,* edited by H. H. Hiatt, J. D. Watson, J. A. Winsten. Book A, *Incidence of Cancer in Humans.* New York: Cold Spring Harbor Laboratory, 1977. *Carcinogenic hydrocarbon pesticides, Table 1, pp. 244–245.*

Epstein, Samuel S., M.D. *The Politics of Cancer.* San Francisco: Sierra Club Books, 1978. *According to Chemical Abstracts Computer Registry, 4,000,000 chemical compounds exist, 33,000 in common use, pp. 32, 34. Minnesota Judge Miles Lord forbade Reserve Mining Co. to dump taconite wastes containing asbestos fibers into Lake Superior, p. 95. Nitrosamines are carcinogenic in more than twenty animal species, p. 283. Paints used by artists and craftsmen contain carcinogenic substances, e.g., metal carcinogens and vinyl chloride, p. 456.*

Epstein, Samuel S., Legator, Marvin S. *The Mutagenicity of Pesticides: Concepts and Evaluation.* Cambridge, Mass.: MIT Press, 1971. *Food additives producing mutations and chromosome aberrations, pp. 17–18.*

Falk, Hans L., Jurgelski, William, Jr. "Health Effects of Coal Mining and Combustion, Number 7: Carcinogens and Cofactors." National Institute of Environmental Health Sciences. April 27, 1979. *Manuscript. Coal effluents reported to combine with other chemicals in air and in animal tissues to form nitrosamines, Section 2C; elemental carcinogens, Table 4; polycyclic and heterocyclic aromatic compounds, Section 2; polynuclear aromatics, Table 3.*

Fine, D. H.; Rounbehler, D. P.; Fan, T.; Ross, R. "Human Exposure to N-Nitroso Compounds in the Environment." In *Origins of Human Cancer,* edited by H. H. Hiatt, J. D. Watson, J. A. Winsten. Book A, *Incidence of Cancer in Humans.* New York: Cold Spring Harbor Laboratory, 1977. *Nitrosamines, notably the carcinogenic N-nitrosodiethylamine, have been reported as industrial air pollutants, pp. 294–295.*

Fisher, G. L.; Chrisp, C. E.; Raabe, O. G. "Physical Factors Affecting the Mutagenicity of Fly Ash from a Coal-Fired Power Plant." *Science 204* (1979). *Respirable coal fly ash particles: fine more mutagenic than coarse, p. 879.*

Flessel, C. Peter. "Metals as Mutagens." In *Inorganic and Nutritional Aspects of Cancer,* edited by G. N. Schrauzer. New York: Plenum, 1978. *Metals, minerals, and/or their compounds which are mutagenic and/or induce chromosomal aberrations, pp. 117, 125–126.*

(FDA) Food and Drug Administration. *Reports to the Press:*

February 10, 1972. (Diethyl pyrocarbonate: DEPC) *HEW News. FDA proposed ban on diethylpyrocarbonate (DEPC), p. 1.*

May 9, 1973. "Polyvinyl Chloride (PVC)." *HEW News. Polyvinyl chloride leaching into bottled alcoholic beverages, p. 1.*

March 25, 1977. "PCBs in Foods." *Talk Paper. Carcinogenic PCBs contaminate foods, pp. 1–2.*

September 27, 1977. (Trichloroethylene) *HEW News. FDA proposes ban on trichloroethylene (TCE), a reported carcinogen, used in drugs, foods and beverages, and as a solvent in instant coffee, p. 1.*

June 8, 1979. (Methapyrilene) *HEW News. Methapyrilene, a drug, carcinogenic, p. 1.*
July 26, 1979. (Medroxyprogesterone acetate) *HEW News. Medroxyprogesterone, a drug, possibly carcinogenic, p. 1.*

(FDA) Food and Drug Administration. "Silver-Plated Hollowware." *Federal Register 40:30* (February 12, 1975). *Lead leaching from silver-plated hollowware, pp. 6523-6524.*

Ford, Robert S. "Drinking Water: New Health Problem." *Science 197* (1977). Letter. *Municipal water tanks, pipelines reported coated with carcinogenic asbestos and coal tar, p. 1322.*

Gegiou, D., Botsivali, M. "Atomic-Absorption Spectrophotometric Determination of Lead in Beverages and Fruit Juices and of Lead Extracted by Their Action on Glazed Ceramic Surfaces." *Analyst 100* (1975), *pp. 234-237.*

(GAO) General Accounting Office. Appendices in "Cancer-Causing Chemicals in Food." Report of the Subcommittee on Oversight and Investigations of the Committee on Interstate and Foreign Commerce, House of Representatives, Ninety-fifth Congress, Second Session. Committee Print 95-67. December 1978. *Mutagenic pesticides, Appendix 1, p. 45.*

———. "Cancer-Causing Chemicals—Part 2: Chemical Contamination of Food." Hearings Before the Subcommittee on Oversight and Investigations of the Committee of Interstate and Foreign Commerce. House of Representatives. Ninety-fifth Congress, Second Session. Serial No. 95-118. February 14, 16, 24, 1978. *Robert Chambers, Testimony: an estimated 30 carcinogens in pesticides, p. 10. GAO: carcinogenic drugs used to treat food animals, p. 198.*

Getschow, George. "Indoor Air Pollution Worries Experts as Buildings Are Sealed to Save Fuel." *Wall Street Journal,* August 15, 1979. *Formaldehyde pollution found in mobile homes, p. 6.*

Gold, Marion D.; Blum, Arlene; Ames, Bruce N. "Another Flame Retardant, Tris(1,3-Dichloro-2-Propyl)-Phosphate, and Its Expected Metabolites Are Mutagens." *Science 200* (1978). *Flame retardant in children's sleepwear can be absorbed through human skin, pp. 785-787.*

Goldman, P.; Ingelfinger, J. A.; Friedman, P. A. "Metronidazole, Isoniazid and the Threat of Human Cancer." In *Origins of Human Cancer,* edited by H. H. Hiatt, J. D. Watson, J. A. Winsten. Book A, *Incidence of Cancer in Humans.* New York: Cold Spring Harbor Laboratory, 1977. *Drugs reported carcinogenic in animals: isoniazid, metronidazole, p. 471.*

Goldstein, B.; Webster, I.; Rendall, R.E.G.; Skikne, M. I. "The Effects of Asbestos-Cement Dust Inhalation on Baboons." *Environmental Research 16* (1978). *Baboons inhaling asbestos dust revealed suggestive signs of bronchiolo-alveolar carcinoma, pp. 216, 224*

Handler, Philip. President, National Academy of Sciences. Letter to the Honorable Joseph A. Califano, Jr., Secretary of Health, Education, and Welfare. Accompanying Part One of the NAS Study of Saccharin and Food Safety Policy. November 6, 1978. *Saccharin reported to produce bladder tumors in male rats at extremely high doses, p. 1.*

(HEW) Department of Health, Education, and Welfare. DHEW Subcommittee on Health Effects of PCBs and PBBs. "General Summary and Conclusions." *Environmental Health Perspectives 24* (1978). *Large portion of U.S. population exposed to PCB's, p. 194.*

———. Interagency Task Force on Ionizing Radiation. "Summary of Work Group Reports." February 27, 1979. *Population exposure estimates, 1978, Table 1, p. 20.*

———. *Survey of Compounds Which Have Been Tested for Carcinogenic Activity.* Vols. I–VII (1974–1976). Cited in Occupational Safety and Health Administration (OSHA). U.S. Department of Labor. *Identification, Classification and Regulation of*

Potential Occupational Carcinogens. Part VII, Book 2. In *Federal Register 45:15* (January 22, 1980). *Of 7,000 chemicals tested between 1974–1976, about 17% were reported tumorigenic, p. 5028.*

————. *We Want You to Know about Television Radiation.* HEW Publication (FDA) 76-8041, 1976. *Ionizing radiation is emitted by television tubes; no exposure without some degree of risk; standards limiting X-ray emissions set by federal government.* Pamphlet.

Heath, Clark W., Jr.; Dumont, Cheryl R.; Gamble, John; Waxweiler, Richard. "Chromosomal Damage in Men Occupationally Exposed to Vinyl Chloride Monomer and Other Chemicals." *Environmental Research 14* (1977). *Vinyl chloride monomer possibly mutagenic, as well as carcinogenic, p. 68.*

Heath, J. C.; Daniel M. R.; Dingle, J. T.; Webb, M. "Cadmium as a Carcinogen." *Nature 193* (1962). *Cadmium, cobalt carcinogenic in rats, pp. 592–593.*

Henderson, Richard W., Andrews D. "Lead Extraction from Aluminum." *Bulletin of Environmental Contamination & Toxicology 13* (1975). *Lead leaches from aluminum products into beverages and foods, p. 330.*

Higgins, G. M.; Levy, Barnet M.; Yollick, Bernard L. "A Transplantable Beryllium-Induced Chondrosarcoma of Rabbits." *Journal of Bone and Joint Surgery 46-A* (1964). *Beryllium compounds cause bone cancer in rabbits, pp. 789–796.*

Hoffmann, Dietrich; Schmeltz, Irwin; Hecht, Stephen S.; Brunnemann, Klaus D.; Wynder, Ernst L. "Volatile Carcinogens: Occurrence, Formation and Analysis." In *Prevention and Detection of Cancer,* edited by Herbert E. Nieburgs. Part 1, *Prevention.* Vol. 2, *Etiology. Prevention Methods.* New York: Marcel Dekker, 1978. *Hydrazine, used in rocket fuel, carcinogenic, Table I, p. 1952.*

Hooper, N. Kim; Ames, Bruce N.; Saleh, Mahmoud Abbas; Casida, John E. "Toxaphene, a Complex Mixture of Polychloroterpenes and a Major Insecticide, Is Mutagenic." *Science 205* (1979). *Toxaphene, a pesticide, reported mutagenic, p. 591.*

(IARC) International Agency for Research on Cancer. *IARC Monographs on the Evaluation of the Carcinogenic Risk of Chemicals to Man.* Lyon: IARC.

Vol. 1. (Untitled monograph.) 1972. *Auramine dye, for textiles, carcinogenic, pp. 70, 72. Benzidine dyestuffs carcinogenic in rodents and man, pp. 81, 84. Beryl, beryllium, beryllium salts, and beryllium sulfate carcinogenic in rats, monkeys, rabbits, p. 25. Carbon tetrachloride carcinogenic in mouse, hamster, rat, p. 57; used as grain fumigant, p. 54. Lead compounds carcinogenic in rats and mice, pp. 47–48; dominantly used in storage batteries and as gasoline additive, p. 42.*

Vol. 6. *Sex Hormones.* 1974. *Drugs (hormones) carcinogenic in animals: diethylstilbestrol, animal carcinogen, p. 69, human carcinogen, p. 70; ethinyloestradiol, pp. 79, 83; progesterone, pp. 137, 143.*

Vol. 7. *Some Anti-Thyroid and Related Substances, Nitrofurans and Industrial Chemicals.* 1974. *Polyvinyl chloride: polyvinyl chloride resins, made from vinyl chloride monomer, are ubiquitous in building and construction industries, pp. 294, 309; polyvinyl chloride resins used in manufacture of records (music), p. 309; vinyl chloride monomer is carcinogenic in rodents and man, p. 305. Other: (MTU) methylthiouracil, a drug, carcinogenic in rodents, pp. 55, 62; PCBs, reported carcinogens, migrating from packaging into foods, pp. 271–272, 281; propylthiouracil, a drug, carcinogenic in rodents, pp. 69, 73.*

Vol. 9. *Some Aziridines, n-, s- & o-Mustards and Selenium.* 1975. *Drugs reported carcinogenic: 2,4,6-tris(1-aziridinyl)-s-triazine, pp. 95, 97, 102; bis(2-chloroethyl) ether, compound used in manufacture of an anesthetic, pp. 119, 121; thiotepa, p. 90; tris(aziridinyl)-para-benzoquinone, pp. 67, 68, 71. Others: 2-methylaziridine, used in petroleum refining and rocket fuel, pp. 62–64; aziridine, used in manufacture of paper, carcinogenic, pp. 39, 43; selenium, used in home-entertainment units, and varied industrial uses of selenium, p. 247.*

Vol. 11. *Cadmium, Nickel, Some Epoxides, Miscellaneous Industrial Chemicals and General Considerations on Volatile Anaesthetics.* 1976. *1,4-dioxane, an oil solvent, carcinogenic, pp. 249, 252; cadmium compounds reported carcinogenic, p. 64; cadmium found in phosphate fertilizers, p. 49; epichlorohydrin, used in resins in manufacture of paper, carcinogenic, pp. 133, 137; isoflurane, an anesthetic, carcinogenic, pp. 285, 289; nickel compounds reported carcinogens, pp. 103, 104, quotation, p. 55; trichloroethylene, an anesthetic, carcinogenic, pp. 285, 271.*

Vol. 12. *Some Carbamates, Thiocarbamates and Carbazides.* 1976. *Diallate, monuron, used as crop controllers, are reported carcinogens, pp. 70, 73, 169, 174; n-propyl carbamate, used in manufacture of durable-press, wash-and-wear fabrics, carcinogenic, pp. 202, 206.*

Vol. 14. *Asbestos.* 1977. *Asbestos causes lung cancer and mesotheliomas in experimental animals (mice, hamsters, rabbits, rats), in workers and their families, p. 80; asbestos filters and asbestos-contaminated talc may be infiltrating manufactured foods. p. 35.*

Vol. 16. *Some Aromatic Amines and Related Nitro Compounds—Hair Dyes, Coloring Agents and Miscellaneous Industrial Chemicals.* 1978. *Food additives reported carcinogenic: Fast Green FCF, pp. 188, 194; guinea green B, banned by FDA, pp. 201, 205; light green SF—may no longer be in use, pp. 211, 216; Rhodamine B, pp. 221-228. Others: Animal data suggest carcinogenicity of N-phenyl-2-naphthylamine, p. 336; N-phenyl-2-naphthylamine contaminated by 2-naphthylamine (NIOSH, 1976), p. 326.*

Janes, Joseph M.; Higgins, George M.; Herrick, J. F. "Beryllium-Induced Osteogenic Sarcoma in Rabbits." *Journal of Bone and Joint Surgery 36-B* (1954), *pp. 543-551.*

Kelly, Henry. "Photovoltaic Power Systems: A Tour Through the Alternatives." *Science 199* (1978). *Arsenic and cadmium compounds used in some solar heating cells, p. 637; quotation, p. 637.*

Kelly, Patrick J.; Janes, Joseph M.; Peterson, Lowell F. A. "The Effect of Beryllium on Bone." *Journal of Bone and Joint Surgery 43-A* (1961). *Beryllium compounds cause bone cancer in rabbits, pp. 829-843.*

Kraybill, Herman F. "Unintentional Additives in Foods." In *Environmental Quality and Food Supply,* edited by Philip L. White, Diane Robbins. Mount Kisco, N.Y.: Futura Publishing Company, 1974. *Classes of synthetic chemicals and compounds which enter the food chain, p. 173; quotation, p. 173.*

Larsen, R. P., Oldham, R. D. "Plutonium in Drinking Water: Effects of Chlorination on its Maximum Permissible Concentration." *Science 201* (1978). *Chlorination reported to be oxidizing plutonium in drinking water, may increase its ingestion, pp. 1008, 1009.*

Lee, Milton L.; Later, Douglas W.; Rollins, David K.; Eatough, Delbert J.; Hansen, Lee D. "Dimethyl and Monomethyl Sulfate: Presence in Coal Fly Ash and Airborne Particulate Matter." *Science 207* (1980). *Chemicals in ash and particulate matter from coal combustion carcinogenic and mutagenic, according to Druckrey, Hollaender, Lowley, and Couch, p. 186; footnote 4, p. 187.*

Lijinsky, William. "Nitrosamines and Nitrosamides in the Etiology of Gastrointestinal Cancer." *Cancer 40:3* (November Supplement) (1977). *N-Nitroso compounds reported to cause almost every type of tumor in almost all organs of laboratory animals, p. 2446; nitrite, used to cure meats, interacts with amines in foods and other sources to produce carcinogenic N-nitroso compounds, pp. 2446-2447.*

Loewengart, Gordon, Van Duuren, Benjamin L. "Evaluation of Chemical Flame Retardants for Carcinogenic Potential." *Journal of Toxicology and Environmental Health 2* (1977). *Pyroset TKP and tetrakis (hydroxymethyl)phosphonium chloride (THPC) are tumor promoters, p. 539.*

Marino, Andrew A., Becker, Robert O. "High Voltage Lines: Hazard at a Distance." *Environment 20* (1978). *Exposure to electric fields produces bone tumors in rats, p. 11.*

Marshall, Eliot. "Governor Ray Relents, Opens Waste Site." *Science* 206 (1979). *One-third of low-level radioactive wastes comes from biomedical research laboratories and hospitals, p. 1165.*

Maugh, Thomas H., II. "Toxic Waste Disposal a Growing Problem." *Science* 204 (1979). *Estimates of different types of sites for waste disposal, p. 819; quotation: elemental carcinogens, e.g., beryllium, cadmium, remain hazards forever, make half-lives of radioactive wastes seem transient, p. 821.*

Maugh, Thomas H., II, Marx, Jean L. *The Seeds of Destruction: The Science Report on Cancer Research.* New York: Plenum, 1975. *1,000 chemicals reported to cause tumors in man or animals, p. 9; quotation, p. 9.*

McCann, Michael. "The Impact of Hazards in Art on Female Workers." *Preventive Medicine* 7 (1978). *Artists work with toxic and sometimes carcinogenic substances, pp. 340-341.*

Merrill, Richard A. "FDA Use of the Delaney Clause." Appendix B in *Food Safety Policy: Scientific and Societal Considerations,* Part 2. Washington, D.C.: Institute of Medicine, NAS, 1979. *Feed animal drugs and chemicals, food additives, in contact with food banned by the FDA, Appendix B, pp. B1-B5.*

Miller, Sanford A. "Additives in Our Food Supply." In *Food and Nutrition in Health and Diseases,* edited by N. Henry Moss and Jean Mayer. *Annals of The New York Academy of Sciences,* Vol. 300. New York: New York Academy of Sciences, 1977. *Classes of food additives, p. 400.*

Morgan, Robert W., Shettigara, P. T. "Occupational Asbestos Exposure, Smoking, and Laryngeal Carcinoma." In *Occupational Carcinogenesis,* edited by Umberto Saffiotti, Joseph K. Wagoner. *Annals of The New York Academy of Sciences,* Vol. 271. New York: New York Academy of Sciences, 1976. *Asbestos causes laryngeal cancer in workers who smoke, pp. 308-310.*

Murthy, G. K., Rhea, U.S. of USHEW and FDA. "Cadmium, Copper, Iron, Lead, Manganese, and Zinc in Evaporated Milk, Infant Products and Human Milk." Submitted to *Journal of Dairy Science,* January 18, 1971. *Cadmium, copper, iron, lead, manganese, and zinc leaching out of tin cans into canned and infant products.*

(NAS) National Academy of Sciences publications: Committee on the Biological Effects of Ionizing Radiations (BEIR). *The Effects on Populations of Exposure to Low Levels of Ionizing Radiation: 1980.* Washington, D.C.: National Academy Press, 1980. *Television sets emit ionizing radiation, p. 57.*

————. Committee on Biologic Effects of Atmospheric Pollutants. *Particulate Polycyclic Organic Matter.* Washington, D.C.: National Academy of Sciences, 1972. *Cigarettes contain such carcinogenic agents as arsenic, nitrosamines, polonium, and polycyclic hydrocarbons, e.g., benzo(a)pyrene, p. 1.*

————. Report by the Panel on Low Molecular Weight Halogenated Hydrocarbons. *Chloroform, Carbon Tetrachloride, and Other Halomethanes: An Environmental Assessment.* Washington, D.C.: National Academy of Sciences, 1978. *Bromoform, bromodichloromethane, chloroform, and dibromochloromethane identified by EPA in U.S. water supplies, pp. 102-103.*

————. Report by the Panel on Nitrates. *Nitrates: An Environmental Assessment.* Washington, D.C.: National Academy of Sciences, 1978. *N-nitroso compounds: reported carcinogenic in every species tested, p. 458; reported to produce tumors in many organs, Table 9.4, p. 455.*

————. Safe Drinking Water Committee. *Drinking Water and Health.* Washington, D.C.: National Academy of Sciences, 1977. *Oxychlordane, a pesticide, causes liver cancer, p. 568; selenium and selenium compound reported carcinogenic in rats, p. 359; trace metals found in 380 samples of finished water supplies in U.S., Table V-6, p. 211.*

(NCRP) National Council on Radiation Protection. 1960. Cited by the X-Radiation Ad Hoc Committee of the Electronics Industries Association. "Evaluation of Television Contribution to the Annual Genetically Significant Radiation Dose of the Population." *Radiological Health Data and Reports*, Vol. 12. Washington, D.C.: EPA, 1971. *Television tubes emit ionizing radiation, tolerated exposures formulated by government, p. 363.*

(NIOSH) National Institute for Occupational Safety and Health. *Suspected Carcinogens*, edited by Herbert E. Christensen, Edward J. Fairchild, Richard J. Lewis, Sr. Cincinnati: NIOSH, 1976. *1,905 chemicals reported carcinogenic, 510 suspected, Foreword by John F. Finklea, p. iii. Reported carcinogens: Actinomycin D, Adriamycin, p. 11; beryllium, p. 47; boric acid, p. 53; busulfan, p. 54; chlorambucil, p. 65; diphenyl, p. 98; diphenyl oxide, p. 99; formaldehyde, p. 116; menthol, mercury, p. 140; mitomycin C, p. 148; nickel compounds, pp. 159–160; nitrogen mustard, p. 161; penicillin, p. 171; phthalate esters, p. 185; prednisone, p. 190; sodium chromate, p. 204; streptozotocin, p. 208; sulfa drugs, pp. 210–211; thio-tepa, p. 217; triethylenemelamine (TEM), p. 226.*

Natusch, D.F.S. "Potentially Carcinogenic Species Emitted to the Atmosphere by Fossil-Fueled Power Plants." *Environmental Health Perspectives 22* (1978). *Classes of carcinogens and suspected carcinogens in the air, including known and suspected carcinogens emitted by burning fossil fuels, Table 1, pp. 80–81; nitrogen oxides are potentiators of carcinogenesis and are found in both urban and rural air, p. 80.*

Nebert, Daniel W.; Levitt, Roy C.; Pelkonen, Olavi. "Genetic Variation in Metabolism of Chemical Carcinogens Associated with Susceptibility to Tumorigenesis." In *Carcinogens: Identification and Mechanisms of Action*, edited by A. Clark Griffin, Charles R. Shaw. New York: Raven, 1979. *TCDD speculative co-carcinogen in mice, p. 166.*

Neill, Robert H.; Youmans, Harry D.; Wyatt, John L. "Estimates of Potential Doses to Various Organs from X-radiation Emissions from Color Television Picture Tubes." *Radiological Health Data and Reports*, Vol. 12. Washington, D.C.: EPA, 1971. *Television tubes emit ionizing radiation, any exposure involves some degree of risk, pp. 1, 4–5.*

The New York Academy of Sciences. *Cancer and the Worker.* 1977. (This popularized book was based on Vol. 271 of the *Annals*, entitled *Occupational Carcinogenesis*, published by New York Academy of Sciences in May 1976.) *Lead salts carcinogenic in experimental animals, p. 35.*

Newberne, Paul M. "Nitrite Promotes Lymphoma Incidence in Rats." *Science 204* (1979), *p. 1079.*

Nicholson, William J. "Cancer Following Occupational Exposure to Asbestos and Vinyl Chloride." *Cancer 39:4* (Supplement) (1977). *Asbestos causes peritoneal and pleural mesothelioma, and colon, esophageal, lung, rectal, and stomach cancer in workers and endangers those exposed to workers and to factories using the fiber, pp. 1792–1793.*

Norseth, T. "Industrial Viewpoints on Cancer Caused by Metals as an Occupational Disease." In *Origins of Human Cancer*, edited by H. H. Hiatt, J. D. Watson, J. A. Winsten. Book A, *Incidence of Cancer in Humans.* New York: Cold Spring Harbor Laboratory, 1977. *Suspected metal carcinogens: antimony, arsenic, cadmium, cobalt, p. 160.*

(OSHA) Occupational Safety and Health Administration. "OSHA Takes Emergency Action to Reduce Worker Exposure to Acrylonitrile." U.S. Department of Labor News (January 16, 1978). *Acrylonitrile, used to produce man-made fibers, is carcinogenic, p. 1.*

Olajos, E. J. "Biological Interactions of N-Nitroso Compounds: A Review." *Ecotoxicology and Environmental Safety 1* (1977). *N-Nitroso compounds mutagenic, p. 175.*

Padgett, Joseph, EPA. Letter to Roger Strelow, Assistant Administrator for Air and Waste Management, November 13, 1975. *Nitrogen oxides (NOx) can interact with amines to form carcinogenic nitrosamines in the air, p. 1.*

Pott, F.; Huth, F.; Friedrichs, K. H. "Tumorigenic Effect of Fibrous Dusts in Experimental Animals." *Environmental Health Perspectives 9* (1974). *Fiberglass and other fibrous dusts produce mesothelioma in rats, pp. 313-315.*

Prival, Michael J.; McCoy, Elena C.; Gutter, Bezalel; Rosenkranz, Herbert S. "Tris(2,-3-Dibromopropyl)Phosphate: Mutagenicity of a Widely Used Flame Retardant." *Science 195* (1977). *Flame retardant in textiles, including children's sleepwear, pp. 76-78.*

Rall, David P. "Researching Health Hazards in the Environment." *American Water Works Association Journal 67* (1975). *10,000 chemicals in commercial use, p. 447.*

Reeves, Andrew L. "Beryllium Carcinogenesis." In *Inorganic and Nutritional Aspects of Cancer,* edited by G. N. Schrauzer. New York: Plenum, 1978. *Beryllium compounds cause bone cancer in rabbits, pp. 13-14; pulmonary adenocarcinoma in rats and monkeys, p. 14.*

Sawicki, E. "Analysis of Atmospheric Carcinogens and Their Cofactors." In *Environmental Pollution and Carcinogenic Risks,* edited by Claude Rosenfeld, Walter Davis. Lyon: IARC Scientific Publications No. 13, 1976. *Concentrations of carcinogenic benzo(a)pyrene and other polycyclic aromatic hydrocarbons reported in airport runways, in asphalts and tars on highways and streets, in automobile exhausts, and in tunnels, pp. 299, 309, Table III, p. 344.*

Schuphan, Ingolf; Rosen, Joseph D.; Casida, John E. "Novel Activation Mechanism for the Promutagenic Herbicide Diallate." *Science 205* (1979). *Diallate, an herbicide, is reported to be promutagenic, p. 1013.*

Selikoff, Irving J. "Cancer Risk of Asbestos Exposure." In *Origins of Human Cancer,* edited by H. H. Hiatt, J. D. Watson, and J. A. Winsten. Book C, *Human Risk Assessment.* New York: Cold Spring Harbor Laboratory, 1977. *Asbestos causes peritoneal mesothelioma in workers in various industries, and exposes families to risk, pp. 1765-1782.*

Selikoff, Irving J., Hammond, E. Cuyler. "Asbestos-Associated Disease in United States Shipyards." *Cancer Journal for Clinicians 28* (1978). *Asbestos carcinogenic in animals, causes peritoneal and pleural mesothelioma, and cancer of colon-rectum, esophagus, kidney, larynx, oropharynx and stomach in man, pp. 87-99.*

Shabad, L. M., Smirnov, G. A. "Aviation and Environmental Benzo(a)pyrene Pollution." In *Environmental Pollution and Carcinogenic Risks,* edited by Claude Rosenfeld, Walter Davis. Lyon: IARC Scientific Publications No. 13, 1976. *Benzo(a)pyrene emerges from turbojet and turboprop engines, p. 53.*

Shibko, Samuel I. "Toxicology of Phthalic Acid Esters." In *Environmental Quality and Food Supply,* edited by Philip L. White, Diane Robbins. Mount Kisco, New York: Futura, 1974. *Phthalate esters reported to migrate from food packaging, p. 219.*

Shimkin, M. B.; Stoner, G. D.; Theiss, J. C. "Lung Tumor Response in Mice to Metals and Metal Salts." In *Inorganic and Nutritional Aspects of Cancer,* edited by G. N. Schrauzer. New York: Plenum, 1978. *Compounds of lead, manganese, molybdenum elicit weakly carcinogenic response in mice, p. 85.*

Shirasu, Y.; Moriya M.; Kato, K.; Lienard F.; Tezuka, H.; Teramoto, S.; Kada, T. "Mutagenicity Screening on Pesticides and Modification Products: A Basis of Carcinogenicity Evaluation." In *Origins of Human Cancer,* edited by H. H. Hiatt, J. D. Watson, J. A. Winsten. Book A, *Incidence of Cancer in Humans.* New York: Cold Spring Harbor Laboratory, 1977. *Mutagenic pesticides, Figure 1, pp. 268, 269.*

Shubik, Philippe. "Identification of Environmental Carcinogens: Animal Test Models." In *Carcinogens: Identification and Mechanisms of Action,* edited by A. Clark Griffin and Charles R. Shaw. New York: Raven, 1979. *Xylitol, a sweetener, reported carcinogenic, p. 44.*

Skougstad, Marvin W. "Minor Elements in Water." In *Environmental Geochemistry in Health and Disease,* edited by Helen L. Cannon, Howard C. Hopps. Boulder, Colorado: Geological Society of America, 1971. *Radioisotopes found in natural water, p. 45; trace metals found in finished drinking water in 100 U.S. cities, p. 51.*

Smith, R. Jeffrey. "Toxic Substances: EPA and OSHA Are Reluctant Regulators." *Science 203* (1979). *According to EPA Administrator Douglas Costle, 70,000 chemicals in commercial use, 20 percent suspected carcinogenic; 25 percent of the 1,500 active ingredients of registered pesticides carcinogenic, p. 28.*

————. "Xylitol: Another Sweetener Turns Sour." *Science 199* (1978). *Xylitol, a sweetener, reported carcinogenic in mice and rats, p. 670.*

Snodin, D. J. "Lead and Cadmium in Baby Foods." *Journal of the Association of Public Analysts 11* (1973). *Cadmium and lead reported leaching from cans into baby foods, p. 112.*

Solon, Leonard R. "A Public Health Approach to Microwave and Radiofrequency Radiation." *Bulletin of the Atomic Scientists 35* (1979). *Microwave and radiofrequency radiation reported to damage central nervous system, impair fetal growth, and cause chromosomal anomalies in hamsters and fruit flies, pp. 51–52.*

Sterling, Theodor D., Kobayashi, Diane M. "Exposure to Pollutants in Enclosed Living Spaces." *Environmental Research 13* (1977). *Indoor carcinogenic air pollutants emerge from a variety of sources and often exceed outdoor pollution, pp. 1–6, 8, 9–12, 16, 17.*

Sunderman, F. William, Jr. "Carcinogenic Effects of Metals." *Federation Proceedings 37:1* (1978). *Metals and/or compounds reported carcinogenic in experimental animals: beryllium, cadmium, chromium, hematite (iron ore), lead, nickel, titanium, zinc, p. 40; reported mutagenic: rhodium and ruthenium, Table 5, p. 44.*

————. "The Current Status of Nickel Carcinogenesis." *Annals of Clinical Laboratory Science 3* (1973). *Nickel carcinogenic to animals and man, pp. 156–175.*

————. "Mechanisms of Metal Carcinogenesis." *Biological Trace Element Research 1* (1979). *Lead a "recognized" carcinogen, p. 77.*

————. "Metal Carcinogenesis in Experimental Animals." *Food and Cosmetics Toxicology 9* (1971). *Metal compounds reported carcinogenic in animals: cadmium, chromium, cobalt, hematite (iron ore), lead, selenium, titanium, zinc, p. 105.*

————. "Pulmonary Carcinogenesis from Exposure to Toxic Agents." In *Laboratory Diagnosis of Diseases Caused by Toxic Agents,* edited by F. William Sunderman, F. William Sunderman, Jr. St. Louis, Missouri: Warren H. Green, 1970. *Nickel, a carcinogen, is reported to be a component of cigarette smoke, and an air pollutant, Table 7, p. 499, Table 9, p. 500; respiratory carcinogens in animal species, Table 3, p. 497.*

————. "A Review of the Carcinogenicities of Nickel, Chromium and Arsenic Compounds in Man and Animals." *Preventive Medicine 5* (1976). *Arsenic compound carcinogenic to mice in experiments by Osswald and Goettler in January 1971, p. 287. Also see footnote 109, p. 292.*

Sundin, David S. National Institute for Occupational Safety and Health. Letter to Rick Grawey. Manpower and Housing Committee. April 14, 1977. *46,000 product formulations on file at NIOSH, p. 2.*

Surgeon General of the United States. *Healthy People: The Surgeon General's Report on Health Promotion and Disease Prevention.* HEW (PHS) 79-55-71. 1979. *Quotation: "over 2,300" chemicals are suspected carcinogens, p. 9–7.*

Thomas, Barry; Edmunds, John W.; Curry, S. Joanne. "Lead Content of Canned Fruit." *Journal of the Science of Food and Agriculture 26* (1975). *Lead leaching out of cans into fruits, p. 1.*

Thomas, Barry; Roughan, John A.; Watters, Evelyn D. "Lead and Cadmium Content of Some Canned Fruit and Vegetables." *Journal of the Science of Food and Agriculture 26* (1973). *Lead and cadmium leaching from cans into fruits and vegetables, p. 447.*

Train, Russell: see EPA, February 26, 1976.

Turk, Amos; Turk, Jonathan; Wittes, Janet T.; Wittes, Robert E. *Environmental Science.* Philadelphia: Saunders, 1978. *Chlorinated hydrocarbons, organophosphates, and carbamates most studied pesticides, p. 359.*

Upton, Arthur C. National Cancer Institute Position Paper. "Human Health Considerations of Carcinogenic Organic Chemical Contaminants in Drinking Water." April 10, 1978. Submitted to Dr. Douglas M. Costle, Administrator of the Environmental Protection Agency. *Federal Register 43:130* (July 6, 1978). *NCI list of carcinogens, suspect carcinogens, and carcinogen promoters in U.S. drinking water, pp. 29148-29150.*

Vaught, J. B., King, C. M. "Phenacetin Studies." *Science 206* (1979). *Phenacetin, a drug, carcinogenic, or can act synergistically to produce tumors in animals, p. 639.*

Vianna, Nicholas J., Polan, Adele K. "Non-Occupational Exposure to Asbestos and Malignant Mesothelioma in Females." *Lancet,* May 20, 1978. *Female relatives of asbestos workers exposed to significant risk of mesothelioma, pp. 1061, 1063.*

Wagner, J.; Berry, Geoffrey; Skidmore, J. W. "Studies of the Carcinogenic Effect of Fibre Glass of Different Diameters Following Intrapleural Inoculation in Experimental Animals." In *Occupational Exposure to Fibrous Glass.* Proceedings of a Symposium Sponsored by the National Institute for Occupational Safety and Health. University of Maryland, June 26-27, 1974. HEW Pub. No. (NIOSH) 76-151. *Fibers in asbestos, as well as fiberglass, cause mesothelioma in rats; the fine fibers are more carcinogenic, p. 193.*

Wildenberg, Judith. "An Assessment of Experimental Carcinogen-Detecting Systems with Special Reference to Inorganic Arsenicals." *Environmental Research 16* (1978). *Arsenic potentially linked to respiratory and skin cancer in humans, pp. 139-151.*

Wolff, Sheldon, Rodin, Brita. "Saccharin-Induced Sister Chromatid Exchanges in Chinese Hamster and Human Cells." *Science 200* (1978). *Saccharin reported mutagenic, p. 543.*

(WHO) World Health Organization. Geneva. *Environmental Health Criteria Series:*
Environmental Health Criteria 2. *Polychlorinated Biphenyls and Terphenyls.* Copyright 1976. *PCBs: may be carcinogenic, p. 64; used in copying paper, p. 26.*

Environmental Health Criteria 3. *Lead.* Copyright 1977. *Lead compounds carcinogenic in mice, rats, p. 94.*

Environmental Health Criteria 5. *Nitrates, Nitrites, and N-Nitroso Compounds.* Copyright 1978. *N-nitroso compounds produce cancer in a variety of organs in rats, Table 3, p. 60.*

Environmental Health Criteria 7. *Photochemical Oxidants.* Copyright 1979. *Ozone from ozonized gasoline is a reported carcinogen found in the air, p. 48.*

(WHO) World Health Organization. *Health Implications of Nuclear Power Production.* Report on a Working Group. Brussels, December 1-5, 1975. Copenhagen: World Health Organization, Regional Office for Europe. WHO Regional Publications, European Series No. 3. Copyright 1977. *Burning coal releases radium decay products, thorium and uranium; more radium released by coal fly ash than by oil-powered generators, p. 61; quotation, p. 61.*

Yoon, Soo-Choon; Krefft, Gerda B.; McLaren, Malcolm G. "Lead Release from Glazes and Glasses in Contact with Acid Solutions." *American Ceramic Society Bulletin 55* (1976). *Lead from glasses and glazes leaching into beverages, p. 508.*

Young, Ronald J.; McKay, William J.; Evans, James M. "Coal Gasification and Occupational Health." *American Industrial Hygiene Association Journal 39* (1978). *Elemental carcinogens, polynuclear aromatics (benzene), p. 991.*

Appendix B

Survey of Natural Carcinogens

REFERENCES

Abraham, S. K., Kesavan, P. C. "Evaluation of Possible Mutagenicity of Ginger, Turmeric, Asafoetida, Clove and Cinnamon Administered Alone and in Combination with Caffeine or Theophylline in *Drosophila melanogaster." Mutation Research 53* (1978). *Abstract 2, p. 142.*

Ackerknecht, Erwin H. *A Short History of Medicine*, rev. ed. New York: Ronald, 1968. *Great reptiles, p. 4; mummies, pp. 6–7.*

Adams, John A. S. "The Geological Origins of Radioactive Anomalies." In *International Symposium on Areas of High Natural Radioactivity*, edited by Academia Brasilera de Ciências. Rio de Janeiro: R. J., 1977. *Primordial nuclides, p. 5.*

Ames, Bruce N. "The Detection of Chemical Mutagens with Enteric Bacteria." In *Chemical Mutagens, Principles and Methods for Their Detection*, edited by Alexander Hollaender, Vol. 1. New York: Plenum, 1971. *UV radiation mutagenic, p. 279.*

———. "Identifying Environmental Chemicals Causing Mutations and Cancer." *Science 204* (1979). *Quotation, p. 591.*

Anaise, D.; Steinitz, R.; Ben Hur, N. "Solar Radiation: A Possible Etiological Factor in Malignant Melanoma in Israel. A Retrospective Study (1960–1972)." *Cancer 42(1):* 299–304; 1978. Cited in *Carcinogenesis Abstracts 16* (1979), Abstract 78-3264.

Anders, A. "Etiology of Cancer as Studied in the Platyfish-Swordtail System." *Biochim Biophys Acta 516(1):* 61–95; 1978. Cited in *Carcinogenesis Abstracts 16* (1979), Abstract 78-6059.

Archer, Victor E.; Gillam, J. Dean; Wagoner, Joseph K. "Respiratory Disease Mortality Among Uranium Miners." In *Occupational Carcinogenesis*, edited by Umberto Saffiotti, Joseph K. Wagoner. Annals of the New York Academy of Sciences, Vol. 271. New York: New York Academy of Sciences, 1976. *Radon, radon daughters, p. 280.*

Arenaz, P., Vig, B. K. "Somatic Mosaicism Induced by Some Carcinogens in Soybean (*Glycine max*). (Meeting abstract)." *Mutat Res 53(2):* 147; 1978. Cited in *Carcinogenesis Abstracts 16* (1979), Abstract 78-5664, *p. 2085.*

Asp, N. G.; Bauer, H.; Dahlqvist, A.; Fredlund, P.; Oste, R. "Dietary Fibre and Experimental Colon Cancer in the Rat." *Nutr Cancer 1(2):* 70–73; 1979. Cited in *Carcinogenesis Abstracts 17* (1979), Abstract 79-3328. *Citrus pectin enhances carcinogenesis.*

Auerbach, C. "History of Research on Chemical Mutagenesis." In *Chemical Mutagens, Principles and Methods for Their Detection*, edited by Alexander Hollaender. Vol. 3. New York: Plenum, 1973. *Mustard oil mutagenic, p. 5; pyrrolizidine alkaloids mutagenic, p. 9.*

Bababunmi, E. A. "Toxins and Carcinogens in the Environment: An Observation in the Tropics." *J Toxicol Environ Health* 4(5/6): 691–699; 1978. Cited in *Carcinogenesis Abstracts 17* (1979), Abstract 79-1231. *Red peppers may be carcinogenic to man.*

Bamburg, James R.; Strong, F. M.; Smalley, E. B. "Toxins from Moldy Cereals." *Journal of Agricultural and Food Chemistry 17* (1969). *Yellow rice contaminated by Penicillium islandicum, pp. 433, 444.*

Battelle Memorial Institute, Dartmouth Medical School. Data cited by Staff of *Chemical & Engineering News.* "Trace Metals: Unknown, Unseen Pollution Threat." *Chemical & Engineering News 49* (1971): 29–33. Reprinted in *Our Chemical Environment,* edited by J. Calvin Giddings, Manus B. Monroe. San Francisco: Canfield, 1972. *Carcinogenic metals: arsenic, beryllium, nickel, selenium, yttrium, Table, p. 132.*

Beauford, W.; Barber, J.; Barringer, A. R. "Heavy Metal Release from Plants into the Atmosphere." *Nature 256* (1975). *Zinc released from pea and broad bean plants and pine-tree seedlings, pp. 35–36.*

———. "Release of Particles Containing Metals from Vegetation into the Atmosphere." *Science 195* (1977). *Lead, zinc released from pea plants and pine-tree seedlings, pp. 571–573.*

Beninson, D. J.; Bouville, A.; O'Brien, B. J.; Snihs, J. O., "Dosimetric Implications of the Exposure to the Natural Sources of Irradiation." In *International Symposium on Areas of High Natural Radioactivity,* edited by Academia Brasilera de Ciências. Rio de Janeiro: R. J., 1977. *External and internal irradiation of man, p. 103; high-altitude exposure to radioactivity, p. 78; potassium-40 required for survival, p. 91; radioactive air, pp. 81, 82, 83, 84, 86, 87, 89; radioactive soil, p. 81; quotation: everything is radioactive, pp. 75, 79; quotation: natural radiation major source of exposure, p. 75.*

Berenblum, Isaac. *Carcinogenesis as a Biological Problem.* North-Holland Research Monographs, *Frontiers of Biology,* edited by A. Neuberger, E. L. Tatum. Vol. 34. New York: Elsevier, 1974. *Natural amines in food, p. 179.*

Bharucha, K. R.; Cross, C. K.; Rubin, L. J. "Mechanism of N-Nitrosopyrrolidine Formation in Bacon." *J Agric Food Chem* 27(1): 63–69; 1979. Cited in *Carcinogenesis Abstracts 17* (1979), Abstract 79-1387. *Carcinogens absent from raw bacon, formed in cooking.*

Bjeldanes, L. F., Chang, G. W. "Mutagenic Activity of Quercetin and Related Compounds." *Science 197* (1977). *Quercetin in fruits and vegetables, p. 577; quercetin mutagenic, pp. 577, 578.*

Blumer, M. "Benzpyrenes in Soil." *Science 134* (1961).

———. "Polycyclic Aromatic Compounds in Nature." *Scientific American 234* (1976). *Quotation, p. 45.*

Blumer, M.; Dorsey, T.; Sass, J. "Azaarenes in Recent Marine Sediments." *Science 195* (1977). *Quotation, p. 284.*

Boyd, Michael R. "Role of Metabolic Activation in Extrahepatic Target Organ Alkylation and Cytotoxicity by 4-Ipomeanol, a Furan Derivative from Moldy Sweet Potatoes; Possible Implications for Carcinogenesis." In *Naturally Occurring Carcinogens—Mutagens and Modulators of Carcinogenesis,* Ninth International Symposium of the Princess Takamatsu Cancer Research Fund, January 23–25, 1979. Tokyo, Japan. *Abstract, p. 15.*

Branda, Richard F., Eaton, John W. "Skin Color and Nutrient Photolysis: An Evolutionary Hypothesis." *Science 201* (1978), *pp. 625–626.*

Brubaker, Paul E.; Moran, John P.; Bridbord, Kenneth; Hueter, F. Gordon. "Noble Metals: A Toxicological Appraisal of Potential New Environmental Contaminants." *Environmental Health Perspectives 10* (1975). *Sulfur dioxide a carcinogen promoter, p. 50.*

Bruce, W. R.; Varghese, A. J.; Furrer, R.; Land, P. C. "A Mutagen in the Feces of Normal Humans." In *Origins of Human Cancer*, edited by H. H. Hiatt, J. D. Watson, J. A. Winsten. Book C, *Human Risk Assessment*. New York: Cold Spring Harbor Laboratory, 1977. *N-nitroso compound discovered in feces, pp. 1641, 1643, 1645–1646.*

Burchfield, H. P., Storrs, Eleanor E. "Organohalogen Carcinogens." In *Advances in Modern Toxicology*, edited by Myron A. Mehlman. Vol. 3, *Environmental Cancer*, edited by H. F. Kraybill, Myron A. Mehlman. Washington, D.C.: Hemisphere, 1977. *Burning trees and wood, cycads, p. 319; quotation: dinosaur cancer, p. 319.*

Busch, F. W.; Seid, D. A.; Wei, E. T. "Mutagenic Activity of Marihuana Smoke Condensates." *Cancer Lett* 6(6): 319–324; 1979. Cited in *Carcinogenesis Abstracts 17* (1980), Abstract 79-5014.

Buys, Donna. "Chinese Scientist Shows Fungus Active in Pharyngeal Carcinoma." *Oncology Times*, May 1980. *Fungi linked to esophageal cancer, pp. 1, 9.*

Campbell, A. D. "Food Mycotoxins Survey and Monitoring Programs." *Pure and Applied Chemistry 49* (1977). *Aflatoxin-contaminated edible nuts, p. 1704.*

Campbell, W. J.; Blake, R. L.; Brown, L. L.; Cather, E. E.; Sjoberg, J. J. *Selected Silicate Minerals and Their Asbestiform Varieties*. Bureau of Mines Information Circular 8751. Washington, D.C.: U.S. Department of the Interior, 1977. *Almost half the crust of U.S. earth asbestiform minerals, p. 2.*

Cannon, Helen L., Anderson, Barbara M. "The Geochemist's Involvement with the Pollution Problem." In *Environmental Geochemistry in Health and Disease*, edited by Helen L. Cannon, Howard C. Hopps. Boulder, Colo: Geological Society of America, Inc., 1971. *Carcinogenic metals in U.S. rivers, p. 171.*

Carcinogenesis Abstracts: A Monthly Publication Sponsored by the National Cancer Institute. Edited by G. P. Studzinski, J. J. Saukkonen. NCI staff consultants, E. Weisburger, J. W. Chase. Philadelphia: Franklin Research Center.

Carter, Luther. "Uncontrolled SO₂ Emissions Bring Acid Rain." *Science 204* (1979). *Burning fossil fuels produces SO_2, p. 1179.*

Chameides, W. L.; Stedman, D. H.; Dickerson, R. R.; Rusch, D. W.; Cicerone, R. J. "NO_x Production in Lightning." *Journal of the Atmospheric Sciences 34* (1977). *Lightning a source of NO_x, pp. 143–149; NO_x, megatons per year, p. 143.*

Cleaver, James. "Mechanisms of DNA Damage and DNA Repair Systems." *Cancer Symposium: An Academic Review of the Environmental Determinants of Cancer Relevant to Prevention*, February 28–March 2, 1979, New York City. In cooperation with the American Cancer Society, Inc. *Manuscript. My copy unpaginated; quotation opens lecture.*

Clement Associates, Inc., Washington, D.C. *Clement's Lists of Carcinogenic Chemicals Found in American Workplaces*. Prepared for Occupational Safety and Health Administration. Washington, D.C.: U.S. Department of Commerce, July 10, 1978. PB-295 978. *Natural sex hormones carcinogenic: estradiol, p. I-6; estrone, p. I-7; progesterone, p. I-11; testosterone, p. I-12.*

Coleman, M. H. "A Model System for the Formation of N-Nitrosopyrrolidine in Grilled or Fried Bacon." *J Food Technol* 13(1): 55–69; 1978. Cited in *Carcinogenesis Abstracts 16* (1979), Abstract 78-2118. *Carcinogens absent from raw bacon, formed in cooking.*

Comar, C. L., Rust, J. H. "Natural Radioactivity in the Biosphere and Foodstuffs." In *Toxicants Occurring Naturally in Foods*, 2nd ed. Washington, D.C.: National Academy of Sciences, 1973. *Radium-226, radon-222, uranium-238 in natural water, pp. 94–95.*

Commoner, Barry; Vithayathil, Antony J.; Dolara, Piero; Nair, Subhadra; Madyastha, Prema; Cuca, Gregory C. "Formation of Mutagens in Beef and Beef Extract During Cooking." *Science 201* (1978), *pp. 913–916.*

Corbett, Thomas H., M.D. *Cancer and Chemicals*. Chicago: Nelson-Hall, 1977. *Garden plants contain co-carcinogens, p. 105.*

Cranmer, Morris F. *Final Report on Saccharin.* Presented to Commissioner, Food and Drug Administration, June 7, 1978. *Sucrose poses carcinogenic risk, p. 0-9.*

Cruse, J. P.; Lewin, M. R.; Ferulano, G. P.; Clark, C. G. "Co-carcinogenic Effects of Dietary Cholesterol in Experimental Colon Cancer." *Nature 276* (1978).

Cruse, Peter; Clark, Charles G.; Lewin, Michael. "Dietary Cholesterol Is Co-carcinogenic for Human Colon Cancer." *Lancet,* April 7, 1979.

Cummings, J. H. "Dietary Factors in the Aetiology of Gastrointestinal Cancer." *J Hum Nutr* 32(16): 455–465; 1978. Cited in *Carcinogenesis Abstracts 17* (1979), Abstract 79-1294. *High-protein diet linked to cancer.*

Debrunner, Peter G. "Oxygen Biochemistry." *Science 208* (1980). *Necessary, yet life-threatening aspects of oxygen, pp. 590-591.*

Deinzer, M. L.; Thomson, P. A.; Burgett, D. M.; Isaacson, D. L. "Pyrrolizidine Alkaloids: Their Occurrence in Honey from Tansy Ragwort (*Senecio jacobaea L.*)." *Science 195* (1977). *Carcinogenic, mutagenic, teratogenic, p. 497.*

Der Marderosian, Ara. "Medicinal Teas—Boon or Bane?" *Drug Therapy,* February 1977. *Phenols, tannin in teas linked to cancer, p. 178.*

DiPaolo, Joseph A., Kotin, Paul. "Teratogenesis—Oncogenesis: A Study of Possible Relationships." *Arch Path 81* (1966). *Oxygen carcinogenic, p. 3.*

Dolara, P.; Commoner, B.; Vithayathil, A.; Cuca, G.; Tuley, E.; Madyastha, P.; Nair, S.; Kriebel, D. "The Effect of Temperature on the Formation of Mutagens in Heated Beef Stock and Cooked Ground Beef." *Mutat Res* 60(3): 231–237; 1979. Cited in *Carcinogenesis Abstracts 17* (1980), Abstract 79-4506. *Higher temperature, greater mutagenicity.*

Dorange, J. L.; Delaforge, M.; Janiaud, P.; Padieu, P. "Mutagenicity of the Epoxide-Diol Metabolites of Safrole and Their Analogs in *Salmonella typhimurium.*" *C R Soc Biol* (Paris) 171(5): 1041–1048; 1977. Cited in *Carcinogenesis Abstracts 16* (1979), Abstract 78-1945.

Dutra, Frank R., Largent, Edward J. "Osteosarcoma Induced by Beryllium Oxide." *American Journal of Pathology 26* (1950). *Footnote, p. 197: discovery in 1940s.*

Ehrenberg, L. "Higher Plants." In *Chemical Mutagens, Principles and Methods for Their Detection,* edited by Alexander Hollaender. Vol. 2. New York: Plenum, 1971. *Auto-oxidizable vegetable oils mutagenic, p. 375.*

Ehrlich, Paul R.; Ehrlich, Anne H.; Holdren, John P. *Ecoscience: Population, Resources, Environment.* San Francisco: Freeman, 1977. *Carbon tetrachloride natural component of atmosphere, p. 675; chemicals required for life, p. 68; radioactive polonium on tobacco, p. 588.*

Eisenbud, Merril. *Environment, Technology, and Health: Human Ecology in Historical Perspective.* New York: New York University Press, 1978. *Exposure to radioactivity varies with terrain, p. 318; most chemical elements in all soils, p. 174; quotation, pp. 314-315.*

———. *Environmental Radioactivity,* 2nd ed. New York: Academic Press, 1973. *Radioactivity: drinking water, p. 173; foods, p. 174; natural, pp. 159-196; radon spas, p. 198; soil, p. 19; quotation: everything is radioactive, p. 159; quotation: exposure to solar flare, p. 193.*

———. Personal communication, 1979, *quotation.*

Eklund, G., Malec, E. "Sunlight and the Incidence of Cutaneous Malignant Melanoma. Effect of Latitude and Domicile in Sweden." *Scand J. Plast Reconstr Surg* 12(3): 231–241; 1978. Cited in *Carcinogenesis Abstracts 17* (1979), Abstract 79-1498.

El-Zawahri, M.; Moubasher, A.; Morad, M.; El-Kady, I. "Mutagenic Effect of Aflatoxin B_1." *Ann Nutr Aliment* 31(4/5/6): 859–866; 1977. Cited in *Carcinogenesis Abstracts 16* (1979), Abstract 78-3680.

Endo, H.; Ishizawa, M.; Endo, T.; Takahashi, K.; Utsunomiya, T.; Kinoshita, N.; Hidaka, K.; Baba, T. "A Possible Process of Conversion of Food Components to Gastric Carcinogens." In *Origins of Human Cancer,* edited by H. H. Hiatt, J. D.

Watson, J. A. Winsten. Book C, *Human Risk Assessment.* New York: Cold Spring Harbor Laboratory, 1977. *Simultaneous ingestion of nitrite and amines produces N-nitroso compounds: carcinogenic, pp. 1591, 1592; mutagenic, pp. 1592, 1602–1604.*

Engel, Ronald E. "Nitrites, Nitrosamines, and Meat." *Journal of the American Veterinary Medical Association 171* (1977). *Carcinogens absent from raw bacon, formed in cooking, p. 1158.*

(EPA) Environmental Protection Agency. *Criteria for Lead.* Summary from "Air Quality Criteria for Lead" published by the Environmental Protection Agency in December 1977. Washington, D.C.: Bureau of National Affairs, 1978. *Forest fires, radon decay, sea salt, volcanic dusts, wind and rain erosion "pollute" air with lead, p. 9.*

————. Office of Water Planning and Standards. *National Water Quality Inventory: 1976 Report to Congress.* Washington, D.C., 1976. *High arsenic content from rocks in Yellowstone River; soil erosion most common natural cause of excess metals in water, p. 10.*

————. *Potential Industrial Carcinogens and Mutagens.* Prepared for the Office of Toxic Substances by Lawrence Fishbein. EPA 560/5-77-005. Washington, D.C., May 1977. *Methyl chloride, p. 163; 2-naphthylamine, pp. 251–252; 2-nitropropane, p. 311; acetaldehyde, p. 114.*

Evans, I. A. "The Bracken Carcinogen." In *Chemical Carcinogens,* edited by Charles E. Searle. Washington, D.C.: American Chemical Society, 1976, *pp. 693–694.*

Falk, Hans L., Jurgelski, William, Jr. *Health Effects of Coal Mining and Combustion.* No. 7, *Carcinogens and Cofactors.* Research Triangle Park, North Carolina: National Institute of Environmental Health Sciences, April 27, 1979. *Manuscript. Carcinogenic compounds in coal, see Table 3, Table 4.*

Ferrando, R.; Guilleux, M. M.; Guerrillot-Vinet, A. "Oestrogen Content of Plants as a Function of Conditions in Culture." *Nature 192* (1961). *Estrogens in carrots comparable to estrogens in diethylstilbestrol, p. 1205.*

Fine, D. H.; Rounbehler, D. P.; Fan, T.; Ross, R. "Human Exposure to N-nitroso Compounds in the Environment." In *Origins of Human Cancer,* edited by H. H. Hiatt, J. D. Watson, J. A. Winsten. Book A, *Incidence of Cancer in Humans.* New York: Cold Spring Harbor Laboratory, 1977. *Nitrosamines: in human blood after eating conventional foods, p. 300; in tobacco smoke, p. 294.*

Fishbein, Lawrence. "Atmospheric Mutagens." In *Chemical Mutagens, Principles and Methods for Their Detection,* edited by Alexander Hollaender. Vol. 4. New York: Plenum, 1976. *Polycyclic aromatic hydrocarbons carcinogens and mutagens, pp. 231–238; quotation: NO_x, p. 227.*

————. "Environmental Sources of Chemical Mutagens. I. Naturally Occurring Mutagens." In *Advances in Modern Toxicology,* edited by Myron A. Mehlman. Vol. 5, *Mutagenesis,* edited by W. Gary Flamm and Myron A. Mehlman. Washington, D.C.: Hemisphere, 1978. *Aflatoxin, p. 180; cycasin, p. 193; NO_2, pp. 219, 224; nitrite in plants, p. 204; ozone, p. 229; SO_2, pp. 218–220.*

Ford, R. E.; Jacobsen, B. J.; White, D. G. "Mycotoxins—Environmental Contaminants in Nature." *Illinois Research,* Winter 1978. *Aflatoxins B_{2a}, G_{2a}, M_1, M_2 carcinogenic, p. 11.*

Freese, Ernst. "Molecular Mechanisms of Mutations." In *Chemical Mutagens, Principles and Methods for Their Detection,* edited by Alexander Hollaender. Vol. 1. New York: Plenum, 1971. *Cycasin activated by intestinal bacteria, p. 38; N-nitroso compounds mutagenic, p. 36; Streptomyces produce carcinogenic and mutagenic N-nitroso compounds, p. 38.*

Friberg, Lars, Cederlöf, Rune. "Late Effects on Air Pollution with Special Reference to Lung Cancer." *Environmental Health Perspectives 22* (1978). *Table, p. 49.*

Friberg, Tom. *Naturally Occurring Volatile Hydrocarbons in the Atmosphere.* Department of Civil Engineering, University of Washington, May 23, 1972. *Manuscript. Quotation, see section "Foliage Emissions."*

Fritz, W. "Contribution of Heat to the Formation of Carcinogenic Hydrocarbons in Food. Part 7. Investigations of Contamination During Smoking." *Arch Geschwulstforsch* 47(8): 685–693; 1977. Cited in *Carcinogenesis Abstracts 16* (1979), Abstract 78-0734. *Benzo(a)pyrene content higher in smoked fish than in meats and sausages.*

Fukuoka, M.; Kuroyanagi, M.; Yoshihira, K.; Natori, S.; Nagao, M.; Takahashi, Y.; Sugimura, T. "Chemical and Toxicological Studies in Bracken Fern, *Pteridum aquilinum Var. Latiusculum.* IV. Surveys on Bracken Constituents by Mutagen Test." *J Pharmacobio Dyn* 1(5): 324–331; 1978. Cited in *Carcinogenesis Abstracts 17* (1980), Abstract 79-4439. *Constituents of bracken mutagenic.*

Furst, Arthur. "Inorganic Agents as Carcinogens." In *Advances in Modern Toxicology*, edited by Myron A. Mehlman. Vol. 3, *Environmental Cancer*, edited by H. F. Kraybill, Myron A. Mehlman. Washington, D.C.: Hemisphere, 1977. *Metal carcinogens: aluminum, mercury, silver, pp. 211, 221.*

——. "An Overview of Metal Carcinogenesis." In *Inorganic and Nutritional Aspects of Cancer*, edited by G. N. Schrauzer. New York: Plenum, 1978. *Metal carcinogens: cadmium, cobalt, nickel, p. 3.*

——. "Trace Elements Related to Specific Chronic Diseases: Cancer." In *Environmental Geochemistry in Health and Disease*, edited by Helen L. Cannon. Howard C. Hopps. Boulder, Colo: Geological Society of America, 1971. *Essential chemicals: copper, iron, magnesium, manganese, molybdenum, zinc, p. 109.*

Fushimi, K; Kato, K.; Kato, T.; Matsubara, N. "Carcinogenicity of Flower Stalks of *Petasites japonicus* Maxim in Mice and Syrian Golden Hamsters." *Toxicol Lett* 1(5/6): 291–294; 1978. Cited in *Carcinogenesis Abstracts 16* (1979), Abstract 78-3077.

Galvan Aguilera, A. S. "Skin Cancer." *Patol Quir Citol Esfoliativa* 4(4): 145–153; 1978. Cited in *Carcinogenesis Abstracts 17* (1979), Abstract 79-0617. *Skin cancer related to skin color and geographical location.*

Gesell, Thomas F., Cook, Lewis M. "Environmental Radioactivity in the South Texas, USA, Uranium District." In *International Symposium on Areas of High Natural Radioactivity*, edited by Academia Brasileira de Ciências. Rio de Janeiro: R. J., 1977. *High radon exposure from South Texas water, p. 184.*

Gibel, W., and others. "Experimental Investigations of the Carcinogenic Effect of Higher Alcohols on the Example of 3-methyl-1-butanol (isoamyl alcohol), *1*-propanol (propyl alcohol) and 2-methyl-*1*-propanol (isobutyl alcohol)." Translation #TT 76-214. *Z. Exper. Chirurg* 7 (1974). *Alcoholic beverages contain carcinogenic and mutagenic oils, p. 5.*

Golberg, Leon. "The Amelioration of Foods: The Milroy Lectures." *Journal of the Royal College of Physicians of London 1* (1967). *Aflatoxins in milk (Nabney, 1967 and Mickelsen, 1964, cited by Golberg), p. 398; coumarin in fruits, p. 400.*

Goldberg, E. D.; Broecker, W. S.; Gross, M. G.; Turekian, K. K. "Marine Chemistry." In *Radioactivity in the Marine Environment*. National Research Council. Washington, D.C.: National Academy of Sciences, 1971. *Ocean contains all elements, pp. 139–140.*

Grasso, P., O'Hare, C. "Carcinogens in Food." In *Chemical Carcinogens*, edited by Charles E. Searle. Washington, D.C.: American Chemical Society, 1976. *Nitrosation by intestinal bacteria, p. 713; polycyclic aromatic hydrocarbons, including benzo(a)pyrene, produced by plants, quotation, p. 707.*

Greden, John F. "Coffee, Tea and You." *Sciences 19* (1979). *Caffeine in cocoa trees, coffee beans, kola nuts, tea leaves, p. 6.*

Green, M., Mackey, J. K. "Are Oncogenic Human Adenoviruses Associated with

Human Cancer? Analysis of Human Tumors for Adenovirus Transforming Gene Sequences." In *Origins of Human Cancer*, edited by H. H. Hiatt, J. D. Watson, J. A. Winsten. Book B, *Mechanisms of Carcinogenesis*. New York: Cold Spring Harbor Laboratory, 1977. *Human adenoviruses carcinogenic in hamsters, p. 1027.*

Grigg, G. W. "Genetic Effects of Coumarins." *Mutat Res* 47(3/4): 161–181; 1978. Cited in *Carcinogenesis Abstracts 16* (1979), Abstract 78-5433. *Coumarin mutagenic.*

Grimmer, Von G., Hildebrandt, A. "Der Gehalt polycyclischer Kohlenwasserstoffe in Kaffee und Tee, Kohlenwasserstoffe in der Umgebung des Menschen, 4. Mitteilung." *Deutsche Lebensmittel-Rundschau*, Heft 1 (1966). *Benzo(a)pyrene emerges from coffee beans and tea leaves at high temperatures, pp. 19–21.*

Griner, L. A. "Neoplasms in Tasmanian Devils (Sarcophilus harrisii)." *J Natl Cancer Inst* 62(3): 589–595; 1979. Cited in *Carcinogenesis Abstracts 17* (1979), Abstract 79-1155.

Gruener, N. "Mutagenicity of Ozonated, Recycled Water." *Bull Environ Contam Toxicol* 20 (4): 522–526; 1978. Cited in *Carcinogenesis Abstracts 16* (1979), Abstract 78-6105.

Hammond, E. Cuyler. *Testimony. Hearings Before the Subcommittee on Labor of the Committee on Human Resources.* United States Senate, Ninety-fifth Congress, First Session. On Examination of the Scope of the Industrial Disease Problem which Confronts Our Society. June 28, 29, 30, 1977. Printed for the use of the Committee on Human Resources. Washington, D.C.: U.S. Government Printing Office, 1978. *Quotation, p. 19.*

Hancock, R. L., Dickie, M. M. "Biochemical, Pathological, and Genetic Aspects of a Spontaneous Mouse Hepatoma." *Journal of the National Cancer Institute 43* (1969). *High-fat diet enhances liver cancer, pp. 407–408.*

Handler, Philip. "Dedication Address." *Northwestern University Cancer Center.* May 18, 1979. *Manuscript. Oxygen mutagenic, p. 15; quotation, p. 15.*

Hardigree, A. A., Epler, J. L. "Mutagenicity of Plant Flavonols in Microbial Systems." *Mutation Research 53* (1978). *Abstract 41. Flavonoid, quercetin mutagenic, p. 89.*

Harley, N. H.; Cohen, B. S.; Pasternack, B.S.; Fisenne, I. M.; Rohl, A. N. "Radioactivity in Asbestos." *Environ Int* 1(4): 161–165; 1978. Cited in *Carcinogenesis Abstracts 17* (1979), Abstract 79-1511, *p. 534.*

Harvey, George R.; Requejo, Adolfo G.; McGillivary, Philip A.; John M. "Observation of a Subsurface Oil-Rich Layer in the Open Ocean." *Science 205* (1979), *pp. 999–1000; quotation, p. 1000.*

(HEW) Department of Health, Education, and Welfare. *Summary of Work Group Reports of the Interagency Task Force on Ionizing Radiation.* Washington, D.C.: Department of Health, Education, and Welfare, February 27, 1979. *Natural radiation, population dose estimates, p. 20.*

Heath, J. C.; Daniel, M. R.; Dingle, J. T.; Webb, M. "Cadmium as a Carcinogen." *Nature 193* (1962). *Cobalt carcinogenic, p. 592.*

Hecht, S. S.; Chen, C. B.; Hirota, N.; Ornaf, R. M.; Tso, T. C.; Hoffmann, D. "Tobacco-Specific Nitrosamines: Formation from Nicotine In Vitro and During Tobacco Curing and Carcinogenicity in Strain A Mice." *J Natl Cancer Inst* 60(4): 819–824; 1978. Cited in *Carcinogenesis Abstracts 16* (1979), Abstract 78-2694.

Hecker, E. "Cocarcinogenic or Conditional Cancer-promoting Factors: New Aspects of the Etiology of Human Tumors and Molecular Mechanisms of Tumor Development." *Naturwissenschaften* 65(12): 640–648; 1978. Cited in *Carcinogenesis Abstracts 17* (1979), Abstract 79-1214. *Teas brewed from plants containing cocarcinogenic diterpene esters.*

———. "Co-carcinogens of the Diterpene Ester Type—Actual New Findings Concerning the Etiology of Human Tumors and the Molecular Mechanism of Carcinogenesis." In *Naturally Occurring Carcinogens—Mutagens and Modulators of*

Carcinogenesis, Ninth International Symposium of the Princess Takamatsu Cancer Research Fund, January 23–25, 1979. Tokyo, Japan. Abstract. *Cocarcinogenic diterpene esters in garden plants, p. 50.*

Henderson, James Stuart, Jenks, Irving Harris. "Guest Editorial: Sun, Light and Human Health." *Photochemistry and Photobiology 29* (1979). *Oxygen a poison, pp. 1–3; ozone mutagenic, p. 3; solar radiation and ozone, p. 3.*

Hendricks, J. D.; Sinnhuber, R. O.; Loveland, P. M.; Pawlowski, N. E.; Nixon, J. E. "Hepatocarcinogenicity of Glandless Cottonseeds and Cottonseed Oil to Rainbow Trout *(Salmo gairdnerii).*" *Science 208* (1980).

Henry, Paul S. "A Simple Description of the 3K Cosmic Microwave Background." *Science 207* (1980). *Big bang creation theory, p. 939.*

Hernberg, S. "Incidence of Cancer in Population with Exceptional Exposure to Metals." In *Origins of Human Cancer,* edited by H. H. Hiatt, J. D. Watson, J. A. Winsten. Book A, *Incidence of Cancer in Humans.* New York: Cold Spring Harbor Laboratory, 1977. *Arsenic, p. 147; beryllium, p. 148; cadmium, p. 149; chromium, p. 150; iron, nickel, p. 151.*

Herriott, Roger M. "Effects on DNA: Transforming Principle." In *Chemical Mutagens, Principles and Methods for Their Detection,* edited by Alexander Hollaender. Vol. 1. New York: Plenum, 1971. *Ultraviolet radiation mutagenic, p. 188.*

Herrmann, W. P. "Melanoma and Solar Radiation." *Dtsch Med Wochenschr* 103(29): 1155–1156; 1978. Cited in *Carcinogenesis Abstracts 16* (1979), Abstract 78-4876. *Ultraviolet radiation possible co-factor in malignant melanoma.*

Hewer, T.; Rose, E.; Ghadirian, P.; Castegnaro, M.; Bartsch, H.; Malaveille, C.; Day, N. "Ingested Mutagens from Opium and Tobacco Pyrolysis Products and Cancer of the Oesophagus." *Lancet* 2(8088): 494–496; 1978. Cited in *Carcinogenesis Abstracts 16* (1979), Abstract 78-5049.

Higginson, John. "Chronic Toxicology—An Epidemiologist's Approach to the Problem of Carcinogenesis." In *Essays in Toxicology.* Vol. 7. Edited by Wayland J. Hayes, Jr. New York: Academic, 1976. *Carcinogenic fossils: anthracene, lignite, petroleum oils, p. 61.*

Hirono, Iwao; Mori, Hideki; Haga, Masanobu; Yamada, Kiyoyuki; Hirata, Yoshimasa. "Edible Plants Containing Carcinogenic Pyrrolizidine Alkaloids in Japan." In *Naturally Occurring Carcinogens—Mutagens and Modulators of Carcinogenesis,* Ninth International Symposium of the Princess Takamatsu Cancer Research Fund, January 23–25, 1979. Tokyo, Japan. Abstract. *Pyrrolizidine alkaloids in food plants: carcinogenic, p. 20; mutagenic, p. 21.*

Ho, J. H. C.; Huang, D. P.; Fong, Y. Y. "Salted Fish and Nasopharyngeal Carcinoma in Southern Chinese." *Lancet,* September 16, 1978. *Salted fish carcinogenic, mutagenic, may be related to cancer, p. 626.*

Hoffmann, D.; Adams, J. D.; Brunnemann, K. D.; Hecht, S. S. "Assessment of Tobacco-specific N-Nitrosamines in Tobacco Products." *Cancer Res* 39(7, part 1): 2505–2509; 1979. Cited in *Carcinogenesis Abstracts 17* (1980), Abstract 79-4409.

Holden, Constance. "Big Future for Synthetics." *Science 208* (1980). *Quotation, p. 576.*

Homburger, F., Boger, Eliahu. "The Carcinogenicity of Essential Oils, Flavors, and Spices: A Review." *Cancer Research 28* (1968). *Oils of grapefruit, lemons, limes, oranges, p. 2372.*

Hopps, Howard C. "Cancer: The Geochemical Environment and Cancer." In *Geochemistry and the Environment.* Vol. III. Washington, D.C.: National Academy of Sciences, 1978. *Carcinogenic metals: arsenic, beryllium, cadmium, chromium, cobalt, copper, iron, lead, mercury, nickel, selenium, silver, titanium, zinc, p. 82; soil particles in air ingested by man, p. 84.*

Howard, John W., Fazio, Thomas. "A Review of Polycyclic Aromatic Hydrocarbons in Foods." *Journal of Agricultural and Food Chemistry 17* (1969). *Benzo(a)pyrene pro-*

duced in heated: amino acids, carbohydrates, fatty acids, starch, p. 530; charred biscuits (Kuratsune, 1956), p. 530; smoking foods, pp. 528–529.

Hueper, Wilhelm C. "Some Comments on the History and the Experimental Exploration of Metal Carcinogens and Cancers." *Journal of the National Cancer Institute* 62 (1979). *Carcinogenic metals: beryllium, cadmium, cobalt, gold, lead, mercury, nickel, selenium, zinc; chromate, first discovery of metal carcinogen, p. 723; quotation, p. 723.*

Il'nitskii, A. P.; Vinogradov, V. N.; Riabchun, V. K.; Mishchenko, V. S.; Gvil'dis, V. Iu.; Chernen'kii, B. I.; Belitskii, G. A.; Shabad, L. M. "Analysis of Prehistoric Levels of Benzo(a)pyrene in Permafrost Soil." *Dokl Akad Nauk SSSR* 245(1): 254–257; 1979. Cited in *Carcinogenesis Abstracts 17* (1979), Abstract 79-2529.

Ilnitsky, A. P.; Belitsky, G. A.; Shabad, L. M. "On the Carcinogenic Polycyclic Aromatic Hydrocarbon Benzo(a)pyrene in Volcano Exhausts." *Cancer Letters 1* (1976).

Ilnitsky, A. P.; Mischenko, V. S.; Shabad, L. M. "New Data on Volcanoes as Natural Sources of Carcinogenic Substances." *Cancer Letters 3* (1977). *Volcanoes "pollute" biosphere with benzo*(a)*pyrene, p. 227.*

Interagency Task Force on Ionizing Radiation, Work Group on Radiation Exposure Reduction. *Draft Report.* Atlanta, Georgia: Center for Disease Control, February 20, 1979. *Radioactive polonium in tobacco plants, pp. 142–143.*

(IARC) International Agency for Research on Cancer. *IARC Monographs on the Evaluation of the Carcinogenic Risk of Chemicals to Man.* Lyon: IARC:

  Vol. 6. *Sex Hormones.* 1974. *Carcinogenic hormones: estradiol, p. 111; estrone, pp. 129–130; progesterone, p. 143; testosterone, p. 245. Metabolism of synthetic and natural hormones same, p. 39. Natural estrogens: estradiol, p. 111; estrone, pp. 129–130; natural hormones, p. 19. Synthetic estrogens: diethylstilbestrol, pp. 69–70; ethinyl estradiol, pp. 83–84.*

  Vol. 7. *Some Anti-thyroid and Related Substances, Nitrofurans and Industrial Chemicals.* 1974. *Acetamide: carcinogenic, p. 201; in overoxidized wine, p. 199. Thiourea: carcinogenic, p. 104; found in laburnum shrubs, p. 99.*

  Vol. 10. *Some Naturally Occurring Substances.* 1976.

  Reported carcinogens emerging from bacteria and fungi: actinomycin D, pp. 31, 37; aflatoxins, pp. 53–54, 63, 64, quotation, pp. 53–54; azaserine, pp. 74, 76; chloramphenicol, pp. 89, 92–93; daunomycin, pp. 147, 150; griseofulvin, pp. 155, 158; mitomycin C, pp. 173–176; patulin, pp. 206, 208; penicillic acid, pp. 212, 214; sterigmatocystin, pp. 246, 249.

  Reported carcinogens emerging from vegetation and trees: carageenan, pp. 181, 187; coumarin, pp. 115, 117; cycasin, p. 129; pyrrolizidine alkaloids, p. 339; tannin, pp. 256, 259.

  Reported carcinogens found in all tissues of higher animals, and in animal fats and oils: cholesterol, p. 101; cholesterol a promoter, p. 103; cholesterol a cocarcinogen, p. 104.

  Vol. 11. *Cadmium, Nickel, Some Epoxides, Miscellaneous Industrial Chemicals and General Considerations on Volatile Anaesthetics.* 1976. *Cadmium in tobacco plant and smoke, p. 48; nickel in tobacco smoke, p. 85; sunflower oil, pp. 176, 179.*

  Vol. 14. *Asbestos.* 1977. *Earth's crust, p. 28; fibrous silicates, p. 11; mineral contaminant, p. 80; talc contaminant, p. 32.*

  Vol. 17. *IARC Monograph on the Evaluation of the Carcinogenic Risk of Chemicals to Humans. Some N-Nitroso Compounds.* 1978. *Streptomyces, a soil microorganism, produces streptozotocin, structurally related to an N-nitroso compound, pp. 35, 339; carcinogenic, p. 344; mutagenic, p. 343; ubiquity of nitrosatable substances in nature, p. 37.*

Ivankovic, S. "Experimental Prenatal Carcinogenesis." In *Transplacental Carcinogen-*

esis, edited by L. Tomatis, U. Mohr. IARC Scientific Publications No. 4. Lyon: IARC, 1973. *Some N-nitroso compounds transplacental carcinogens, pp. 97-98.*

――――. "Gastric Cancer in Rats after Chronic Intraperitoneal Application of Sap of Green Parts of Potatoes (*Solanum tuberosum L.*)." *Experientia* 34(5): 645; 1978. Cited in *Carcinogenesis Abstracts 16* (1979), Abstract 78-6210.

Jones, C. Allan, Rasmussen, Reinhold A. "Production of Isoprene by Leaf Tissue." *Plant Physiology 55* (1975), *p. 982.*

Joseph, A. B.; Gustafson, P. F.; Russell, I. R.; Schuert, E. A.; Volchok, H. L.; Tamplin, A. "Sources of Radioactivity and Their Characteristics." In *Radioactivity in the Marine Environment.* Washington, D.C.: National Academy of Sciences, 1971. *Ocean contains all cosmic and terrestrial radioactive nuclides, pp. 7-9.*

Jukes, T. H. "Des in Beef Production: Science, Politics, and Emotion." In *Origins of Human Cancer*, edited by H. H. Hiatt, J. D. Watson, J. A. Winsten. Book C, *Human Risk Assessment.* New York: Cold Spring Harbor Laboratory, 1977. *Animal, plant, vegetable estrogens are comparable to diethylstilbestrol, pp. 1657-1658.*

Kahn, H. "Toxicity of Oil Shale Chemical Products. A Review." *Scand J Work Environ Health* 5(1): 1-9; 1979. Cited in *Carcinogenesis Abstracts 17* (1980), Abstract 79-4246. *Shale oil carcinogenic.*

Kakvan, M., Greenberg, S. D. "Cigarette Smoking and Cancer of the Lung: A Review." *RI Med J* 60(12): 588-591, 606; 1977. Cited in *Carcinogenesis Abstracts 16* (1979), Abstract 78-0610. *Hydrocarbons in cigarette smoke tar carcinogenic.*

Kapadia, Govind J.; Chung, E. B.; Ghosh, B.; Shukla, Y. N.; Basak, S. P.; Morton, J. F.; Pradhan, S. N. "Carcinogenicity of Some Folk Medicinal Herbs in Rats." *Journal of the National Cancer Institute 60* (1978). *Extracts of plants carcinogenic, p. 684.*

Karler, Ralph. "Toxicological and Pharmacological Effects." In *Marijuana Research Findings: 1976*, edited by Robert C. Petersen. Rockville, Md.: U.S. Department of Health, Education, and Welfare; National Institute on Drug Abuse, July 1977. *Marijuana smoke has greater carcinogenic hydrocarbon content than tobacco smoke, p. 67.*

Keller, Edward A. *Environmental Geology.* Columbus, Ohio: Charles E. Merrill, 1976. *Volcanoes eject selenium, p. 283; volcanoes, locations, products, pp. 151-152.*

Kessler, I. I. *Journal of the National Cancer Institute 44* (1970). Cited in H. F. Kraybill, "The Question of Benefits and Risks." In *Sweeteners, Issues and Uncertainties.* Washington, D.C.: National Academy of Sciences, 1975. *Diabetics susceptible to pancreatic cancer, Table, p. 72.*

Kihlman, B. A. "Root Tips for Studying the Effects of Chemicals on Chromosomes." In *Chemical Mutagens, Principles and Methods for Their Detection*, edited by Alexander Hollaender. Vol. 2. New York: Plenum, 1971. *Caffeine mutagenic, p. 507.*

Kimura, Shuichi; Suwa, Junichi; Ito, Michiko; Sato, Haruo. "Experimental Studies on the Development of Malignant Goiter with Defatted Soybean." In *Naturally Occurring Carcinogens—Mutagens and Modulators of Carcinogenesis*, Ninth International Symposium of the Princess Takamatsu Cancer Research Fund, January 23–25, 1979. Tokyo, Japan. Abstract. *Soybeans contain carcinogens, mutagens. p. 24.*

Klein, D.; Gaconnet, N.; Poullain, B.; Debry, G. "Effect of a Nitrate Test Meal on Salivary and Gastric Nitrite Levels in Humans." *Food Cosmet Toxicol* 16(2): 111–115; 1978. Cited in *Carcinogenesis Abstracts 16* (1979), Abstract 78-3111. *Bacterial reduction of nitrate to nitrite in saliva.*

Kraybill, Herman F. "Carcinogenesis Induced by Trace Contaminants in Potable Water." *Bulletin of the New York Academy of Medicine 54* (1978). *Natural oil seepage into ocean; southern California coast, p. 415.*

――――. "Conceptual Approaches to the Assessment of Nonoccupational Environmental Cancer." In *Advances in Modern Toxicology*, edited by Myron A. Mehlman. Vol. 3, *Environmental Cancer*, edited by H. F. Kraybill, Myron A. Mehlman. Washington, D.C.: Hemisphere, 1977. *Carcinogenic drugs derived from bacteria and fungi: actinomycin D, griseofulvin, mitomycin C, penicillin, Table, p. 53.*

―――. "The Question of Benefits and Risks." In *Sweeteners, Issues and Uncertainties*. Washington, D.C.: National Academy of Sciences, 1975. *Sucrose entails potential pancreatic cancer risk among diabetics, pp. 61, 72.*

Kroes, R. "Food: A Carcinogenic Hazard?" In *Prevention and Detection of Cancer*, edited by Herbert E. Nieburgs. Part I, *Prevention*. Vol. 1, *Etiology*. New York: Marcel Dekker, 1977. *High-protein diet linked to cancer in man, p. 660; nitrate in leeks, purslane, spinach, pp. 659–660; smoking foods produces benzo(a)pyrene, p. 661.*

Kröplien, Udo. "Monosaccharides in Roasted and Instant Coffees." *Journal of Agricultural and Food Chemistry 22* (1974). *Coffee contains fructose, p. 110.*

Kubota, J.; Holmgren, George S.; Lakin, Hubert W. "Soils: Their Distribution, Uses and Trace-Element Concentration." In *Geochemistry and the Environment*. Vol. III. Washington, D.C.: National Academy of Sciences, 1978. *Trace elements common in soil and living organisms, Table 10, p. 55.*

Kuczuk, Maureen H.; Benson, Paul M.; Heath, Harry; Hayes, A. Wallace. "Evaluation of the Mutagenic Potential of Mycotoxins Using *Salmonella Typhimurium* and *Saccharomyces Cerevisiae*." *Mutation Research 53* (1978). *Aflatoxin B_1 and sterigmatocystin mutagenic, pp. 17–18.*

Kuhlmann, Wilhelm; Fromme, Hans-Georg; Heege, Eva-Maria; Ostertag, Wolfram. "The Mutagenic Action of Caffeine in Higher Organisms." *Cancer Research 28* (1968). *Caffeine is mutagenic in bacteria*, Drosophila, *fungi, human cells* in vitro, *mice, plants; evidence for carcinogenicity, p. 2375.*

Laqueur, G. L. "Oncogenicity of Cycads and Its Implications." In *Advances in Modern Toxicology*, edited by Myron A. Mehlman. Vol. 3, *Environmental Cancer*, edited by H. F. Kraybill, Myron A. Mehlman. Washington, D.C.: Hemisphere, 1977. *Cycads carcinogenic, pp. 231, 242–250; mutagenic, pp. 255–256.*

Laqueur, G. L., Spatz, Maria. "Transplacental Induction of Tumours and Malformations in Rats with Cycasin and Methylazoxymethanol." In *Transplacental Carcinogenesis*, edited by L. Tomatis, U. Mohr. IARC Scientific Publications No. 4. Lyon: IARC, 1973. *Cycasin: carcinogenic, p. 59; transplacental carcinogen, see whole paper.*

Laqueur, G. L., Spatz, M. "Toxicology of Cycasin." *Cancer Research 28* (1968). *Cycads carcinogenic, pp. 2263–2264; mutagenic, p. 2265.*

Lave, Lester B., Seskin, Eugene P. *Air Pollution and Human Health*. Baltimore: Johns Hopkins University Press, 1977. *Volcanoes eject sulfur oxides, p. 3; quotation, p. 3.*

Lee, D. J.; Wales, J. H.; Ayres, J. L.; Sinnhuber, R. O. "Synergism between Cyclopropenoid Fatty Acids and Chemical Carcinogens in Rainbow Trout (*Salmo gairdneri*)." *Cancer Research 28* (1968). *S. foetida oil a carcinogen promoter, p. 2312.*

Lee, L. S., Weinstein, I. B. "Tumor-promoting Phorbol Esters Inhibit Binding of Epidermal Growth Factor to Cellular Receptors." *Science* 202(4365): 313–315; 1978. Cited in *Carcinogenesis Abstracts 16* (1979), Abstract 78-6306. *Phorbol esters and related plant diterpenes are tumor promoters.*

Léonard, Alain. "Observations on Meiotic Chromosomes of the Male Mouse as a Test of the Potential Mutagenicity of Chemicals in Mammals." In *Chemical Mutagens, Principles and Methods for Their Detection*, edited by Alexander Hollaender. Vol. 3. New York: Plenum, 1973. *Caffeine causes chromosome breakage, p. 47.*

Leopold, A. Carl, Ardrey, Robert. "Toxic Substances in Plants and the Food Habits of Early Man." *Science 176* (1972). *Cooking plant foods a recent evolutionary development, quotation p. 512.*

Levin, W.; Lu, A. Y. H.; Ryan, D.; Wood, A. W.; Kapitulnik, J.; West, S.; Huang, M.-T; Conney, A. H.; Thakker, D. R.; Holder, G.; Yagi, H.; Jerina, D. M. "Properties of the Liver Microsomal Monoxygenase System and Epoxide Hydrase: Factors Influencing the Metabolism and Mutagenicity of Benzo(a)pyrene." In *Origins of Human Cancer,* edited by H. H. Hiatt, J. D. Watson, J. A. Winsten. Book B, *Mechanisms of Carcinogenesis.* New York: Cold Spring Harbor Laboratory, 1977. *Quotation, p. 659.*

Lewis, Walter H., Elvin-Lewis, Memory P. F. *Medical Botany: Plants Affecting Man's Health.* New York: Wiley, 1977. E. coli *produces ethionine, p. 118; mineral oil, p. 116; red pepper (chili), p. 121.*

Liener, Irvin E. "Miscellaneous Toxic Factors." In *Toxic Constituents of Plant Foodstuffs,* edited by Irvin E. Liener. New York: Academic, 1969. *Estrogens in cereals, fruits, plant oils and vegetables, p. 411.*

Lijinsky. W., Shubik, P. "Benzo(a)pyrene and Other Polynuclear Hydrocarbons in Charcoal-Broiled Meat." *Science 145* (1964). *Polynuclear hydrocarbons in charcoal-broiled steaks, see Table 1, p. 54.*

Lijinsky, William, Shubik, Philippe. "The Detection of Polycyclic Aromatic Hydrocarbons in Liquid Smoke and Some Foods." *Toxicology and Applied Pharmacology 7* (1965). *Smoked haddock, salmon contain benzo(a)pyrene, p. 341.*

Lindroth, S., Niskanen, A. "Comparison of Potential Patulin Hazard in Home-made and Commercial Apple Products." *J Food Sci* 43(2): 446–448; 1978. Cited in *Carcinogenesis Abstracts 16* (1979), Abstract 78-2128. *Homemade apple jam and apple juices contaminated by patulin.*

Lorenz, O. A.; Weir, B. L. "Nitrate Accumulation in Vegetables." In *Environmental Quality and Food Supply,* edited by Philip L. White, Diane Robbins. Mount Kisco, N.Y.: Futura, 1974. *Nitrates in vegetables, p. 95.*

Lovelock, James, Epton, Sidney. "The Quest for Gaia." *New Scientist 65* (1975). *Carbon tetrachloride, a natural substance, p. 305; role of oxygen in evolution, p. 305.*

Lovelock, James E.; Maggs, R. J.; Wade, R. J. "Halogenated Hydrocarbons in and over the Atlantic." *Nature 241* (1973). *Carbon tetrachloride produced by nature, pp. 194–196.*

MacDonald, Gordon A., Hubbard, Douglass H. *Volcanoes of the National Parks in Hawaii.* Honolulu, Hawaii: Tongg, 1970. Rev. ed. *Carcinogenic metals, sulfur dioxide a carcinogen promoter, Table, p. 10.*

Macgregor, J. T., Jurd, L. "Mutagenicity of Plant Flavonoids: Structural Requirements for Mutagenic Activity in Salmonella typhimurium." *Mutat Res* 54(3): 297–309; 1978. Cited in *Carcinogenesis Abstracts 17* (1979), Abstract 79-0149. *Kaempferol, quercetin mutagenic.*

Magee, P. N. "Mechanisms of Transplacental Carcinogenesis by Nitroso Compounds." In *Transplacental Carcinogenesis,* edited by L. Tomatis, U. Mohr. IARC Scientific Publications No. 4. Lyon: IARC, 1973. *Transplacental nitroso compounds, p. 143.*

———. "N-Nitrosodiethanolamine." In *Some N-Nitroso Compounds.* IARC Monographs on the Evaluation of the Carcinogenic Risk of Chemicals to Humans. Vol. 17. 365 pp.; 77–82; 1978. Cited in *Carcinogenesis Abstracts 16* (1979), Abstract 78-4823. N-*Nitrosodiethanolamine in tobacco.*

Magee, P. N.; Montesano, R.; Preussmann, R. "N-Nitroso Compounds and Related Carcinogens." In *Chemical Carcinogens,* edited by Charles E. Searle. Washington, D.C.: American Chemical Society, 1976. N-*Nitroso carcinogenic, p. 491;* N-*Nitroso transplacental carcinogens, p. 502; ubiquitous natural amines in foods, p. 587.*

Mancuso, Thomas F. "Prevention and Control of Occupational Exposures: An Overview." In *Prevention and Detection of Cancer,* edited by Herbert E. Nieburgs. Part I, *Prevention.* Vol. 2, *Etiology · Prevention Methods.* New York: Marcel Dekker, 1978. *Quotation, p. 1851.*

Mandel, M.; Ichinotsubo, D.; Mower, H. "Nitroso Group Exchange as a Way of Activation of Nitrosamines by Bacteria." *Nature* 267 (1977). *Intestinal bacteria (E. coli) interact with amines and amides, may cause mutation and cancer, p. 249.*

Markus, R. L. "Fern Leaves and Cancer." (Letter to Editor.) *Chem Eng News* 56(15): 4; 1978. Cited in *Carcinogenesis Abstracts 16* (1979), Abstract 78-1134. *Fern leaves eaten in Japan and Wales are carcinogenic.*

Marshall, Eliot. "Carcinogens in Scotch." *Science 205* (1979). *Nitrosamines discovered in Scotch and beer, p. 768; beet juice and carrot juice linked to nitrosamines, p. 769.*

Matsumoto, Hiromu. "Metabolic and Carcinogenic Effects of Methylazoxymethanol (MAM), MAM-Glucoside (Cycasin), and MAM-Glucosiduronic Acid." In *Naturally Occurring Carcinogens—Mutagens and Modulators of Carcinogenesis*, Ninth International Symposium of the Princess Takamatsu Cancer Research Fund, January 23–25, 1979. Tokyo, Japan. Abstract. *Cycads contain carcinogenic cycasin, p. 18.*

Mayer, Vernon W., Legator, Marvin S. "Production of Petite Mutants of *Saccharomyces cerevisiae* by Patulin." *Journal of Agricultural and Food Chemistry 17* (1969). *Patulin produces chromosomal abnormalities and mutations, pp. 454–456.*

Mayneord, W. V., Radley, J. M., and Turner, R. C. (1958). "The Alpha-Ray Activity of Humans and Their Environment." *Proc. 2nd Int. Conf. Peaceful Uses At. Energy*, 1958. United Nations, N. 4. *Radium in foods.* (Also see: Eisenbud.)

McKey, Doyle; Waterman, Peter G.; Mbi, C. N.; Gartlan, J. Stephen; Struhsaker, T. T. "Phenolic Content of Vegetation in Two African Rain Forests: Ecological Implications." *Science 202* (1978). *Flavonoids, polyphenols, tannins, p. 61; quotation, p. 61.*

McLean, A. E. M. "Diet and the Chemical Environment as Modifiers of Carcinogenesis." In *Host Environment Interactions in the Etiology of Cancer in Man*, edited by R. Doll and I. Vodopija. IARC Scientific Publications No. 7. Lyon: IARC, 1973. *Less protein reduces cancer incidence in animals, p. 224.*

McMillian, W. W.; Tifton, G. A.; Wilson, D. M.; Widstrom, N. W. "Insect Damage, *Aspergillus flavus* Ear Mold and Aflatoxin Contamination in South Georgia Corn Fields in 1977." *J Environ Qual* 7(4): 564–566; 1978. Cited in *Carcinogenesis Abstracts 17* (1979), Abstract 79-0551. *Pre-harvest corn samples in Georgia, 90 percent contaminated by aflatoxin.*

Meins, F. "Reversal of the Neoplastic State in Plants." *Amer J Pathol* 89(3): 687–702; 1977. Cited in *Carcinogenesis Abstracts 16* (1978), Abstract 78-0066. *Plant tumors, mechanisms.*

Miller, B., Strohmeyer, G. "Diverticulosis and Carcinoma of the Large Intestine as Fiber Deficiency Diseases: Fact or Hypothesis?" *Internist* (Berlin) 20(4): 195–200; 1979. Cited in *Carcinogenesis Abstracts 17* (1980), Abstract 79-4314. *Bacteria plus bile acids and cholesterol co-carcinogenic.*

Miller, Elizabeth C., Miller, James A. "The Mutagenicity of Chemical Carcinogens: Correlations, Problems and Interpretations." In *Chemical Mutagens, Principles and Methods for Their Detection*, edited by Alexander Hollaender. Vol. 1. New York: Plenum, 1971. *Carbon tetrachloride carcinogenic, p. 89.*

Miller, James A. "Concluding Remarks on Chemicals and Chemical Carcinogenesis." In *Carcinogens: Identification and Mechanisms of Action*, edited by A. Clark Griffin, Charles R. Shaw. New York: Raven, 1979. *Quotation: carcinogens may have played a role in evolution of life forms, p. 456.*

———. "Naturally Occurring Substances That Can Induce Tumors." In *Toxicants Occurring Naturally in Foods*, 2nd ed. Washington, D.C.: National Academy of Sciences, 1973. *Benzo(a)pyrene naturally synthesized by bacteria, pp. 525–526; ergot, rye contaminant, p. 515.*

Miller, James A., Miller, Elizabeth C. Interviewed by Jane Brody. *New York Times*, March 13, 1979. *Plant estrogens compared to diethylstilbestrol, p. C2.*

Miller, James A.; Swanson, Anne B.; Miller, Elizabeth C. "The Metabolic Activation of Safrole and Related Naturally Occurring Compounds in Relation to Carcinogenesis." In *Naturally Occurring Carcinogens—Mutagens and Modulators of Carcinogenesis*, Ninth International Symposium of the Princess Takamatsu Cancer Research Fund, January 23–25, 1979. Tokyo, Japan. Abstract. *Safrole is a carcinogen, p. 26.*

Mohr, U. "Effects of Diethylnitrosamine on Fetal and Suckling Syrian Golden Hamsters." In *Transplacental Carcinogenesis*, edited by L. Tomatis, U. Mohr. IARC Scientific Publications No. 4. Lyon: IARC, 1973. *Diethylnitrosamine a transplacental carcinogen, pp. 65–69.*

Moore, W. E.; Cato, E. P.; Holdeman, L. V. "Some Current Concepts in Intestinal Bacteriology." *Am J Clin Nutr* 31(10): S33–S42; 1978. Cited in *Carcinogenesis Abstracts 16* (1979), Abstract 78-6033. *Intestinal bacteria metabolize carcinogens.*

Morton, I. D. "Toxic Substances in Foods." *Journal of Human Nutrition 31* (1977). *Benzo(a)pyrene synthesized by bacteria, lentils and soybeans, p. 55.*

Mottram, D. S.; Patterson, R. L.; Edwards, R. A.; Gough. T. A. "The Preferential Formation of Volatile *N*-Nitrosamines in the Fat of Fried Bacon." *J Sci Food Agric* 28(11): 1025–1029; 1977. Cited in *Carcinogenesis Abstracts 16* (1979), Abstract 78-1436. *Frying raw bacon produces volatile nitrosamines.*

Muir, C. S., Nectoux, Janine. "Epidemiology of Cancer of the Testis and Penis." Presented at the Second Symposium of Epidemiology and Cancer Registries in the Pacific Basin, Maui, Hawaii, January 16–20, 1978. *National Cancer Institute Monograph 53.* 1979. *Carcinogenicity of human smegma needs assessment, p. 157; horse smegma carcinogenic in mice, p. 163.*

Nagao, Minako; Honda, Masako; Seino, Yuko; Yahagi, Takie; Sugimura, Takashi. "Mutagenicities of Smoke Condensates and the Charred Surface of Fish and Meat." *Cancer Letters 2* (1977). *Extracts of charred surfaces of broiled fish and meat mutagenic, p. 221.*

Nagao, Minako; Sugimura, Takashi; Matsushima, Taijiro. "Environmental Mutagens and Carcinogens." *Annual Review of Genetics 12* (1978). *Mutagens and/or carcinogens: Drugs derived from bacteria—daunomycin, mitomycin C, actinomycin D, p. 133. Extracts of bracken fern (cows, rats), p. 125. Flavonoids in fruits, plants, vegetables, p. 126. High-temperature cooking—amino acids, beef, fish, garlic, onion, proteins, vegetables, sugars, pp. 128–130. Malonaldehyde, p. 127. Pyrrolizidine alkaloids in plants, p. 125. Safrole in spices, p. 127. Hydrazines in tobacco, pp. 126, 127; hydrazines in mushrooms, pp. 126, 127.*

Nagao, Minako; Yahagi, Takie; Kawachi, Takashi; Seino, Yuko; Honda, Masako; Matsukura, Norio; Sugimura, Takashi; Wakabayashi, Keiji; Tsuji, Kuniro; Kosuge, Takuo. "Mutagens in Foods, and Especially Pyrolysis Products of Proteins." In *Progress in Genetic Toxicology*, edited by D. Scott, B. A. Bridges, F. H. Sobels. New York: Elsevier/North-Holland: Biomedical Press, 1977. *Mutagenic tars from amino acids, Table 3, p. 261.*

———. "On Mutagens in Foods, Especially on Compounds from Pyrolysis of Protein." *Mutation Research 53* (1978). Abstract 155. *Cooked carbohydrates and vegetable oil not mutagenic, p. 239.*

(NAS) National Academy of Sciences publications: Committee on Biologic Effects of Atmospheric Pollutants. *Particulate Polycyclic Organic Matter.* Washington, D.C.: National Academy of Sciences, 1972. *Nature vs. man: aerosols in the atmosphere, p. 37; polyaromatic hydrocarbons: potency, pp. 5, 6, 9, 10; terpenes from vegetation major source of atmospheric aerosols, p. 36.*

———. Committee on Food Protection, Food and Nutrition Board. *Radionuclides in Food.* Washington, D.C.: National Academy of Sciences, 1973. *Largest natural radiation exposure to man from potassium-40 in food, p. 17.*

————. Panel on Nitrates of the Coordinating Committee for Scientific and Technical Assessments of Environmental Pollutants. *Nitrates: An Environmental Assessment.* Washington, D.C.: National Academy of Sciences, 1978. *Forest fires toxic, p. 282. Inhaled nitrosamines, p. 32. Lightning: may produce 50 percent of world NO_x (Chameides' estimate), produces ozone in local air, p. 282. Measurements of NO, NO_2, p. 275. N-Nitroso compounds carcinogenic, mutagenic, pp. 454, 455, 458. NO_x produced by atmospheric inflow, burning, forest fires, lightning, volcanoes, p. 276. Nitrate, nitrite, nitrogen oxides, and N-nitroso compounds are bacterial, plant products, pp. 36, 37. Nitric oxide produced by cosmic radiation, lightning, p. 68. Vegetable supply 90 percent of nitrate inake, pp. 436, 438. UV radiation and fair skin, p. 461. Forest burning, pp. 282-283.*

————. Workshop on Inputs, Fates, and the Effects of Petroleum in the Marine Environment. *Petroleum in the Marine Environment.* Washington, D.C.: National Academy of Sciences, 1975. *Carcinogenic classes of hydrocarbons same in crude and refined petroleums, p. 20; polynuclear aromatic hydrocarbons naturally synthesized by bacteria, land and sea plants, vegetables, p. 20; quotation: ubiquity of polynuclear aromatic hydrocarbons, p. 20.*

————. Safe Drinking Water Committee. *Drinking Water and Health.* Washington, D.C.: National Academy of Sciences, 1977. *Acetaldehyde major metabolite of liquor, p. 687. Animals, fish, insects, plants get cancer, p. 53; quotation, p. 53. Carcinogenic asbestos fibers in natural water, p. 152; carcinogenic metals enter drinking water from decaying vegetation and rain filtering through soil, p. 205; carcinogenic metals identified in samplings of U.S. drinking water, pp. 207, 209, 210, 211, 212, 301-343. Nitrate in celery juice, p. 416; nitrite-plus-amine = N-Nitroso compounds in stomach, pp. 421-422. Potassium-40, largest source radioactivity in drinking water, p. 896.*

————. Workshop on Tropospheric Transport of Pollutants to the Ocean Steering Committee. *The Tropospheric Transport of Pollutants and Other Substances to the Oceans.* Washington, D.C.: National Academy of Sciences, 1978. *Crustal and sea salt flux, pp. 135, 136; inadequate data on human contribution, pp. 1, 2, 5, 6; metals in air, plant metal particulates, p. 134; radionuclides in air, p. 17; SO_2 in air, p. 182; volcanic metal particulates, pp. 132, 133; quotation, p. 135.*

(NCRP) National Council on Radiation Protection and Measurements. *Natural Background Radiation in the United States.* NCRP Report No. 45. Washington, D.C.: National Council on Radiation Protection and Measurements. Issued November 15, 1975. *Cosmogenic radionuclides and half-lives, Table, p. 27; cosmogenic radionuclides significantly affecting man (carbon-14, tritium (3_H), beryllium-7, sodium-22), p. 25. Man absorbs radionuclides from atmosphere and soil, p. 54. Man absorbs radionuclides from atmosphere and soil, p. 66, and from galaxy, pp. 6-7, 17-22, 24, 25, 41-43. Potassium-40 found in many foods required for survival, p. 91. Radioactivity in air, pp. 66-89; animal tissues, pp. 40-41; food, pp. 42-43, 91-93; human tissues, pp. 25, 41-43, 62, 90-111; plant tissues, pp. 37, 39, 40, 56; rocks, pp. 49-59; soil, pp. 54-59, 79-81; ubiquitous, pp. 2, 3, 42, 44, 60; water, pp. 56-58, 91-93. Radioactivity measured by air, pp. 66, 67-74. Quotation: natural radiation major source of human exposure, p. 1.*

(NIOSH) National Institute for Occupational Safety and Health. *Suspected Carcinogens*, 2nd ed. Edited by Herbert Christensen, Edward J. Fairchild, Richard J. Lewis, Sr. Cincinnati, Ohio: National Institute for Occupational Safety and Health, 1976. *Acetone, p. 8; aflatoxin G_1, G_2, B, B_1, B_2, pp. 11-12; amaranth, p. 13; aniline, p. 17; arsenic, p. 23; benzo(a)pyrene, p. 44; beryl, beryllium, p. 47; bracken fern, p. 53; cadmium, p. 57; carbon tetrachloride (CCL_4), p. 63; carageenan, Irish moss gelose, p. 64; chlorite, p. 65; cholesterol, p. 69; chromite (iron chromate), chromium, p. 70; cobalt, p. 73; corn oil, Mazola, courmarin, p. 74; croton—resin and oil, crude oil, p. 76; crystalline silica (agate, amethyst, chalcedony, flint, onyx, pure quartz, rose quartz, sand), p. 204; daunomycin, p. 80; derris, p. 81; ethyl alcohol (eth-*

anol), *p. 109; fructose, p. 117; hematite (iron ore), p. 122; insulin lente (insulin), p. 131; iron III oxide (bauxite residues, burnt sienna, burnt umber, natural iron oxides, ocher, rouge, sienna, yellow oxide of iron), p. 132; lactose, laraha, p. 136; limonite (brown hematite, brown iron ore, brown ironstone clay), p. 137; magnetite (black gold, black iron oxide, iron black, micaceous iron ore), maltose, p. 138; menthol, mercury, p. 140; methyl chloride, 3-methylbutan-1-ol, p. 145; 2-methylpropan-1-ol, p. 147; naphthalene, p. 149; nicotine, p. 160; ozone, patulin, p. 171; penicillin, pp. 13, 171; petroleum, p. 172; phenol, p. 173; 2-phenylethanol, p. 178; raton, p. 199; safrole, sali, p. 201; sodium chloride: salt and types of salt, p. 204; sand, silica (crystalline), pp. 201, 204; silver, p. 204; sorsaka, p. 205; tantalum, p. 213; terpenes, p. 214; o-toluidine, p. 220; urea, p. 229; watapama shimaron, p. 234.*

Natusch, D. F. S. "Potentially Carcinogenic Species Emitted to the Atmosphere by Fossil-Fueled Power Plants." *Environmental Health Perspectives 22* (1978). *Fossil fuels release radionuclides when burned; nitrogen oxides and sulfur oxides may promote cancer, pp. 79, 80.*

Nawar, M. M., Hamza, H. A. "Effects of Mixtures of Ethyl Methanesulfonate and Caffeine or Maleic Hydrazine on Lethal Frequencies in *Drosophila melanogaster.*" *Mutation Research 53* (1978). Abstract 157. *Caffeine mutagenic, p. 240.*

Nesheim, S., Trucksess, M. W. "Mycotoxins. Thin Layer Chromatographic Determination of Aflatoxin B_1 in Eggs; Collaborative Study." *J Assoc of Anal Chem* 61(3): 569–573; 1978. Cited in *Carcinogenesis Abstracts 16* (1979), Abstract 78-4958. *Aflatoxin B_1-contaminated eggs.*

Newberne, P. M. "The Influence of a Low Lipotrope Diet on Response of Maternal and Fetal Rats to Lasiocarpine." *Cancer Research 28* (1968). *Pyrrolizidine alkaloids, including genera Senecio, carcinogenic, p. 2327.*

Nishizuka, Y. "Biological Influence of Fat Intake on Mammary Cancer and Mammary Tissue: Experimental Correlates." *Prev Med* 7(2): 218–224; 1978. Cited in *Carcinogenesis Abstracts 16* (1979), Abstract 78-5025. *High-fat diet promotes mammary cancer.*

Norseth, T. "Industrial Viewpoints on Cancer Caused by Metals as an Occupational Disease." In *Origins of Human Cancer*, edited by H. H. Hiatt, J. D. Watson, J. A. Winsten. Book A, *Incidence of Cancer in Humans.* New York: Cold Spring Harbor Laboratory, 1977. *Metals, established or suspected carcinogens: antimony, arsenic, beryllium, cadmium, cobalt, nickel, pp. 160–161 (see Table 1).*

Oberley, Larry W., Buettner, Garry R. "Role of Superoxide Dismutase in Cancer: A Review." *Cancer Research 39* (1979). *Superoxide radicals linked to cancer, pp. 1141, 1143–1144.*

Office of Consumer Inquiries, FDA. "Consumer Information and Questions About . . . Food Additives." Rockville, Md., 1978. *Nitrates in cabbage and broccoli, p. 3.*

O'Sullivan, Dermot A. "Air Pollution." In *Our Chemical Environment*, edited by J. Calvin Giddings and Manus B. Monroe. San Francisco: Canfield, 1972. *Terpenes and other natural substances produce blue haze over forests, p. 46.*

Pamukcu, A. M. "Bracken Fern (BF), A Natural Urinary Bladder Carcinogen." In *Naturally Occurring Carcinogens—Mutagens and Modulators of Carcinogenesis*, Ninth International Symposium of the Princess Takamatsu Cancer Research Fund, January 23–25, 1979. Tokyo, Japan. Abstract. *Bracken has produced cancer in cows, rats, mice, guinea pigs and Japanese quail, pp. 22–23.*

Panel on Chemicals and Health of the President's Science Advisory Committee. *Chemicals and Health.* Report. Science and Technology Policy Office. National Science Foundation, September 1973. *Carcinogenic polycyclic aromatic hydrocarbons, including benzo(a)pyrene, in vegetables, quotation, p. 64.*

Patterson, J. M.; Haidar, N. F.; Smith, W. T.; Benner, J. F.; Burton, H. R.; Burdick, D. "Benzo(a)pyrene Formation in the Pyrolysis of Selected Amino Acids, Amines, and Maleic Hydrazide." *J Agric Food Chem* 26(1): 268–270; 1978. Cited in *Carcinogenesis Abstracts 16* (1979), Abstract 78-0735.

Pearson, David. *The Chemical Analysis of Foods*, 7th ed. New York: Chemical Publishing, 1977. *Chemicals present in significant amounts in common liquors, p. 335.*

Pitts, J. N.; Van Cauwenberghe, K. A.; Grosjean, D.; Schmid, J. P.; Fitz, D. R.; Belser, W. L.; Knudson, G. B.; Hynds, P. M. "Atmospheric Reactions of Polycyclic Aromatic Hydrocarbons: Facile Formation of Mutagenic Nitro Derivatives." *Science* 202(4367): 515–519; 1978. Cited in *Carcinogenesis Abstracts, 16* (1979), Abstract 78-5568. *Benzo(a)pyrene and real or simulated photochemical smog form mutagenic nitro derivatives.*

Pool, R. A. F. "Determination of Patulin in Apple Juice Products as the 2,4-Dinitrophenylhydrazone Derivative." *Journal of Agricultural and Food Chemistry 25* (1977). *Patulin in apple juice, p. 1220.*

Price, J. M. Pamukcu, A. M. "The Induction of Neoplasms of the Urinary Bladder of the Cow and the Small Intestine of the Rat by Feeding Bracken Fern (*Pteris aquilina*)." *Cancer Research 28* (1968), p. 2247.

Rapp, Fred, Howett, Mary K. "Oncogenesis and Viruses." In *Proceedings of the Eleventh Canadian Cancer Research Conference.* Preprint. Sponsored by the National Cancer Institute of Canada. Toronto, Ontario, May 6–8, 1976. *Cancer and viruses in animals, Table 1, pp. 177–179.*

Rasmussen, R. A. "Emission of Biogenic NO from Soil." *EOS Transactions American Geophysical Union 56* (1975). *Natural sources of nitric oxide, p. 176.*

Rasmussen, R. A., Holdren, M. W. "Analysis of C_5 to C_{10} Hydrocarbons in Rural Atmospheres." For Presentation at the 65th Annual Meeting of the Air Pollution Control Association. Miami Beach, Florida, June 18–22, 1972. *Volatile terpenes and other organic volatiles emerge from plant tissues, p. 3.*

Rasmussen, Reinhold A. Cited in "Volcanoes May Emit Chemicals Believed to Harm Ozone Layer," *New York Times*, December 17, 1978. *Kilauea eruption produced methyl chloride, p. 83.*

———. "What Do the Hydrocarbons from Trees Contribute to Air Pollution?" *Journal of the Air Pollution Control Association 22* (1972). *Terpenes: eastern and western forests, p. 540; global hydrocarbon production, p. 537.*

Rasmussen, Reinhold A., Went, F. W. "Volatile Organic Material of Plant Origin in the Atmosphere." *Proceedings of the National Academy of Sciences 53* (1965). *Terpenes as cause of blue haze, natural photochemical smog, pp. 215, 218; terpenes from: autumn leaf litter, pp. 218, 219; drying hay, p. 220; trees, pp. 215, 216.*

Rawson, R. W. "Inorganic Carcinogens." In *Prevention and Detection of Cancer. Proceedings of the Third International Symposium on Detection and Prevention of Cancer Held by the International Study Group for the Detection and Prevention of Cancer in New York, April 26–May 1, 1976.* Vol. 2 (part 1), 2404 pp.; 1893–1906; 1978. Cited in *Carcinogenesis Abstracts 16* (1979), Abstract 78-6631. *Potential metallic carcinogens: arsenic, beryllium, cadmium, chromium, lead, nickel.*

Rhodes, Martha E. " 'Natural' Food Myth." *Sciences 19* (1979). *Coffee contains acetaldehyde, p. 30.*

Rodricks, Joseph V. "Food Hazards of Natural Origin." *Federation Proceedings 37* (1978). *Contaminants in meat and milk products: bracken fern, estrogenic plants and fungi, patulin, pyrrolizidine alkaloids, p. 2589; patulin-contaminated apples, apple products, report 37 percent contamination, patulin reported carcinogenic, p. 2591.*

Rose, Elizabeth F. "The Role of Demographic Risk Factors in Carcinogenesis." In *Prevention and Detection of Cancer*, edited by Herbert E. Nieburgs. Part II, *Detection.* Vol. 1, *High Risk Markers: Detection Methods and Management.* New York: Marcel Dekker, 1978. *Quotation, p. 31.*

Sadeghi, Ahmad; Behmard, Shahla; Vesselinovitch, Stan D. "Opium: A Potential Urinary Bladder Carcinogen in Man." *Cancer 43* (1979). *Eating, smoking opium linked to cancer, p. 2315.*

Sander, Johannes. "The Formation of N-Nitroso Compounds in the Stomach of Animals and Man and in the Diet." In *Transplacental Carcinogenesis*, edited by L. Tomatis, U. Mohr. IARC Scientific Publications No. 4. Lyon: IARC, 1973. *Bacteria in stomach: produce carcinogenic nitrosamines, pp. 159, 160, 161; reduce nitrate to nitrite, p. 161.*

Sax, Karl, Sax, Hally J. "Radiomimetic Beverages, Drugs, and Mutagens." *Proceedings of the National Academy of Sciences 55* (1966). *Caffeine mutagenic, p. 1433.*

Schoental, R. "Toxicology and Carcinogenic Action of Pyrrolizidine Alkaloids." *Cancer Research 28* (1968). *Pyrrolizidine alkaloids liver carcinogens in animals, p. 2237.*

Schopf, J. William. "The Evolution of the Earliest Cells." *Scientific American 239* (1978). *Appearance of oxygen in Precambrian evolution, p. 111.*

Schwartz, Morton K. "Role of Trace Elements in Cancer." *Cancer Research 35* (1975). *Chemicals required for life: cobalt, copper, chromium, fluorine, iodine, iron, manganese, molybdenum, selenium, tin, vanadium, zinc; "and possibly silicon and nickel," p. 3481; chromium, lead, nickel, titanium and manganese found in asbestos, p. 3485.*

Scott, E. L., Straf, M. L. "Ultraviolet Radiation as a Cause of Cancer." In *Origins of Human Cancer*, edited by H. H. Hiatt, J. D. Watson, J. A. Winsten. Book A, *Incidence of Cancer in Humans*. New York: Cold Spring Harbor Laboratory, 1977. *Geography, skin color, factors in skin cancer, p. 530.*

Seifter, E.; Rettura, G.; Liu, S.; Levenson, S. M. "Citral Promotes BW10232 Tumor Growth: Vitamin A Antagonizes This (Meeting Abstract)." *Fed Proc* 38(3, part 1): 714; 1979. Cited in *Carcinogenesis Abstracts 17* (1979), Abstract 79-2084.

Seino, Y.; Nagao, M.; Yahagi, T.; Sugimura, T.; Yasuda, T.; Nishimura, S. "Identification of a Mutagenic Substance in a Spice, Sumac, as Quercetin." *Mutat Res* 58(2/3): 225–229; 1978. Cited in *Carcinogenesis Abstracts 17* (1979), Abstract 79-0151.

Seitz, H. K.; Garro, A. J.; Lieber, C. S. "Effect of Chronic Ethanol Ingestion on Intestinal Metabolism and Mutagenicity of Benzo(a)pyrene." *Biochem Biophys Res Commun* 85(3): 1061–1066; 1978. Cited in *Carcinogenesis Abstracts 17* (1979), Abstract 79-0888. *Ethanol a carcinogen promoter in rats; may be linked to cancer incidence in alcoholics.*

Selikoff, Irving J. "Occupational Lung Diseases." In *Environmental Factors in Respiratory Disease*, edited by Douglas H. K. Lee. New York: Academic, 1972. *Quotation: much of earth's crust silicate, p. 201.*

Shabad, L. M. "Data on Environmental Carcinogenic Polycyclic Aromatic Hydrocarbons." *Magy Onkol* 23(1):3–11; 1979. Cited in *Carcinogenesis Abstracts 17* (1979), Abstract 79-2405. *Polynuclear aromatic hydrocarbons, including benzo(a)pyrene, generated by germinating plants.*

Shamberger, Raymond J. "Antioxidants and Cancer VII. Presence of Malonaldehyde in Beef and Other Meats and Its Epidemiological Significance." In *Trace Substances in Environmental Health—XI*, Proceedings of University of Missouri's 11th Annual Conference on Trace Substances in Environmental Health, edited by Delbert D. Hemphill. Columbia, Mo.: University of Missouri-Columbia, June 7, 8, and 9, 1977. *Malonaldehyde: carcinogenic and mutagenic, p. 36; cooking affects amount, pp. 36–39; fat contains small amount, p. 38; found in cheeses, chopped walnuts, dried raisins, peanut butter, seafood, p. 40; found in lean raw meats and fowl, p. 38; table, p. 39.*

Shepard, Thomas H. *Catalog of Teratogenic Agents*, 2nd ed. Baltimore, Md.: Johns Hopkins University Press, 1976. *Teratogenic metals: antimony, p. 18; arsenic, p. 19; barium, p. 24; bismuth, p. 27; cadmium, p. 33; cesium, p. 40; chromium, p. 51; cobalt, p. 54; fluorine, p. 102; iodine, p. 130; indium, p. 126; lead, p. 135; lithium, p. 137; mercury, p. 146; nickel, p. 164; rhodium, p. 197; selenium, p. 204; tellurium, p. 214; thallium, p. 221. Too much oxygen (hyperoxia) can cause birth defects, p. 120. Quotation: Introduction, p. xiii.*

Shimkin, M. B.; Stoner, G. D.; Theiss, J. C. "Lung Tumor Response in Mice to Metals and Metal Salts." In *Inorganic and Nutritional Aspects of Cancer*, edited by G. N. Schrauzer. New York: Plenum, 1978. *Carcinogenic metals: chromium, cobalt, selenium, zinc, pp. 90–91.*

Shubik, Philippe. "Identification of Environmental Carcinogens: Animal Test Models." In *Carcinogens: Identification and Mechanisms of Action*, edited by A. Clark Griffin, Charles R. Shaw. New York: Raven, 1979. *Xylitol carcinogenic, p. 44.*

Singleton, V. L., Kratzer, F. H. "Plant Phenolics." In *Toxicants Occurring Naturally in Foods*, 2nd ed. Washington, D.C.: National Academy of Sciences, 1973. *Tannin carcinogenic, p. 329.*

Smith, R. Jeffrey. "Xylitol: Another Sweetener Turns Sour." *Science 199* (1978). *Xylitol carcinogenic to rats, p. 670.*

Soos, K.; Fritz, W. "Comparative Studies of the Carcinogenic Polycyclic Aromatic Hydrocarbon Levels in Smoked Foodstuffs in Hungary and in East Germany." *Egeszsegtudomany* 21(3): 277–285; 1978. Cited in *Carcinogenesis Abstracts 16* (1979), Abstract 78-5555. *Smoked cheese and fish contain benzo(a)pyrene.*

Sorrell, Charles A. *Minerals of the World.* New York: Golden, 1973. *Periodic Table, pp. 271–273.*

Stedman, R. L. "The Chemical Composition of Tobacco and Tobacco Smoke." *Chemical Reviews 68* (1968). *Tobacco leaf and smoke: phenolics and related compounds, p. 174; radioactive substances, p. 186; reportedly carcinogenic metals, p. 183; sugars, p. 180.*

Stein-Werblowsky, R. "On the Etiology of Cancer of the Prostate." *Eur Urol* 4(5): 370–373; 1978. Cited in *Carcinogenesis Abstracts 16* (1979), Abstract 78-7142. *Sperm penetrating into prostatic tissue of rats causes cancer.*

———. "On the Etiology of Testicular Tumors. An Experimental Study." *Eur Urol* 4(1): 57–59; 1978. Cited in *Carcinogenesis Abstracts 16* (1979), Abstract 78-7143. *Sperm penetrating into testicular tissues of rats causes cancer.*

Stephany, R. W., Schuller, P. L. "The Intake of Nitrate, Nitrite and Volatile *N*-Nitrosamines and the Occurrence of Volatile *N*-Nitrosamines in Human Urine and Veal Calves." In *Environmental Aspects of N-Nitroso Compounds*, edited by E. A. Walker, L. Gricuite, M. Castegnaro, R. E. Lyle. IARC Scientific Publications No. 19. Lyon: IARC, 1978. *Salivary nitrite linked to nitrate in vegetable consumption, pp. 450, 457.*

Stob, Martin, "Estrogens in Foods." In *Toxicants Occurring Naturally in Foods*, 2nd ed. Washington, D.C.: National Academy of Sciences, 1973. *Estrogens in damaged vegetables, p. 554; quotation: carcinogenicity a function of dose, p. 554; zearalenone, p. 553.*

Sugimura, Takashi. "Carcinogens in Foods and Food Products." In *Proceedings of the Eleventh Canadian Cancer Research Conference.* Sponsored by the National Cancer Institute of Canada. Toronto, Ontario, May 6–8, 1976. *Salt, Vitamin A enhance carcinogenesis, p. 72.*

———. "Naturally Occurring Genotoxic Carcinogens." In *Naturally Occurring Carcinogens—Mutagens and Modulators of Carcinogenesis*, Ninth International Symposium of the Princess Takamatsu Cancer Research Fund, January 23–25, 1979. Tokyo, Japan. Abstract. *Maize plants contain mutagens, pyrrolizidine alkaloids mutagenic, p. 49.*

Sugimura, Takashi; Kawachi, Takashi; Nagao, Minako; Yahagi, Takie; Seino, Yuko; Okamoto, Toshihiko; Shudo, Koichi; Kosuge, Takuo; Tsuji, Kuniro; Wakabayashi, Keiji; Iitaka, Yoichi; Itai, Akiko. "Mutagenic Principle(s) in Tryptophan and Phenylalanine Pyrolysis Products." *Proceedings of the Japan Academy 53* (1977). *Pyrolized carbohydrates, vegetable oil nonmutagenic, pyrolized protein mutagenic, p. 58.*

Sugimura, T.; Nagao, M.; Kawachi, T.; Honda, M.; Yahagi, T.; Seino, Y.; Sato, S.; Matsukura, N.; Matsushima, T.; Shirai, A.; Sawamura, M.; Matsumoto, H. "Mutagen-Carcinogens in Food, with Special Reference to Highly Mutagenic Pyrolytic Products in Broiled Foods." In *Origins of Human Cancer,* edited by H. H. Hiatt, J. D. Watson, J. A. Winsten. Book C, *Human Risk Assessment.* New York: Cold Spring Harbor Laboratory, 1977. *Charred beef and fish mutagenic, p. 1567; cooking protein at high temperature mutagenic, p. 1568.*

Sunderman, F. William, Jr. "The Current Status of Nickel Carcinogenesis." *Annals of Clinical Laboratory Science 3* (1973). *Carcinogenic nickel in cigarette smoke, p. 156.*

————. "Mechanisms of Metal Carcinogenesis." *Biological Trace Element Research 1* (1979). *Metals reactive in bacterial and cellular tests, p. 77; "recognized" metal carcinogens: arsenic, beryllium, cadmium, chromium, cobalt, lead, manganese, nickel, zinc, p. 77.*

————. "Metal Carcinogenesis in Experimental Animals." *Food and Cosmetics Toxicology 9* (1971). *Metallic carcinogens: lead, selenium, p. 115.*

————. "Pulmonary Carcinogenesis from Exposure to Toxic Agents." In *Laboratory Diagnosis of Diseases Caused by Toxic Agents,* edited by F. William Sunderman, F. William Sunderman, Jr. St. Louis: Warren H. Green, 1970. *Carcinogenic nickel and other trace metals constituents of chrysotile types of asbestos, p. 499.*

Suskind, Raymond R. "Environment and the Skin." *Environmental Health Perspectives 20* (1977). *Ultraviolet radiation and types of cancer, p. 32.*

Szepsenwol, J. "Carcinogenic Effect of Egg White, Egg Yolk and Lipids in Mice." *The Proceedings of the Society for Experimental Biology and Medicine 112* (April 1963), pp. 1073, 1075–1076.

Szepsenwol, J.; Fletcher, J.; Toro-Goyco, E. "Mammary Cancer in Mice Receiving Weekly Subcutaneous Injections of Sesame Oil (Meeting Abstract)." *Proc Am Assoc Cancer Res 20*: 56; 1979. Cited in *Carcinogenesis Abstracts 17* (1980), Abstract 79-4450, *p. 1736.*

Tannenbaum, S. R. "Steven Tannenbaum Replies." *Sciences,* May/June, 1980. *N-Nitrosopyrrolidine formed by frying bacon, p. 3.*

Tannenbaum, S. R.; Archer, M. C.; Wishnok, J. S.; Correa, P.; Cuello, C.; Haenszel, W. "Nitrate and the Etiology of Gastric Cancer." In *Origins of Human Cancer,* edited by H. H. Hiatt, J. D. Watson, J. A. Winsten. Book C, *Human Risk Assessment.* New York: Cold Spring Harbor Laboratory, 1977. *Most nitroso compounds carcinogenic, p. 1609.*

Tannenbaum, Steven R.; Archer, Michael C.; Wishnok, John S.; Bishop, Walter W. "Nitrosamine Formation in Human Saliva." *Journal of the National Cancer Institute 60* (1978). *Bacterial reduction of nitrate to nitrite by saliva, p. 251.*

Tannenbaum, S. R.; Fett, D.; Young, V. R.; Land, P. D.; Bruce, W. R. "Nitrite and Nitrate Are Formed by Endogenous Synthesis in the Human Intestine." *Science 200* (1978). *Bacterial reduction of nitrate to nitrite, production of N-nitroso compounds, pp. 1487–1488.*

Tannenbaum, S. R.; Sinskey, A. J.; Weisman, M.; Bishop, W. "Nitrite in Human Saliva. Its Possible Relationship to Nitrosamine Formation." *Journal of the National Cancer Institute 53* (1974). *Bacteria produce nitrite in saliva, pp. 79–81.*

Temcharoen, P.; Anukarahanonta, T.; Bhamarapravati, N. "Influence of Dietary Protein and Vitamin B_{12} on the Toxicity and Carcinogenicity of Aflatoxins in Rat Liver." *Cancer Res 38*(7): 2185–2190; 1978. Cited in *Carcinogenesis Abstracts 16* (1979), Abstract 78-5470. *Vitamin B_{12} may potentiate or promote carcinogens.*

Thomas, Lewis. *The Lives of a Cell: Notes of a Biology Watcher.* New York: Bantam, 1975. *Oxygen-metabolizing mutants, p. 172; quotation, p. 3.*

Toth, Bela. "The Large Bowel Carcinogenic Effects of Hydrazines and Related Compounds Occurring in Nature and in the Environment." *Cancer 40* (1977). *Carcinogenic hydrazines: in commonly eaten mushrooms, in tobacco plant, p. 2427.*

———. "Mushroom Hydrazines: Occurrence, Metabolism, Carcinogenesis and Environmental Implications." In *Naturally Occurring Carcinogens—Mutagens and Modulators of Carcinogenesis*, Ninth International Symposium of the Princess Takamatsu Cancer Research Fund, January 23-25, 1979. Tokyo, Japan. Abstract. *Commonly eaten mushrooms contain carcinogenic hydrazine compounds, pp. 16-17.*

Toth, Bela, Nagel, D. "Mushroom Toxin: N-Methyl-N-formylhydrazine (MFH) Carcinogenesis in Mice (Meeting Abstract)." *Proc Am Assoc Cancer Res* 19: 42; 1978. Cited in *Carcinogenesis Abstracts 16* (1979), Abstract 78-1906.

Trefil, James S. "Missing Particles Cast Doubt on Our Solar Theories." *Smithsonian 8* (1978). *Gigantic fusion "reactor" inside sun's core, p. 75.*

Turk, Amos; Turk, Jonathan; Wittes, Janet T.; Wittes, Robert E. *Environmental Science*, 2nd ed. Philadelphia: Saunders, 1978. *Natural air "contaminants:" dust from volcanic eruptions, p. 402; salt from sea spray, soil particles, sulfur dioxide from volcanic eruptions, p. 400.*

Underwood, E. J. "Trace Elements." In *Toxicants Occurring Naturally in Foods*, 2nd ed. Washington, D.C.: National Academy of Sciences, 1973. *Foods containing: cobalt, p. 54; copper, p. 51; iron, p. 49; lead, p. 61; manganese, p. 57; mercury, p. 67; nickel, p. 55; selenium, p. 60.*

———. *Trace Elements in Human and Animal Nutrition.* New York: Academic, 1971. *Foods containing: chromium, p. 262; copper, p. 100; zinc, p. 240. Leguminous plants rich in cobalt, copper, iron, nickel, zinc, p. 468.*

(United Nations) Report of the United Nations Scientific Committee on the Effects of Atomic Radiation. General Assembly Official Records. Seventeenth Session. Supplement No. 16 (A/5216). New York: United Nations, 1962. *Quotation, p. 208.*

Upadhyay, R. R.; Bakhtavar, F.; Ghaisarzadeh, M.; Tilabi, J. "Cocarcinogenic and Irritant Factors of *Euphorbia Esula* L. Latex." *Tumori* 64(1): 99–102; 1978. Cited in *Carcinogenesis Abstracts 16* (1979), Abstract 78-2608. *Ingenol-3-dodecanoate cocarcinogenic component of plant.*

Upton, A. C. "Radiation Effects." In *Origins of Human Cancer*, edited by H. H. Hiatt, J. D. Watson, J. A. Winsten. Book A, *Incidence of Cancer in Humans.* New York: Cold Spring Harbor Laboratory, 1977. *Ultraviolet radiation linked to skin color and geographical location, Figure 1, p. 478.*

Van Duuren, B. L. "Tobacco Carcinogenesis." *Cancer Research 28* (1968). *Carcinogens in cigarette tars, Table 3, p. 2359; aromatic hydrocarbons in cigarette smoke: carcinogens and carcinogen promoters, p. 2358.*

Varghese, A. J.; Land, P. C.; Furrer, R.; Bruce, W. R. "Non-Volatile N-Nitroso Compounds in Human Feces." *IARC Sci Publ* (19): 257–264; 1978. Cited in *Carcinogenesis Abstracts 16* (1979), Abstract 78-5629.

Vithayathil, Antony J.; Commoner, Barry; Nair, Subhadra; Madyastha, Prema. "Isolation of Mutagens from Bacterial Nutrients Containing Beef Extract." *Journal of Toxicology and Environmental Health 4* (1978). *Mutagens in nutrient broth containing beef extract enhance mutation rate of* Salmonella *bacteria, p. 189.*

Vizthum, Otto G.; Werkhoff, Peter; Hubert, Peter. "New Volatile Constituents of Black Tea Aroma." *Journal of Agricultural and Food Chemistry 23* (1975). *Black tea contains aniline and o-toluidine, Table 1, pp. 1000-1001.*

Vogel, E., Sobels, F. H. "The Function of *Drosophila* in Genetic Toxicology Testing." In *Chemical Mutagens, Principles and Methods for Their Detection*, edited by Alexander Hollaender. Vol. 4. New York: Plenum, 1976. *Mutagenic pyrrolizidine alkaloids: echinatine, echimidine, fulvine, heliotrine, jacobine, lasiocarpine, monocrotaline, platyphylline, retrorsine, senecionine, supinine, Table 5, p. 111.*

von Nieding, Giselher. "Possible Mutagenic Properties and Carcinogenic Action of the Irritant Gaseous Pollutants NO_2, O_3, and SO_2." *Environmental Health Perspectives* 22 (1978). *Ozone mutagenic, NO_2 possibly mutagenic, p. 91.*

Wagoner, Joseph K.; Miller, Robert W.; Lundin, Frank E.; Fraumeni, Joseph F.; Haij, Marian E. "Unusual Cancer Mortality Among a Group of Underground Metal Miners." *New England Journal of Medicine* 269 (1963). *Inhalation of carcinogenic air in mines linked to cancer, p. 288.*

Waldbott, George L. *Health Effects of Environmental Pollutants,* 2nd ed. St. Louis: Mosby, 1978. *Carcinogenic or co-carcinogenic contaminants of natural air: Crystallized silicates in sand, 42.5 percent crystallized silicates in rural air, p. 18. Meteoritic metal particles, p. 17. NO produced by microorganisms in seawater, p. 18. Salt from sea spray, billion tons salt fall on continent, pp. 17-18. Volcanic dusts, aerosols, p. 17.*

Wang, T.; Kakizoe, T.; Dion, P.; Furrer, R.; Varghese, A. J.; Bruce, W. R. "Volatile Nitrosamines in Normal Human Faeces." *Nature* 276 (1978). *Consumption of nitrites plus amines produces nitrosamines in intestines, p. 280; mutagenic N-nitroso compounds found in healthy human feces, pp. 280-281.*

Ward, Barbara, Dubos, René. *Only One Earth: The Care and Maintenance of a Small Planet.* New York: Norton, 1972. *Emergence of oxygen on earth allowed development of complex life forms, p. 37.*

Weinberger, M. A.; Friedman, L.; Farber, T. M.; Moreland, F. M.; Peters, E. L.; Gilmore, C. E.; Khan, M. A. "Testicular Atrophy and Impaired Spermatogenesis in Rats Fed High Levels of the Methylxanthines, Caffeine, Theobromine, or Theophylline." *J Environ Pathol Toxicol* 1(5): 669–688; 1978. Cited in *Carcinogenesis Abstracts 16* (1979), Abstract 78-6123.

Weisburger, Elizabeth K. "Natural Carcinogenic Products." *Environmental Science 13* (1979). *Carcinogenic ergot contaminates rye crops, p. 281; fermented foods contain carcinogenic ethyl carbamate or urethane, p. 280.*

Weisburger, John H. "Bioassays and Tests for Chemical Carcinogens." In *Chemical Carcinogens,* edited by Charles E. Searle. Washington, D.C.: American Chemical Society, 1976. *Carcinogenic metals: beryllium, cadmium, chromium, cobalt, lead, manganese, nickel, titanium, p. 3.*

Went, F. W. "Organic Matter in the Atmosphere, and Its Possible Relation to Petroleum Formation." *Proceedings of the National Academy of Sciences 46* (1960). *Terpenes and other isoprene derivatives in vegetation form blue haze, pp. 212-217.*

———. "Plants and the Chemical Environment." In *Chemical Ecology,* edited by Ernest Sondheimer, John B. Simeone. New York: Academic, 1970. *Plants develop tumors caused by other life forms, pp. 79-81.*

Whanger, P. D.; Weswig, P. H.; Stoner, J. C. "Arsenic Levels in Oregon Waters." *Environmental Health Perspectives 19* (1977). *High arsenic levels due to volcanic deposits, pp. 139-140.*

Whittaker, R. H. "The Biochemical Ecology of Higher Plants." In *Chemical Ecology,* edited by Ernest Sondheimer, John B. Simeone. New York: Academic, 1970. *Terpenes emerge from leaves into atmosphere, p. 45.*

Winter, Ruth A. *A Consumer's Dictionary of Food Additives.* Rev. ed. New York: Crown, 1978. *Acetaldehyde in fruits, p. 18.*

Wogan, G. N. "Naturally Occurring Carcinogens." In *The Physiopathology of Cancer.* Vol 1, *Biology and Biochemistry.* Basel: S. Karger, 1974. *Cholesterol reported carcinogen, carcinogen promoter, p. 98; safrole carcinogenic, p. 95; safrole in oils of ginger, mace, star anise, p. 95.*

Wong, C. S. "Atmospheric Input of Carbon Dioxide from Burning Wood." *Science 200* (1978). *More forest fires caused by lightning than by man, Table 1, p. 197.*

Wood, H. N.; Binns, A. N.; Braun, A. C. "Differential Expressions of Oncogenicity and Nopaline Synthesis in Intact Leaves Derived from Crown Gall Teratomas of Tobacco." *Differentiation 11(3): 175–180; 1978. Cited in Carcinogenesis Abstracts 17* (1979), Abstract 79-0146. *Tobacco gets cancer.*

(WHO) World Health Organization, Geneva; Environmental Health Criteria Series: Environmental Health Criteria 1. *Mercury.* 1976. *Volcanic gases source of mercury in atmosphere, p. 42; quotation, p. 42.*

Environmental Health Criteria 3. *Lead.* 1977. *Air "polluted" by lead from variety of natural sources, volcanic aerosols eject lead, p. 32.*

Environmental Health Criteria 4. *Oxides of Nitrogen, 1977. NO and NO₂ produced by bacteria, lightning, volcanoes, p. 10; natural NO and NO₂ far greater than man-produced, pp. 10–11.*

Environmental Health Criteria 5. *Nitrates, Nitrites, and N-Nitroso Compounds.* Copyright 1978. *Bacterial reduction of nitrate to nitrite in plants, p. 14; in storage of fresh vegetables, p. 36; most N-Nitroso compounds mutagenic, p. 18; NOₓ possible nitrosating agents, p. 19; nitrosamines in tobacco and its products, p. 49.*

(WHO) World Health Organization. *Health Hazards of the Human Environment.* Geneva: World Health Organization. 1972. *Benzo(a)pyrene most studied polynuclear carcinogen, combustion produces benzo(a)pyrene, p. 222; shale oil, p. 220; quotation, p. 222.*

Wyllie, Thomas D., Morehouse, Lawerence G., eds. *Mycotoxic Fungi, Mycotoxins, Mycotoxicoses: An Encyclopedic Handbook.* Vol. 1, *Mycotoxic Fungi and Chemistry of Mycotoxins.* 1977. Vol. 2, *Mycotoxicoses of Domestic and Laboratory Animals, Poultry, and Aquatic Invertebrates and Vertebrates.* 1978. Vol. 3, *Mycotoxicoses of Man and Plants: Mycotoxin Control and Regulatory Aspects.* 1978. New York: Marcel Dekker. *Aflatoxin-contaminated eggs, Vol. 1, p. 195; aflatoxin-contaminated foods, Vol. 1, pp. 190–196; ergot-contaminated grains and pasture grasses, Vol. 1, pp. 84–85; Vol. 2, p. 150; Vol. 3, p. 2.*

Yamazaki, H.; Minami, J.; Ichikawa, T.; Kondo, M. "Analysis of Polycyclic Aromatic Hydrocarbons in Raw and Broiled Fishes." *J Food Hyg Soc Jpn* 18(4): 368–374; 1977. Cited in *Carcinogenesis Abstracts 17* (1979), Abstract 79-0894.

Yang, M. G., Mickelsen, O. "Cycads." In *Toxic Constituents of Plant Foodstuffs,* edited by Irvin E. Liener. New York: Academic, 1969. *Cycads used in foods on most continents, pp. 159–163; cycasin a carcinogen and mutagen, pp. 163–164.*

Yoshida, D.; Matsumoto, T.; Yoshimura, R.; Matsuzaki, T. "Mutagenicity of Amino-α-Carbolines in Pyrolysis Products of Soybean Globulin." *Biochemical and Biophysical Research Communications* 83 (1978). *Protein in shredded tobacco correlates with mutagenicity of cigarette smoke, p. 915.*

Yoshihira, K.; Fukuoka, M.; Kuroyanagi, M.; Natori, S.; Umeda, M.; Moroshi, T.; Enomoto, M.; Saito, M. "Chemical and Toxicological Studies on Bracken Fern, *Pteridium aquilinum Var. Latiusculum.* I. Introduction. "Extraction and Fractionation of Constituents, and Toxicological Studies Including Carcinogenicity Tests." *Chem Pharm Bull* (Tokyo) 26(8): 2346–2364; 1978. Cited in *Carcinogenesis Abstracts 16* (1979), Abstract 78-6717. *Extracts of fronds of bracken fern carcinogenic.*

Yudkin, John. *Sweet and Dangerous.* New York: Wyden, 1972. *Sucrose consumption potentially linked to human cancer, p. 141.*

Appendix C

FACT SHEET: ATLAS OF CANCER MORTALITY FOR U.S. COUNTIES: 1950–1969

U.S. Department of Health, Education, and Welfare
National Institutes of Health
National Cancer Institute
Bethesda, MD 20014

The National Cancer Institute (NCI) has published an *Atlas of Cancer Mortality for U.S. Counties; 1950–1969* showing geographic variation in cancer death rates across the U.S. for 35 anatomic sites of cancer.

NCI scientists believe the *Atlas* provides clues to occupation and other environmental factors that contribute to cancer causation. The *Atlas* can be used to identify communities or areas of the U.S. where additional studies may pinpoint these factors.

Authors of the *Atlas* are Thomas J. Mason, Ph.D., Frank W. McKay, Robert Hoover, M.D., William J. Blot, Ph.D., and Joseph F. Fraumeni, Jr., M.D. of NCI's Epidemiology Branch.

The *Atlas* contains maps of 16 common cancer sites on a county-by-county basis. The other 19 sites, for which fewer deaths occurred during 1950–1969, are mapped by state economic area (SEA). The SEA is a unit defined by the U.S. Bureau of the Census as a single county or group of counties with similar economic and social characteristics. SEAs usually are intermediate in size between counties and states.

The maps are based on average annual cancer death rates (deaths per 100,000 population) computed after tabulation of cancer deaths in the U.S. during 1950–1969. This information, obtained from data provided by HEW's National Center for Health Statistics, is based on death certificates. The rates were computed separately for whites and nonwhites and for males and females. The data were adjusted to correspond to the distribution by age of the U.S. population in 1960. The resulting 729-page volume of cancer death rates was published by NCI in 1974.

The new maps of career mortality show geographic patterns separately for males and females and describe cancer only in whites. The smaller numbers of nonwhites in the U.S. make modification of the mapping technique necessary to assure reliable results. Another mapping study now under way will examine in detail geographic differences in cancer death rates for nonwhites.

The maps are followed by summary tables for each cancer site, listing a percentile ranking of both mortality rates and numbers of deaths. Using these tables, together with the volume of county-by-county tabulations, a reader may assess the relative impact of a particular cancer for any county. Other tables in the *Atlas* list death rates for each cancer site for consecutive five-year age groups.

NCI scientists suggest the chief value of the maps will be to stimulate scientists and other health professionals to conduct studies of intriguing cancer patterns in their own locales. Similar geographic patterns for both males and females for a particular cancer suggest that common environmental factors may contribute to causation; markedly different patterns for the sexes might suggest effects of occupational factors.

For some sites such as melanoma (a rare form of skin cancer), the NCI scientists found predictable geographic patterns. Melanoma deaths occurred predominantly in the southern U.S. In areas of the Southwest bordering Mexico, rates were somewhat lower. Scientists have known for many years that sunlight is a major cause of skin cancer, and that darker-skinned persons are less susceptible.

Cancers of the colon and rectum, believed to be related to diet were found in both sexes at above average rates in the Northeast (New Jersey, southern New York, Connecticut, Rhode Island, Massachusetts) and in urban areas along the Great Lakes (Buffalo, Cleveland, Detroit, Chicago, Milwaukee). Low rates were found in the southern and central parts of the U.S. Surprisingly, breast cancer showed a similar pattern, suggesting that this disease may have an environmental factor in common with cancers of the large intestine.

High rates in the Northeast for cancers of the esophagus, larynx, mouth and throat, and bladder were limited to males, suggesting the influence of occupational factors. In a correlation study, the NCI scientists identified high rates of cancers of the lung, liver and bladder in counties with significant employment in the chemical industry. Additional studies are needed to clarify any occupational risks.

It is nearly certain, the NCI scientists believe, that industrial exposures have produced the striking geographic concentrations of bladder cancer deaths in males in the East.

The NCI scientists also found above-average lung cancer death rates in counties where a significant percentage of the work force is engaged in smelting and refining of copper, lead and zinc ores. Arsenic, a known human cancer-producing agent, is an airborne byproduct of the smelting operation for these ores. Above-average rates were found for females as well as males in these counties, suggesting spread of an occupational risk to the surrounding community.

High mortality rates for lung cancer were found along the Gulf Coast from Texas to the Florida Panhandle. Of Louisiana's 64 counties, 38 are in the highest 10 percent of all U.S. counties ranked for rates of male lung cancer mortality. Thirteen Louisiana counties are in the top one percent, as are an additional seven counties along the Gulf Coast and along the Atlantic Coast from northern Florida to Charleston, South Carolina. This pattern suggests that environmental factors, in addition to cigarette smoking, may be contributing to lung cancer deaths in these predominantly rural and seaport areas.

High rates of stomach cancer were found in the North Central States (the Dakotas, Minnesota, Wisconsin, upper Michigan). NCI scientists believe ethnic factors are responsible for this pattern. The high rates in both sexes correspond closely with the geographic concentration of persons with ancestors from Austria, the Soviet Union, and Scandinavia. Stomach cancer rates in these countries are also higher than the U.S. average.

The NCI scientists noted an unexpected concentration of above-average rates for cancers of the lip and mouth/throat among women in the South. There were no clearly discernible patterns in the U.S. for several forms of cancer, including cancers of the pancreas, brain, salivary gland, nose, and sinuses.

The authors of the mapping study caution that the maps should not be used alone to ascribe cancer mortality to hazards in specific areas. For example, mortality rates in specific areas sometimes may reflect environmental exposures from entirely different parts of the United States due to population movements such as retirement. However, the geographic patterns are compatible with known risk factors for several cancer sites, a fact that gives the scientists confidence in the geography of cancers for which little has been known.

Notes

PREFACE

[1] Ernest Nagel, *The Structure of Science: Problems in the Logic of Scientific Explanation* (New York: Hackett and Harcourt, Brace and World, 1961), pp. 445–446.

[2] Ann Mozley Moyal, "Studies of Science," *Science 200* (1978): 755.

[3] Bernard D. Davis, "Limits in the Regulation of Scientific Research," in *Ethics for Science Policy: Report from a Nobel Symposium,* edited by Torgny Segerstedt (New York: Pergamon, 1978), p. 213.

[4] Philip H. Abelson, "Scientific Communication," *Science 209* (1980): 61–62.

[5] Philip Handler, "Public Doubts About Science," *Science 208* (1980): 1093.

[6] James D. Watson, speaking at the J. M. Foundation and Grantmakers in Health Cancer Forum, "Cancer Research, Current and Future Scientific Prospects," held at Rockefeller University, New York, N.Y., May 27, 1982.

[7] Roy E. Albert, Letter, *Science 219* (1983): 796.

CHAPTER 1

[1] J. O'M. Bockris, "Environmental Chemistry," in *Environmental Chemistry,* edited by J. O'M. Bockris (New York: Plenum Press, 1977), p. 6.

[2] William D. Carey, "A Very Human Business," *Science 199* (1978): 1161.

[3] Irving J. Selikoff, "Perspectives in the Investigation of Health Hazards in the Chemical Industry," Meeting of the Scientific Committee on Occupational Medicine, Milan, December 12, 1975 (Sezione: Medicina del Lavoro, Igiene Ambientale; Comitato Scientifico, Fondazione Carlo Erba), p. 79.

[4] Carl C. Craft, "Cancer-Environment," *Associated Press,* January 13, 1976; Bill Richards, "U.S. Action Urged to Curb Cancer-Causing Agents," *Washington Post,* January 13, 1976, p. A-2.

[5] Ibid.

[6] Russell Train, in a speech to the National Press Club, February 26, 1976, in Washington, D.C., quoted in *Environmental News,* U.S. Environmental Protection Agency, February 26, 1976; incorporated into Toxic Substances Control Act, P.L. 94–469, Senate Report No. 94–698, Legislative History, March 16, 1976.

[7] Thomas H. Corbett, M.D., *Cancer and Chemicals* (Chicago: Nelson-Hall, 1977), introductory essay by Corbett inside cover, and p. 12.

[8] John Cairns, *Cancer: Science and Society* (San Francisco: Freeman, 1978), p. 164.

[9] Samuel S. Epstein, M.D., *The Politics of Cancer* (San Francisco: Sierra Club Books, 1978), p. 21; Corbett, *Cancer and Chemicals,* p. x.

[10] Dr. Elizabeth Whelan, *Preventing Cancer* (New York: Norton, 1977), pp. 38–39.

[11] Philip M. Boffey, *The Brain Bank of America: An Inquiry Into the Politics of Science* (New York: McGraw-Hill, 1975), p. xii.

[12] Philip Handler, interviewed in "The Enemies of Growth," *In Search of the Real America,* produced for PBS by WGBH-TV, Boston, Mass., June 1, 1978; *transcript.*

[13] David L. Sills, "The Environmental Debate," prepared for delivery before the American Association for the Advancement of Science, in Washington, D.C., February 13, 1978; *manuscript,* pp. 1–2.

[14] Paul R. Ehrlich, Anne H. Ehrlich, and John P. Holdren, *Ecoscience: Population, Resources, Environment* (San Francisco: Freeman, 1977), pp. 819–820.

[15] Robert Cameron Mitchell, "Silent Spring/Solid Majorities," *Public Opinion,* August/September 1979. The article was adapted from two reports written by the author which appeared earlier in the *Resources for the Future* newsletter, *Resources.* Mitchell reported that polls show continued strong public support for environmental protection.

[16] Margaret Mead, a passage from a book review on the cover of the paperback edition of Rachel Carson, *Silent Spring* (Greenwich, Conn.: Fawcett, 1962).

[17] Barry Commoner, *Science and Survival* (New York: Viking Press, 1963), reprinted under the title "To Survive on the Earth." in *The Ecological Conscience: Values for Survival,* edited by Robert Disch (Englewood Cliffs, N.J.: Prentice-Hall, 1970), pp. 118–119.

[18] Lynn White, Jr., "The Historical Roots of Our Ecologic Crisis," *Science 155* (1967): 1204, 1206.

[19] Don K. Price, "Purists and Politicians," *Science 163* (1969): 31.

[20] Alan W. Watts, "The Individual as Man/World," in *The Subversive Science: Essays Toward an Ecology of Man,* edited by Paul Shepard, Daniel McKinley (Boston: Houghton Mifflin, 1969), p. 142.

[21] Lewis Mumford, *The Pentagon of Power: The Myth of the Machine* (New York: Harcourt Brace Jovanovich, Inc., 1970), p. 413.

[22] Robert Disch, in *The Ecological Conscience,* pp. xiii–xiv.

[23] Ralph Nader, Introduction, *Ecotactics: The Sierra Club Handbook for Environmental Activists,* edited by John G. Mitchell and Constance L. Stallings (New York: Simon and Schuster, 1970), p. 13.

[24] Senator Gaylord Nelson, quoted by Tony Wagner, "The Ecology of Revolution," in *Ecotactics,* p. 43.

[25] Murray Bookchin, "Toward an Ecological Solution," *Ramparts,* May 1970, pp. 10, 14.

[26] G. Evelyn Hutchinson, "The Biosphere," *Scientific American 223* (1970): 53.

[27] Lee Loevinger, quoted in Melvin J. Grayson, Thomas R. Shepard, Jr., *The Disaster Lobby: Prophets of Ecological Doom and Other Absurdities* (Chicago: Follett, 1973), pp. 133–134.

[28] Michael McCloskey, Foreword in *Ecotactics,* p. 11.

[29] William O. Douglas, *The Three Hundred Year War: A Chronicle of Ecological Disaster* (New York: Random House and Alfred A. Knopf, 1972), p. 225.

[30] Charles E. Lindblom, *Politics and Markets: The World's Political-Economic Systems* (New York: Basic Books, 1977), p. 3.

[31] Albert Szent-Györgyi, "Snakes Do It. So Must Man," *New York Times,* March 29, 1975, Op Ed page.

[32] P. B. Medawar, J. S. Medawar, *The Life Science: Current Ideas of Biology* (New York: Harper and Row, 1977), p. 173.

[33] Albert Schweitzer, quoted on frontispiece of Rachel Carson, *Silent Spring* (Greenwich, Conn.: Fawcett, 1962).

[34] Carson, *Silent Spring,* pp. 13–15.

[35] Ibid., pp. 157, 158, 160.

[36] Ibid., pp. 164–165.

[37] Ibid., pp. 16–17.

[38] Ibid., p. 24.

[39] Ibid., p. 30.

[40] Ibid., pp. 157–165.

[41] Ibid., p. 167.

[42] Ibid., p. 22.

[43] Ibid., p. 19.

[44] Ibid., p. 261.

[45] Ibid., pp. 168–169.

[46] Dr. Paul R. Ehrlich, *The Population Bomb* (New York: Ballantine, 1968), pp. 21, 44.

[47] Ibid., pp. 18–19.

[48] Ibid., p. 38.

[49] Ibid., pp. 37–38.

[50] Ibid., pp. 48, 47, 51, 60–62.

[51] Ibid., pp. 66–67.

[52] Ibid., pp. 166–167.

[53] Ibid., pp. 138, 135, 136, 137.

[54] Ibid., p. 131.

[55] Ibid., pp. 158–161.

[56] Ibid., pp. 170–171.

[57] Ehrlich, Ehrlich, and Holdren, *Ecoscience*, pp. 846, 850.

[58] Paul R. and Anne H. Ehrlich, article in *Stanford Magazine*, quoted in "Notable and Quotable," *Wall Street Journal*, July 24, 1978.

[59] Paul R. Ehrlich, quoted in Fred Warshofsky, *Doomsday: The Science of Catastrophe* (New York: Reader's Digest, 1977), p. 229.

[60] "To Establish a Select Senate Committee on Technology and the Human Environment," Hearings before the Subcommittee on Intergovernmental Relations of the Committee on Government Operations, United States Senate, Ninety-first Congress, First Session, March 4, 5, and 6, April 24, and May 7, 1969. Commoner, pp. 222–250; Ferry, pp. 250–261.

[61] Background paper prepared for the 13th National Conference of the U.S. National Commission for UNESCO, 1969. It also appeared, under the title "The Ecological Facts of Life," in *The Ecological Conscience*, p. 16.

[62] Barry Commoner, *The Poverty of Power: Energy and the Economic Crisis* (New York: Alfred A. Knopf, 1976), p. 262.

[63] Rae Goodell, *The Visible Scientists* (Boston: Little, Brown, 1977), especially pp. 60–69.

[64] René Dubos, *Man Adapting* (New Haven: Yale University Press, 1965), pp. 366–367. Dubos' own summary of his thesis in *Man Adapting* appears in his book *Of Human Diversity* (Worcester, Mass.: Clark University Press with Barre Publishers, 1974), p. 58.

[65] René Dubos, "The Limits of Adaptability," in *The Environmental Handbook*, Garrett DeBell, comp. (New York: Ballantine, 1970), p. 28.

[66] René Dubos, quoted in Ehrlich et al., *Ecoscience*, p. 805.

[67] René Dubos, "A Theology of the Earth," *Audubon*, July 1972, p. 34.

[68] René Dubos, *A God Within* (New York: Scribner's, 1972), pp. 40–41.

[69] Ibid., p. 266.

[70] Ibid., p. 289.

[71] Maurice Strong, Preface to Barbara Ward and René Dubos, *Only One Earth: The Care and Maintenance of a Small Planet* (New York: Norton, 1972), p. vii.

[72] Ward and Dubos, *Only One Earth*, p. 11.

[73] Ibid., pp. 40–43.

[74] Ibid., p. 44.

[75] Ibid., p. 45.

[76] Ibid.

[77] Ibid., p. 28.

[78] Ibid., pp. 92–93.

[79] Ibid., p. 20.

[80] Ibid., pp. 142–143.

[81] Foreword by William Watts, President of Potomac Associates, publisher of Donella H. Meadows, Dennis L. Meadows, Jørgen Randers, William W. Behrens III, *The Limits to Growth: A Report for the Club of Rome's Project on the Predicament of Mankind* (New York: A Potomac Associates Book, New American Library, 1974), pp. ix–x.

[82] Meadows et al., *The Limits to Growth*, p. 29.

[83] Ibid., pp. 194–195.

[84] "Club of Rome Revisited," *Time*, April 26, 1976, p. 56.

[85] Charles Horner, "Redistributing Technology," *Commentary*, January 1979, p. 52. Charles Horner was senior legislative assistant to Senator Daniel P. Moynihan.

[86] George Wald, "There Isn't Much Time," *Progressive*, December 1975, pp. 22–23.

[87] Ibid., p. 24.

[88] Ibid.

[89] Ibid.

[90] *Man's Impact on the Global Environment: Assessment and Recommendations for Action*, Report of the Study of Critical Environmental Problems (SCEP), sponsored by the Massachusetts Institute of Technology (Cambridge, Mass.: MIT Press, 1970), pp. xi–xii, xiv.

[91] Ibid., pp. 6–7.

[92] Ibid., p. 47.

[93] Ibid., p. 13.
[94] Ibid., p. 15.
[95] Ibid., pp. 15–16.
[96] Ibid., p. 18.
[97] Ibid., p. 19.
[98] Ibid., p. 27.
[99] Ibid., p. 117.
[100] Ibid., pp. 168–170.
[101] Ibid., pp. 17, 136.
[102] Ibid., p. 11.
[103] Ehrlich, Ehrlich, and Holdren, *Ecoscience*, p. 731.
[104] Norman Macrae, quoted in *The Disaster Lobby*, p. 135.
[105] Gunnar Myrdal, "Economics of an Improved Environment," in *Who Speaks for Earth?*, based on the series of distinguished lectures sponsored by International Institute for Environmental Affairs in cooperation with Population Institute held in Stockholm concurrently with the United Nations Conference on the Human Environment, June 1972, edited by Maurice F. Strong (New York: Norton, 1973), pp. 70–71, 76.
[106] *Models of Doom*, edited by H. Cole, C. Freeman, M. Jahoda, K. Pravitt (New York: Universe Books, 1973), cited in *Ecoscience*, p. 733.
[107] M. Mesarovic and E. Pestel, "Mankind at the Turning Point: The Second Report to the Club of Rome," 1974, cited in *Ecoscience*, p. 733.
[108] Lord Zuckerman, "Science, Technology, and Environmental Management," in *Who Speaks for Earth?*, pp. 138–139.
[109] Ward and Dubos, *Only One Earth*, p. xi.
[110] Ibid., p. 202.
[111] Ibid., p. 193.
[112] Ibid., p. 194.
[113] Ibid., p. xiv.
[114] Ibid.
[115] Ibid., p. 86.
[116] Ibid., pp. xiv, xvi.
[117] Ibid., p. xii.
[118] Ibid., p. 213.
[119] Barbara Ward, "Only One Earth: Speech for Stockholm," in *Who Speaks for Earth?*, pp. 23–24.
[120] René Dubos, quoted by Gunnar Myrdal, "Economics of an Improved Environment," in *Who Speaks for Earth?*, pp. 70–71.
[121] Dubos, *A God Within*, p. 288.
[122] Ibid., p. 289.
[123] Ehrlich, Ehrlich, and Holdren, *Ecoscience*, p. 170.
[124] Ernest Nagel, *The Structure of Science: Problems in the Logic of Scientific Explanation* (New York: Hackett and Harcourt, Brace and World, 1961), pp. 445–446.
[125] Loren Eiseley, *The Star Thrower* (New York: Times Books, 1978). According to Eiseley, Charles Darwin speculated that "animals, our fellow brethren in pain, disease, suffering and famine—our slaves in the most laborious works, our companions in our amusements—they may partake of our origin in one common ancestor—we may be all netted together." Eiseley, citing Darwin, elaborated: "we may be all netted together in one gigantic mode of experience . . . we are in a mystic sense one single diffuse animal. . . ." (p. 187).
[126] Dr. James Lovelock, F.R.S., Dr. Sidney Epton, "The Quest for Gaia," *New Scientist* 65 (1975). Lovelock hypothesized that "living matter, the air, the oceans, the land surface were parts of a giant system which was able to control temperature, the composition of the air and sea, the pH of the soil and so on so as to be optimum for survival of the biosphere. The system seemed to exhibit the behaviour of a single organism, even a living creature. One having such formidable powers deserved a name to match it; William Golding, the novelist, suggested Gaia—the name given by the ancient Greeks to their Earth goddess." (p. 304).
[127] Eric Ashby, *Reconciling Man with the Environment* (Stanford, Calif.: Stanford University Press, 1978), pp. 82, 84, 86, 87.
[128] Ibid., pp. 82–83.
[129] Ibid., p. 85.

[130] Ibid., p. 83.

[131] Ibid.

[132] Ibid., p. 13.

[133] James E. Krier and Edmund Ursin, *Pollution and Policy: A Case Essay on California and Federal Experience with Motor Vehicle Air Pollution 1940–1975* (Berkeley, Calif.: University of California Press, 1977), pp. 299–300.

[134] Ward, "Only One Earth: Speech for Stockholm," in *Who Speaks for Earth?*, pp. 21–22.

[135] John Denver, *Rocky Mountain Suite* (*Cold Nights in Canada*), Cherry Lane Music Co., 1973.

[136] Daniel Patrick Moynihan, "United States in Opposition," in *The First World and the Third World: Essays on the New International Economic Order*, edited by Karl Brunner (Rochester, N.Y.: University of Rochester Policy Center Publications, 1978), pp. 119, 131.

[137] Paul Johnson, *Enemies of Society* (New York: Atheneum, 1977), p. 88.

[138] Charles Frankel, "Sociobiology and Its Critics," *Commentary*, July 1979, p. 39.

[139] Charles Kadushin, "Who Are the Elite Intellectuals?," *Public Interest*, Fall 1972, p. 114; also see footnote, p. 117.

[140] Edward O. Wilson, *On Human Nature* (Cambridge, Mass.: Harvard University Press, 1978), p. 203.

[141] Occupational Safety and Health Act of 1970, P.L. 91–596, Senate Report No. 91–1282, "Legislative History, Background," p. 5178.

[142] Clean Air Act as Amended, 1977, P.L. 95–95, Part A Section 101, Part B Section 151.

[143] Toxic Substances Control Act of 1976, P.L. 94–469, Section 2(a), Section 3(5).

[144] Endangered Species Act of 1973, P.L. 93–205, Section 2.

[145] This tally has never been made before. In order to arrive at estimated figures, I had to collect and read all the press releases of the EPA, FDA, CPSC, and OSHA from 1967, or from the date of the founding of the agency, to 1977.

[146] U.S. Department of Health, Education and Welfare, *HEW News*, April 8, 1970.

[147] U.S. Environmental Protection Agency, "EPA Reports Seizure of Two Pesticide Products," *Environmental News*, February 13, 1972.

CHAPTER 2

[1] Samuel S. Epstein, M.D., "Cancer and the Environment," *Bulletin of the Atomic Scientists*, March 1977, p. 22.

[2] Lewis Thomas, *The Medusa and the Snail: More Notes of a Biology Watcher* (New York: Viking Press, 1979), p. 48.

[3] TELEVISION

CBS Reports: "The American Way of Death," October 15, 1975.

CBS News: "Face the Nation," Guest: Russell E. Train, Administrator, Environmental Protection Agency, April 18, 1976.

CBS Reports Special: "The Politics of Cancer," June 22, 1976.

NBC News: "What Is This Thing Called Food?," September 8, 1976.

MAGAZINES

Samuel S. Epstein, M.D., "Cancer and the Environment," *Bulletin of the Atomic Scientists*, March 1977.

"The Chemicals Around Us," *Newsweek*, August 21, 1978.

BOOKS

Larry Agran, *The Cancer Connection: And What We Can Do About It* (New York: St. Martin's, 1977).

John Cairns, *Cancer: Science and Society* (San Francisco: Freeman, 1978).

Thomas H. Corbett, M.D., *Cancer and Chemicals* (Chicago: Nelson-Hall, 1977).

Samuel S. Epstein, M.D., *The Politics of Cancer* (San Francisco: Sierra Club Books, 1978).

Samuel S. Epstein, M.D., *The Politics of Cancer*, rev. ed. (Garden City, N.Y.: Anchor Press/Doubleday, 1979).

CONFERENCE FOR LAYMEN

Environmental Cancer: Causes, Victims, Solutions, A Summary of Proceedings of a Conference held March 21 and 22, 1977, sponsored by the Urban Environment Conference, Inc., and primarily funded by the National Cancer Institute, as well as the National Institute for Environmental Health Sciences and the Environmental Protection Agency (Washington, D.C.: Urban Environment Conference, Inc., 1978).

[4] Dan Rather, "The American Way of Death," CBS, 1975, *transcript*.

[5] James Bishop, Jr., panelist on "Face the Nation," CBS, 1976, *transcript*.

[6] Agran, *The Cancer Connection*, p. xv.

[7] "The Chemicals Around Us," *Newsweek*, August 21, 1978, p. 25.

[8] Anthony Mazzocchi in "The Politics of Cancer," CBS, 1976, *transcript*.

[9] Rather, "The American Way of Death," CBS, 1975, *transcript*.

[10] Lesley Stahl, "The Politics of Cancer," CBS, 1976, *transcript*.

[11] Betty Furness, "What Is This Thing Called Food?," NBC, 1976, *transcript*.

[12] Agran, *The Cancer Connection*, p. xvi.

[13] Corbett, *Cancer and Chemicals*, Corbett's essay on inside cover, and p. 7.

[14] Barry Commoner, "The Carcinogen Problem," Urban Environment Conference, pp. 35, 37, 38.

[15] Samuel Epstein, M.D., "Proposed Scientific and Societal Response," Urban Environment Conference, pp. 21-22.

[16] Corbett, *Cancer and Chemicals*, p. x.

[17] Douglas Costle, quoted in "The Chemicals Around Us," *Newsweek*, August 21, 1978, p. 28.

[18] Epstein, *The Politics of Cancer* (1978), p. 21.

[19] Agran, *The Cancer Connection*, back cover.

[20] Miles Lord quoted on back cover of Corbett, *Cancer and Chemicals*.

[21] Miles Lord, "Political Issues," Urban Environment Conference, pp. 33, 34.

[22] George Wald, Nobel Laureate, Harvard University: "A superb book on a subject of vital public and medical concern." On front cover of Samuel Epstein, *The Politics of Cancer* (revised, 1979).

[23] Corbett, *Cancer and Chemicals*, pp. x, 15.

[24] Douglas Costle, quoted in "The Chemicals Around Us," *Newsweek*, August 21, 1978, p. 26.

[25] Epstein, *The Politics of Cancer* (1978), p. 24.

[26] Marvin Legator, "What Is This Thing Called Food?," NBC, 1976, *transcript*.

[27] David Rall, "Extrapolating Animal and Microbiological Tests to Humans," Urban Environment Conference, p. 9.

[28] Russell Train, "Face the Nation," CBS, 1976, *transcript*.

[29] David Rall in "The Politics of Cancer," CBS, 1976, *transcript*.

[30] Rall, "Extrapolating Animal and Microbiological Tests to Humans," Urban Environment Conference, pp. 8-9.

[31] Marvin Schneiderman in "The American Way of Death," CBS, 1975, *transcript*.

[32] ". . . scientists at the National Cancer Institute . . ." to Lesley Stahl, "The Politics of Cancer," CBS, 1976, *transcript*.

[33] Marvin Schneiderman, Ph.D., "Extrapolating Animal and Microbiological Tests to Humans," Urban Environment Conference, p. 10.

[34] Eula Bingham, Ph.D., "Regulatory Issues," Urban Environment Conference, p. 31.

CHAPTER 3

[1] Umberto Saffiotti, "Risk-Benefit Considerations in Public Policy on Environmental Carcinogenesis," Proceedings of the Eleventh Canadian Cancer Research Conference, sponsored by the National Cancer Institute of Canada in affiliation with the Canadian Cancer Society, Toronto, Ontario, May 6-8, 1976, p. 135.

[2] "The Chemicals Around Us," *Newsweek*, August 21, 1978, p. 26.

[3] Samuel S. Epstein, M.D., *The Politics of Cancer* (San Francisco: Sierra Club Books, 1978), p. 24.

[4] Jacqueline Verrett and Jean Carper, *Eating May Be Hazardous to Your Health* (Garden City, N.Y.: Anchor/Doubleday, 1975), p. 101.

[5] Ibid., pp. 2-3, 101.

[6] Umberto Saffiotti, "Risk-Benefit Considerations in Public Policy on Environmental Carcinogenesis," Proceedings of the Eleventh Canadian Cancer Research Conference. See

footnote 1, in which Saffiotti identifies J. Sontag, N. Page, and himself as authors of *Guidelines for Carcinogenesis Bioassay in Small Rodents,* National Cancer Institute Carcinogenesis Technical Report Series No. 1, 1976.

[7] Epstein, *The Politics of Cancer* (1978), pp. 254, 267–268.

[8] Saffiotti, "Risk-Benefit Considerations in Public Policy on Environmental Carcinogenesis," *Proceedings of the Eleventh Canadian Cancer Research Conference,* pp. 13–14.

[9] Larry Agran, *The Cancer Connection: And What We Can Do About It* (New York: St. Martin's, 1977), p. 195.

[10] Bil Gilbert, "All in Favor of Cancer, Say 'Aye,' " *Audubon,* March 1979, p. 60.

[11] Saffiotti, "Risk-Benefit Considerations in Public Policy on Environmental Carcinogenesis," *Proceedings of the Eleventh Canadian Cancer Research Conference,* pp. 15–16.

[12] David P. Rall, "Researching Health Hazards in the Environment," *American Water Works Association Journal 67* (1975): 447.

[13] Saffiotti, "Risk-Benefit Considerations in Public Policy on Environmental Carcinogenesis," *Proceedings of the Eleventh Canadian Cancer Research Conference,* p. 21.

[14] CBS Reports Special, "The Politics of Cancer," June 22, 1976, *transcript.*

[15] "The Chemicals Around Us," *Newsweek,* p. 26.

[16] Umberto Saffiotti, "The Laboratory Approach to the Identification of Environmental Carcinogens," in *Proceedings of the Ninth Canadian Cancer Research Conference 1971,* edited by P. G. Scholefield (University of Toronto Press, 1972), pp. 23–26; cited in *Federal Register 42:192* (October 4, 1977): 54152.

[17] Office of Science and Technology Policy, Executive Office of the President, *Identification, Characterization, and Control of Potential Human Carcinogens. A Framework for Federal Decision-Making,* February 1, 1979, p. 8. (This staff report, an adaptation of the formal document, was prepared for publication in the *Journal of the National Cancer Institute 64* 1980, and was signed by D. R. Calkins, R. L. Dixon, C. R. Gerber, G. S. Omenn and D. Zarin.)

[18] Ibid., p. 9.

[19] (NAS) Committee on Biologic Effects of Atmospheric Pollutants, *Particulate Polycyclic Organic Matter* (Washington, D.C.: National Academy of Sciences, 1972), p. 91.

[20] Umberto Saffioti, "Comments on the Scientific Basis for the 'Delaney Clause,' " *Preventive Medicine 2* (1973): 127.

[21] Ibid., pp. 127–128.

[22] R. E. Albert and F. J. Burns, "Carcinogenic Atmospheric Pollutants and the Nature of Low-level Risks," in *Origins of Human Cancer,* edited by H. H. Hiatt, J. D. Watson, J. A. Winsten, Book A, *Incidence of Cancer in Humans* (New York: Cold Spring Harbor Laboratory, 1977), pp. 289, 291, 292.

[23] Epstein, *The Politics of Cancer* (1978), pp. 60–61.

[24] Verrett and Carper, *Eating May Be Hazardous to Your Health,* pp. 148–149.

[25] Arthur M. Langer and Mary S. Wolff, "Asbestos Carcinogenesis," *Inorganic and Nutritional Aspects of Cancer,* edited by G. N. Schrauzer (New York: Plenum, 1978), p. 29.

[26] General Accounting Office, Report by the Comptroller General of the United States, *Does Nitrite Cause Cancer? Concerns About Validity of FDA-Sponsored Study Delay Answer,* January 31, 1980, p. 29.

[27] Report to the Surgeon General, USPHS, April 22, 1970, Ad Hoc Committee on the Evaluation of Low Levels of Environmental Chemical Carcinogens, National Cancer Institute, *Evaluation of Environmental Carcinogens.* Exhibit 10 in "Chemicals and the Future of Man," Hearings before the Subcommittee on Executive Reorganization and Government Research of the Committee on Government Operations, United States Senate, Ninety-second Congress, First Session, April 6 and 7, 1971, p. 181. According to Samuel Epstein, who reproduced this report in Appendix II of *The Politics of Cancer* (1978, p. 475), it was also published in "Federal Environmental Pesticide Control Act," Hearings before the Subcommittee on Agricultural Research and General Legislation of the Committee on Agriculture and Forestry, United States Senate, March 23–26, 1971.

[28] Saffiotti, "Comments on the Scientific Basis for the 'Delaney Clause,' " p. 130.

[29] Report to the Surgeon General, USPHS, April 22, 1970, Ad Hoc Committee on the Evaluation of Low Levels of Environmental Chemical Carcinogens, Exhibit 10 in "Chemicals and the Future of Man," Hearings, United States Senate, p. 180.

[30] Verrett and Carper, *Eating May Be Hazardous to Your Health,* pp. 50–51.

[31] Office of Science and Technology Policy, *Identification, Characterization, and Control*

of Potential Human Carcinogens: A Framework for Federal Decision-Making, adapted by Calkins et al., p. 9.

[32] General Accounting Office, Report by the Comptroller General of the United States, *Does Nitrite Cause Cancer? Concerns About Validity of FDA-Sponsored Study Delay Answer,* p. 72.

[33] Barry Commoner, "Hiroshima at Home," *Hospital Practice,* April 1978, p. 63.

[34] Samuel S. Epstein, M.D., *The Politics of Cancer,* rev. ed. (Garden City, N.Y.: Anchor/Doubleday, 1979), p. 510.

[35] Irving Selikoff, quoted in Gilbert, "All in Favor of Cancer, Say 'Aye,' " p. 59.

CHAPTER 4

[1] Barry Commoner, *The Closing Circle: Nature, Man and Technology* (New York: Bantam, 1972), p. 37.

[2] Wilhelm Hueper, cited in Rachel Carson, *Silent Spring* (Greenwich, Conn.: Fawcett, 1962), pp. 213–215; Hueper checks Carson manuscript; see: Frank Graham, Jr., *Since Silent Spring* (Boston: Houghton Mifflin, 1970), p. 33.

[3] Carson, *Silent Spring,* p. 195.

[4] Ibid., p. 17.

[5] Ibid., p. 195.

[6] Ibid., p. 16.

[7] Ibid., p. 17.

[8] Ibid., p. 213.

[9] Ibid., pp. 162–167.

[10] Ibid., p. 17.

[11] Ibid., pp. 27–28.

[12] Ibid., pp. 71–72.

[13] Ibid., p. 71.

[14] Ibid., pp. 213–215.

[15] Ibid., p. 215

[16] Ibid., pp. 213, 216.

[17] Commoner, *The Closing Circle,* p. 37.

[18] Ibid., p. 39.

[19] Ibid., p. 40.

[20] Ibid.

[21] Ibid., pp. 138–144.

[22] Barry Commoner, *The Poverty of Power: Energy and the Economic Crisis* (New York: Alfred A. Knopf, 1976), pp. 262–263.

[23] Barry Commoner, "The Carcinogen Problem," *Environmental Cancer: Causes, Victims, Solutions,* a summary of Proceedings of a Conference held March 21 and 22, 1977, sponsored by the Urban Environment Conference, Inc., and primarily funded by the National Cancer Institute, as well as the National Institute for Environmental Health Sciences and the Environmental Protection Agency (Washington, D.C.: Urban Environment Conference, Inc., 1978), pp. 36–38.

[24] In *Since Silent Spring,* Frank Graham, Jr., provided a detailed review of the controversies that followed the publication of *Silent Spring.* None pertained to its major premise— the "axiom" of nature's noncarcinogenicity.

[25] John R. Quarles, Jr., Testimony, "Toxic Substances Control Act," Hearings before the Subcommittee on Consumer Protection and Finance of the Committee on Interstate and Foreign Commerce, House of Representatives, Ninety-fourth Congress, First Session, on H.R. 7229, H.R. 7548, and H.R. 7664, June 16, July 9, 10, and 11, 1975, Serial No. 94-41, p. 213.

[26] "From Microbes to Men: The New Toxic Substances Control Act and Bacterial Mutagenicity/Carcinogenicity Tests," *Environmental Law Reporter* 6 (1976): 10251–10252.

[27] *Point of View:* "DDT and the Limits of Toxicology," a portion of the testimony of Samuel S. Epstein, who appeared on behalf of the Environmental Defense Fund at the Environmental Protection Agency Hearing on DDT, *Science 175* (1972): 610; Charles F. Wurster, "DDT Proved Neither Essential Nor Safe," *BioScience 23* (1973): 106; William D. Ruckelshaus, *Consolidated DDT Hearings: Opinion and Order of the Administrator,* Environ-

mental Protection Agency, *Federal Register 37:131* (July 7, 1972): 13369–13371, especially p. 13371.

[28] William D. Ruckelshaus, *Consolidated DDT Hearings; Opinion and Order of the Administrator*, Environmental Protection Agency, p. 13371.

[29] Ralph Nader, cited in Thomas C. Hunter, *Beginnings* (New York: T. Y. Crowell, 1978), pp. 187–188.

[30] Natural Resources Defense Council, Inc., "Cancer: The Price of Technological Advancement?" *NRDC Newsletter 5(2)* (Summer 1976), cited by Merril Eisenbud, *Environment, Technology, and Health: Human Ecology in Historical Perspective* (New York: New York University Press, 1978), p. 187.

[31] Lawrence Fishbein, "Environmental Metallic Carcinogens: An Overview of Exposure Levels," *Journal of Toxicology and Environmental Health 2* (1976): 77.

[32] Norton Nelson, Director, Institute of Environmental Medicine, New York University Medical Center, "Introduction," *Research in Environmental Health Sciences,* Fourteenth Annual Report of Progress to the National Institute for Environmental Health Sciences Center under NIEHS Grant ES00260, December 31, 1977, p. 1.

[33] Gene Lyons, "Politics in the Woods," *Harper's,* July 1978, p. 27.

[34] Thomas H. Corbett, M.D., "Naturally Occurring Carcinogens," Chapter 8, *Cancer and Chemicals* (Chicago: Nelson-Hall, 1977), pp. 103–107.

[35] Samuel S. Epstein, M.D., *The Politics of Cancer,* rev. ed. (Garden City, N.Y.: Anchor/Doubleday, 1979), pp. 18–20, 486–487, 522–525.

[36] Ibid., p. 18.

[37] Larry Agran, *The Cancer Connection* (New York: St. Martin's, 1977), p. xiv.

[38] Ibid., p. xv.

[39] Minako Nagao, Takashi Sugimura, and Taijiro Matsushima, "Environmental Mutagens and Carcinogens," *Annual Review of Genetics 12* (1978): 118.

[40] Marvin Schneiderman, quoted by Judith Randal, "This Rat Died in a Cancer Lab to Save Lives," reprint from *Washington Post* "Outlook," July 22, 1979, circulated by the United States Environmental Protection Agency, OPA 15/80, January 1980. My copy unpaginated; see paragraph 4 of article.

[41] R. Jeffrey Smith, "Toxic Substances: EPA and OSHA Are Reluctant Regulators," *Science 203* (1979): 28.

[42] Randal, "This Rat Died in a Cancer Lab to Save Lives." My copy unpaginated; see paragraphs 2 and 3.

[43] H. F. Kraybill and Myron A. Mehlman, Preface to *Advances in Modern Toxicology,* edited by Myron A. Mehlman, Vol. 3, *Environmental Cancer,* edited by H. F. Kraybill, Myron A. Mehlman (Washington: Hemisphere, 1977), p. xi.

[44] Ibid.

[45] (NAS) Panel on Low Molecular Weight Halogenated Hydrocarbons of the Coordinating Committee for Scientific and Technical Assessments of Environmental Pollutants, *Chloroform, Carbon Tetrachloride, and Other Halomethanes: An Environmental Assessment* (Washington, D.C.: National Academy of Sciences, 1978), pp. 97, 117–119.

[46] Ibid., p. 6; James Lovelock and Sidney Epton, "The Quest for Gaia," *New Scientist 65* (1975): 305; J. E. Lovelock, R. J. Maggs, and R. J. Wade, "Halogenated Hydrocarbons in and over the Atlantic," *Nature 24* (1973): 195.

[47] A. M. Pamukcu, "Bracken Fern (BF). A Natural Urinary Bladder Carcinogen," *Naturally Occurring Carcinogens—Mutagens and Modulators of Carcinogenesis,* Ninth International Symposium of the Princess Takamatsu Cancer Research Fund, Tokyo, Japan, January 23–25, 1979, Abstract, pp. 22, 23.

[48] George Claus and Karen Bolander, *Ecological Sanity* (New York: McKay, 1977), p. 511; William Tucker, "Of Mites and Men," *Harper's,* August 1978, p. 54.

[49] Tom Friberg, Department of Civil Engineering, Air and Water Resources, University of Washington, "Naturally Occurring Volatile Hydrocarbons in the Atmosphere," May 23, 1972, *manuscript,* my copy unpaginated; Reinhold A. Rasmussen, "Isoprene: Identified as a Forest-Type Emission to the Atmosphere," *Environmental Science and Technology 4* (1970): 667; F. W. Went, "Organic Matter in the Atmosphere, and Its Possible Relation to Petroleum Formation," *Proceedings of the National Academy of Science 46* (1960): 213.

[50] E. K. Weisburger (National Cancer Institute), "Carcinogenic Natural Products," in *Structural Correlates of Carcinogenesis and Mutagenesis. A Guide to Testing Priorities?,* Pro-

ceedings of the Second Food and Drug Administration Office of Science Summer Symposium held in Annapolis, August 31–September 2, 1977, Office of Science, FDA (Annapolis, MD), HEW Publication No. (FDA) 78-1046: 241 pp. 184–192; 1978, cited in *Carcinogenesis Abstracts: A Monthly Publication Sponsored by the National Cancer Institute 17,* edited by G. P. Studzinski, J. J. Saukkonen; NCI Staff Consultants, E. Weisburger, J. W. Chase (Philadelphia, Pennsylvania: Franklin Research Center, 1979), Abstract 79-0045.

[51] Samuel I. Shibko, "Toxicology of Phthalic Acid Ester," in *Environmental Quality and Food Supply,* edited by Philip L. White, Diane Robbins (Mount Kisco, New York: Futura, 1974), p. 207; Paul R. Graham, "Phthalates: A Story in the Making," in *Environmental Quality and Food Supply,* pp. 204–205.

[52] Irving Selikoff, cited in Bil Gilbert, "All in Favor of Cancer Say 'Aye,' " *Audubon,* March 1979, p. 59.

CHAPTER 5

[1] Frederick F. Becker, "Keynote Address: Evolution, Chemical Carcinogenesis, and Mortality: The Cycle of Life," in *Carcinogens: Identification and Mechanisms of Action,* edited by A. Clark Griffin, Charles R. Shaw (New York: Raven, 1979), p. 5.

[2] Lewis Thomas, *The Lives of a Cell: Notes of a Biology Watcher* (New York: Bantam, 1975), p. 119.

[3] Gary Flamm, Lecture, *Seminar on Government Regulation of Cancer-Causing Chemicals,* sponsored by the National Center for Administrative Justice, Washington, D.C., December 7–8, 1978.

[4] Umberto Saffiotti, "Carcinogenesis, 1957–77: Notes for a Historical Review," *Journal of the National Cancer Institute 59:2* (Supplement) (1977): 618; P. N. Magee, "Metabolic Activation," Proceedings of the Eleventh Canadian Cancer Research Conference, sponsored by the National Cancer Institute of Canada in affiliation with the Canadian Cancer Society, Toronto, Ontario, May 6–8, 1976, p. 135; P. N. Magee, "Extrapolation of Cellular and Molecular Level Studies to the Human Situation," *Journal of Toxicology and Environmental Health 2* (1977): 1418.

[5] Elizabeth C. Miller and James A. Miller, "Biochemical Mechanisms of Chemical Carcinogenesis," in *The Molecular Biology of Cancer,* edited by Harris Busch (New York: Academic, 1974), pp. 382–383.

[6] Ibid., p. 382.

[7] Ibid., p. 391.

[8] Norbert P. Page, "Concepts of a Bioassay Program in Environmental Carcinogenesis," in *Advances in Modern Toxicology,* edited by Myron A. Mehlman, Vol. 3, *Environmental Cancer,* edited by H. F. Kraybill, Myron A. Mehlman (Washington: Hemisphere, 1977), p. 117.

[9] Stephen L. DeFelice, M.D., *Drug Discovery: The Pending Crisis* (New York: Medcom Learning Systems, 1972), p. 49.

[10] Knut Schmidt-Nielsen, "Energy Metabolism, Body Size, and Problems of Scaling," *Federation Proceedings 29* (1970): 1524.

[11] David P. Rall, "Problems of Low Doses of Carcinogens," *Journal of the Washington Academy of Sciences 64* (1974): 65.

[12] Richard R. Johnston, Thomas H. Cromwell, Edmond I. Eger II, David Cullen, Wendell C. Stevens, and Thomas Joas, "The Toxicity of Fluroxene in Animals and Man," *Anesthesiology 38* (1973): 313; W. M. Wardell, "Fluroxene and the Penicillin Lesson," *Anesthesiology 38* (1973): 309.

[13] Wardell, "Fluroxene and the Penicillin Lesson," p. 310.

[14] Curtis C. Harris, Statement before the United States Department of Labor, Occupational Safety and Health Administration, *OSHA Docket No. 090,* Washington, D.C., April 4, 1978, p. 6; D. B. McGregor, "Cotton Rat Anomaly," *Nature 274* (1978): 21.

[15] A. L. Reeves, "Beryllium Carcinogenesis," *Adv Exp Med Biol,* 91: 13–27; 1977, cited in *Carcinogenesis Abstracts: A Monthly Publication Sponsored by the National Cancer Institute 16,* edited by G. P. Studzinski, J. J. Saukkonen, NCI Staff Consultants, E. Weisburger, J. W. Chase (Philadelphia: Franklin Research Center, 1979), Abstract 78-0637.

[16] J. R. Cabral, R. K. Hall, S. A. Bronczyk, and P. Schubik, "A Carcinogenicity Study of

the Pesticide Dieldrin in Hamsters," *Cancer Lett,* 6(4): 241–246; 1979, cited in *Carcinogenesis Abstracts 17* (1979), Abstract 79-3720, p. 1441.

[17] Environmental Protection Agency, *Potential Industrial Carcinogens and Mutagens,* prepared for the Office of Toxic Substances by Lawrence Fishbein (Washington, D.C.: May 5, 1977), p. 149.

[18] D. P. H. Hsieh, J. J. Wong, Z. A. Wong, C. Michas, and B. H. Ruebner, "Hepatic Transformation of Aflatoxin and Its Carcinogenicity," in *Origins of Human Cancer,* edited by H. H. Hiatt, J. D. Watson, J. A. Winsten, Book B, *Mechanisms of Carcinogenesis* (New York: Cold Spring Harbor Laboratory, 1977), p. 705.

[19] H. L. Marks, R. D. Wyatt, "Genetic Resistance to Aflatoxin in Japanese Quail," *Science 206* (1979): 1329.

[20] John H. Weisburger, "Bioassays and Tests for Chemical Carcinogens," in *Chemical Carcinogens,* edited by Charles E. Searle (Washington, D.C.: American Chemical Society, 1976), p. 8.

[21] Marvin A. Schneiderman and Charles C. Brown, "Estimating Cancer Risks to a Population," *Environmental Health Perspectives 22* (1978): 117.

[22] P. Shubik and D. B. Clayson, "Application of the Results of Carcinogen Bioassays to Man," in *Environmental Pollution and Carcinogenic Risks,* edited by Claude Rosenfeld, Walter Davis (Lyon: IARC Scientific Publications No. 13, 1976), p. 244.

[23] Isaac Berenblum, "Carcinogenicity Testing for Control of Environmental Tumor Development in Man," *Israel Journal of Medical Science 15* (1979): 476.

[24] H. Nagasawa, "The Cause of Species Differences in Mammary Tumorigenesis: Significance of Mammary Gland DNA Synthesis," *Med Hypotheses,* 5(4): 499–509; 1979, cited in *Carcinogenesis Abstracts 17* (1979), Abstract 79-3046.

[25] Benjamin L. Van Duuren, "Carcinogenicity of Hair Dye Components," *Cancer Symposium, An Academic Review of the Environmental Determinants of Cancer Relevant to Prevention,* held in cooperation with the American Cancer Society, Inc., New York City, February 28, March 1–2, 1979, *manuscript,* p. 6.

[26] OSHA, *Federal Register 45:15* (January 22, 1980): 5067.

[27] David P. Rall, "Role of Pharmacological Disposition in Drug Action," in *Importance of Fundamental Principles in Drug Evaluation,* edited by David H. Tedeschi, Ralph E. Tedeschi (New York: Raven, 1968), p. 175.

[28] David P. Rall, "Difficulties in Extrapolating the Results of Toxicity Studies in Laboratory Animals to Man," *Environmental Research 2* (1969): 361.

[29] David P. Rall, "Pharmacokinetic and Other Factors Related to Mutagenicity Testing: Quantitative Analysis of the Testing Procedures," *Environmental Health Perspectives,* Experimental Issue Number Six, December 1973, p. 67.

[30] Rall, "Problems of Low Doses of Carcinogens," p. 65.

[31] R. T. Williams, "Species Variations in the Pathways of Drug Metabolism," *Environmental Health Perspectives 22* (1978): 133.

[32] Ibid., p. 134.

[33] Marcus M. Reidenberg, "Species Similarities and Differences in Drug Metabolism," *Hospital Pharmacy 10* (1975): 256.

[34] P. N. Magee, "Thoughts on the Prevention of Cancer," in *Fundamentals in Cancer Prevention,* edited by Peter N. Magee, Shozo Takayama, Takashi Sugimura, Taijiro Matsushima (Baltimore: University Park Press, 1976), p. 2; Weisburger, "Bioassays and Tests for Chemical Carcinogens," in *Chemical Carcinogens,* p. 3.

[35] Isaac Berenblum, "Sequential Aspects of Chemical Carcinogenesis: Skin," in *Cancer: A Comprehensive Treatise,* edited by Frederick F. Becker, Vol. 1, *Etiology: Chemical and Physical Carcinogenesis* (New York: Plenum, 1975), p. 336.

[36] H. Bartsch, "Mutagenicity Tests in Chemical Carcinogenesis," in *Environmental Pollution and Carcinogenic Risks,* p. 229.

[37] Charles Heidelberger, "Mammalian Cell Transformation and Mammalian Cell Mutagenesis (*in vitro*)," *Cancer Symposium, An Academic Review of the Environmental Determinants of Cancer Relevant to Prevention, manuscript,* p. 5.

[38] H. V. Malling cited by Bryn A. Bridges, "Short Term Screening Tests for Carcinogens," *Nature 261* (1976): 196.

[39] Bruce N. Ames, William E. Durston, Edith Yamasaki, and Frank D. Lee, "Carcinogens Are Mutagens: A Simple Test System Combining Liver Homogenates for Activation and Bacteria for Detection," *Proceedings of the National Academy of Sciences 70* (1973): 2281.

[40] Joyce McCann, Edmund Choi, Edith Yamasaki, and Bruce N. Ames, "Detection of Carcinogens as Mutagens in the *Salmonella*/Microsome Test: Assay of 300 Chemicals," *Proceedings of the National Academy of Sciences 72* (1975): 5135.

[41] Magee, "Extrapolation of Cellular and Molecular Level Studies to the Human Situation," p. 1420.

[42] Thomas H. Maugh II and Jean L. Marx, *Seeds of Destruction: The Science Report on Cancer Research* (New York: Plenum, 1975), p. 12.

[43] Center for the Biology of Natural Systems, Washington University, St. Louis, Mo., *News Summary,* May 16, 1978, p. 2; "Realiability of Bacterial Mutagenesis Techniques to Distinguish Carcinogenic and Noncarcinogenic Chemicals," prepared by Barry Commoner and associates at the Center for the Biology of Natural Systems, Washington University, for the Environmental Protection Agency, Washington, D.C., Office of Health and Ecological Effects (U.S. Department of Commerce, National Technical Information Service, PB-259 934), April 1976, p. 43.

[44] T. Sugimura, "Review of Submammalian Systems for Detecting Mutagens and Carcinogens," *Mutation Research 53* (1978), Abstract 204, pp. 270–271.

[45] Minako Nagao, Takashi Sugimura, Taijiro Matsushima, "Environmental Mutagens and Carcinogens," *Annual Review of Genetics 12* (1978): 144.

[46] James E. Trosko and Chia-Cheng Chang, "Environmental Carcinogenesis: An Integrative Model," *Quarterly Review of Biology 53* (1978): 121–123.

[47] Richard B. Setlow, quoted by Jean L. Marx, "New Clues to Cancer's Causes," *New York Times Magazine,* November 25, 1979, p. 138.

[48] Magee, "Thoughts on the Prevention of Cancer," in *Fundamentals in Cancer Prevention,* p. 2.

[49] Flamm, Lecture, *Seminar on Government Regulation of Cancer-Causing Chemicals.*

[50] Bruce N. Ames, "The Detection of Chemical Mutagens with Enteric Bacteria," in *Chemical Mutagens: Principles and Methods for Their Detection,* edited by Alexander Hollaender, Vol. 1 (New York: Plenum, 1971), p. 271.

[51] Lee W. Wattenberg, "Inhibition of Chemical Carcinogenesis by Antioxidants and Some Additional Compounds," in *Fundamentals In Cancer Prevention,* p. 154; I. Berenblum, "The Modifying Influence of Dichloroethyl Sulphide on the Induction of Tumours in Mice by Tar," in *Journal of Pathology and Bacteriology,* The Official Journal of the Pathological Society of Great Britain and Ireland, edited by A. E. Boycott, Volume Thirty-two, Part I (Edinburgh: Oliver and Boyd, 1929).

[52] Wattenberg, "Inhibition of Chemical Carcinogenesis by Antioxidants and Some Additional Compounds," in *Fundamentals in Cancer Prevention,* p. 154.

[53] Ibid., pp. 154–156.

[54] Lee W. Wattenberg, "Inhibition of Chemical Carcinogenesis," *Journal of the National Cancer Institute 60* (1978): 11.

[55] Lee Wattenberg, "Inhibitors of Chemical Carcinogens," *Cancer Symposium, An Academic Review of the Environmental Determinants of Cancer Relevant to Prevention,* manuscript, p. 1.

[56] Wattenberg, "Inhibitors of Carcinogenesis," in *Carcinogens: Identification and Mechanisms of Action,* p. 312.

[57] H. L. Falk, "Anticarcinogenesis—an Alternative," in *Progress in Experimental Tumor Research,* edited by F. Homburger, Vol. 14, *Inhibition of Carcinogenesis,* edited by B. L. van Duuren, B. A. Rubin (Basel: S. Karger, 1971), p. 119.

[58] Ibid., p. 108.

[59] Thomas H. Maugh II, "Vitamin A: Potential Protection from Carcinogens," *Science 186* (1974): 1198.

[60] Wattenberg, "Inhibition of Chemical Carcinogenesis by Antioxidants and Some Additional Compounds," in *Fundamentals in Cancer Prevention,* p. 155.

[61] Michael Sporn, "Retinoids in Cancer Prevention," *Cancer Symposium, An Academic Review of the Environmental Determinants of Cancer Relevant to Prevention,* manuscript, Table 4.

[62] Wattenberg, "Inhibition of Chemical Carcinogenesis by Antioxidants and Some Additional Compounds," in *Fundamentals in Cancer Prevention,* p. 155.

[63] Sporn, "Retinoids in Cancer Prevention," *Cancer Symposium, An Academic Review of the Environmental Determinants of Cancer Relevant to Prevention,* manuscript, Table 4.

[64] Maugh, "Vitamin A: Potential Protection from Carcinogens," p. 1198.

[65] Elizabeth W. Chu and Richard A. Malmgren, "An Inhibitory Effect of Vitamin A on the Induction of Tumor of Forestomach and Cervix in the Syrian Hamster by Carcinogenic Polycyclic Hydrocarbons," *Cancer Research 25* (1965): 884.

[66] Ilse Lasnitzki and DeWitt S. Goodman, "Inhibition of the Effects of Methylcholanthrene on Mouse Prostate in Organ Culture by Vitamin A and Its Analogs," *Cancer Research 34* (1974): 1564.

[67] Michael B. Sporn, Robert A. Squire, Charles C. Brown, Joseph M. Smith, Martin L. Wenk, and Stephen Springer, "13-*cis*-Retinoic Acid: Inhibition of Bladder Carcinogenesis in the Rat," *Science 195* (1977): 487.

[68] B. T. Mossman, J. E. Craighead, and B. V. MacPherson, "Asbestos-Induced Epithelial Changes in Organ Cultures of Hamster Trachea: Inhibition by Retinyl Methyl Ether," *Science 207* (1980): 311.

[69] Sporn, "Retinoids in Cancer Prevention," *Cancer Symposium, An Academic Review of the Environmental Determinants of Cancer Relevant to Prevention, manuscript,* Table 4.

[70] Maugh, "Vitamin A: Potential Protection from Carcinogens," p. 1198.

[71] J. H. Weisburger and G. M. Williams, "Metabolism of Chemical Carcinogens," in *Cancer: A Comprehensive Treatise,* Vol. 1, p. 197.

[72] Wattenberg, "Inhibition of Chemical Carcinogenesis," p. 11.

[73] Isaac Berenblum, "Historical Perspective," in *Carcinogenesis: A Comprehensive Survey,* Vol. 2, *Mechanisms of Tumor Promotion and Cocarcinogenesis,* edited by T. J. Slaga, A. Sivak, R. K. Boutwell (New York: Raven, 1978), p. 1.

[74] Sanford A. Miller, quoted in "Who Decides What We Eat?," *Technology Review,* March/April, 1980, p. 72.

[75] M. Nagao, T. Kawachi, T. Yahagi, Y. Takahashi, O. Tsuda, T. Sugimura, T. Matsushima, K. Umezawa, T. Kawakami, A. Shirai, and M. Sawamura, "Our View on the Relation Between Mutagens and Carcinogens," *Naturally Occurring Carcinogens—Mutagens and Modulators of Carcinogenesis,* Ninth International Symposium of the Princess Takamatsu Cancer Research Fund, January 23–25, 1979, Tokyo, Japan, Abstract, p. 63.

[76] John Higginson and Calum S. Muir, "The Role of Epidemiology in Elucidating the Importance of Environmental Factors in Human Cancer," *Cancer Detection and Prevention 1* (1976): see "Summary."

[77] Wattenberg, "Inhibitors of Chemical Carcinogens," *Cancer Symposium, An Academic Review of the Environmental Determinants of Cancer Relevant to Prevention, manuscript,* p. 5.

[78] Joseph V. Rodricks, "Measurement of Exposure," Lecture, *Seminar on Government Regulation of Cancer-Causing Chemicals.*

[79] Flamm, Lecture, *Seminar on Government Regulation of Cancer-Causing Chemicals.*

[80] Maugh, "Vitamin A: Potential Protection from Carcinogens," p. 1198.

[81] Jean L. Marx, "Tumor Promoters: Carcinogenesis Gets More Complicated," *Science 201* (1978): 515.

[82] Berenblum, "Historical Perspective," in *Carcinogenesis: A Comprehensive Survey,* Vol. 2, p. 1; also see footnotes, p. 7.

[83] Berenblum, "Sequential Aspects of Chemical Carcinogenesis: Skin," in *Cancer: A Comprehensive Treatise,* Vol. 1, p. 323.

[84] Ibid., p. 324.

[85] Marx, "Tumor Promoters: Carcinogenesis Gets More Complicated," p. 515.

[86] OSHA, *Federal Register 45:15* (January 22, 1980): 5150.

[87] Benjamin L. Van Duuren, "Tumor-Promoting and Co-Carcinogenic Agents in Chemical Carcinogenesis," in *Chemical Carcinogens,* p. 25.

[88] Erich Hecker, "Cocarcinogenic Principles from the Seed Oil of *Croton tiglium* and from Other Euphorbiaceae," *Cancer Research 28* (1968): 2338.

[89] I. Berenblum, "Cocarcinogenesis," *British Medical Bulletin,* edited by N. Howard-Jones, Vol. 4 (1946–1947) (London: British Council, 1947), p. 344.

[90] Berenblum, "Sequential Aspects of Chemical Carcinogenesis: Skin," in *Cancer: A Comprehensive Treatise,* Vol. 1, p. 324.

[91] *British Medical Journal,* Leading Article [editorial], "Is Cancer Irreversible?," August 26, 1978, p. 585.

[92] OSHA, *Federal Register 45:15* (January 22, 1980): 5150.

[93] Berenblum, "Sequential Aspects of Chemical Carcinogenesis: Skin," in *Cancer: A Comprehensive Treatise,* Vol. 1, pp. 323–324.

[94] Ibid.

[95] Berenblum, "Cocarcinogenesis," in *British Medical Bulletin*, Vol. 4, p. 344; Berenblum, "Sequential Aspects of Chemical Carcinogenesis: Skin," in *Cancer: A Comprehensive Treatise*, Vol. 1, p. 324.

[96] Berenblum, "Sequential Aspects of Chemical Carcinogenesis: Skin," in *Cancer: A Comprehensive Treatise*, Vol. 1, p. 327.

[97] Van Duuren, "Tumor-Promoting and Co-carcinogenic Agents in Chemical Carcinogenesis," in *Chemical Carcinogens*, pp. 30–31.

[98] Berenblum, "Sequential Aspects of Chemical Carcinogenesis: Skin," in *Cancer: A Comprehensive Treatise*, Vol. 1, p. 327.

[99] Van Duuren, "Tumor-Promoting and Co-carcinogenic Agents in Chemical Carcinogenesis," in *Chemical Carcinogens*, pp. 31–32.

[100] Marx, "Tumor Promoters: Carcinogenesis Gets More Complicated," p. 515; Van Duuren, "Tumor-Promoting and Co-carcinogenic Agents in Chemical Carcinogenesis," in *Chemical Carcinogens*, pp. 24–25.

[101] Berenblum, "Sequential Aspects of Chemical Carcinogenesis: Skin," in *Cancer: A Comprehensive Treatise*, Vol. 1, p. 332.

[102] Van Duuren, "Tumor-Promoting and Co-carcinogenic Agents in Chemical Carcinogenesis," in *Chemical Carcinogens*, p. 27.

[103] R. E. Albert and F. J. Burns, "Carcinogenic Atmospheric Pollutants and the Nature of Low-level Risks," in *Origins of Human Cancer*, Book A, p. 291.

[104] *British Medical Journal*, "Is Cancer Irreversible?," p. 585.

[105] Berenblum, "Historical Perspective," in *Carcinogenesis: A Comprehensive Survey*, Vol. 2, p. 3.

[106] Charles Heidelberger and Sukdeb Mondal, "In Vitro Chemical Carcinogenesis," in *Carcinogens: Identification and Mechanisms of Action*, pp. 88–89.

[107] Neal K. Clapp, "Interactions of Ionizing Radiation, Nitrosamines, Sulfonoxyalkanes and Antioxidants as They Affect Carcinogenesis and Survival in Mice," *American Industrial Hygiene Association Journal 39* (1978): 448.

[108] R. Lee Clark, "Introduction of the Ernst W. Bertner Memorial Award Recipients," in *Carcinogens: Identification and Mechanisms of Action*, pp. 21–23.

[109] "Names in the News," *Oncology Times*, September 1980, p. 11.

[110] Van Duuren, "Tumor-Promoting and Co-carcinogenic Agents in Chemical Carcinogenesis," in *Chemical Carcinogens*, p. 24.

[111] Berenblum, "Historical Perspective," in *Carcinogenesis: A Comprehensive Survey*, Vol. 2, p. 2.

[112] P. Armitage and R. Doll, "The Age Distribution of Cancer and a Multi-Stage Theory of Carcinogenesis," *British Journal of Cancer*, Vol. VIII, No. 1 (1954), p. 9.

[113] Berenblum, "Sequential Aspects of Chemical Carcinogenesis: Skin," in *Cancer: A Comprehensive Treatise*, Vol. 1, p. 330.

[114] Armitage and Doll, "The Age Distribution of Cancer and a Multi-Stage Theory of Carcinogenesis," p. 9.

[115] Berenblum, "Sequential Aspects of Chemical Carcinogenesis: Skin," in *Cancer: A Comprehensive Treatise*, Vol. 1, p. 330.

[116] Ibid., p. 330.

[117] Richard Peto, "Epidemiology, Multi-stage Models and Short-term Mutagenicity Tests," in *Origins of Human Cancer*, Book C, *Human Risk Assessment*, p. 1418.

[118] Ibid., p. 1415.

[119] *British Medical Journal*, "Is Cancer Irreversible?," p. 585.

[120] Marx, "Tumor Promoters: Carcinogenesis Gets More Complicated," p. 518.

[121] *British Medical Journal*, "Is Cancer Irreversible?," p. 585.

[122] Ibid.

[123] R. Peto, "Epidemiology, Multi-stage Models and Short-term Mutagenicity Tests," in *Origins of Human Cancer*, Book C, p. 1415.

[124] Berenblum, "Sequential Aspects of Chemical Carcinogenesis: Skin," in *Cancer: A Comprehensive Treatise*, Vol. 1, p. 328.

CHAPTER 6

[1] Bruce N. Ames, William E. Durston, Edith Yamasaki, and Frank D. Lee, "Carcinogens Are Mutagens: A Simple Test System Combining Liver Homogenates for Activation and Bacteria for Detection," *Proceedings of the National Academy of Sciences 70* (1973): 2281.

[2] William Lijinsky, Statement before the United States Department of Labor, Occupational Safety and Health Administration, *OSHA Docket No. 090,* April 4, 1978, p. 18.

[3] Frederick F. Becker, "Keynote Address: Evolution, Chemical Carcinogenesis, and Mortality: The Cycle of Life," in *Carcinogens: Identification and Mechanisms of Action,* edited by A. Clark Griffin, Charles R. Shaw (New York: Raven, 1979), pp. 6–7.

[4] John Higginson, "Multiplicity of Factors Involved in Cancer Patterns and Trends," *Cancer Symposium, An Academic Review of the Environmental Determinants of Cancer Relevant to Prevention,* held in cooperation with the American Cancer Society, Inc., New York City, February 28, March 1–2, 1979, *manuscript,* p. 4.

[5] Occupational Safety and Health Administration (OSHA), U.S. Department of Labor, *Identification, Classification and Regulation of Potential Occupational Carcinogens,* Part VII, Book 2, in *Federal Register 45:15* (January 22, 1980): 5169; Bryn A. Bridges, "Short Term Screening Tests for Carcinogens," *Nature 261* (1976): 196; H. S. Rosenkranz and L. A. Poirier, "Evaluation of the Mutagenicity and DNA-Modifying Activity of Carcinogens and Noncarcinogens in Microbial Systems," *J Natl Cancer Inst,* 62(4): 873–892 (1979), cited in *Carcinogenesis Abstracts: A Monthly Publication Sponsored by the National Cancer Institute 17,* edited by G. P. Studzinski, J. J. Saukkonen, NCI Staff Consultants, E. Weisburger, J. W. Chase (Philadelphia: Franklin Research Center, 1979), Abstract 79–2512; T. Sugimura, "Review of Submammalian Systems for Detecting Mutagens and Carcinogens," *Mutation Research 53* (1978); Abstract 204, p. 721; L. A. Poirier, F. J. de Serres, "Initial National Cancer Institute Studies on Mutagenesis as a Prescreen for Chemical Carcinogens: An Appraisal," *J Natl Cancer Inst,* 62(4): 919–926 (1979), cited in *Carcinogenesis Abstracts 17* (1979), Abstract 79–2513; Bridges, "Short Term Screening Tests for Carcinogens," p. 198; I. Chouroulinkov, "Experimental Carcinogenesis and Mutagenesis," *Ann Mines,* 184(7/8): 51–56 (1978), cited in *Carcinogenesis Abstracts 16* (1979), Abstract 78–5418; Joyce McCann, Edmund Choi, Edith Yamasaki, Bruce N. Ames, "Detection of Carcinogens as Mutagens in the *Salmonella*/Microsome Test: Assay of 300 Chemicals," *Proceedings of the National Academy of Sciences 72* (1975): 5135; OSHA, *Federal Register 45:15* (January 22, 1980): 5169; Center for the Biology of Natural Systems, Washington University, St. Louis, Mo., *News Summary,* May 16, 1978, p. 2; "Reliability of Bacterial Mutagenesis Techniques to Distinguish Carcinogenic and Noncarcinogenic Chemicals," prepared by Barry Commoner and associates at the Center for the Biology of Natural Systems, Washington University, for the Environmental Protection Agency, Washington, D.C., Office of Health and Ecological Effects (U.S. Department of Commerce, National Technical Information Service, PB-259 934), April 1976, p. 43.

[6] Thomas H. Maugh II, "Chemical Carcinogens: The Scientific Basis for Regulation," *Science 201* (1978): 1203.

[7] OSHA, *Federal Register 45:15* (January 22, 1980): 5169–5170.

[8] Ibid., p. 5169.

[9] Gary Flamm cited by Wil Lepkowski, "Extrapolation of Carcinogenesis Data," *Environmental Health Perspectives 22* (1978): 174.

[10] T. Sugimura, cited by Frederick J. de Serres, "Strength and Weaknesses of Microbial Test Results for Predicting Human Response," *Journal of Environmental Pathology and Toxicology 1* (1977): 46.

[11] Bruce N. Ames, "Identifying Environmental Chemicals Causing Mutations and Cancer," *Science 204* (1979): 589.

[12] OSHA, *Federal Register 45:15* (January 22, 1980): 5171.

[13] International Agency for Research on Cancer, IARC Monographs on the Evaluation of Carcinogenic Risk of Chemicals to Humans, Vol. 17, *Some N-Nitroso Compounds* (Lyons: IARC, 1978), p. 27.

[14] McCann et al, "Detection of Carcinogens as Mutagens in the *Salmonella*/Microsome Test: Assay of 300 Chemicals," p. 5135; Chouroulinkov, "Experimental Carcinogenesis and Mutagenesis," cited in *Carcinogenesis Abstracts 17* (1979), Abstract 78-5418; Bridges, "Short Term Screening Tests for Carcinogens," p. 198; Rosenkranz et al., "Evaluation of the Muta-

genicity and DNA-Modifying Activity of Carcinogens and Noncarcinogens in Microbial Systems," cited in *Carcinogenesis Abstracts 17* (1979), Abstract 79–2512.

[15] J. McCann, B. N. Ames, "The *Salmonella*/Microsome Mutagenicity Test: Predictive Value for Animal Carcinogenicity," in *Origins of Human Cancer,* edited by H. H. Hiatt, J. D. Watson, J. A. Winsten, Book C, *Human Risk Assessment* (New York: Cold Spring Harbor Laboratory, 1977), pp. 1436, 1443.

[16] OSHA, *Federal Register 45:15* (January 22, 1980): 5168–5169.

[17] McCann et al., "Detection of Carcinogens as Mutagens in the *Salmonella*/Microsome Test: Assay of 300 Chemicals," pp. 5138, 5135.

[18] OSHA, *Federal Register 45:15* (January 22, 1980): 5169.

[19] Ibid., p. 5165.

[20] H. V. Malling, "Laboratory of Environmental Mutagenesis: Summary Statement," *Environmental Health Perspectives 20* (1977): 206.

[21] "Edited Transcript" of the Public Information Meeting on the preliminary findings of the International Program for the Evaluation of Short-Term Tests for Carcinogenicity, held at the National Institutes of Health, Bethesda, Md., December 3, 1979, p. 5.

[22] *Oncology Times,* "Short-Term Tests for Carcinogenicity Seen Needed," January 1980, p. 8.

[23] "Edited Transcript" of preliminary findings of the International Program for the Evaluation of Short-Term Tests for Carcinogenicity, see title page and "Agenda."

[24] Ibid., pp. 14–15, 16–18.

[25] "Edited Transcript" of the Public Information Meeting on the preliminary findings of the International Program for the Evaluation of Short-Term Tests for Carcinogenicity, p. 13.

[26] Ibid., pp. 28–30, 46.

[27] Ibid., p. 33.

[28] Preliminary report distributed at the Public Information Meeting on the findings of the International Program for the Evaluation of Short-Term Tests for Carcinogenicity, December 3, 1979, "Conclusions," p. 3.

[29] Ibid.

[30] Ibid., and "Edited Transcript" on preliminary findings of the International Program for the Evaluation of Short-Term Tests for Carcinogenicity, p. 52.

[31] de Serres, "Strength and Weaknesses of Microbial Test Results for Predicting Human Response," pp. 46–47.

[32] OSHA, *Federal Register 45:15* (January 22, 1980): 5168.

[33] Bridges, "Short Term Screening Tests for Carcinogens," p. 198.

[34] Bernard D. Davis, "Frontiers of the Biological Sciences," *Science 209* (1980). The entire article reviews the year's achievements in biology. The section pertaining to achievements in cancer is revealingly short (only one paragraph) and consists primarily of a list of unanswered questions.

[35] L. Fishbein, cited in N. Bishun, N. Smith, and D. Williams, "Mutations, Chromosome Aberrations and Cancer," *Clinical Oncology 4* (1978): 257.

[36] McCann et al., "The *Salmonella*/Microsome Mutagenicity Test: Predictive Value for Animal Carcinogenicity," in *Origins of Human Cancer,* Book C, p. 1447.

[37] *Banbury Report 1, Assessing Chemical Mutagens: The Risk to Humans,* edited by Victor K. McElheny, Seymour Abrahamson (New York: Cold Spring Harbor Laboratory, 1977), p. xii.

[38] Ibid., p. 217.

[39] Ibid., pp. 225–227.

[40] Ibid., pp. 229–230.

[41] H. P. Burchfield, Eleanor E. Storrs, "Organohalogen Carcinogens," in *Advances in Modern Toxicology,* edited by Myron A. Mehlman, Vol. 3, *Environmental Cancer,* edited by H. F. Kraybill, Myron A. Mehlman (Washington: Hemisphere, 1977), p. 328.

[42] P. N. Magee, "The Relationship Between Mutagenesis, Carcinogenesis and Teratogenesis," in *Progress in Genetic Toxicology,* edited by D. Scott, B. A. Bridges, F. H. Sobels (New York: Elsevier/North-Holland Biomedical Press, 1977), p. 19.

[43] James Cleaver, "Mechanisms of DNA Damage and DNA Repair Systems," *Cancer Symposium, An Academic Review of the Environmental Determinants of Cancer Relevant to Prevention,* manuscript, p. 6.

[44] Magee, "The Relationship Between Mutagenesis, Carcinogenesis and Teratogenesis," in *Progress in Genetic Toxicology,* p. 15.

[45] F. Meins, "Reversal of the Neoplastic State in Plants," *American Journal of Pathology,* 89(3): 687–702; 1977, cited in *Carcinogenesis Abstracts 16* (1978), Abstract 78–0066, p. 13.

[46] A. C. Braun, "Cancer as a Problem in Development," *Cancer Outlaw Cell,* 47–59; 1978, cited in *Carcinogenesis Abstracts 17* (1980), Abstract 79–4296.

[47] Magee, "The Relationship Between Mutagenesis, Carcinogenesis and Teratogenesis," in *Progress in Genetic Toxicology,* p. 24.

[48] Ibid., and James E. Trosko and Chia-Cheng Chang, "Environmental Carcinogenesis: An Integrative Model," *Quarterly Review of Biology 53* (1978): 126.

[49] Trosko et al., "Environmental Carcinogenesis: An Integrative Model," p. 126.

[50] A. Z. Bluming, "Cancer: The Eighth Plague—A Suggestion of Pathogenesis," *Isr J Med Sci,* 14(1): 192–200; 1978, cited in *Carcinogenesis Abstracts 16* (1979), Abstract 78–0660.

[51] I. Berenblum, "Established Principles and Unresolved Problems in Carcinogenesis," *Journal of the National Cancer Institute 60* (1978): 725.

[52] John Cairns, *Cancer: Science and Society* (San Francisco: Freeman, 1978), p. 96.

[53] Berenblum, "Established Principles and Unresolved Problems in Carcinogenesis," p. 725.

[54] Trosko et al., "Environmental Carcinogenesis: An Integrative Model," p. 126.

[55] Ibid., and James E. Trosko and Chia-Cheng Chang, "Genes, Pollutants and Human Diseases," *Quarterly Reviews of Biophysics II* (1978): 609.

[56] Magee, "The Relationship Between Mutagenesis, Carcinogenesis and Teratogenesis," in *Progress in Genetic Toxicology,* p. 16.

[57] Isaac Berenblum, "Historical Perspective," in *Carcinogenesis—A Comprehensive Survey,* Vol. 2, *Mechanisms of Tumor Promotion and Carcinogenesis,* edited by T. J. Slaga, A. Sivak, R. K. Boutwell (New York: Raven, 1978), p. 3.

[58] Cairns, *Cancer: Science and Society,* pp. 91, 94.

[59] Berenblum, "Established Principles and Unresolved Problems in Carcinogenesis," p. 723.

[60] Elizabeth C. Miller and James A. Miller, "Biochemical Mechanisms of Chemical Carcinogenesis," in *The Molecular Biology of Cancer,* edited by Harris Busch (New York: Academic, 1974), pp. 394–395.

[61] Takashi Sugimura, Shigeaki Sato, Minako Nagao, Takie Yahagi, Taijiro Matsushima, Yuko Seino, Micko Takeuchi, and Takashi Kawachi, "Overlapping of Carcinogens and Mutagens," in *Fundamentals in Cancer Prevention,* edited by Peter N. Magee, Shozo Takayama, Takashi Sugimura, Taijiro Matsushima (Baltimore: University Park, 1976), p. 209.

[62] Bishun et al., "Mutations, Chromosome Aberrations and Cancer," p. 252.

[63] Higginson, "Multiplicity of Factors Involved in Cancer Patterns and Trends," *Cancer Symposium, An Academic Review of the Environmental Determinants of Cancer Relevant to Prevention, manuscript,* p. 4.

[64] William Lijinsky, Statement before the United States Department of Labor, Occupational Safety and Health Administration, April 4, 1978, *OSHA Docket No. 090,* pp. 18, 19.

[65] Ibid., pp. 16, 17.

[66] Frederick F. Becker, "Keynote Address: Evolution, Chemical Carcinogenesis, and Mortality," in *Carcinogens: Identification and Mechanisms of Action,* pp. 5–7.

[67] Lewis Thomas, *The Lives of a Cell: Notes of a Biology Watcher* (New York: Bantam, 1975), pp. 135–137.

[68] Isaac Berenblum, "Cancer Research in Historical Perspective: An Autobiographical Essay," *Cancer Research 37* (1977): 4.

[69] OSHA, *Federal Register 45:15* (January 22, 1980): 5007.

CHAPTER 7

[1] Occupational Safety and Health Administration (OSHA), U.S. Department of Labor, *Identification, Classification and Regulation of Potential Occupational Carcinogens,* Part VII, Book 2, in *Federal Register 45:15* (January 22, 1980): 5059, 5154, 5158, 5118, 5093, 5067, 5075, 5078, 5083, 5105, 5159, etc., etc.

[2] Richard A. Merrill, "Regulation of Toxic Chemicals; I. Background: The Growing Importance of Toxic Chemical Regulation," an analysis of contemporary regulatory theory and

practice in an essay reviewing and discussing *A Nation of Guinea Pigs,* by Marshall Shapo, Professor of Law at Northwestern University, *Texas Law Review 58:463* (1980): 465, 466.

[3] Ibid., p. 465, footnote 8.

[4] OSHA, *Federal Register 45:15* (January 22, 1980): 5154, 5158.

[5] Ibid., pp. 5161, 5022, 5152.

[6] Ibid., pp. 5170, 5172.

[7] Ibid., pp. 5024–5025.

[8] Ibid., p. 5024.

[9] Hans Falk, "Biologic Evidence for the Existence of Thresholds in Carcinogenesis," Extrapolation Conference, Pinehurst, N.C., March 10–12, 1976, *manuscript;* my copy unpaginated.

[10] OSHA, *Federal Register 45:15* (January 22, 1980): 5172.

[11] Ibid., pp. 5129, 5024, 5150.

[12] Ibid., pp. 5023–5024.

[13] Ibid., p. 5024.

[14] Safe Drinking Water Committee, *Drinking Water and Health* (Washington, D.C.: National Academy of Sciences, 1977), pp. 37–38.

[15] OSHA, *Federal Register 45:15* (January 22, 1980): 5152.

[16] Ibid., p. 5023.

CHAPTER 8

[1] General Accounting Office, Report by the Comptroller General of the United States, *Does Nitrite Cause Cancer? Concerns about Validity of FDA-Sponsored Study Delay Answer,* January 31, 1980, p. 24.

[2] Ibid., p. 36.

[3] Umberto Saffiotti, "Scientific Bases of Environmental Carcinogenesis and Cancer Prevention: Developing an Interdisciplinary Science and Facing Its Ethical Implications," *Journal of Toxicology and Environmental Health 2* (1977): 1445.

[4] International Agency for Research on Cancer, "IARC: Working Towards the Prevention of Cancer," *WHO Chronicle 32* (1978): 142.

[5] H. F. Kraybill, "Assessment of Current Approaches in the Evaluation of Carcinogenicity in Animal Models and Their Relevance to Man," scheduled for inclusion as Chapter VII in Monograph on Environmental Carcinogenesis, edited by R. E. Olson (New York: Marcel Dekker, Inc.), *manuscript,* received from Kraybill, 1980, pp. 4, 79; also see H. F. Kraybill, "By Appropriate Methods: The Delaney Clause," in *Regulatory Aspects of Carcinogenesis and Food Additives: The Delaney Clause* (New York: Academic, 1979), pp. 61–80.

[6] Charles Heidelberger, "Mammalian Cell Transformation and Mammalian Cell Mutagenesis (in vitro)," *Cancer Symposium, An Academic Review of the Environmental Determinants of Cancer Relevant to Prevention,* held in cooperation with the American Cancer Society, Inc., New York City, February 28, March 1–2, 1979, *manuscript,* p. 7.

[7] Toxic Substances Strategy Committee, *Toxic Chemicals and Public Protection,* A Report to the President, 1980, p. xxxiv.

[8] Steven D. Jellinek, "On the Inevitability of Being Wrong," *Technology Review,* August/September 1980, pp. 8–9.

[9] Office of Science and Technology Policy, Executive Office of the President, *Identification, Characterization, and Control of Potential Human Carcinogens: A Framework for Federal Decision-Making,* February 1, 1979, p. 21.

[10] National Cancer Institute, *Everything Doesn't Cause Cancer* (Washington, D.C.: U.S. Department of Health, Education, Welfare, Public Health Service, National Institutes of Health, NIH Pub. No. 79–2039, September 1979), pp. 5–6.

[11] R. Jeffrey Smith, "Creative Penmanship in Animal Testing Prompts FDA Controls," *Science 198* (1977): 1227.

[12] Melvin Reuber, cancer researcher, and Jeffrey Howard, Frank Sizemore, and William Reukauf, lawyers for the EPA, on CBS Reports Special, "The Politics of Cancer," June 22, 1976, *transcript;* Sen. Gaylord Nelson on NBC Documentary, "What Is This Thing Called Food?," September 8, 1976, *transcript;* Russell Train, Administrator, EPA, on CBS, "Face the Nation," April 18, 1976, *transcript;* William Wells, EPA, and Robert Harris, Environmental Defense fund, on MacNeil/Lehrer Report, "DBCP," October 20, 1977, *transcript.*

[13] Sen. Edward Kennedy, quoted by Smith, "Creative Penmanship in Animal Testing Prompts FDA Controls," p. 1227.

[14] Miles W. Lord, "Political Issues," *Environmental Cancer: Causes, Victims, Solutions,* a summary of Proceedings of a Conference held March 21 and 22, 1977, sponsored by the Urban Environment Conference, Inc. and primarily funded by the National Cancer Institute, as well as the National Institute for Environmental Health Services and the Environmental Protection Agency (Washington, D.C.: Urban Environment Conference, Inc., 1978), p. 33 and "Acknowledgments."

[15] Saffiotti, "Scientific Bases of Environmental Carcinogenesis and Cancer Prevention: Developing an Interdisciplinary Science and Facing Its Ethical Implications," p. 1445.

[16] Samuel S. Epstein, *The Politics of Cancer* (San Francisco: Sierra Club Books, 1978), pp. 300–302.

[17] Smith, "Creative Penmanship in Animal Testing Prompts FDA Controls," p. 1227.

[18] Ibid.

[19] Ibid., p. 1228.

[20] Ibid., p. 1229.

[21] Ibid.

[22] Ibid.

[23] Ibid.

[24] Ibid.

[25] Lynne McTaggart, "Putting Drug Testers to the Test," *New York Times Magazine,* December 7, 1980, pp. 176–178.

[26] Ewan A. Whitaker, "Galileo's Lunar Observations," *Science 208* (1980): 446.

[27] Walter Reich, "The Force of Diagnosis," *Harper's,* May 1980, pp. 26–28; William J. Broad, "Fraud and the Structure of Science," *Science 212* (1981): 140.

[28] Constance Holden, "FDA Tells Senators of Doctors Who Fake Data in Clinical Drug Trials," *Science 206* (1979): 432.

[29] William J. Broad, "Would-Be Academician Pirates Papers," *Science 208* (1980): 1438–1440; William J. Broad, "Jordanian Accused of Plagiarism Quits Job," *Science 209* (1980): pp. 886–887.

[30] Michael Knight, "Doctor at Harvard Quit After Faking Research Data," *New York Times,* June 28, 1980, p. 22; Nicholas Wade, "A Diversion of the Quest for Truth," *Science 211* (1981): 1022.

[31] Nicola Di Ferrante, "*N*-Acetylglucosamine-6-Sulfate Sulfatase Deficiency Reconsidered," *Science 210* (1980): 448.

[32] (Name withheld), "Veteran Labsman Unhappy over the New Grantsmanship," *Oncology Times,* April 1980, p. 22.

[33] Philip M. Boffey, "Piltdown Papers," *New York Times,* August 18, 1980, p. A-14.

[34] William J. Broad, "The Case of the Unmentioned Malignancy," *Science 210* (1980): 1229; Paul S. Furcinitti, Paul Todd, Letter, "Gamma Rays and the Concept of a Threshold Dose," *Science 210* (1980): 806–807; Paul S. Furcinitti, Paul Todd, Letter, "Radiosensitivity of Human Cells in vitro," *Science 212* (1981): 6; W. A. Nelson-Rees, D. W. Daniels, and R. R. Flandermeyer, "Cross-Contamination of Cells in Culture," *Science 212* (1981): 446–452; Michael Gold, "The Cells That Would Not Die," *Science 81,* April 1981, pp. 29–35.

[35] Occupational Safety and Health Administration (OSHA), U.S. Department of Labor, *Identification, Classification and Regulation of Potential Occupational Carcinogens,* Part VII, Book 2, in *Federal Register 45:15* (January 22, 1980); 5002–5003.

[36] John Cairns, *Cancer: Science and Society* (San Francisco: Freeman, 1978), p. 101.

[37] R. Peto, "Epidemiology, Multistage Models, and Short-term Mutagenicity Tests," *Origins of Human Cancer,* edited by H. H. Hiatt, J. D. Watson, J. A. Winsten, Book C, *Human Risk Assessment* (New York: Cold Spring Harbor Laboratory, 1977), p. 1413.

[38] Robert N. Butler, Testimony, "Frontiers in Cancer Research for the Elderly," Hearings before the Select Committee on Aging, House of Representatives, Ninety-sixth Congress, First Session, June 19, 20, and 21, 1979 (Comm. Pub. No. 96–188), p. 323.

[39] Kraybill, "Assessment of Current Approaches in the Evaluation of Carcinogenicity in Animal Models and Their Relevance to Man," p. 19; also: "By Appropriate Methods: The Delaney Clause," p. 70.

[40] Safe Drinking Water Committee, *Drinking Water and Health* (Washington, D.C.: National Academy of Sciences, 1977), p. 36.

[41] William Lijinsky, Statement before the United States Department of Labor, Occupational Safety and Health Administration, *OSHA Docket No. 090*, April 4, 1978, p. 15.

[42] John H. Weisburger and David P. Rall, "Do Animal Models Predict Carcinogenic Hazards for Man?," *Environment and Cancer* (Baltimore: Williams and Wilkins, 1972), p. 439.

[43] Isaac Berenblum, "Carcinogenicity Testing for Control of Environmental Tumor Development in Man," *Israel Journal of Medical Sciences 15* (1979): 473.

[44] Marvin A. Schneiderman and Charles C. Brown, "Estimating Cancer Risks to a Population," *Environmental Health Perspectives 22* (1978): 118.

[45] Norbert P. Page, "Concepts of a Bioassay Program in Environmental Carcinogenesis, in *Advances in Modern Toxicology*, edited by Myron A. Mehlman, Vol. 3, *Environmental Cancer*, edited by H. F. Kraybill, Myron A. Mehlman (Washington: Hemisphere, 1977), p. 113.

[46] Ibid., p. 111.

[47] OSHA, *Federal Register 45:15* (January 22, 1980), p. 5064.

[48] Kraybill, "Assessment of Current Approaches in the Evaluation of Carcinogenicity in Animal Models and Their Relevance to Man," p. 98; also "By Appropriate Methods: The Delaney Clause," p. 63.

[49] Office of Science and Technology Policy, *Identification, Characterization, and Control of Potential Human Carcinogens: A Framework for Federal Decision-Making*, p. 13.

[50] OSHA, *Federal Register 45:15* (January 22, 1980): 5116–5117.

[51] Ibid., p. 5117.

[52] Ibid., p. 5118.

[53] Page, "Concepts of a Bioassay Program in Environmental Carcinogenesis," in *Advances in Modern Toxicology*, Vol. 3, *Environmental Cancer*, p. 146; Kraybill, "Assessment of Current Approaches in the Evaluation of Carcinogenicity in Animal Models and Their Relevance to Man," p. 38; also Kraybill, "By Appropriate Methods: The Delaney Clause," pp. 66–67.

[54] Page, "Concepts of a Bioassay Program in Environmental Carcinogenesis," in *Advances in Modern Toxicology*, Vol. 3, *Environmental Cancer*, p. 146.

[55] Philippe Shubik, "Identification of Environmental Carcinogens: Animal Test Models," in *Carcinogens: Identification and Mechanisms of Action*, edited by A. Clark Griffin, Charles R. Shaw (New York: Raven, 1979), p. 43.

[56] OSHA, *Federal Register 45:15* (January 22, 1980): 5069–5070.

[57] International Agency for Research on Cancer, IARC Monographs on the Evaluation of the Carcinogenic Risk of Chemicals to Humans, Vol. 17, *Some N-Nitroso Compounds* (Lyon: IARC, 1978), p. 21.

[58] OSHA, *Federal Register 45:15* (January 22, 1980): 5075–5076.

[59] Ibid., p. 5076.

[60] Ibid., pp. 5071, 5074, 5076, 5077; L. Tomatis, "The Value of Long-term Testing for the Implementation of Primary Prevention," in *Origins of Human Cancer*, Book C, p. 1354.

[61] OSHA, *Federal Register 45:15* (January 22, 1980): 5075.

[62] Tomatis, "The Value of Long-term Testing for the Implementation of Primary Prevention," in *Origins of Human Cancer*, Book C, pp. 1349–1350.

[63] Wil Lepkowski, "Extrapolation of Carcinogenesis Data," *Environmental Health Perspectives 22* (1978): 175.

[64] Kraybill, "Assessment of Current Approaches in the Evaluation of Carcinogenicity in Animal Models and Their Relevance to Man," p. 15.

[65] Tomatis, "The Value of Long-term Testing for the Implementation of Primary Prevention," in *Origins of Human Cancer*, Book C, p. 1349.

[66] Schneiderman et al., "Estimating Cancer Risks to a Population," p. 117.

[67] Ibid.

[68] H. F. Kraybill, "Conceptual Approaches to the Assessment of Nonoccupational Environmental Cancer," in *Advances in Modern Toxicology*, Vol. 3, *Environmental Cancer*, pp. 35–36; also "By Appropriate Methods: The Delaney Clause," pp. 70–73.

[69] Kraybill, "Assessment of Current Approaches in the Evaluation of Carcinogenicity in Animal Models and Their Relevance to Man," p. 14.

[70] Ibid., pp. 57–58.

[71] Ibid., Table 3.

[72] H. F. Kraybill, "Biochemical Intermediates as Research Probes in Carcinogenesis Methodology," presented at December 19, 1977, meeting of the Clearinghouse of Environmental Carcinogens, Chemical Selection Subgroup, *manuscript*, p. 3.

[73] Kraybill, "Assessment of Current Approaches in the Evaluation of Carcinogenicity in Animal Models and Their Relevance to Man," p. 58; also "By Appropriate Methods: The Delaney Clause," pp. 74–78.

[74] Kraybill, "Assessment of Current Approaches in the Evaluation of Carcinogenicity in Animal Models and Their Relevance to Man," p. 23; also "By Appropriate Methods: The Delaney Clause," p. 75.

[75] OSHA, *Federal Register 45:15* (January 22, 1980): pp. 5084–5087, 5090, 5093–5094.

[76] Ibid., p. 5085.

[77] Page, "Concepts of a Bioassay Program in Environmental Carcinogenesis," in *Advances in Modern Toxicology*, Vol. 3, *Environmental Cancer*, pp. 126, 137.

[78] Office of Science and Technology Policy, *Identification, Characterization, and Control of Potential Human Carcinogens: A Framework for Federal Decision-Making*, pp. 8, 9.

[79] Richard Peto, "Distorting the Epidemiology of Cancer: The Need for a More Balanced Overview," *Nature 284*, p. 300.

[80] I. C. Munro, Lecture, *Seminar on Government Regulation of Cancer-Causing Chemicals*, sponsored by the National Center for Administrative Justice, Washington, D.C., December 7–8, 1978; I. C. Munro, "Considerations in Chronic Toxicity Testing: The Chemical, The Dose, The Design," *Journal of Environmental Pathology and Toxicology 1* (1977): 183–197.

[81] D. Schmähl, "Problems of Dose-Response Studies in Chemical Carcinogenesis with Special Reference to N-Nitroso Compounds," *CRC Critical Reviews in Toxicology 6* (1979): 268.

[82] Thomas H. Maugh II, "Chemical Carcinogens: The Scientific Basis for Regulation," *Science 201* (1978): 1201.

[83] OSHA, *Federal Register 45:15* (January 22, 1980): 5085.

[84] "Remarks by Assistant Secretary Eula Bingham at Cancer Policy News Briefing," OSHA News Release reprinted in *Federal Regulation of Carcinogens in the Workplace: OSHA's Cancer Policy*, chairmen Peter Barton Hutt, Anson M. Keller (New York: Law & Business, Inc., Harcourt Brace Jovanovich, 1980), p. 51.

[85] National Cancer Institute, *Everything Doesn't Cause Cancer*, pp. 6–7.

[86] Maugh, "Chemical Carcinogens: The Scientific Basic for Regulation," p. 1201.

[87] Sidney Wolfe, Testimony, "National Cancer Program, 1979," Hearings before the Subcommittee on Health and Scientific Research of the Committee on Labor and Human Resources, United States Senate, Ninety-sixth Congress, First Session, Washington, D.C., March 5, 7, 1979, p. 195.

[88] OSHA, *Federal Register 45:15* (January 22, 1980): p. 5140.

[89] Ibid., pp. 5138, 5139.

[90] Page, "Concepts of a Bioassay Program in Environmental Carcinogenesis," in *Advances in Modern Toxicology*, Vol. 3, *Environmental Cancer*, p. 118.

[91] Ibid.

[92] "General Criteria for Assessing the Evidence for Carcinogenicity of Chemical Substances: Report of the Subcommittee on Environmental Carcinogenesis, National Cancer Advisory Board," *Journal of the National Cancer Institute 58* (1977): 462.

[93] H. E. Kraybill in *Human Epidemiology and Laboratory Correlations in Chemical Carcinogenesis*, edited by F. Coulston and P. E. Shubik (Norwood, N.J.: Ablex, 1980), cited by G. B. Gori, "The Regulation of Carcinogenic Hazards," *Science 208* (1980): 258, 261; see also Kraybill, "Assessment of Current Approaches in the Evaluation of Carcinogenicity in Animal Models and Their Relevance to Man."

[94] Page, "Concepts of a Bioassay Program in Environmental Carcinogenesis," in *Advances in Modern Toxicology*, Vol. 3, *Environmental Cancer*, p. 118.

[95] Kraybill, "Assessment of Current Approaches in the Evaluation of Carcinogenicity in Animal Models and Their Relevance to Man," p. 2; also "By Appropriate Methods: The Delaney Clause," p. 63.

[96] D. Mark Hegsted, "Relevance of Animal Studies to Human Disease," *Cancer Research 35* (1975): 3539.

[97] J. R. Sabine, "Susceptibility to Cancer and the Influence of Nutrition," *Nutr Cancer,*

1(3): 52–57; 1979, cited in *Carcinogenesis Abstracts: A Monthly Publication Sponsored by the National Cancer Institute 17*, edited by G. P. Studzinski, J. J. Saukkonen; NCI Staff Consultants, E. Weisburger, J. W. Chase (Philadelphia: Franklin Research Center, 1980), Abstract 79–6026.

[98] Kraybill, "Assessment of Current Approaches in the Evaluation of Carcinogenicity in Animal Models and Their Relevance to Man," p. 29; also "By Appropriate Methods: The Delaney Clause," pp. 67–69.

[99] Food and Drug Administration Advisory Committee on Protocols for Safety Evaluation: Panel on Carcinogenesis Report on Cancer Testing in the Safety Evaluation of Food Additives and Pesticides, *Toxicology and Applied Pharmacology 20* (1971): 427; cited by Gori, "The Regulation of Carcinogenic Hazards," pp. 258, 261.

[100] H. P. Burchfield, Eleanor E. Storrs, and E. E. Green, "Role of Analytical Chemistry in Carcinogenesis Studies," in *Advances in Modern Toxicology*, Vol. 3, *Environmental Cancer*, p. 184.

[101] R. Jeffrey Smith, "Nitrosamines Found in NIH-Approved Animal Feed," *Science 202* (1978): 192.

[102] Joseph J. Knapka, Letter, "Laboratory Animal Feed," *Science 204* (1979): 1367.

[103] R. Schoental, "Mycotoxins in Food and the Variations in Tumor Incidence Among Laboratory Rodents," *Nutr and Cancer,* 1(1): 13–14; 1978, cited in *Carcinogenesis Abstracts 17* (1979), Abstract 79-0552, p. 125.

[104] J. R. Sabine, B. J. Horton, M. B. Wicks, "Spontaneous Tumors in C3H-A^{vy} and C3H-A^{vy}fB Mice: High Incidence in the United States and Low Incidence in Australia," *Journal of the National Cancer Institute 50* (1973): 1237; George Vlahakis, "Possible Carcinogenic Effects of Cedar Shavings in Bedding of C3H-A^{vy}fB Mice," *Journal of the National Cancer Institute 58* (1977): 149; W. E. Heston, "Testing for Possible Effects of Cedar Wood Shavings and Diet on Occurrence of Mammary Gland Tumors and Hepatomas in C3H-A^{vy}fB Mice," *Journal of the National Cancer Institute 54* (1975): 1011; James G. Fox, "Clinical Assessment of Laboratory Rodents on Long Term Bioassay Studies," *Journal of Environmental Pathology and Toxicology 1* (1977): 203; P. N. Magee, "Extrapolation of Cellular and Molecular Level Studies to the Human Situation," *Journal of Toxicology and Environmental Health 2* (1977): 1420.

[105] Vernon Riley, Darrel H. Spackman, George A. Santisteban, Gilbert Dalldorf, Ingegerd Hellstrom, Karl-Eric Hellstrom, Eugene M. Lance, K.E.K. Rowson, B.W.J. Mahy, Peter Alexander, C. Chester Stock, Hans O. Sjogren, Vincent P. Hollander, and M.C. Horzinek, "The LDH Virus: An Interfering Biological Contaminant," *Science 200* (1978); Abner L. Notkins, "Lactic Dehydrogenase Virus," *Bacteriological Reviews 29* (1965); Abner Louis Notkins, Suellen Mahar, Christina Scheele, and Joel Goffman, "Infectious Virus-Antibody Complex in the Blood of Chronically Infected Mice," *Journal of Experimental Medicine 124* (1966).

[106] E. B. Sansone and A. M. Losikoff, "Potential Contamination from Feeding Test Chemicals in Carcinogen Bioassay Research: Evaluation of Single- and Double-Corridor Animal Housing Facilities," *Toxicol Appl Pharmacol,* 50(1): 115–121, 1979, cited in *Carcinogenesis Abstracts 17* (1980), Abstract 79–6263.

[107] Antony J. Vithayathil, Barry Commoner, Subhadra Nair, and Prema Madyastha, "Isolation of Mutagens from Bacterial Nutrients Containing Beef Extract," *Journal of Toxicology and Environmental Health 4* (1978): 190.

[108] OSHA, *Federal Register 45:15* (January 22, 1980): 5166.

[109] Smith, "Nitrosamines Found in NIH-Approved Animal Feed," 192.

[110] Ibid.

[111] Exchange of letters: William Lijinsky, "Nitrosamines in Animal Feed," *Science 202* (1978): 1034; and Gordon S. Edwards and James G. Fox, "Significance of Nitrosamines in Animal Diets," *Science 203* (1979): 6.

[112] Vernon Riley, "Stress and Cancer: Fresh Perspectives," in *Prevention and Detection of Cancer,* edited by Herbert E. Nieburgs, Part I, *Prevention,* Vol. 2, *Etiology: Prevention Methods* (New York: Marcel Dekker, 1978), p. 1771; also see Vernon Riley, "Psychoneuroendocrine Influences on Immunocompetence and Neoplasia," *Science 212* (1981): 1100–1101; Vernon Riley, Darrel Spackman, "Melanoma Enhancement by Viral-Induced Stress," in *Pigment Cell,* Series Editor V. Riley, Vol. 2, *Melanomas: Basic Properties and Clinical Behavior,* edited by V. Riley (Basel: S. Karger, 1976), pp. 163–164.

[113] Robert M. Nerem, Murina J. Levesque, and J. Frederick Cornhill, "Social Environment as a Factor in Diet-Induced Atherosclerosis," *Science 208* (1980): 1475–1476.

[114] *Guidelines for Carcinogen Bioassay in Small Rodents,* National Cancer Institute, Carcinogenesis Technical Report Series No. 1 (Washington, D.C.: U.S. Department of Health, Education and Welfare, February 1976), pp. 52–53.

[115] Ibid., pp. 53–56.

[116] Maugh, "Chemical Carcinogens: The Scientific Basis for Regulation," p. 1200.

[117] Judith Randal, "This Rat Died in a Cancer Lab to Save Lives," reprinted in *Washington Post* "Outlook," July 22, 1979, circulated by the U.S. Environmental Protection Agency, OPA 15/80, January, 1980. My copy unpaginated; see section entitled "Bad News in a Rush."

[118] Select Committee on GRAS Substances, Life Sciences Research Office, Federation of American Societies for Experimental Biology, "Evaluation of Health Aspects of GRAS Food Ingredients: Lessons Learned and Questions Unanswered," *Federation Proceedings 36* (1977): 2535.

[119] William Kruskal, cited by Ida R. Hoos, "Problems in Futures Research," in *The Study of the Future: An Agenda for Research,* edited by Wayne I. Boucher (Washington, D.C.: National Science Foundation, NSF-RA-770036, 1977), p. 124.

[120] Eliot Marshall, "Nuclear Fuel Account Books in Bad Shape," *Science 211* (1981): 147–148.

[121] Hoos, "Problems in Futures Research," in *The Study of the Future: An Agenda for Research,* p. 125.

[122] Kraybill, "Conceptual Approaches to the Assessment of Nonoccupational Environmental Cancer," in *Advances in Modern Toxicology,* Vol. 3, *Environmental Cancer,* p. 57.

[123] "Edited Transcript" of the Public Information Meeting on the preliminary findings of the International Program for the Evaluation of Short-term Tests for Carcinogenicity, held at the National Institutes of Health; Bethesda, Md., December 3, 1979, p. 52.

[124] Office of Science and Technology Policy, *Identification, Characterization, and Control of Potential Human Carcinogens: A Framework for Federal Decision-Making,* p. 13.

[125] Thomas R. Fears, Robert E. Tarone and Kenneth C. Chu, "False-Positive and False-Negative Rates for Carcinogenicity Screens," *Cancer Research 37* (1977): 1941.

[126] OSHA, *Federal Register 45:15* (January 22, 1980): 5140.

[127] Roy Albert, Lecture, *Seminar on Government Regulation of Cancer-Causing Chemicals.*

[128] R. E. Albert, R. E. Train, E. Anderson, "Rationale Developed by the Environmental Protection Agency for the Assessment of Carcinogenic Risks," *Journal of the National Cancer Institute 58* (1977): 1537.

[129] Schneiderman et al., "Estimating Cancer Risks to a Population," p. 117.

[130] Umberto Saffiotti and Norbert P. Page, "Releasing Carcinogenesis Test Results: Timing and Extent of Reporting," *Medical and Pediatric Oncology 3* (1977): 159.

[131] Ibid., p. 165.

[132] Marvin Moser, New York Medical College, H. Mitchell Perry, Washington University School of Medicine, and W. McFate Smith, University of California School of Medicine, "The Dangers of the Early Release of Drug Study Data," letter, *New York Times,* July 24, 1979, p. A-14.

[133] Kraybill, "Conceptual Approaches to the Assessment of Nonoccupational Environmental Cancer," in *Advances in Modern Toxicology,* Vol. 3, *Environmental Cancer,* p. 57.

[134] Philip H. Abelson, "Scientific Communication," *Science 209* (1980): 61–62.

[135] J. M. Ziman, "The Proliferation of Scientific Literature: A Natural Process," *Science 208* (1980): 371.

[136] Ibid., pp. 369, 370.

[137] Derek J. De Solla Price, *Little Science, Big Science* (New York: Columbia University Press, 1963), p. 86.

[138] Ibid., pp. 83–86.

[139] Walter H. Stockmayer, "Data Evaluation: A Critical Activity," *Science 201* (1978): p. 9.

[140] Charles S. Tidball, "Data Evaluation in Biology," *Science 202* (1978): 576.

[141] Committee on Data Needs, *National Needs for Critically Evaluated Physical and Chemical Data* (Washington, D.C.: National Academy of Sciences, 1978), p. 3.

[142] Richard A. Carpenter, "Scientific Information, Expert Judgment and Political Decision Making," *Journal of Occupational Medicine 18* (1976): 293.

[143] Environmental Protection Agency, "EPA and the Academic Community: Partners in Research" (EPA-600/8-80-010), December 1979, p. 11.

[144] George S. Innis, "Statistical Quality," *Science 204* (1979): 242.

[145] Joseph V. Rodricks, Lecture, "Measurement of Exposure," *Seminar on Government Regulation of Cancer-Causing Chemicals.*

[146] Kenneth W. Gardiner, Professor, University of California, Riverside, Department of Soil and Environmental Sciences, *personal correspondence,* September 12, 1978.

[147] Marvin W. Skougstad, "Minor Elements in Water," *Environmental Geochemistry in Health and Disease,* edited by Helen L. Cannon, Howard C. Hopps (Boulder, Colo.: Geological Society of America, 1971), p. 49.

[148] Judge F. W. Winner, Memorandum Opinion: The Anaconda Company vs. William D. Ruckelshaus, EPA, filed in the United States District Court for the District of Colorado, Denver, Colo., December 19, 1972, p. 10.

[149] John K. Taylor, "The Status of Chemical Analysis in Environmental Research and Control," August 31, 1978, *manuscript,* p. 11. The paper was prepared in response to a request of the U.S. National Bureau of Standards by the journal *Lung.*

[150] John K. Taylor, "The Role of Analytical Measurements in the Environmental Regulatory Process," comments at the 1978 Engineering Foundation Conference, *Examination of the Scientific Basis for Government Regulations,* Franklin Pierce College, Rindge, N.H., July 10, 1978, p. 2.

[151] Taylor, "The Status of Chemical Analysis in Environmental Research and Control," p. 11.

[152] Toxic Substances Strategy Committee, *Toxic Chemicals and Public Protection,* A Report to the President, 1980, p. 21.

[153] Ibid., p. 27.

[154] Gregory Ahart, GAO, Testimony, "Occupational Diseases, 1977," Hearings before the Subcommittee on Labor of the Committee on Human Resources, United States Senate, Ninety-fifth Congress, First Session, June 28, 29, and 30, 1977, p. 104.

[155] Gregory Ahart, GAO, Testimony, "Cancer-Causing Chemicals—Part 2: Chemical Contamination of Food," Hearings before the Subcommittee on Oversight and Investigations of the Committee on Interstate and Foreign Commerce, House of Representatives, Ninety-fifth Congress, Second Session, February 14, 16, and 24, 1978, p. 120.

[156] Gregory Ahart, GAO, letter to Representative Henry A. Waxman, U.S. House of Representatives, March 30, 1979, Enclosure II, p. 14.

[157] Ibid., p. 15.

[158] Ibid., p. 19.

[159] Ibid.

[160] Ibid.

[161] Ibid., p. 27.

[162] Ibid., p. 29.

[163] Ibid.

[164] R. Jeffrey Smith, "Congress Says Bioassay Reports Are Stalled," *Science 204* (1979): 1288.

[165] Ibid.

[166] Phyllis J. Mullenix, Remarks before the Air Quality Conference in San Francisco, California, January 16, 1979, *manuscript,* p. 3.

[167] Ibid., pp. 4–7.

[168] Ibid., p. 5.

[169] John Walsh, "EPA and Toxic Substances Law: Dealing with Uncertainty," and "Office of Toxic Substances' Spot on the Learning Curve," *Science 202* (1978): 598, 601.

[170] "Remarks by Assistant Secretary Eula Bingham at Cancer Policy News Briefing," OSHA News Release, reprinted in *Federal Regulation of Carcinogenesis in the Workplace: OSHA's Cancer Policy,* p. 49.

[171] OSHA, *Federal Register 45:15* (January 22, 1980): 5005.

[172] Philip M. Boffey, "Color Additives: Botched Experiment Leads to Banning of Red Dye No. 2," *Science 191* (1976): Philip M. Boffey, "Death of a Dye," *New York Times Magazine,* February 29, 1976.

[173] Boffey, "Death of a Dye," p. 9.

[174] Ibid., p. 49.

[175] Ibid.

[176] Ibid., pp. 49–50.

[177] Boffey, "Color Additives: Botched Experiment Leads to Banning of Red Dye No. 2," p. 450.

[178] Epstein, *The Politics of Cancer* (1978), p. 183.

[179] *Environmental Law Reporter*, "D.C. Circuit Sustains Food and Drug Administration's 'Anticipatory' Ban of Red No. 2," Vol. 6, 1976, p. 10198.

[180] General Accounting Office, Report by the Comptroller General of the United States, *Does Nitrite Cause Cancer? Concerns About Validity of FDA-Sponsored Study Delay Answer*, p. 72.

[181] OSHA, *Federal Register 45:15* (January 22, 1980): 5140.

[182] Ibid.

[183] Boffey, "Death of a Dye," p. 9.

[184] *Environmental Law Reporter*, "D.C. Circuit Sustains Food and Drug Administration's 'Anticipatory' Ban on Red No. 2," pp. 10197–10198.

[185] Wilhelm Hueper, cited by Rachel Carson, *Silent Spring* (Greenwich, Conn.: Fawcett, 1962), p. 200.

[186] Charles F. Wurster, "DDT Proved Neither Essential Nor Safe," *BioScience 23* (1973): 106.

[187] Ibid.

[188] Lorenzo Tomatis and Vladimir Turusov, "Studies on the Carcinogenicity of DDT," *GANN Monograph on Cancer Research*, No. 17, *Recent Topics in Chemical Carcinogenesis*, edited by Shigeyoshi Odashima, Shozo Takayama, Haruo Sato; Japanese Cancer Association (Baltimore-London-Tokyo: University Park Press, 1975), p. 219.

[189] Thomas H. Corbett, M.D., *Cancer and Chemicals* (Chicago: Nelson-Hall, 1977), pp. 82–83.

[190] National Institute for Occupational Safety and Health (NIOSH), Division of Criteria, Documentation and Standards Development, *Special Occupational Hazard Review for DDT* (Rockville, Md.: U.S. Department of Health, Education and Welfare, Public Health Services, Center for Disease Control, September 1978), p. ix.

[191] *Bioassays of DDT, TDE, and p,p'-DDE for Possible Carcinogenicity*, National Cancer Institute, Carcinogenesis Technical Report Series No. 131 (Washington, D.C.: U.S. Department of Health, Education and Welfare, 1978), pp. vii–viii.

[192] T. Syrowatka, E. Tyrkiel, and T. Nazarewicz, "Effect of Simultaneous Administration of DDT on the Toxicity of Dimethylnitrosamine in Rats in a Long-term Experiment," *Rocz Panstw Zakl Hig*, 30(1): 67–69; 1979, cited in *Carcinogenesis Abstracts 17* (1980), Abstract 79-4375.

[193] Kraybill, "Conceptual Approaches to the Assessment of Nonoccupational Environmental Cancer," in *Advances in Modern Toxicology*, Vol. 3, *Environmental Cancer*, p. 37.

[194] Wurster, "DDT Proved Neither Essential Nor Safe," p. 106.

[195] H. P. Burchfield and Eleanor E. Storrs, "Organohalogen Carcinogens," in *Advances in Modern Toxicology*, Vol. 3, *Environmental Cancer*, pp. 355–356.

[196] Ibid., p. 356.

[197] Ibid.

[198] Corbett, *Cancer and Chemicals*, p. 83.

[199] Kraybill, "Assessment of Current Approaches in the Evaluation of Carcinogenicity in Animal Models and Their Relevance to Man," p. 80.

[200] R. Jeffrey Smith, "Nitrites: FDA Beats a Surprising Retreat," *Science 209* (1980): 1100.

[201] Ibid.

[202] Karen DeWitt, "U.S. Will Not Seek to Ban Nitrite from Foods as a Cause of Cancer," *New York Times*, August 20, 1980, p. 1.

[203] General Accounting Office, Report by the Comptroller General of the United States, *Does Nitrite Cause Cancer? Concerns About Validity of FDA-Sponsored Study Delay Answer*, January 31, 1980, p. 36.

[204] Ibid.

[205] Ibid., p. 69.

[206] Ibid., p. 70.

[207] Ibid., p. 68.

[208] Ibid., pp. 70–71.

[209] Ibid., pp. 71–72.

[210] Ibid., p. 73.

[211] Ibid.

[212] Ibid., p. 75.

[213] Ibid., pp. 76–77.

[214] Ibid., p. 14.

[215] Ibid., pp. 14, 19.

[216] Ibid., pp. 14, 16.

[217] Ibid., p. 16.

[218] Ibid.

[219] Ibid., p. 18.

[220] Ibid., Introduction.

[221] Ibid., pp. 22–24.

[222] Ibid., pp. 21, 24, 26.

[223] Ibid., pp. 21–22.

[224] Ibid., pp. 24–25.

[225] Ibid., p. 25.

[226] Ibid.

[227] *FDA Talk Paper*, "Nitrite Update," April 27, 1979.

[228] General Accounting Office, Report by the Comptroller General of the United States, *Does Nitrite Cause Cancer? Concerns About Validity of FDA-Sponsored Study Delay Answer*, p. 66.

[229] Ibid.

[230] Ibid., p. 59.

[231] Ibid., pp. 59–60.

[232] Ibid., p. 60.

[233] Ibid., Letter from Paul Newberne, pp. 88–89.

[234] Ibid., p. 89.

[235] Ibid., Letter from Paul Newberne, p. 24.

CHAPTER 9

[1] Anonymous, "Animal Models in Cancer Research," *Lancet 2* (1974); quoted by Mark Hegsted, "Relevance of Animal Studies to Human Disease," *Cancer Research 35* (1975), p. 3537.

[2] L. Tomatis, "The Value of Long-Term Testing for the Implementation of Primary Prevention," in *Origins of Human Cancer*, Book C, *Human Risk Assessment*, edited by H. H. Hiatt, J. D. Watson, J. A. Winsten (New York: Cold Spring Harbor Laboratory, 1977), p. 1349.

[3] William Lijinsky, Statement before the United States Department of Labor, Occupational Safety and Health Administration, *OSHA Docket No. 090*, April 4, 1978, p. 23.

[4] National Cancer Institute, *Everything Doesn't Cause Cancer* (Washington, D.C.: U.S. Department of Health, Education and Welfare, Public Health Service, National Institutes of Health, NIH Pub. No. 79-2039, September 1979), p. 6.

[5] "Edited Transcript" of the Public Information Meeting on the preliminary findings of the International Program for the Evaluation of Short-term Tests for Carcinogenicity, held at the National Institutes of Health, Bethesda, Md., December 3, 1979, p. 15.

[6] J. McCann and B. N. Ames, "The *Salmonella*/Microsome Mutagenicity Tests: Predictive Value for Animal Carcinogenicity," in *Origins of Human Cancer*, Book C, p. 1436.

[7] Ibid., p. 1443.

[8] William Lijinsky, Statement before the United States Department of Labor, Occupational Safety and Health Administration, *OSHA Docket No. 090*, April 4, 1978, pp. 22–23.

[9] Occupational Safety and Health Administration (OSHA), U.S. Department of Labor, *Identification, Classification and Regulation of Potential Occupational Carcinogens*, Part VII, Book 2, in *Federal Register 45:15* (January 22, 1980): 5028.

[10] Umberto Saffiotti, "Carcinogenesis, 1957–77: Notes for a Historical Review," *Journal of the National Cancer Institute 59:2* (Supplement) (1977): 618.

[11] S. S. Epstein, "The Carcinogenicity of Organochlorine Pesticides," in *Origins of Human Cancer*, Book A, *Incidence of Cancer in Humans*, p. 263.

[12] OSHA, *Federal Register 45:15* (January 22, 1980): 5028.

[13] Norbert P. Page, "Concepts of a Bioassay Program in Environmental Carcinogenesis," in *Advances in Modern Toxicology*, edited by Myron A. Mehlman, Vol. 3, *Environmental Cancer*, edited by H. F. Kraybill, Myron A. Mehlman (Washington: Hemisphere, 1977), p. 110.

[14] Matthew S. Meselson, Statement before the United States Department of Labor, Occupational Safety and Health Administration, *OSHA Docket No. 090*, April 4, 1978, pp. 3–4.

[15] National Cancer Institute, *Everything Doesn't Cause Cancer*, p. 7.

[16] Judith Randal, "This Rat Died in a Cancer Lab to Save Lives," reprinted in *Washington Post* "Outlook," July 22, 1979, circulated to the press by the United States Environmental Protection Agency, OPA 15/80, January 1980. My copy unpaginated; see two concluding paragraphs of section entitled "Bad News in a Rush."

[17] Ibid. See footnote, second page.

[18] Ibid. See two opening paragraphs of article.

[19] Sidney Wolfe, Testimony, "National Cancer Program, 1979," Hearings before the Subcommittee on Health and Scientific Research of the Committee on Labor and Human Resources, United States Senate, Ninety-sixth Congress, First Session, March 5 and 7, 1979, p. 195.

[20] OSHA, *Federal Register 45:15* (January 22, 1980): 5029; *Proposed Rulemaking: Identification, Classification and Regulation of Toxic Materials Posing a Potential Occupational Cancer Risk to Workers*, Occupational Safety and Health Administration, January 1977, cited in *Toxic Substances Control Sourcebook*, edited by Alexander McRae, Leslie Whelchel (Germantown, Md.: Aspen Systems Corporation, Center for Compliance Information, 1978), pp. 325–329, quotation, p. 328.

[21] National Cancer Institute, *Everything Doesn't Cause Cancer*, p. 7; OSHA, *Federal Register 45:15* (January 22, 1980): 5028; Epstein, "The Carcinogenicity of Organochlorine Pesticides," in *Origins of Human Cancer*, Book A, p. 263; Page, "Concepts of a Bioassay Program in Environmental Carcinogenesis," in *Advances in Modern Toxicology*, Vol. 3, *Environmental Cancer*, p. 110; Matthew S. Meselson, Statement before the U.S. Department of Labor, Occupational Health and Safety Administration, *OSHA Docket No. 090*, April 4, 1978, pp. 3–4.

[22] Richard Peto, "Distorting the Epidemiology of Cancer: The Need for a More Balanced Overview," *Nature 284* (1980): 300.

[23] Isaac Berenblum, cited in OSHA, *Federal Register 45:15* (January 22, 1980): 5028.

[24] Page, "Concepts of a Bioassay Program in Environmental Carcinogenesis," in *Advances in Modern Toxicology*, Vol. 3, *Environmental Cancer*, pp. 159, 156.

[25] OSHA, *Federal Register 45:15* (January 22, 1980): 5028.

[26] Umberto Saffiotti, "Comments on the Scientific Basis for the 'Delaney Clause,'" *Preventive Medicine 2* (1973): 131.

[27] Umberto Saffiotti, "Risk-Benefit Considerations in Public Policy on Environmental Carcinogenesis," Proceedings of the Eleventh Canadian Cancer Research Conference, sponsored by the National Cancer Institute of Canada in affiliation with the Canadian Cancer Society, Toronto, Ontario, May 6–8, 1976, p. 16.

[28] OSHA, *Federal Register 45:15* (January 22, 1980): 5098.

[29] Ibid., p. 5004.

[30] A. L. Brown, "Evaluation of Environmental Carcinogens for Cancer in Man," *Oncology 33* (1976): 59.

[31] Richard A. Carpenter, "Scientific Information, Expert Judgment and Political Decision Making," *Journal of Occupational Medicine 18* (1976): 294.

[32] Statement by Sir Richard Doll, read in his absence by Dr. Philip Cole, Department of Epidemiology, Harvard School of Public Health, at *Congressional Briefing on Saccharin*, Rayburn House Office Building, Room 2123, Washington, D.C., September 15, 1977, transcript, p. 32.

[33] Richard Peto, "Carcinogenic Effects of Chronic Exposure to Very Low Levels of Toxic Substances," *Environmental Health Perspectives 22* (1978): 158.

[34] OSHA, *Federal Register 45:15* (January 22, 1980): 5081.

[35] Ibid., p. 5051.

[36] Brian MacMahon, "Strengths and Limitations of Epidemiology," in *Current Issues and Studies*, the National Research Council, 1979, excerpted under the title "Epidemiology's Strengths and Weaknesses in Environmental Health Issues," *News Reports*, a monthly register of activities of the National Academy of Sciences, National Academy of Engineering, Institute of Medicine, and National Research Council, April 1980, p. 5.

[37] OSHA, *Federal Register 45:15* (January 22, 1980): 5048.

[38] Ibid., p. 5080.

[39] Umberto Saffiotti, "Identifying and Defining Chemical Carcinogens," in *Origins of Human Cancer*, Book C, p. 1314.

[40] OSHA, *Federal Register 45:15* (January 22, 1980): 5156.

[41] Joyce McCann on furyl furamide, cited in OSHA, *Federal Register 45:15* (January 22, 1980): 5081; Umberto Saffiotti on DB(a,c)A, in a discussion following a paper by Bruce N. Ames and Joyce McCann, "Carcinogens Are Mutagens: A Simple Test System," in *Screening Tests in Chemical Carcinogenesis*, edited by R. Montesano, H. Bartsch, L. Tomatis (Lyon: IARC Scientific Publications No. 12, 1976), pp. 503–504.

[42] Interagency Regulatory Liaison Group (IRLG), Work Group on Risk Assessment, representing the Consumer Product Safety Commission, the Environmental Protection Agency, the Food and Drug Administration, and the Occupational Safety and Health Administration, "Scientific Bases for Identification of Potential Carcinogens and Estimation of Risks," *Journal of the National Cancer Institute 63* (1979): 248.

[43] OSHA, *Federal Register 45:15* (January 22, 1980): 5145.

[44] Umberto Saffiotti, "Validation of Short-Term Bioassays as Predictive Screens for Chemical Carcinogens," in *Screening Tests in Chemical Carcinogenesis*, p. 9.

[45] OSHA, *Federal Register 45:15* (January 22, 1980): 5144.

[46] Ibid.

[47] Ibid., p. 5148.

[48] Ibid., p. 5149.

[49] Ibid., p. 5142.

[50] Ibid., p. 5143.

[51] Ibid., p. 5142.

[52] Ibid., p. 5149.

[53] Ibid., p. 5079.

[54] General Criteria for Assessing the Evidence for Carcinogenicity of Chemical Substances: Report of the Subcommittee on Environmental Carcinogenesis, National Cancer Advisory Board," *Journal of the National Cancer Institute 58* (1977): 463.

[55] Office of Science and Technology Policy, Executive Office of the President, *Identification, Characterization, and Control of Potential Human Carcinogens: A Framework for Federal Decision-Making*, February 1, 1979, p. 9.

[56] OSHA, *Federal Register 45:15* (January 22, 1980): 5068.

[57] Ibid., pp. 5079, 5080.

[58] IRLG, *Identification of Potential Carcinogens and Risk Estimation*, p. 258.

[59] Ibid., p. 252.

[60] Ibid., p. 253.

[61] OSHA, *Federal Register 45:15* (January 22, 1980): 5079.

[62] Ibid., pp. 5038, 5036.

[63] "General Criteria for Assessing the Evidence for Carcinogenicity of Chemical Substances: Report of the Subcommittee on Environmental Carcinogenesis, National Cancer Advisory Board," p. 463.

[64] IRLG, *Identification of Potential Carcinogens and Risk Estimation*, p. 255.

[65] Irving I. Kessler, "Putting Reason into Regulation" (Rochester, New York: Center for the Study of Drug Development, University of Rochester Medical Center, School of Medicine and Dentistry, Publication Series 7705, October 1977), see Section 5.

[66] OSHA, *Federal Register 45:15* (January 22, 1980): 5037.

[67] H. F. Kraybill, "Assessment of Curent Approaches in the Evaluation of Carcinogenicity in Animal Models and Their Relevance to Man," scheduled for inclusion as Chapter VII in Monograph on Environmental Carcinogenesis, edited by R. E. Olson (New York: Marcel Dekker), *manuscript*, received from Kraybill, 1980, p. 21.

[68] OSHA, *Federal Register 45:15* (January 22, 1980): 5145.

[69] "Toxic Substances Control Act," Hearings before the Subcommittee on Consumer Protection and Finance, Committee on Interstate and Foreign Commerce, House of Representatives, Ninety-fourth Congress, First Session, June 16, July 9, 10, and 11, 1975, p. 2.

[70] OSHA, *Federal Register 45:15* (January 22, 1980): 5168–5169.

[71] Ibid., p. 5165.

[72] McCann and Ames, "The *Salmonella*/Microsome Mutagenicity Test: Predictive Value for Animal Carcinogenicity," in *Origins of Human Cancer*, Book C, p. 1436.

CHAPTER 10

[1] Department of Health and Human Services, U.S.A., *First Annual Report on Carcinogens*, Vol. 1, July 1980, p. v.

[2] James A. Miller, "Concluding Remarks on Chemicals and Chemical Carcinogenesis," in *Carcinogens: Identification and Mechanisms of Action*, edited by A. Clark Griffin, Charles R. Shaw (New York: Raven, 1979), pp. 457–459.

[3] Norbert P. Page, "Concepts of a Bioassay Program in Environmental Carcinogenesis," in *Advances in Modern Toxicology*, edited by Myron A. Mehlman, Vol. 3, *Environmental Cancer*, edited by H. F. Kraybill, Myron A. Mehlman (Washington: Hemisphere, 1977), p. 95.

[4] Thomas H. Maugh II, "Who Chooses Chemicals for Testing?," *Science 201* (1978): 1202.

[5] Miller, "Concluding Remarks on Chemicals and Chemical Carcinogenesis," in *Carcinogens: Identification and Mechanisms of Action*, p. 456.

[6] Tamas E. Doszkocs, Barbara A. Rapp, and Harold M. Schoolman, "Automated Information Retrieval in Science and Technology," *Science 208* (1980): 26.

[7] Ibid., p. 25.

[8] John S. Wassom, "The Literature of Chemical Mutagenesis," in *Chemical Mutagens: Principles and Methods for Their Detection*, edited by Alexander Hollaender, Vol. 2 (New York: Plenum, 1973), p. 282.

[9] Interviews by Pamela Wharton Blanpied, Research Assistant to Edith Efron, October 10 and 14, 1980.

[10] Roy Albert, Lecture, *Seminar on Government Regulation of Cancer-Causing Chemicals*, sponsored by the National Center for Administrative Justice, Washington, D.C., December 7–8, 1978.

[11] *Clement's Lists of Carcinogenic Chemicals Found in American Workplaces*, U.S. Department of Commerce National Technical Information Service, PB-295 978. Covering letter to Grover C. Wrenn, Director, Health Standards Programs, Occupational Safety and Health Administration, from Jay Turim, Vice President, Clement Associates, Inc., Washington, D.C., July 10, 1978, p. ii.

[12] Ibid., p. iii.

[13] Samuel S. Epstein, M.D., *The Politics of Cancer*, rev. ed. (Garden City, N.Y.: Anchor/Doubleday, 1979), p. 375; L. Embler, "OSHA on the Move," *Environ. Sci, Technol.*, 11(13): 1142–1147; 1977, cited in *Carcinogenesis Abstracts: A Monthly Publication Sponsored by the National Cancer Institute 16*, edited by G. P. Studzinski, J. J. Saukkonen; NCI Staff Consultants E. Weisburger, J. W. Chase (Philadelphia: Franklin Research Center, 1979), Abstract 78–0811.

[14] Epstein, *The Politics of Cancer*, pp. 374, 375.

[15] U. Saffiotti, "Validation of Short-Term Bioassays as Predictive Screens for Chemical Carcinogens," in *Screening Tests in Chemical Carcinogenesis*, edited by R. Montesano, H. Bartsch, L. Tomatis (Lyon: IARC Scientific Publications No. 12, 1976), pp. 6–7.

[16] Ibid., p. 7.

[17] S. S. Epstein, "The Carcinogenicity of Organochlorine Pesticides," in *Origins of Human Cancer*, edited by H. H. Hiatt, J.D. Watson, J. A. Winsten, Book A, *Incidence of Cancer in Humans* (New York: Cold Spring Harbor Laboratory, 1977), p. 263.

[18] Umberto Saffiotti, "Carcinogenesis, 1957–77: Notes for a Historical Review," *Journal of the National Cancer Institute 59:2* (Supplement) (1977): 618.

[19] Thomas H. Maugh II, "Chemical Carcinogens: The Scientific Basis for Regulation," *Science 201* (1978): 1200.

[20] George F. Will, "The Mind Reels," *Newsweek*, December 25, 1978, p. 13.

[21] Umberto Saffiotti, "Experimental Identification of Chemical Carcinogens, Risk Eval-

uation, and Animal-to-Human Correlations," *Environmental Health Perspectives 22* (1978): 108.

[22] Luther J. Carter, "Yearly Report on Carcinogens Could Be a Potent Weapon in the War on Cancer," *Science 203* (1979): 525; *Public Law 95-622, Section 262, Part E,* November 9, 1978 (Amendment to Section 301 (b)(4) of the Public Health Service Act), 92 STAT. 3435.

[23] Carter, "Yearly Report on Carcinogens Could Be a Potent Weapon in the War on Cancer," p. 525.

[24] Ibid.

[25] Department of Health and Human Services, U.S.A., *First Annual Report on Carcinogens,* p. v.

[26] Ibid.

[27] Ibid., p. vi.

[28] Ibid., p. 9.

[29] Ibid., p. 8.

[30] John H. Weisburger, "Chemical Carcinogenesis," in *Toxicology: The Basic Science of Poisons,* edited by Louis J. Casarett, John Doull (New York: Macmillan, 1975), p. 333.

[31] Department of Health and Human Services, U.S.A., *First Annual Report on Carcinogens,* pp. 8, 10.

[32] Lorenzo Tomatis, Claus Agthe, Helmut Bartsch, James Huff, Ruggero Montesano, Rodolfo Saracci, Ernest Walker and Julian Wilbourn, "Evaluation of the Carcinogenicity of Chemicals: A Review of the Monograph Program of the International Agency for Research on Cancer (1971–1977)," *Cancer Research 38* (1978), Table 3, pp. 882–883.

[33] Ibid., p. 881. The "almost 65 percent" is my own calculation. Since Tomatis provides the numbers, the reader can confirm the percentage for himself.

[34] Ibid., p. 881.

CHAPTER 11

[1] CBS Reports Special, "The Politics of Cancer," June 22, 1976, *transcript.*

[2] John Higginson, "Overview," in *Environmental Cancer: Causes, Victims, Solutions,* A Summary of Proceedings of a Conference held March 21 and 22, 1977, sponsored by the Urban Environment Conference, Inc., and primarily funded by the National Cancer Institute, as well as the National Institute for Environmental Health Sciences and the Environmental Protection Agency (Washington, D.C., Urban Environment Conference, Inc., 1978), p. 2.

[3] Occupational Safety and Health Administration (OSHA), U.S. Department of Labor, *Identification, Classification and Regulation of Potential Occupational Carcinogens,* Part VII, Book 2, in *Federal Register 45:15* (January 22, 1980): 5168.

[4] International Agency for Research on Cancer, IARC Monographs on the Evaluation of the Carcinogenic Risk of Chemicals to Humans, Vol. 17, *Some N-Nitroso Compounds* (Lyon: IARC, 1978), p. 12.

[5] CBS Reports Special, "The Politics of Cancer," June 22, 1976, *transcript.*

[6] Safe Drinking Water Committee [*Drinking Water and Health* (Washington, D.C.: National Academy of Sciences, 1977)], cited in OSHA, *Federal Register 45:15* (January 22, 1980): 5066.

[7] IARC Monographs, Vol. 1 (untitled), 1972, p. 6.

[8] IARC Monographs on the Evaluation of the Carcinogenic Risk of Chemicals to Man, Vol. 1–16, 1972–1978.

[9] Lorenzo Tomatis, Claus Agthe, Helmut Bartsch, James Huff, Ruggero Montesano, Rodolfo Saracci, Ernest Walker and Julian Wilbourn, "Evaluation of the Carcinogenicity of Chemicals: A Review of the Monograph Program of the International Agency for Research on Cancer (1971 to 1977)," *Cancer Research 38* (1978): 883.

[10] Ibid., p. 884.

[11] Ibid., p. 883.

[12] IARC Monographs, Vol. 17, p. 20.

[13] *Chemicals and Industrial Processes Associated with Cancer in Humans: IARC Monographs, Volumes 1 to 20,* Supplement 1, Report of an IARC ad hoc Working Group which met in Lyon, 15–17 January 1979, prepared by Ralph Althouse, James Huff, Lorenzo Tomatis and Julian Wilbourn (Lyon: IARC, September 1979).

[14] Report of an IARC Working Group, prepared by Ralph Althouse, James Huff,

Lorenzo Tomatis and Julian Wilbourn, International Agency for Research on Cancer, "An Evaluation of Chemicals and Industrial Processes Associated with Cancer in Humans Based on Human and Animal Data: IARC Monographs Volumes 1 to 20," *Cancer Research 40* (1980).

[15] *Chemicals and Industrial Processes Associated with Cancer in Humans: IARC Monographs, Volumes 1 to 20,* Supplement 1, prepared by Ralph Althouse et al., pp. 9–10.

[16] Ibid., pp. 10–11.

[17] Ibid., p. 4.

[18] Ibid., pp. 4–8.

[19] Ibid., p. 4.

[20] Ibid., pp. 11–14.

[21] Ibid., Table 3, pp. 15–18.

[22] Ibid., p. 3.

[23] Ibid., p. 11.

[24] Ibid.

[25] Ibid.

[26] OSHA, *Federal Register 45:15* (January 22, 1980): 5066.

[27] IARC Monographs, Vol. 17, p. 20.

[28] OSHA, *Federal Register 45:15* (January 22, 1980): 5012–5013.

[29] IARC Monographs, Vol. 17, p. 21.

[30] "The National Cancer Institute," cited in R. E. Albert, R. E. Train, and E. Anderson, "Rationale Developed by the Environmental Protection Agency for the Assessment of Carcinogenic Risks," *Journal of the National Cancer Institute 58* (1977): 1538.

[31] Arthur C. Upton, "Progress in the Prevention of Cancer," *Preventive Medicine 7* (1978): 483.

[32] Curtis C. Harris, Umberto Saffiotti and Benjamin F. Trump, "Carcinogenesis Studies in Human Cells and Tissues," *Cancer Research 38* (1978): 474.

[33] Umberto Saffiotti, "Scientific Bases of Environmental Carcinogenesis and Cancer Prevention: Developing an Interdisciplinary Science and Facing Its Ethical Implications," *Journal of Toxicology and Environmental Health 2* (1977): 1440.

[34] Thomas H. Maugh II, "Chemical Carcinogens: The Scientific Basis for Regulation," *Science 201* (1978): 1201.

[35] Ibid., Albert et al., "Rationale Developed by the Environmental Protection Agency for the Assessment of Carcinogenic Risks," p. 1538.

[36] Albert et al., "Rationale Developed by the Environmental Protection Agency for the Assessment of Carcinogenic Risks," p. 1538.

[37] P. B. Medawar, "Advice to a Young Scientist," excerpt published in *Harper's,* September 1979, p. 44.

[38] Ibid., p. 43.

[39] OSHA, *Federal Register 45:15* (January 22, 1980): 5061.

[40] Samuel S. Epstein, "Regulatory Aspects of Occupational Carcinogens: Contrasts with Environmental Carcinogens, in *Environmental Pollution and Carcinogenic Risks,* edited by Claude Rosenfeld, Walter Davis (Lyon: IARC Scientific Publications No. 13, 1976), p. 393.

[41] Upton, "Progress in the Prevention of Cancer," p. 482.

[42] William Lijinsky, "U.S. Health Will Be Jeopardized if Delaney Clause Is Abandoned," *Chemical & Engineering News,* June 27, 1977, pp. 26–27.

[43] D. P. Rall, "The Role of Laboratory Animal Studies in Estimating Carcinogenic Risks for Man," in *Carcinogenic Risks: Strategies for Intervention,* edited by W. Davis, C. Rosenfeld (Lyon: IARC Scientific Publications No. 25, 1979), pp. 183–184; David Rall, "Extrapolating Animal and Microbiological Tests to Humans," Urban Environment Conference, p. 8; D. P. Rall, "Species Differences in Carcinogenesis Testing," in *Origins of Human Cancer,* edited by H. H. Hiatt, J. D. Watson, J. A. Winsten, Book C, *Human Risk Assessment* (New York: Cold Spring Harbor Laboratory, 1977), p. 1389.

[44] OSHA, *Federal Register 45:15* (January 22, 1980): 5063.

[45] Gus Speth, "Science and Prudence in Cancer Prevention," *New York Times,* March 9, 1978, p. A-21.

[46] Toxic Substances Strategy Committee, *Toxic Chemicals and Public Protection,* A Report to the President, 1980, p. xxxviii.

[47] L. Tomatis, "The Predictive Value of Rodent Carcinogenicity Tests in the Evaluation of Human Risks," *Annual Review of Pharmacology and Toxicology 19* (1979): 516.

[48] Renate D. Kimbrough, Statement before the United States Department of Labor, Occupational Safety and Health Administration, *OSHA Docket No. 090,* April 4, 1978, p. 4.

[49] John H. Weisburger, "Bioassays and Tests for Chemical Carcinogens," in *Chemical Carcinogens,* edited by Charles E. Searle (Washington, D.C.: American Chemical Society, 1976), p. 7.

[50] Cesare Maltoni, "Occupational Chemical Carcinogenesis: New Facts, Priorities and Perspectives," in *Environmental Pollution and Carcinogenic Risks,* p. 128.

[51] Lijinsky, "U.S. Health Will Be Jeopardized if Delaney Clause Is Abandoned," p. 26.

[52] Ibid., p. 27.

[53] OSHA, *Federal Register 45:15* (January 22, 1980): 5061.

[54] Epstein, "Regulatory Aspects of Occupational Carcinogens: Contrasts with Environmental Carcinogens," in *Environmental Pollution and Carcinogenic Risks,* p. 393.

[55] Safe Drinking Water Committee [*Drinking Water and Health* (Washington, D.C.: National Academy of Sciences, 1977)], cited in OSHA, *Federal Register 45:15* (January 22, 1980): p. 5066.

[56] H. F. Kraybill, "Assessment of Current Approaches in the Evaluation of Carcinogenicity in Animal Models and Their Relevance to Man," scheduled for inclusion as Chapter VII in Monograph on Environmental Carcinogenesis, edited by R. E. Olson (New York: Marcel Dekker), *manuscript,* received from Kraybill, 1980, p. 76.

[57] Office of Science and Technology Policy, Executive Office of the President, *Identification, Characterization, and Control of Potential Human Carcinogens: A Framework for Federal Decision-Making,* February 1, 1979, p. 12.

[58] OSHA, *Federal Register 45:15* (January 22, 1980): 5061.

[59] L. Tomatis, "The Value of Long-Term Testing for the Implementation of Primary Prevention," in *Origins of Human Cancer,* Book C, p. 1353; Ruggero Montesano and Lorenzo Tomatis, "Legislation Concerning Chemical Carcinogens in Several Industrialized Countries," *Cancer Research 37* (1977).

[60] Tomatis, "The Value of Long-Term Testing for the Implementation of Primary Prevention," in *Origins of Human Cancer,* Book C, pp. 1353–1354.

[61] In January 1981, my inquiry addressed to Dr. Tomatis for more recent information was answered with a copy of the same study by Montesano and Tomatis from which the generalizations were drawn.

[62] John H. Weisburger and Gary M. Williams, "Carcinogen Testing: Current Problems and New Approaches," *Science 214* (1981): 406, 407.

CHAPTER 12

[1] Occupational Safety and Health Administration (OSHA), U.S. Department of Labor, *Identification, Classification and Regulation of Potential Occupational Carcinogens,* Part VII, Book 2, in *Federal Register 45:15* (January 22, 1980): 5155.

[2] Ibid., p. 5122.

[3] Lawrence Garfinkle, quoted by Malcolm W. Browne, "How Tiny Chemical Traces Are Found," *New York Times,* August 14, 1979, pp. C1, C2; quotation p. C2.

[4] Alexander Schmidt quoted by T. H. Jukes, "DES in Beef Production: Science, Politics, and Emotion," *Origins of Human Cancer,* edited by H. H. Hiatt, J. D. Watson, J. A. Winsten, Book C, *Human Risk Assessment* (New York: Cold Spring Harbor Laboratory, 1977), pp. 1658–1659.

[5] Gary Flamm, First Meeting of the Chemical Selection Subgroup of the Clearinghouse on Environmental Carcinogens, held at the National Institutes of Health, Bethesda, Md., November 8, 1976, *transcript,* pp. 173–174; Arthur L. Robinson, "Analytical Chemistry: Using Lasers to Detect Less and Less," *Science 199* (1978): 1191, 1193; Mitchell H. Bradley, "Zero—What Does It Mean?," *Science 208* (1980): 7; Richard C. Atkinson, "Environmental Regulation," *Science 209* (1980): 969; H. F. Kraybill, "Assessment of Current Approaches in the Evaluation of Carcinogenicity in Animal Models and Their Relevance to Man," scheduled for inclusion as Chapter VII in Monograph on Environmental Carcinogenesis, edited by R. E. Olson (New York: Marcel Dekker), *manuscript,* received from Kraybill, 1980, p. 88.

[6] OSHA, *Federal Register 45:15,* (January 22, 1980): 5119.

[7] Office of Science and Technology Policy, Executive Office of the President, *Identification, Characterization, and Control of Potential Human Carcinogens: A Framework for Federal Decision-Making,* February 1, 1979, Appendix B, "Summary of Comments Received Regarding October 20, 1978 Draft Staff Discussion Paper," p. 28.

[8] Ibid., p. 32.

[9] Thomas H. Maugh II, "Chemical Carcinogens: How Dangerous Are Low Doses?" *Science 202* (1978): 37.

[10] Charles C. Brown, Thomas R. Fears, Mitchell H. Gail, Marvin A. Schneiderman, Robert E. Tarone and Nathan Mantel, letter, "Models for Carcinogenic Risk Assessment," *Science 202* (1978): 1105.

[11] OSHA, *Federal Register 45:15* (January 22, 1980): 5155.

[12] Ibid., p. 5123.

[13] Ibid.

[14] Ibid., p. 5122.

[15] Ibid.

[16] Ibid., p. 5119

[17] Ibid.

[18] Interagency Regulatory Liaison Group (IRLG), Work Group on Risk Assessment, representing the Consumer Product Safety Commission, the Environmental Protection Agency, the Food and Drug Administration, and the Occupational Safety and Health Administration, "Scientific Bases for Identification of Potential Carcinogens and Estimation of Risks," *Journal of the National Cancer Institute 63* (1979): 265.

[19] Samuel S. Epstein, M.D., *The Politics of Cancer,* rev. ed. (Garden City, N.Y.: Anchor/Doubleday, 1979), p. 359.

[20] R. Truhaut, "An Overview of the Problem of Thresholds for Chemical Carcinogens," in *Carcinogenic Risks: Strategies for Intervention,* edited by W. Davis, C. Rosenfeld (Lyon: IARC Scientific Publications No. 25, 1979), p. 192; D. Hoel, R. Peto and L. Tomatis, cited in OSHA, *Federal Register 45:15* (January 22, 1980): 5023; Edward P. Radford, "Statement Concerning the Current Version of Cancer Risk Assessment in the Report of the Advisory Committee on the Biological Effects of Ionizing Radiations, (BEIR III Committee)," in *The Effects on Populations of Exposure to Low Levels of Ionizing Radiation: 1980,* Committee on the Biological Effects of Ionizing Radiations (Washington, D.C.: National Academy, 1980), p. 231; OSHA, *Federal Register 45:15* (January 22, 1980): 5137.

[21] Bruce N. Ames and Charles Yanofsky, "The Detection of Chemical Mutagens with Enteric Bacteria," in *Chemical Mutagens: Principles and Methods for Their Detection,* edited by Alexander Hollaender, Vol. 1 (New York: Plenum, 1971), p. 271; Jacqueline Verrett and Jean Carper, *Eating May Be Hazardous to Your Health* (Garden City, N.Y.: Anchor/Doubleday, 1975), pp. 148–149; Safe Drinking Water Committee, *Drinking Water and Health* (Washington, D.C.: National Academy of Sciences, 1977), pp. 37–38; Eula Bingham, "Regulatory Issues," in *Environmental Cancer: Causes, Victims, Solutions,* A Summary of Proceedings of a Conference held March 21 and 22, 1977, sponsored by the Urban Environment Conference, Inc., and primarily funded by the National Cancer Institute, as well as the National Institute for Environmental Health Sciences and the Environmental Protection Agency (Washington, D.C., Urban Environment Conference, Inc., 1978), p. 31; OSHA, *Federal Register 45:15* (January 22, 1980): p. 5024.

[22] Umberto Saffiotti, "Scientific Bases of Environmental Carcinogenesis and Cancer Prevention: Developing an Interdisciplinary Science and Facing Its Ethical Implications," *Journal of Toxicology and Environmental Health 2* (1977): 1437–1439; Truhaut, "An Overview of the Problem of Thresholds for Chemical Carcinogens," in *Carcinogenic Risks: Strategies for Intervention,* p. 192; OSHA, *Federal Register 45:15* (January 22, 1980), see "The Nature of the Disease," H. Stewart, I. N. Dubin, E. Farber, and OSHA, pp. 5016–5017.

[23] OSHA, *Federal Register 45:15* (January 22, 1980), M. Schneiderman, p. 5119; A. Upton, R. Squire, p. 5125; E. Farber, p. 5129; OSHA, pp. 5024, 5025.

[24] Samuel S. Epstein, M.D., *The Politics of Cancer* (San Francisco: Sierra Club Books, 1978), p. 61; William Lijinsky, Statement before the United States Department of Labor, Occupational Safety and Health Administration, *OSHA Docket No. 090,* April 4, 1978, p. 15; I. Selikoff, R. Griesemer, R. Squire cited in OSHA, *Federal Register 45:15* (January 22, 1980): p. 5136.

[25] Arthur C. Upton, "Progress in the Prevention of Cancer," *Preventive Medicine 7*

(1978): 482; OSHA, *Federal Register 45:15* (January 22, 1980), M. Meselson, p. 5135; D. Kennedy, p. 5137; W. Lijinsky, p. 5137; D. Kaufman, p. 5137; D. Rall, pp. 5136, 5137; OSHA, p. 5137.

[26] Umberto Saffiotti, "Identifying and Defining Chemical Carcinogens," *Origins of Human Cancer,* Book C, p. 1315; OSHA, *Federal Register 45:15* (January 22, 1980), R. Peto, p. 5136; OSHA, p. 5138.

[27] OSHA, *Federal Register 45:15* (January 22, 1980): 5137.

[28] Truhaut, "An Overview of the Problem of Thresholds for Chemical Carcinogens," in *Carcinogenic Risks: Strategies for Intervention,* pp. 191–202.

[29] P. N. Magee, "Extrapolation of Cellular and Molecular Level Studies to the Human Situation," *Journal of Toxicology and Environmental Health 2* (1977): 1422; Hans L. Falk "Biologic Evidence for the Existence of Thresholds in Chemical Carcinogenesis," *Environmental Health Perspectives 22* (1978): 167; Philip Handler, Dedication Address. Northwestern University Cancer Center, May 18, 1979, *manuscript,* p. 13; H. F. Kraybill, "Assessment of Current Approaches in the Evaluation of Carcinogenicity in Animal Models and Their Relevance to Man," p. 46; Gio Batta Gori, "The Regulation of Carcinogenic Hazards," *Science 208* (1980): 257.

[30] D. Henschler, "New Approaches to a Definition of Threshold Values for Irreversible Toxic Effects," *Archives of Toxicology 32* (1974): 63–67, cited by Kraybill, "Assessment of Current Approaches to the Evaluation of Carcinogenicity," p. 51; Falk, "Biologic Evidence for the Existence of Thresholds in Chemical Carcinogenesis" (1978), pp. 167–170; R. Olson, cited in OSHA, *Federal Register 45:15* (January 22, 1980): 5131.

[31] John Higginson, interviewed by Thomas H. Maugh II, "Cancer and Environment: Higginson Speaks Out," *Science 205* (1979): 1364.

[32] H. B. Jones and A. Grendon, "Environmental Factors in the Origin of Cancer and Estimation of the Possible Hazard to Man," *Food and Cosmetics Toxicology 13* (1975): 251; John Cairns, *Cancer: Science and Society* (San Francisco: Freeman, 1978), p. 132.

[33] H. F. Kraybill, "Biochemical Intermediates as Research Probes in Carcinogenesis Methodology," presented at December 19, 1977, *Meeting of the Clearinghouse on Environmental Carcinogens, Chemical Selection Subgroup, manuscript,* p. 2; Norbert P. Page, "Concepts of a Bioassay Program in Environmental Carcinogenesis," in *Advances in Modern Toxicology,* edited by Myron A. Mehlman, Vol. 3, *Environmental Cancer,* edited by H. F. Kraybill, Myron A. Mehlman (Washington, D.C.: Hemisphere, 1977), p. 135.

[34] K. Kay, "Occupational Cancer Risks for Pesticide Workers," *Environmental Research 7* (1974), cited by H. F. Kraybill, "Conceptual Approaches to the Assessment of Nonoccupational Environmental Cancer," in *Advances in Modern Toxicology,* Vol. 3, *Environmental Cancer, p. 46; K*raybill, "Assessment of Current Approaches in the Evaluation of Carcinogenicity in Animal Models and Their Relevance to Man," p. 92; Jerome Cornfield, "Carcinogenic Risk Assessments," *Science 198* (1977): 695; Nathan Mantel, "Letter to the Editor," *Cancer Research 38* (1978): 1835; Higginson, interview by Maugh, "Cancer and Environment," p. 1364.

[35] R. Kroes, G. J. Van Esch and J. W. Weiss, "Philosophy of 'No Effect Level' for Chemical Carcinogens," in *Proceedings of an International Symposium on Nitrite in Meat Products, Zeist,* 1973, p. 230; Hans L. Falk, "Biologic Evidence for the Existence of Thresholds in Carcinogenesis," Extrapolation Conference, Pinehurst, N.C., March 10–12, 1976, *manuscript,* my copy unpaginated; D. Schmahl and M. Habs, "Experimental Carcinogenesis of Antitumour Drugs," *Cancer Treat Rev* 5(4): 175–184; 1978, cited in *Carcinogenesis Abstracts: A Monthly Publication Sponsored by the National Cancer Institute 17,* edited by G.P. Studzinski, J. J. Saukkonen; NCI Staff Consultants, E. Weisburger, J. W. Chase (Philadelphia: Franklin Research Center, 1979), Abstract, 79–1819.

[36] Raymond J. Shamberger, cited by Maugh, "Chemical Carcinogens: How Dangerous Are Low Doses?," p. 40.

Kraybill, "Assessment of Current Approaches in the Evaluation of Carcinogenicity in Animal Models and Their Relevance to Man," p. 83; also see Kraybill, "Conceptual Approaches to the Assessment of Nonoccupational Environmental Cancer," in *Advances in Modern Toxicology,* Vol. 3, *Environmental Cancer,* p. 46.

[37] David P. Rall, "Thresholds?," *Environmental Health Perspectives 22* (1978): 163.

[38] Lijinsky, Statement before the United States Department of Labor, Occupational Safety and Health Administration, *OSHA Docket No. 090,* pp. 30–31.

[39] OSHA, *Federal Register 45:15* (January 22, 1980): p. 5138.

[40] Ibid., p. 5124.

[41] Ibid., p. 5128.

[42] Ibid.

[43] Ibid., p. 5136.

[44] Paracelsus, translation from German by John A. Zapp, "An Acceptable Level of Exposure," Herbert E. Stokinger Lecture 1977, *American Industrial Hygiene Association Journal* 38 (1977): 426.

[45] Ibid.

[46] Frontispiece, in *Toxicology: The Basic Science of Poisons*, edited by Louis J. Casarett, John Doull (New York: Macmillan, 1975).

[47] D. Schmähl, "Problems of Dose-Response Studies in Chemical Carcinogenesis with Special Reference to N-Nitroso Compounds," *CRC Critical Reviews in Toxicology 6* (1979): 258.

[48] Louis J. Casarett, "Toxicologic Evaluation," in *Toxicology: The Basic Science of Poisons*, pp. 17–18, p. 24.

[49] Ibid., p. 18.

[50] Ibid., p. 24.

[51] Ibid.

[52] Ibid., p. 27.

[53] Lijinsky, Statement before The United States Department of Labor, Occupational Health and Safety Administration, *OSHA Docket No. 090*, pp. 13–14.

[54] Jerzy Neyman, "Public Health Hazards from Electricity-Producing Plants," *Science 195* (1977): 755.

[55] Henry C. Pitot, "Relationships of Bioassay Data on Chemicals to Their Toxic and Carcinogenic Risk for Humans," *Cancer Symposium, An Academic Review of the Environmental Determinants of Cancer Relevant to Prevention*, held in cooperation with the American Cancer Society, Inc., New York City, February 28, March 1–2, 1979, *manuscript*, p. 13.

[56] Saffiotti, "Identifying and Defining Chemical Carcinogens," in *Origins of Human Cancer*, Book C, p. 1311.

[57] Ibid., pp. 1311–1312. Saffiotti was speaking at the fourth of the "Conferences on Cell Proliferation" conducted by Cold Spring Harbor Laboratory. That conference was subsequently published by Cold Spring Harbor Laboratory, in 1977, under the broad title *Origins of Human Cancer*, edited by H. H. Hiatt, J. D. Watson, J. A. Winsten.

[58] Richard Wilson, Testimony before the Food and Drug Administration of the Department of Health, Education, and Welfare, in the Matter of: *Acrylonitrile Copolymers Used to Fabricate Beverage Containers, Exhibit M-90, Docket No. 76N-0070;* Peter Barton Hutt, "Monsanto: Important for Food, Cosmetic Problems," *Legal Times of Washington*, Vol. II, No. 25, November 26, 1979, reprinted in *Federal Regulation of Carcinogens in the Workplace: OSHA's Cancer Policy*, chairmen Peter Barton Hutt, Anson M. Keller (Law & Business, Inc., Harcourt Brace Jovanovich, 1980), pp. 158–159.

[59] George B. Koelle, "The Zero-Tolerance Concept," *Perspectives in Biology and Medicine 20* (1977): 507.

[60] Wilson, Statement before the Food and Drug Administration of the Department of Health, Education, and Welfare, *Exhibit M-90, Docket No. 76N-0070*, p. 21.

[61] Hutt, "Monsanto: Important for Food, Cosmetic Problems," p. 159.

[62] Ibid., pp. 160–161. For original Court opinion see: Monsanto Co. v. Kennedy, United States Court of Appeals, District of Columbia Circuit. Argued March 15, 1979. Decided November 6, 1979, 613 F.2d 947 (1979). Note especially Sections 1, 3, 7, 8, 9, 10.

[63] Hutt, "Monsanto: Important for Food, Cosmetic Problems," pp. 160–161.

CHAPTER 13

[1] Robert Bensetler, "Re-counting Ghosts," letter of August 11, 1980, in *New York Times*, published August 18, 1980, p. A22.

[2] F. Winsor and M. Parry, quoted by Jeff Masten in "Epistemic Ambiguity and the Calculus of Risk: Ethyl Corporation vs. Environmental Protection Agency," *South Dakota Law Review 21* (Spring 1976).

[3] David Bazelon, "Science, Technology, and the Court," *Science 208* (1980): 661.

[4] John Higginson, "Multiplicity of Factors Involved in Cancer Patterns and Trends," *Cancer Symposium, An Academic Review of the Environmental Determinants of Cancer Relevant to Prevention*, held in cooperation with the American Cancer Society, Inc., New York City, February 28, March 1–2, 1979, *manuscript, p. 3.*

[5] H. F. Kraybill, "Assessment of Current Approaches in the Evaluation of Carcinogenicity in Animal Models and Their Relevance to Man," scheduled for inclusion as Chapter VII in Monograph on Environmental Carcinogenesis, edited by R. E. Olson (New York: Marcel Dekker), *manuscript*, received from Kraybill, 1980, see Table 18.

[6] Richard Gallagher, *Diseases That Plague Modern Man* (Dobbs Ferry, N.Y.: Oceana, 1969), pp. 176–177.

[7] Ibid., pp. 123, 125, 129, 131.

[8] David G. Hoel, Statement before the United States Department of Labor, Occupational Safety and Health Administration, *OSHA Docket No. 090*, April 4, 1978, pp. 1–2.

[9] William Lijinsky, Statement before the United States Department of Labor, Occupational Safety and Health Administration, *OSHA Docket No. 090*, April 4, 1978, p. 19.

[10] D. P. Rall, "The Role of Laboratory Animal Studies in Estimating Carcinogenic Risks for Man," in *Carcinogenic Risks: Strategies for Intervention*, edited by W. Davis, C. Rosenfeld (Lyon: IARC Scientific Publications No. 25, 1979), p. 184.

[11] L. Tomatis, "The Predictive Value of Rodent Carcinogenicity Tests in the Evaluation of Human Risks," *Annual Review of Pharmacology and Toxicology 19* (1979): 522.

[12] Office of Science and Technology Policy, Executive Office of the President, *Identification, Characterization, and Control of Potential Human Carcinogens: A Framework for Federal Decision-Making*, February 1, 1979, p. 14.

[13] Wilhelm Hueper, quoted by Eula Bingham, Richard W. Niemeier, and Jon B. Reid, "Multiple Factors in Carcinogenesis," *Annals of The New York Academy of Sciences*, Vol. 271, *Occupational Carcinogenesis*, edited by Umberto Saffiotti, Joseph K. Wagoner (New York: New York Academy of Sciences, 1976), see footnote, p. 14.

[14] Ibid.

[15] Judith Randal, "This Rat Died in a Cancer Lab to Save Lives," reprinted in *Washington Post* "Outlook," July 22, 1979, circulated by the EPA, OPA 15/80, January 1980, my copy unpaginated, see fourth paragraph.

[16] H. O. Hartley and R. L. Sielken Jr., "Estimation of 'Safe Doses' in Carcinogenic Experiments," address invited by the President, Eastern North American Region, Biometric Society for Regional Meeting, March 8–10, 1976, *manuscript*, my copy unpaginated, see discussion following table called "Contributions to Likelihood."

[17] H. L. Falk, "Anticarcinogenesis—an Alternative," in *Progress in Experimental Tumor Research*, edited by F. Homburger, Vol. 14, *Inhibition of Carcinogenesis*, edited by B. L. Van Duuren, B. A. Rubin (Basel: S. Karger, 1971), p. 107.

[18] Ad Hoc Committee on Testing for Environmental Chemical Carcinogens, NCI, quoted by Harold L. Stewart, Statement before the United States Department of Labor, Occupational Safety and Health Administration, *OSHA Docket No. 090*, April 4, 1978, p. 2.

[19] Sidney Weinhouse, "Conference on Extrapolation of Data from Animals to Man," *Cancer Research 36* (1976): 3854.

[20] Umberto Saffiotti, "Identifying and Defining Chemical Carcinogens," in *Origins of Human Cancer*, edited by H. H. Hiatt, J. D. Watson, J. A. Winsten, Book C, *Human Risk Assessment* (New York: Cold Spring Harbor Laboratory, 1977), pp. 1315, 1320–1321.

[21] John Higginson and Calum S. Muir, "The Role of Epidemiology in Elucidating the Importance of Environmental Factors in Human Cancer," *Cancer Detection and Prevention, I,* 1976, p. 81.

[22] John Higginson, "Overview," in *Environmental Cancer: Causes, Victims, Solutions*, A Summary of Proceedings of a Conference held March 21, 22, 1977, sponsored by the Urban Environment Conference, Inc., and primarily funded by the National Cancer Institute, as well as the National Institute for Environmental Health Sciences and the Environmental Protection Agency (Washington, D.C., Urban Environment Conference, Inc., 1978), p. 2.

[23] Pesticide Information, Review and Evaluation Committee (NAS, 1977), cited in Occupational Safety and Health Administration (OSHA), U.S. Department of Labor, *Identification, Classification and Regulation of Potential Occupational Carcinogens*, Part VII, Book 2, in *Federal Register 45:15* (January 22, 1980): 5182.

[24] Lijinsky, Statement before the United States Department of Labor, Occupational

Safety and Health Administration, *OSHA Docket No. 090,* April 4, 1978, p. 22; Lijinsky, cited in OSHA, *Federal Register 45:15* (January 22, 1980): 5182.

[25] Arthur C. Upton, "Progress in the Prevention of Cancer," *Preventive Medicine 7* (1978): 483.

[26] Samuel Epstein cited in OSHA, *Federal Register 45:15* (January 22, 1980): 5194.

[27] Richard Griesemer cited in OSHA, *Federal Register 45:15* (January 22, 1980): 5181.

[28] Harold L. Stewart, Statement before the United States Department of Labor, Occupational Safety and Health Administration, *OSHA Docket No. 090,* April 4, 1978, pp. 4–5.

[29] Umberto Saffiotti and Curtis C. Harris, "Carcinogenesis Studies on Organ Cultures of Animal and Human Respiratory Tissues," *Carcinogens: Identification and Mechanisms of Action,* edited by A. Clark Griffin, Charles R. Shaw (New York: Raven, 1979), p. 66.

[30] OSHA *Federal Register 45:15* (January 22, 1980): 5200.

[31] Charles C. Brown, "Statistical Aspects of Extrapolation of Dichotomous Dose-Response Data," *Journal of the National Cancer Institute 60* (1978): 101.

[32] Interagency Regulatory Liaison Group (IRLG), Work Group on Risk Assessment, representing the Consumer Product Safety Commission, the Environmental Protection Agency, the Food and Drug Administration, and the Occupational Safety and Health Administration, "Scientific Bases for Identification of Potential Carcinogens and Estimation of Risks," *Journal of the National Cancer Institute 63* (1979): 259; Roy E. Albert and Bernard Altshuler, "Considerations Relating to the Formulation of Limits for Unavoidable Population Exposures to Environmental Carcinogens," in *Radionuclide Carcinogenesis,* edited by C. L. Sanders, R. H. Busch, J. E. Ballou, D. D. Mahlum, Proceedings of the Twelfth Annual Hanford Biology Symposium at Richland, Washington, May 10–12, 1972, sponsored by Battelle Memorial Institute, Pacific Northwest Laboratories, U.S. Atomic Energy Commission (Published by U.S. Atomic Energy Commission Office of Information Services, Conf-720505, June 1973), p. 244.

[33] IRLG, "Scientific Bases for Identification of Potential Carcinogens and Estimation of Risks," p. 264.

[34] David Rall, "Extrapolating Animal and Microbiological Tests to Humans," Urban Environment Conference, p. 9; Kraybill, "Assessment of Current Approaches in the Evaluation of Carcinogenicity in Animal Models and Their Relevance to Man," p. 19.

[35] OSHA, *Federal Register 45:15* (January 22, 1980): 5122.

[36] Henry C. Pitot, "Relationships of Bioassay Data on Chemicals to Their Toxic and Carcinogenic Risk for Humans," *Cancer Symposium, An Academic Review of the Environmental Determinants of Cancer Relevant to Prevention, manuscript,* see Table 5.

[37] Hoel, Statement before the United States Department of Labor, Occupational Safety and Health Administration, *OSHA Docket No. 090,* p. 2; OSHA, *Federal Register 45:15* (January 22, 1980): 5184, see No. 3, "Methods of extrapolating dose-response data to low dose-levels."

[38] Committee for a Study of Saccharin and Food Safety Policy (NAS, 1978) quoted in OSHA, *Federal Register 45:15* (January 22, 1980): 5184.

[39] Pitot, "Relationships of Bioassay Data on Chemicals to Their Toxic and Carcinogenic Risk for Humans," *Cancer Symposium, An Academic Review of the Environmental Determinants of Cancer Relevant to Prevention, manuscript,* pp. 18–19; Richard Peto, cited in OSHA, *Federal Register 45:15* (January 22, 1980): 5136.

[40] Rall, "The Role of Laboratory Animal Studies in Estimating Carcinogenic Risks for Man," in *Carcinogenic Risks: Strategies for Intervention,* pp. 184–186; quotation, p. 186. In the text of this paper Rall refers to this report as "the NAS/NRC (1975) report." A full and more readily available reference for the report appears in his Cold Spring Harbor paper "Species Differences in Carcinogenesis Testing," in *Origins of Human Cancer,* Book C, see bibliography, p. 1390: *National Academy of Sciences (NAS) NRC Environmental Studies Board, 1975. "Contemporary pest control practices and prospects: The Report of the Executive Committee. I. Pest control: An assessment of present and alternative technologies." NAS, Washington, D.C.* In the literature, this report, so thickly encrusted with titles, is referred to briefly in several ways, e.g., "The Meselson Committee," "The Meselson Report," "The Pest Control Committee," "The NAS Analysis," and as an analysis "published as part of the NAS Pest Control Report" by Matthew Meselson (Harvard University) and Dr. Donald Kennedy (Commissioner, FDA). (See notes 41, 42, 43 below.)

[41] Rall, "Species Differences in Carcinogenesis Testing," in *Origins of Human Cancer,*

Book C, pp. 1388–1389; Marvin Schneiderman of the NCI, cited by Weinhouse, "Conference on Extrapolation of Data from Animals to Man," p. 3854; Pitot, "Relationships of Bioassay Data on Chemicals to Their Toxic and Carcinogenic Risk for Humans," *Cancer Symposium, An Academic Review of the Environmental Determinants of Cancer Relevant to Prevention, manuscript,* p. 4.

[42] OSHA, *Federal Register 45:15* (January 22, 1980): 5189–5190; D. B. Clayson, cited by Weinhouse, "Conference on Extrapolation of Data from Animals to Man," p. 3854.

[43] M. Schneiderman, H. L. Falk, D. Clayson, D. Rall, and J. M. Brown, cited by Weinhouse, "Conference on Extrapolation of Data from Animals to Man," p. 3854.

[44] Rall, "Extrapolating Animal and Microbiological Tests to Humans," Urban Environment Conference, p. 9.

[45] Safe Drinking Water Committee [*Drinking Water and Health* (Washington, D.C.: National Academy of Sciences, 1977)], quoted in OSHA, *Federal Register 45:15* (January 22, 1980): 5120; R. E. Albert and F. J. Burns, "Carcinogenic Atmospheric Pollutants and the Nature of Low-level Risks," in *Origins of Human Cancer*, Book A, *Incidence of Cancer in Humans*, p. 290; Arthur C. Upton, "Radiation," *Bulletin of the New York Academy of Medicine 54* (1978): 429.

[46] Committee on the Biological Effects of Ionizing Radiations (BEIR), *The Effects on Populations of Exposure to Low Levels of Ionizing Radiation: 1980* (Washington, D.C.: National Academy Press, 1980), see section "The Experience of the Atomic Bomb Survivors as a Source of Data on the Late Somatic Effects of Ionizing Radiation," pp. 150–157.

[47] IRLG, *Scientific Bases for Identification of Potential Carcinogens and Estimation of Risks*, p. 259.

[48] Thomas H. Maugh II, "Chemical Carcinogens: How Dangerous Are Low Doses?," *Science 202* (1978): 37.

[49] See Chapter VII for OSHA's incorporation of the no-threshold/one-molecule theory derived from radiation theory into the agency's postulated etiology of malignancy; speculation taken from (NAS) Safe Drinking Water Committee, *Drinking Water and Health*, pp. 37–38.

[50] W. Gary Flamm, "The Need for Quantifying Risk from Exposures to Chemical Carcinogens," *Preventive Medicine 5* (1976): 5.

[51] Kraybill, "Assessment of Current Approaches in the Evaluation of Carcinogenicity in Animal Models and Their Relevance to Man," p. 49.

[52] Marvin Schneiderman, Lecture, *Seminar on Government Regulation of Cancer-Causing Chemicals*, sponsored by the National Center for Administrative Justice, Washington, D.C., December 7–8, 1978.

[53] REVIEWS OF STATISTICAL THEORIES: GENERAL

David G. Hoel, David W. Gaylor, Ruth L. Kirschstein, Umberto Saffiotti, Marvin A. Schneiderman, "Estimation of Risks of Irreversible, Delayed Toxicity," *Journal of Toxicology and Environmental Health 1* (1975).

C. C. Brown, "Mathematical Aspects of Dose-Response Studies in Carcinogenesis—The Concept of Thresholds," *Oncology 33* (1976).

D. G. Hoel, "Some Problems in Low-dose Extrapolation," *Origins of Human Cancer*, edited by H. H. Hiatt, J. D. Watson, J. A. Winsten, Book C, *Human Risk Assessment* (New York: Cold Spring Harbor Laboratory, 1977).

Marvin A. Schneiderman, Charles C. Brown, "Estimating Cancer Risks to a Population," *Environmental Health Perspectives 22* (1978).

E. Scherer, P. Emmelot, "Multihit Kinetics of Tumor Cell Formation and Risk Assessment of Low Doses of Carcinogen," in *Carcinogens: Identification and Mechanisms of Action*, edited by A. Clark Griffin, Charles R. Shaw (New York: Raven, 1979).

Interagency Regulatory Liaison Group (IRLG), Work Group on Risk Assessment, representing the Consumer Product Safety Commission, the Environmental Protection Agency, the Food and Drug Administration, and the Occupational Safety and Health Administration, "Scientific Bases for Identification of Potential Carcinogens and Estimation of Risks," *Journal of the National Cancer Institute 63* (1979): 258–265.

Occupational Safety and Health Administration (OSHA), U.S. Department of Labor, *Identification, Classification and Regulation of Potential Occupational Carcinogens*, Part VII, Book 2, in *Federal Register 45:15* (January 22, 1980): 5184–5188.

PRACTICAL THRESHOLDS: THE MANTEL-BRYAN THEORY

Nathan Mantel, W. R. Bryan, " 'Safety' Testing of Carcinogenic Agents," *Journal of the National Cancer Institute 27* (1961).

Committee on Safe Drinking Water [*Drinking Water and Health* (Washington, D.C.: National Academy of Sciences, 1977)], quoted in OSHA, *Federal Register 45:15* (January 22, 1980): 5120–5121.

Joyce McCann, quoted in OSHA, *Federal Register 45:15* (January 22, 1980): 5186.

Adrian M. Gross, FDA, quoted in OSHA, *Federal Register 45:15* (January 22, 1980): 5186–5187.

H. F. Kraybill, "Assessment of Current Approaches in the Evaluation of Carcinogenicity in Animal Models and Their Relevance to Man," scheduled for inclusion as Chapter VII in Monograph on Environmental Carcinogenesis, edited by R. E. Olson (New York: Marcel Dekker), *manuscript*, received from Kraybill, 1980, pp. 46–48. Also see: H. F. Kraybill, "By Appropriate Methods: The Delaney Clause," in *Regulatory Aspects of Carcinogenesis and Food Additives: The Delaney Clause* (New York: Academic, 1979), pp. 61–80.

PRACTICAL THRESHOLDS: THE H. DRUCKREY THEORY

H. Druckrey, "Quantitative Aspects in Chemical Carcinogenesis," in *Potential Carcinogenic Hazards from Drugs: Evaluation of Risks*, edited by Rene Truhaut, UICC Monograph Series, Vol. 7 (New York: Springer-Verlag, 1967).

H. B. Jones and A. Grendon, "Environmental Factors in the Origin of Cancer and Estimation of the Possible Hazard to Man," *Food and Cosmetics Toxicology 13* (1975).

Harry A. Guess, David G. Hoel, "The Effect of Dose on Cancer Latency Period," *Journal of Environmental Pathology and Toxicology 1* (1977).

Hardin Jones, "Dose-Effect Relationships in Carcinogenesis and the Matter of Threshold of Carcinogenesis," *Environmental Health Perspectives 22* (1978).

Marvin Schneiderman quoted in OSHA, *Federal Register 45:15* (January 22, 1980): 5134–5135.

David Hoel, quoted in OSHA, *Federal Register 45:15* (January 22, 1980): 5134.

Richard Peto, quoted in OSHA, *Federal Register, 45:15* (January 22, 1980): 5134.

[54] Jerome Cornfield, "Carcinogenic Risk Assessment," *Science 198* (1977): 695.

[55] Kraybill, "Assessment of Current Approaches in the Evaluation of Carcinogenicity in Animal Models and Their Relevance to Man," p. 45; Edward E. Pochin, cited by Maugh, "Chemical Carcinogens: How Dangerous Are Low Doses?," p. 37.

[56] John Cairns, *Cancer: Science and Society* (San Francisco: Freeman, 1978), p. 104.

[57] Memorandum from Daniel G. Greathouse, Water Supply Research Laboratory, NERC, EPA, to David Hoel, National Institute of Environmental Health Sciences, Review of Document Prepared by the Carcinogen Testing Subcommittee, April 10, 1974, p. 3.

[58] Leo Friedman, "A Proposed Procedure for the Assessment of Health Hazards of Carcinogens at Very Low Levels of Exposure," "Annex" to Report of a WHO Scientific Group, *Assessment of the Carcinogenicity and Mutagenicity of Chemicals*, Technical Report Series 546 (Geneva: World Health Organization, 1974), p. 18.

[59] Report of a WHO Scientific Group, *Assessment of the Carcinogenicity and Mutagenicity of Chemicals*, p. 13.

[60] Hoel et al., "Estimation of Risks of Irreversible, Delayed Toxicity," p. 145.

[61] R. L. Dixon, "Problems in Extrapolating Toxicity Data for Laboratory Animals to Man," *Environmental Health Perspectives 13* (1976): 43, 45.

[62] Lorenzo Tomatis, "THE IARC Program on the Evaluation of the Carcinogenic Risk of Chemicals to Man," in *Annals of The New York Academy of Sciences,* Vol. 271, *Occupational Carcinogenesis*, p. 401.

[63] Norton Nelson, "Comments on Extrapolation of Cancer Response from High Dose to Low Dose," *Environmental Health Perspectives 22* (1978): 94.

[64] Schneiderman et al., "Estimating Cancer Risks to a Population," p. 122.

[65] Gary Flamm, Lecture, *Seminar on Government Regulation of Cancer-Causing Chemicals.*

[66] International Agency for Research on Cancer, IARC Monographs on the Evaluation of the Carcinogenic Risk of Chemicals to Humans, Vol. 17, *Some N-Nitroso Compounds* (Lyon: IARC, 1978), p. 20.

[67] David B. Clayson, cited by Maugh, "Chemical Carcinogens: How Dangerous Are Low Doses?," p. 37.

[68] D. B. Clayson, "Chemical Carcinogenesis: Dose-Response Extrapolation," *Science 203* (1979): 1068, 1069.

[69] Philip Handler, "Dedication Address, Northwestern University Cancer Center," May 18, 1979, *manuscript*, p. 6.

[70] Philip Handler, "Basic Research in the United States," *Science 204* (1979): 477.

[71] Pitot, "Relationships of Bioassay Data on Chemicals to Their Toxic and Carcinogenic Risk for Humans," *Cancer Symposium, An Academic Review of the Environmental Determinants of Cancer Relevant to Prevention, manuscript*, pp. 17, 20.

[72] Office of Science and Technology Policy, *Identification, Characterization, and Control of Potential Human Carcinogens: A Framework for Federal Decision-Making*, p. 14.

[73] Gio Batta Gori, "The Regulation of Carcinogenic Hazards," *Science 208* (1980): 259.

[74] Joseph V. Rodricks, "Regulation of Carcinogens in Food," presented at New York Academy of Sciences *Workshop on Management of Assessed Risk for Carcinogens*, New York, March 17, 18, 19, 1980, reprinted in *Federal Regulation of Carcinogens in the Workplace: OSHA's Cancer Policy*, chairman Peter Barton Hutt, Anson M. Keller (New York: Law & Business, Inc., Harcourt Brace Jovanovich, 1980), p. 67.

[75] OSHA, *Federal Register 45:15* (January 22, 1980): 5200.

[76] Ibid., p. 5198.

[77] Philip Handler, NAS, prefatory letter to Douglas Costle, EPA, July 22, 1980, transmitting *The Effects on Populations of Exposure to Low Levels of Ionizing Radiation: 1980*, prepared by the Committee on the Biological Effects of Ionizing Radiations under contract with EPA's Office of Radiation Programs (Washington, D.C.: National Academy Press, 1978), pp. iii–iv.

CHAPTER 14

[1] "Leon Rosenberg on the 'Human Life' Bill," excerpt from Rosenberg's testimony before the U.S. Senate on bill S.158, April 23–24, 1981, *Science 212* (1981): 907.

[2] Umberto Saffiotti, "Identifying and Defining Chemical Carcinogens" in *Origins of Human Cancer*, edited by H. H. Hiatt, J. D. Watson, J. A. Winsten, Book C, *Human Risk Assessment* (New York: Cold Spring Harbor Laboratory, 1977), pp. 1314, 1320–1321.

[3] David B. Clayson, "Overview, Fact, Myth and Speculation," *Journal of Environmental Pathology and Toxicology 2* (1978): 1.

[4] L. Tomatis, "The Value of Long-term Testing for the Implementation of Primary Prevention," in *Origins of Human Cancer*, Book C, p. 1352.

[5] Philip H. Abelson, "The Tris Controversy," *Science 197* (1977): 113.

[6] Robert H. Harris, "The Tris Ban," letter, *Science 197* (1977): 1132–1133.

[7] Ian Munro, Lecture, *Seminar on Government Regulation of Cancer-Causing Chemicals*, sponsored by National Center for Administrative Justice, Washington, D.C., December 7–8, 1978.

[8] Irving Selikoff, quoted by William E. Burrows, "The Cancer Safety Controversy," *New York Times Magazine*, March 25, 1979, p. 85.

[9] Letter from Irving Selikoff to E. I. Eger II at the University of California Medical Center, San Francisco, discussing certain studies conducted by Thomas Corbett, March 13, 1975, quoted in Thomas H. Corbett, *Cancer and Chemicals* (Chicago: Nelson-Hall, 1977), pp. 186–188.

[10] Richard Peto, "Distorting the Epidemiology of Cancer: The Need for a More Balanced Overview," *Nature 284* (1980): 300.

[11] Gio Batta Gori, "The Regulation of Carcinogenic Hazards," *Science 208* (1980): 257–258, quotation, p. 257.

[12] Jerome Cornfield, "Carcinogenic Risk Assessment," *Science 198* (1977): 695–696.

[13] Gary Flamm, Lecture, *Seminar on Government Regulation of Cancer-Causing Chemicals*.

[14] Tomatis, "The Value of Long-term Testing for the Implementation of Primary Prevention in *Origins of Human Cancer*, Book C, pp. 1341–1342, quotation, p. 1341.

[15] D. P. Rall, "The Role of Laboratory Animal Studies in Estimating Carcinogenic Risks

for Man," in *Carcinogenic Risks: Strategies for Intervention,* edited by W. Davis, C. Rosenfeld (Lyon: IARC Scientific Publications No. 25, 1979), pp. 179–184, quotation p. 184.

[16] Lewis Thomas, "Tolerance Issue Bedevils Scientists, Solons," original article published by the Department of Public Affairs, Memorial Sloan-Kettering Cancer Center, Winter, 1979, excerpted by *Oncology Times,* April 1980, editorial page.

[17] Elizabeth C. Miller, "Some Current Perspectives on Chemical Carcinogenesis in Humans and Experimental Animals: Presidential Address," *Cancer Research 38* (1978): 1491.

[18] Samuel S. Epstein, Statement before the United States Department of Labor, Occupational Safety and Health Administration, *OSHA Docket No. 090,* April 4, 1978, p. 34.

CHAPTER 15

[1] Lewis H. Lapham, "The American Courtier," *Harper's,* October 1978, p. 16.

[2] Aaron Wildavsky, quoted in "Scientists Debate Acceptable Risk" (unsigned article), *New York Times,* February 27, 1979, p. C1.

[3] Norio Matsukura, Takashi Kawachi, Kazuhide Morino, Hiroko Ohgaki, Takashi Sugimura and Shozo Takayama, "Carcinogenicity in Mice of Mutagenic Compounds from a Tryptophan Pyrolyzate," *Science 213* (1981).

[4] Isaac Berenblum, "Author's Preface," *Frontiers of Biology,* edited by A. Neuberger, E. L. Tatum, Vol. 34, *Carcinogenesis as a Biological Problem* (New York: Elsevier, 1974).

[5] John Higginson, "Multiplicity of Factors Involved in Cancer Patterns and Trends," *Cancer Symposium, An Academic Review of the Environmental Determinants of Cancer Relevant to Prevention,* held in cooperation with the American Cancer Society, Inc., February 28, March 1, 2, 1979, New York City, *manuscript,* p. 1.

[6] Paul Seabury, quoted by Rael Jean Isaac and Erich Isaac, "Sanctifying Revolution: Protestantism's New Social Gospel," *American Spectator,* May 1981, p. 11.

[7] Ross Hume Hall, interviewed in "What Is This Thing Called Food?," NBC News, September 8, 1976, *transcript.*

[8] Frank N. Rauscher, Director, National Cancer Program, letter to Philippe Shubik, Director, Eppley Institute for Research in Cancer, conclusion of "General Criteria for Assessing the Evidence of Chemical Substances: Report of the Subcommittee on Environmental Carcinogenesis, National Cancer Advisory Board," *Journal of the National Cancer Institute 58* (1977): 464.

[9] David Rall, Testimony, "Toxic Substances Control Act," Hearings before the Subcommittee on the Environment of the Committee on Commerce, United States Senate, Ninety-fourth Congress, First Session on S.776, March 3, 5, 10, and April 15, 1975, Serial No. 94-24, p. 222.

[10] Ibid., pp. 222–223.

[11] Thomas H. Maugh II and Jean L. Marx, *Seeds of Destruction: The Science Report on Cancer Research* (New York: Plenum, 1975), p. 9.

[12] Gary Flamm, First Meeting of the Chemical Selection Subgroup of the Clearinghouse on Environmental Carcinogens, National Institutes of Health, Bethesda, Md., November 8, 1976, *transcript,* p. 175.

[13] John Walsh, "EPA and Toxic Substances Law: Dealing with Uncertainty," *Science 202* (1978): 598.

[14] Isaac Berenblum, "Carcinogenicity Testing for Control of Environmental Tumor Development in Man," *Israel Journal of Medical Science 15* (1979): 474.

[15] Toxic Substances Strategy Committee, *Toxic Chemicals and Public Protection,* A Report to the President, 1980, p. 16.

[16] Ibid., p. xxvi.

[17] Maugh and Marx, *Seeds of Destruction,* p. 20.

[18] Ibid.

[19] Thomas H. Maugh II, "Chemical Carcinogens: The Scientific Basis for Regulation," *Science 201* (1978): 1202.

[20] Ibid.

[21] Gregory J. Ahart, Director, Human Resources Division, General Accounting Office, letter March 30, 1979 (B-164031(2)) to The Honorable Henry A. Waxman, U.S. House of Representatives, Enclosure I of report on program operations, pp. 8–9.

[22] H. L. Falk, "Anticarcinogenesis—an Alternative," in *Progress in Experimental Tumor*

Research, edited by F. Homburger, Vol. 14, *Inhibition of Carcinogenesis,* edited by B. L. van Duuren, B. A. Rubin (Basel: S. Karger, 1971), p. 106.

[23] U.S. Department of Health, Education, and Welfare, *HEW News,* November 13, 1978.

[24] Ibid.

[25] Norbert P. Page, "Concepts of a Bioassay Program in Environmental Carcinogenesis," in *Advances in Modern Toxicology,* edited by Myron A. Mehlman, Vol. 3, *Environmental Cancer,* edited by H. F. Kraybill, Myron A. Mehlman (Washington, D.C.: Hemisphere, 1977), pp. 104–106.

[26] "Needs for Environmental Research: Which Are Most Important?," an analysis of a report by the Committee on Environmental Research and Development, Environmental Studies Board, Commission on Natural Resources, National Research Council, to the Director, Office of Science and Technology Policy, Executive Office of the President, May 31, 1979; in *News Report,* a monthly register of activities of the National Academy of Sciences, National Academy of Engineering, Institute of Medicine, and National Research Council, September 1979, p. 6.

[27] Gary Flamm, Lecture, *Seminar on Government Regulation of Cancer-Causing Chemicals,* sponsored by National Center for Administrative Justice, Washington, D.C., December 7–8, 1978.

[28] Joyce McCann, Edmund Choi, Edith Yamasaki, and Bruce N. Ames, "Detection of Carcinogens as Mutagens in the *Salmonella*/Microsome Test: Assay of 300 Chemicals," *Proceedings of the National Academy of Sciences 72* (1975): 5135.

[29] J. McCann and B. N. Ames, "The Salmonella/Microsome Mutagenicity Test: Predictive Value for Animal Carcinogenicity," in *Origins of Human Cancer,* edited by H. H. Hiatt, J. D. Watson, J. A. Winsten, Book C, *Human Risk Assessment* (New York: Cold Spring Harbor Laboratory, 1977), p. 1447.

[30] Bruce N. Ames, "Identifying Environmental Chemicals Causing Mutations and Cancer," *Science 204* (1979): 587, 591.

[31] Ibid., p. 591.

[32] M. Meselson and K. Russell, "Comparisons of Carcinogenic and Mutagenic Potency," *Origins of Human Cancer,* Book C, pp. 1474, 1479.

[33] Bruce Ames and Kim Hooper, "Does Carcinogenic Potency Correlate with Mutagenic Potency in the Ames Assay?," *Nature 274* (1978): 19.

[34] Occupational Safety and Health Administration (OSHA), U.S. Department of Labor, *Identification, Classification and Regulation of Potential Occupational Carcinogens,* Part VII, Book 2, in *Federal Register 45:15* (January 22, 1980): 5181, 5194.

[35] Ibid., p. 5194.

[36] Ibid., p. 5181.

[37] Ibid., p. 5180.

[38] Flamm, Lecture, *Seminar on Government Regulation of Cancer-Causing Chemicals.*

[39] Thomas H. Maugh II, "Estimating Potency of Carcinogens Is an Inexact Science," *Science 202* (1978): 38.

[40] Umberto Saffiotti, Lecture, "Seminar on Government Regulations of Cancer-Causing Chemicals."

[41] Isaac Berenblum, "Carcinogenicity Testing for Control of Environmental Tumor Development in Man," *Israel Journal of Medical Sciences 15* (1979): 476.

[42] OSHA, *Federal Register 45:15* (January 22, 1980): 5193.

[43] Berenblum, "Carcinogenicity Testing for Control of Environmental Tumor Development in Man," p. 476; Isaac Berenblum, *Frontiers of Biology,* Vol. 34, *Carcinogenesis as a Biological Problem,* p. 335.

[44] OSHA, *Federal Register 45:15* (January 22, 1980): 5184.

[45] Saffiotti, Lecture, *Seminar on Government Regulation of Cancer-Causing Chemicals.*

[46] Donald V. Lassiter, "Occupational Carcinogenesis," in *Advances in Modern Toxicology,* Vol. 3, *Environmental Cancer,* p. 75; H. F. Kraybill, "Assessment of Current Approaches in the Evaluation of Carcinogenicity in Animal Models and Their Relevance to Man," scheduled for inclusion as Chapter VII in Monograph on Environmental Carcinogenesis, edited by R. E. Olson (New York: Marcel Dekker), *manuscript,* received from Kraybill, 1980, pp. 11, 73.

[47] Office of Science and Technology Policy, Executive Office of the President, *Identifica-*

562 NOTES

tion, Characterization, and Control of Potential Human Carcinogens: A Framework for Federal Decision-Making, February 1, 1979, pp. 14, 15, 16.

[48] L. Tomatis, "The Value of Long-Term Testing for the Implementation of Primary Prevention," *Origins of Human Cancer,* Book C, p. 1352.

[49] OSHA, *Federal Register 45:15* (January 22, 1980): 5197.

[50] Ibid., p. 5208.

[51] Ibid.

[52] Ibid., p. 5209.

[53] "Risks in Exposure to Mutagens," *News Report,* a monthly register of activities of the National Academy of Sciences, National Academy of Engineering, Institute of Medicine, and National Research Council, January 1980, p. 1.

[54] Gerald S. Schatz, "Pesticides, Benefit-Cost Analysis, and the Burden of Regulation," *News Report,* a monthly register of activities of the National Academy of Sciences, National Academy of Engineering, Institute of Medicine, and National Research Council, August 1980, p. 5.

[55] Victor K. McElheny, "Foreword," *Banbury Report 1, Assessing Chemical Mutagens: The Risk to Humans,* edited by Victor K. McElheny, Seymour Abrahamson (New York: Cold Spring Harbor Laboratory, 1979), p. xii.

[56] Schatz, "Pesticides, Benefit-Cost Analysis, and the Burden of Regulation," *News Report,* p. 4.

[57] Ibid., p. 5.

[58] John H. Weisburger and Gary M. Williams, "Carcinogen Testing: Current Problems and New Approaches," *Science 214* (1981): 402.

[59] Ibid., p. 403.

[60] Ibid., pp. 403–404.

[61] Eliot Marshall, "EPA's High-Risk Carcinogen Policy," *Science 218* (1982): 975.

[62] Ibid..

[63] Ibid.

[64] Ibid.

[65] Weisburger and Williams, "Carcinogen Testing: Current Problems and New Approaches," p. 401.

[66] Ibid., p. 402.

[67] Ibid., p. 405.

[68] John W. Drake, "Some Guidelines for Determining Maximum Permissible Levels of Chemical Mutagens," in *Advances in Modern Toxicology,* edited by Myron A. Mehlman, Vol. 5, *Mutagenesis,* edited by W. G. Flamm, Myron A. Mehlman (Washington, D.C.: Hemisphere, 1978), p. 17.

[69] *Banbury Report 1, Assessing Chemical Mutagens: The Risk to Humans,* published discussion by geneticists in which James Neel stresses the need for human data, pp. 20, 217, 225; J. V. Neel, T. O. Tiffany, N. G. Anderson, "Approaches to Monitoring Human Populations for Mutation Rates and Genetic Disease," in *Chemical Mutagens: Principles and Methods for Their Detection,* edited by Alexander Hollaender, Vol. 3 (New York: Plenum, 1973), p. 121.

[70] James F. Crow, "Human Population Monitoring," in *Chemical Mutagens: Principles and Methods for Their Detection,* Vol. 2 (1971), p. 591.

[71] Drake, "Some Guidelines for Determining Maximum Permissible Levels of Chemical Mutagens," in *Advances in Modern Toxicology,* Vol. 5, *Mutagenesis,* p. 17.

[72] Ibid., pp. 18–23, quotation p. 22.

[73] E. K. Weisburger, "Carcinogenic Natural Products," in *Structural Correlates of Carcinogenesis and Mutagenesis. A Guide to Testing Priorities? Proceedings of the Second Food and Drug Administration Office of Science Summer Symposium held in Annapolis, August 31–September 2, 1977.* Office of Science, FDA (Annapolis, Md.), HEW Publication No. (FDA)78-1046: 241 pp.; 184–192; 1978, cited in *Carcinogenesis Abstracts: A Monthly Publication Sponsored by the National Cancer Institute 17,* edited by G. P. Studzinski, J. J. Saukkonen; NCI Staff Consultants, E. Weisburger, J. W. Chase (Philadelphia: Franklin Research Center, 1979), Abstract 79-0045.

[74] Letter from Russell W. Peterson, Chairman, Council on Environmental Quality, Executive Office of the President, to Wallace H. Johnson, Assistant Attorney General, Land and Natural Resources Division, U.S. Department of Justice, July 16, 1974, inserted into the record, "Burdens of Proof in Environmental Litigation," Hearing before the Subcommittee

on Environment of the Committee on Commerce, United States Senate, Ninety-third Congress, Second Session on S. 1104 Amendment No. 1814, November 19, 1974, Serial No. 93-126, pp. 8-10, quotation, p. 10.

[75] Safe Drinking Water Committee, *Drinking Water and Health* (Washington, D.C.: National Academy of Sciences, 1977), pp. 152-153.

[76] Walter Sullivan, "Radiation Danger Seen in Seepage of Radon in Homes," *New York Times,* October 7, 1980, pp. C1, C4.

[77] Morton K. Schwartz, "Role of Trace Elements in Cancer," *Cancer Research 35,* (1975): 3481; OSHA, *Federal Register 45:15* (January 22, 1980), see discussion of bionutrients, pp. 5129-5131.

[78] International Agency for Research on Cancer, IARC Monographs on the Evaluation of the Carcinogenic Risk of Chemicals to Humans, Vol. 17, *Some N-Nitroso Compounds* (Lyon: IARC, 1978), p. 36.

[79] Steven R. Tannenbaum, "Ins and Outs of Nitrites," *Sciences,* January 1980, p. 7.

[80] Hans L. Falk, "Biologic Evidence for the Existence of Thresholds in Chemical Carcinogenesis," *Environmental Health Perspectives, 22,* 1978, p. 169.

[81] Kraybill, "Assessment of Current Approaches in the Evaluation of Carcinogenicity in Animal Models and Their Relevance to Man," p. 60.

[82] OSHA, *Federal Register 45:15* (January 22, 1980): 5130.

[83] Ibid.

[84] Thomas H. Maugh II, "Chemical Carcinogens: How Dangerous Are Low Doses?," *Science 202* (1978): 39.

[85] OSHA, *Federal Register 45:15* (January 22, 1980): 5130.

[86] Ibid., p. 5129.

[87] Elizabeth C. Miller, "Some Current Perspectives on Chemical Carcinogenesis in Humans and Experimental Animals: Presidential Address," *Cancer Research 38* (1978): 1491.

[88] Kraybill, "Assessment of Current Approaches in the Evaluation of Carcinogenicity in Animal Models and Their Relevance to Man," p. 84.

[89] Rosalyn S. Yalow cited in Petr Beckmann, "Nuclear Notes," *Access to Energy,* March 1980; Rosalyn S. Yalow, "Fear of Radiation," *New York Times,* January 31, 1981, p. 28.

[90] R. H. Mole, "Anxieties and Fears About Plutonium," *British Medical Journal 2* (1977): 743.

[91] Petr Beckmann, "Protecting the Environment," *Access to Energy,* March 1979.

[92] Diane Ravitch, "The Schools We Deserve," *New Republic,* April 18, 1981, p. 25.

[93] Joseph V. Rodricks, "Food Hazards of Natural Origin," Symposium: *Principal Hazards in Food Safety and Their Assessment, Federation Proceedings 37* (1978): 2587.

[94] T. Sugimura, M. Nagao, T. Kawachi, M. Honda, T. Yahagi, Y. Seino, S. Sato, N. Matsukura, T. Matsushima, A. Shirai, M. Sawamura, H. Matsumoto, "Mutagen-carcinogens in Food, with Special Reference to Highly Mutagenic Pyrolytic Products in Broiled Foods," in *Origins of Human Cancer,* Book C, pp. 1561-1574.

[95] Peter Barton Hutt, "Public Policy Issues in Regulating Carcinogens in Food," *Food Drug Cosmetic Law Journal 33:10* (1978): 548-549.

[96] James and Elizabeth Miller, interviewed by Jane E. Brody, "Two Biochemists Did Pioneering Work the Hard Way," *New York Times,* March 13, 1979, p. C2.

[97] Peter Barton Hutt, "Hair Dye Regs: A Narrowing of FDA 'No Risk' Policy, *Legal Times of Washington 2:22* (1979), reprinted in *Federal Regulation of Carcinogens in the Workplace: OSHA's Cancer Policy,* chairmen: Peter Barton Hutt, Anson M. Keller (New York: Law & Business, Inc., Harcourt Brace Jovanovich, 1980), pp. 155-156; Richard A. Merrill, "Regulation of Toxic Chemicals," *Texas Law Review 58:463* (1980): pp. 478-479.

[98] Food and Drug Administration, 21 CFR Part 740 (Docket No. 77P-0353), FDA Cosmetic Product Warning Statements; Coal Tar Hair Dyes Containing 4-Methoxy-M-Phenylenediamine (2, 4-Diaminoanisole) or 4-Methoxy-*M*-Phenylenediamine Sulfate (2, 4-Diaminoanisole Sulfate), *Federal Register 44:201* (October 16, 1979): 59513.

[99] Merrill, "Regulation of Toxic Chemicals," *Texas Law Review,* p. 479.

[100] Sugimura et al., "Mutagen-Carcinogens in Food with Special Reference to Highly Mutagenic Pyrolytic Products in Broiled Foods," in *Origins of Human Cancer,* Book C, p. 1574.

[101] Joseph V. Rodricks, "Regulation of Carcinogens in Food," presented at New York Academy of Sciences *Workshop on Management of Assessed Risk for Carcinogens,* March 17,

18, 19, 1980. Reprinted in *Federal Regulation of Carcinogens in the Workplace: OSHA's Cancer Policy*, pp. 71–72.

[102] Neil E. Spingarn, Hiroshi Kasai, Loretto L. Vuolo, Susumu Nishimura, Ziro Yamaizumi, Takashi Sugimura, Taijiro Matsushima, and John H. Weisburger, "Formation of Mutagens in Cooked Foods. III. Isolation of a Potent Mutagen From Beef," *Cancer Letters 9* (1980): 177.

[103] Ibid., pp. 182–183.

[104] Hiroshi Kasai, Ziro Yamaizumi, Tomoko Shiomi, Shigeyuki Yokoyama, Tatsuo Miyazawa, Keiji Wakabayashi, Minako Nagao, Takashi Sugimura, and Susumu Nishimura, "Structure of a Potent Mutagen Isolated from Fried Beef," *Chemistry Letters*, The Chemical Society of Japan, 1981, p. 485.

[105] Ibid.

[106] Norio Matsukura, Takashi Kawachi, Kazuhide Morino, Hiroko Ohgaki, Takashi Sugimura, and Shozo Takayama, "Carcinogenicity in Mice of Mutagenic Compounds from a Tryptophan Pyrolyzate," *Science 213* (1981): 347.

[107] Ibid.

[108] "Names in the News," Takashi Sugimura, *Oncology Times*, April 1981, p. 24. Even the anonymous "Names in the News" writer appeared to be unaware of the universality of the findings of Sugimura and his colleagues, e.g., that broiling and frying beef produces mutagens and carcinogens. Sugimura, the writer said, had discovered natural carcinogens in food "that were enhanced by traditional styles of Japanese cooking."

[109] Harold M. Schmeck, Jr., "4 Cancer Researchers Win General Motors Awards," *New York Times*, June 17, 1981, p. A18.

[110] I wrote to Dr. Takashi Sugimura, Director of the Japanese National Cancer Center Research Institute, on December 22, 1981; he replied on January 4, 1982, telling me that the Vice-Director of the Institute, Dr. Takashi Kawachi would check the survey on natural carcinogens and mutagens. On January 13, 1982, I wrote to Dr. Kawachi and received two letters from him, one sent on April 12, 1982, and one (undated) sent in May 1982.

[111] Shoichi Katayama, Emerich Fiala, Bandaru S. Reddy, Abraham Rivenson, Jerald Silverman, Gary M. Williams, and John H. Weisburger, "Prostate Adenocarcinoma in Rats: Induction by 3,2'-Dimethyl-4-aminobiphenyl," *Journal of the National Cancer Institute 68* (1982): 867.

[112] John W. Berg, "Can Nutrition Explain the Pattern of International Epidemiology of Hormone-dependent Cancers?," *Cancer Research 35* (1975): 3345–3347; H. T. Lynch, A. J. Krush, and H. Guirgis, "Genetic Factors in Families with Combined Gastrointestinal and Breast Cancer," *American Journal of Gastroenterology 59* (1973): 31–40.

[113] Katayama et al., "Prostate Adenocarcinoma in Rats," p. 867.

[114] John H. Weisburger, Neil E. Spingarn, Yi Y. Wang, and Loretto L. Vuolo, "Assessment of the Role of Mutagens and Endogenous Factors in Large Bowel Cancer," *Cancer Bulletin 33* (1981): 126.

[115] Committee on Diet, Nutrition, and Cancer, National Research Council, *Diet, Nutrition and Cancer* (Washington, D.C.: National Academy Press, 1982). This study was announced to the press in *News from the National Research Council*, "Interim Guidelines Recommended for Reducing Risks through Diet," January 16, 1982. The press release contained no reference to laboratory data.

[116] Bruce N. Ames, "Dietary Carcinogens and Anticarcinogens: Oxygen Radicals and Degenerative Diseases," *Science, 221,* September 23, 1983, pp. 1256–1264.

[117] Wildavsky, quoted in *New York Times*, February 27, 1979, p. C1.

EPILOGUE

[1] James Bishop, Jr., panelist on "Face the Nation," CBS, 1976, *transcript.*

[2] Dan Rather, "The American Way of Death," CBS, 1975, *transcript.*

[3] Larry Agran, *The Cancer Connection: And What We Can Do About It* (New York: St. Martin's, 1977), p. xvi.

[4] *Time,* "The Disease of the Century," October 20, 1975, cited by Senator John Tunney, statement in "Toxic Substances Control Act," *Hearing Before the Subcommittee on the Environment of the Committee on Commerce,* United States Senate, Ninety-fourth Congress, October 24, 1975, Part 2, Serial No. 94–24, p. 1.

[5] Rather, "The American Way of Death," *transcript.*

[6] *Time,* "The Disease of the Century," October 20, 1975, reprinted in "Toxic Substances Control Act," *Hearing,* October 24, 1975, p. 2.

[7] I. Berenblum, *Israel Journal of Medical Sciences 4* (1968): 466.

[8] John Higginson, "Distribution of Different Patterns of Cancer," *Israel Journal of Medical Sciences 4* (1968): 460.

[9] Doll, Payne and Waterhouse, eds., *Cancer Incidence in Five Continents, A Technical Report* (Berlin: Springer, 1966, 1970, 1976); Segi's series of reports on *Cancer Mortality for Selected Sites in 24 Countries* (Segi, 1960; Segi and Kurihara, 1962, 1964, 1966; Segi et al., 1969), (Tokyo: Japan Cancer Society); World Health Organization, *Mortality from Malignant Neoplasms,* 1955–1965, *Number of Deaths by Site, Sex, and Age,* Vols. I and II (Geneva: WHO, 1970).

[10] Higginson, "Distribution of Different Patterns of Cancer," p. 459.

[11] *Syncrisis: The Dynamics of Health, An Analytic Series on the Interactions of Health and Socioeconomic Development, XII: Thailand,* Government Document OS 74-50008 (Washington, D.C.: U.S. Department of Health, Education and Welfare, 1974), p. 2.

[12] Higginson, "Distribution of Different Patterns of Cancer," section entitled "Theoretical Implications of Prevention," following Table 4.

[13] John Higginson, "Present Trends in Cancer Epidemiology," in *Canadian Cancer Conference: Proceedings of the Eighth Canadian Cancer Research Conference,* Ontario, 1968 (New York: Pergamon, 1969), p. 43.

[14] Richard Doll, "Strategy for Detection of Cancer Hazards to Man," *Nature 263* (1977): 589.

[15] C. S. Muir, "Epidemiological Identification of Cancer Hazards," in *Prevention and Detection of Cancer,* Part II, Vol. 1, edited by Herbert E. Nieburgs (New York: Marcel Dekker, 1978), p. 6.

[16] John Higginson, "Population Studies in Cancer," *ACTA,* Unio Internationalis Contra Cancrum, *16* (1960): 1668–1669.

[17] Ibid., p. 1669.

[18] Muir, "Epidemiological Identification of Cancer Hazards," p. 6.

[19] Richard Doll, *Prevention of Cancer: Pointers from Epidemiology* (Nuffield Provincial Hospitals' Trust, 1967), p. 33.

[20] World Health Organization, *Mortality from Malignant Neoplasms,* 1955–1965, *Number of Deaths by Site, Sex, and Age,* Vols. I and II (Geneva: WHO, 1970).

[21] Johannes Clemmesen, *Statistical Studies in Malignant Neoplasms, I. Review and Results* (Copenhagen: Munksgaard, 1965).

[22] Doll, *Prevention of Cancer: Pointers from Epidemiology.*

[23] William Haenszel and Minoru Kurihara, "Studies of Japanese Migrants: I. Mortality from Cancer and Other Diseases Among Japanese in the United States," *Journal of the National Cancer Institute 40* (1968): 43–68; also see Muir, "Epidemiological Identification of Cancer Hazards," pp. 8–9.

[24] Richard Doll, "The Epidemiology of Cancer," *Cancer 45* (1980): 2477.

[25] Elizabeth C. Miller, "Some Current Perspectives on Chemical Carcinogenesis in Humans and Experimental Animals: Presidential Address," *Cancer Research 38* (1978): 1491.

[26] John Higginson, interviewed by Thomas H. Maugh II, "Cancer and Environment: Higginson Speaks Out," *Science 205* (1979): 1363.

[27] John Higginson, interviewed by Daniel S. Greenberg, "Cancer: The Difference Life-Style Makes," *Washington Post,* July 17, 1979, p. A-17.

[28] Umberto Saffiotti, quoted in "The Disease of the Century," *Time,* October 20, 1975, reprinted in "Toxic Substances Control Act," *Hearing,* October 24, 1975.

[29] Susan S. Devesa and Marvin A. Schneiderman, "Increase in the Number of Cancer Deaths in the United States," *American Journal of Epidemiology 106* (1977): 1–2.

[30] Ibid., p. 4; also see Susan S. Devesa and Debra T. Silverman, "Cancer Incidence and Mortality Trends in the United States: 1935–74," *Journal of the National Cancer Institute 60* (1978): 545, Tables, pp. 555–558; for another source, see *1977 Cancer Facts and Figures,* American Cancer Society, Trends, 1952–54 to 1972–74, p. 13; *1978 Cancer Facts and Figures,* American Cancer Society, Trends, 1953–55 to 1973–75, p. 13.

[31] Lawrence K. Altman, "W.H.O. Study Finds Lung Cancer Deaths Are Rising," *New York Times,* October 9, 1977; also John Higginson, "Multiplicity of Factors Involved in

Cancer Patterns and Trends," *Cancer Symposium, An Academic Review of the Environmental Determinants of Cancer Relevant to Prevention,* held in cooperation with the American Cancer Society, Inc., New York City, February 28, March 1–2, 1979, *manuscript,* pp. 4–5.

[32] *Proceedings of the Conference on the Decline in Coronary Heart Disease Mortality,* National Heart, Lung and Blood Institute, National Institutes of Health, Bethesda, Md., October 24–25, 1978, NIH publication No. 79-1610, Table 1, Trends 1920–1976, prepared by Division of Vital Statistics, National Center for Health Statistics, June 1978.

[33] *Cancer Facts and Figures,* 1979, American Cancer Society, p. 6.

[34] *Health, United States: 1980, with Prevention Profile,* U.S. Department of Health and Human Services, DHHS Publication (PHS) 81-1232, 1980.

[35] "Lung Cancer Rates Rising Rapidly," *The Nation's Health,* the official newspaper of the American Public Health Association, April 1982, p. 12.

[36] "Interim Guidelines Recommended for Reducing Cancer Risks through Diet," *News from the National Research Council,* January 16, 1982, p. 4.

[37] Lesley Stahl, "The Politics of Cancer," CBS, 1976, *transcript.*

[38] "Fighting Cancer in the Work Place," Sunday Review of the Week, *New York Times,* January 20, 1980.

[39] Marvin A. Schneiderman, statement before the United States Department of Labor, Occupational Safety and Health Administration, *OSHA Docket No. 090,* April 4, 1978, p. 3.

[40] Earl S. Pollack and John W. Horm, "Trends in Cancer Incidence and Mortality in the United States, 1969–76," *Journal of the National Cancer Institute 64* (1980): 1095.

[41] Brian E. Henderson, "Descriptive Epidemiology and Geographic Pathology," delivered at *Cancer 1980: Achievements, Challenges and Prospects,* Symposium sponsored by Memorial Sloan-Kettering Cancer Center, co-sponsored by American Cancer Society, New York City, September 13–18, 1980, *manuscript,* pp. 5–6.

[42] *Cancer Incidence and Mortality in the United States,* SEER, 1973–1976, prepared by Biometry Branch, Division of Cancer Cause and Prevention, National Cancer Institute, edited by John L. Young, Jr., Ardyce J. Asire, Earl S. Pollack, DHEW Publication No. (NIH) 78-1837 (Bethesda, Md.: National Cancer Institute), Introduction, p. ii.

[43] Ibid., p. i.

[44] *Health, United States: 1978,* U.S. Department of Health, Education and Welfare, DHEW Publication (PHS) 78-1232, 1978, p. 232.

[45] *Toxic Chemicals and Public Protection, A Report to the President by the Toxic Substances Strategy Committee* (Washington, D.C.: U.S. Government Printing Office, 1980), pp. 146–153.

[46] Ibid., p. 153.

[47] "Government Says Cancer Rate Is Increasing. But Are the Data Really There? and Are Chemicals Really the Cause?," *Science 209* (1980): 998–999.

[48] *Cancer Facts and Figures, 1980,* American Cancer Society, p. 4.

[49] *Cancer Facts and Figures, 1981,* American Cancer Society, p. 4.

[50] Richard Doll and Richard Peto, "Avoidable Risks of Cancer in the U.S.," *Journal of the National Cancer Institute 66* (1981): 1210, 1274–1276, 1280–1281; also see JNCI essay reprinted under the title *The Causes of Cancer* (New York: Oxford, 1981), same pagination.

[51] Ibid., *Abstract,* p. 1194.

[52] Philip M. Boffey, "Cancer Experts Lean Toward Steady Vigilance, but Less Alarm, on Environment," *New York Times,* March 2, 1982, pp. C-1, C-2.

[53] John Berg, statement before the United States Department of Labor, Occupational Safety and Health Administration, *OSHA Docket No. 090,* April 4, 1978, pp. 4, 5, 6.

[54] Doll and Peto, "Avoidable Risks of Cancer in the U.S.," pp. 1256, 1274–1277.

[55] SEER, *Incidence and Mortality Data:* 1973–1977; National Cancer Institute Monograph No. 57 (Washington, D.C.: Department of Health and Human Services, 1981); Emil Frei III, John Cairns and Peter Boyle, letters, *Science 220* (1983): 252–256.

[56] Draft Summary, "Estimates of the Fraction of Cancer Incidence in the United States Attributable to Occupational Factors," National Cancer Institute and National Institute of Environmental Health Sciences. This mimeographed document was a press release, and a release date was published on its first page: "Not for use before 3:30 P.M. EDT, September 11, 1978."

[57] Ibid., pp. 1–3.

[58] Ibid., p. 4.

[59] Ibid., pp. 1–2.

[60] I. J. Selikoff, "Cancer Risks of Asbestos Exposure," in *Origins of Human Cancer,* Book C, *Human Risk Assessment,* edited by H. H. Hiatt, J. D. Watson, J. A. Winsten (New York: Cold Spring Harbor Laboratory, 1977), Table 11, p. 1777.

[61] *Remarks of Secretary Joseph A. Califano, Jr., Department of Health, Education and Welfare, to the AFL-CIO National Conference on Occupational Safety and Health,* Sheraton Park Hotel, Washington, D.C., September 11, 1978, p. 3. This was a mimeographed speech, with a first-page release date for the press: "Not for use before 3:30 P.M. EDT, September 11, 1978."

[62] Ibid., p. 2.

[63] Ibid., pp. 13–14.

[64] "Estimates of the Fraction of Cancer in the United States Related to Occupational Factors," prepared by National Cancer Institute, National Institute of Environmental Health Sciences, National Institute of Occupational Safety and Health, *mimeographed manuscript,* Table 2, p. 33.

[65] Ibid., p. 1.

[66] Letter to my research assistant, Henry Constantine, from James F. Foster, Chief, News Media Services, U.S. Department of Labor, Occupational Safety and Health Administration, October 19, 1978.

[67] "Estimates of the Fraction of Cancer in the United States Related to Occupational Factors," pp. 5–7.

[68] Clemmesen, "Statistical Studies in Malignant Neoplasms," pp. 177–178.

[69] Doll, *Prevention of Cancer: Pointers from Epidemiology,* pp. 63, 64, 67, 100; Doll, "Strategy for Detection of Cancer Hazards to Man," *Nature 265* (1977).

[70] J. Higginson and C. S. Muir, "The Role of Epidemiology in Elucidating the Importance of Environmental Factors in Human Cancer," *Cancer Detection and Prevention 1:* 86.

[71] L. M. Shabad, "Methodology of the Study of Carcinogens in Human Populations," *Journal of Toxicology and Environmental Health 4* (1978): 638.

[72] David L. Levin, Susan S. Devesa, J. David Godwin II, and Debra T. Silverman, *Cancer Rates and Risks,* 2nd ed., 1974, DHEW Publication No. (NIH) 76-691, p. 73.

[73] Guy R. Newell, "A Case for the Support of Treatment and Prevention Research in the Control of Cancer," *Journal of the National Cancer Institute 59* (1977): 1581–1582.

[74] Doll, "Strategy for Detection of Cancer Hazards to Man," p. 591.

[75] Robert Flamant, "Epidemiological Research on the Relationship between Tobacco, Alcohol and Cancer," *Prog. Biochem. Pharmacol.,* Vol. 14 (Basel: Karger, 1978), p. 45.

[76] Ernst L. Wynder, "Dietary Habits and Cancer Epidemiology," *Cancer 43* (May Supplement, 1979): 1955.

[77] Paul M. Newberne, "Diet and Nutrition," in *Cancer Epidemic? A Symposium on Carcinogens,* held by Blue Cross and Blue Shield of Greater New York at the New York Academy of Medicine, May 25, 1977, published in *Bulletin of the New York Academy of Medicine 54* (1978): 385.

[78] Papers asssociating cervix cancer with infection, venereal infection, or, specifically, with Herpes type 2 infection: I. D. Rotkin, "A Comparison Review of Key Epidemiological Studies in Cervical Cancer Related to Current Searches for Transmissible Agents," *Cancer Research 33* (1973); Andre J. Nahmias, Zuher M. Naib, and William E. Josey, "Epidemiological Studies Relating Genital Herpetic Infection to Cervical Carcinoma," *Cancer Research 34* (1974); Clark W. Heath, Glyn G. Caldwell, and Paul C. Feorino, "Viruses and Other Microbes," in *Persons at High Risk of Cancer,* edited by Joseph F. Fraumeni, Jr. (New York: Academic, 1975), pp. 243–244; Michael Shimkin, "Overview," in *Persons at High Risk of Cancer,* 1975, p. 438; J. W. Berg, "World-Wide Variations in Cancer Incidence as Clues to Cancer Origins," in *Origins of Human Cancer,* Book A, *Incidence of Cancer in Humans,* p. 16; Laure Aurelian, Bruce C. Strnad, and Marie F. Smith, "Immunodiagnostic Potential of a Virus-Coded, Tumor-Associated Antigen (AG-4) in Cervical Cancer," *Cancer 39* (April Supplement, 1977); Richard Doll, "Introduction," in *Origins of Human Cancer,* Book A, p. 9; Doll, "An Epidemiological Perspective of the Biology of Cancer," *Cancer Research 38* (1978): 3575.

[79] Papers and books linking breast cancer to a lack of childbirth: Clemmesen, *Statistical Studies in Malignant Neoplasms,* 1965, pp. 253–256, 261–266, 271; Doll, *Prevention of Cancer: Pointers from Epidemiology,* 1967, p. 40; Levin, Devesa, Godwin, and Silverman, *Cancer*

Rates and Risks, 1974, pp. 55, 57, 58, 68; Shimkin, "Overview," in *Persons at High Risk of Cancer,* 1975, p. 437; Higginson and Muir, "The Role of Epidemiology in Elucidating the Importance of Environmental Factors in Human Cancer," 1976, p. 98.

[80] Papers linking prostate cancer to infection and nutrition disease: R. Steele. R. Lees, A. S. Kraus et al., "Sexual Factors in the Epidemiology of Cancer of the Prostate," *J. Chron. Dis. 24* (1971); L. Krain, "Epidemiologic Variables in Prostatic Cancer," *Geriatrics 28* (1973); Brian Henderson, "Sexual Factors and Pregnancy," in *Persons at High Risk of Cancer,* 1975, p. 277; H. K. Armenian, A. M. Lilienfeld, E. L. Diamond, and I. D. J. Bross, "Epidemiologic Characteristics of Patients with Prostatic Neoplasms," *American Journal of Epidemiology 102* (1975); Berg, "World-Wide Variations in Cancer Incidence as Clues to Cancer Origins," 1977, p. 18; Berg, "Can Nutrition Explain the Pattern of International Epidemiology of Hormone-Dependent Cancers?," *Cancer Research 35* (1975): 3349.

[81] Thomas H. Maugh II, "Industry Council Challenges HEW on Cancer in the Workplace," *Science 202* (1978): 602.

[82] Ibid., p. 602.

[83] Ibid., p. 603.

[84] Ibid., p. 604.

[85] *Conference on Cancer Prevention—Quantitative Aspects,* sponsored by Office of the Director, National Cancer Institute, Sheraton International Conference Center, Reston, Va., September 26, 1978. The mimeographed transcript is prefaced with these words: "Informal transcript of the discussion of the paper 'Estimates of the Fraction of Cancer in the United States Related to Occupation,' which occurred in the afternoon of September 26. The recording of the discussion begins on tape 10A and concludes on tape 11A."

[86] Ibid., p. 4.

[87] Ibid., pp. 9–10, p. 12.

[88] Ibid., p. 11.

[89] Ibid., pp. 20–21.

[90] Ibid., p. 25.

[91] Ibid., pp. 27–28.

[92] Ibid., p. 2.

[93] Ibid., p. 21.

[94] Ibid., pp. 25–26.

[95] Ibid., pp. 18–19.

[96] "Cancer and Government," unsigned editorial, *Washington Post,* August 13, 1981, p. C-1.

[97] William Havender, "Politicians Make Bad Scientists," *American Enterprise Institute Journal on Government and Society,* November–December 1981, p. 47.

[98] "Needed: Better Studies of Links to Cancer," *Chemical Week,* February 14, 1979, quotation from Philippe Shubik, p. 39.

[99] Ibid.

[100] Ibid.

[101] Ibid.

[102] Clive Cookson, "OSHA and Industry Clash on Workplace Safety," and ". . . Rall Defends Carcinogenesis Estimates," *Science and Government Report 9,* October 1, 1979, pp. 4–5.

[103] Philip H. Abelson, "Cancer—Opportunism and Opportunity," Editorial, *Science, 206* (1979).

[104] Truhaut quoted in a protest letter to Gus Speth, Chairman, Council on Environmental Quality, from Richard Wilson, Energy and Environmental Policy Center, Harvard University, September 26, 1979, pp. 5, 9.

[105] Richard Peto, "Distorting the Epidemiology of Cancer: The Need for a More Balanced Overview," *Nature, 284,* 1980, p. 299.

[106] Ibid., p. 299.

[107] Ibid., p. 298.

[108] Ibid., p. 297.

[109] Ibid., p. 300.

[110] Ibid.

[111] Ibid.

[112] Ibid., pp. 297–300.

[113] John Higginson, "Proportion of Cancers Due to Occupation," *Preventive Medicine, 9,* 1980, pp. 180–188.

[114] Ibid., p. 180.

[115] Ibid., p. 184.

[116] Ibid., p. 187.

[117] Doll and Peto, "Avoidable Risks of Cancer in the United States," p. 1240.

[118] Ibid.

[119] Ibid., pp. 1240–1241.

[120] Ibid., p. 1305.

[121] Ibid., p. 1241.

[122] Ibid. (tobacco), p. 1222; (diet), p. 1235; (industrial products), p. 1251; (air pollution), p. 1248; (occupational exposures), p. 1245; table of estimates, p. 1256.

[123] David Rall, in Occupational Safety and Health Administration (OSHA), U.S. Department of Labor, *Identification, Classification and Regulation of Potential Occupational Carcinogens,* Part VII, Book 2, in *Federal Register, 45:15,* January 22, 1980, p. 5044.

[124] Ibid., p. 5028.

[125] Kessler quoted in "Needed: Better Studies of Links to Cancer," p. 39.

[126] Guy R. Newell, "Prevention of Cancer," *Preventive Medicine, 9,* 1980, p. 317.

[127] *Cancer Facts and Figures for Black Americans 1979,* American Cancer Society, table, "Cancer Around the World, 1973," source: M. Segi's Age Adjusted Death Rates for Cancer for Selected Sites in 52 Countries in 1973, p. 25.

[128] *Cancer Statistics, 1977,* American Cancer Society, table, "Cancer Around the World, 1970–1971," source: *World Health Statistics Annual, 1970–1971,* pp. 16–17.

[129] *Cancer Statistics, 1979,* American Cancer Society, table, "Cancer Around the World," 1972–1973, source: *World Health Statistics Annual, 1972–1973,* pp. 18–19.

[130] C. S. Muir, "International Variations in High-Risk Populations," Proceedings of a Conference, Key Biscayne, Florida, December 10–12, 1974, sponsored by the National Cancer Institute and the American Cancer Society, published under the title, *Persons at High Risk of Cancer: An Approach to Cancer Etiology and Control,* edited by Joseph F. Fraumeni, Jr. (New York: Academic Press, 1975), pp. 295–296.

[131] Richard Doll, Calum Muir, J. A. H. Waterhouse, editors, *Cancer Incidence in Five Continents* (Berlin: Springer Verlag, 1970), cited by John Berg in "World-Wide Variations in Cancer Incidence," in *Origins of Human Cancer,* Book A, p. 15.

[132] John Berg, "Diet," in *Persons at High Risk of Cancer,* p. 216.

[133] Sidney J. Cutler and John L. Young, Jr., "Demographic Pattern of Cancer Incidence in the United States," in *Persons at High Risk of Cancer,* pp. 310, 312–321.

John Weisburger, "Cancer Prevention," *Chemtech, 7,* 1977. See table, "Estimated Deaths for All Sites" (based E. Silverburg and A. Holleb, "Major Trends in Cancer: 25-Year Survey," *Cancer Journal for Clinicians, 25,* 1975), p. 735; Bruce Armstrong and Richard Doll, "Environmental Factors and Cancer Incidence and Mortality in Different Countries with Special Reference to Dietary Practices," *International Journal of Cancer, 15,* 1975, pp. 617–637; John Berg, "Can Nutrition Explain the Patterns of International Epidemiology of Hormone-dependent Cancers?," *Cancer Research, 35,* 1975, pp. 3348–3349; Brian Henderson, Veeba R. Gerkins, and Malcolm C. Pike, "Sexual Factors and Pregnancy," in *Persons at High Risk of Cancer,* p. 267.

[134] J. N. P. Davies, "Overview: Geographic Opportunities and Demographic Leads," in *Persons at High Risk of Cancer,* p. 375.

[134a] Marvin Schneiderman, "Sources, Resources and Tsouris," speaking at the 1974 Conference identified in note 130, published in *Persons at High Risk of Cancer,* p. 462.

[135] Robert Hoover, "Cancer Epidemiology," in *Environmental Cancer; Causes, Victims, Solutions,* a summary of proceedings of a conference held March 21 and 22, 1977, sponsored by the Urban Environmental Conference, Inc., and funded by the National Cancer Institute, p. 5.

[136] Peter T. Bernstein, "Cancer Pollution Link Is Seen," *Washington Post,* February 16, 1975, reprinted in "Toxic Substances Control Act," *Hearings before the Subcommittee on the Environment of the Committee on Commerce,* United States Senate, Ninety-fourth Congress, First Session on S. 776, March 3, 5, 10 and April 15, 1975, Serial No. 94–24, p. 223.

[137] Senator John Tunney, in "Toxic Substances Control Act," *Hearing,* October 24, 1975, p. 1.

[138] "The Disease of the Century," *Time,* October 20, 1975, reprinted in "Toxic Substances Control Act," *Hearing,* October 24, 1975, p. 2.

[139] Carl C. Craft, "Cancer-Environment," Associated Press, January 13, 1976; Bill Richards, "U. S. Action Urged to Curb Cancer-Causing Agents," *Washington Post,* January 13, 1976.

[140] James Bishop, Jr., panelist on "Face the Nation," CBS, 1976, *transcript.*

[141] Larry Agran, *The Cancer Connection: And What We Can Do About It* (New York: St. Martin's Press, 1977), p. xvi.

[142] Thomas Corbett, *Cancer and Chemicals* (Chicago: Nelson-Hall, 1977), p. x.

[143] Samuel Epstein, *The Politics of Cancer,* rev. ed. (New York: Anchor Books, 1979), p. 26, and Acknowledgments.

[144] *Health, United States 1980, with a Prevention Profile,* U.S. Department of Health and Human Services, DHHS Publication No. (PHS) 81-1232, p. 292.

[145] Malcolm C. Pike, Robert J. Gordon, Brian E. Henderson, Herman R. Menck, and Jennie Soohoo, "Air Pollution," in *Persons at High Risk of Cancer,* p. 225.

[146] John Berg, "Diet," in *Persons at High Risk of Cancer,* p. 209.

[147] C. R. Buncher, R. J. Kuzma, and C. M. Forcade, "Drinking Water as an Epidemiologic Risk Factor for Cancer," in *Origins of Human Cancer,* Book A, p. 347.

[148] Brian MacMahon, "Epidemiology's Strengths, Weaknesses in Environmental Health Issues," excerpted from "Strengths and Limitations of Epidemiology" in The National Research Council, *Current Issues and Studies,* 1979, published in *News Report,* a monthly register of the National Academy of Sciences, National Academy of Engineering, Institute of Medicine, and National Research Council, Vol. XXX, No. 4, April 1980.

[149] E. Cuyler Hammond and Lawrence Garfinkel, "General Air Pollution and Cancer in the United States," *Preventive Medicine, 9,* 1980, pp. 206–211.

[150] Johannes Clemmesen, "Parameters for Identification of High-Risk Groups," delivered at International Symposium on Detection and Prevention of Cancer, New York, 1976; published in *Prevention and Detection of Cancer,* edited by Herbert E. Nieburgs (New York: Marcel Dekker, 1978), p. 1514.

[151] See note 130 for full description of conference, and of *Persons at High Risk of Cancer.*

[152] See note 72 for full description of *Cancer Rates and Risks.*

[153] *Cancer Questions—And Answers About Rates and Risks,* based on *Cancer Rates and Risks,* 2nd ed., prepared by the Biometry Branch of the National Cancer Institute, DHEW Publication No. (NIH) 76-1040 (formerly PHS Publication No. 1514). Revised 1975; US DHEW, Public Health Service, National Institutes of Health.

[154] Symposium Sponsored by the American Cancer Society and National Cancer Institute, *Nutrition in the Causation of Cancer,* held at Key Biscayne, Florida, May 19–22, 1975; papers published in *Cancer Research, 35,* Part 2, November 1975.

[155] Michael B. Shimkin, "Overview: Preventive Oncology," in *Persons at High Risk of Cancer,* p. 441.

[156] *Cancer Questions—And Answers About Rates and Risks,* p. 11.

[157] Cutler and Young, "Demographic Patterns of Cancer Incidence in the United States," in *Persons at High Risk of Cancer,* pp. 310, 312–321; John Weisburger, "Cancer Prevention," table, p. 735.

[158] Armstrong and Doll, "Environmental Factors and Cancer Incidence and Mortality in Different Countries with Special Reference to Dietary Practices," pp. 617–637.
Henderson et al., "Sexual Factors and Pregnancy," in *Persons at High Risk of Cancer,* p. 267.

[159] Cutler and Young, "Demographic Patterns of Cancer Incidence in the United States," in *Persons at High Risk of Cancer,* p. 339; John L. Young, Jr., Susan S. Devesa, and Sidney J. Cutler, "Incidence of Cancer in U.S. Blacks," *Cancer Research, 35,* 1975, p. 3524.

[160] Isidro Martinez, Raquel Torres, and Zenaida Frias, "Cancer Incidence in the United States and Puerto Rico," *Cancer Research, 35,* 1975, p. 3265; Nelson A. Fernandez, "Nutrition in Puerto Rico," *Cancer Research, 35,* 1975, p. 3289.

[161] John Wakefield, "Education of the Public," in *Persons at High Risk of Cancer,* p. 417; Herman R. Menck, "Cancer Incidence in the Mexican American," *National Cancer Institute Monograph No. 47,* 1977, p. 103.

[162] Robert Hoover, Thomas J. Mason, Frank W. McKay and Joseph F. Fraumeni, Jr.,

"Geographic Patterns of Cancer Mortality in the United States," in *Persons at High Risk of Cancer*, p. 352.

[163] *Cancer Questions—And Answers About Rates and Risks*, p. 17.

[164] Cedric Davern, *Summary, Banbury Report 4, Cancer Incidence in Defined Populations* (New York: Cold Spring Harbor Laboratory, 1980), pp. 453, 455.

[165] Irving Kessler, Lecture, *Seminar on Government Regulation of Cancer-Causing Substances*, sponsored by the National Center for Administrative Justice, December 7–8, 1978, Washington, D.C.

[166] C. S. Muir, "Epidemiological Identification of Cancer Hazards," in *Prevention and Detection of Cancer*, p. 11.

[167] Kessler, Lecture, *Seminar on Government Regulation of Cancer-Causing Substances.*

[168] Brian MacMahon, "Epidemiology's Strengths, Weaknesses in Environmental Health Issues," p. 6.

[169] Richard Doll, *Comments for Congressional Briefing*, Rayburn House Office Building, Washington, D.C., September 15, 1977.

[170] Marvin Schneiderman, "Sources, Resources and Tsouris," in *Persons at High Risk of Cancer*, p. 465.

[171] Irving Selikoff and E. Cuyler Hammond, "Multiple Risk Factors in Environmental Cancer," in *Persons at High Risk of Cancer*, p. 474.

[172] John Higginson, "Cancer Etiology and Prevention," in *Persons at High Risk of Cancer*, pp. 389, 391.

[173] Schneiderman, "Sources, Resources and Tsouris," in *Persons at High Risk of Cancer*, p. 464.

[174] John Higginson, in "Discussion," following A. C. Templeton, "Acquired Diseases," in *Persons at High Risk of Cancer*, p. 84.

[175] Schneiderman, "Sources, Resources and Tsouris," in *Persons at High Risk of Cancer*, p. 464.

[176] Seymour Jablon, "Radiation," in *Persons at High Risk of Cancer*, p. 161.

[177] John Mulvihill, "Congenital and Genetic Diseases," in *Persons at High Risk of Cancer*, pp. 4–15, 16.

[178] David E. Anderson, "Familial Susceptibility," in *Persons at High Risk of Cancer*, p. 40.

[179] Bruce S. Schoenberg, "Multiple Primary Neoplasms," in *Persons at High Risk of Cancer*, pp. 106–108, 111.

[180] *Cancer Questions—And Answers About Rates and Risks*, p. 15.

[181] A. C. Templeton, "Acquired Diseases," in *Persons at High Risk of Cancer*, pp. 70–72, 75.

[182] E. Cuyler Hammond, "Tobacco," p. 133; Hoover et al., "Geographic Patterns of Cancer Mortality in the United States," p. 352; Muir, "International Variation in High-Risk Populations," p. 300; Shimkin, "Preventive Oncology," p. 437; Schneiderman, "Sources, Resources and Tsouris," p. 452; Selikoff and Hammond, "Multiple Risk Factors in Environmental Cancer," pp. 468, 470; Ernst Wynder, "Discussion," after Hammond, "Tobacco," p. 138; Brian MacMahon, "Environmental Factors," pp. 286–287—all in *Persons at High Risk of Cancer*.

[183] Kenneth J. Rothman, "Alcohol," pp. 140–144; Hammond, "Tobacco," p. 132; Templeton, "Acquired Diseases," p. 71—all in *Persons at High Risk of Cancer;* Joseph J. Vitale and Leonard S. Gottlieb, "Alcohol and Alcohol-Related Deficiencies as Carcinogens," *Cancer Research, 35*, 1975, p. 3336.

[184] E. L. Wynder, L. Hyams and T. Shigematsu, "Correlations of International Cancer Rates: An Epidemiological Exercise," *Cancer, 20*, 1967, pp. 113–126.

[185] Schneiderman, "Sources, Resources and Tsouris," in *Persons at High Risk of Cancer*, p. 452.

[186] Brian Henderson, "Sexual Factors in Pregnancy," in *Persons at High Risk of Cancer*, pp. 274, 275; Berg, "Can Nutrition Explain the Patterns of International Epidemiology of Hormone-dependent Cancers?," *Cancer Research, 35*, 1975, pp. 3348–3349; Berg, "Diet," in *Persons at High Risk of Cancer*, pp. 215–216.

[187] Armstrong and Doll, "Environmental Factors and Cancer Incidence and Mortality in Different Countries with Special Reference to Dietary Practices," pp. 617–637.

[188] William Haenszel, "Migrant Studies," in *Persons at High Risk of Cancer*, p. 366.

[189] Henderson et al., "Sexual Factors and Pregnancy," in *Persons at High Risk of Cancer,* p. 270.

[190] B. MacMahon, P. Cole, and J. Brown, "Etiology of Human Breast Cancer: A Review," *Journal of the National Cancer Institute, 50,* 1973, pp. 21–42; B. MacMahon, P. Cole, T. M. Lin, et al., "Age at First Birth and Breast Cancer Risk," *Bulletin of the World Health Organization, 43,* 1973, pp. 209–221.

[191] Henderson et al., "Sexual Factors and Pregnancy," p. 274; Berg, "Diet," p. 213; Templeton, "Acquired Diseases," p. 71—all in *Persons at High Risk of Cancer.*

[192] Clark W. Heath, "Viruses and Other Microbes," pp. 243–244; Henderson et al., "Sexual Factors and Pregnancy," pp. 274–275; Shimkin, "Preventive Oncology," p. 438—all in *Persons at High Risk of Cancer.*

[193] Henderson et al., "Sexual Factors and Pregnancy," in *Persons at High Risk of Cancer,* p. 275.

[194] Henderson et al., "Sexual Factors and Pregnancy," in *Persons at High Risk of Cancer,* p. 277; Berg, "Can Nutrition Explain the Patterns of International Epidemiology of Hormone-dependent Cancers?," pp. 3348–3349.

[195] Berg, "Can Nutrition Explain the Patterns of International Epidemiology of Hormone-dependent Cancers?," pp. 3348–3349; Armstrong and Doll, "Environmental Factors and Cancer Incidence and Mortality in Different Countries with Special Reference to Dietary Practices," pp. 617–637.

[196] Robert Hoover and Joseph Fraumeni, Jr., "Drugs," in *Persons at High Risk of Cancer,* p. 187.

[197] Selikoff and Hammond, "Multiple Risks in Environmental Cancer," in *Persons at High Risk of Cancer,* p. 478.

[198] Philip Cole and Marlene Goldman, "Occupation," in *Persons at High Risk of Cancer,* pp. 172–176, 178.

[199] Hoover, Mason, McKay, and Fraumeni, "Geographic Patterns of Cancer Mortality in the United States," in *Persons at High Risk of Cancer,* pp. 355–358.

[200] Pike et al., "Air Pollution," in *Persons at High Risk of Cancer,* pp. 225–234, 236.

[201] Alfred G. Knudson, Jr., "Towards the Understanding and Control of Cancer," in *Persons at High Risk of Cancer,* pp. 506–507.

[202] Weisburger, "Cancer Prevention," table, p. 735.

[203] W. J. Blot, T. J. Mason, R. Hoover, and J. F. Fraumeni, Jr., "Cancer by County: Etiologic Implications," in *Origins of Human Cancer,* Book A, p. 29.

[204] Ibid., p. 25.

[205] Ibid.

[206] Ibid.

[207] Selikoff and Hammond, "Multiple Risk Factors in Environmental Cancer," in *Persons at High Risk of Cancer,* p. 468.

[208] Blot et al., "Cancer by County: Etiologic Implications," in *Origins of Human Cancer,* Book A, p. 26.

[209] Hoover et al., "Geographic Patterns of Cancer Mortality in the United States," in *Persons at High Risk of Cancer,* p. 344.

[210] Robert Hoover, "Cancer Epidemiology," delivered at the Urban Environment Conference, *Environmental Cancer: Causes, Victims, Solutions,* a summary of proceedings of a conference held March 21–22, 1977, pp. 4–6; William J. Blot, Joseph F. Fraumeni, Jr., and B. J. Stone, "Geographic Correlates of Pancreas Cancer in the United States," *Cancer, 42,* 1978, pp. 373–380 (the paper was accepted for publication on September 12, 1977).

[211] Robert Hoover, Thomas J. Mason, Frank W. McKay, and Joseph Fraumeni, Jr., "Geographic Pattern of Cancer Mortality in the United States," in *Persons at High Risk of Cancer,* pp. 355, 359; W. J. Blot, T. J. Mason, R. Hoover, J. F. Fraumeni, Jr., "Cancer by County: Etiologic Implications," in *Origins of Human Cancer,* Book A, p. 21; Joseph F. Fraumeni, Jr., "Epidemiological Studies of Cancer," in *Carcinogens: Identification and Mechanisms of Action,* edited by A. Clark Griffin and Charles R. Shaw (New York: Raven Press, 1979), p. 53.

[212] Robert Hoover and Joseph F. Fraumeni, Jr., "Cancer Mortality in U.S. Counties with Chemical Industries," *Environmental Research, 9,* 1975, pp. 196, 205.

[213] Thomas J. Mason, "Cancer Mortality in U.S. Counties with Plastics and Related Industries," *Environmental Health Perspectives,* June, 1975, pp. 79, 83.

[214] William J. Blot and Joseph F. Fraumeni, Jr., "Geographic Patterns of Lung Cancer: Industrial Correlations," *American Journal of Epidemiology, 103,* 1976, pp. 539, 549.

[215] W. J. Blot, T. J. Mason, R. Hoover, and J. F. Fraumeni, Jr., "Cancer by County: Etiologic Implications," in *Origins of Human Cancer,* Book A, p. 25.

[216] *Cancer and the Worker* (New York: New York Academy of Sciences, 1977), p. 67. (*Cancer and the Worker* is a popular volume based on *Occupational Carcinogens,* Volume 271 of the Annals of the New York Academy of Sciences, 1976, a collection of papers delivered at a 1975 conference chaired by Umberto Saffiotti of the National Cancer Institute and by Joseph Wagoner of NIOSH. Saffiotti was one of the "chief" reviewers of the popularized version.)

[217] B. J. Stone, W. J. Blot, J. F. Fraumeni, Jr., "Geographic Patterns of Industry in the United States," *Journal of Occupational Medicine, 20,* 1978, p. 477.

[218] Pike et al., "Air Pollution," in *Persons at High Risk of Cancer,* pp. 229–230.

[219] Fraumeni, "Epidemiological Studies of Cancer," in *Carcinogens: Identification and Mechanisms of Action,* p. 53.

[220] Irving Kessler, quoted in "Needed: Better Studies of Links to Cancer," *Chemical Week,* February 14, 1979, p. 39.

[221] John Higginson, "Overview," delivered at the Urban Environment Conference, *Environmental Cancer: Causes, Victims, Solutions,* a summary of proceedings of a conference held March 21–22, 1977, p. 3.

[222] J. H. Weisburger, L. A. Cohen, and E. L. Wynder, "On the Etiology and Metabolic Epidemiology of the Main Human Cancers," in *Origins of Human Cancer,* Book A, p. 567.

[223] Umberto Saffiotti, paraphrased by scientific rapporteur Vincent Guinee, following delivery of "Education of the Public" by John Wakefield in *Persons at High Risk of Cancer,* p. 434.

[224] Saffiotti, quoted in "The Disease of the Century," *Time,* October 20, 1975.

[225] Saffiotti, "Risk-Benefit Considerations in Public Policy on Environmental Carcinogenesis." Proceedings of the Eleventh Canadian Cancer Research Conference, sponsored by the National Cancer Institute of Canada in affiliation with the Canadian Cancer Society, Toronto, Ontario, May 6–8, 1976, p. 135.

[226] Philip Handler, "Public Doubts About Science," *Science, 208,* 1980, p. 1093. Excerpt from a speech, "Science and the American Future," delivered at Duke University, Durham, North Carolina, March 6, 1980.

[227] J. Fletcher, "Ethical Considerations in Biomedical Research Involving Human Beings," in *Proceedings of the International Conference on the Role of the Individual and the Community in the Research, Development, and Use of Biologicals* (Geneva: World Health Organization, 1976).

[228] Bernard Davis, "Limits in the Regulation of Scientific Research," in *Ethics for Science Policy: Report from a Nobel Symposium* (New York: Pergamon Press, 1978), pp. 206–208, 212–213.

[229] Doll and Peto, "Avoidable Risks of Cancer," p. 1203.

[230] Davis, "Limits in the Regulation of Scientific Research," p. 208.

INDEX

(*Continued from page 4*)